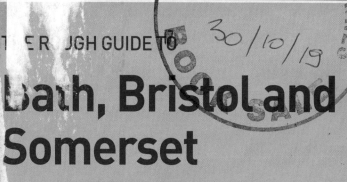

THE ROUGH GUIDE TO

30/10/19

Bath, Bristol and
Somerset

INCLUDES SALISBURY AND STONEHENGE

written and researched by

Robert Andrews and Keith Drew

ROUGH
GUIDES

roughguides.com

Contents

OPPOSITE SHEEP GRAZING ON GLASTONBURY TOR **PREVIOUS PAGE** CLIFTON SUSPENSION BRIDGE, BRISTOL

Introduction to

Bath, Bristol and Somerset

Somerset – the very name, seemingly derived from the Anglo-Saxon for "people dwelling in a summer pasture", evokes a picture of bucolic bliss, a soft undulating landscape grazed by sheep and populated by straw-chewing yokels speaking in a quaint "zummerzet" drawl. Early railway posters traded on the cliché, portraying thatched cottages, tottering hayricks and castellated church towers. And while the modern reality is much more complex and nuanced, parts of the caricature are still identifiable today, where rounding a bend will bring you face to face with a heart-stoppingly lovely picture of quiet lanes meandering through hushed valleys, landscapes essentially unchanged for centuries, and yes, even a castellated church tower or two in the distance.

As counties go, Somerset is fairly unique in England for its breadth and diversity. The distance from the Wiltshire border in the east to the Devon border in the west stretches some seventy miles, within which every kind of landscape features, from limestone gorges to marshy flatlands, and from lush meadows to windswept moorland. There are forty miles of coastline, ranging from busy and brash holiday resorts to bleakly beautiful wetland reserves. Populous towns and cities give way to one-horse villages, and the historical traces take in stone circles, ruined castles and Renaissance palaces.

Where to go

The Romans knew a good thing when they saw it, and in **Bath**, in the northeast corner of the county, they hit gold. Possessing Britain's only natural hot springs, the town quickly developed as a home from home for the baths-loving Romans, and it was the presence of these thermal waters that came to define Bath throughout its subsequent history. Visitors from far and wide came to wallow in the healing waters, with the town reaching its greatest glory in the eighteenth century, when fashion and great architecture came together to create the apotheosis of the Georgian urban centre. Today, Bath has plenty to offer: some of the finest museums outside London, inviting shops and a vibrant cultural life that belies its size – all contained within a compact area that makes for easy strolling, often through traffic-free lanes.

Within easy distance of Bath are a cluster of towns and villages on the Somerset-Wiltshire border that make alluring day-trips: **Bradford-on-Avon**, with its medieval bridge and terraces of ex-weavers' cottages; **Lacock**, whose abbey-turned-stately home incorporates a museum of photography; and **Corsham**, with its prized collection of Old Masters at Corsham Court.

West of Bath, **Bristol**, while not technically part of Somerset, is one of the dominant centres in the region and shares some of Bath's best features, such as its Georgian architecture and the River Avon winding through. Here, though, the tidal Avon was harnessed, and the city's skyline owes much to the riches that were funnelled through its harbour, fuelled by the transatlantic trade of tobacco, sugar and slaves. With its fierce creative energy and urban bustle, Bristol takes in more extremes, and has more of a contemporary, cosmopolitan view of life than Bath. Its verve and panache is expressed in everything from genre-defying music and eye-catching street art to cutting-edge design and technology, not to mention a dynamic range of bars, restaurants and clubs. The newly opened M-Shed museum celebrates Bristol's rich history and cultural diversity,

which you can explore further in the city's galleries and collections, its venerable churches and miscellaneous markets.

South of the Bath-Bristol axis, the countryside soon takes over, and some of Somerset's most appealing small towns are nestled among its rolling hills and sweeping marshland. **Wells** has one of the earliest and finest English Gothic cathedrals, and lies within easy reach of the **Mendip Hills**. Cutting through the country, they're not particularly high, but they are wilder than you'd expect, and surprisingly dramatic in parts, most jaw-droppingly so at **Cheddar Gorge**.

A short distance down the road, **Glastonbury** is distinguished for the ruins of its once-mighty abbey, but resonates among the New Age crowd for its tangled knot of Arthurian links and other mystical associations. Even the most cynical of sceptics would find it hard to deny that there's a certain aura about the town, not least in the peculiar

WHERE THE WILD THINGS ARE

Somerset isn't all rolling green fields and rich fertile pasture. From gorse-covered moors to towering sea cliffs, dry valleys to reed-swathed marshland, its varied landscapes cover a wide spectrum of habitats that are home to all creatures great and small. In the **Quantock Hills**, Somerset has the country's first Area of Outstanding Natural Beauty, a compact outcrop of upland heath and wooded combes harbouring adders, nightjars and red deer. The Quantocks share similar flora and fauna with nearby **Exmoor**, the region's only national park and the other destination for deer spotters. The more pronounced hills of the **Mendips**, another AONB to the north, are riddled with caves and cut through by two dramatic gorges, most famously at Cheddar, and are a great place to see badgers, bats and peregrine falcons. Lying between the two ranges, the mesmerizing wetlands of the **Somerset Levels** provide hands-down the best bird-watching in the South West, particularly among the reed beds and former peat-bogs of the Avalon Marshes; a number of the waders and migrants that call in here can also be seen in the estuaries, sand dunes and cliffs that make up Somerset's **coast**.

TOP 5 NATURE RESERVES

Exmoor Strikingly scenic national park abutting the Bristol Channel, blanketed in heather and gorse and home to herds of majestic red deer. See p.252

Shapwick Heath This vast reserve – the largest in the Somerset Levels – is rich in birdlife and makes a great place to watch otters swimming among the reeds. See p.179

Ubley Warren Former mining landscape, now buzzing with a variety of butterflies and birdlife. See p.158

West Sedgemoor Migrant waders out on the wet meadows and a huge heronry in the Swell Wood section. See p.185

Westhay Moor Brilliant bird-watching, and a reliable spot to catch the winter starling migration. See p.180

WHAT'S IN A NAME?

Somerset, perhaps more than any other county in England, is blessed with some truly spectacular **place names**. Where else would you find such intriguing-sounding villages as Nempnett Thrubwell, Furzy Knaps, Charlton Mackrell and Haselbury Plucknett? Many of these can be traced back to their **Celtic origins** – *crug*, the old Celtic word for "hill", for example, is buried away in names like Crewkerne and Cricket St Thomas. Others are derived from **Anglo-Saxon words**, such as Huish Episcopi, the prefix of which stems from *hus*, or "house", the suffix recalling the time when the Bishop of Bath and Wells played landlord to much of the county.

You'll see Currys (from *cwr*, meaning "border" or "edge"), Camels (a combination of *cant* and *mel*, which literally translates as "bare district") and Chews (a stream or river), but nothing crops up quite as much as Combe. From Monkton Combe to the extravagantly named Nyland cum Batcombe, it indicates a hollow or valley and is most often linked to the Celtic word *cwm*, though it also appears in Saxon, Norse and Irish languages.

promontory that is **Glastonbury Tor**. From the Tor, you can survey the **Somerset Levels** stretching out to the west – a captivating latticework of rhynes and ditches that's excellent terrain for walkers, cyclists and birders.

Continuing south, you'll come to a mix of modern and ancient sights around the unassuming towns of **Yeovil** and **Chard**, ranging from **Cadbury Castle** (another place recalling the mythology of King Arthur) and the Renaissance mansion of **Montacute House** to collections of cars and aeroplanes – though the pretty little hamstone hamlets and orchards heavy with cider apples are just as much of a draw. To the west lies **Taunton**, home to the new **Museum of Somerset**, a must for visitors to the region, and **Bridgwater**, with its Civil War memories. Either place would make a good departure point for forays into the **Quantock Hills**, perfect country for gentle hikes and home to some of Somerset's most exquisite churches.

In the far west of the region, straddling the Devon border, the wide open spaces of **Exmoor** beckon, traversed by a good network of walking routes. The moor reaches all the way to the coast, with high cliffs affording unforgettable vistas, and a string of picturesque villages providing shelter and refreshment. If it's seaside fun you're after, however, you'd do better to let your hair down in Somerset's coastal resorts, the biggest of which, **Weston-super-Mare** and **Minehead**, offer all the fun of the fair, though the smaller centres of **Clevedon** and **Burnham-on-Sea** have a more low-key, old-fashioned charm of their own.

At the other end of the region, East Somerset has an almost industrial feel around **Radstock** – once a booming coal-mining centre – but reverts to a more rural theme in places nearby, such as **Iford Manor**, where a gorgeous Italian Renaissance garden has been created, or along the **Colliers Way** cycle and walking route. The distant past can be explored in the remote **Stoney Littleton Long Barrow**, while two ruined fortresses – **Farleigh**

CLOCKWISE FROM TOP LEFT FROME; GUILD SHOP, BRISTOL; LYNMOUTH HARBOUR; WESTON SAND SCULPTURE FESTIVAL

SOMERSET SPECIALITIES

The pastoral landscape that constitutes much of Somerset provides a wealth of high-quality **produce**, the majority of it making the short journey from field to local farm shop, market stall or restaurant menu. The region is well known for its tangy cheeses and punchy ciders – all of which would make a gourmand giddy – but it's also worth sampling a few less familiar dishes. Here are five to try…

Bath chap Pigs' cheeks (and sometimes jawbones), salted, smoked and covered in breadcrumbs, served cold.

Chew Valley trout Brown trout, freshly hooked out of Chew Valley Lake, is a regional speciality, at its best when the cook lets the fish do the talking.

Eels Svelte and silky in texture, and delicious when smoked over beech and apple wood, as they are at Brown & Forrest in the Somerset Levels (see p.187).

Salt-marsh lamb Tender meat that owes its sweet, unusually aromatic taste to the variety of herbs and wild grasses that the lambs feed on in the low-tide marshes of the Severn Estuary.

Spelt Nutritious organic grain from Sharpham Park near Glastonbury that's finding its way onto more and more regional menus, in risottos, flans, home-baked breads and the like.

Hungerford Castle and **Nunney Castle** – recall a time of medieval strife. Close to Nunney, the vibrant shops and thriving cultural scene of **Frome** have placed this small town firmly on the map in recent years, and two nearby country piles across the Wiltshire border, **Longleat** and **Stourhead**, present a hoard of magnificent treasures – paintings, furniture and assorted gewgaws of every description. Longleat also boasts a panoply of family amusements and a safari park, while Stourhead has some of England's finest landscaped grounds.

Venturing further into Wiltshire, you can make easy excursions to **Salisbury**, one of England's greatest cathedral cities, and to one of the country's most iconic prehistoric sites, **Stonehenge**; much more than the famous stone circle, the site encompasses a range of archeological splendours that demand prolonged exploration.

When to go

If you're aiming to hit the beaches in and around Somerset's coastal resorts, you'll want to catch the hottest months between June and September, but if it's peace you're after, avoid the hectic **school summer holidays** (late July to early Sept), when accommodation can be hard to find and tough on the wallet. Otherwise, the region doesn't have much in the way of a seasonal pattern – any time of the year is a good time to visit. **Weekends and bank holidays**, however, can be busy in Bristol, Bath, and, to a lesser extent, Wells, where early booking of accommodation is recommended and (in Bath particularly) there will often be a minimum-stay requirement of a couple of nights. If you're intent on pursuing **outdoor activities**, the increased likelihood of cold and rainy days in **winter** can make a trip at this time of year risky, especially on Exmoor, which attracts more rain than the rest of the region, not to mention fog and wind.

Author picks

Our authors have spent years living, working and travelling in Bath, Bristol and Somerset, delighting in the region's hidden gems as much as its heavyweight sights. Here are a few of their unsung heroes...

Hidden in the City Tucked away down Bristol's Broad Street, the striking facade of the former Everard's Printing Works is one of the most startling in the city, even when you know it's there. p.87

Cider I Up Pulling in at Land's End Farm on the edge of the Wedmore plateau and sampling a generous taster of Roger Wilkins' farmhouse cider makes you feel like you've truly arrived in Somerset. p.181

Lord of the Manor Rambling *Brympton House* makes a gloriously quirky place to stay, with rooms accessed via winding turrets, a medieval breakfast hall and various wildfowl roaming the grounds. p.204

Making a Comeback Cranes have returned to the Somerset Levels (p.183), otters are out in force and the rare bittern is breeding again in Ham Wall National Nature Reserve (p.179), showing that conservation can work given half the chance.

Holier Than Thou Once you get the church bee in your bonnet, it quickly becomes an obsession. Somerset's churches are especially renowned for their pinnacled towers and amazing oak bench-ends, for example at Crowcombe (p.229) and Combe Florey (p.228) in the Quantocks.

Arts and Crafts Marvels abound at Tyntesfield, a flamboyant mansion outside Bristol that's being painstakingly returned to its glory days of Gothic grandeur. p.238

> Our author recommendations don't end here. We've flagged up our favourite places – a perfectly sited hotel, an atmospheric café, a special restaurant – throughout the guide, highlighted with the ★ symbol.

FROM TOP CRANES, SOMERSET LEVELS; EVERARD'S PRINTING WORKS; ORCHARD; WILKINS' CIDER FARM

23

things not to miss

It's not possible to see everything that Somerset has to offer in one trip – and we don't suggest you try. What follows, in no particular order, is a selective taste of the region's highlights, from beautiful beaches and outstanding national parks to fascinating wildlife encounters and unforgettable urban experiences. All highlights have a page reference to take you straight into the Guide, where you can find out more. Coloured numbers refer to chapters in the Guide.

1

1 CIDER
Page 29
Tasting traditional farmhouse cider straight from the barrel, and fresh from the surrounding orchards, is a quintessential Somerset experience.

2 THERMAE BATH SPA
Page 47
Take the waters at this cutting-edge facility in the UK's original spa town.

3 GLASTONBURY FESTIVAL
Page 176
The legendary musical mud bath in a field near Glastonbury has become a modern-day rite of passage.

4 BRISTOL INTERNATIONAL BALLOON FIESTA
Page 136
Night glows, novelty inflatables and the uplifting sight of a hundred hot-air balloons taking flight over the city.

18 BRIDGWATER CARNIVAL
Page 227

The culmination of Somerset's carnival season, with a train of floats so brightly illuminated they can allegedly be seen from space.

19 EXMOOR
Page 252

Ruggedly beautiful national park of rolling moorland, cloaked with heather and roamed by stocky ponies.

20 STONEHENGE
Page 307

The most famous stone circle in the world, and an unforgettable sight, either from the perimeter path or from within the sarsens themselves.

21 CHEDDAR GORGE
Page 155

Whether hiking the clifftop path or exploring the caves below, the deepest gorge in Britain makes for a singularly scenic day out.

22 BIRD-WATCHING ON THE SOMERSET LEVELS
Page 177

The rhynes and ditches of this striking marshland provide a spectacular backdrop for the best inland birding in the country, especially in winter, when the skies fill with millions of starlings.

23 MONTACUTE HOUSE
Page 200

Etched out of golden hamstone and full of period furnishings, this magnificent stately pile is set in acres of wooded parkland.

Itineraries

The following itineraries will take you right across the region, from the urbane delights of Bath and Bristol to longer stays in the countryside beyond. Dipping into Somerset's varied landscapes and exploring its rich tradition of folklore, they take in major destinations such as Glastonbury and Exmoor, as well as lesser-known gems like the island of Steep Holm.

A WEEKEND IN BATH

FRIDAY

Pulteney Bridge Take an introductory amble along the river and over Robert Adam's graceful bridge. **See p.49**

Dinner Sample some Moorish fennel *urid walis* at veggie restaurant *Demuths*. **See p.63**

SATURDAY

Roman Baths You'll need a whole morning for the informative showpiece that gives Bath its name. **See p.46**

Bath Abbey It's a short stroll across bustling Abbey Churchyard to the towering abbey and its superb vaulted ceiling. **See p.45**

Shopping Wander the Upper Town's warren of lanes, crammed with antique shops. **See p.67**

Dinner Treat yourself to a refined meal at the *Olive Tree*. **See p.64**

SUNDAY

Thermae Bath Spa Relax at this state-of-the-art spa, complete with indoor bath, steam rooms and a rooftop pool. **See p.47**

The Circus and the Royal Crescent Admire John Wood the Elder's architectural masterpiece, before taking in his son's majestic crescent, just a few steps away. **See p.54**

A WEEKEND IN BRISTOL

FRIDAY

M Shed Start with a thought-provoking rundown of Bristol and the people that make it tick. **See p.98**

Dinner Tuck into an *assiette* of pork terrines, scallops with salt-cod ravioli and other organic goodies at *Bordeaux Quay*. **See p.120**

SATURDAY

St Nicholas Market Browse the eclectic stalls in the Exchange before grabbing brunch in the Glass Arcade. **See p.87**

Park Street and Clifton Have a nose round Bristol Cathedral (**see p.103**) on your way up to Clifton (**see p.106**), where you can join a tour of the dramatic Suspension Bridge.

Dinner More meat than you can eat at *The Cow Shed* (**see p.123**) or trendy poolside dining at *Lido* (**see p.123**).

Afters Follow a slice of boho Berlin at *Hausbar* (**see p.128**) with a cool cocktail or two at *Hyde & Co* (**see p.128**).

SUNDAY

ss Great Britain Jump on a ferry down to the Great Western Dockyard and spend the morning exploring Brunel's beautifully restored iron ship. **See p.98**

ABOVE FROM LEFT BALLOONING OVER BRISTOL; THERMAE BATH SPA

THE GREAT OUTDOORS

The best of Mother Nature, from up among the clouds to hundreds of feet below ground. Allow a week to tick off all the walking, climbing and caving, including a couple of days on Exmoor – and another week to recover in a spa afterwards.

❶ Ballooning in Bristol Pick a still, sunny morning and float up, up and away, past the Suspension Bridge, over Bristol Harbour and across the city beyond. **See p.135**

❷ Bath Skyline Walk The six-mile circuit above Bath cuts through meadows and woodland, and affords fantastic views over its mellow terraced crescents. **See p.59**

❸ Cheddar Gorge The country's biggest gorge is the region's best activity centre, whether climbing, abseiling, caving or walking – or all of the above. **See p.155**

❹ Steep Holm Take a boat trip out into the Bristol Channel to this island nature reserve with its population of Muntjac deer. **See p.242**

❺ Westhay Moor National Nature Reserve Whether out on the trails or at a poolside hide, you'll spot plenty of birdlife at this tranquil reserve in the heart of the Avalon Marshes. **See p.180**

❻ Exmoor Expansive national park that sprawls across the border into Devon: join a red-deer safari, hit the bridleways on the back of a horse or set off on a windswept walk along Britain's tallest cliffs. **See p.252**

MYTHS AND LEGENDS

There should be enough intrigue here to keep you busy for a week or so, more if you want to tackle all of Glastonbury's legends or explore the landscape around Stonehenge.

❶ Stanton Drew The third-largest stone circle in the country is actually a ring of petrified locals, punished for celebrating on the Sabbath – or so they say. **See p.138**

❷ Jack and Jill Hill Take care climbing to the hilltop well in the village of Kilmersdon – people have been known to break their crown up here. **See p.291**

❸ Wookey Hole Cast into stone, the figure of the Wookey Hole Witch awaits visitors who venture underground at this network of atmospheric caverns. **See p.153**

❹ Glastonbury Take your pick, from Joseph of Arimathea to King Arthur, by way of holy thorns, fairy kings and the final resting place of the Cup of Christ. **See p.166**

❺ Burrow Mump Allegedly part of the fort that once sheltered Alfred from the Danes, the "mump" overlooks the marshland where the king charred his cakes. **See p.183**

❻ Cadbury Castle Soak up the spectacular views from this Iron Age hill fort, reputedly the sixth-century site of King Arthur's fabled Camelot. **See p.195**

❼ Stonehenge The enigmatic circle of sarsens is one of those rare places that can still send a shiver down your spine. **See p.307**

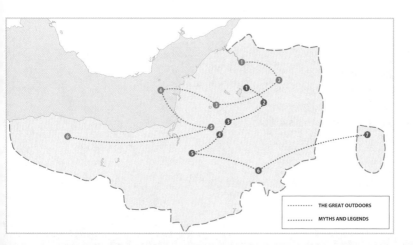

········· THE GREAT OUTDOORS

·········· MYTHS AND LEGENDS

TRAIN ON THE WEST SOMERSET RAILWAY

Basics

Getting there

Somerset's main centres – Bristol, Bath and Taunton – are well integrated into the UK's transport infrastructure, easily accessible by air, road and rail. Domestic and foreign flights use Bristol Airport, eight miles south of the city, while Exeter International Airport and Southampton Airport are also useful arrival points from elsewhere in the UK or from abroad, Exeter only an hour or so from Somerset's western reaches, Southampton with good links to Salisbury.

Bristol, Bath, Taunton and some other towns (such as Bradford-on-Avon, Bridgwater, Yeovil and Salisbury) are on the main rail network, while National Express and a few other private companies run bus services connecting these to all the UK's major cities. Drivers can access the region along the M4 motorway between London and Wales (passing close to Bristol and Bath) and the M5 between Birmingham and Exeter (good for Bristol, Glastonbury, the Quantock and Mendip hills and the coast).

Flights

Bristol International Airport (Ⓦ bristolairport.co.uk) is the West Country's busiest airport, with regular **flights** from Leeds-Bradford, Edinburgh, Glasgow, Aberdeen, Belfast and Newcastle in the UK, and from Rome, Milan, Madrid, Barcelona, Malaga, Prague, Dublin, Cork, Amsterdam, Paris, Nice, Berlin, Hannover, Dusseldorf and Brussels in Europe. On the south coast, **Southampton Airport** (Ⓦ southamptonairport.com) has regular flights from Leeds-Bradford, Edinburgh, Glasgow, Aberdeen, Belfast, Manchester and Newcastle in the UK, and from such European centres as Dublin, Amsterdam, Paris, Hannover, Dusseldorf and Brussels. In Devon, **Exeter International Airport** (Ⓦ exeter-airport.co.uk) has flight connections to Leeds-Bradford, Edinburgh, Glasgow, Aberdeen, Belfast, Manchester and Newcastle in the UK, and international connections to Paris, Rennes, Bergerac, Dublin, Amsterdam, Malaga, Alicante and Faro. There are also seasonal flights to and from a range of other European towns and cities from these airports, as well as summer connections between Bristol and Orlando, Florida. Operators include budget airlines and smaller companies such as easyJet and flybe, with single fares as low as £50, dependent on season and demand.

There are frequent **bus connections** from Bristol Airport to Bristol (see p.114), less frequent services to Weston-super-Mare, but none at all to Bath. If you're arriving at London's Heathrow Airport, you'll find direct connections to Bristol and Bath on National Express buses.

By train

First Great Western (Ⓦ firstgreatwestern.co.uk) is the main **train** company serving the region, with twice-hourly services to Bath and Bristol from London Paddington, the journey to Bath taking around 1hr 30min, to Bristol 1hr 45min. There are also frequent services to Bristol from Cardiff, Birmingham and Exeter, and direct services from London Paddington and Reading to Westbury, Castle Cary and Taunton. South West Trains (Ⓦ southwesttrains.co.uk) operate from London Waterloo to Salisbury, leaving twice hourly and taking about 1hr 25min, with some trains continuing to Westbury and Yeovil. There are regular connections between Salisbury, Bath and Bristol, stopping at Westbury and Bradford-on-Avon en route. For other stations on the rail network (Weston-super-Mare, Highbridge & Burnham, Avoncliff, Frome and Bruton) you'll usually need to change at Bristol or Westbury. Megatrain (Ⓦ megatrain.com) runs budget train services to Salisbury, Yeovil, Bath and Bristol from London Waterloo, with limited timetables and sometimes longer journey times.

Train **tickets** in the UK are notoriously expensive, but you can find relatively cheap fares by booking early. As a rule, the earlier you buy them, the cheaper they will be, but the more subject to restrictions; the most expensive ones are those sold on the day of travel and those with more flexibility. Rail cards and concessionary fares are available (see p.24).

By bus

National Express (Ⓦ nationalexpress.com), covering most of the UK's long-distance **bus** routes, has direct services from London's Victoria Coach Station to Bath, Bristol, Salisbury and Taunton. The journey from London to Bristol takes around 2hr 45min, to Bath 3hr 20min. Bristol also has direct links with Birmingham, Swansea, Cardiff, Manchester and Southampton, while Salisbury has connections from Southampton and Portsmouth. The budget bus service Megabus (Ⓦ megabus.com) runs coaches to Bristol from London, Birmingham, Exeter, Cardiff, Manchester and Leeds. Berry's Coaches (Ⓦ berryscoaches.co.uk) operates a service two or three times daily from London's Hammersmith Bus Station to Yeovil, Bridgwater, Taunton, Wellington

24 **BASICS** GETTING AROUND

and Wincanton. As with trains, National Express and Megabus **tickets** bought on the day cost more.

Getting around

Getting from A to B is one of the pleasures of Somerset. Inevitably, however, the way isn't always smooth. Drivers will face motorway snarl-ups and slow-moving traffic on minor roads, while negotiating Bath and Bristol by car can be a nightmare. Users of public transport will find high fares and limited networks, and even walkers and cyclists will occasionally despair at the ubiquity of motor traffic. Nonetheless, public transport will get you to the vast majority of places mentioned in the Guide, and driving, cycling and walking will enable you to reach everywhere else. For all public transport routes and timetables, contact Traveline (see box below).

By train

Trains provide the easiest means of moving between Bath and Bristol (taking less than 15min), and are useful for reaching some points further afield – the snag is that there aren't that many places in the area that you can reach by train. Heading southwest from Bristol, you can get to Weston-super-Mare, Highbridge & Burnham (for Burnham-on-Sea), Bridgwater, Taunton and Tiverton (for Exmoor); from Bath there are trains to Avoncliff, Bradford-on-Avon, Westbury and Salisbury, and from Westbury you can board a train to Frome, Bruton, Castle Cary and Yeovil. And that's about it. Of the two heritage train routes in the region – both seasonal – the **West Somerset Railway** (see p.230)

is moderately useful for exploring the western flank of the Quantock Hills and the coast to Minehead, though the stations are often quite far from the villages and the best walking country. Elsewhere, train stations are fairly well placed for town centres, and the services that exist are usually punctual.

Cyclists should be aware that they won't always find space for bikes on trains, though places can be booked at least 24hr before travel. For all reservations and information on services, contact **National Rail Enquiries** (see box below).

Tickets can be bought at the station or online, or onboard if a station is unstaffed; otherwise, ticketless travel can result in having to pay the maximum fare for the journey. On all rail journeys, under-5s travel free and children aged 5–15 normally qualify for a fifty percent discount of the full fare. If you're travelling exclusively in Somerset and for a limited period, it probably won't be worth investing in one of the various **rail cards** available, which give a year's discounted travel over the national train network to families, travellers with disabilities, those aged 16–25 and those aged 60 or over (the National Rail website has full details of these). More useful for limited periods is the **Freedom Travel Pass** offered by First, valid for travel on all First trains and most First bus routes in Bristol, Bath and North Somerset, and available from bus drivers, train conductors and stations. A one-day Freedom Pass costs £7.80/8.30 for off-peak/anytime travel in Bristol, £10/10.60 for Bristol and Bath; a one-week Freedom Pass costs £37 for Bristol; £47 for Bristol and Bath; £57 for Bristol, Bath and Weston-super-Mare. Monthly passes are also available.

By bus

Somerset's **bus** network is infinitely more comprehensive than the train one, though even buses don't reach some of the remoter corners of the county, particularly on Exmoor. The main operator

---

PUBLIC TRANSPORT CONTACTS

Berry Coaches ☎01823 331356,
ⓦberrycoaches.co.uk
First ☎0845 602 0156, ⓦfirstgroup.com
National Express ☎08717 818178,
ⓦnationalexpress.com
National Rail Enquiries ☎08457 484950,
ⓦnationalrail.co.uk
Nippy Bus ☎01935 823888,
ⓦnippybus.co.uk
Quantock Motor Services ☎01823 430202,

ⓦquantockmotorservices.co.uk
South West Coaches ☎01963 33124,
ⓦsouthwestcoaches.co.uk
Stagecoach South West ☎01392 427711,
ⓦstagecoachbus.com
Traveline ☎0871 200 2233,
ⓦtravelinesw.com
Travelplus ⓦtravelplus.acislive.com
WebberBus ☎0800 096 3039,
ⓦwebberbus.com

in the region is First, though Stagecoach South West, WebberBus and Quantock Motor Services also operate some services. Summaries of schedules and routes are given in every chapter of the Guide; bear in mind that these normally only refer to direct services, and many more places than those listed are reachable by bus with a change or two. Services on Sundays drop sharply, and winter also sees a reduction of routes and frequencies.

Tickets are purchased on boarding the bus. Return tickets are normally cheaper than two singles. Children under 5 travel free and those aged 5–15 get a discount of around a third depending on the route. Apart from journeys made during peak times (Mon–Fri before 9am), free travel is available for those aged 60 and over and for travellers with disabilities on presentation of a concessionary pass, available from the local authority where you reside.

Dedicated bus travellers can benefit from **travel passes**. First offers a FirstDay pass, valid for one day's travel on most First bus routes throughout the region (£7.50, with separate prices for children, students, seniors and families). For longer journeys you might consider AvonPlus, allowing a week's travel in Bristol, Somerset and West Wiltshire (£32), or AvonPlus FirstTen, valid for any ten journeys on the region's bus network (£38). Stagecoach, with a much more limited network in Somerset, offers a Dayrider valid for travel on all Stagecoach services on one day (£4.50), and a Megarider Gold for travel over a week (£23). There's also the Freedom Travel Pass (see opposite), which also applies to train travel.

Traveline provides full information on all services. **Travelplus** may also be useful, providing live updates on schedules in Bristol, Bath and North Somerset.

By car

Touring Somerset **by car** may free you of the limitations of the public transport network but it does have its downsides. Most of the county's roads were originally designed for horses and carts, and the M5 motorway, while providing an easy way to cover the distance between Bristol and West Somerset, can get horrifically jammed, especially during school holidays and on bank holiday weekends. Somerset's "A" roads – mostly single-carriageway – are subject to long hold-ups too, as a result of roadworks, farm traffic and slow-moving caravans. Drivers should keep alert for constantly changing speed limits (speed cameras are fairly ubiquitous, particularly around Bristol and Bath) and, on Exmoor above all, should be aware of sheep and ponies wandering onto the roads (including at night) – game birds can also be a hazard.

Lastly, a car can prove an encumbrance when visiting towns and villages. The only way to get acquainted with many of the places covered in this Guide is on foot, and the first thing drivers should do on arrival is to find somewhere to stow the car. Consequently, **parking** can be a constant preoccupation, and you'll save a lot of time by either heading straight for a central car park, or, where it exists, locating a **Park & Ride** (Wparkandride.net), where free car parks on the periphery of towns are connected to the centre by frequent buses. Bristol, Bath, Salisbury and Taunton all have Park & Ride schemes. For other car parks, keep a bundle of change handy; Bristol and Bath are more expensive, but elsewhere you'll pay around £1 for an hour; parking at meters will be more expensive and time restricted.

If you want to **rent a car**, all the main rental companies have branches in Somerset, mostly in Bristol and Bath. You'll normally pay around £30 for a day, £50 for a weekend, and from £120 for a week; check out Wcarrentals.co.uk for the best deals.

In the event of an **emergency breakdown**, contact the RAC (T0844 774 7279 or 0800 828282, Wrac.co.uk), the AA (T0800 887766 or 0121 275 3746, Wtheaa.com) or Green Flag (T0800 051 0636, Wgreenflag.com) for roadside assistance – though this will be expensive unless you're already a member. They also provide **route-planning** information and notice of traffic conditions.

Walking and cycling

Hilly Somerset might not be the first place that springs to mind when it comes to getting about **on foot** or **by bike**, but the county has an impressive range of shared-use walking and cycling routes, some of them along old rail lines and canal towpaths, that make legwork comparatively painless. The obvious examples are the **Bristol and Bath Railway Path**, the **Avon & Kennet Canal**, connecting Bath and Bradford-on-Avon, and the **Bridgwater & Taunton Canal**. As for terrain, the **Somerset Levels** are, as the name suggests, as flat as you could wish, making for easy walking and riding in the area between Glastonbury and the Quantock Hills. For walkers, the **South West Coast Path** is the most satisfying way of exploring Exmoor's seaboard, though this can be arduous in parts. A few other long-distance trails also cross Somerset – for more on waking and cycling in Somerset generally and on the various routes, see p.31. **Bike rental** shops are available in Bristol (see p.116), Bath (p.61), Bradford-on-Avon (p.72), Glastonbury (p.173), Taunton (p.221), Langport (p.186) and Minehead (p.251). Rates are around £10–20 per day.

Accommodation

Somerset has every kind of accommodation, with options to suit all tastes and budgets. The choice is of course widest in Bath and Bristol, and the seaside resorts of Weston-super-Mare and Minehead also have a good selection, while village inns, farmhouse B&Bs and campsites add to the stock outside the towns.

However, even this wide choice can narrow down drastically at certain times. Accommodation in Bath is scarce at weekends and during festivals, seaside resorts get booked up early over the summer, and vacancies are at a premium in and around places like Glastonbury during the Glastonbury Festival, and Shepton Mallet while the Royal Bath & West Show is on. Moreover, some places impose conditions, such as a minimum stay of two nights in Bath at weekends and up to a week in the seaside resorts in summer. For greater availability and lower rates, it's always worth considering other options close by: Bradford-on-Avon instead of Bath, for example, or Dunster rather than Minehead. Most tourist offices keep abreast of local vacancies and provide a free booking service.

Hotels, inns and B&Bs

Hotels in Somerset range from luxurious country-house retreats to seedy seaside dives with peeling wallpaper. At the top end, with rates starting from around £150 per room per night, you can expect every comfort, with a decent restaurant, good leisure facilities and spacious rooms, perhaps overlooking acres of grounds. Many have the air of exclusive clubs, with deliberately old-fashioned

---

ACCOMMODATION PRICES

For all accommodation reviewed in the Guide, we provide approximate prices **in high season** (roughly July–Sept), referring to the lowest price for one night's stay in a **double or twin room** in a hotel or B&B, the price of a bed in **dorm accommodation** in a hostel (and of a double room if available), and of a **pitch** in a campsite (sites sometimes charge per person, instead of, or in addition to the pitch price). Prices in hotels and B&Bs may be lower between Sunday and Thursday and for stays of more than a couple of days; it's often worth looking online for the best deals.

---

style and trappings; others might come into the "boutique hotel" category, with dark colours, sleek bathrooms and a blend of traditional and contemporary design. At the lower end of the scale, starting from around £80 a night, hotels are pretty indistinguishable from B&Bs (the legal distinction is largely technical) – a few rooms, perhaps with parking spaces and a part-time reception desk. That's not to say the cheaper places are necessarily tawdry; many smaller hotels offer heaps of character as well as the most attentive service.

Increasingly, **room rates** are determined according to demand, with prices generally higher at weekends and other peak periods. In any case, it's always worth looking online for cheaper deals than the official tariffs, and sites such as Ⓦlastminute .com will often throw up top-notch hotels at rock-bottom prices.

Somerset has a rich selection of **inns**, or pubs with rooms, which at their best are traditional old coaching inns, thatched and rickety, and often found in the most out-of-the-way places. They're not all wonderful, but the best ones are worth seeking out for a bit of authentic period atmosphere and a decent pint to boot. Choose your room carefully, though – you may not want to stay directly above the bar.

B&Bs, starting from around £50 per double room per night, are ubiquitous throughout Somerset and come in every shape and hue. The majority are just two or three simple rooms in a modestly sized house with minimal facilities, though most places now offer either en-suite or separate but private bathrooms. Grander ones, or "boutique B&Bs", may have a lot more style, more space and generous gardens, sometimes with a swimming pool or spa facilities as an added draw. A substantial number of B&Bs have free wi-fi connections, but note that many don't accept credit cards (we've mentioned where this is the case).

"**Restaurants with rooms**" also come into this category, where a quality restaurant, usually in a rural area, offers two or three well-appointed guest rooms in a traditional setting. These places will often appeal to foodies unwilling to move very far from the table after a gastronomic blow-out, but they're usually smart and well maintained, making them a good option.

Hostels

Somerset has six **hostels** belonging to the Youth Hostels Association (YHA; Ⓦyha.org.uk), in Bath, Bristol, Street, Exford, Cheddar and Minehead, and

---

SOMERSET'S QUIRKIEST ACCOMMODATION

Gypsy Caravan Breaks, Pitney Discover your inner gypsy in this cosy caravan parked in an apple orchard. See p.186.

Harptree Court, Chew Valley Wake with the birds (literally) in a fully equipped treehouse. See p.139.

Kildare Lodge, Minehead An eccentric, Lutyens-influenced version of Tudor architecture. See p.251.

Pack o' Cards Inn, Combe Martin As the name says, the building is modelled on a pack of cards. See p.277.

Yarlington Yurt, near Wincanton Glamping with a twist – a yurt furnished in eighteenth-century French style. See p.197.

---

the area of Wiltshire covered by the Guide has two, in Salisbury and Cholderton, near Stonehenge. Modernized and less institutionalized than they once were, YHA hostels – affiliated to the global Hostelling International network and open to non-members with a £3 surcharge – often have a choice of rooms catering to individuals, couples and families, as well as cooking facilities and canteens. Prices fluctuate according to demand, but might be £20–30 per person in high summer. Book early, as these places often fill up with groups.

As well as these, the region has a handful of independent or **backpacker hostels** in the region (most in Bath and Bristol), usually cheaper than YHA hostels, but often scruffier too, and with fewer restrictions. However, all have catering facilities and wi-fi connections, and are ideal for meeting up with other travellers.

Most hostels have single-sex dorms of 4 to 8 beds, and many also have en-suite doubles and family rooms; listings in the Guide show prices for individual beds and, where they exist, double rooms.

Campsites

Camping makes a great alternative to fully serviced accommodation, whether under canvas or in a motorhome or caravan. Somerset has a range of campsites, ranging from farmers' fields with basic washing facilities to mega-sites equipped for family holidays in or near the seaside resorts. Larger sites have shops, restaurants and evening entertainment, and even smaller places may have laundries, shops, swimming pools, playgrounds and other children's amusements. Areas holding tents are usually separated from parts reserved for motorhomes or caravans, and many of the larger sites offer static caravans to rent on a weekly basis. Most campsites close in the winter months, though dates tend to be flexible, varying according to the weather and demand. **Prices** for tent pitches start at around £5 per person per night in low season

rising to around £12 in summer, depending on the facilities. You'll find descriptions and reviews of most sites at Ⓦ ukcampsite.co.uk.

On Exmoor there are also one or two **camping barns**, amounting to little more than barns or large rooms with sleeping platforms and basic cooking and washing facilities. Some of these are managed by or affiliated to the YHA, and can be booked through their website; prices are in the region of £6–12 a night. Unlike on Dartmoor, wild camping on Exmoor is illegal.

Rented accommodation

Rented accommodation in self-catering cottages or apartments can prove a more satisfying and economical option. Some places, such as those managed by the Landmark Trust and the National Trust, are in historic buildings with plenty of character. Most rentals are only available by the week (usually Friday to Friday or Saturday to Saturday), and the best ones are often booked up months in advance, especially on the coast, but it's always worth checking for cancellations, and shorter stays are often available in low season. Prices begin from around £350 for a week's stay in a one-bedroom property in high season. Local tourist offices can supply lists of properties.

HOLIDAY PROPERTY AGENCIES

Classic Cottages ☎ 01326 555555, Ⓦ classic.co.uk. Rural properties in the West Country, with a small selection in Somerset.

Helpful Holidays ☎ 01647 433593, Ⓦ helpfulholidays.com. A range of cottage rentals throughout the West Country, including several on Exmoor.

Hoseasons ☎ 0844 847 1356, Ⓦ hoseasons.co.uk. Nationwide company whose Somerset properties include cottages, cabins with hot tubs and caravans, including in the Chew Valley, the Quantocks and Exmoor.

Landmark Trust ☎ 01628 825925, Ⓦ landmarktrust.org.uk. Stay in historic properties, including Bath's Beckford's Tower, a priory near Weston-super-Mare and the attic rooms of a regimental museum in

Salisbury's Cathedral Close.

National Trust Holiday Cottages ☎ 0844 800 2070,
ⓦ nationaltrustcottages.co.uk. Lodgings in 18 National Trust properties in
Somerset and Wiltshire, including on the Tyntesfield and Stourhead
estates and in the Trust-owned villages of Lacock and Selworthy.

Rural Retreats ☎ 01386 701177, ⓦ ruralretreats.co.uk. Upmarket
accommodation in restored historic buildings, including a Georgian
apartment in Bath and a former toll house in Nether Stowey.

Food and drink

In recent decades, Somerset – and particularly Bristol – has embraced the Slow Food Movement, with seemingly even the simplest café now sourcing its products locally, and using seasonal (and often organic) ingredients where possible. Cutting-edge cocktail bars are generally limited to Bristol and, to a lesser extent, Bath, though traditional pubs are still going strong, in many cases with a slight tweak of philosophy that sees them now combining Real Ales and refined food.

You'll be spoilt for choice in the big cities, with their huge range of independent cafés and innovative restaurants catering for every taste and budget. It's here (and in Castle Combe and the Chew Valley) that you'll find the region's four **Michelin-star** restaurants – *Casamia* (see p.126), *Lucknam Park* (see p.64), *Manor House* (see p.77) and *The Pony and Trap* (see p.139) – and the best **vegetarian** restaurants, such as *Café Maitreya* (see p.125) and *Demuths* (see p.63).

There are some great **community cafés** elsewhere in the county, with teashops in notable abundance in Exmoor, though the traditional restaurant has faded of late, and in many smaller towns and villages, you'll generally find the best chefs running the kitchens of **gastropubs**. The menus at many of these are often built around "Modern British" cuisine, which at its best memorably marries local, seasonal produce with ingredients and techniques from the Mediterranean and Southeast Asia.

No matter where you eat, though, the unifying factor throughout is Somerset itself, whose rich pastures provide a bounty of **meat** (particularly Mendip lamb and Exmoor horned sheep) and **dairy products** (good-quality Somerset brie and goat's cheese in addition to Exmoor blue and its world-famous Cheddar). There's also fruit from its plentiful **orchards**, while sharing a border with Devon means freshly caught **seafood** (scallops, mussels, hake and the like) is a given on most menus.

Markets and farm shops

Somerset's rich agricultural heritage is celebrated at numerous weekly or monthly **farmers' markets** and other showcase events: the Levels' Best market at Montacute House near Yeovil (see p.200), Bristol's monthly Slow Food Market (see p.88) and Bath's

FARMERS' MARKETS

Axbridge	First Sat 9am–1pm	**Highbridge**	First Fri 9am–noon
Bath	Every Sat 9am–1.30pm	**Lynton**	First Sat 10am–12.30pm
Bradford-on-Avon	Third Thurs 9am–1.30pm	**Martock**	Second Sat 10am–1pm
Brent Knoll	Every Tues 10am–4pm	**Midsomer Norton**	First Sat 9am–1pm
Bridgwater	Second Fri 9am–2pm	**Minehead**	Every Fri 8.30am–2.30pm
Bristol	Every Wed 9.30am–2.30pm	**Taunton**	Every Thurs 9am–3pm
Burnham-on-Sea	Last Fri 9am–1pm	**Watchet**	Every Wed 10am–4pm
Chard	Every Sat 9am–2pm	**Wellington**	First & third Sat 9am–1pm
Cheddar	Third Sat 9am–1pm	**Wells**	Every Wed & Sat 9am–2.30pm
Crewkerne	Third Sat 9am–1pm	**Weston-super-Mare**	Second Sat 9am–12.30pm
Dulverton	Every Fri 9.30am–1pm	**Wincanton**	First Fri 9am–1pm
Frome	Second & last Sat 9am–1pm		
Glastonbury	Last Sat 9am–1pm		

DRINK UP YE CIDER

I am a cider drinker / I drinks it all of the day
I am a cider drinker / It soothes all me troubles away
Ooh arrh, ooh arrh ay / Ooh arrh, ooh arrh ay   I am a Cider Drinker, The Wurzels

Nothing is quite as synonymous with Somerset as **cider**, a drink ingrained in the regional identity and one that – in some parts of the country, at least – still carries clichéd connotations of a sozzled yokel dozing in a hayfield with an empty flagon hanging from his hand. While the image is encouraged to some extent by Scrumpy & Western groups like The Wurzels, the market has moved on. Cider has enjoyed something of a renaissance in recent years, thanks largely to Irish firm Magners, who poured their cider over ice and marketed it to the masses as a refreshing summer tipple.

Traditional farmhouse cider is made with a variety of **cider apples** (usually a mix of bittersweets and bittersharps) and nothing more. The apples are harvested in the autumn, a process also known as a "scrump" from the nineteenth-century practice of stealing apples from a neighbouring orchard – and from where "scrumpy" derives its name. They're pulped, mixed with straw and racked into layers (or "cheeses") to be pressed and then naturally fermented in oak barrels for between eight months and two years. The fermented juice is blended – the key to achieving a well-balanced cider in terms of sweetness and acidity – filtered, and sweetened if necessary (all cider apples press out dry).

Farmhouse cider is **dry, medium or sweet** (medium is usually a blend of the other two) and, more often than not, still rather than sparkling. What constitutes scrumpy varies between producers and can signify a rough, sharp and often potent cider, or simply draught (unpasteurized) cider served straight from the barrel; either way, it's always cloudy. In recent years, several producers have started creating single-variety ciders using just one of Somerset's 85 different types of cider apple, such as Yarlington Mill, Stoke Red, Dabinett or, perhaps most famously, Kingston Black. Burrow Hill (see p.206) also make a bottle-fermented sparkling cider, which is developed in the same way as champagne, as well as a highly regarded cider brandy.

You can learn more about the cider-making process at **cider farms** such as Sheppey's near Taunton (see p.220) and Perry's in Dowlish Wake near Ilminster (see p.209).

Guildhall Market (see p.69), which is becoming increasingly popular with foodies.

On a smaller scale, you can stock up on self-catering supplies or pick up a tasty souvenir or two at the resourceful little **farm shops** that dot the region, where the ciders are local, the chutneys home-made and the eggs still warm; we've highlighted some of the best ones in the Guide.

FOOD FESTIVALS

Love Food Festival Throughout the year Seasonal festivals – mostly in Bristol but also in Bath and the odd regional venue such as Dyrham Park – championing local produce and producers.
🌐 lovefoodfestival.com

Exmoor Food Festival Sept & Oct Week-long platter of culinary events, food trails and one-off menus at restaurants throughout the region. 🌐 exmoorfoodfestival.co.uk

Organic Food Festival Sept Bristol's Harbourside hosts Europe's first (and foremost) organic extravaganza, with livestock and live bands combining in a real festival atmosphere. 🌐 organicfoodfestival.co.uk

South Somerset Food Festival Sept & Oct Fifty events – mainly food markets and fairs – spread over nine days and held at venues such as Montacute House and East Lambrook Manor Gardens.

Drink

Somerset has a wealth of public houses, with a wide variety of contemporary **bars** and ancient coaching **inns** in Bath and Bristol, and some gloriously **traditional pubs** and **cider houses** in the countryside beyond: cosy, oak-beamed taverns with open fires that offer a fine range of hand-pumped Real Ales and local ciders from a barrel.

As well as the region's famous farmhouse **ciders**, there are also plenty of very good **apple juices** available, with some cider-producers making up to twenty varieties.

Cider and perry

Herefordshire folk may argue to the contrary, but if the apples haven't been freshly picked from a dew-kissed Somerset orchard then it isn't really **cider**. It's widely recognized that England has three vintage areas for growing cider apples – and all of them are in Somerset. Consequently, the region is home to large-scale, supermarket-savvy producers like Gaymers (makers of Blackthorn) and Brothers, though the gap between their offerings and a pint of traditional Somerset farmhouse cider is so big that they're virtually a different drink.

There are around forty cider producers in Somerset, and most pubs will have at least one variety of **Thatchers** (see p.161) and **Ashton Press** on tap, with bottles of **Orchard Pig** in the fridge; some will have half a dozen or so barrels out the back – specialist cider houses considerably more – with a good percentage coming from local producers such as **Wilkins** (see p.181) and **Hecks** (see p.173).

Most cider producers will also make a **perry** (pear cider) or two, a slightly sweeter drink produced using pretty much the same method; it's been growing in popularity in recent years but is still difficult to find in pubs.

Beer

Although somewhat overshadowed by their fruity cousins, Somerset's good local **beers** stand up well in comparison to any of the brews produced in more renowned centres like Yorkshire and Kent. The vast majority are **Real Ales**, many of them CAMRA award-winners; CAMRA, the Campaign for Real Ale (Ⓦ camra.org.uk), also recognizes pubs that contribute to the survival of this brewing craft, of which the county has many.

The biggest local breweries, **Bath Ales** and **Butcombe Bitter**, own their own pubs – *The Salamander* in Bath (see p.66) is a great place to sample the former, *The Lamb* in Axbridge (see p.161) the latter – though an independent "freehouse" is best if you want to try a range of local beers. Breweries to look out for include: **Cheddar Ales**, with their zippy Potholer golden ale; **Moor Beer** (from Pitney on the Somerset Levels), who do a particularly good chocolatey porter; **Cotleigh** (from Wiveliscombe, on the edge of Exmoor National Park), notable for their Honey Buzzard, heavy with local honey; the **Quantock Brewery**, whose rich Royal Stag is a traditional IPA; **RCH** (from West Hewish, near Weston-super-Mare), makers of the citrusy Pitchfork; **Exmoor Ales** (another Wiveliscombe brewer), creators of the first golden ale in the country, Exmoor Gold; and **Glastonbury Ales**, whose Mystery Tor is perhaps best appreciated in Glastonbury itself.

Regional brewers making lagers and stouts are harder to come by, though Bristol has a couple of recommended outfits: **Zerodegrees** microbrewery, who produce both their pilsner and black lager – as well as fruit beers and a German-style wheat beer – on site (see p.127); and **Bristol Beer Factory**, who stock Hefe (also a wheat beer) and their multi-

award-winning Milk Stout at their floating pub, *The Grain Barge* (see p.127).

Sports and outdoor activities

Football and rugby are popular in Somerset – the former more so in the cities, the latter in the countryside – though perhaps cricket is the quintessential Somerset pastime. The county's rolling hills, dramatic coastline and network of trails make it classic walking and horseriding territory, while some of the best fishing in the country is to be had in its lakes, ponds, rivers and streams.

Spectator sports

Somerset sports fans have enjoyed a mixed time of it in recent years, with the fortunes of the local rugby and cricket teams ebbing and flowing, while Bristol City, the region's main football team, have flirted with promotion to the Premiership but never quite yet made the leap.

Football

Football is the main sporting passion in Somerset's towns, particularly in Bristol, though as in the rest of the South West the Premier League has yet to be graced by a team from this neck of the woods. Bristol City (see p.135) were just one game shy of reaching the Promised Land in 2008, and currently try to repeat the feat each year in the Championship (despite the name, football's second tier); Yeovil Town play in League One (the third tier); Bristol Rovers (see p.135), established in 1883 and the oldest club in the region, in League Two (the fourth tier); and Bath City, a semi-professional team, just outside the Football League, in the Blue Square Bet Premier.

Rugby

Bath's sporting strength lies in **rugby**, and its rugby union team – known as Bath Rugby since the game turned professional in 1996 – play in the Aviva Premiership (☎ 0844 448 1865, Ⓦ bathrugby.com; tickets from £20, £13 for under-17s). The club were the dominant force in English rugby during the mid-1980s and 1990s, winning 17 trophies during that time, including the Heineken Cup in 1998. Their star has faded somewhat in the professional era, though, with the European Challenge Cup win of 2008 their only silverware since. Bristol – also known as Bristol Rugby (see p.135) – have always toiled in the shadow of their more illustrious neighbours and currently play in the second-tier Championship.

Cricket

The soundtrack of Somerset sport is the thwack of willow on leather, and **cricket** is the most popular game out in the countryside – there are over 75 cricket grounds in the county, with a dozen in Taunton alone. Cricket was first played here over 260 years ago, although it wasn't until 1875 that Somerset County Cricket Club was formed, when the "Gentlemen of Somerset" beat their opponents from Devon. The County Ground in Taunton (see p.218) has seen plenty of high and low points since, though recent form (the 2010 season was one of the most successful in the club's history) bodes well for the future. Ironically, Gloucestershire County Cricket Club play most of their games in Bristol (see p.135).

Walking

Somerset's lush pastures and rolling hills make for glorious walking country – the Mendips, Quantocks and Blackdown Hills provide some particularly memorable hikes, while Exmoor National Park alone is blessed with over six hundred miles of footpaths and bridleways. There are countless rambles around the county's lakes and reservoirs, and gentle loops leading out from most country villages (check with local tourist offices or see ⓦ visitsomerset.com).

Waymarked walks are often the best way of exploring a region, and Somerset is no exception. The **River Avon Trail** (23 miles; ⓦ riveravontrail.org .uk), which heads upstream from Pill through the Avon Gorge to Pulteney Bridge, is a great introduc-

tion to Bristol and Bath; the fifty-mile **West Mendip Way** (see box, p.153) joins together the highlights of the Mendips; the Somerset Levels are at their finest along the fifty-mile **River Parrett Trail** (see box, p.208) – as are parts of South Somerset, with the best of the rest revealed on the **Leland Trail** (28 miles), a rolling route from the Alfred Tower east of Bruton to Stoke-sub-Hamdon; the 36-mile **Quantock Greenway** (see box, p.229) links the prettiest villages in that range; while Exmoor is essentially one big path-laden park.

Hardcore hikers will be pleased to note that England's longest National Trail, the **South West Coast Path** (see box, p.249), kicks off at Minehead, finishing some 630 miles (and around 55 days) later in Poole Harbour. A couple of other long-distance cross-country routes run through the region: the **Monarch's Way** (615 miles; ⓦ themonarchsway .com), which follows King Charles II's escape route from the Battle of Worcester down to Shoreham in Sussex, spends more time in Somerset than any other county, while the **Macmillan Way** (290 miles; ⓦ macmillanway.org), from Boston in Lincolnshire to Abbotsbury in Dorset, cuts down past Bath and Bradford-on-Avon to Castle Cary, where Douglas Macmillan, the charity's founder, was born; a branch path from here, the **Macmillan Way West** (102 miles), heads across the Somerset Levels, the Quantocks and Exmoor to Barnstaple on the North Devon coast.

There are several further "linking" routes across the county, including the **Liberty Trail** (28 miles), which follows in the footsteps of the Monmouth Rebellion, from Ham Hill to Lyme Regis in Dorset, and connects the Leland Trail with the South West Coast Path; the **Limestone Link** (36 miles), which joins the Cotswold Way and the West Mendip Way; and the **Somerset Way** (116 miles), connecting the South West Coast Path with the Cotswold Way. Trail

---

TOP 5 WALKS

Bath Skyline Walk Six-mile circuit around the surrounding hills; meandering though woodlands and across peaceful meadows, it takes in a variety of sites, including an Iron Age fort and the eighteenth-century folly of Sham Castle. See p.59.
Charterhouse Numerous trails in a striking former mining landscape, across lovely little nature reserves, past World War II bunkers and around the remnants of Roman and Victorian lead workings. See p.157.
Cheddar Gorge Walk Three-mile circuit

around Cheddar Gorge's precipitous cliffs, with great views over the towering rock faces and opportunities to strike off on longer hikes over the Mendips. See p.156.
Lynmouth to Watersmeet Two-mile riverside ramble, tracing the East Lyn inland to picturesque Watersmeet, where it "meets" Hoar Oak Water. See p.272.
Wills Neck Follow the easy path from Dead Woman's Ditch to the equally oddly named Wills Neck, the highest point on the Quantocks. See p.228.

maps for all walks are available online, and it's worth buying a map to take with you if you plan to do a lot of walking (see p.36).

Cycling

Bristol is the home of Sustrans, the **National Cycle Network** (Ⓦ sustrans.org.uk), whose first route – now called Route 4 – was the Bristol and Bath Railway Path (see box, p.116). Bristol was also named the UK's first Cycling City in 2008, and is consequently pretty geared up for cyclists, with plenty of cycle lanes and green spaces.

Of the five other Sustrans routes that run through Somerset, **The West Country Way**, a regional section of Route 3, gives the best overview of the area: leaving Devon, it traverses Exmoor and follows canal towpaths to Bridgwater, before heading across the Somerset Levels – a great place for recreational cycling thanks to its pancake-flat terrain – and up to Bristol via Glastonbury, Wells, the Mendips and the Chew Valley. Otherwise, **Route 33** runs for 33 miles from Chard to Ilminster and Bridgwater, taking in Barrington (for Barrington Court), South Petherton, Langport (Muchelney Abbey) and Burrowbridge (Burrow Mump) along the way, and tracing the River Parrett for some of its journey; part of this route is combined with routes 26 and 30 to form the waymarked eighty-mile **South Somerset Cycle Route**, looping between Yeovil, Castle Cary, Somerton, South Petherton, Ilminster and Montacute. Route 24, **The Colliers Way**, runs from Frome to Radstock and the Dundas Aqueduct (see box, p.283); Route 26, **The Strawberry Line**, connects Yatton with Cheddar but may be extended north to Clevedon; while what's rather dramatically titled **The Ride to the North Somerset Coast** follows the Avon Gorge out of Bristol to the open-air lido at Portishead, along routes 33 and 41.

You can download leaflets and **route maps** for all of these from the Sustrans website, who also produce a more-detailed series of waterproof maps (1:100,000). See Ⓦ somersetcycling.com for a list of bike shops in the area and other recommended routes.

Fishing

The best fishing in all of Somerset is on the **Chew Valley lakes** (see box, p.138), where Blagdon makes a superlative **fly-fishing** destination for trout, and Chew Valley itself serves up king-size pike. The county's numerous waterways provide some great **coarse fishing**, particularly on the **Somerset**

Levels, where bream, tench and carp can be found in King Sedgemoor Drain, the Huntspill River and Combwich Ponds (see Ⓦ bridgwaterangling.co.uk), and 30lb pike stalk the waters of the River Brue and River Tone. **Exmoor** is the place to head for wild salmon and trout fishing, notably the River Barle and River Exe. See Ⓦ go-fish.co.uk/somerset.htm for the details of nearly seventy fisheries, ponds, rivers, lakes reservoirs and drains on which to cast a line. **Sea fishing** in the Bristol Channel can yield flounder bass, wrasse and conger; try the seafront at **Weston-super-Mare** or **Burnham-on-Sea** or charter a boat for the day with a company like Seafire, in **Watchet** (Ⓣ 01984 634507, Ⓦ seafirefishing.co.uk).

Horseriding

Exmoor is a fantastic place for **horseriding**, with open heather-clad moors stretching as far as the eye can see – though, as with walking, the Mendips and Quantocks are also criss-crossed with a number of bridleways worth following. There are around twenty riding schools across the county (see Ⓦ epony.co.uk), if you fancy giving it a go for the first time or are interested in improving your technique, while several companies offer riding holidays here, mostly in the national park. Some guesthouses (mostly those on farms) can provide stables for those bringing their own horses on holiday with them.

Rock-climbing and caving

Somerset's best area for both **rock-climbing** and **caving** is the Mendip Hills, where the limestone walls of Cheddar Gorge and Burrington Combe are etched with a variety of challenging routes, as well as shorter ascents suitable for beginners (see box, p.155), and numerous sinkholes and cave systems provide plenty of opportunities for potholers (see box, p.154). Climbers can also tackle the deep quarry at Ham Hill in South Somerset, though it is forbidden to insert climbing gear into the rock face here.

SPECIALIST OPERATORS

Bath & West Country Walks Ⓣ 01761 233807, Ⓦ bathwestwalks.com. Guided and self-guided walking holidays around Bath, the Mendips and Exmoor, plus a Historic Mendips trip that includes Wells and Glastonbury.

Contours Ⓣ 01629 821900, Ⓦ contours.co.uk. Walking holidays and self-guided hikes, including the Mendip Way, the South West Coast Path and the Tarka Trail, which dips into Exmoor from Devon.

Cycle Dorset Ⓦ cycledorset.com. Despite the name, over half of their organized routes are in Somerset, including a five-day ride across the

Levels and a tour of National Trust properties in South Somerset.

Cycle Tours UK ☎ 01962 870616, ⊛ cycletoursuk.com. Cycle trips taking in rural villages in South Somerset, plus Stourhead.

Footpath Holidays ☎ 01985 840049, ⊛ footpath-holidays.com. Good selection of guided, self-guided and tailor-made itineraries on Exmoor and the Quantocks.

Let's Go Walking ☎ 01837 880075, ⊛ letsgowalking.com/walking_holidays_somerset.html. UK walking specialists, organizing self-guided holidays on the South West Coast Path, Coleridge Way, Macmillan Way West, River Parrett Trail, Leland Trail and Liberty Trail.

Spirit of Exmoor ☎ 01598 753318, ⊛ spiritofexmoor.com. Week-long or short-break horseriding holidays and courses (classical riding, horse-whispering, etc) in Exmoor National Park, for all abilities.

Festivals and events

As the cultural capitals of the South West, Bath and Bristol have an active calendar packed with festivals, events and seasonal celebrations, a love of a good party that spreads into the Somerset countryside in the form of music festivals, agricultural shows and village fêtes. The following is a varied selection of the best of these, from ancient livestock fairs to fledgling music festivals; for details on every local listing, either contact the tourist office or ⊛ visitbath.co.uk, ⊛ visitbristol.co.uk or ⊛ visitsomerset.co.uk.

JANUARY TO MARCH

Wassail Jan 17 (region-wide) Cider-soaked ceremony dedicated to the health of apple trees and their forthcoming crop, dating back to Saxon times – the word comes from the Saxon wes hal, "good health" – and held on the old (Julian calendar) Twelfth Night. You can join in the tradition at the Somerset Rural Life Museum in Glastonbury (see p.170) and Barrington Court (see p.206), among other places.

Bath Literature Festival Late Feb to early March Two-week topical lit-fest that regularly attracts Nobel and Booker Prize winners, poet laureates and political heavyweights to a number of historic venues across the city. ⊛ bathlitfest.org.uk

APRIL, MAY AND JUNE

Mayfest May (Bristol) Wacky, challenging festival of contemporary theatre that lasts a month and still manages to turn up something new every day, be it physical theatre, magic or storytelling. ⊛ mayfestbristol.co.uk

Dot To Dot Late May (Bristol) Multi-venue music fest with a well-earned reputation for staging up-and-coming bands and soon-to-be big names. ⊛ dottodotfestival.co.uk

Igfest Late May (Bristol) Surreal, ultra-creative schedule of street games, ranging from simple wiffle-hurling to the role-playing Cowgirl Cowhunt and zombie chase game 2.8 Hours Later (⊛ 2.8hourslater.com). ⊛ igfest.org

newmusicwells Late May to early June (Wells) Spread over six days and a great chance to hear choral music and organ recitals in beautiful Wells Cathedral. See box, p.147. ⊛ wellscathedral.org.uk/music-the-choir/new-music-wells

Bath International Music Festival Late May to early June Well-respected twelve-day event mostly featuring classical music but also contemporary jazz, world and folk, and with some freebie outdoor performances. ⊛ bathmusicfest.org.uk

Bath Fringe Festival Late May to early June Seventeen days of genre-defying performances across the city – in big venues, small cafés and on the streets in between. ⊛ bathfringe.co.uk

Royal Bath & West Show Late May/early June (Shepton Mallet) Weighty agricultural show with loads of livestock, numerous displays, and the biggest cheese and cider competitions in the country. ⊛ bathandwest.com/royal-bath-west/97/

Sunrise Celebration Early June (Bruton) Four-day, super-relaxed "Festival of Organic Arts and Culture" that blends music, cabaret and slam poetry with healing sanctuaries and alternative-technology workshops. ⊛ sunrisecelebration.com

We The People Early June (Bristol) Urban-influenced music festival running over two days down on the waterfront, featurely mostly rap, reggae, dance and dub. ⊛ wethepeoplefestival.co.uk

Summer solstice Mid- or late June (Stonehenge) A mixed bag of druids, pagans, hippies and general partygoers gather to watch the sun rise over the Heel Stone on the longest day of the year. See box, p.310. ⊛ www.english-heritage.org.uk

Weston-super-Mare Sand Sculpture Festival Mid-June to early Sept Brilliant, summer-long themed competition that will make your bucket-castle efforts look truly inept in comparison. Past creations include King Kong, Cinderella and the Sagrada Família. See box, p.240. ⊛ westonsandsculpture.co.uk

Glastonbury Festival Late June The music festival against which all other music festivals are measured, attracting the biggest names in the industry – and some 180,000 people to watch them. See box, p.176. ⊛ glastonburyfestivals.co.uk

JULY AND AUGUST

RNAS Yeovilton Air Day Early July Huge air show at one of the largest airfields in Europe, with acrobatic displays, flybys from historic aircraft, flight simulators and various military demonstrations. ⊛ royalnavy.mod.uk

Priddy Folk Festival Early July Billing itself as the "friendliest folk festival in England", this well-respected event is focused around its pretty village green. ⊛ priddyfolk.org

St Pauls Carnival Early July (Bristol) A day-long parade of over-the-top costumes and elaborate floats forms the focus of this raucous celebration of Bristol's West Indian heritage. See box, p.136. ⊛ stpaulscarnival.co.uk

Frome Festival Early July This artsy East Somerset town ups the ante for ten days of open studios, various exhibitions, cabaret, theatre and impromptu street performances. ⊛ fromefestival.co.uk

Lowland Games Late July (Thorney) The Highland Games with a Somerset Levels twist, so wellies are thrown instead of hammers and

A CARNIVAL ATMOSPHERE

Somerset is rightly famous for its annual illuminated **carnivals**, a lightbulb-laden roadshow of spectacular floats and "squibbing" displays that date back to 1605, when the people of a predominantly Protestant Somerset took to the streets on torch-lit hay carts to celebrate the failure of the Gunpowder Plot. Between September and November each year (see ⓦ cispp.org. uk for exact dates), fourteen towns from four different carnival federations put on their own one-night-only parade – **Bridgwater Carnival** (see box, p.227) is the one to catch, the biggest of its kind in the world, and renowned for its 100ft-long monster floats.

ferret-racing replaces Scottish dancing. ⓦ thelowlandgames.co.uk

Bristol Harbour Festival Late July Water-based Harbourside event, the biggest in the city's calendar, with music, circus and plenty of bobbing boats. See box, p.136. ⓦ bristolharbourfestival.co.uk

Taunton Flower Show Early Aug Vivary Park makes a suitably bucolic setting for the biggest flower show in the South West, with designer gardens, arena events and more. ⓦ tauntonflowershow.co.uk

Bath Folk Festival Mid-Aug A medley of concerts, ad-hoc amateur gigs and informal sessions at venues across the city. ⓦ bathfolkfestival .org

Bristol International Balloon Fiesta Mid-Aug Atmospheric "night glows" and a battalion of odd-shaped balloons all trying to take to the sky at once make for one of the city's most unusual festivals. See box, p.136. ⓦ bristolballoonfiesta.co.uk

Ladies Day Mid-Aug (Bath) Posh frocks and fancy hats at Bath racecourse's seminal event, with live music, fireworks and a bit of horseracing thrown in for good measure. ⓦ bath-racecourse.co.uk

Priddy Sheep Fair Nearest Wed to Aug 21 Classic country livestock fair (sheep auction, horse-trading) that's been going strong since 1348, when the Black Death forced it out of Wells. ⓦ priddysomerset.org

RNLI Raft Race Late Aug (Minehead) Watch the fancy-dress hop across Minehead Bay or the five-mile race from Blue Anchor – both finishing at pretty Minehead Harbour – in what is the biggest event of its kind in the country. ⓦ mineheadlifeboat.org.uk

SEPTEMBER AND OCTOBER

The National Gardening Show Early Sept (Shepton Mallet) Green-fingered gathering with a variety of inspirational garden displays, plus TV celebrities and gardening experts on hand for the latest tips. ⓦ bathandwest.com/national-gardening/95/

Bristol International Festival of Kites and Air Creations Early Sept Two-day event for little kids (and big ones), with a mixture of novelty kites and extreme sports displays in the attractive surrounds of Ashton Court Estate. See box, p.136. ⓦ www.kite-festival.org.uk

Heritage Open Days Mid-Sept (region-wide) An annual opportunity to spend the weekend nosing around historic buildings not normally open to the public. ⓦ heritageopendays.org.uk

Jane Austen Festival Mid-Sept (Bath) Celebrate the work of one of England's favourite authors at a variety of Austen-focused events, beginning with a costumed parade through the city. ⓦ janeausten. co.uk/festival/index.ihtml

BrisFest Mid-Sept (Bristol) Youthful part performance art, part rave city festival that has proven a popular combination of see and do. See box, p.136. ⓦ brisfest.co.uk

Somerset Art Weeks Mid-Sept to early Oct (region-wide) The best place to catch local art and artists, with more than a hundred venues hosting various events and exhibitions of the visual arts. ⓦ somersetartworks.org.uk

Power Tool Drag Racing Championships Late Sept (Yeovilton) You'll never look at a Black & Decker leaf blower in the same way again if you catch this unusual event, focused around the "art" of engineering hand-held power tools into machines capable of racing down a 75ft track. ⓦ silverlinetools.com/ptdr

Cooler Jazz and Blues Festival Early Oct (Bath) Ten days of jazz and blues sessions culminates in an all-day gig at the city's Green Park Station. ⓦ coolerfestivals.co.uk

Halloween Oct 31 (region-wide) Take the trick-or-treating to the next level on a "Spooktacular" at Wookey Hole caves (see p.153) or a late-night ghost tour around Dunster Castle (see p.266), where even the gift shop is supposedly haunted.

NOVEMBER AND DECEMBER

Bath Film Festival Mid-Nov The region's premier film fest screening new documentaries and short films, plus classic reissues, at various venues across the city. ⓦ bathfilmfestival.org.uk

Bath Mozart Fest Mid-Nov Nine days of Mozart and Mozart-influenced music in historic venues that do justice to his work, and that of his contemporaries. ⓦ bathmozartfest.org.uk

Bath Christmas Market Late Nov to mid-Dec Wooden chalets fill Abbey Churchyard for this popular annual Yuletide market, which gets visitors in the festive spirit. ⓦ bathchristmasmarket.co.uk

Travellers with disabilities

Somerset, and particularly Bath and Bristol, caters well for travellers with disabilities. All new public buildings – including museums and galleries – must provide wheelchair access, train stations are generally fully accessible and many buses have easy-access boarding ramps.

There are Shopmobility schemes (ⓦ www.shop mobilityuk.org) in **Bristol** (Cabot Circus and The Mall in Broadmead) and **Bath** – as well as in Taunton and Yeovil (Quedam) – which lend or rent out wheelchairs and/or powered scooters, while both cities have open-top bus tours with disabled access, though you'll need to contact Bristol's in advance for the schedule of its low-floor, step-free vehicle (see p.115). Dropped kerbs and signalled crossings are the rule, while the cities' big attractions also score highly on accessibility: Thermae Bath Spa, for example, has assistance chairs that give access to the baths, and lends lightweight shower wheelchairs, while the *ss Great Britain* has won awards for its accessibility.

Getting around some of **Somerset**'s smaller villages (many of which don't even have pavements) can be more problematic, however, as can negotiating the county's many historic buildings. That said, properties belonging to both the National Trust and English Heritage generally have decent accessibility, details of which can be found in their latest Access Guides (ⓦnationaltrust org.uk/accessforall and ⓦwww.english-heritage. org.uk/publications/access-guide). Other more accessible attractions out in the country include **Haynes International Motor Museum** in South Somerset, whose owner has installed ramps throughout; **Ham Hill** near Yeovil, where you can whizz round two designated routes for free on an off-road scooter (Mon–Fri; call ☎01935 823617 or see ⓦwww.southsomersetcountryside.com) and **Montacute House**, which although steeply stepped, has tactile images for the blind of every painting in its top-floor Long Gallery.

Unfortunately, much of the finest **walking** (the Mendips and the Quantocks, for example) is up in the hills and across challenging terrain. The **nature reserves** in the Avalon Marshes, though, are particularly geared towards travellers with disabilities, with Shapwick Heath, Ham Wall and Catcott Lows all featuring accessible trails and boardwalks, some running to hides and viewing screens; furthermore, Double-Gate Farm (see p.181), six miles from both Shapwick Heath and Ham Wall, is a former AA Accessible Hotel of the Year.

RESOURCES

As well as the online resources listed below, *The Rough Guide to Accessible Britain* has detailed accounts of major attractions in the area – reviewed by writers with disabilities – with more places given the once-over by fellow travellers at ⓦ accessibleguide.co.uk.

Accessible South West ⓦ accessiblesouthwest.co.uk. Searchable directory of accommodation and restaurants, plus fairly detailed listings outlining the accessibility of local attractions.

Caravanable ⓦ caravanable.co.uk. Listings of accessible campsites and caravan parks, plus a handful of accessible beaches around Burnham-on-Sea, Weston-super-Mare and Minehead.

Door-to-Door ⓦ dptac.independent.gov.uk/door-to-door.

Travel website offering basic information and advice, plus details of concession schemes.

Need a Loo? ⓦ needaloo.org. Online directory of accessible toilets in Bath, Bristol and nearly seventy other cities, towns and villages across Somerset.

RADAR ⓦ radar.org.uk. Campaigning organization with links and advice.

Tourism for All ⓦ tourismforall.org.uk. Excellent resource, with advice, listings and useful information.

Travel essentials

Costs

Although Bath and Bristol rank among the most expensive English cities outside London, Somerset is generally not much costlier than anywhere else in southwest England. What you spend depends entirely on your **budget**: buying your own food, staying on campsites or hostels, and walking or cycling everywhere might allow you to get by on as little as £30 per person per day, plus whatever you spend on sightseeing, while a couple staying in a B&B or modest hotel and eating out once a day can easily double this expenditure – after that, the sky's the limit. Your biggest expense will always be **accommodation**, which usually costs £60–120 per night for a double or twin room (singles cost around 75 percent of the full price of a double).

Admission prices for attractions given in the Guide are the full adult charges. The majority of fee-charging attractions have reductions for senior citizens, the unemployed, full-time students, under-26s and under-18s, with under-5s being admitted free almost everywhere; teachers, too, are sometimes given discounts. Anyone qualifying for reduced rates for attractions or travel should carry documentary proof.

Many of Somerset's **historic sites** – from long barrows to castles, abbeys and great houses – come under the aegis of the private **National Trust** (ⓦnationaltrust.org.uk) or the state-run **English Heritage** (ⓦwww.english-heritage.org.uk), whose properties are denoted in the Guide with "NT" or "EH" respectively. Both bodies charge an entry fee for the majority of their historic properties, and these can be quite high, especially for the grander National Trust estates – though the expense can be partly offset at most NT properties by reductions for anyone arriving on foot, by bike or by public transport. If you think you'll be visiting more than half a dozen places owned by the National Trust or more than a dozen owned by English Heritage, it's worth taking out annual membership (around £50), which allows free entry to the organizations' respective properties.

Privately owned **stately homes** tend to charge £5–10 for admission to edited highlights of their domain. Attractions owned by the local authorities – municipal galleries and **museums**, for example – charge lower admission or are free, while private collections always have fees. The **cathedrals** in Bath, Bristol, Wells and Salisbury request a voluntary donation of £2–6 and charge a small fee for a photographic permit.

Health

Although Somerset does not present particular **health hazards** that are exclusive to this region of the country, there are some tips that are worth remembering whether or not you are covered by health insurance. Remember that the sun can be deceptively strong in the South West, especially (but not only) in the summer months, and ensure that you use a suitable **sunscreen** (sun factor 30+ is recommended). On beaches, the wearing of "jelly shoes" – available at many seaside shops – is a good safeguard against the **weaver fish**, which lurk under the sand at low tide and can cause painful stings from the venomous spines along their dorsal fins.

On Exmoor and other areas where there is woodland and thick vegetation (for instance bracken), beware of **ticks**, which are brushed (or fall) onto exposed skin and burrow down to suck blood. Covering bare flesh on walks is the best protection; if you find ticks in your skin, seek professional advice – yanking them out can leave traces behind. Other possible hazards on moorland include **toxocara**, a small parasite carried in the faeces of some animals, and **adders** (or vipers), distinguished by a zigzag stripe along their backs; they're quite rare, and if you should be unlucky enough to be bitten, it is extremely unlikely to be fatal, though you should seek medical attention as soon as possible.

More generally, it's worth checking what your health insurance covers (if you have it) and packing

any prescription medication that you normally take, as well as carrying contact details of your own doctor. Should health issues arise, you can consult **NHS Direct** (**☎** 0845 4647, **🔇** www.nhsdirect.nhs. uk), a 24-hour service offering advice for most problems; the website is packed with information on the most common ailments and provides details of local doctors (GPs), dentists, pharmacies and walk-in centres, where you can receive attention on a first-come first-served basis. **Pharmacies** can advise on a range of health topics.

Internet

Most hotels, B&Bs and hostels, and some campsites, are fully connected to the **internet**, usually using wi-fi – though connectivity may be confined to public rooms, especially in older properties. **Public internet points** can be found in all towns and villages in Somerset where there are public libraries, offering free access at specific times, for which booking is advisable to avoid a wait. See **🔇** www.somerset.gov. uk/libraries, **🔇** bathnes.gov.uk/libraries, **🔇** bristol.gov. uk/libraries and **🔇** www.n-somerset.gov.uk/libraries for lists of the region's libraries and opening times. Increasing numbers of pubs and cafés offer free wireless connections, and many tourist offices also offer access for a small fee. Larger towns have internet cafés, charging around £1 for twenty minutes.

Maps

The best general **map** of Somerset is Philip's Somerset Navigator, which reproduces the county at a scale of two miles to the inch (1:125,000), with town plans of Bristol, Bath and Taunton, and showing cycle tracks and major footpaths. Philip's (**🔇** octopusbooks.co.uk/philips-map) also publish a 1:100,000 map covering the whole southwest region as far east as Salisbury, which also has some visitor information. **Walkers** and **cyclists**, however, should get hold of maps published by Ordnance Survey (**🔇** ordnancesurvey.co.uk), either the 1:50,000 Landranger series (pink) or the more detailed

---

PUBLIC AND BANK HOLIDAYS

January 1	**Last Monday in May**
Good Friday (late March or early April)	**Last Monday in August**
Easter Monday (as above)	**December 25**
First Monday in May	**December 26**

Note that if January 1 or December 25 or 26 falls on a Saturday or Sunday, the next weekday becomes a public holiday.

1:25,000 Explorer series (orange), available in regular or more expensive weather-proof versions. You can also consult these maps online. AA (Ⓦtheaa.com) and Geographers' A–Z (Ⓦa-zmaps.co.uk) produce useful road atlases for drivers, and Harvey's (Ⓦharveymaps.co.uk) 1:40,000 maps cover the South West Coast Path. All the above are on sale at outdoors stores and bookshops in the region or from dedicated **map outlets** such as Stanfords (see p.133), who offer a mail-order service. It's also worth checking online maps at Ⓦisharemaps.bathnes.gov.uk, Ⓦmaps.google.co.uk and Ⓦstreetmap.co.uk.

Opening hours

Opening hours of all attractions, cafés, restaurants and pubs are given in the Guide, though as these change regularly it's recommended to check before making any long excursions. Many paying attractions stop admitting visitors 45 minutes or an hour before closing. Larger and more important **churches** are almost always open during daylight hours, but you'll often find country churches locked up unless they're particular tourist attractions – most in any case close at 4 or 5pm.

Shops generally open from 9am to 5.30pm Monday to Saturday, with many shops in Bath and Bristol open on Sunday as well, along with supermarkets and some bigger stores everywhere. When all else is closed, you can normally find a garage selling basic items. In summer, food shops in tourist areas often stay open until 10 or 11pm. **Banks** are usually open Monday to Friday from 9am to 4pm, and larger branches are also open on Saturday mornings; most **post offices** are open Monday to Friday from 9am to 5.30pm, Saturday 9am to 12.30 or 1pm, with main branches open on Saturday afternoons and smaller branches closed at lunchtimes and/or Wednesday afternoons. Banks, post offices and most shops close on bank holidays (see box opposite).

Phones

Public telephone kiosks are fairly ubiquitous in towns and villages throughout Somerset, though most do not accept coins; instead, swipe a credit or debit card, or use a phone card available from the post office (£5, £10 or £20), for which you must dial

> For all **emergencies**, including police, fire, ambulance and coastguard, dial ☎999.

an access number followed by the card's PIN number. **Mobile phones** are not always to be relied upon in rural areas – large parts of Exmoor and the Mendip and Quantock hills, for example, are out of range or have only a weak signal.

Dial ☎100 for the **operator**, ☎155 for the **international operator**. Calling **directory enquiries** (available at a variety of numbers, for example ☎118500) is expensive; you can look up numbers online at Ⓦbtexchanges.com and Ⓦyell.com.

Tourist information

Somerset's **regional tourist body**, Visit Somerset, has an office at the Sedgemoor service station (Roadchef) on the M5 southbound between junctions 21 and 22 (Easter–Oct Mon–Fri 9.15am–4.30pm, also weekends in summer; ☎01934 750833, Ⓦvisitsomerset.co.uk). There's also a branch dedicated to South Somerset in the Cartgate picnic area on the A303, near Stoke-sub-Hamdon (daily 10am–5pm, Oct–Easter Mon & Fri only; ☎01935 829333, Ⓦvisitsouthsomerset.com). The equivalent body in Wiltshire, Visit Wiltshire (Ⓦvisitwiltshire.co.uk), has no walk-in office. While regional offices can supply maps and general information, the local tourist offices listed in the Guide have their ears closer to the ground and are better placed for practical information.

The staff are knowledgeable and helpful as a rule, and well supplied with details of public transport, local attractions and accommodation – though it's worth noting that much of the material relates only to places that have paid for their entries and listings in the official brochures. All the same, it's worth grabbing whatever free literature and maps are available, and perusing their stock of books and leaflets for sale.

Opening hours for most tourist offices are Monday to Saturday 9am to 5pm; in high summer many are open daily, while in winter some are open at weekends only or else close altogether. Most offices will book accommodation, and many also sell tickets for tours, ferries and National Express buses.

Bath and around

BATH ABBEY

1

Bath and around

Water, stone and wool are the elements that have shaped the history and appearance of the city of **Bath**: the thermal waters that underpinned the city's growth; the soft oolitic limestone that fashioned its elegant Palladian architecture; and wool, the foundation of the region's wealth, without which the grand vision and ambitions of its leading personalities could not have been realised. Bath's **hot springs** alone set the city apart from anywhere else in the UK, but it is the aesthetic experience of its buildings and crescents that make the greatest impression – the eighteenth-century city par excellence, Bath is in many ways a collection of urban set pieces, a visual feast best appreciated at a leisurely pace. And it's not just the buildings that appeal to the senses: the acres of parkland between the Georgian developments and the green landscape of the surrounding hills contribute equally to the spacious, measured feel of modern Bath, simultaneously soothing and exhilarating.

It is also a city that repays digging beneath its operatic surface, which you can do in some of the most rewarding **museums and galleries** to be found anywhere in the country. As well as the artistic attractions displayed in these, Bath offers a dynamic cultural life in other areas – in the arts **festivals** that punctuate the year, and in the diversity of **restaurants** and **bars** that cater more strictly to the flesh. In the world of retail too, Bath has a multitude of small **shops** and **markets** that distinguish it from the majority of Britain's mid-size towns.

On the flip side, Bath has never lost its exclusive air, and it ranks among the country's most expensive cities. This doesn't deter the constant flow of visitors who throng its attractions, hotels and restaurants year round, however. While it's sometimes a challenge to rein in the expenditure, it's not hard to find respite from the hubbub, either in the parks or walks outside the centre and further afield. Bath may have a veritable surfeit of attractions, but there is much to be seen and enjoyed within a short ride. Upstream, **Bradford-on-Avon** delivers further architectural delights and has a cluster of engrossing historical remains. To the northeast, you can get a taste of the Cotswolds in the villages of **Lacock** and **Castle Combe**, both oozing charm.

Any of these places would make less pricey alternatives to Bath when you're seeking **accommodation**, though **public transport** links to Lacock and Castle Combe are sketchy.

Bath

A glance at a map might suggest that the city of **BATH**, with a population of 84,000, might have its identity completely submerged by that of metropolitan Bristol, England's sixth most populous city, just twelve miles away. Nothing could be less true, for Bath is distinctive and independent from its neighbour in every way – a harmonious, leisurely, compact, rather complacent city, richly endowed with historical and literary associations, its smart, prosperous centre abuzz with shops and cafés. While there's something undeniably patrician in Bath's prevailing tone, it lacks the snooty pretensions of that other great West Country spa town, Cheltenham, while the quirky

ROMAN BATHS

Highlights

❶ Roman Baths They're what Bath is all about – the source of its fame and fashionability – but this thermal complex is also an imaginative and engaging insight into Roman Britain. **See p.46**

❷ Thermae Bath Spa Relive the rituals of past generations in Bath while pampering your body with treatments and a rooftop bathe at this twenty-first-century spa establishment. **See p.47**

❸ Holburne Museum In a newly renovated Palladian mansion, this collection gathers together exquisite examples of ceramics, silverware and sculpture. **See p.50**

❹ Royal Crescent This graceful Palladian masterpiece is the most jaw-dropping of Bath's architectural highlights, best experienced in the early morning or at sunset. **See p.54**

❺ Building of Bath Collection Unearth the secrets of Georgian building design – an invaluable preliminary to appreciating Bath's architecture at first hand. **See p.57**

❻ Corsham Court Hidden away in the winsome village of Corsham, this place is a wonderful find – a treasure-trove of European masterpieces from the sixteenth and seventeenth centuries. **See p.74**

❼ Lacock Abbey Not just an eighteenth-century manor house superimposed on sixteenth-century ruins, this was the home of "father of photography" William Fox Talbot, and holds an excellent museum of his work. **See p.75**

HIGHLIGHTS ARE MARKED ON THE MAP ON P.42

1

details, architectural oddities and fragments of delicate rococo ornamentation you'll come across when you look closely undermine any overweening tendencies. In long shot, with its architectural integrity and amphitheatre-like setting, Bath is the most Italianate of British towns, with theatrical vistas at every turn. Jane Austen set *Persuasion* and *Northanger Abbey* here, it is where Gainsborough established himself as a portraitist and landscape painter, and the city's elegant crescents and Georgian buildings are studded with plaques naming the eminent inhabitants and visitors associated with the place from its heyday as a spa resort.

Inevitably it is the **Roman Baths** that make up the city's most essential sight, and one that lives up to the hype, but visually it is Bath's Georgian character that constitutes the real pleasure of a visit. The showpieces are the **Circus** and the **Royal Crescent**, intensely satisfying architectural ensembles, closely followed by **Pulteney Bridge** and **Pulteney Street**. You can absorb more of the same – but without the crowds – in the stately crescents of the aristocratic **Lansdown** neighbourhood, and learn how these projects were brought to fruition in the instructive **Building of Bath Collection**. Housed in a Neoclassical mansion, the **Holburne Museum** displays some of the artistic treasures of the period, while the **Herschel Museum of Astronomy**, dedicated to one of the outstanding scientists of the era, illuminates the scientific achievements of the time, as well as revealing aspects of ordinary life in the eighteenth century.

Offering relief from the city's insistent evocations of Georgian Bath are a couple of wildly differing collections: the **Museum of East Asian Art** and the **Museum of Bath at Work**, while, outside town, the **American Museum** presents a thoroughly enjoyable slice of the history and culture of the USA from colonial times.

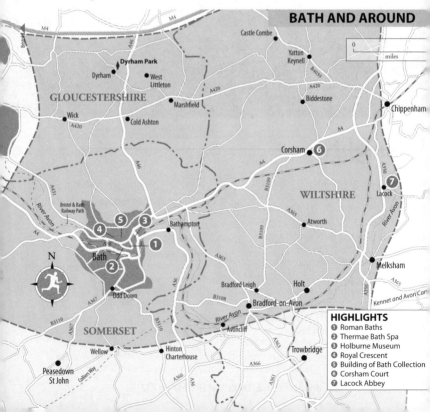

BATH AND AROUND

HIGHLIGHTS
❶ Roman Baths
❷ Thermae Bath Spa
❸ Holburne Museum
❹ Royal Crescent
❺ Building of Bath Collection
❻ Corsham Court
❼ Lacock Abbey

1

Brief history

Bath owes its name and fame to its **hot springs** – the only ones in the country – which made it a place of reverence for the local Celtic population, the **Dobunni**, who dedicated the waters here to the goddess Sul. Numerous traces of Iron Age settlements have been found on the surrounding hills, including – east of the present city – on Solsbury Hill, the place immortalized in Peter Gabriel's eponymous song. But the place had to wait for Roman technology before a fully fledged bathing establishment could be created in the first century AD. The Romans identified the local deity Sul, or Sulis, with their own Minerva, and renamed the settlement **Aquae Sulis** ("Waters of Sulis"). Alongside the baths, a temple and probably a theatre and administrative buildings were established, the core of a thriving market town which was a stop on the great Fosse Way that ran between Lincoln and Exeter.

With the departure of the Romans, the baths quickly declined, but the town regained its importance under the **Saxons**, its abbey seeing the coronation of Edgar as king of all England in 973. All the same, a hundred years later, the Domesday Book recorded that Bath had a scarcely greater population than a large village today. The transfer of the seat of the bishopric of Somerset here (this was later reversed) and the Norman rebuilding of the Saxon cathedral 1090–1170 helped to stimulate the town, but in the centuries that followed it became increasingly overshadowed by the developing port and trading centre of Bristol.

A new bathing complex was built in the sixteenth century, popularized by the visit of Elizabeth I in 1574 and Anne of Denmark, James I's queen, in 1616, who came to find a cure for her dropsy. Following Charles II's visit in 1663, pumps were installed to encourage visitors to imbibe the waters, but it was not until after visits by Queen Anne in 1702 and 1703 and the reorganization of the town's social scene by **Beau Nash** (see box, p.57) that the city reached its fashionable zenith. And it was at this time – Bath's "**Golden Age**" – that the city acquired its ranks of Palladian mansions and townhouses, all of them built in the local **Bath stone**, which is still Bath's leitmotif today. The two John Woods – father and son – are the names most associated with the Georgian reconstruction of the city, but many other architects made significant contributions, among them Thomas Baldwin, John Eveleigh, John Palmer and John Pinch, whose works were predominantly Palladian and Neoclassical in style but made detours into the wilds of Georgian Gothic and Baroque.

Bath's heyday was over by the beginning of the **nineteenth century**. The currents of fashion had drawn people instead to such coastal resorts as Brighton and Weymouth, or to more exotic European climes, newly accessible following the end of the Napoleonic Wars. Now, elderly spinsters and retired military men made up the majority of the city's residents – none with much money to spend. The construction of the **Kennet and Avon Canal** in 1810 to link Bath with London via Newbury and the River Thames helped to revive the local economy, as did Brunel's extension of the Great Western Railway to Bath in 1841, but the Industrial Revolution largely passed the city by, and it assumed the character of a slightly faded, slightly twee provincial resort that it has never entirely shaken off.

BATH'S LEGENDARY BIRTH

According to legend, Bath was founded by **Bladud**, a prince who suffered from some form of leprosy-like skin condition, for which he was banished from court by his father, Hudibras. Bladud survived by wandering from place to place and tending pigs, which themselves contracted the disease. Camped in what is now the Avon Valley, Bladud noticed that the lesions on their skins appeared to recede after his pigs wallowed in the warm mud in the valley, and he too was healed after wading in the mud. Returning to the court of Hudibras, he was accepted once more as his father's heir, and when he became king, Bladud formally recognised the sacred nature of the springs. His son, the legend goes, was Lear, Shakespeare's tragic hero.

CENTRAL BATH

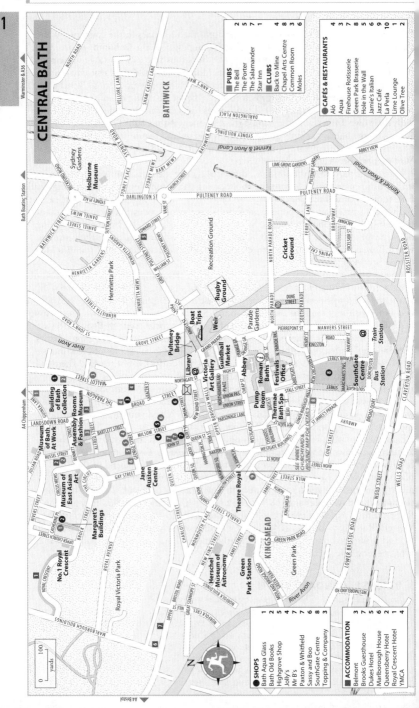

PUBS
The Bell	2
The Porter	5
The Salamander	7
Star Inn	1

CLUBS
Back to Mine	4
Chapel Arts Centre	8
Common Room	3
Moles	6

CAFÉS & RESTAURANTS
Aïo	4
Aqua	3
Firehouse Rotisserie	7
Green Park Brasserie	8
Hole in the Wall	5
Jamie's Italian	6
Jazz Café	9
La Perla	10
Lime Lounge	1
Olive Tree	2

SHOPS
Bath Aqua Glass	1
Bath Old Books	5
Highgrove Shop	4
Jolly's	7
Mr B's	6
Paxton & Whitfield	7
Sassy and Boo	8
SouthGate Centre	2
Topping & Company	3

ACCOMMODATION
Belmont	3
Brooks Guesthouse	7
Dukes Hotel	5
Marlborough House	6
Queensberry Hotel	2
Royal Crescent Hotel	1
YMCA	4

1

Spas were back in vogue in the late nineteenth century, and it was during a renovation of the King's Bath in 1878–9 that the remains of the old Roman Baths were discovered and excavated. The subsequent Victorian additions to the baths drew a new wave of tourism.

Bath didn't escape bombardment during **World War II**, with the Assembly Rooms among the buildings destroyed in 1942 (they were faithfully rebuilt). In 1964, the **University of Bath** was founded above the city on Claverton Down, bringing a much-needed infusion of youth culture to the staid city. The university has established a good reputation for its science and technology departments, while **Bath Spa University**, inaugurated in 2006, focuses on the humanities.

Bath Abbey

Abbey Churchyard • April–Oct Mon–Sat 9am–6pm, Sun 1–2.30pm & 4.30–5.30pm; Nov–March Mon–Sat 9am–4.30pm, Sun 1–2.30pm & 4.30–5.30pm • Requested donation £2.50 **Tower tour** Mon–Sat: April, May, Sept, & Oct 10am–4pm hourly; June–Aug 10am–5pm hourly; Nov & Jan–March 11am, noon & 2pm; check the website for December opening • £5 • Ⓦ bathabbey.org

Dominating the pedestrianized **Abbey Churchyard**, whose two interlocking squares are usually a mélée of buskers, tourists and traders, **Bath Abbey** commands attention. The site of a Roman temple and, in the seventh century, an Anglo-Saxon convent, the abbey is essentially a sixteenth-century replacement of a Norman construction erected between 1090 and 1170 and with a length of 106m compared with 67m today. This hugely over-ambitious Norman building ultimately turned out too big for the under-resourced monks to maintain adequately, and it was practically in ruins by the end of the fifteenth century when the new Bishop of Bath and Wells, Oliver King, in collaboration with Prior William Birde commenced the formidable task of dismantling and rebuilding, incorporating the Norman foundations and much of the surviving stone. The bishop was said to have been inspired by a vision of angels ascending and descending a ladder to heaven, which the present **facade** recalls on the turrets flanking the central window. The west front also features the founder's signature in the form of carvings of olive trees surmounted by crowns, a play on his name.

King died shortly after work began, and the rebuilding project was further interrupted by the destruction of the abbey monastery in 1539 under Henry VIII, but significant restoration took place in the years following, with Henry's daughter, Elizabeth I, playing a large part in the repairs following her visit in 1574.

The interior

The abbey's **interior** is predominantly Perpendicular in style – this was in fact England's last major building to be built in this idiom – though much of it in a restrained manner, with relatively spare decoration. The glaring exception is the splendid **ceiling**, not properly completed until the nineteenth century when the great Victorian architect Sir George Gilbert Scott faithfully modelled the fan vaulting of the nave on the sixteenth-century ceilings of the choir and its aisles. The huge **east window** too, depicting 56 events in the life of Christ, is Victorian – it was restored after bomb damage during World War II.

Below the east window, to the right of the high altar, you can see traces of the grander Norman building in the **Gethsemane Chapel** (also called the Norman Chapel). Outside it, in a separate enclosure next to the altar, is the **chantry chapel of William Birde**, intricately decorated with its own little fan vault and carved with Birde's initials and, referencing his name, little birds. Elsewhere the abbey's floor and walls are crammed with elaborate monuments and memorials, including, in the **South Aisle** just before the transept, a wall tablet commemorating the renowned Master of Ceremonies Beau Nash (see box, p.57). The **North Aisle** holds memorials to Thomas Malthus (1766–1834), the prophet of over-population, and shorthand pioneer Sir Isaac Pitman (1813–1897).

On most days you can join a 45-minute **tower tour** to see the massive bells, clock and bell-pulling machinery, and can enjoy a bird's-eye view of Bath – but be prepared for the 212 spiral steps. An mp3 download of an **audio tour** is available from the abbey's website.

1

The Roman Baths

Abbey Churchyard • Daily: March–June, Sept & Oct 9am–6pm; July & Aug 9am–10pm; Nov–Feb 9.30am–5.30pm; last entry 1hr before closing • £12, £12.50 in July & Aug, £15.50 combined ticket with Fashion Museum • ☎ 01225 477785, ⒲ romanbaths.co.uk

Even more than the abbey, the **Roman Baths** are the focal point of Bath, as they have been on and off since Roman times. Although ticket prices are high, there's two or three hours' worth of well-balanced, informative entertainment here, with hourly guided tours lasting about 45 minutes and audioguides available (both free) – the English version comes with three different commentaries, including one for kids and one by Bill Bryson, offering a more personal take. Allow up to three hours to get the most of this attraction, but come early in the day or in the evening – after 7pm in July and August – to avoid the crowds. Visiting after dark gives the bonus of viewing the complex lit by flaming torches.

The architecture

Essentially, the baths complex visible today is the product of three eras – the Roman construction, much more extensive than what has survived today; the Norman-era reconstruction, when monks from Bath Abbey built a bath-house on top of the Roman remains; and the Victorian additions, mostly in a cod-Roman style. The Roman structure dates from the mid-60s, just a few decades after the Romans first occupied the area, and remained in use for some 350 years thereafter, falling into disrepair in around 410. Successive constructions were erected over the rubble of the Roman site, by Saxon times buried some 5m below. Saxon monks created a rudimentary bathing complex after the eighth century, which was augmented by Norman engineers. In subsequent centuries residential housing and even a tennis court were built over the site, but in the 1850s subsidence in the area led to investigations by city planners and the eventual discovery of the Roman site, far below street level. Excavations and restoration work continued until the grand opening of the Roman Baths to the public in 1897, since when there have been few alterations.

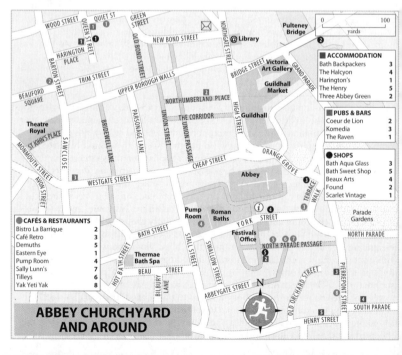

Visiting the baths

Among the highlights of a visit today are the **Sacred Spring**, part of the temple of the local deity Sulis Minerva, where water still bubbles up at a constant 46.5°C. The **Great Bath** is now open-air, but was originally covered by a barrel-vaulted roof. Its vaporous waters are surrounded by pillars, terraces and statues of Roman emperors and generals, all from the nineteenth-century restoration. Most of what you'll see at ground level is Roman, however, including a length of original lead piping and fragments of the arched roof showing the hollowed-out bricks. Following a conduit of iron-red water off one end of the bath brings you to the covered **Circular Bath**, where bathers cooled off, and, opposite, the open-air Norman **King's Bath**, placed over the hot spring and surrounded by original Roman arches and iron rings placed here in the sixteenth century to help bathers get in and out. This section was used for bathing up until 1978, when the waters were declared unsafe, mainly due to the presence of bacteria – much of it from the accumulation of pigeon droppings.

Throughout the complex, projections showing Roman-era characters help to recreate the atmosphere of the baths in their heyday, and there are generally a few actors dressed up in Roman garb offering information and posing for photos.

The exhibits

The museum **exhibits** include a plethora of Roman finds, among them a quantity of coins, jewellery and sculpture. The most impressive items are a bronze head of Sulis Minerva and a grand, Celtic-inspired gorgon's head from the temple's pediment, but less ostentatious items such as the scraps of graffiti salvaged from the Roman era – mainly curses and boasts – are equally evocative, giving a nice personal slant on the range of people who frequented this antique leisure centre. There's plenty of background on the Roman Baths, their origins and their rediscovery and restoration, and models of the complex at its greatest extent give some idea of the awe which it must have inspired. Ask at the ticket counter about free hourly **tours** of the baths.

The Pump Room

You can get a free glimpse of the Roman baths from the next-door **Pump Room**, one of the social hubs of the Georgian spa community and still redolent of that era. Built in 1706, the Pump Room was enlarged and remodelled in the 1790s by Thomas Baldwin and John Palmer, two of the principal architects of Bath's Golden Age. Today, the building houses a formal tearoom and restaurant where lunches and teas are served in a period setting (see p.64). It's all a bit self-conscious and touristy, but the interior is worth a glance even if you don't want to order anything, and there's the opportunity to sample the filtered but still distinctly unpleasant spa waters – free for Baths ticket-holders (keep your ticket receipt), 50p a glass for everyone else. Note the Greek quotation from Pindar picked out in gold lettering above the entrance, roughly translated as "Water is the greatest essence".

Thermae Bath Spa

Hot Bath St • Daily 9am–10pm, last entry at 7.30pm **New Royal Bath** £25 for 2hr, £35 for 4hr, £50 for full day; treatments range in price, starting from £38 for a 30min facial **Cross Bath** £15 for 90min • Children under 16 are not admitted into the New Royal Bath, under-12s cannot use the Cross Bath, and you must be 18 or over to book a spa treatment **Visitor Centre** April–Oct Mon–Sat 10am–5pm, Sun 11am–4pm • Free • ☎ 0844 888 0844, ⊛ thermaebathspa.com

At the bottom of the elegantly colonnaded Bath Street, **Thermae Bath Spa** allows you to take the local waters in much the same way that visitors to Bath have done since Roman times, but with state-of-the-art spa facilities. The complex is heated by the city's thermal waters and offers both pool and shower sessions and a variety of treatments from massages to dry flotation. The centrepiece is the **New Royal Bath**, a sleekly futuristic "glass cube" designed by Nicholas Grimshaw, incorporating the curving indoor Minerva Bath, fragrant steam rooms and a **rooftop pool** with glorious views.

TAKING THE WATERS

"I assure you, Miss Woodhouse, where the waters do agree it is quite wonderful the relief they give. In my Bath life, I have seen such instances of it!" Mrs Elton, in Jane Austen's *Emma*

Bath's natural thermal springs are its *raison d'être*, an object of worship for the local Celtic population, a social ritual for the Romans and a fashionable fad for the Georgians, who congregated here by the carriage-load to "**take the waters**". The spa water was historically claimed to assuage gout and skin conditions as well as promote fecundity – hence the decision of Charles II to bring his queen, Catherine of Braganza, here in 1663, in the (vain) hope of producing a legitimate male heir. The most usual therapy consisted of immersion in the water, but drinking it became popular in the eighteenth century: "The water should always be drunk hot from the pump, or else at your lodgings as warm as it can possibly be procured," instructed the Bath Guide of 1800. "The water is generally drank in the morning fasting, between the hours of six and ten, that it may have time to pass out of the stomach; though some drink a glass about noon. The quantity generally drunk in a day is from one pint to three, though some drink two quarts; few constitutions require more."

Health-giving properties are still attributed to the water, which mostly fell as rain 6000–10,000 years ago in the Mendip Hills, was warmed by geothermal heat and rose through fissures in the limestone beneath Bath. It contains some thirty different **minerals**, including sodium, calcium, magnesium, sulphate and iron – in fact it is slightly radioactive and, with so much dissolved lime, extremely hard. Today, various spa treatments are offered at some of Bath's swisher hotels such as the *Royal Crescent* (see p.63), but the only place to experience the natural thermal waters to the full is at the modern Thermae Bath Spa complex (see p.47).

The tourist office (see p.61) offers a **Spas Ancient and Modern** package that includes a ticket to the Roman Baths, a voucher for a three-course lunch or champagne afternoon tea in the Pump Room, and a voucher for a two-hour spa session at Thermae Bath Spa, costing £61.50 per person.

Across from the entrance, the **Cross Bath** is in a separate building, a smaller, oval, open-air pool on a site once used by the Celts and Romans and rebuilt by Thomas Baldwin and John Palmer in the eighteenth century, when it was the most fashionable of the city's baths for its more intimate setting (bathers at the time were serenaded by musicians). The Cross Bath is open for spa sessions, though it has more rudimentary facilities than the New Royal Bath. All the baths have a depth of 1.35m and a water-temperature of around 33.5 degrees Celsius.

Note that treatments can (and must) be booked at the ticket desk or by phone, but pool sessions cannot be booked in advance. Weekdays are the quietest time to visit. Towels, robes and slippers can be rented, but you'll need a bathing costume. The building also houses *Springs*, an excellent **café-restaurant** with nourishing (but fairly pricey) soups and salads. You can also book a Roman Baths/Thermae Bath Spa package (see box above). Next to the Cross Bath outside the entrance, a small **Visitor Centre** shows displays relating to Bath's thermal waters and a brief film. Audioguides (£2) can be rented from here to learn more about the exterior of the complex.

The Guildhall

High St

Just north of Bath Abbey, the main part of the **Guildhall** was the work of Thomas Baldwin in 1775–78, though the Victorians made additions at each end and the dome is twentieth-century. The Guildhall's centrepiece is the grand **Banqueting Room** adorned with ornate chandeliers and portraits of some of Bath's chief movers and shakers – including the local general and MP Marshall Wade and the quarry magnate Ralph Allen (see box, p.55) – as well as national figures such as George III, Frederick, Prince of Wales and Pitt the Elder. The room is now used for civic ceremonies and is one of the main venues of Bath's music and literature festivals.

The rest of the building holds the council chamber and register office, while adjacent is the **Guildhall Market**, a small indoor area mainly selling household goods, with another entrance on Grand Parade (🅦 bathguildhallmarket.co.uk).

Sally Lunn's

4 North Parade Passage • Museum Mon–Sat 10am–6pm, Sun 11am–6pm • 30p, free for diners • ☎ 01225 461634, 🅦 sallylunns.co.uk

One of Bath's oldest houses, **Sally Lunn's** is named after a Huguenot refugee – possibly Solange Luyon originally – who arrived in Bath in 1680, worked in this building and is said to have invented the Bath Bun, a sort of soft-doughed brioche, here called the Sally Lunn Bun. The building, which may date back to 1482 but incorporates remains of much earlier dwellings, now houses a rather twee tearoom and restaurant (see p.64) where various permutations of the bun take centre stage on the menu. In the basement, originally the ground-floor kitchen, a tiny **museum** reveals the Roman and medieval foundations of the various buildings that have occupied the site, and shows the reconstructed eighteenth-century kitchen and some bits and pieces unearthed during excavations.

Parade Gardens

Grand Parade • March–Sept 10am–7pm, Oct–Easter 10am–5pm or dusk • £1, winter free • 🅦 paradegardens.co.uk

Abutting the west bank of the Avon, the **Parade Gardens** were once an orchard belonging to the abbey's monks and were formally laid out as ornamental gardens by John Wood the Elder in 1737. The tidy, flower-bordered lawns are furnished with deck chairs and make a peaceful refuge from bustling Bath and a great picnic venue – not least when the traditional brass band strikes up from the bandstand (May to mid-Sept most Sunday afternoons from 3pm). Among the gardens' numerous commemorative plaques and statues is the original "Angel of Peace" sculpture from c.1910, copied in parks and gardens all over the country, and an image of Bladud, Bath's legendary founder, with one of his pigs who helped reveal the presence of therapeutic springs here (see box, p.43). You'll also see a sundial from 1916 and a Victorian pet cemetery, and there's also a café (Easter–Sept).

There are great views over the Avon and the two bridges – Pulteney Bridge and North Parade Bridge, an iron structure built in 1836 and encased in Bath stone a century later. Overlooking the gardens on the west is **The Empire**, a rather hideous Victorian hotel (now retirement flats) that was taken over by the Admiralty when the latter was relocated outside London at the start of World War II. Rather bizarrely, its roof is variously made up to resemble carved cottages, a townhouse, a gabled manor house and a castle – said to represent the different classes of Victorian customer who were apparently welcomed at the hotel.

Victoria Art Gallery

Bridge St • Tues–Sat 10am–5pm, Sun 1.30–5pm • Free • ☎ 01225 477233, 🅦 victoriagal.org.uk

At the top of Grand Parade, the **Victoria Art Gallery**, built in the 1890s, has temporary exhibitions on the ground floor and an impressive exhibition space upstairs where you can see works by artists who worked locally, including Gainsborough. Beau Nash appears among the subjects of the numerous portraits, while twentieth-century works include Rex Whistler's *The Foreign Bloke* and Walter Sickert's *London Street, Bath*.

Pulteney Bridge and Great Pulteney Street

The flow of the River Avon through Bath is interrupted by a graceful V-shaped weir, just below the Palladian, shop-lined **Pulteney Bridge**. This Italianate structure from

1

around 1760, inevitably calling to mind Florence's Ponte Vecchio, was designed by the Scottish Robert Adam, best known for his work on house interiors, and is now one of Bath's most iconic landmarks.

On the far side of the bridge, the handsome, broad avenue of **Great Pulteney Street** was begun in 1788, planned to be the nucleus of a large residential quarter. The project ran into financial difficulties, however, which is why the roads running off it stop short after a few yards. Nonetheless, the street (the work of Thomas Baldwin) makes a striking impression, with Corinthian pilasters, impressive detail around the first-floor windows and a lengthy vista to the grand classical facade of the Holburne Museum at the end of the street.

Holburne Museum

Great Pulteney St • Mon–Sat 10am–5pm, Sun 11am–5pm • Free • ☎ 01225 388588, ⓦ holburne.org

The imposing columned and pedimented Georgian mansion at the far end of Great Pulteney Street began life as Sydney House, a coffee house and ballroom that backed onto pleasure gardens where Bath's leisured classes were wont to promenade (Jane Austen, who lived at nearby 4 Sydney Place in the autumn of 1801, enthusiastically described the public breakfasts here). Started by Thomas Baldwin and finished by his pupil Charles Harcourt Masters, the building later became a hotel and hydropathic establishment, and since 1916 has housed the **Holburne Museum**, Bath's primary exhibition space for the fine arts. The core of the collection was created by Sir William Holburne (1793–1874), a naval officer who had fought at Trafalgar as an 11-year-old and whose private collection of paintings, silverware and porcelain was bequeathed to the city after his death. It has since been greatly augmented, and in 2011 the interior was completely redesigned, allowing much more light into the rooms, and the building acquired a startlingly modern extension at the back.

First floor

On the first floor, the regal **Ballroom** holds the kernel of Sir William Holburne's collection with numerous later additions: among the ceramics, silver, paintings and a rich collection of sixteenth-century Italian maiolica, highlights include the gracefully contorted *Crouching Venus*, a sculpture attributed to the Florentine Antonio Susini (1572–1608). Some treasures need to be sought out – in the room opposite, for example, drawers open to reveal a collection of miniature spoons and a miniature tea set.

The rest of the museum

The **mezzanine** floor displays items relating to Bath's eighteenth-century "consumer society" – statuettes, plates and some eye-catching vases suspended on cords – while the **top floor** has hilarious caricatures of some of the fashionable visitors to the city of the time, and an impressive gallery showing paintings by Stubbs, Angelika Kauffman and Gainsborough, among others. The latter's most famous work here is the *Byam Family*, his biggest portrait, which originally showed a typical well-to-do couple of the time but was later modified to include the addition of their daughter – her shy presence softening the haughty and slightly austere attitude of her parents. The gallery also includes works that formed part of Somerset Maugham's collection of theatrical paintings, bequeathed to the Holburne, among them a portrait of the eighteenth-century actor-manager David Garrick by Johan Zoffany. Look out too for some minor works by Turner, a couple of pieces by Pieter Brueghel the Younger and a miniature portrait of Beau Nash.

1

Sydney Gardens and the canal

Behind Holburne House, **Sydney Gardens** make a quiet, elegant and shady expanse in which to take a breather. Today, the gardens' slopes are cut through by the railway and the **Kennet and Avon Canal**, whose towpath runs through a couple of short tunnels and beneath two ornate cast-iron bridges overhead. It's a pleasant one-and-a-half mile saunter east along the canal to *The George* pub (see p.66), beyond which you can walk or cycle the whole way to Bradford-on-Avon (see p.69), around ten miles in all. Alternatively, you can **rent a dayboat** for cruises along the canal from Sydney Wharf, near Bathwick Bridge (£60–75 for half-day, £100–120 for full day; ☎01225 447276, ⓦbath-narrowboats.co.uk).

Theatre Royal

Tours Usually Sept–June first Wed and the following Sat of the month 11am; booking not required, but call to confirm the tour is taking place • £4 • ☎ 01225 448844, ⓦ theatreroyal.org.uk

West of the abbey, Westgate Street leads into the largely traffic-free **Sawclose**, once the site of a timber yard. The city's master of ceremonies, Beau Nash, had his first house in Bath here from 1743, in what is now the foyer of the **Theatre Royal**. Opened in 1805, the theatre is one of the country's finest surviving Georgian theatres; it was originally entered from round the corner in Beauford Square, where its monumental facade is preserved. You can join one of the twice-monthly **tours** to view the interior, or book tickets for a play here (see p.67). Next door is Beau Nash's second home in Bath, where he spent his last years, now a *Strada* restaurant.

Queen Square

North of Sawclose, Barton Street leads to the graceful **Queen Square** (1736), a fenced-in pocket of greenery holding a few gravelly areas for games of boules. Now rather besieged by the circulating traffic, the square was the first Bath venture of the architect **John Wood the Elder**, whose home at no. 9 (not no. 24 as a tablet there mistakenly asserts) afforded him a vista of the palatial northern terrace, with its pediment and Corinthian columns and pilasters. Wood had originally planned for the square to contain formal gardens, with a circular pool in the centre from which an obelisk rose; the pool is gone but the obelisk remains, erected in honour of a visit to Bath by Frederick, Prince of Wales in 1738, at the instigation of Beau Nash, who also persuaded Alexander Pope to write the rather lacklustre inscription (Pope was no fan of the Prince). The physician and philanthropist William Oliver (see box, p.55) lived on the square's west side, in a grand house that's now disappeared.

Jane Austen Centre

40 Gay St • April–Oct daily 9.45am–5.30pm, July & Aug Thurs–Sat till 7pm; Nov–March Mon–Fri & Sun 11am–4.30pm, Sat 9.45am–5.30pm • £7.45 • ☎ 01225 443000, ⓦ janeausten.co.uk

North of Queen Square, the **Jane Austen Centre** helps to tie Bath's various Austen threads together with an overview of the author's connections with the city, illustrated by extracts from her writings, contemporary costumes, furnishings and household items. Visitors are given a useful fifteen-minute introductory talk before viewing the exhibits, which also include stills from films and TV adaptations. There's nothing here that Austen obsessives won't already know, but for all others it's an entertaining whirl around life in Bath circa 1800, shedding light on the social and domestic context of the two Austen novels largely set in the city, *Persuasion* and *Northanger Abbey*.

The top floor holds the period-furnished *Regency Tea Rooms* (open to non-visitors to the museum), while the ground-floor shop has all the novels as well as lace, needlepoint and stationery for sale.

JANE AUSTEN'S BATH

Jane Austen paid two long visits to Bath, at the end of the eighteenth century and between 1801 and 1806, setting most of **Northanger Abbey** and much of **Persuasion** here. In fact, Austen wasn't entirely enamoured of the city, expressing relief to be leaving in letters to her sister Cassandra, though it is thought that she fell in love while in Bath, possibly receiving her only known offer of marriage here.

The only place in the city devoted to the author is the **Jane Austen Centre** (see opposite), a Georgian house at 40 Gay Street a few steps up from no. 25, where the writer lived in 1805 – one of a number of places the Austen family inhabited while in Bath. The Jane Austen Festival (see box, p.67) in late September features a promenade through town in Regency costume led by a town crier, and there are banquets, country dances and readings.

Herschel Museum of Astronomy

19 New King St • Feb to mid-Dec Mon, Tues, Thurs & Fri 1–5pm, Sat & Sun 11am–5pm; also open Wed during school hols • £5 • ☎ 01225 446865, ⓦ bath-preservation-trust.org.uk

Five minutes' walk west of Queen Square, a surprisingly modest Bath townhouse was the home of the astronomer Sir William Herschel (1738–1822), who, in collaboration with his sister Caroline, was the first to identify the planet Uranus. The building is now the **Herschel Museum of Astronomy**, celebrating this great achievement as well as the Herschels' other significant breakthroughs: the detection of two of Saturn's and two of Uranus's moons; the discovery of infra-red radiation in sunlight; the cataloguing of nebulae and of the behaviour of binary stars; and – last but not least – the discovery of the disc-like structure of the Milky Way itself. It's an absorbing collection, with knowledgeable and helpful staff ready to answer questions; an audioguide (£1) is worth investing in.

Formerly a German soldier in a Hannoverian regiment, and later an itinerant music teacher in the north of England, William Herschel arrived in Bath in 1766 to take up a post as organist at the Octagon Chapel, off Milsom Street. In 1772, he invited his sister Caroline to join him from Germany, and the couple moved into this building five years later. They left Bath when William Herschel was appointed "King's Astronomer" to George III in 1782, moving to Datchet, near Windsor.

Although both Herschels earned their living in Bath primarily as music teachers, it was astronomy that claimed most of their free time, and was the field in which they made the most lasting impact. Accordingly the museum focuses mostly on their scientific careers, though you don't need to be an astronomy buff to appreciate the collection. The Georgian furnishings and personal knick-knacks of the Herschels in the ground-floor **dining room** give insights into life in contemporary Bath, while cartoons and pictures scattered around the house lend a flavour of the time.

The ground floor and basement

The former **drawing room** displays a replica of the 7ft telescope with which Uranus was identified in 1781, and more instruments are displayed in the basement of the building, where Herschel's preserved **workshop** holds the treadle lathe he used to make parts for his own home-made telescopes. Also here are the **kitchen** and a **cinema** that shows a ten-minute film of Herschel's life and career narrated by the astronomer Sir Patrick Moore. The tiny – once larger – back **garden** was where the telescopes were wheeled out and where the significant discoveries were made. Now it holds a Bath stone statue of William and Caroline from 1988 and a modern stainless steel representation of Uranus.

The first floor

Upstairs, the **Science Room** holds notebooks, letters, examples of eyepieces and such items as a brass orrery, or model of the solar system, and an Indian astrolabe. The adjacent **Music Room** displays a few musical instruments of the Georgian era and usually has a decorous soundtrack of pieces composed by William Herschel. On one

1

wall is a copy of the famous wildly dramatic photographic portrait by Julia Margaret Cameron of John Herschel, William's son and a renowned astronomer in his own right.

The Circus

Up from Queen Square, at the end of Gay Street, the elder John Wood created his masterpiece, **The Circus** (1754–1767), Britain's first circular street. Consisting of three crescents arranged in a tight circle of three-storey houses, this architectural *pièce de resistance* has been compared to an inverted Colosseum and to Stonehenge (which shares roughly the same diameter). A closer look reveals a wealth of detail suggesting other influences, notably in the carved frieze running round the entire circle, where, among a range of arcane, possibly masonic symbols, acorns recall the mythical story of Bath's founding – how Prince Bladud discovered the health-giving waters here with the help of pigs rooting for acorns.

Wood died soon after laying the foundation stone for the "King's Circus", as it was then known, and the job was finished by his son. The centre was originally paved, and the elder Wood had planned for it to be occupied by an equestrian statue of George II, though this was never realised (the towering plane trees were first planted decades later). The painter **Thomas Gainsborough** lived at no. 17 from 1760 to 1774.

Royal Crescent and Victoria Park

The Circus is connected by Brock Street to the **Royal Crescent** (1767–1774), Bath's grandest architectural statement, and said to be the country's first crescent. Built by the younger John Wood, the design reflected the new taste for "picturesque" landscaping, with the stately arc of thirty houses set off by a spacious sloping lawn with a ha-ha (sudden drop), from which a magnificent vista extends to green hills and distant ribbons of honey-coloured stone. The houses themselves, embellished with 114 Ionic columns, are austere in their simplicity and almost indistinguishable from each other, even the house at the centre of the arc, marked by coupled columns, which now fronts the five-star *Royal Crescent Hotel* (see p.63), though lacking any outward advertising of the fact. According to some, the Royal Crescent's design may have been inspired by the older John Wood's belief in the existence of an arc-shaped Druid temple dedicated to the moon that once stood near Stonehenge, though there is no firm evidence for this link.

No. 1 Royal Crescent

Mid-Feb to late Oct Tues–Sun 10.30am–5pm; late Oct to mid-Dec Tues–Sun 10.30am–4pm • £6.50 • ☎ 01225 428126, ⓦ bath-preservation-trust.org.uk

Though rigidly uniform in outward appearance, the interiors of the houses on the Royal Crescent reveal great variations in planning and decoration. You can get a close-up look at one of these, **No. 1 Royal Crescent**, on the corner with Brock Street. The first house to be completed on the crescent, when it was leased to John Wood and Thomas Brock (probably Wood's father-in-law), it has been restored to reflect as closely as possible its original Georgian appearance at the end of the eighteenth century. All furnishings, pictures and other items on display are authentic of the period or else – in the case of the wallpaper – faithful recreations, as explained by the highly informative attendants providing commentaries in each room. Highlights are the sumptuous drawing room hung with green damask silk, the study with its card table, the dining room with its mahogany table laid for dessert, the sepia-toned bedroom and the basement kitchen, which shows an example of a dog wheel, in which a dog was made to run in order to turn a spit. Note that the restoration of the adjacent service building should be complete by 2013, when the kitchen will be restored to its original position and the space currently holding the kitchen will be an educational centre.

1

BATH'S GOLDEN AGE

Covering the first four decades of the eighteenth century, Bath's **Golden Age** was dominated by a handful of individuals who laid down the rules in architecture and social style. Among the arbiters of etiquette, none enjoyed greater prestige than **Beau Nash** (see box, p.57), but Nash's reforms could not have made any lasting impact on the city without the construction of suitably theatrical settings for his social functions. A building boom and a new market in "speculation" – investment in building developments to accommodate the city's seasonal floods of fashionable visitors – was encouraged, in a style commensurate with Bath's grand aspirations. The greatest examples of Bath's distinctive Georgian architecture were largely the work of a father-and-son team, both called John Wood, and both champions of the Neoclassical Palladianism that originated in Renaissance Italy. **John Wood the Elder** (c.1704–1754) retired to his native Bath in 1727 armed with a vision to restore the city to its Roman glory, using the Palladian idiom but incorporating ancient British pagan symbols. His son and collaborator **John Wood the Younger** (1728–1782) continued his work after his death, and towards the end of his life interested himself in improving the sanitation and living conditions of poor labourers.

The "speculative developments" of the Woods and others were constructed in the oolitic limestone, locally called Bath stone, much of which came from local quarries belonging to **Ralph Allen** (c.1694–1764), another prominent figure of the period. A deputy postmaster who made a fortune by improving England's postal routes, and later from Bath's building boom, Allen was nicknamed "the man of Bath", and is best remembered for Prior Park, the mansion he built outside the city based on the elder Wood's designs (see p.59), and for his association with Pope, Fielding and other luminaries who were frequent visitors.

Lastly, the name of **William Oliver** should not be forgotten in the story of Georgian Bath. A physician and philanthropist, Oliver did more than anyone to boost the city's profile as a therapeutic centre, thanks to publications such as his *Practical Essay on the Use and Abuse of Warm Bathing in Gouty Cases* (1751), and by founding the Bath General Hospital to enable the poor to make use of the waters. He is remembered today by the Bath Oliver biscuit, which he invented, apparently as an alternative to the Bath Bun for his liverish patients.

Royal Victoria Park

At the bottom of the Royal Crescent, Royal Avenue leads onto **Royal Victoria Park**, the city's largest open space, containing copious flower displays, an obelisk dedicated to Victoria and Albert, an aviary and nine acres of **botanical gardens**, including a replica Roman temple that was the city's contribution to the British Empire Exhibition in Wembley in 1924. The western end of the gardens, alongside Upper Bristol Road, holds a large, well-equipped children's **play area**, with climbing apparatus, skateboard ramp, zip-lines and tyre-swings.

The park has an old-fashioned bandstand with performances by brass bands on summer Sundays (May–Sept), and the lawns below the Royal Crescent and further west are used for balloon launches (around dawn and towards sunset) and events spilling over from Bath's various festivals. At its east end, the park has a bowling green, **tennis courts** (£4 per person per hour for the outdoor courts, £14 for the indoor ones) and "**adventure golf**" (£4).

Museum of East Asian Art

12 Bennett St • Tues–Sat 10am–5pm, Sun noon–5pm; last admission at 4.30pm • £5 • ☎ 01225 464640, ⓦ www.meaa.org.uk

The private **Museum of East Asian Art** is based on the collection of a retired solicitor who spent more than 35 years in Hong Kong. The pieces are spread over three floors, and include delicate ceramics, a diverse haul of snuff bottles, ivory figurines from the sixteenth century, bronze weaponry and lots of jade – for centuries one of the most highly valued materials in China. The **ground floor** is taken up with wide-ranging exhibitions on such themes as Chinese calligraphy and Japanese kimonos. Among the highlights on the **first floor** are shadow puppets from Thailand and Indonesia and,

1

protected behind a yellow curtain, a gruesome series of nineteenth-century watercolours depicting the Chinese idea of hell, mainly consisting of graphic illustrations of torture (specific methods were accorded to different sins). Also here, in a rare meeting between oriental craftsmen and Bath's high society, you can view examples of armorial porcelain made in China for aristocratic families in England in the eighteenth century.

The Assembly Rooms

Bennett St • Daily: March–Oct 10.30am–6pm, Nov–Feb till 5pm; last admission 1hr before closing • Assembly Rooms £2, Assembly Rooms and Fashion Museum £7.25; £15.50 with the Roman Baths; NT • ☎ 01225 477789, Ⓦ museumofcostume.co.uk

From the time they opened in 1771, the younger John Wood's **Assembly Rooms** were, together with the Pump Room, the centre of Bath's social scene. Here, subscription-holders gathered to play cards, drink tea and engage in polite conversation, no doubt spiced with generous helpings of flirtation and social climbing. The various rooms were used for specific activities, with the centrepiece being, naturally, the stately **Ball Room**, elegantly coved and chandeliered, and still the largest eighteenth-century room in Bath, where genteel minuets and more sprightly country dances were performed. The **Octagon and Card Rooms** were the venues for gambling and card-playing (and organ recitations on a Sunday), and the **Tea Room** for refreshment and music. Jane Austen described evenings in the Assembly Rooms in *Northanger Abbey* and *Persuasion*, while Dickens, another visitor to Bath, wrote in *The Pickwick Papers* how "the hum of many voices, and the sound of many feet, were perfectly bewildering. Dresses rustled, feathers waved, lights shone, and jewels sparkled".

The Assembly Rooms saw tough times in the nineteenth century, with competition from the newly enlarged Pump Room, and in the twentieth century they even briefly housed a cinema before suffering savage bombing in World War II, leaving the structure roofless. A faithful restoration eventually left the Rooms as we see them today, largely following the original eighteenth-century decor and colour scheme. The nine chandeliers are authentic, however, having been safely sequestered during the war. The Rooms are open to view whenever they are not in use for functions, and host **exhibitions and concerts** – ask at the desk about forthcoming events.

The Fashion Museum

Assembly Rooms • Assembly Rooms and Fashion Museum £7.25; £15.50 with the Roman Baths; NT • ☎ 01225 477789, Ⓦ museumofcostume.co.uk

The basement of the Assembly Rooms now houses the **Fashion Museum**, a well-presented and entertaining review of clothing from the Stuart era to the latest Milanese designs. Apart from anything, it's an excellent opportunity to see how the Georgians dressed, showing, for example, the hoops worn under the dresses of society ladies, which they were obliged to remove in designated apartments before joining in the dances at balls. Regular exhibitions focus on different aspects of dress through the ages

---

THE PERFECT LOCATION: BATH IN THE MOVIES

Given their well-preserved state and theatrical panache, it's no surprise that the Georgian buildings and streets of Bath have been used for a plethora of **film locations**, including in such recent titles as *Persuasion* (1995 and 2007), *Vanity Fair* (2004), *The Duchess* (2008) and *The Other Boleyn Girl* (2008). Less predictably, episodes of *Buffy the Vampire Slayer* were filmed here in 2002. The most popular settings are the Assembly Rooms and Royal Crescent. Nearby, scenes from the Charles Darwin biopic, *Creation* (2009) were filmed in Bradford-on-Avon, while Castle Combe and Lacock have also been seen in a steady stream of films, notably *Dr Dolittle* (1967), *Stardust* (2007) and *War Horse* (2011) in Castle Combe, and the Harry Potter series (2001–2009) in Lacock. Groups can arrange for a **tour** of Bath's film and TV locations with Clapperboard Tours (£60 for up to 12 people; ☎ 01225 477773, Ⓦ www.clapperboardtours.co.uk).

BEAU NASH

Bath's social renaissance in the eighteenth century was largely due to one man, **Richard "Beau" Nash** (1674–1761), a Welsh ex-army officer, ex-lawyer, dandy and gambler, who became Bath's Master of Ceremonies in 1704. Determined to rescue the city from the neglect and squalor into which it had fallen, Nash wielded dictatorial powers over dress and behaviour, for instance banning smoking in Bath's public rooms – an early example of health awareness at a time when pipe-smoking was a general pastime among men, women and children – and, most radical of all, forbidding the wearing of swords in public places. (This injunction was referred to in Sheridan's play *The Rivals*, in which Captain Absolute declares: "A sword seen in the streets of Bath would raise as great an alarm as a mad dog.") Less philanthropically, Nash encouraged gambling – in fact his wealth depended on his cut from the bank's takings. Nonetheless, he was generally held in high esteem, his influence even extending to cover road improvements and the design of buildings. Most important of all, the public balls he conducted were of an unprecedented splendour, though rigidly orchestrated – white aprons were banned, scandalmongers were shunned and each function had to begin at six (opening with a minuet "danced by two persons of the highest distinction present") and end at eleven. Nash also exercised his skills in the spa town of Tunbridge Wells, but his fortunes changed when new gambling restrictions were introduced in 1739 and 1745, and long before his death in Bath at the ripe age of 87 he had lost his influence and was reduced to shabby poverty.

– from the evolution of wigs to sportswear, while current and past "Dresses of the Year" are also displayed – a holder of this title has been acquired and shown every year since 1963. An audio guide is included in the ticket price.

Museum of Bath at Work

Julian Rd • April–Oct daily 10.30am–5pm; Nov & Jan–March Sat & Sun only; last entry at 4pm • £5 • ☎01225 318348, ⓦ bath-at-work.org.uk

This down-to-earth collection makes a refreshing antidote to Bath's prevailing tone of high-society hedonism. Installed in a Real Tennis court from 1777, the **Museum of Bath at Work** is largely given over to a recreation of a soft drinks factory and engineering workshop that operated in Bath from 1872, and also includes material on different aspects of the city's industrial, manufacturing and mining history. The ground floor displays reconstructions of a cabinet-maker's workshop and a quarry face, together with an original manually operated crane and the various mining tools used for the extraction of Bath stone, while the top floor holds a pristine Horstmann car, made in Bath in 1914, a self-winding clock also invented by Gustav Horstmann, and a copy of *The Hound of the Baskervilles* written in Pitman shorthand (locally born Isaac Pitman lived on Royal Crescent in the 1890s). Also here is the "velocipede" – a sort of pedal-cart – belonging to entrepreneur J.B. Bowler, whose factory is reconstructed on the museum's middle floor. It features a crowded assemblage of bottling devices, carbonating machines for such fizzy concoctions as Cherry Punch and Orange Champagne, numerous lathes, a brass foundry and even the firm's office, together offering a fascinating insight into the working life of Bath, far removed from the flighty gossip of the Pump Room. Audioguides (included in the ticket price) provide full explanations for all the exhibits.

Building of Bath Collection

The Vineyards, The Paragon • Mid-Feb to Nov Mon, Sat & Sun 10.30am–5pm • £4 • ☎01225 333895, ⓦ bath-preservation-trust.org.uk

Accessed from a raised pavement, the graceful Georgian-Gothic Countess of Huntingdon's Chapel from 1765 now contains the **Building of Bath Collection**, an absorbing exploration of the construction and architecture of Bath. This should ideally be an early stop on your wanderings around the city, with special appeal for anyone interested in the finer points of Palladian architecture. Explaining and illustrating the evolution of the city, the museum focuses on the architectural features that you'll see

1

with examples of everything from the kind of facades associated with the two John Woods, Baldwin, Palmer and others, to such details as balustrades, door designs and sash windows.

The exhibition also focuses on aspects of interior ornamentation, for example marbling, stencilling and japanning (European imitations of oriental lacquer-work). A huge 1:500 scale model of the city allows you to view Bath in long shot.

Lansdown

North of the centre, Lansdown Road ascends to the salubrious heights of **Lansdown**, an aristocratic neighbourhood mostly laid out in the 1790s. Off the lower end of Lansdown Road, it's worth taking a look at **Camden Crescent**, designed by John Eveleigh and with a splendid prospect over city and valley. It's a typically Palladian composition, with Corinthian pilasters and a pediment with a tympanum displaying the arms of Lord Camden, lawyer, MP and Lord Chancellor – the elephant heads over the doorways are his Pratt family crest.

Lansdown's most pleasing groups of buildings, however, lie further up Lansdown Road. With its broad pavements and graceful iron lampholders, **Lansdown Crescent**, the work of John Palmer, is considered one of the city's greatest glories – William Beckford, the eccentric builder of Beckford's Tower (see p.60) lived at nos. 19 and 20. Close by, the quiet and secluded **Somerset Place** is another design by John Eveleigh;

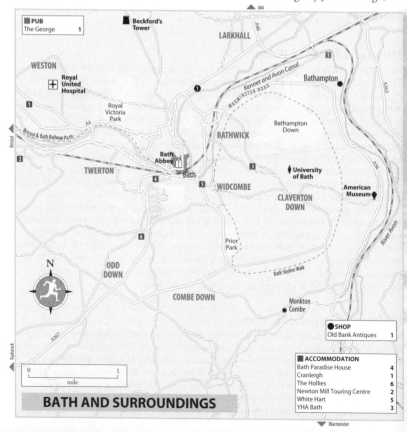

BATH AND SURROUNDINGS

BATH SKYLINE WALK

The streets and lanes of Bath are perfect for gentle ambling, but you can really stretch your legs on the heights to the east of the city by following the **Bath Skyline Walk**, a six-mile trail laid out by the National Trust. The waymarked circular route takes in woods, meadows and two of Bath's sights – Prior Park and the American Museum – as well as **Sham Castle**, a battlemented architectural folly erected in 1762 at the expense of local entrepreneur Ralph Allen, supposedly to improve the view from his townhouse; it's located below the university campus on Bathwick Hill. Needless to say, the vistas of the towers, spires and crescents of Bath from here and numerous other points on the route are superb.

The easiest access points for the Skyline Walk are Cleveland Walk, Bathwick (near the Holburne Museum and the canal), or, higher up, from the University of Bath campus at Claverton (buses #8, #18 or #U18), from where it's signposted alongside a golf course. You can download a free route description and map from the National Trust website (Ⓦ nationaltrust.org.uk), and a leaflet is available from the tourist office and Prior Park.

like Lansdown Crescent it looks out over a fabulous skyline. West of Somerset Place, **Sion Hill Place**, a simple and elegant construction, was the work of one of the last of Bath's great Georgian architects, John Pinch the Elder, in around 1820. Bath Spa University has one of its campuses here.

Prior Park

Ralph Allen Drive • Mid-Feb to Oct daily 11am–5.30pm or dusk; early Nov to mid-Feb Sat & Sun only; last entry 1hr before closing • £5; NT • ☎ 01225 833422, Ⓦ nationaltrust.org.uk/priorpark • Bus #1

One of the leading lights of Bath's Golden Age, Ralph Allen, who made his wealth by providing the stone for the city's rebuilding (see box, p.55), commissioned John Wood the Elder to construct a grand home for himself on a hill southeast of the centre in around 1738. The Palladian mansion, where he entertained such guests as Alexander Pope, Henry Fielding and Samuel Richardson, is now a school and closed to the public. You can, however, pass a pleasurable hour or two in the landscaped grounds, **Prior Park**, part-designed by Capability Brown and draped picturesquely along a valley that was chosen to provide the best views over the Georgian city. A circular path takes in wooded areas, cow pastures and the artificial lake that is the centrepiece of the ensemble, crossed by a perfect Palladian bridge. There are benches for secluded panoramic picnics, and a pleasant garden tea-house halfway along the route.

Note that the walk from the centre is an uphill trudge or cycle-ride along a busy road, and that the limited car parking is reserved for people with disabilities. Everybody else coming from town should consider either taking a taxi or bus from the bus station; Prior Park is also a stop on the hop-on hop-off City Sightseeing service (see box, p.68) and part of Bath's Skyline Walk (see box above).

The American Museum

Claverton, 2 miles east of Bath centre • Mid-March to Oct Tues–Sun noon–5pm, daily in Aug; late Nov to mid-Dec Tues–Sun noon–4.30pm • £8 • ☎ 01225 460503, Ⓦ americanmuseum.org • Free shuttle bus to the museum from Terrace Walk, off Orange Grove, leaving late July to early Sept at noon, 1pm, 2pm, 3pm & 4pm or university buses #8, #18 and #U18 run frequently every day to The Avenue (the stop at the entrance to the campus), from where it's a 10min walk to the museum; alternatively, combine a visit here with other stops on a City Sightseeing Skyline Tour bus (see p.68), which also stops on The Avenue

Built on a high wooded slope in the Greek-Revival style, the early nineteenth-century Claverton Manor was where Winston Churchill made his maiden political speech in 1897. Since 1961 it has been home to the **American Museum**, the first collection of Americana to be established outside the US, with a particular focus on folk and

1

decorative arts. American culture from the seventeenth to the twentieth centuries is illustrated via a series of reconstructed rooms, such as a seventeenth-century "keeping room" (a "hearth" or family room off the kitchen) from Massachusetts and a richly red New Orleans bedroom from the 1860s. Special sections are devoted to textiles, whaling, Native Americans, the opening of the West and Hispano-American culture, while other galleries display rugs, quilts, porcelain and the minimalist furniture associated with the Shaker sect.

Even without the museum, the lovely **grounds** of Claverton Manor make the trek here worthwhile, with sweeping views across the Limpley Stoke valley. The gardens contain a replica of George Washington's garden at Mount Vernon, Virginia, a wigwam, an arboretum and assorted other relics resembling items from a movie set. A separate building houses exhibitions – Marilyn Monroe was a recent subject.

Beckford's Tower

Lansdown Rd, 2 miles north of Bath centre • Sat & Sun 10.30am–5pm • £3 • ⓦ bath-preservation-trust.org.uk • Bus #2

High above the city, aloof from its conventionalities, **Beckford's Tower** is the eccentric creation of one of England's true originals, a soaring flight of fancy concocted in 1827 in order to take advantage of "the finest prospect in Europe". William Beckford (1760–1844) was used to making grand statements: the traveller, collector and author, aged 21, of *Vathek* – an Oriental Gothic romance written in French – was previously known for his *grande folie*, Fonthill Abbey, a vast neo-Gothic palace built in collaboration with the architect James Wyatt, whose central 280ft tower spectacularly collapsed in 1825. Beckford had already sold the ungainly building by this time, and, now a recluse, had moved to Lansdown Crescent in Bath. From here, working with the architect H. E. Goodridge, he directed the construction of his new project, a 120ft-tall Neoclassical tower, Italianate in style, and topped by a belvedere commanding distant views (according to legend, it was from here that Beckford discovered the collapse of Fonthill Abbey's tower, some 25 miles away in Wiltshire).

Beckford passed most of his remaining life in this retreat, riding out from the city to spend his hours in solitary contemplation and study. Fire and rebuilding work have removed his Scarlet and Crimson drawing rooms, the Sanctuary and two libraries, but on the first storey of the tower you can view some of Beckford's preserved *objets* and furniture, along with paintings of the original rooms, a model of Fonthill Abbey and further items relating to Beckford's colourful life. An earthy-pink spiral staircase of 154 steps leads to a small viewing room at the top (the tower's highest section is closed to the public).

Beckford himself is buried in a raised and moated granite sepulchre in the **cemetery** that spreads around the base of the tower, an attractively overgrown site that also holds the tombs of Goodridge (who designed the cemetery's imposing gateway), Sir William Holburne (see p.50) and Beckford's dog.

Dyrham Park

Dyrham, 7 miles north of Bath on the A46 **House** Mid-Feb to early March (servants' quarters only) Mon, Tues & Fri–Sun 11am–4pm; early March to June, Sept & Oct Mon, Tues & Fri–Sun 11am–5pm; July & Aug daily 11am–5pm; early Nov to mid-Dec (servants' quarters only) Sat & Sun 11am–4pm, with grounds **Grounds** Same days 10am–4/5pm • £4.20 **Park** Daily 10/11am–5pm or dusk • £2.90 (on days when house closed) ; NT • ☎ 0117 937 2501, ⓦ nationaltrust.org.uk

The landscape north of Bath is a scenic patchwork of verdant slopes, offering a far-reaching panorama at the top of Tog Hill, near the intersection of the A46 with the A420. A couple of miles north of here, **Dyrham Park** stands on the site of a calamitous defeat of the Celtic Britons by the Saxons in 577. While the extensive parkland affords grand vistas, the house – a late seventeenth-century Baroque mansion – shelters within a dip in the valley, its grand east front presenting a magnificent sight as it swings into view at the end of a long curving drive.

Within the house is a finely decorated but rather sombre succession of rooms panelled in oak, cedar, walnut and gilt leather or else draped in Flemish and English tapestries. Alongside furniture used by the diarists Pepys and Evelyn, many of the contents reflect the career of the first owner William Blathwayt, a diplomat who collected Delftware from Holland, and fine wood from North America for Dyrham's staircases and abundant panelling. Later additions include rows of portraits of the Blathwayt family, who occupied the house for nearly three centuries, and a good painting by Murillo, as well as a copy of the same by Gainsborough.

The name Dyrham means "deer enclosure", and the surrounding 268 acres of parkland are still grazed by fallow deer – and afford marvellous views as far as the Welsh hills. Drama productions are staged every summer in the gardens or courtyard of the house: call ☎0117 937 2501 for details. From the entrance at the top of the drive, you can either walk downhill to the house (about 10min) or take the shuttle bus.

ARRIVAL AND DEPARTURE   BATH

There are no public transport links to Bristol Airport (see p.114); the best option is to take a shuttle bus into Bristol and catch a train from there. A taxi to Bath from the airport would cost £30–40.

By train First Great Western trains stop at Bath Spa station, five minutes' walk from the centre at the bottom of Manvers St.

Destinations Bradford-on-Avon (Mon–Sat 2 hourly, Sun hourly; 15min); Bristol (2–4 hourly; 15min); Chippenham (Mon–Sat every 30min, Sun hourly; 10min); Frome (Mon–Sat 12 daily, Sun 3 daily; 40min); London Paddington (every 30min–1hr; 1hr 40min); Salisbury (every 30min–1hr; 1hr–1hr 50min); Trowbridge (Mon–Sat 2–3 hourly, Sun hourly; 20min).

By bus Bath's bus station is located next to the train station on Dorchester St.

Destinations Bradford-on-Avon (Mon–Sat every 30min, Sun 8 daily; 35–45min); Bristol (Mon–Sat every 12min, Sun every 30min; 55min); Corsham (Mon–Sat 3–5 hourly, Sun 14 daily; 35–50min); Frome (Mon–Sat 2 hourly; 45min–1hr); London Paddington (10 daily; 3–4hr); Salisbury (Mon–Sat every 30min with change, Sun 1 daily; 1hr 25min–2hr 30min); Wells (Mon–Sat hourly, Sun 6 daily; 1hr 20min).

By bike If you're coming from Bristol, you can cycle all the way along the Bristol & Bath Railway Path (see box, p.116), following the route of a disused railway line and the course of the Avon.

INFORMATION AND ACTIVITIES

Tourist office Abbey Churchyard (Mon–Sat 9.30am–6pm, Oct–May till 5.30pm, Sun 10am–4pm; ☎0906 711 2000, ⓦvisitbath.co.uk). Telephone calls cost 50p/minute from land lines. Tickets for some attractions and tours can be purchased here, and a free accommodation-booking service is offered.

Boating Skiffs, punts and canoes for leisurely rides on the

River Avon can be hired from Bath Boating Station at the end of Forester Rd, north of Sydney Gardens (Easter–Sept daily 10am–6pm; £7 per person for 1hr, then £3 per hour; ☎01225 312900, ⓦbathboating.co.uk). On the Kennet and Avon Canal, Bath Narrowboats at Sydney Wharf, off Bathwick Hill, rent day-boats (£60–100 for half-day, £90–165 per full day; ☎01225 447276, ⓦbath-narrowboats.co.uk).

GETTING AROUND

There are few English cities in which **walking** is such an integral part of the experience as Bath. With architectural idiosyncrasies at every corner, walking allows you to take everything in at the pace for which the city was designed. However, to visit some of the more far-flung corners of the city – especially those lying at the top of steep hills – there are good local transport links. For Claverton (for the American Museum and the Bath Skyline Walk), Beckford's Tower and Prior Park, **bus services** are detailed in the Guide.

By bike Hilly Bath is not ideal for biking but the canal towpath is ideal for leisurely excursions. Bike in Bath (ⓦbikeinbath.com) is a council-run cycle-rental scheme, with bikes available for use within the city for up to four hours a day. After registering online or directly at the tourist office (£9 for a day, £13 for a weekend), you get the first 30min free, the

second 30min costs £1, then it's £3 per hour. Bikes can be collected from and deposited at racks at Orange Grove, Holburne Museum, Bath Spa station and Green Park Station. For straightforward bike rental in Bath, try Bath Bike Hire, Bath Narrowboats, Sydney Wharf, Bathwick Hill (£13 for half-day, £19 full day: ☎01225 447276, ⓦbathbikehire.com).

1

By car Cars are simply a hindrance in Bath, and parking is expensive; drivers should use one of the Park-and-Ride car parks (w bathnes.gov.uk) on the periphery of town at Newbridge, off the A4 Bristol road; Lansdown Road, northeast of the centre; Odd Down, southwest of town on the A367 Radstock road; and – Saturdays only – at the University of Bath campus, east of the city off the A36 Warminster road. Two of the most useful car parks are on Charlotte Street, near Queen Square, and Green Park Road west of the stations.

By taxi Ranks at Orange Grove, near the abbey, Bath Spa train station and South Parade, or call Abbey Taxis ☎ 01225 444444 or V Cars ☎ 01225 464646.

ACCOMMODATION

Bath is chock-full of **hotels and B&Bs**, but they do fill up in busy periods. It's always worth booking early, especially at weekends when most places demand a two-night minimum – and prices rise. There's also a choice of good-value, centrally located **hostels**, and there's a decent **campsite** a short distance outside town. Note that the centre can get quite noisy at night, so choose a room away from the street for an undisturbed sleep. As an alternative to staying in Bath, consider Bradford-on-Avon (see p.69), a brief train ride away, with generally lower rates and greater availability.

HOTELS AND B&BS

★ **Bath Paradise House** 88 Holloway ☎ 01225 317723, w paradise-house.co.uk; map p.58. The inspiring views over the city justify the ten-minute uphill trudge from the centre to this Georgian villa, where some rooms have four-posters and three open straight onto the lush garden. In summer, you can try your hand at croquet or boules, and open fires add atmosphere and warmth in winter. Wi-fi available. From **£120**

Belmont 7 Belmont, Lansdown Rd ☎ 01225 423082, w belmontbath.co.uk; map p.44. In the upper town, this simple B&B has large doubles (the single's a bit pokey), most with tiny but clean and modern en-suite bathrooms. The house was designed by the younger John Wood. No credit cards. From **£50**

Brooks Guesthouse 1 Crescent Gardens ☎ 01225 425543, w brooksguesthouse.com; map p.44. Capacious place near Royal Victoria Park, blending traditional and modern elements in mostly good-sized rooms (avoid the cramped attic). Breakfasts are outstanding – abundant, with a huge variety of options. Wi-fi available. From **£80**

Cranleigh 159 Newbridge Hill ☎ 01225 310197, w cranleighguesthouse.com; map p.58. A mile or so west of the centre, this period Victorian house has spacious rooms – three with four-poster beds – and valley views from the back. Nine breakfast options are offered, including pancakes, salmon and fresh fruit salad, and the garden has a hot tub where you can wallow for £12.50 per person for two hours. Wi-fi available. Buses #14, #17, #319 and #332 (#632 Sun). From **£105**

Dukes Hotel 53–54 Great Pulteney St ☎ 01225 787960, w www.dukesbath.co.uk; map p.44. This classic Georgian hotel provides lashings of period atmosphere and occupies a prime location on one of Bath's most characteristic streets. Some rooms have good views and the basement restaurant and bar has a secluded patio. From **£121**

The Halcyon 2–3 South Parade ☎ 01225 444100, w thehalcyon.com; map p.46. Boutiquey hotel with small, smart rooms, some with cooking facilities. Breakfast is extra, at £6.50 per person (or £12 for a cooked option at weekends). The basement bar provides great cocktails and has pavement seating, and there's wi-fi in the bar/reception area. **£125**

Harington's Queen St ☎ 01225 461728, w haringtonshotel.co.uk; map p.46. Central hotel in a converted townhouse with modern, well-equipped rooms, mostly quite small, and some at the top of steep steps. Breakfasts are superlative, food is available throughout the day, service is friendly and there's wi-fi. **£145**

The Henry 6 Henry St ☎ 01225 424052, w thehenry .com; map p.46. Handy guesthouse for the stations and central sights, with seven large, clean and wi-fi-enabled rooms, most with en-suite bathrooms. Cheaper rooms are at the top of the house, and there's a family room on the first floor and a separate apartment. Laundry service available. From **£95**

The Hollies Hatfield Rd ☎ 01225 313366, w theholliesbath.co.uk; map p.58. A fifteen-minute walk south of the stations, off Wellsway (A367), this B&B from 1850 has three meticulously decorated rooms, a cluttered library and a lovely garden overlooked by the neighbouring church. Wi-fi available. No under-16s. **£85**

Marlborough House 1 Marlborough Lane ☎ 01225 318175, w marlborough-house.net; map p.44. Close to the Royal Crescent, this Victorian B&B on a busy road has quiet and elegant rooms with period furnishings, fridges and complimentary sherry. Breakfasts are organic and vegetarian, with options for vegans and those on special diets. From **£95**

★ **Queensberry Hotel** Russel St ☎ 01225 447928, w thequeensberry.co.uk; map p.44. Occupying four Georgian townhouses built for the eponymous marquis, Bath's most luxurious boutique hotel lays on the chic charm, with tastefully minimalist white-walled rooms, a walled garden and a superb basement restaurant, *The Olive Tree* (see p.64). From **£130**

Royal Crescent Hotel 16 Royal Crescent ☎01225 823333, ⓦwww.royalcrescent.co.uk; map p.44. For that special occasion, Bath's most palatial lodging has rooms and suites with sofas, old paintings, fireplaces and bookcases. Bodily needs are taken care of in the gym, spa and top-notch restaurant, where evening set-price menus come to £50 or £60. From **£199**

★ **Three Abbey Green** 3 Abbey Green ☎01225 428558, ⓦthreeabbeygreen.com; map p.46. Classy B&B in a beautifully renovated Georgian house a stone's throw from the abbey. The airy, spotless rooms are wi-fi-enabled; the larger ones overlooking a peaceful square are more expensive but occasionally suffer from street noise. From **£110**

HOSTELS AND CAMPSITE

Bath Backpackers 13 Pierrepont St ☎01225 446787, ⓦhostels.co.uk; map p.46. This central but rather run-down place has location, low rates and a sociable common room in its favour. There's free luggage deposit, a large kitchen, limited wi-fi, laundry service, a "party dungeon" and no curfew or lockout. Beds are in 4– to 10-bed mixed or single-sex dorms. Breakfast extra. Dorms from **£15**

Newton Mill Touring Centre Newton St Loe ☎01225 333909, ⓦnewtonmillpark.co.uk; map p.58. The nearest campsite to the city lies two miles west of the centre (bus #5 to Newton Mill), with the Bristol–Bath cycleway nearby. Facilities are clean and there's a laundry, bar-restaurant and shop. Pitches **£20**

★ **White Hart** Widcombe Hill ☎01225 313985, ⓦwhitehartbath.co.uk; map p.58. The comfiest of Bath's hostels has a kitchen, a first-class bar-restaurant and a spacious courtyard. There are clean doubles and twins available, some with ensuites. Midnight curfew. Dorms **£15**, doubles **£50**

YHA Bath Bathwick Hill ☎0845 371 9303, ⓔbath@ yha.org.uk; map p.58. An elegant Italianate mansion houses this hostel a mile above the centre, with gardens and panoramic views. Most rooms are in a shabby back annexe. Evening meals and a kitchen available. Bus #18 or #U18. Dorms **£16.50**, doubles **£36**

YMCA International House, Broad St ☎01225 325900, ⓦwww.bathymca.co.uk; map p.44. Clean, central and spacious, this place has dorms, singles and doubles, with reductions for weekly stays; all rates include breakfast (but there's no kitchen). Dorms **£18**, doubles **£53**

EATING

Bath has a huge range of places to eat, from inexpensive **cafés** and **tapas bars** to pricey gourmet **restaurants**. Booking in the evening is advisable at most of them, essential at weekends. Many places offer excellent-value set-price meals at certain times, usually at lunchtime and before 7pm. Check out ⓦthepigguide.com for up-to-date news and reviews.

Aió 7 Edgar Buildings, George St ☎01225 443900, ⓦaiorestaurant.co.uk; map p.44. From the bread and olives or spiced sardines for starters to the *fregola* (semolina pasta) and fish skewers, this modern and relaxed place dedicated to Sardinian cuisine has the smack of authenticity. The antipasti to share are also delicious, and all portions are generous. Mains are around £15. Mon–Sat 9.30am–10.30pm, Sun 10am–10pm; food served noon–3.30pm & 5–10pm, Sun till 9.30pm.

Aqua 88 Walcot St ☎01225 471371, ⓦaqua-restaurant .com; map p.44. In a converted Arts and Crafts church house, this atmospheric Italian eatery has chandeliers suspended from the high-beamed roof and a gallery. The menu ranges from pastas and pizzas (£8–14) to char-grilled fillet steak (£20), and the desserts are luscious. Fixed-price menus available at £11.50 before 7pm. Mon–Thurs & Sun 11am–10pm, Fri & Sat 11am–10.30pm.

Bistro La Barrique 31 Barton St ☎01225 463861, ⓦbistrolabarrique.co.uk; map p.46. This place has cornered the market in "French tapas", or *petits plats*, ideal for grazing on such dishes as mushroom flan, bean cassoulet with onions, and braised ox cheek, each costing £5.75–7. There's a walled garden for eating alfresco. Mon–Sat noon–2.30pm & 5.30–10.30pm, Sun noon–2.30pm & 5.30–10pm.

★ **Café Retro** 18 York St ☎01225 339347, ⓦcaferetro.co.uk; map p.46. This congenial spot near the abbey with check tablecloths and a continental air is ideal for a cappuccino and a bite accompanied by a mellow soundtrack. Hot meals such as ratatouille or organic burgers cost around £8, and there are set-price menus on Saturday evening (£12 and £15). The *Retro-to-Go* takeaway next door sells rolls and salads. Mon–Fri 9am–5pm, Sat 9am–9.30pm, Sun 10am–5pm.

★ **Demuths** 2 North Parade Passage ☎01225 446059, ⓦdemuths.co.uk; map p.46. Bath's favourite veggie and vegan restaurant offers original and delicious dishes in an unruffled, arty environment. Choices range from "quick bites" at lunchtime (2 for £12.50) to more substantial "world food" concoctions (£10–15). Beers and wines are organic. Mon–Fri & Sun noon–3pm & 5–9.30pm, Sat 11.30am–3.30pm & 5–9.30pm.

Eastern Eye 8 Quiet St ☎01225 422323, ⓦeasterneye .com; map p.46. This designer curry house occupies a Georgian bank, and has a spectacular vaulted ceiling and huge frescoes. The wide-ranging menu includes such dishes as Sultan Puri Pillau, a zesty lamb, nuts and rice dish; most mains are around £10, or pay £8 for three courses at lunchtime. Mon–Sat noon–2.30pm & 6–11.30pm, Sun noon–11.30pm.

Firehouse Rotisserie 2 John St ☎01225 482070,

1

Ⓦfirehouserotisserie.co.uk; map p.44. Delicious, thin-crusted Californian pizzas (from £11) and grills (mostly £13–15) are the mainstay of this busy place with pleasant staff and a woody interior. Upstairs is smaller and more subdued. Mon–Sat noon–11pm, Sun noon–10pm.

Green Park Brasserie Green Park Station ☎01225 338565, Ⓦgreenparkbrasserie.com; map p.44. Spacious and laidback café-restaurant housed in the old ticket office of a restored train station, with a well-stocked bar, live jazz (Wed–Sat eves), free wi-fi and some outdoor seating. Paninis, cakes and full meals are served (evening mains £11–17, Early Diner menus £10–15). Mon 10.30am–3pm, Tues–Sat 10.30am–11pm, Sun noon–2.45pm (last orders).

Hole in the Wall 16 George St ☎01225 425242, Ⓦtheholeinthewall.co.uk; map p.44. This candlelit subterranean bistro makes a quiet, civilized place to unwind after a day on the hoof. The Modern British dishes are locally sourced and seasonal (most mains £13–19). There are good lunch and early evening deals, and a long wine list. Mon 6–9.45pm, Tues–Sat noon–3pm & 6–9.45pm, Sun noon–3pm.

Jamie's Italian 10 Milsom Place, off Milsom St and Broad St ☎01225 432340, Ⓦjamieoliver.com/italian/bath; map p.44. There's a constant buzz in this large, affable brasserie hidden away in a smart shopping precinct, so you may need to wait for a table at busy times (bookings are not taken). The menu features Mediterranean-style dishes such as Tuscan wild boar sausages and lamb *spiedini* (mains £11–17). Mon–Sat noon–11pm, Sun noon–10.30pm.

Jazz Café 1 Kingsmead Square ☎01225 329002, Ⓦbathjazzcafe.co.uk; map p.44. "Jazz breakfasts", toasted sandwiches, tortillas and mezzes in two sizes (£4.25 and £7.50) are served at this boho hangout. Beers and wines, newspapers and free wi-fi are on hand, and there's some outside seating. Mon–Sat 8.30am–5pm, Sun 10.30am–4pm.

La Perla 12a North Parade ☎01225 463626, Ⓦla-perla.co.uk; map p.44. This Spanish restaurant and tapas bar occupies atmospheric vaults with outdoor seating below pavement level. Most dishes are £5–7, including *calamares* and *bacalao frito*, though the authentic paellas are £12.50 and £14. Even if you're not eating, it's a great place to wind up the day over a glass of wine. Mon–Sat 8am–late, Sun 10am–late.

Lime Lounge 11 Margaret's Buildings ☎01225 421251, Ⓦlimeloungebath.co.uk; map p.44. Small, lively and friendly café-bistro near the Royal Crescent that includes baguettes, home-made soups, tasty burgers, risotto and "posh fish and chips" on the menu. Most dishes are £12–15 (lunchtime is cheaper), and there's a two-for-one deal on mains (Sun–Thurs 5–7pm). Breakfasts and weekend brunches are popular. Mon–Sat 8am–late, Sun 10am–late.

Lucknam Park Colerne, six miles northeast of Bath, off A420 ☎01225 742777, Ⓦlucknampark.co.uk/dining. The restaurant of this luxury hotel in a Palladian mansion has scooped a Michelin star under the direction of chef Hywel Jones, who creates Modern British dishes using the best of seasonal and local produce, some of it from the hotel's own kitchen garden. Set-price menus are £70 for three courses, £80 for four. There's also a less formal brasserie offering a simpler range of dishes from the same kitchen, with mains around £18 and alfresco dining in summer. Restaurant Tues–Sat 6.30–10pm, Sun 12.30–2.30pm; brasserie daily 7.30am–10.30pm.

Olive Tree Russel St ☎01225 447928, Ⓦthequeensberry.co.uk; map p.44. In the basement of the *Queensberry Hotel*, this is one of Bath's top restaurants, offering a contemporary ambience, discreetly attentive service and French-inspired dishes. The changing menu might list crab risotto, squab pigeon and roast venison, and some delectable desserts. Set-price lunches are £16–20, otherwise count on £40–60 per person. Mon 7–10pm, Tues–Sat noon–2pm & 7–10pm, Sun 12.30–2pm & 7–10pm.

Pump Room Abbey Churchyard ☎01225 444477, Ⓦromanbaths.co.uk; map p.46. Splash out on a champagne breakfast, sample the excellent lunchtime menu or succumb to a Bath bun or a range of cream teas, all accompanied by a pianist or classical trio. It's a bit hammy and overpriced, and you may have to queue, but you get a good view of the Baths. When they're available, evening menus list mains at £12–17 (book ahead). Daily 9.30am–4.30pm; July, Aug, Dec & major festivals 9.30am–9pm (last orders).

Sally Lunn's 4 North Parade Passage ☎01225 461634, Ⓦsallylunns.co.uk; map p.46. Trading on the great age of its premises and on what is said to be the original Bath bun, this tearoom and restaurant gets packed, but it's a good opportunity to sample the famous Sally Lunn bun, served here with a choice of more than forty sweet and savoury toppings (£10–11). There are set-price deals, and daytime diners can view the small kitchen museum in the cellar (see p.49). Mon–Sat 10am–10pm, Sun 11am–10pm.

Tilleys 3 North Parade Passage ☎01225 484200, Ⓦtilleysbistro.co.uk; map p.46. The menu in this traditional French bistro includes everything from *escargots* and onion soup to vegetable tart and *boeuf bourguignon*. Dishes come in three sizes, ranging from £6 to 19. It's a bit cramped but there's a downstairs dining area too. Mon–Sat noon–2.30pm & 6.30–10.30pm.

★ Yak Yeti Yak 12 Pierrepont St ☎01225 442299; map p.46. Nepalese restaurant in a series of cellar rooms with a choice of chairs or floor cushions. Meat dishes are stir-fried or spicily marinated, and there's a good vegetarian selection, all £5.50–9. Mon–Sat noon–2.30pm & 5–10.30pm, Sun noon–2.30pm & 5–10pm.

1

DRINKING

★ **The Bell** 103 Walcot St ☎01225 460426, ⓦ walcotstreet.com; map p.44. Easy-going, slightly grungy tavern with a great juke box, live music (Mon & Wed eve, plus Sun lunchtime) and DJs (Fri, Sat & Sun). There's bar billiards and a beer garden with table footy. Mon–Sat 11.30am–11pm, Sun noon–10.30pm.

Coeur de Lion 17 Northumberland Place ☎01225 463568, ⓦ coeur-de-lion.co.uk; map p.46. Centrally located tavern on a flagstoned shopping alley, with a few tables outside (and more upstairs), this is one of three pubs belonging to the local Abbey Ales brewery. It's also Bath's smallest boozer and a regular tourist stop, but persevere for the good lunchtime food and the Victorian trappings, including some nice stained glass. Mon–Sat 10.30am–11.30pm, Sun till 10.30pm, food served noon–6pm.

The George Mill Lane, Bathampton ☎01225 425079, ⓦ chefandbrewer.com; map p.58. Popular canalside pub 20min walk from the centre, with local ales and better-than-average bar food. There's plenty of outside seating. By car it's off the Warminster road, at the bottom of Bathampton Lane. Mon–Sat 11am–11pm, Sun noon–10.30pm.

The Porter 2 Miles Buildings, George St ☎01225 424104, ⓦ theporter.co.uk; map p.44. Very relaxed café/pub serving good beer, coffees and all-veggie food until 9pm, with free wi-fi. There are tables outside and nightly music and comedy events in the *Cellar Bar* (see below) Mon–Wed noon–midnight, Thurs noon–2am, Fri & Sat noon–3am, Sun noon–11.30pm.

The Raven 7 Queen St ☎01225 425045 ⓦ theravenofbath.co.uk; map p.46. Civilized watering hole with first-rate local ales (try the Raven Gold), serve both downstairs and in the less-crowded upstairs room Food available, including renowned pies. Mon–Thurs 11.30am–11pm, Fri & Sat 11.30am–midnight, Sun noon–10.30pm.

The Salamander 3 John St ☎01225 428889 ⓦ bathales.com; map p.44. Bath Ales pub with woody decor and good food at the bar or in the upstairs restaurant It's a laidback kind of place, with a quiet local clientele Mon–Thurs 10am–11pm, Fri 10am–midnight, Sat 9am–midnight, Sun 9am–10.30pm; food served Mon–Sat 9/10am–3pm & 6–9/9.30pm, Sun 9am–4pm.

★ **Star Inn** 23 The Vineyards, The Paragon ☎01225 425072, ⓦ star-inn-bath.co.uk; map p.44. First licensed in 1760, this Bath stalwart has a classic Victorian interior uncompromised by modern intrusions. It's run by the local Abbey Ales, serving such beers as the award-winning Bellringer and draught Bass from a jug. Mon–Fri noon–2.30pm & 5.30–11pm, Sat noon–11pm, Sun noon–10.30pm.

NIGHTLIFE AND ENTERTAINMENT

The two or three **theatres** in town often stage productions before or after their London run, but most of the fare is fairly mainstream. Bath's **music scene** is lively, especially during the festival (see box opposite), while its small but relaxed **clubbing scene**, overshadowed by the proximity of Bristol, takes place mostly in unventilated basements. See the free monthly magazine *Venue* (ⓦ venue.co.uk) or the website ⓦ whatsonbath.co.uk for listings and events.

Back to Mine The Paragon ☎01225 425677, ⓦ backtomineclub.co.uk; map p.44. For a slightly older, more laidback crowd – there's even a back room for real conversation – this club plays everything from retro to reggae. Mon–Sat 10pm–2am.

Chapel Arts Centre St James Memorial Hall, Lower Borough Walls ☎01225 461700, ⓦ chapelarts.org; map p.44. Nice little venue for all kinds of performing arts, with an emphasis on jazz, blues and folk. Arrive early to get one of the cabaret-style tables.

The Common Room 2 Saville Row ☎01225 425550. A bit like someone's front room, this is an intimate spot for late-night chat and chilled sounds, though things get a bit more raucous at weekends. There's a small dancefloor and a quieter room with sofas upstairs. Sun–Thurs 8pm–2am, Fri & Sat 8pm–3am.

Komedia 22–23 Westgate St ☎0845 293 8480, ⓦ komedia.co.uk/bath; map p.46. Cabaret, comedy, punk and ska bands, tribute acts and more are all staged at this venue. Saturdays and most Fridays see the popular Krater Comedy Club, after which you can stay on for club nights. Meals also available.

★ **Moles** George St ☎01225 404445, ⓦ moles.co.uk map p.44. This Bath institution hosts a mix of live music and DJs. The cramped basement can get pretty hot and sweaty – not for claustrophobes. Sun & Mon 11am–midnight, Tues & Wed 11am–2am, Thurs 11am–3am, Fri & Sat 11am–4am.

The Porter Cellar Bar 2 Miles Buildings, George St ☎01225 424104, ⓦ theporter.co.uk; map p.44. Below *The Porter* pub (see above), the *Cellar Bar* has free live music (Mon–Thurs) and DJs (Fri & Sat). Comedy nights (Sun) £7 Mon–Wed noon–midnight, Thurs noon–2am, Fri & Sat noon–3am, Sun noon–11.30pm.

Rondo Theatre St Saviours Rd, off London Rd ☎01225 463362, ⓦ rondotheatre.co.uk. You can get close to the action at this intimate place northeast of the centre, which hosts drama productions, comedy, jazz and folk. Buy tickets at the Festivals Box Office (see box opposite), or at the theatre 30min before start of show.

1

BATH'S FESTIVALS

Bath has a rich range of **festivals** throughout the year, featuring talks, gigs and other events in often sumptuous surroundings. If you're visiting during one of these occasions, you'll find the city's mellow pace livened up a notch or two, but accommodation gets scarce and restaurants fill up. The main events are listed below, but there are a few others scattered throughout the year. For information, call ☎01225 463362, see ⓦ bathfestivals.org.uk, visit the festivals office at 2 Church St, Abbey Green, or check out the individual websites. Tickets for events in most of the festivals can be purchased from the festivals office or the website ⓦ bathboxoffice.org.uk.

Bath Comedy Festival Ten days, usually starting on April Fool's Day (April 1). Stand-up routines from mainstream to left-field in various venues, plus walks and other events (ⓦ bathcomedy.com).

Bath Film Festival Ten days in late Oct or early Nov. Previews, new releases from around the world plus talks (ⓦ bathfilmfestival.org).

Bath Folk Festival A week in early to mid-August. Live music and workshops around the city (ⓦ bathfolkfestival.org).

Bath Fringe Festival From late May to mid-June, with the accent on art and performance (ⓦ bathfringe.co.uk).

Bath International Dance Festival Three days in early May. Great range of classical and modern dance performances, plus taster classes from African to ballet (ⓦ bathdancefest.org.uk).

Bath International Music Festival Twelve days in late May and early June. Features big names in classical music, jazz, folk and world, plus a fireworks display and lots of busking (ⓦ bathmusicfest.org.uk).

Bath Literature Festival Ten days in February/March. Literary big-hitters and others give talks and readings, and participate in discussions (ⓦ bathlitfest.org.uk).

Bath Mozartfest Ten days in mid-November. Classical performances, mainly at the Guildhall and Assembly Rooms (ⓦ bathmozartfest.org.uk).

Jane Austen Festival Last full week of September. Walks, talks and a parade in Georgian costume (ⓦ janeausten.co.uk).

Theatre Royal Sawclose ☎01225 448844, ⓦ theatreroyal.org.uk; map p.46. Theatre and ballet fans should check out what's showing at this historic venue, if only for the atmosphere. More experimental productions are staged in its Ustinov Studio. Book as early as you can.

SHOPPING

Retail therapy is always close at hand in Bath, where **shopping** has been a major pastime at least since Austen's day. As in every British town, **chain stores** are much in evidence, but Bath's strength lies in its range of independent, chic **boutiques**, speciality food shops and galleries. There's a concentration of these squeezed into the tiny lanes north of the abbey, and you'll find more clusters in and around Bartlett Street (near the Assembly Rooms), and Brock Street (near the Royal Crescent), while Milsom Street, where Jane Austen's contemporaries once patronized millinery shops and dressmakers, still holds some of Bath's smartest stores.

INDEPENDENT SHOPS

Bath Aqua Glass 1–2 Orange Grove & 105–107 Walcot St ☎01225 428146, ⓦ bathaquaglass.com; map p.44 & p.46. Glass objets of every description are sold here, including delicate jewellery. There are nods to the locale, in the addition of copper oxide to the molten glass to produce an aquamarine effect reminiscent of Bath's thermal waters, and in the "Georgian Range" which includes Jane Austen goblets. You can watch the glass being blown in the Walcot St branch, with demonstrations at 11.15am and 2.15pm, and courses are available. Orange Grove Mon–Sat 9.30am–6pm, Sun noon–6pm; Walcot St Mon–Sat 9.30am–5pm.

Bath Old Books 9c Margaret's Buildings ☎01225 422244; map p.44. Maps, prints and antiquarian books are sold at this classic old shop, one of very few of the kind remaining in the city. Bargains to be found.

Mon–Sat 10am–5pm.

Bath Sweet Shop 8 North Parade Passage ☎01225 428040; map p.46. The oldest sweet shop in town sells all your granny's favourites – mint humbugs, dolly mixtures, lemon sherberts and liquorice. Sugar-free alternatives are available too. Mon–Sat 10am–5.30pm, Sun till 5pm.

Beaux Arts 12–13 York St ☎01225 464850, ⓦ beauxartsbath.co.uk; map p.46. There's always plenty to admire among the contemporary sculptures and ceramics in this smart gallery near the abbey – thought-provoking canvases, beautifully executed bronze statuettes and richly coloured pottery by world-class artisans. It's the sister-gallery of Beaux Arts in Cork Street, London – the three- and four-figure price tags may daunt, however. Mon–Sat 10am–5pm.

⭐ **Found** 17 Argyle St ☎01225 422001, ⓦ foundbath.co.uk; map p.46. As well as lovely views over the weir, this

1

boutique on Pulteney Bridge offers a quirkily original selection of dresses, contemporary satchels and shoes, plus a range of gifts from prints to notebooks. Mon–Sat 10am–6pm, Sun noon–4pm.

The Highgrove Shop 38 Milsom St ☎01225 445125, ⓦhighgroveshop.com; map p.44. The merchandise in this high-quality gift shop selling Prince Charles's own Highgrove brand has a predictable flavour – fancy crockery, tweed caps, gardening knick-knacks, organic wines – but you'll find the odd ethically produced lotion or horticultural book that appeals. Mon–Sat 9.30am–5.30pm, Sun 10.30am–5pm.

★ **Mr B's** 14–15 John St ☎01225 331155, ⓦmrbsemporium.co.uk; map p.44. Lovely independent bookshop on three floors, with armchairs and fresh coffee for browsers. It's strong on fiction, travel writing and children's literature, and has an inspiring local-interest section. Mr B's was Independent Bookshop of the Year in 2008 and 2011. Mon–Sat 9.30am–6.30pm.

Old Bank Antiques Centre 14–17 Walcot Buildings, London Rd ☎01225 469282, ⓦoldbankantiquescentre .com; map p.58. Antique shops are thick on the ground in Bath, but this complex of eleven dealers has a wider selection, fewer airs and graces, and lower prices than most.

The shops specialize in Georgian and Victorian silver, ceramic and furniture, but you'll also find 1970s retro, lighting and brassware. Mon–Sat 10am–6pm, Sun 11am–5pm.

Paxton & Whitfield 1 John St ☎01225 466403, ⓦpaxtonandwhitfield.co.uk; map p.44. Cheeses galore and everything to do with cheese, are available in this corne shop, where you'll encounter an array of goat's and sheep's cheeses, Cornish blues, Somerset bries and Frenc camemberts among the 100-plus varieties, not to mention local ciders and apple juices, and some very handsome olive wood boards. Mon 10am–6pm, Tues–Sat 9.30am–6pm.

Sassy & Boo 9 Green St ☎01225 447938 ⓦsassyandboo.com; map p.44. New and vintage dres designs, modern jewellery, handmade leather bags, glove and belts are all available in this boudoir-like store – a chandeliers, mirrors and dressing tables. Also specializes in hand-sewn frocks and accessories reproduced from the 1920s. Mon–Sat 9.30am–5.30pm, Sun 11am–4pm.

★ **Scarlet Vintage** 5 Queen St ☎01225 338677 ⓦscarletvintage.co.uk; map p.46. This tiny vintage sho packs a lot in. The great choice of clothes and accessorie runs from glamorous Charleston-era handbags to 1950 brooches and 1970s sequined disco dresses. Mon–Sa

---

TOURS IN AND AROUND BATH

A **tour** with an informative and/or entertaining commentary can be the best way to take in a lot of Bath in a short time. For orientation and insider's knowledge, you can't beat the free **walking tours** conducted by the Mayor of Bath's Honorary Guides; these cover the main architectural sites, with heaps of historical detail and insight that reveal the guides' genuine passion for the city. The walks leave daily from Abbey Churchyard at 10.30am and 2pm (☎01225 477411, ⓦbathguides.org.uk; no 2pm tour on Sat; May–Sept also Tues & Fri 7pm; 2hr). If you want to go at your own pace, you can **download a walking tour** in mp3 format from ⓦvisitbath.co.uk, either in its entirety or in individual chapters.

Bizarre Bath With the emphasis on entertainment rather than information, Bizarre Bath offers "comedy walks" around the city, offering an irreverent and idiosyncratic take on the city with magic tricks thrown in, taking place every evening from April to October (☎01225 335124, ⓦbizarrebath.co.uk; 1hr 30min; £8); meet at 8pm outside the *Huntsman Inn* on North Parade Passage.

Ghost Walks For fans of the macabre and gruesome, two-hour ghost walks leave from outside the *Garrick's Head* pub next to the Theatre Royal at 8pm (☎01225 350512, ⓦghostwalksofbath.co.uk; Thurs–Sat; £7).

Jane Austen walks The Jane Austen Centre arranges ninety-minute walks in the author's footsteps, leaving from Abbey Churchyard (☎01225 443000, ⓦjaneausten.co.uk; Sat & Sun all year at 11am, also July & Aug Fri & Sat at 4pm; £6).

Bus tours There is a plethora of open-top bus tours with commentaries available all year, leaving from

Grand Parade or the bus station (all-day tickets £11.50), for example City Sightseeing (☎01225 444102, ⓦcity-sightseeing.com), which operates both city and skyline tours – the latter taking in the higher reaches of the city around Claverton Down.

Boat tours Between Easter and October, hour-long river trips can be made from Pulteney Bridge; operators include Pulteney Cruisers (March–Sept 1–3 hourly; £8; ☎01225 312900, ⓦbathboating.com) and Avon Cruising (April–Oct 5–7 daily; £8; ☎07791 910650, ⓦwww.pulteneyprincess.co.uk).

Outside Bath Mad Max Tours offers half- or full-day minibus excursions with commentaries to the villages of Lacock and Castle Combe, Stonehenge, Avebury and the Cotswolds, using minor roads wherever practical (☎07990 505970, ⓦmadmaxtours.co.uk; £17.50–35), while Scarper Tours conducts daily trips to Stonehenge lasting three hours, including at least an hour at the site (☎07739 644155, ⓦscarpertours.com; £15).

1

10.30am–5.30pm.

Topping & Company The Paragon ☎ 01225 428111, ⓦ toppingbooks.co.uk; map p.44. This book-lover's bookshop has a huge range of titles, including a great travel section with an excellent selection of maps. Check the website for regular author talks. Daily 9am–8pm.

MARKETS AND SHOPPING CENTRES

Green Park Station Green Park Rd ⓦ greenparkstation. co.uk; map p.44. Formerly a terminus of the now-defunct Midland Railway, in use between 1870 and 1960, this refurbished station has a few permanent shops selling food and crafts Monday to Saturday, but is best known for its various markets, including Bath's Farmers' Market every Saturday morning, and a vintage and antiques market on the last Sunday of the month. The *Green Park Brasserie* provides refreshments (see p.63).

Guildhall Market Between High St and Grand Parade ⓦ bathguildhallmarket.co.uk; map p.46. The dome of this indoor market, which has been in operation since 1770, is one of Bath's landmarks. It's worth a rummage for its delicatessens, craft shops and general bric-a-brac. Mon–Sat 8am–5.30pm.

Jolly's 13 Milsom St ☎ 0844 800 3704, ⓦ houseoffraser. co.uk; map p.44. Bath's oldest department store is now part of the House of Fraser group, but hasn't lost its idiosyncratic style nor its maze-like layout. There's something for everyone among its gents' suits, ladieswear, perfumes and handbags, with top brands represented. Mon–Thurs 9.30am–5.30pm, Fri 8am–8pm, Sat 9am–6pm, Sun 10.30am–5pm.

SouthGate Centre Between Southgate St and Manvers St ⓦ www.southgatebath.com; map p.44. Part covered, part broad avenues, this modern precinct opened in 2010 has big-name megastores including Debenhams and H&M as well as independent stores (Avon Valley Cyclery), brand outlets (Karen Millen, Tommy Hilfiger and Calvin Klein) and modern galleries (Whitewall Gallery). Mon–Wed & Fri 9am–7pm, Thurs till 8pm, Sat till 6pm, Sun till 5pm.

DIRECTORY

Cinemas Little Theatre Cinema, Bath's only independent cinema, St Michael's Place (☎ 0871 902 5735, ⓦ picturehouses.co.uk); Odeon, James St West, Kingsmead Leisure Complex (☎ 0871 224 4007, ⓦ odeon.co.uk).

Hospital Royal United Hospital (Combe Park, ☎ 01225 428331, ⓦ www.ruh.nhs.uk) has an emergency department.

Internet @ Internet, 13 Manvers St (daily 9am–9pm); Library, 19 The Podium, Northgate St (Mon 9.30am–6pm, Tues–Thurs

9.30am–7pm, Fri & Sat 9.30am–5pm, Sun 1–4pm).

Laundry Coin-operated washers at Spruce Goose, 4 Margaret's Buildings, until 7pm daily. Service washes also available.

Left luggage @ Internet (see above) accepts bags for £2.50–6.50 each according to size, while *Bath Backpackers* (see p.63) charges £3 per item per day.

Post office 27 Northgate Street (Mon–Sat 9/9.30am–5.30pm).

Around Bath

Bath has plenty to occupy your time, but it also makes a useful base or starting point for expeditions across the county border into Wiltshire. River, canal and train line run together to **Bradford-on-Avon**, which, with its old tithe barn and rows of cloth-workers' cottages interspersed with handsome merchants' mansions, makes an enticing destination in its own right, and is also a viable alternative to staying in Bath itself. With its homogeneous pale stone architecture, Bradford has more than a whiff of the Cotswolds about it, a sensation that grows stronger in such meticulously preserved villages as **Lacock**, once home to the photography pioneer William Fox Talbot, whose work is showcased in the museum attached to local crowd-puller **Lacock Abbey**. Further off the beaten track, the villages of **Corsham** and **Castle Combe** are equally well preserved, and boast an outstanding collection of Old Masters in **Corsham Court**.

There are good **transport** connections from Bath to Bradford-on-Avon and Corsham, but nothing direct to Lacock or Castle Combe, for which it's easiest to take a train to Chippenham and catch a bus from there.

Bradford-on-Avon

Just over the border in Wiltshire's northwest corner, eight miles east of Bath, **BRADFORD-ON-AVON** is an appealing small town with buildings of mellow fawn-coloured stone, many in a striking style sometimes described as vernacular Baroque, and reminiscent of the architecture of Bath and the nearby Cotswolds. Sheltering against a steep wooded slope, the town takes its name from its "broad ford" across the River Avon, and for six centuries Bradford – like its Yorkshire namesake – made its living from the mills that once lined the river, powering its wool and cloth trade. The local textiles industry was revolutionized by the arrival of Flemish weavers in 1659, and much of the town's architecture reflects the prosperity of this period – both the splendid stone houses owned by the rich wool manufacturers and the humbler cottages of the spinners and weavers working from home. The impact on the town of the gradual decline of Britain's cloth manufacture was partially offset in the last century by the growth of a rubber industry, with many of the tall mills adapted for use for the production of rubber components, though this too ended in 1992. More recently, Bradford has evolved as a local cultural and shopping centre, with a vibrant local arts scene and small independent stores in and around the pedestrianized **Shambles**, just up from the bridge off Silver Street.

The town's long history is reflected in its tithe barn and its rich heritage of churches, most significant of which is **St Laurence**, dating from Saxon times. A short distance outside town lies **Great Chalfield Manor**, a well-preserved fifteenth-century house.

The town bridge

Bradford's original fording place was replaced in the thirteenth century by a **bridge** that was in turn largely rebuilt in the seventeenth century, and which is still the focal point of the town. The small domed structure at its southern end, the **Blind House**, is a quaint old lock-up, or jail for the drunk and disorderly, converted from a chapel in the seventeenth century. Its weather vane is topped with a golden gudgeon, or fish, an early Christian symbol.

Looking west along the river from the bridge you'll see **Abbey Mill** from 1857, the last woollen mill to be built in Bradford and now containing retirement apartments.

Bradford-on-Avon Museum

Library, Bridge St • Mon–Fri 10am–5pm, Sat & Sun 10am–6pm • Free • bradfordonavonmuseum.co.uk

A brief walk east from the bridge along Bridge Street will bring you to Bradford's **museum**, housed above the library. It's a strictly local collection, an entertaining diversion worth a few minutes for its diminutive Roman sarcophagus, a reconstructed Victorian pharmacy and various war mementoes. Among the curiosities are photographs of the underground mushroom crops that were once harvested from a nearby quarry, and a couple of **Moulton bicycles** – the revolutionary small-wheeled bike that was all the rage in the 1960s was designed and built in Bradford by Dr Alex Moulton, still a local resident.

Saxon church of St Laurence

Church St • Usually daily 9.30am–5pm, stays open longer in summer, closes earlier in winter • Free

Bradford's most significant building is the tiny church of **St Laurence**, an outstanding example of Saxon church architecture. Tall and narrow with small windows, its exact age is uncertain; though it has been suggested that it dates back to the eighth century, the architecture points to an early eleventh-century construction. Later used as a school and a simple dwelling, it was reworked by a local vicar in the 1860s and the west wall was rebuilt. Its only decoration is two carved angels flying across the nave's east wall. The north entrance has photographs and documents relating to the Saxon church.

Holy Trinity

Church St • Open for services & mid-June to early Sept daily 2.30–4pm • Free

Tall as it is, St Laurence is almost dwarfed by the much larger medieval church of **Holy Trinity** standing below it. Originally twelfth-century, the parish church was much rebuilt in later times. Inside are various memorials and brasses connected to the wool industry, and what is claimed to be England's longest "squint", or opening through the wall allowing people in peripheral parts of the church a view of the altar.

St Mary Tory

Off Newtown • Usually daily 9.30am–5pm, stays open longer in summer, closes earlier in winter • Free

From Holy Trinity, a steep uphill path brings you to the **Tory** neighbourhood (from *tor*, meaning "hill", the loftiest part of Bradford with bird's-eye views over town and river stretching as far east as the Marlborough Downs. Nestled among the cottages, accessed along footpaths, the fifteenth-century chapel of **St Mary Tory** once served the needs of pilgrims en route to Glastonbury. Heavily renovated in the nineteenth century, it's a very simple affair, the interior illuminated by beautiful stained-glass windows from 1999. The adjoining former hospice is now a private dwelling.

Northeast of St Mary Tory, past prosperous houses once belonging to managers and high-ranking specialists in the cloth industry, **Zion Baptist Chapel** dating from 1698, is worth a glance, though it's rarely open.

The Tithe Barn

Daily 10am–5pm • Free

Heading down narrow Barton Orchard from Holy Trinity church, or following the river southwest from Bradford's town bridge, you'll come to the medieval **Barton Packhorse Bridge** across the Avon, a pretty and serene sight, untroubled by traffic. East of the bridge stands Bradford's **Tithe Barn**, a magnificently preserved example of buildings used by religious houses to store food (a "tithe" was a tenth of a tenant's produce). This one, dating from the fourteenth century, was owned by Shaftesbury Abbey – once the richest nunnery in the country – and boasts a fine cruck roof, made from curved timbers extending to the ground, and the old threshing floor.

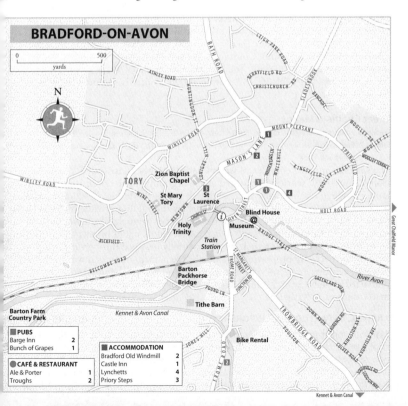

BRADFORD-ON-AVON

PUBS	
Barge Inn	2
Bunch of Grapes	1

CAFÉ & RESTAURANT	
Ale & Porter	1
Troughs	2

ACCOMMODATION	
Bradford Old Windmill	2
Castle Inn	1
Lynchetts	4
Priory Steps	3

1

THE WEALTH OF WOOL

The wealth of northeast Somerset and the Cotswold region was founded on the huge growth in England's **wool trade** and cloth industry in the Middle Ages. Compared to continental breeds, English sheep were small and neat, with long, soft fleeces, and they thrived on the verdant, well-watered uplands of the Cotswolds to the north. The proximity of these grazing pastures combined with the abundant and fast-flowing rivers to power the fulling mills (where woven cloth was felted to make it thick and strong) generated a good deal of wealth in the area around Bath and Bradford-on-Avon. Much of the trade was owned and run by the great religious houses, such as Bath Priory, one of the richest houses in the southwest, while its beneficiaries embraced the whole gamut of society, including such people as Chaucer's Wife of Bath, who lived "bisyde Bath", probably in the important weaving village of Twerton, now a Bath suburb. Bradford's cloth industry flourished in the seventeenth and eighteenth centuries, dwindling to almost nothing by 1900, though, like nearby Castle Combe, the town preserves its picturesque rows of weavers' and cloth-workers' cottages.

On the east side of the farmyard, the restored granary now holds a shop. Note the dovecote on the rear wall of the farmhouse, a source of meat during winter. The old cow byres surrounding the main building now house craft shops, workshops, galleries and a tea garden (ⓦ www.tithebarnartscrafts.co.uk).

Along the canal to Avoncliff

Extending west of the Tithe Barn, the **Barton Farm Country Park** offers wooded walks and picnic areas between the river and canal. The towpath along the **Kennet and Avon Canal** offers the possibility of easy walks or cycle rides, either thirteen miles east to Devizes, or a mile and a quarter west to **Avoncliff**, a lovely spot where the canal crosses the river on a graceful viaduct. There's a pub with riverside seating here, and a good café-restaurant (see opposite). Continuing north will bring you to another viaduct at **Dundas**, and eventually to Bath. You can **rent bikes** from TT Bikes, where Frome Road crosses the canal (☏ 01225 867187, ⓦ towpathtrail.co.uk; £10–15 per day); they also rent out **canoes**.

Great Chalfield Manor

Near Holt, 2.5 miles northeast of Bradford House • **Guided tours** April–Oct Tues–Thurs 11am, noon, 2pm, 3pm & 4pm, Sun 2pm, 3pm & 4pm • £7.80 **Garden** April–Oct Tues–Thurs 11am–5pm, Sun 2–5pm • £5 • NT • ☏ 01225 782239, ⓦ nationaltrust.org.uk • Zig Zag bus to Holt (not Sun), then walk 1 mile

The splendid moated complex of **Great Chalfield Manor** consists of a house dating from about 1480, sensitively restored at the beginning of the twentieth century as a family home, plus an equally ancient church and outbuildings. The house has the typical exterior of a Cotswold manor, all gables and mullions, while its **Great Hall** is overlooked by a minstrels' gallery from which three gargoyle-like masks gaze down into the hall, the eyes cut away so that the womenfolk could inspect the proceedings below without jeopardizing their modesty. Briefly besieged during the Civil War, the modest but perfectly proportioned house has remained much as it was in the late fifteenth century, a rare survival of the period and genre. The interior of the pinnacled **church** features some fifteenth-century wall paintings depicting the martyrdom of St Katherine.

ARRIVAL, DEPARTURE AND INFORMATION
BRADFORD-ON-AVON

By train Bradford's train station, with regular connections to Salisbury, Dorchester, Bath and Bristol, is close to the town centre on St Margaret's Street.
Destinations Bath (Mon–Sat 2 hourly, Sun hourly; 15min); Bristol (1–2 hourly; 30–40min); Chippenham (1–2 hourly

with change; 35min); Salisbury (1–2 hourly; 45min–1hr).
By bus Most buses stop on Silver Street, St Margaret's Street and Frome Road.
Destinations Bath (Mon–Sat every 30min, Sun 8 daily; 35–45min); Chippenham (Mon–Sat 1–2 hourly with

change; 1hr–1hr 40min); Corsham (Mon–Sat 4 daily; 55min); Lacock (Mon–Sat 2–3 hourly with change; 2hr); Salisbury (Mon–Sat hourly with change; 2hr).

By bike or on foot The canal towpath offers a pain-free way to reach Bradford from Bath; it's about 9 miles.

Tourist office 50 St Margaret's St (April–Oct Mon–Sat 10am–5pm, Sun 10am–4pm; Nov–March Mon–Sat 10am–4pm, Sun 11am–3pm; ☎01225 865797, ⓦ bradfordonavon.co.uk).

ACCOMMODATION

Bradford Old Windmill 4 Mason's Lane ☎01225 866842, ⓦ bradfordoldwindmill.co.uk. The three rooms in this unusual B&B include one with a waterbed and a spa bath, though the best views are from the Fantail suite. There are seven choices of breakfast, and "ethnic" vegetarian evening meals can be pre-arranged (Mon, Wed, Thurs & Sat only; £25). 2nt minimum stay at weekends. Closed Nov–Feb. From **£100**

Castle Inn 10 Mount Pleasant ☎01225 865657, ⓦ flatcappers.co.uk. Four boutiquey rooms with thick carpets, contemporary designs and generous bathrooms are available at this excellent inn at the top of town. First-class food and real ales are served in the flagstone bar, and there's a large garden. From **£100**

★ **Lynchetts** 15 Woolley St ☎01225 866400, ⓦ lynchetts.co.uk. This handsome Georgian B&B is in the centre of town, but you might as well be in the country for its peace and quiet, not least in the huge garden which includes a croquet lawn (mallets available) and orchards that provide the fresh fruits, jams and honey served at breakfast. If you don't mind the stairs, the attic room offers most space as well as seclusion. Wi-fi and parking available. No credit cards. From **£75**

★ **Priory Steps** Newtown ☎01225 862230, ⓦ priorysteps.co.uk. Above the centre, with great views over the rooftops from all rooms, this spacious family home was converted from seventeenth-century weavers' cottages. The owners are friendly, the elegant rooms come with modern bathrooms and dinners are available with notice (£28). **£55**

EATING, DRINKING AND ENTERTAINMENT

★ **Ale & Porter** 25 Silver St ☎01225 868135, ⓦ aleandporter.co.uk. This open-plan space with contemporary art on the walls makes a great spot for delicious pastries, organic coffees, snack lunches or something fuller, for example fishcakes with roasted Mediterranean vegetables or wild mushroom risotto. Prices are reasonable, with set-price meals around £14.50 for two courses, £18.50 for three. Tues & Wed 9am–5pm, Thurs–Sat 9am–3.30pm & 6–11pm, last orders 9pm.

Barge Inn 17 Frome Rd ☎01225 863403. Relax by the canal in this freehouse with various eating areas and a large garden. Melksham and other local beers are on tap, and the menu includes baguettes as well as such dishes as steak and ale pie and quiche (mostly £9–14). Daily 11.15am–late, food noon–9pm.

Bunch of Grapes 14 Silver St ☎01225 863877, ⓦ grapespub.com. Cosily old-fashioned pub with good wines, beers and meals – notably steaks and a renowned range of pies (all £13–17). Mon & Tues 6–11pm, Wed &

Thurs noon–2.30pm & 5–11pm, Fri noon–2.30pm & 5pm–midnight, Sat noon–midnight, Sun noon–10.30pm; food served Mon 6–8pm, Tues 6–9.30pm, Wed & Thurs noon–2pm & 6–9.30pm, Fri & Sat noon–2.30pm & 6–10pm, Sun noon–4pm & 5–8pm.

★ **Troughs** Avoncliff ☎01225 868123, ⓦ troughsatavoncliff.co.uk. Whether it's a crusty cheddar sandwich, mushrooms on toast with parsley and parmesan or mutton tagine, everything on the menu at this simple café-restaurant tastes fresh and zingy. Hot dishes cost around £8. Most of the tables are outside, and local juices, wines, beers and ciders are also available. It's worth booking on summer evenings. Daily 9am–5pm, closes 8pm during summer school hols.

Wiltshire Music Centre Ashley Rd ☎01225 860100, ⓦ wiltshiremusic.org.uk. High up on the outskirts of town (on the Bath side of Bradford), this arts centre hosts music and other cultural events throughout the year, specializing in world, folk, classical and jazz.

Corsham

Like Bradford-on-Avon, **CORSHAM**, about seven miles northeast of Bath and the same distance north of Bradford, grew rich on the manufacture of cloth, and its nearby quarries were also a source of building stone. It's a friendly, low-key village, thankfully free of traffic and bustle, with a concentration of well-preserved historic buildings as well as a good range of small, independent shops, pubs and cafés to amble around, all on or close to the central, part-pedestrianized High Street. The street holds buildings of every period, including Corsham's elegant **town hall** dating

1

from 1783 (rebuilt a century later), and, at the bottom of the street, a row of **Flemish Buildings** where weavers fleeing Catholic persecution settled in the seventeenth century.

Corsham Court

Mid-March to Sept Tues–Thurs, Sat & Sun 2–5.30pm; Oct, Nov & Jan to mid-March Sat & Sun 2–4.30pm • £7, gardens only £2.50 • ☎ 01249 712214, Ⓦ www.corsham-court.co.uk

Corsham's star attraction is unquestionably **Corsham Court**, accessible from Church Street off the High Street. Though the house dates from Elizabethan times, major rebuilding in the eighteenth century by Lancelot "Capability" Brown, John Nash and Humphrey Repton effaced most of the Tudor construction, and a further radical remodelling by Thomas Bellamy in the 1840s replaced most of Nash's work. The interior was furnished by Thomas Chippendale and Robert and James Adam among others, while the landscaped grounds, designed initially by Brown, were completed forty years later by Repton. House and gardens have featured in such films as *The Remains of the Day* and in the BBC adaptation of *Tess of the D'Urbervilles*.

For the Methuen family, who took possession of the property in 1745, the house was first and foremost a showcase for the magnificent collection of sixteenth- and seventeenth-century art originally assembled by Sir Paul Methuen, an ambassador to Portugal. The centrepiece is Capability Brown's long **Picture Gallery**, still covered in the original rich, red damask silk wall-hangings and topped by an intricate plaster ceiling. Works displayed here include paintings by Van Dyck, Guercino and Guido Reni; other rooms contain pieces by Rubens, Andrea del Sarto, Turner, Lely and Reynolds. Among the stand-outs are an Annunciation by Fra Filippo Lippi in the **Cabinet Room** and, in the **State Bedroom**, an allegorical painting of Elizabeth I in old age and a pair of gaudy but gracefully carved eighteenth-century wall mirrors of English design.

After viewing these masterpieces, take time to stroll around the gardens, which include a Gothic Bath House, the joint work of Capability Brown and John Nash, a host of strutting peacocks and, in spring, a splendid display of magnolias. The six hundred acres of parkland include a lake created by Repton.

Hungerford Almshouses

Corner of Pound Pill & Lacock Rd • Feb, March, Oct & Nov Sat 1–3pm; April–Sept Tues & Wed 11am–4pm, Fri & Sat 1.30–4pm • £3 • ☎ 01249 701414, Ⓦ corshamalmshouses.org.uk

Opposite the original main gateway to Corsham Court, a brief walk from the High Street, **Hungerford Almshouses** is one of Corsham's most revered buildings, a heavily gabled complex built in 1668 for "6 poor people" and "10 needy scholars" by Lady Margaret Hungerford, wife of a commander of Parliamentary forces during the English

---

BOX TUNNEL AND CORSHAM'S QUARRIES

When **Isambard Kingdom Brunel** (see box, p.100) extended the Great Western Railway in the 1830s, he was confronted by a massive obstacle in the form of **Box Hill**, a couple of miles west of Corsham. His solution was simply to bore through it, creating what was then the longest **railway tunnel** in the world, at nearly two miles. In recognition of the achievement, the western entrance to the tunnel was given an imposing Neoclassical style (though the embellishment is invisible to rail passengers). The excavations revealed large new deposits of quality **limestone** (or Bath stone) which spurred the local underground quarrying business and boosted the local economy. The **quarries** were used in the 1930s and during World War II to store ammunition and even contained a munitions factory, and in the 1950s they were earmarked as a regional seat of government in the event of nuclear war, to accommodate up to four thousand people. The centre was decommissioned in 1991 and declassified in 2004.

Civil War who lived in Corsham Court. The well-preserved exterior displays the flamboyant Hungerford coat of arms, and at the back the Pentice, or cloister, still holds cottages for homeless or needy locals. Inside you can tour the original schoolroom, with a gallery, pulpit and seventeenth-century benches still showing ancient graffiti, and an exhibition room with explanatory panels.

ARRIVAL AND INFORMATION   CORSHAM

By bus There are bus stops on Newlands Road and Pickwick Road, close to the High Street.
Destinations Bath (Mon–Sat 4–5 hourly, Sun 1–2 hourly; 35–50min); Bradford-on-Avon (Mon–Sat 4 daily; 50min–1hr); Castle Combe (Mon–Sat 5 daily with change; 40min–1hr); Lacock (Mon–Sat 1–2 hourly, most with change;

15min–1hr).
Tourist office 31 High St (Mon–Sat 10am–4pm; ☎01249 714660, ⓦcorshamheritage.org.uk). A free accommodation-booking service is offered. The historic building also houses a heritage centre, focusing on the local cloth and quarrying industries.

ACCOMMODATION

The Garden House 46a High St ☎01249 701166, ⓔmail@rowanhousecorsham.co.uk. Friendly and central B&B above a sculpture-strewn yard, offering just two smart en-suite doubles. It's not huge, but it's got loads of character. No credit cards. **£80**

Methuen Arms 2 High St ☎01249 717060, ⓦthemethuenarms.com. This pub offers chic, contemporary rooms in dark brown and grey tones, and bathrooms with rainforest showers and free-standing baths. Good food and drink are served in the bar. **£120**

EATING AND DRINKING

The Century Martingate Centre ☎01249 701400, ⓦthecentury.co.uk. In a shopping precinct just off the High Street, an old chapel house has been sympathetically converted into a modern café-bar and restaurant, serving breakfasts, doorstep sandwiches and staples such as gammon steak, lasagne with garlic bread and gourmet burgers with sweet chilli and mozzarella – most mains are £9–10. If you don't want to eat, just come for a coffee or evening drink – there's outdoor seating. Daily

8.30am–11pm, food served until 9pm.
Cinnamon 8 High St ☎01249 701190. With its cottagey interior and friendly atmosphere, this place is ideal for a coffee and pastry, a snack lunch or a candlelit supper. The soup of the day might be spicy sweet potato and coconut, evening mains (around £15) include grilled mackerel fillets with pesto, and there's a brasserie menu (Mon–Thurs eves with dishes £5–8). Mon–Sat 9am–4pm & 7–9/9.30pm, meals served noon–2pm & 7–9pm.

Lacock

With its lime-washed, half-timbered stone houses, **LACOCK**, four miles southeast of Corsham, is a perfectly preserved if highly gentrified version of an English feudal village. The National Trust owns all but three houses here – a curious state of affairs, but one that has ensured Lacock's survival in a relatively pristine and tack-free state. As an established coach stop, however, the village is besieged by tourists all summer, many of them here to view the settings of the various period dramas and movies that have been filmed in the village and its abbey, including scenes from the Harry Potter films. The wealth accumulated from the wool trade is still evident in Lacock's well-to-do houses and fine church, and some historic inns and excellent B&Bs provide added incentives for a detour here.

In the village, the Lady Chapel in the fifteenth-century church of **St Cyriac** contains Sir William Sharington's opulent tomb beneath a splendid lierne-vaulted roof where traces of paint testify to its once brightly coloured appearance. Three panels on the front of the tomb show Sharington's crest with a scorpion in each.

Lacock Abbey

House Early Jan to early Feb, Nov & Dec daily noon–4pm; mid-Feb to late Oct daily except Tues 11am–5pm • £10.70, with museum, cloisters & grounds; NT **Cloisters, grounds & museum** Early Jan to early Feb, Nov & Dec daily 11am–4pm; early Feb to Oct daily 10.30am–5.30pm • £7.90; NT • ☎01249 730459, ⓦnationaltrust.org.uk

Standing gracefully aloof within its grounds at one end of Lacock village, **Lacock Abbey** consists mainly of an eighteenth-century neo-Gothic stately home, but a few monastic

1

fragments survive from the nunnery founded in 1232 by Ela, Countess of Salisbury, including the original cloisters, chapter house and sacristy. The rest was levelled during and after the Dissolution of the Monasteries in 1539, when the abbey passed to Sir William Sharington; ten years later Sharington was arrested for colluding with Thomas Seymour, Treasurer of the Mint, in a plot to subvert the coinage. Sharington narrowly escaped with his life by shopping his partner in crime – who was beheaded – and after a period of disgrace managed to buy back his estates. Furniture and paintings owned by later generations of the family are now displayed in a series of rooms, culminating in the lofty **Great Hall**, its walls studded with terracotta figures in niches (look out for the sugar lump on the nose of a goat, first placed here in 1919).

The Fox Talbot Museum

Appropriately for such a regular TV and film location, the grounds of Lacock Abbey hold a fascinating museum dedicated to the founding father of photography, **William Henry Fox Talbot** (1800–1877), a scion of the Sharingtons and the first person to produce a photographic negative, in 1834 (five years before the announcement of the discovery of the daguerreotype process in France). The **Fox Talbot Museum**, in a sixteenth-century barn by the abbey gates, captures something of the excitement he must have experienced as the dim outline of an oriel window in the abbey's south gallery slowly imprinted itself on a piece of silver nitrate paper. A copy of the postage-stamp-sized result is on display in the museum (the original is in the National Media Museum in Bradford, Yorkshire). Fox Talbot enjoyed a reputation in many other fields, and some of the exotic trees in the abbey were planted by him.

ARRIVAL AND DEPARTURE LACOCK

By bus Almost all bus routes go via Chippenham; Lacock's stop is outside *The George* pub on West Street.
Destinations Bath (Mon–Sat 3 hourly with change; 1hr 10min–1hr 40min); Bradford-on-Avon (Mon–Sat hourly with change; 40min–1hr 10min); Castle Combe (Mon–Sat 5 daily with change; 40min–1hr 20min); Chippenham (Mon–Sat 2 hourly, 20min); Corsham (Mon–Sat 1–2 hourly, most with change; 15min–1hr).

ACCOMMODATION, EATING AND DRINKING

At the Sign of the Angel 6 Church St ☎ 01249 730230, ⓦ lacock.co.uk. This hostelry has all the low ceilings, beams and sloping floors you could wish for. Each room is different – those in the main house have more medieval character, ones in the annexe across the garden are cheaper. The restaurant also has plenty of atmosphere, and garden seating amid an orchard and stream; sandwiches are £7, set-price two-course meals are £14 at lunch and £18 at dinner. Food served Mon 7–9pm, Tues–Sun 12.30–2pm & 7–9pm. **£130**
George Inn 4 West St ☎ 01249 730263, ⓦ wadworth .co.uk. Dating from 1361, this Wadworth pub has beams, a fireplace, a dog-wheel (once used for turning a spit) and a range of food, from baguettes (£4.50–6) to venison steak (mains around £12.50). Some outdoor seating. Mon–Sat 9am–11pm, Sun 10am–10.30pm; food served noon–2pm & 6–9pm.
★ **Lacock Pottery** The Tanyard, Church St ☎ 01249 730266, ⓦ lacockbedandbreakfast.com. Lovely old B&B overlooking St Cyriac's, with antiques, a warming fire in winter and fresh produce from the garden for breakfast. Rooms are quiet and comfortable – the more expensive Governor's House has its own entrance – and the gallery showing the owner's pottery is also worth a look. **£84**

Castle Combe

Set in a wooded valley four miles north of Lacock, **CASTLE COMBE** is a quintessential Cotswold hamlet, all pale-gold houses grouped around a fourteenth-century market cross and an even older church largely financed by wealthy wool merchants. The church can also be accessed from the local manor house, which in the early fifteenth century was the property of Sir John Fastolf, on whom Shakespeare based his comically villainous character Falstaff. In fact, the real Fastolf – who never actually came to Castle Combe – was said to be a loyal and respected follower of Henry V, fighting with him at Agincourt. Hidden within its grounds, the house is now a swanky hotel with a Michelin-starred restaurant (see opposite).

Mills once lined the Bybrook stream running through the village, but the cloth industry folded in the eighteenth century after an unexplained drop in the river's level, the last mill closing in the early 1800s. The town, which had far outstripped nearby Chippenham in size and influence, dwindled to a set-in-aspic village, which now trades largely on the golf course attached to the hotel in the old manor house and the racetrack located a short distance outside.

St Andrew's

Dating back to the thirteenth century, the richly endowed church of **St Andrew's** shows traces from most subsequent periods, including examples of Early English, Decorated and Perpendicular windows. In the north aisle lies the effigy and tomb (from 1270) of the Norman baron, Walter de Dunstanville, who is said to have built the original castle from which the village takes its name. At the back of the church, at the base of the bell tower, you can admire the workings of a seventeenth-century faceless clock – though it's now electrically powered.

Castle Combe Circuit

Three quarters of a mile southeast of Castle Combe on the B4039 • ☎ 01249 782417, ⓦ castlecombecircuit.co.uk

Back in the twenty-first century, Castle Combe is best known for the **Castle Combe Circuit** racing track, though it's well out of sight of the village, with noise levels rigidly controlled. Race days for Formula Fords, GTs, sports cars, classic saloons from the 1950s and 1960s, and motor bikes take place on selected Saturdays, Sundays and Mondays between March and October, with tickets £12–15. On Action Days and Track Days you can take a turn at the wheel yourself, with prices ranging from £35 for a circuit (plus £10 admission) to £170 per day.

ARRIVAL AND DEPARTURE   CASTLE COMBE

By bus The only bus services in Castle Combe are #35, #35A and #75 to Chippenham (Mon–Sat 4 daily; 25–40min).

ACCOMMODATION, EATING AND DRINKING

Castle Inn ☎ 01249 783030, ⓦ castle-inn.info. In keeping with the dominant tone of the village, this is a romantic but posh bolthole, with small, smart rooms and modern bathrooms. Bar snacks and full meals (£10–20) are available downstairs 11.30am–2.45pm & 6.15–9pm (bar open all day until 11pm). From **£115**

Manor House Hotel ☎ 01249 782206, ⓦ manorhouse. co.uk. One of the most luxurious hotels in the region, this place wears its history on its sleeve, stuffed with oak panelling, antique furnishings and old paintings. Some of the rooms have Elizabethan fireplaces but the cheaper ones are in blander cottage annexes. The setting is magnificent, with a tennis court and golf course in the ample grounds. The Michelin-starred *Bybrook* restaurant, with chef Richard Davies at the helm, is well worth investigating, at £60 for three courses. From **£190**

Bristol and around

STREET ART IN STOKES CROFT

2

Bristol and around

The South West's de facto capital and one of the most vibrant urban centres outside of London, dynamic, cosmopolitan Bristol has harmoniously blended its mercantile roots and rich maritime history with an innovative, modern culture, fuelled by a lively arts and music scene. While not as immediately attractive as nearby Bath, a simple stroll round the medieval quarter, along the rejuvenated waterfront or through the gorgeous suburb of Clifton will gradually reveal the Bristol that John Betjeman once declared "the most beautiful, interesting and distinguished city in England."

Up snug against the borders of Gloucestershire and Somerset, Bristol is defined by the River Avon, which weaves through the centre and forms part of a system of waterways that once made the city a great inland port. The revitalized **Harbourside** remains a focal point, home to heavyweight attractions such as M Shed and the *ss Great Britain*, part of Brunel's illustrious impact on the city's landscape and, along with his Suspension Bridge, one of its greatest monuments.

The tongue of land that juts out into the harbour holds picturesque Queen's Square and historic King Street, southern highlights of the compact **Old City**, a blend of medieval churches, merchants' houses and lively markets. A short walk from here leads to the celebrated religious sites of cockeyed **Temple Church** and striking **St Mary Redcliffe**, each the focus of its eponymous neighbourhood, or, in the other direction, Bristol Cathedral, at the foot of shop-lined **Park Street**. Some of the city's best restaurants and bars can be found here, towards the top of the hill, in the surrounding streets of the **West End** and on Whiteladies Road.

Whiteladies acts as the eastern boundary of **Clifton**, Bristol's most refined neighbourhood. Running west to the very edge of the Avon Gorge, it is famously home to some beautiful Georgian housing, as well as the Downs, trumped only by the estates of Ashton Court and Blaise Castle in the city's leafy ensemble of attractive parks and green spaces.

CLIFTON SUSPENSION BRIDGE

Highlights

❶ St Nicholas Markets Browse for bargains at historical St Nick's, stock up on fresh produce at the Wednesday Farmers' Market or catch the ground-breaking monthly Slow Food extravaganza. **See p.87**

❷ Street art Nelson Street showcases the work of some of the best street artists in the world, while Stokes Croft's ever-evolving cityscape includes Banksy's most famous mural. **See p.89 & p.110**

❸ ss Great Britain Moored in the dock in which she was built, the iconic ship is now an iconic museum, an interactive insight into life aboard a nineteenth-century steamer. **See p.98**

❹ Clifton Fine Georgian mansions and a buzzing café culture make the crescents of

Clifton well worth a wander. **See p.106**

❺ Clifton Suspension Bridge Brunel's "darling" soars above the ragged edges of the dramatic Avon Gorge. **See p.106**

❻ Eating out Bristol's restaurants are the best in the West, with "local" and "seasonal" the buzzwords on most of the city's menus. **See pp.118–126**

❼ Bristol International Balloon Fiesta Memorable four-day festival held in the wooded grounds of Ashton Court Estate. **See p.136**

❽ The Chew Valley Attractive lakes, country pubs and a ring of ancient standing stones, set in verdant countryside just a few miles from Bristol. **See p.137**

HIGHLIGHTS ARE MARKED ON THE MAP ON P.83

2

ARK AT EE! THE RUFF GUYED TO SPEEKEN BRIZZLE

One of the warmest and most rhythmic of local dialects, **Bristolian** or Bristolese (or, to use the local lingo, Brizzle), is proudly spoken throughout the city, and particularly by *Bemmies* and *Meaders* – residents of Bedminster and Broadmead, respectively.

"Celebrated" by Little Britain's Vicky Pollard (Matt Lucas studied in Bristol), it can roughly be characterized by a confusion of **ownership** and the **first- and third-person singular**, and the **addition of an "l"** to words ending with a vowel – which is how the Anglo-Saxon city of Brycgstow ultimately became "Bristol". A proper Bristolian can cram them all into one single sentence, with bewildering effect: "*I luvs ASDAwl, I does; are muh done, mind*" or "I like ASDA but my mum doesn't".

The below words and phrases should start you off, but for a handy on-the-street **reference**, check out *A Dictionary of Bristle* by Harry Stoke and Vinny Green (£5.95).

BASIC WORDS AND PHRASES

Macky	*mack-ee*	Big
Gert macky	*guRt mack-ee*	Very big
Gert macky biggun	*guRt mack-ee big-en*	Enormous
Proper job	*pRahp-eR jaahb*	Nice work
Gert lush	*guRt luush*	Very nice
Alright my lover?	*awlRite moi luvveR?*	How's it going?
How be on young 'un?	*ow bee-yon young ern?*	How's it going?
Ow bis me babber?	*ow biss mee babbeR?*	How's it going?
Where's ee to?	*wuRz ee two?*	Where is he?
Cheers then drive	*chuRz en droive*	Thanks for the lift
Laters!	*lay-uRz!*	See you!
That's mint, innit?	*thas menn, en-et?*	It's good
Ark at ee!	*aRk at eeeee!*	Listen to you!
I'll have two of they	*oil aave tua they*	Two of those, please
Don't tell I, tell ee!	*doughn tell aye, tell ee!*	It's not my problem
Zider I up	*zydeR aye up*	A pint of cider please
Forn or fatch?	*fawRn oaR faatch?*	What kind of cider would you like, Dry Blackthorn or Thatchers?

Conservative Clifton contrasts sharply with **East Bristol**, where the city's reputation for free thinking is alive and kicking in Stokes Croft, the artsy area of Montpelier and the slowly resurgent, West Indian-influenced district of St Pauls. Across the Avon in **South Bristol**, Southville – drolly referred to as "Lower Clifton'" due to its gentrification over the last decade or so – is centred around the hub of bars, delis and chilled-out cafés that is North Street, and has seen its fortunes revived by the Tobacco Factory, a neighbourhood-defining theatre and arts centre.

Somerset begins just beyond the suburbs, and it's a short hop down the A37 or A38 to the picturesque **Chew Valley**, a scenic taster of the verdant fields and rolling hills that await to the south.

Brief history

Legend points to Bristol being founded in the sixth century by **Brennus**, a descendant of Brutus, the mythical King of Britain, but the earliest known settlements here were the **Iron Age hill forts** at Blaise Castle, Burwalls and Stokeleigh (in Leigh Woods), and at Clifton Camp on the opposite side of the Avon Gorge.

The Anglo-Saxon trading centre of **Brycgstow** – the first recorded reference to the city we know today as Bristol – grew up around Bristol Bridge (*Brycgstow* means "Place of the Bridge"), on the high ground, away from the far-reaching tides of the River Avon, that is now Castle Park. The natural protection afforded by the Avon (and from the River Frome) was supplemented by stout city walls and, under the Normans, a castle,

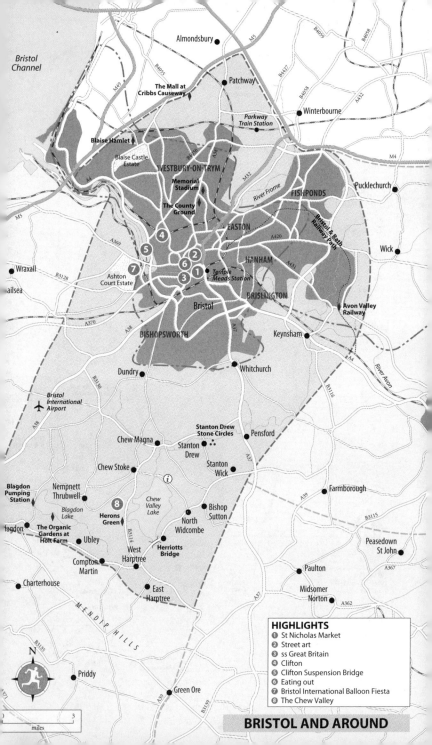

Bristol Channel

Almondsbury

The Mall at
Cribbs Causeway

Patchway

Winterbourne

*Parkway
Train Station*

Blaise Hamlet

Blaise Castle
Estate

WESTBURY-ON-TRYM

Memorial
Stadium

FISHPONDS

Pucklechurch

River Frome

The County
Ground

EASTON

Bristol & Bath
Railway Path

Wick

④

⑤

HANHAM

② ⑥ ① ⑦

*Temple
Meads Station*

③

Wraxall

Ashton Court Estate

BRISLINGTON

ailsea

Bristol

Avon Valley
Railway

BISHOPSWORTH

Keynsham

River Avon

Dundry

Whitchurch

*Bristol
International
Airport*

Stanton Drew
Stone Circles

Pensford

Chew Magna

Stanton
Drew

Chew Stoke

Stanton
Wick

ⓘ

Farmborough

Blagdon
Pumping
Station

Nempnett
Thrubwell

*Chew Valley
Lake*

⑧

Herons
Green

Bishop
Sutton

Blagdon Lake

Peasedown
St John

lagdon

The Organic
Gardens at
Holt Farm

Ubley

North
Widcombe

Compton
Martin

West
Harptree

Herriotts
Bridge

Paulton

Charterhouse

East
Harptree

Midsomer
Norton

M E N D I P   H I L L S

N

Priddy

Green Ore

0   3
miles

HIGHLIGHTS

① St Nicholas Market
② Street art
③ ss Great Britain
④ Clifton
⑤ Clifton Suspension Bridge
⑥ Eating out
⑦ Bristol International Balloon Fiesta
⑧ The Chew Valley

BRISTOL AND AROUND

2

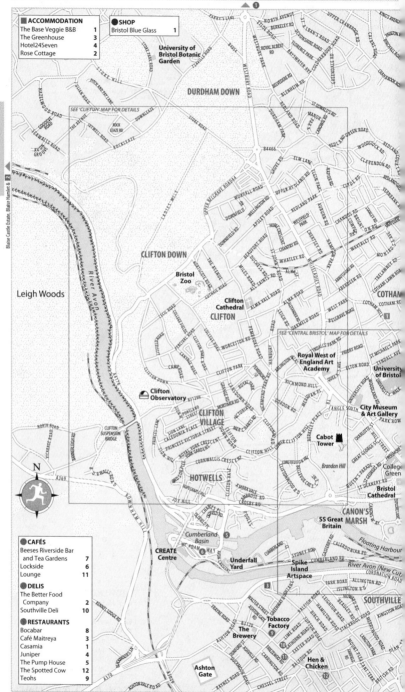

■ ACCOMMODATION

The Base Veggie B&B	1
The Greenhouse	3
Hotel24Seven	4
Rose Cottage	2

● SHOP

| Bristol Blue Glass | 1 |

● CAFÉS

Beeses Riverside Bar and Tea Gardens	7
Lockside	6
Lounge	11

● DELIS

| The Better Food Company | 2 |
| Southville Deli | 10 |

● RESTAURANTS

Bocabar	8
Café Maitreya	3
Casamia	1
Juniper	4
The Pump House	5
The Spotted Cow	12
Teohs	9

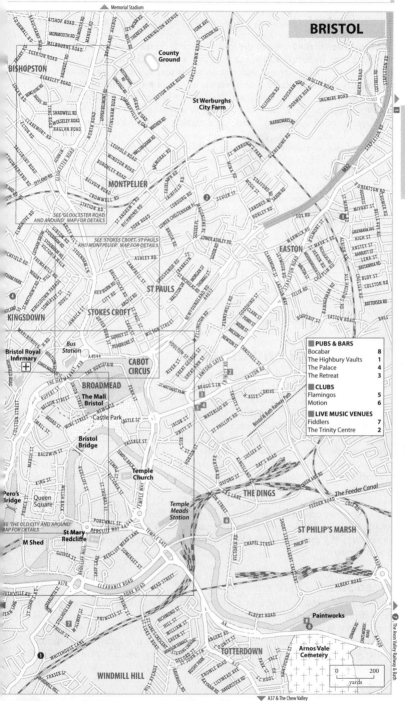

BRISTOL

Memorial Stadium

BISHOPSTON

County
Ground

St Werburghs
City Farm

MONTPELIER

EASTON

SEE 'GLOUCESTER ROAD
AND AROUND' MAP FOR DETAILS

SEE 'STOKES CROFT, ST PAULS
AND MONTPELIER' MAP FOR DETAILS

ST PAULS

KINGSDOWN

STOKES CROFT

Bristol Royal
Infirmary

Bus
Station

CABOT
CIRCUS

BROADMEAD

The Mall
Bristol

Castle Park

Bristol
Bridge

Pero's
Bridge

Queen
Square

Temple
Church

SEE 'THE OLD CITY AND AROUND'
MAP FOR DETAILS

M Shed

St Mary
Redcliffe

Temple
Meads
Station

THE DINGS

The Feeder Canal

ST PHILIP'S MARSH

Paintworks

Arnos Vale
Cemetery

TOTTERDOWN

WINDMILL HILL

A37 & The Chew Valley

■ PUBS & BARS	
Bocabar	8
The Highbury Vaults	1
The Palace	4
The Retreat	3
■ CLUBS	
Flamingos	5
Motion	6
■ LIVE MUSIC VENUES	
Fiddlers	7
The Trinity Centre	2

0   200
yards

later enhanced with a huge keep – the ruins of which just about survive today in Castle Park.

The **diversion of the Frome** in the mid-thirteenth century increased the nascent harbour's capacity for trade, and the granting of a **Royal Charter** a hundred years later enhanced the city's power and widened its boundaries to include previously separate settlements such as Redcliffe. But it was the advent of **transatlantic trade** – sparked by John Cabot's discovery of America in 1497 – that helped Bristol really boom, the trading of tobacco, sugar and most notably **slaves** bringing enormous wealth and privilege to the city's merchant classes and making it the busiest commercial centre outside of London.

Much of this money helped fund the building of modern-day Bristol: Temple Meads station, the Suspension Bridge and the graceful Georgian houses that stagger down Clifton, to name a few. The area around the Old City would be just as grand were it not for the heavy bombing it sustained during **World War II**, a particularly brutal Blitz that wiped out more than a quarter of medieval Bristol. The rise of some hideous postwar architecture around Broadmead and Temple coincided with the commercial demise of the harbour, marking a shift towards technology-based businesses, such as the aerospace industry (**Concorde** was built at Filton), and the fields of computing, communications and design. Today, the city increasingly serves as a testbed for **eco** entrepreneurs – it's home to the Soil Association; Sustrans, the charity behind the UK's National Cycle Network; and the world's first Slow Food Market – and was recently voted the UK's most sustainable city. Even the Council House, the seat of local government, uses recycled rainwater. Bristol has become that kind of a place.

The Old City and around

The church-cluttered wedge that constitutes the **Old City** is a compact lesson in Bristol's history. Heading south from Castle Park, it starts at the centre of the initial Saxon settlement and leads, via narrow alleyways and ancient markets, to the historic buildings of cobbled **King Street** and grand merchants' houses of **Queen Square**, whose tranquil air belies its turbulent past.

The harbour may have brought much of Bristol's wealth, but trade was established here long before that. The church of St Mary le Port in **Castle Park**, one of the oldest in the city, was originally known as St Mary de Foro ("of the Market"), and the mercantile classes had been striking deals for centuries before they packed up their tables and moved into the grander surroundings of the Exchange – a practice that continues today in the form of **St Nicholas Markets**. The Castle District, the biggest commercial centre of recent times, was all but flattened during World War II, though the shopping tradition survives in the ugly, postwar development of **Broadmead**, and the later, more sympathetically designed **Cabot Circus**, one of the largest inner-city retail centres in the South West.

Broad Street

Crowned with churches and leading down to the old city wall, condensed **Broad Street** gives perhaps the best impression of how medieval Bristol once looked – along with High Street, Wine Street and Corn Street, it is one of the city's four original thoroughfares. Interest today lies in its range of architectural styles, which run the gamut from the Greek Doric former **Bank of England**, at nos. 13–14, to the **Guildhall** next door, the earliest Gothic town hall in England.

Christ Church

Broad St • Wed 1.10–1.45pm • Free • ⓦ christchurchcitybristol.org

Standing at the very heart of the Old City, eighteenth-century **Christ Church** is most notable for its little tunic-clad quarterjacks, who strike their bells outside the clock every quarter of an hour; you can only get a glimpse of the elaborate interior on Wednesday lunchtimes when the church is open for organ recitals, piano concerts and other musical events.

Everard's Printing Works

37–38 Broad St

2

The stunning Art Nouveau facade of the former **Everard's Printing Works** can come as a bit of a shock, standing back from the street as it does, and hidden behind the neighbouring buildings. Designed by W. J. Neatby in 1901, and made using Carrara-Ware tiles, the lavish mural depicts Johannes Gutenberg (spelled "Gutenburg" here) and William Morris – the fathers of modern printing – separated by the Spirit of Literature and presided over by a woman holding a lamp (representing Light) and a mirror (Truth). Everard's name, spanning the two arches below, is written in a typeface he designed himself. Nothing survives of Henry Williams's interior, which is now home to a bank.

St John the Baptist

Broad St • Tues, Wed & Thurs 10am–1pm • Free • ⓦ visitchurches.org.uk

The striking church of **St John the Baptist** is unique in Bristol, the last of five churches that were built into the city walls, its slim tower and spire straddling the archway of St John's Gate. The side passages were added in 1828, but the carved statues on either side of the gate are much older: Brennus, legendary founder of the city, and his brother Belinus.

It ceased to be a working church long ago, but it's worth venturing into what is effectively the city wall for a peek inside the spooky vaulted **crypt**, and to admire the rather grand **monument of Walter Frampton**, the three-time Mayor of Bristol who founded St John in the fourteenth century.

Corn Street

Running at a right angle to Broad Street, Corn Street is home to the excellent St Nicholas Markets, the majority of it occupying John Wood the Elder's eighteenth-century **Exchange**, arguably his finest public building. It was designed specifically to house the merchants who were blocking up the surrounding streets – they settled their debts on the four flat-topped **brass pillars** (or nails) outside, hence the expression to "pay on the nail". The **clock** above the entrance has two minute-hands: "Bristol Time" and, just over ten minutes ahead, "Railway Time" (GMT), adopted by the city in 1852 following the advent of Brunel's London–Bristol line the decade before.

St Nicholas Markets

Corn St • Mon–Sat 9.30am–5pm, also first Sun of month 11am–5pm • ⓦ stnicholasmarketbristol.co.uk

Bustling **St Nicholas Market** is the largest collection of independent retailers in the city, over sixty traders peddling just about everything you might ever want to rummage through. Head to the **Exchange** and the **Covered Market** for clothes (see p.134), jewellery, records (see p.133) and general gifts, and to the **Glass Arcade** for lunchtime snacks such as Portuguese stews, Caribbean curries, sausage baps (see p.118) and chunky *Pieminister* pies (see p.118).

Corn Street and neighbouring Wine Street also play host to a number of other markets, which together form "St Nicholas Markets": the award-winning, produce-laden **Bristol Farmers' Market** (Wed 9.30am–2.30pm); **The Nails Market** (Fri & Sat 10am–5pm), specializing in arts, crafts and clothing; the **Arts Market**, in the Glass

Arcade at St Nick's and **Bristol Book Market** (both first Sun of the month 10am–4pm), which can be rich hunting grounds for bargain browsers; and, most interesting of all, an excellent **Slow Food Market** (first Sun of the month 10am–3pm), whose locally sourced goods made it the first regular slow-food market in the world.

The Centre and around

Away from the heart of the original settlement, **The Centre** links the Old City with the Harbourside and Park Street but is little more than a concrete island surrounded by a sea

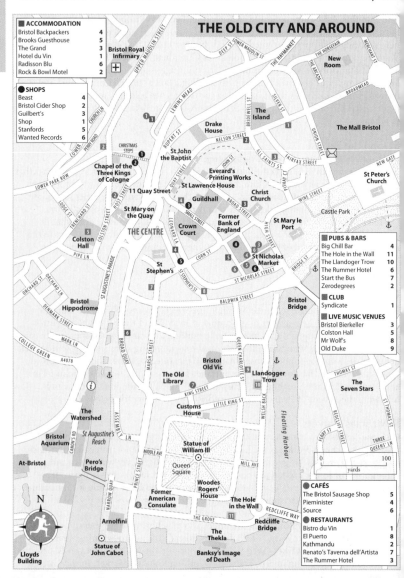

THE OLD CITY AND AROUND

■ ACCOMMODATION
Bristol Backpackers	4
Brooks Guesthouse	5
The Grand	3
Hotel du Vin	1
Radisson Blu	6
Rock & Bowl Motel	2

● SHOPS
Beast	4
Bristol Cider Shop	2
Guilbert's	3
Shop	1
Stanfords	5
Wanted Records	6

■ PUBS & BARS
Big Chill Bar	4
The Hole in the Wall	11
The Llandoger Trow	10
The Rummer Hotel	6
Start the Bus	7
Zerodegrees	2

■ CLUB
Syndicate	1

■ LIVE MUSIC VENUES
Bristol Bierkeller	3
Colston Hall	5
Mr Wolf's	8
Old Duke	9

● CAFÉS
The Bristol Sausage Shop	5
Pieminister	4
Source	6

● RESTAURANTS
Bistro du Vin	1
El Puerto	8
Kathmandu	2
Renato's Taverna dell'Artista	7
The Rummer Hotel	3

SEE NO EVIL: THE RENAISSANCE OF NELSON STREET

In August 2011, over 35 graffiti artists from around the globe descended on **Nelson Street**, just off The Centre, to turn its dreary, run-down office blocks and high-rises into a gallery of stunning street art. The phenomenal three-day-long event, dubbed **See No Evil**, created some of the largest murals in the world: **Nick Walker**'s banker pours paint down the side of eleven-storey St Lawrence House, while **Aryz**'s wolf in a lumberjack shirt covers the entire length of Drake House. Partly funded by the city council, See No Evil's guest list read like a *Who's Who* of international graffers, with the likes of LA artist **El Mac** daubing a huge photo-realistic mural of a woman and baby on the side of 11 Quay St, and the **Tats Cru**, from the Bronx in New York, filling a wall above *Café Central* with their "Welcome to Bristol" aerosol sign. The project was organized by local graffiti legend **Inkie**, whose evidently considerable powers of persuasion managed to secure the Royal Bank of Scotland, the Unite building and – with presumable irony for Bristol-based artists such as **SEPR**, **Paris**, **Cheo** and **Epok** – the police station and old juvenile courts, though these two have since been redeveloped.

2

of traffic – it only became known as such thanks to the Tramways Centre terminus that used to exist here. The harbour once covered all this area, as evidenced by the name of the stout church on the western side of St Augustine's Parade: St Mary on the Quay.

The drab network of roads running off The Centre's eastern end was given a revolutionary facelift in 2011 when **Nelson Street** and its continuation, **Quay Street**, were transformed by some of the world's best street artists (see box above).

Christmas Steps

Leading off the western end of Colston Avenue, higgledy-piggledy **Christmas Steps**, "steppered done and finished September 1669", leaps straight off the pages of a Dickens novel. The specialist little shops that line both sides (see p.134) help break the stiff climb, as do the sedilia near the top, moved here from the Chapel of the Three Kings of Cologne that stands in the grounds of nearby John Foster Almshouse.

St Stephen's

21 St Stephen's St • Daily 9.30am–4pm • Café Mon–Fri 10am–3.30pm, also Sat in summer • Free • ⓦ saint-stephens.com

Hemmed in by public buildings, **St Stephen's** might easily be missed but for its slender spire towering over the surrounding office blocks. One of Bristol's oldest churches, it was established in the thirteenth century and has some flamboyant tombs inside, mainly of various members of the mercantile class who were the church's main patrons: look out for the Flemish mercer **Edmund Blanket**, in the north wall, who supposedly gave his name to the stitched woollen bedspread – though it was more likely the other way around. The surprisingly funky **café** does bagels, salads and Middle East-inspired dishes.

King Street

King Street, a short walk southeast from The Centre, was laid out on marshland in 1663 (the "King" in question being Charles II) and still holds a cluster of fine historic buildings, among them the **Old Library**, at no 30 King St, one of the first in England (now a Chinese restaurant). Opened in 1766, the nearby **Bristol Old Vic** is home to the **Theatre Royal**, the oldest working theatre in the country, which preserves many of its original Georgian features.

The Llandoger Trow

1–3 King St

Built in 1664, the timber-framed **Llandoger Trow** pub (see p.127) was traditionally the haunt of seafarers and smugglers and is laden with maritime lore: it was reputed to

2

> ## I PREDICT A RIOT: QUEEN SQUARE, 1831
>
> Bristol has a long history of **violent protest**, from the food riots of 1709 to the disturbances in Stokes Croft in April and August 2011. None, however, has been quite as ferocious as the riots that erupted in genteel **Queen Square** in October 1831, which were some of the worst civil disturbances ever seen in England.
>
> At the time, just five percent of Bristol's population was able to vote, and so when local magistrate **Sir Charles Wetherall** arrived to open the new Assize Courts – having just played a key role in initially overturning the **Reform Act** that would have brought greater democracy to the city – the touch paper was lit. Angry mobs chased him to the **Mansion House** in Queen Square, and in the violence that followed over the next three days a hundred buildings were destroyed, including the Bishop's Palace, the Mansion House itself, the Customs House and most of the jail. It was eventually suppressed when the 3rd Dragoon Guards charged the square, their swords drawn, cutting down the rioters, driving them into burning buildings and killing and wounding 130 people in the process.

have been the meeting place of Daniel Defoe and Alexander Selkirk, the model for Robinson Crusoe, and is also said to be the basis for the *Admiral Benbow* in Robert Louis Stevenson's *Treasure Island*. The pub derives its unique name from the flat-bottomed barges that were used to trade between Bristol and the Welsh coast.

Queen Square

South of King Street, **Queen Square** is an elegant grassy area with a statue of William III by Flemish sculptor John Michael Rysbrack at its centre, reckoned to be the best equestrian statue in the country. The square was home to some of Bristol's wealthiest merchants, including, on the site of nos. 33–35, **Woodes Rogers**, the privateer who rescued Alexander Selkirk from four years of solitude on the Juan Fernandez Islands; many of these grand houses were targeted in the **Reform riots** (see box above), during which much of the northern and western sides were razed. Further along the relatively untouched southern side, a plaque at no. 37 recalls how the first **American Consulate** in Britain was established here in September 1792.

The **Hole in the Wall** pub (see p.127) on the southeastern corner is named after the tiny spy house that served as a lookout for press-gang recruitment drives, and was another *Treasure Island* inspiration.

The New Room

36 The Horsefair, Broadmead • Mon–Sat 10am–4pm • Free • Ⓦ newroombristol.org.uk

One of the few buildings in Broadmead to have survived World War II, the **New Room** was the country's first Methodist chapel, established by **John Wesley** in 1739. Access is from both the central strip of Broadmead and from the Horsefair, though the former gives a more immediate impression of this neatly austere but strangely captivating little place – bar the addition of pews, it is very much as Wesley left it, with a double-deck pulpit beneath a hidden upstairs window, from which the evangelist could observe the progress of his trainee preachers.

The top-floor **living quarters** are similarly perfunctory and contain Wesley's bedroom and study – he somehow managed to find time to publish over two hundred works between the estimated forty thousand or so sermons he delivered during his life. The truly committed can also book tours of **Charles Wesley's house** on Charles Street here (£5, £8 with tour of the New Room); Wesley's brother shared his appetite for hard work, penning over nine thousand religious poems and hymns, an obsessive feat that earned him the nickname of the "Poet Preacher".

Castle Park

The open expanse of **Castle Park** is effectively a grassy shortcut to the Harbourside. Crowded on sunny days with picnicking office workers, it can seem quite bleak otherwise, littered with the ghosts of Bristol past: the scant remains of the city's Norman **castle**, demolished after the Civil War; the ruined tower of **St Mary le Port**, abandoned behind a boarded-up 1970s eyesore; and the roofless shell of **St Peter's Church**, the city's oldest. Until German bombers came calling in late 1940 (see box below), the medieval area formed part of the Old City and – hard as it is to imagine today – was a bustling network of narrow lanes that constituted Bristol's busiest shopping district.

Temple and Redcliffe

South of the Old City, just across Bristol Bridge, **Temple**'s blend of 1960s office blocks and modern quayside developments is a legacy of the pounding it received during the Blitz, the drab ensemble making for a rather ignominious introduction to the city for visitors emerging from **Temple Meads Railway Station**. German bombers destroyed most of the buildings around here – with one direct hit on St Philip's Bridge during the Good Friday raid of April 1941 effectively ending the city's tramway system – though the quirky fourteenth-century **Temple Church** just about survived the Luftwaffe.

Like Temple, which wasn't incorporated into Bristol until after the Reformation, neighbouring **Redcliffe** developed as a separate settlement outside the city walls, becoming a suburb of the city only by default, when Edward II included it as part of the new county of Bristol in 1373. Also like Temple, the one reminder of the area's medieval past is its church, magnificent **St Mary Redcliffe**, which is second only to Bristol Cathedral as the city's most beautiful place of worship.

Opposite the church, Redcliffe Parade leads down to the Floating Harbour, where you can best see the **red cliffs** that lend the district its name. The sandstone "**caves**" here, extending over a dozen acres underground, were quarried for use in Bristol's many glassworks; the skyline of both Redcliffe and Temple was at one time studded with conical glass kilns, though the only reminder of this once-thriving industry is the 25ft stub of the city's last remaining kiln, which has been converted into the restaurant of the nearby *Ramada Bristol City* hotel.

Temple Church

Temple St, Temple • Closed to the public • ⓦ english-heritage.org.uk

Gutted by bombing during World War II, and its interior off-limits to the public, **Temple Church** is still well worth a visit thanks to its extraordinary leaning tower, which totters some 5ft to the side – it seems to be slowly submerging into the pavement as a result of the soft clay foundations on which it was built. The 114ft tower was

---

BRISTOL IN THE BLITZ

The significance of Bristol's docks was not lost on Adolf Hitler, and between November 24, 1940 and April 11, 1941, the city was on the receiving end of six **major bombing raids**. Despite the best efforts of surrounding "Starfish" sites (see box, p.159), the Luftwaffe were able to navigate into the very heart of the city (using moonlight reflecting off the River Avon) and in five months of severe bombing put paid to the entire **Castle District**, including St Mary le Port and St Peter's Church, **Broadmead**, and large parts of **Temple** and **Park Street**. Areas as far afield as **Filton** (targeted for its aircraft manufacturing industry) were also damaged – though, ironically, the docks were not. St Peter's now acts as a memorial to the 1300 civilians killed in the raids, the names of which are remembered on a plaque outside the church's western entrance.

2

constructed in stages throughout the fourteenth and fifteenth centuries, the top added seventy years after the bottom, once it appeared to have stopped leaning; the additional weight, however, exacerbated the angle, and the tower was never finished, hence the absence of any pinnacles or other ornamental finishes to its crown.

You're restricted to peeking through the window-less frames, but you should be able to make out the circular plan of the original twelfth-century church built by the **Knights Templar**, the religious military order who gave the current church – and the area – its name. Its design matched that of the Church of the Holy Sepulchre in Jerusalem, which the knights were ordained to protect. The few artefacts to survive the bombs have been scattered across the city: a pair of fourteenth-century brasses went to St Mary Redcliffe and the chapel screens to the Lord Mayor's Chapel, while the medieval chandelier now hangs in Bristol Cathedral.

The church's **cemetery** is today a tranquil public garden, from where you can get a real sense of just how far out the tower veers from the nave behind.

Temple Meads Railway Station

Temple Gate, Temple • Old Station closed to the public

Bristol's Old Station stands outside **Temple Meads Railway Station**, the original terminus of the Great Western Railway linking London and Bristol. The terminus, like the line itself, was designed by Isambard Kingdom Brunel in 1840, and was the first great piece of railway architecture. Brunel's Tudor-style offices fronted a large passenger shed, topped by a decorative hammerbeam roof, and platforms built over vast brick vaults – only twenty years previously, this area was fertile water meadows (or *meads*), and the station was constructed on a viaduct to raise it above the River Avon. It was expanded into what is today's Temple Meads by Brunel's colleague, Sir Matthew Digby Wyatt, in the early 1870s.

Trains stopped running to the Old Station itself in 1965, and since the closure of the British Empire and Commonwealth Museum in 2008 it has become an events venue and is inaccessible to the general public for most of the year.

St Mary Redcliffe

Redcliffe Way, Redcliffe • Mon–Sat 8.30am–5pm, Sun 8am–8pm • Free • ⓦ stmaryredcliffe.co.uk

"The fairest, goodliest and most famous parish church in England".

Queen Elizabeth I

Dominating its eponymous parish, the richly decorated church of **St Mary Redcliffe** was largely paid for and used by merchants and mariners, who would pray to the Virgin Mary and leave offerings for a safe voyage in its intricately carved north porch. The present building was begun at the end of the thirteenth century, though it was added to in subsequent centuries, much of it by **William Canynges**, a wealthy medieval shipping magnate and five times Mayor of Bristol who swapped commerce for the cloth and is buried in a canopied altar tomb in the south transept. The soaring spire, though, which provides one of the distinctive features of the city's skyline, dates from 1872, the original having been destroyed in a storm some four hundred years before.

The Handel Window and Penn Memorial

Of St Mary's many memorials and tombs, the **Handel Window** in the north choir aisle – installed in 1859 on the centenary of the death of Handel, who composed on the magnificent organ here – is perhaps the most interesting, and the funerary achievements of **Admiral Sir William Penn** the most dramatic. As reformer of the Royal Navy, Penn was arguably the instigator of what became the British Empire but is better known as the father of the founder of Pennsylvania; his arms and armour, complete with lion-crested helmet and hefty-looking gauntlets, hang high up on the north nave wall.

THOMAS CHATTERTON: THE MARVELLOUS BOY

Born in 1752, **Thomas Chatterton** grew up in the shadows of St Mary Redcliffe, where his family had held the office of sexton for nearly two hundred years – his childhood home still stands, isolated, on the opposite side of busy Redcliffe Way (with the facade of his old school clumsily tacked onto its southern end in 1939). He received a distinguished education at Colston's School, but there was nothing to suggest that the brilliant poems he "discovered" – distributed as the work of a fifteenth-century monk named **Thomas Rowley**, a chaplain of William Canynges – could be anything but authentic. They were, however, dazzling fakes, penned instead by the teenager himself.

Exposed and discredited, Chatterton committed suicide aged just 17, and was buried in an unmarked grave in the Shoe Lane Workhouse cemetery in London, thereby supplying English literature with one of its most glamorous stories of self-destructive genius and providing the inspiration for the **Romantic Movement** that followed – William Wordsworth, who described Chatterton as a "marvellous boy" and a "sleepless soul that perished in his pride", made pilgrimages to St Mary's; John Keats dedicated *Endymion* to him; while both Samuel Taylor Coleridge and Robert Southey chose to be married in the church, within six weeks of each other in 1795.

The Chapel of St John, the muniment room and the cemetery

William Edney's elegant wrought-iron gates, fashioned to separate the west end from the pews of the nave, open into the **Chapel of St John**, which features St Mary's only remaining medieval stained glass and, more prominently, a whalebone said to have been brought back from Newfoundland by John Cabot. The wooden statue of Queen Elizabeth I here commemorates her famous admiration of the church.

Heading back through the north door leads to the inner porch, the oldest part of the church, from which a spiral staircase leads up to the **muniment room**, where **Thomas Chatterton** claimed to have found a trove of medieval manuscripts that were later revealed as forgeries (see box above).

Chatterton is remembered by a memorial stone in the south transept, and there is another one to his family, who were long associated with the church, in the **cemetery** – the Chattertons' rather odd bedfellows include Tom, the church cat (1912–1927), and up near the railings on Colston Parade, a chunk of tramline, hurled here by a bomb explosion on Redcliffe Hill in 1941 and still protruding from the grass like a rusting javelin.

Harbourside

The Old City may be the historical centre of Bristol, but the **Harbourside** is its heart. Lined with restaurants and bars and home to marquee attractions such as the **ss Great Britain**, the whole harbour area has undergone a remarkable transformation. Rundown, neglected and on the verge of being swept over with concrete in the late 1960s, its **regeneration** epitomizes Bristol's ambitious development of recent years. Old warehouses, once crumbling and derelict, now boast arts centres and museums, cinemas and cafés, a trend that started with the conversion of Bush House into the **Arnolfini** in 1961 and continues today with **M Shed**, the city's innovative new history museum.

Developed at the lowest bridging point on the River Avon, the harbour was already well established by the mid-eleventh century, and for the next nine hundred years swelled the city's coffers with a wealth built on tea and tobacco, sugar and slaves. Goods were traded first with Ireland and the Severn ports, then Iceland and the Mediterranean, and ultimately – following John Cabot's discovery of America in 1497 and the subsequent expansion of the Atlantic slave trade (see box, p.105) – the colonies and the Caribbean.

The creation of the **Floating Harbour** extended Bristol's eminence, and in its heyday it was one of the busiest ports in the country, second only to London. The harbour ceased operating commercially in 1975, but its trading past is writ large in the names

2

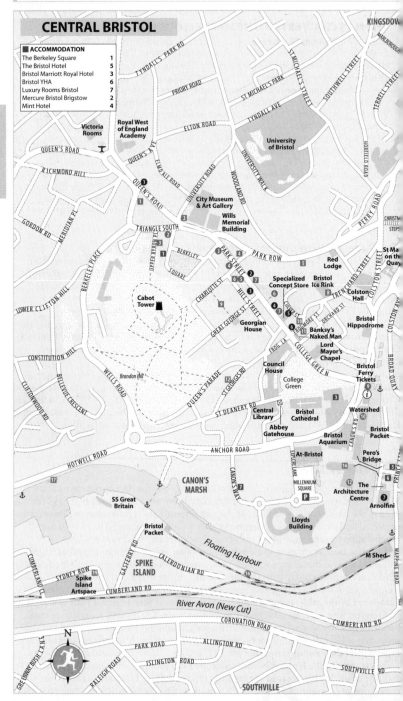

CENTRAL BRISTOL

■ ACCOMMODATION

The Berkeley Square	1
The Bristol Hotel	5
Bristol Marriott Royal Hotel	3
Bristol YHA	6
Luxury Rooms Bristol	7
Mercure Bristol Brigstow	2
Mint Hotel	4

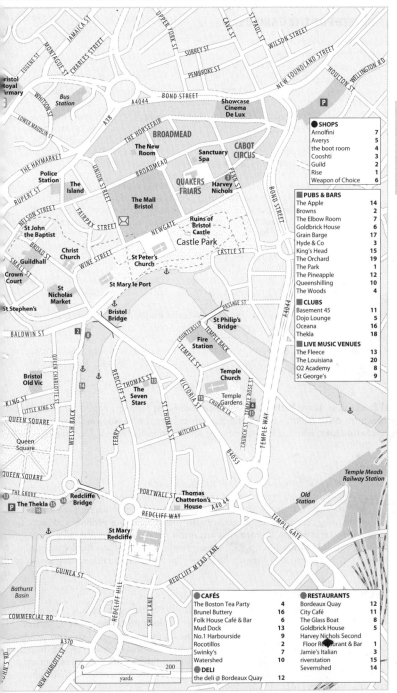

● SHOPS

Arnolfini	7
Averys	5
the boot room	4
Cooshti	3
Guild	2
Rise	1
Weapon of Choice	6

■ PUBS & BARS

The Apple	14
Browns	2
The Elbow Room	7
Goldbrick House	6
Grain Barge	17
Hyde & Co	3
King's Head	15
The Orchard	19
The Park	1
The Pineapple	12
Queenshilling	10
The Woods	4

■ CLUBS

Basement 45	11
Dojo Lounge	5
Oceana	16
Thekla	18

■ LIVE MUSIC VENUES

The Fleece	13
The Louisiana	20
O2 Academy	8
St George's	9

● CAFÉS

The Boston Tea Party	4
Brunel Buttery	16
Folk House Café & Bar	6
Mud Dock	13
No.1 Harbourside	9
Rocotillos	2
Swinky's	7
Watershed	10

● DELI

the deli @ Bordeaux Quay	12

● RESTAURANTS

Bordeaux Quay	12
City Café	11
The Glass Boat	8
Goldbrick House	5
Harvey Nichols Second Floor Restaurant & Bar	1
Jamie's Italian	3
riverstation	15
Severnshed	14

0   200
yards

2

PIRATES OF THE CARIBBEAN

"Fifteen men on the dead man's chest--
Yo-ho-ho, and a bottle of rum!
Drink and the devil had done for the rest--
Yo-ho-ho, and a bottle of rum!"

Treasure Island, Robert Louis Stevenson

In the early eighteenth century, Bristol was a hotbed of **piracy**. The burgeoning trade between Africa, the Caribbean and Europe meant rich pickings were to be had at sea, and the city's docks were rife with smugglers, pirates and privateers intent on getting their share of the spoils – it was no coincidence that when Robert Louis Stevenson penned his quintessential pirate tale, he made **Long John Silver** the landlord of a Bristol tavern – inspired by *The Hole in the Wall* pub (see p.90) – and had his characters set sail from the city's harbour.

The most famous Bristol pirate, indeed of all pirates, was Edward Teach, allegedly born in Redcliffe and better known as **Blackbeard**. Teach was feared across the Caribbean, a reputation he encouraged by tying lit canon fuses to his hair so that his thick black beard fizzled "like a frightful meteor". Legend has it that he marooned a mutinous crew on Dead (Man's) Chest Island, in the British Virgin Islands, leaving them each with just "a bottle of rum" and a cutlass for company; pirates will be pirates, and by the time he returned, only a few ("fifteen") were still alive. Blackbeard's reign of terror caught up with him, however, and he was killed in a battle off Ocracoke Island, North Carolina in 1718.

The most successful pirate in history also sailed from Bristol: Bartholomew Roberts, or **Black Bart**, who captured over 450 vessels in raids off the coasts of Brazil, West Africa and the Caribbean before his death in 1722.

Ironically, though, it was another Bristolian, **Woodes Rogers**, who proved instrumental in the ultimate demise of piracy. Rogers, who was born in Bristol in 1679 and lived on Queen Square (see p.90), was made Governor of the Bahamas with the sole mandate of ridding the islands of their two-thousand-strong pirate contingent. That he did, and his maxim "Piracy expelled, commerce restored" remained the motto of the Bahamas until they gained independence in 1973.

that adorn its quays: **Welsh Back**, the departure point for boats bound for Swansea and Newport; **Baltic Wharf**, whose warehouses once heaved with Russian timber; and **Bordeaux Quay**, where crates of fine wine arrived from the vineyards of western France.

Arnolfini

16 Narrow Quay • Tues–Sun 11am–6pm • Free • ☎ 0117 917 2300, ⊛ arnolfini.org.uk

Occupying a former tea warehouse at the head of the Floating Harbour, the **Arnolfini** – named after Jan van Eyck's fifteenth-century painting, *The Arnolfini Portrait* – is Bristol's leading centre for contemporary arts, with a history of probing and sometimes controversial exhibitions, performance art, music, art-house films and talks.

The attached **bookshop** (see p.133) has an excellent range of arty books and magazines, and there's also a trendy little café-bar, with harbourside seating in summer.

Architecture Centre

Narrow Quay • Tues–Fri 11am–5pm, Sat & Sun noon–5pm • Free • ☎ 0117 922 1540, ⊛ architecturecentre.co.uk

Housed in an eighteenth-century sail loft, the **Architecture Centre** is a bijou gallery, resource room and gift shop offering a window into the workings of this independent organization. Regular exhibitions, workshops and talks tackle issues ranging from the architectural impact of the slave trade on Bristol to the best in local contemporary design – a timely topic, given the concern in some quarters over the Harbourside's growing number of identikit developments.

At-Bristol

Anchor Rd • Daily 10am–5pm, Sat, Sun & hols till 6pm • Live Lab sessions daily 11am–noon, Sat, Sun & hols till 3pm • £11.35, under-15s £7.25, under-3s free • ☎ 0845 345 1235, ⓦ at-bristol.org.uk

Although chiefly aimed at families, the engaging **At-Bristol** packs in a good half-day's worth of wizardry for everyone. It's all very interactive and hands-on, and doesn't shy away from real science – one of the exhibits features a human brain and a **Live Lab** where experiments include DNA extraction and dissections.

A good place to start is **All About Us**, with opportunities to view the blood in your veins and play music through your "headbones" – a clever little gadget that uses your jaw as a sound conductor. Many visitors also make a beeline for the **Curiosity Zone**, on the floor above, where you can freeze your shadow, shake hands with yourself and stand in the eye of a tornado.

The adjoining exhibition, and one of At-Bristol's star attractions, the brilliant **Animate It!** was made with input from Bristol-based Aardman Animations (Wallace and Gromit, Shaun the Sheep) and gives you the chance to create your own short films, from storyboarding through to frame-by-frame shooting at touch-screen Animation Stations; apply the finishing touches at the Edit Stations or save your work and refine it on your computer at home.

The spherical, stainless-steel **planetarium** attached to the complex has regular shows illustrating the night sky – make sure you book a slot when you buy your entry tickets (50p/£1 extra).

Bristol Aquarium

Anchor Rd • Daily 10am–5pm, Sat, Sun & school hols till 6pm • £13.50, under-14s £9.20, under-3s free, £2 discount if booked online • ☎ 0117 929 8929, ⓦ bristolaquarium.co.uk

Just around the corner from At-Bristol, the deceptively large **Bristol Aquarium** allows you to get face to fin with a fabulous array of native and tropical marine life, from seahorses to stingrays. Displays range from sunken ships to the Amazon, though the huge Coral Sea tank, with its underwater tunnel and circling sharks, is the most impressive. It's worth catching one or more of the feedings (you can return throughout the day), which feature piranhas and the resident giant octopus, and an educational talk or show at the Learning Lab, a sort of aquatic nursery. Entry to the four-storey **IMAX 3D cinema,** which gives you a good idea of what a 40ft-tall shark might look like, is included in the price.

THE DISCOVERY OF "AMERYKA"

The Italian explorer **John Cabot** (Giovanni Cabboto), whose statue gazes wistfully across the water from outside the Arnolfini, set sail from Bristol in 1497 in the belief that a shortcut to the East lay in fact to the West. He landed his ship, *The Matthew* (a replica of which is sometimes moored outside the *ss Great Britain*), at Newfoundland, thus "discovering" North America in the process.

Of this, there is no doubt. More contentious, however, is the name his new continent acquired. History points to its stemming from **Amerigo Vespucci**, the Italian navigator who explored the New World at the end of the fifteenth century and whose name was marked on maps depicting the Americas. But records show that Cabot's transatlantic trip was mostly funded by one **Richard Ameryk**, Sheriff of Bristol and the King's Custom Officer, and who, as the principal patron of the voyage, was likely to have had any new-found lands named after him.

So is it, in fact, the Bristolian politician from whom "America" is derived? We'll never know for sure, but when weighing up the evidence consider this: the Stars and Stripes, the flag of the United States, is based on the design of Ameryk's coat of arms…

M Shed

Princes Wharf, Wapping Rd • Tues–Fri 10am–5pm, Sat, Sun & bank hols 10am–6pm • Free, £2 donation suggested • Boat and harbour railway rides on selected days throughout the year; £3–5 • ☎ 0117 352 6600, ⓦ mshed.org

It's difficult to miss **M Shed**, Bristol's newest museum, which opened in June 2011, a good four and a half years after the Industrial Museum it replaced closed its doors for the last time. Marked by four huge cargo cranes, the three-storey transit shed dominates the harbour's eastern end, and is an altogether different beast to the city's other museums.

Its three galleries, spread across the first two floors (the top floor hosts changing exhibitions), are devoted totally to Bristol: its **people**, their **history**, their **common identity**, now and in the past. In a way, it's perhaps of most interest to locals – the first gallery is usually busy with residents trying to pick out their homes on the satellite map covering the floor – but the everyday details and the novel way in which they're delivered, with personal snippets from those who were there and opinionated feedback from those who weren't, offers the best official insight into what makes Bristol Bristol.

Bristol Places

On the ground floor, **Bristol Places** charts the city's changing face, from the Triassic period of Thecodontosaurus antiquus – or the "socket-toothed lizard of antiquity", better known as the Bristol Dinosaur – through its development as a port and the hardships of World War II, epitomized by an old Anderson air-raid shelter, one of forty thousand erected across the city during the Blitz (see box, p.91). Interactive touch-screens let you find out more and – perhaps most importantly, given the museum's philosophy – have your say.

Bristol People and Bristol Life

Bristol People, on the floor above, and the adjoining **Bristol Life**, look at the (often ordinary) folk who have shaped the city. There's an excellent – and long overdue – display on the slave trade in Bristol, where the copious visitor feedback can be equally as interesting, and others depicting music, art and protest in the city, all constantly questioning, probing and asking visitors to think that little bit more about what they're looking at.

ss Great Britain

Great Western Dockyard • Daily 10am–5.30pm, Nov–March till 4.30pm • £12.50, under-16s £6.25, under-4s free • ☎ 0117 926 0680, ⓦ ssgreatbritain.org

Harbourside's major draw, and one of Bristol's iconic sights, the **ss Great Britain** was the first propeller-driven, ocean-going iron ship in the world, built by Brunel in 1843. She initially ran between Liverpool and New York, then between Liverpool and Australia, circumnavigating the globe 32 times and chalking up more than a million miles at sea. Her ocean-going days ended in 1886 when she was caught in a storm off Cape Horn and abandoned in the Falkland Islands. Salvaged and returned to Bristol in 1970, she is now berthed in the same dry dock in which she was built.

The Dry Dock

Visits start in the mammoth **Dry Dock**, purpose-built to house the *ss Great Britain* during four years of construction. Enclosed under a striking "glass sea" that acts as a giant dehumidification chamber and keeps her iron panels from rusting any further, you can stand beneath the mighty hull and its enormous replica propeller – the original is in the Dockyard Museum – and admire the sheer scale of what was, in its time, the largest ship in the world.

Look out for the series of puncture marks in the hull's port side, which were made when she was scuttled in Sparrow Cove in the Falklands in 1937.

CLOCKWISE FROM TOP M SHED; AT-BRISTOL'S PLANETARIUM (P.97); THE CLIFTON ARCADE (P.132) >

The Dockyard Museum

The ship itself is accessed through the **Dockyard Museum**, which traces her history from ocean liner to emigrant clipper and finally windjammer through a variety of interactive exhibits and historical tidbits, including original tickets and a 130-year-old ship's biscuit.

ISAMBARD KINGDOM BRUNEL

"The commercial world thought him extravagant; but although he was so, great things are not done by those who sit down and count the cost of every thought and act."   The Diaries of Sir Daniel Gooch, 1892

The most celebrated of British engineers, **Isambard Kingdom Brunel** (1806–1859) was a man who dealt in superlatives. During a prolific career of permanent planning and relentless construction, the "Little Giant" – a nickname his colleagues bestowed on him thanks to his bold ideas but diminutive stature (he was just five foot, three inches tall) – built the first major railway in Britain, the fastest vessel to cross the Atlantic, record-breaking bridges and tunnels, and the world's largest ship, three times in a row.

Born in Portsmouth on April 9, 1806, the only son of a French engineer, Brunel was educated at the Lycée Henri-IV in Paris before joining his father on a project to link Rotherhithe with Wapping in East London. The **Thames Tunnel** was to set the tone for his career. A remarkable feat of engineering – it was described as the Eighth Wonder of the World when it opened in 1843 – the tunnel was beset by financial difficulties and took eighteen years to complete.

The project was hampered by a spate of accidents, and it was during a flood that destroyed part of the tunnel that Brunel himself was badly injured. He was sent to convalesce in the healing waters of **Hotwells** (see box, p.109), and so began a relationship with Bristol that was to last the rest of his life. Brunel's impact on the city was immense, but it was his first (and, ultimately, his last) design that remains his most iconic. Begun in 1831, the monumental **Clifton Suspension Bridge** (see p.106), which Brunel referred to as "my first child, my darling", soars over the River Avon, spanning the 702ft gap between the two sides of the Avon Gorge. It, too, was plagued with economic problems, and Brunel oversaw only the building of the towers at either end during his lifetime.

Within a couple of years of starting work in Clifton, aged just 27, Brunel was appointed chief engineer of the **Great Western Railway** (GWR), a train line conceived to connect London with Bristol and bring rail travel to the people. It was a project that would shape his career and leave his greatest legacy. Brunel designed the dramatic stations that bookend the line – **Temple Meads** in 1840 (see p.92) and **Paddington** in 1849 – and planned every inch of the 118-mile route, creating imposing viaducts at Hanwell and Chippenham, groundbreaking bridges at Maidenhead and Chepstow, and the unerringly straight, two-mile-long **Box Tunnel** outside Bath (see box, p.74), the longest in the world at the time. More controversially, he lined the route with broad-gauge tracks, which could take faster trains but were (unsurprisingly) more expensive – ultimately, they were changed to the narrower standard gauge championed by George Stephenson and used throughout the rest of the country.

Brunel married Mary Horsley in 1836, with whom he had three children (his son, Henry, was a structural engineer on Tower Bridge), but his focus remained resolute, and he worked eighteen-hour days in order to satisfy his increasingly ambitious plans. Despite the enormity of the GWR, Brunel considered it only one stage in the linking of London and New York – his three "great" ships, two of them built in a harbour he helped design (see box, p.102), would provide the other. When the **ss Great Western** was launched in 1837, she was the largest steamship in the world and the first to provide a service across the Atlantic. The **ss Great Britain**, which followed six years later, was bigger and faster, making the journey to New York in just fourteen days. Brunel's final ship, the **ss Great Eastern**, was the largest of them all, but also the least successful. Designed in an unhappy alliance with John Scott Russell, the *Great Eastern* was easily the biggest ship ever built when she launched in 1859, but like his most audacious assignments before, ran over budget and behind schedule. The project took its toll, and Brunel died of a stroke on board on September 15, 1859, shortly before her maiden voyage. He was buried, like his father, at Kensal Green Cemetery in London.

Perhaps the most resonant displays are those on her salvage and ultimately triumphant **return to Bristol**: thousands lined the Avon to watch her stubby, mastless frame being towed up river – ironically, one of the trickiest stretches of her eight-thousand-mile journey home (see box, p.102) – and the attention this focused on the harbour was instrumental in its eventual regeneration.

The Ship

The immersion in Victorian life continues on board, pepped by the smell of freshly baked bread and a smoky engine. Strolling the **Weather Deck** gives a good idea of her record-breaking length, all 322ft of it, while beneath the funnel you can peer into the immense **engine room** (with its working engine) and see the restored **cabins**, their bunks occupied by eerily breathing mannequins. Compact but comfortable, their contrast with the crowded steerage accommodation is reflected in the eating arrangements on board: pease soup and stale biscuits for the latter, grouse, pigeon and veal for the former, served in some style in the sumptuous first-class **dining saloon**.

Brunel Institute

Tues–Sat 10.30am–4.30pm • Free • ID required• ☎ 0117 926 0680, Ⓦ brunelinstitute.org

For a detailed insight into Brunel's work – and of British maritime history in general – pop into the **Brunel Institute**, built on the site of his former steam-engine factory (its exterior is designed to look like the original) that adjoins the *ss Great Britain*. This research-centric library holds the National Brunel Archive, which includes some two thousand ship plans, a hundred ship models, Brunel's diaries and drawing instruments, and correspondence from the passengers and crew of the famous ship itself.

Spike Island Artspace

133 Cumberland Rd • Tues–Sun 11am–5pm; café Mon–Fri 8.30am–5pm, Sat & Sun 11am–5pm • Free • ☎ 0117 929 2266, Ⓦ spikeisland.org.uk

There's a creative buzz about **Spike Island Artspace**, which enjoys a similar set-up to the Arnolfini – a former tea-packing factory turned contemporary arts venue, with a relaxed café attached – but is also home to artists' studios and commercial workspaces. It's not as extensive as its forerunner, though the huge central galleries provide plenty of scope for the variety of (often leftfield) exhibitions and events that run here throughout the year.

Underfall Yard

Cumberland Rd • Ⓦ underfallboatyard.co.uk

Built on land formed by the creation of the Floating Harbour in the early nineteenth century (see box, p.102), **Underfall Yard** offers a rare glimpse into the goings-on of a working boatyard. When it's open, you can walk among the traditional boat-builders, blacksmiths and riggers that still operate out of their original workshops, and there's often some kind of historical vessel perched on top of the restored slipway awaiting repairs.

The yard is named after the **sluices**, or "underfalls", designed by Brunel to control the level of water in the docks – you can just about make them out through the window of the Sluice Room, draining water and silt from the harbour under Cumberland Road and into the New Cut behind – and its **engine house**, the chimney-topped building behind the slipway, continues to serve as the operational centre for the harbour's entire network of swing bridges and locks.

CREATE Centre

Smeaton Rd, Cumberland Basin • Mon–Fri 8.30am–5pm, Sat 10am–4pm • Café Mon–Fri 8.30am–2pm, Sat 11am–3pm • Free • ☎ 0117 925 0505, Ⓦ createbristol.org

The **CREATE Centre**, at the western tip of Spike Island, is a neat little red-brick

2

THE FLOATING HARBOUR

For over five hundred years, Bristol's harbour flourished thanks to the ebb and flow of the Severn Estuary and the River Avon's tides. Ships used the extraordinary **tidal range**, the second largest in the world, to carry them the six miles between the mouth of the river and into the city's docks. But these same waters grounded them in the harbour when the tide went out – or worse, stranded them in the mud halfway up the receding Avon – often resulting in damaged hulls and ruined cargo. (The consequential custom of building the ships more robustly, and of carefully stowing their loads, led sailors elsewhere to regard them as being "**Bristol fashion**", a term that was later co-opted into the phrase "ship-shape and Bristol fashion" to indicate that everything was in good order.)

As trade increased, so did the number of ships waiting on each high tide. There was not enough room at the quay, and many had already turned to the larger and more accessible docks at Liverpool by the time the **Floating Harbour** opened in 1809. Eventually designed by William Jessop, the harbour was forty years in the planning but only took five years to build. It worked by trapping over eighty acres of river behind a system of **dams** and **locks** around the Cumberland Basin, the level of water maintained at first by a weir and then later by a set of Brunel-designed **sluices**; together, the locks and sluices enabled quayside ships to stay "afloat" at all times. The locks are still in use – though the current one dates to 1873 – and the gates and sluices are still operated from **Underfall Yard** (see p.101).

Two man-made waterways completed the Floating Harbour. The **New Cut**, which carries the River Avon south of the harbour, was dug so that smaller vessels could bypass the main locks and instead access the docks at Bathurst Basin, closer to their berths – the Bathurst lock was blocked during World War II to prevent the harbour from draining were it hit by a bomb. The **Feeder Canal**, east of Temple Meads, maintains its water level by "feeding" the harbour and provided a way for barges to rejoin the Avon above the weir at Netham Lock.

Over the next two centuries, the city's docks flourished again. The Floating Harbour, however, could do nothing about the navigability of the Avon, and as ocean-going ships grew ever bigger, they began to use the docks further out at **Avonmouth**, developed in the late nineteenth century. The harbour closed its lock gates to commercial shipping for the last time in 1975, and the closure two years later of Charles Hill & Sons, the oldest shipbuilders in the country, truly marked the end of an era.

metaphor for Bristol. Occupying a former WD & HO Wills factory, it has effectively replaced tobacco production with environmental concerns and is now the city's hub for sustainable development. In addition to seasonal exhibitions that explore recycled fashion, slow food and the like, workshops (every Sat) cover topics from making gifts out of hand-me-downs to organic wine tasting. The onsite **café** serves breakfast and simple meals – fair trade, organic and locally sourced, of course.

Ecohome
Mon–Fri noon–3pm, Sat 11am–3.30pm • Free

Bruges Tozer's low-impact **Ecohome** is the undoubted highlight of CREATE, a poster child for sustainable living that can make guilty viewing for anyone who thinks they're doing their bit for the environment with a fortnightly trip to the bottle bank. The obvious points are covered – low-energy light bulbs in every room, solar panels on the roof – as well as more creative ways of cutting down your carbon footprint, which will have you sticking a "Sava Plug" in your fridge and a "Hippo" in your toilet the minute you get home.

Park Street and the West End

Originally the preserve of monied merchants and the well-to-do, the graceful residential premises of **Park Street** gradually succumbed to traders, and since the 1820s it has been one of Bristol's most popular destinations for an afternoon's shopping. A few big names re creeping in, but it essentially remains an enclave of quirky boutiques and offbeat independents, an eclectic collection mirrored by the area's variety of cafés and bars.

Park Street climbs steeply from **College Green** and the medieval lines of **Bristol Cathedral**, on the way passing one of the more central of Banksy's works, *The Naked Man* (see box, p.112), unfortunately now partially vandalized. A stiff uphill hike from here leads to the traffic-ringed "**Triangle**", marking the move towards Clifton.

The surrounding Georgian streets loosely form what's known as the **West End**, more a marketing tag than any physically recognisable area; much of it forms the precinct of Bristol University, which stretches back behind the towering **Wills Memorial Building** and includes the **Victoria Rooms**, a dramatic-looking concert hall that hosts regular lunchtime recitals (w bris.ac.uk/music).

2

Bristol Cathedral

College Green • Mon–Fri 8am–6pm, Sat & Sun 8am–5pm • **Evensong** Mon–Fri 5.15pm, Sat & Sun 3.30pm • Free • **Guided tours** Sat 1.30am, sometimes also 1.30pm • w bristol-cathedral.co.uk

Founded around 1140 as an abbey on the supposed spot of St Augustine's convocation with Celtic Christians in 603, **Bristol Cathedral** became a cathedral church with the Dissolution of the Monasteries in the mid-sixteenth century. Among the many later additions are the two towers on the west front, erected in the nineteenth century, eleven years after the nave was rebuilt to its medieval design.

The choir and the Elder Lady Chapel

The cathedral's interior is a unique example among Britain's cathedrals of a German-style "hall church", in which the aisles, nave and choir rise to the same height; the immense **choir** – its arches stretching to more than 50ft, making it the highest in England – offers one of the country's most exquisite illustrations of the early Decorated Gothic style.

The adjoining thirteenth-century **Elder Lady Chapel** contains some fine tombs and eccentric carvings of animals, including (between the arches on the right) a monkey playing the bagpipes accompanied by a ram on the violin.

The Eastern Lady Chapel

The **Eastern Lady Chapel** at the far end of the cathedral was restored in 1935 and gives a good indication of how the abbey would once have been decorated. Paul Bush, who in 1542 became Bristol's first bishop, is entombed here; he was expelled twelve years later for marrying and, as fate would have it, is buried near the grave of his wife. The two silver candles were pilfered from the Spanish by Woodes Rogers and given to the cathedral in thanks for the safe return of *The Duke* and *The Duchess* (and of Alexander Selkirk) from the Juan Fernandez Islands (see p.90).

The south transept and the Chapter House

The thousand-year-old stone bas-relief of the *Harrowing of Hell* in the **south transept** – showing Christ plucking Eve from the devil's clutches – is one of the most important Saxon sculptures in the world; it was discovered under the Chapter House floor, where it was being used as a coffin lid.

From the south transept, a door leads through to the **Chapter House** itself, a richly carved piece of late Norman architecture that, for its majority, is little changed from when it was built in 1165.

Around College Green

Dominated by the crescent-shaped 1950s **Council House**, the grassy expanse of **College Green** was created in the twelfth century, when pastoral land at the bottom of what is now Park Street was enclosed to form the precincts of St Augustine's Abbey – the later conversion of which into a collegiate church gives the green its name. Aside from the chapels inside Bristol Cathedral, the old **Abbey Gatehouse**, opposite, is one of the abbey's few remains that are accessible to the public, the rest being incorporated into the various buildings of Bristol Cathedral School.

Central Library

College Green • Mon, Tues & Thurs 9.30am–7.30pm, Wed 10am–5pm, Fri & Sat 9.30am–5pm, Sun 1–5pm • Free

The **Central Library**, adjoining the Abbey Gatehouse, was built in 1906 to house the collection of the Old Library on King Street, one of the first public libraries in the country and a frequent port of call for Samuel Taylor Coleridge and Robert Southey; it preserves one of the original rooms, complete with rich wooden panelling and period furniture.

Lord Mayor's Chapel

College Green • Wed–Sat 10am–noon & 1–4pm • Free

Across College Green, and conspicuous by its large Perpendicular window, the **Lord Mayor's Chapel** is crammed with a bewildering array of monuments and memorials, all painstakingly explained in some of the most enthusiastic signage in the city. The only civic church in England, the chapel's nave is lined with the **funeral hatchments** of six of the former mayors that lend it its name – the large wooden boards were hung outside the deceased's door before being carried to the church for burial.

Look out for the striking effigies of the thirteenth-century founders of the hospital of which the church once formed a part, and for the family crest in the Poyntz Chapel that incorporates Richard Ameryk's familiar-looking coat-of-arms (see box, p.97).

Georgian House

7 Great George St • Easter–Oct Wed, Thurs, Sat & Sun 10.30am–4pm, July & Aug also Tues & Fri • Free • ☎ 0117 921 1362, ⓦ bristol.gov .uk/museums

Built in 1791, the deceptively large, six-storey **Georgian House** is the former home of local sugar merchant John Pinney, its spacious and faithfully restored rooms filled with sumptuous examples of period furniture. The basement gives particular insight into domestic times past, with "speaking tubes" for summoning workers in the kitchen, and in the room opposite, Pinney's remarkable stone cold-water plunge bath.

Upstairs, illustrated panels tell the engrossing story of the family's dealings in the West Indies, including their involvement in **slavery** – Pinney's slave, Pero, was commemorated in iron in 1999 with the opening of the horned Pero's Bridge down in the harbour, a rare acknowledgement of the impact the slave trade had in shaping modern Bristol.

Brandon Hill and Cabot Tower

Daily dawn–dusk • Free

From Great George Street, or from Berkeley Square further up the hill, you can access the attractive parkland of **Brandon Hill**, a conservation area that's home to the landmark **Cabot Tower**, built in 1897 to commemorate the four-hundredth anniversary of John Cabot's voyage to America.

You can climb the 105ft tower for the city's best panorama, with far-reaching views over the cathedral and down across the harbour below.

Wills Memorial Building

The imposing Neo-Gothic **Wills Memorial Building** that crowns the top of Park Street was built by George and Henry Wills in honour of their father, the tobacco magnate

THE SLAVE TRADE IN BRISTOL

Over two hundred years after the abolition of the British **slave trade**, Bristol is still haunted by the instrumental part it played in the trafficking of African men, women and children to the New World – indeed, it was Bristol-born Sir John Yeamans, a Barbados planter, who effectively introduced slavery to North America.

The slave trade in Britain was monopolized by the London-based Royal African Company until 1698 when, following pressure from Bristol's powerful **Society of Merchant Venturers** (see box, p.107), the market was opened to all. For the next hundred years, the city's merchants were able to participate in the "**triangular trade**" whereby brass pots, glass beads and other manufactured goods were traded for slaves on the coast of West Africa, who were then shipped to plantations in the Americas, the vessels returning to Europe with cargoes of sugar, cotton, tobacco and other slave-labour-produced commodities. By the 1730s, Bristol had become – along with London and Liverpool – one of the main beneficiaries of the trade, sending out a total of more than two thousand ships in search of slaves on the African coast; in 1750 alone, Bristol ships transported some eight thousand of the twenty thousand slaves sent that year to colonies in the Caribbean and America. The direct profits, together with the numerous spin-offs, helped to finance some of the city's finest Georgian architecture.

Bristol's primacy in the trade had been long supplanted by Liverpool by the time **opposition to slavery** began to gather force: first the Quakers (remembered in a plaque outside *The Seven Stars* pub on St Thomas Street) and Methodists, then more powerful forces, voiced their discontent. By the 1780s, the Anglican Dean Josiah Tucker and the Evangelical writer Hannah More had become active abolitionists, and Samuel Taylor Coleridge made a famous anti-slavery speech in Bristol in 1795.

The British slave trade was finally abolished in 1807, but its legacy is still felt strongly in the city, particularly in the divisive figure of **Edward Colston**. The eighteenth-century sugar magnate is revered by many as a great philanthropist – his name given to numerous buildings, streets and schools in Bristol – but reviled by more as a leading light in the Royal African Company. His statue in The Centre has more than once been the subject of graffiti attacks and calls for its removal, and Massive Attack still refuse to play the Colston Hall because of the connotations of its name.

Henry Overton Wills, who founded the University of Bristol and was its first chancellor. Its bold, near-faultless design earned its architect, Sir George Oatley, a knighthood in 1925.

You can access the entrance hall, directly underneath the 215ft Wills Tower, to see the double staircase and lofty, ornate ceiling, though only university students are allowed into the heart of the building itself.

City Museum and Art Gallery

Queen's Rd • Daily 10.30am–5pm, Wed till 8pm • Free • ☎ 0117 922 3571, ⓦ bristol.gov.uk/museums

The labyrinthine **City Museum and Art Gallery** has sections on local archeology, geology and natural history that you'd expect in a provincial museum, but its scope is occasionally surprising – it has an important collection of Chinese porcelain and some magnificent Assyrian reliefs carved in the eighth century BC.

Aptly enough, though, the piece that immediately catches your attention in the light-filled atrium is Banksy's *Paint Pot Angel*, donated from his pioneering **Banksy v Bristol Museum** exhibition in 2009, by far the most popular art exhibition ever held here (and for which he received a £1 fee); another of his works, *London New York Bristol*, a former piece of graffiti depicting a monkey "surfing" a bomb, is displayed among the succinct Modern British Art collection on the top floor.

Still on the ground floor, the themed walk-throughs of the interactive **Egyptology** collection feature a number of mummies and their elaborately decorated coffins, but its appeal lies in the detail, in the intricate clay fertility figures and the compactly mummified cats – looking for all the world like pharaonic sock puppets – which were given to the gods as gifts.

It's worth a brief stop on the first floor to take in the series of **historical maps** that plot Bristol's growth as a port before heading up to the top floor, where **artworks** by the Bristol School and French Impressionists are mixed in with some choice older pieces, including a portrait of Martin Luther by Cranach the Elder and Giovanni Bellini's unusual *Descent into Limbo*.

Red Lodge

Park Row • Easter–Oct Wed, Thurs, Sat & Sun 10.30am–4pm, July & Aug also Tues & Fri • Free • ☎ 0117 921 1360, ⓦ bristol.gov.uk /museums

The **Red Lodge** was a merchant's home when built in the sixteenth century, and was later England's first girls' reform school; its undoubted highlight is the Great Oak Room, featuring a splendid carved stone fireplace and lavish oak panelling. From the Great Oak Room's windows, you can see Colston Hall, occupying the site of the "Great House" that the lodge was originally created for; the barn-like building in the Elizabethan-style knot garden below is the Wigwam, home of the Bristol Savages society (see box opposite).

Clifton

Perched on a hillside overlooking the Avon Gorge, elegant, leafy **Clifton** (from "Cliff Town", after its dramatic setting) has always felt somewhat removed from the chaotic commerce of the city down below. Bristol's most attractive quarter, its slopes lined with honeyed Georgian terraces, Clifton started life as an aloof spa resort, and it wasn't until the late eighteenth century – when wealthy merchants started building mansions up here, away from the dirty and densely populated city centre – that Clifton became the desirable address that it remains today.

It's a sizeable suburb, spreading east to bar-laden **Whiteladies Road** and north to **Bristol Zoo**, but by far the most enjoyable area to wander is the select enclave of **Clifton Village**, centred on The Mall and close to **Royal York Crescent**, the longest Georgian crescent in the country; upmarket boutiques abound, and there are plenty of restaurants and coffee shops to detain you along the way.

North of the Village lies Brunel's mighty **Clifton Suspension Bridge**, and above that, the vast expanse of **the Downs** (Clifton Downs and the much larger Durdham Down), a popular spot for picnicking couples and kite-flying kids.

Clifton Suspension Bridge

Free, 50p for vehicles **Interpretation Centre** Daily 10am–5pm **Free guided tours** April–Oct Sat & Sun 3pm • ⓦ cliftonbridge.org.uk

Spanning the Avon Gorge, 702ft long and poised 245ft high above water, **Clifton Suspension Bridge** is Bristol's most famous symbol. Money was first put forward for a bridge to link Clifton with the opposite cliffs by a Bristol wine merchant in 1754, though it was not until 1829 that a competition was held for a design, won by Isambard Kingdom Brunel on a second round, and not until 1864 that the bridge was completed, five years after Brunel's death. The tradition of illuminating the bridge at night dates back to its opening ceremony.

Hampered by financial difficulties, the Suspension Bridge never quite matched the engineer's original ambitious design, which included Egyptian-style towers topped by sphinxes on each end, although it was still ingenious in its execution – in 2002, the bridge's solid-looking abutments were revealed to be hollow, instead containing

HIGH SOCIETY: MERCHANTS, RINGERS AND SAVAGES

The attractive **Merchants Hall** on Clifton Down Road – grand, yes, but no grander than any of the other fine Georgian mansions that fringe the Downs – is home to arguably the most powerful organization in Bristol. Established by royal charter in 1552 to protect and promote trade in the city, the **Society of Merchant Venturers** (W merchantventurers.com) effectively controlled Bristol's docks (and therefore the city itself) for three hundred lucrative years, monopolizing trade with the New World and amassing a vast fortune from slavery.

Merchant money lay behind many of the city's major civic achievements – they helped finance Cabot's voyage to Newfoundland, established the Floating Harbour, set up the Great Western Railway, provided the means to build the Clifton Suspension Bridge and founded Bristol University and the University of the West of England. In 1686, the Merchants bought the manor of Clifton; Clifton Down, which the Hall overlooks, is still Merchant property. Merchants continue to dominate Bristol business, and the society remains an invite-only, predominantly male enclave, but it adopts a far more philanthropic approach these days, running almshouses and contributing to numerous community charities.

Membership of the Merchants historically overlaps with that of another, mysterious-sounding group, the **Antient Society of St Stephen's Ringers** (W saintstephensringers.org .uk), dedicated to the upkeep of St Stephen's Church (see p.89). Starting out in 1620 as a collection of campanologists, the Ringers quickly progressed to secret drunken feasts and a bizarre procession featuring a stuffed fox and a model of Queen Elizabeth I's death mask, though nowadays settle for a rather lively annual dinner instead.

That dinner is traditionally held in the Red Lodge's Wigwam, the meeting place since 1904 of another invite-only (and male-only) society, the **Bristol Savages** (W bristol-savages.org). Essentially an elite art club, the thirty or so "Brothers of the Brush" meet once a week during winter, the Red Feathers (artists) sketching or painting before being entertained by the Blue Feathers (musicians).

a latticework of vaulted chambers that reduced construction costs without weakening the bridge.

You can see copies of Brunel's drawings in the **Interpretation Centre**, located at the far side of the bridge, alongside other designs proposed by Brunel's rivals, some of them frankly bizarre.

The weekend **guided tours** that depart from the tollbooth at the Clifton end (45min; no booking required) cover its history, construction and maintenance – it was designed to carry a few horse-drawn carriages at a time but currently handles around twelve thousand vehicle crossings a day.

Clifton Observatory

Litfield Place, Observatory Hill • Weather permitting Easter–Sept daily 10.30am–5.30pm; Oct–Easter Sat & Sun 10.30am–4.30pm • **Camera obscura** £2, children £1 **Giant's Cave** £1, children 50p • ☎ 0117 974 1242, W www.cliftonobservatory.co.uk

Set on the slopes of an Iron Age hillfort, the medieval-looking tower of **Clifton Observatory** is home to one of only two **camera obscuras** in the country still open to the public – it uses mirrors to reflect a panorama of the surrounding area, so achieves the best results in sunny weather.

From the tower, a passage leads down to the **Giant's Cave**, site of an ancient hermitage (it's also known as St Vincent's Cave), and to a viewing platform perched 250ft above the Avon, with giddy vistas of the Suspension Bridge and the gorge below.

Clifton Cathedral

Clifton Park • Mon–Fri 6.15am–7pm, till 6pm in winter, Sat 8am–7.15pm & Sun 7.15am–7.15pm • Free • W cliftoncathedral.org.uk

The pink granite Roman Catholic Cathedral Church of Saints Peter and Paul, otherwise known as **Clifton Cathedral**, is unlike any other house of worship in the city. Described as "a sermon in concrete", it was completed in May 1973, its dramatically stark interior accommodating a thousand people around a hexagonal-shaped sanctuary, creatively designed so that it bathes in reflected natural light. Cutting-edge acoustics, one of the finest Neoclassical organs in Europe and a highly regarded cathedral choir (who normally sing at the 11am Sunday Mass) also make this a great place to catch **liturgical music**; see ⓦcliftonms.com for details of concerts and other events. The cathedral's ultra-modern design is reflected in the contemporary thinking of the diocese itself, whose website features a downloadable parish podcast, the award-winning "Let Us Pod".

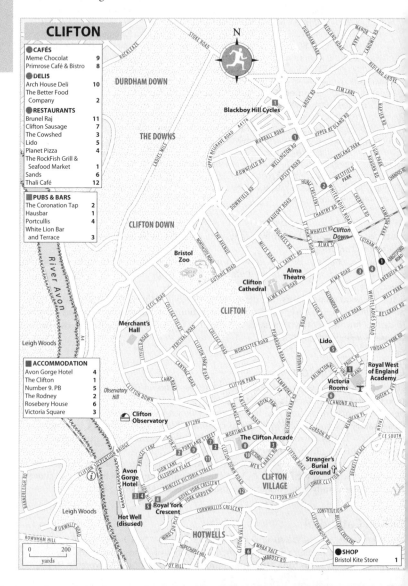

CLIFTON

● CAFÉS
Meme Chocolat	9
Primrose Café & Bistro	8

● DELIS
Arch House Deli	10
The Better Food Company	2

● RESTAURANTS
Brunel Raj	11
Clifton Sausage	7
The Cowshed	3
Lido	5
Planet Pizza	4
The RockFish Grill & Seafood Market	1
Sands	6
Thali Café	12

■ PUBS & BARS
The Coronation Tap	2
Hausbar	1
Portcullis	4
White Lion Bar and Terrace	3

■ ACCOMMODATION
Avon Gorge Hotel	4
The Clifton	1
Number 9. PB	5
The Rodney	2
Rosebery House	6
Victoria Square	3

● SHOP
Bristol Kite Store	1

SPA AND AWAY

It's strange to think that the rather nondescript area of **Hotwells** that lies at the base of Clifton is largely responsible for the affluent neighbourhood of sweeping crescents above. As early as the fifteenth century, people were drinking the **spring waters** that revealed themselves in the river here at low tide, but its potential was only realized in the late seventeenth century, when the Society of Merchant Venturers purchased the "hot wells", along with the manor of Clifton itself. Spring water was pumped into Hotwell House – and later to the Clifton Grand Spa and Hydropathic Institution, now the *Avon Gorge Hotel* – and **Hotwell Spa** took off, a smaller summer complement to Bath's winter season. Indeed, so popular was its water that Bristol's glass-making industry was born out of the demand for it to be bottled.

By the end of the eighteenth century, though, with prices (and pollution) on the rise, the spa went into decline and Hotwells became the preserve of the **terminally ill** seeking one last chance of a cure. Despite some "success" (the waters allegedly rid John Wesley of tuberculosis), the stay for the majority of visitors was a permanent one – with the church graveyards filled to capacity, many were interred in the **Strangers' Burial Ground** at the foot of Lower Clifton Hill.

2

Royal West of England Academy

Queen's Rd • Mon–Sat 10am–5.30pm, Sun 2–5pm • £4, under-16s free, free on third Sat of every exhibition; exhibitions in the New Gallery and Friends Gallery free • ☎ 0117 973 5129, ⓦ www.rwa.org.uk

The first art gallery in Bristol, the **Royal West of England Academy** (RWA) has amassed some 1300 pieces in its permanent fine-art collection, including works by Elizabeth Blackadder, Julian Trevelyan and the nonagenarian Mary Fedden, believed to be Bristol's oldest working artist. But it's the wide-ranging and thought-provoking programme of temporary displays that is the real draw here, from photography and sculpture to woodblock prints and street art; recent exhibitions have included local studio group Jamaica Street Artists and Damien Hirst's 22ft-high bronze statue based on the 1970s Spastic Society's charity box.

Bristol Zoo

Zoo Daily 9am–5.30pm, Nov to mid-March till 5pm • £14, under-14s £8.50, under-3s free **ZooRopia** Daily 10am–4pm, Nov to mid-March Sat, Sun & school hols only • £7.50, under-14s £6.40, no under-5s • ☎ 0117 974 7300, ⓦ www.bristolzoo.org.uk

One of the oldest zoological gardens in the world, ever-popular **Bristol Zoo** is home to over 450 different species of squawking, swinging and slithering animals. The **enclosures** in its dozen acres of gardens range from the Monkey Jungle to the walk-through Butterfly Forest and from Gorilla Island to the Twilight World – an update of the world's first nocturnal house – but it's hard to beat the award-winning Seal and Penguin Coasts, where underwater walkways prove just how much more adept African penguins are in the water than out of it.

The zoo is renowned for its animal **conservation** work and has a strong track record in breeding endangered species in captivity, including Asiatic lions (in the enclosure just left of the entrance) and Livingstone's fruit bats (in Twilight World). It also provides a home to several slightly less glamorous critters – such as the Partula snail and the Potosi pupfish – that are now extinct in the wild. Numerous talks, feeds and animal encounters can easily extend your visit into a full-on day-trip, as can **ZooRopia**, a primate-themed aerial obstacle course that ends in a zip wire onto the main lawn.

University of Bristol Botanic Garden

The Holmes, Stoke Park Rd, Stoke Bishop • April–Oct Wed–Fri & Sun, June–Sept also Sat 10am–4.30pm; Nov–March Wed–Fri 10am–4.30pm • £3.50, under-16s free • ☎ 0117 331 4906, ⓦ bristol.ac.uk/Depts/BotanicGardens

The **University of Bristol Botanic Garden** near Durdham Down cultivates some 4500 plant species, including several you won't see outside these walls. It's not your average botanical garden: science-centric displays trace the evolution of land plants and reflect modern theories on how different species are in fact related through their DNA. There are also Chinese and European medicinal herb gardens, a number of glasshouses that contain floral gems such as giant Amazon water lilies and South Africa *fynbos* and, closer to home, collections of threatened native species like the Bristol onion, the pinky-purple flowers of which you may see sprouting out of the rocks in the Avon Gorge.

2

East Bristol

Down-at-heel and rough around the edges, the vibrant areas that make up **East Bristol** are some of the most culturally diverse in the city. United by their resilient, resourceful communities (and historically by their less-than-savoury reputations), **Stokes Croft** and **St Pauls** are uncompromisingly creative quarters that are quite unlike anywhere else in the city – Clifton Village this is not.

North of Stokes Croft, The Arches mark the start of **Gloucester Road**, a buzzing stretch of independent shops, restaurants and bars; while heading east leads into the bohemian district of **Montpelier**, centred round foodie Picton Street and looking like a slightly wearier version of Clifton thanks to its shabby-chic Georgian terraces.

Although it has claims to be the birthplace of the Industrial Revolution – Britain's first brass works were established here at Baptist Mills (now under the M32) in 1702 – **Easton**, on the other side of the motorway, is better known these days for its notorious Stapleton Road, allegedly the most dangerous street in the UK. It's only likely to crop up on your itinerary if you book a table at what is arguably the best vegetarian restaurant in the country (see p.125).

Stokes Croft

Fiercely independent **Stokes Croft**, the area (and road) immediately north of the bus station, is one of the most dynamic neighbourhoods in Bristol, an exercise in collective ownership and one of the best places to explore the city's thriving **street art** scene, most obvious on the arches of E. W. Lewin's **Carriage Works** and along the sides of the **Magpie Squat** on Ashley Road. Longer-lasting murals include *The Wave*, on the corner of Jamaica and Hillgrove streets; *Boycott Tesco*, at the junction of Stokes Croft and Sydenham Road; and, of course, a number of **Banksy**s – look out for the *Rose & Mousetrap*, on St Thomas Street North; *Take the Money and Run*, a collaboration that adorns a health-centre wall on Bath Buildings in nearby Montpelier; and, on Stokes Croft itself, the striking *Mild, Mild West* (see box, p.112).

POWER TO THE PEOPLE

The **People's Republic of Stokes Croft** (ⓦprsc.org.uk) is a community action group with a difference. Charged with promoting Stokes Croft and protecting it from "the blandification of conventional development", the PRSC has had a pretty significant impact judging by the number of new cafés, restaurants and bars that have opened up in this once-neglected neighbourhood since it was formed in September 2007. Often taking a tongue-in-cheek approach – note the "adapted" street signs around Stokes Croft and the "National Trust" plaque on Turbo Island – they have an admirable ethic of working with former drug addicts and running workshops for the homeless. The PRSC's long-running but as yet unsuccessful campaign to keep Tesco out of Stokes Croft (ⓦnotesco.wordpress.com) gained national attention in April 2011, when the newly opened **Tesco Express** on Cheltenham Road was attacked by protestors in the city's first riots since the 1980s.

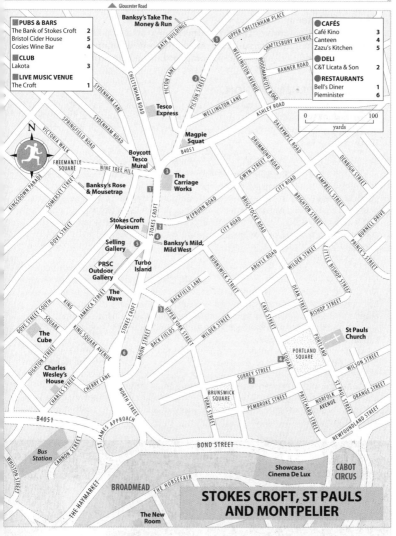

▲ Gloucester Road

■ PUBS & BARS	
The Bank of Stokes Croft	2
Bristol Cider House	5
Cosies Wine Bar	4
■ CLUB	
Lakota	3
■ LIVE MUSIC VENUE	
The Croft	1

● CAFÉS	
Café Kino	3
Canteen	4
Zazu's Kitchen	5
● DELI	
C&T Licata & Son	2
● RESTAURANTS	
Bell's Diner	1
Pieminister	6

0   100
yards

STOKES CROFT, ST PAULS AND MONTPELIER

Selling Gallery

35 Jamaica St • Mon–Sat 11am–6pm • Ⓦ sellinggallery.wordpress.com

The **Selling Gallery** is the headquarters of the People's Republic of Stokes Croft, and as such is less of a shop than a series of political statements. Focused around changing exhibitions of local artists whose works are sold by Dutch auction, the gallery also helps fund the PRSC by selling Godwin-inspired "art furniture" constructed from recycled cast-offs and a range of China mugs and plates, made on their own kiln in the **New Gallery** next door (same hours) and bearing slogans such as "Think Local, Boycott Tesco" and "Control Tax and Regulate All Drugs". The adjoining **PRSC Outdoor Gallery**, which serves as a controlled canvas for local street artists, is a changing exhibition in itself.

Stokes Croft Museum

81–83 Stokes Croft • Wed–Fri 11am–3pm, Sat noon–4pm • £1, children free

In keeping with the area's alternative approach, the "world famous" **Stokes Croft Museum** is a museum only by name. Tapping into the neighbourhood's recent

2

THE BANKSY PHENOMENON

Shrouded in mystery despite his fame and dividing opinion because of his art, the street artist known as **Banksy** has spray-painted walls in London, Detroit, Melbourne and the Middle East, but it was in the graffiti-hotbed of Bristol that he developed the stencil style that defines his work.

Street art comes and goes but several of Banksy's key murals remain, dotted around the city, all exhibiting the dry wit that undercuts his social message. The most iconic, and the first stop on any Banksy trail, is **Mild, Mild West** (1999), at the junction of Stokes Croft and Jamaica Street. Showing a wobbly white teddy bear pitching a Molotov cocktail at advancing riot police, it was seen by many as a reference to the St Pauls riots of 1980 (which were ignited by a police raid on a café in nearby Grosvenor Road), though is actually a reaction to the crackdown on the city's "free parties", a late-twentieth-century Bristol phenomenon where scores of people broke into abandoned warehouses. The piece took three days to paint and even went through a couple of drafts – look closely and you can see the outlines of the policemen have been slightly adjusted.

Mild, Mild West was chosen as the city's alternative landmark in a local radio poll in 2007, and there's similar affection for Banksy's image of **Death** (2003) on the waterline of the *Thekla*, a nightclub boat moored in the harbour. His original tag was removed by the city's harbourmaster (the club wanted to keep it, and subsequently sued for criminal damage), prompting Banksy to return and paint a Grim Reaper figure rowing in the same spot. The stencil is based on *The Silent Highwayman*, an illustration depicting The Great Stink that appeared in *Punch* in July 1858.

Arguably the most famous of Banksy's works lies a short walk northwest from here, off the bottom of Park Street. Secretly created beneath sheet-covered scaffolding, **The Naked Man** (2006), an adulterous lover hanging from a window (it's ironically painted on the side of a sexual-health clinic), was saved thanks to a petition from a Lib Dem councillor. Finally acknowledging public opinion, it was the first official recognition of Banksy's rising role in the city's cultural profile and paved the way for his wildly successful exhibition in the City Museum and Art Gallery in 2009 (see p.105).

resurgence and do-it-yourself attitude, it charts (very) local history in a single room through a busy mixture of art installation, montage and unusual displays – the adults-only, hands-on Toss exhibit is certainly something you won't find elsewhere. The sense of being slighted by the establishment manifests itself in a bit of fun-poking – signs read "Britain in Bloom Winner 2015" and "Twinned with Wan Chai, Hong Kong" – but you're ultimately left in little doubt as to the message in its medium.

St Pauls

The embattled neighbourhood of **St Pauls** still struggles to shake off the stigma of the 1980 riots. While its reputation for crime is hardly undeserved – it's not *that* long ago that even the police refused to venture beyond the notorious "Frontline" of Grosvenor Road – this is one of Bristol's most cosmopolitan neighbourhoods, with a very real and tangible community spirit, fostered here perhaps more than elsewhere as a direct result of thirty years of social prejudice. St Pauls has been shaped by Caribbean migrants, whose lasting legacy is the hugely popular **St Pauls Carnival**, which snakes through the streets each July (see box, p.136).

St Pauls Church
Portland Square

Standing proud over the eastern side of eighteenth-century Portland Square, **St Pauls Church** encapsulates the progress that's slowly changing the wider area – boarded up and abandoned in the 1990s, it has now been restored to its former glory, and thanks to a novel initiative with the Churches Conservation Trust, provides a dramatic home to Circomedia, one of only two circus schools in the country. Designed by Daniel Hague in 1789, the church is thought to be the most important example of provincial Gothic architecture in Bristol.

If you drop in during Circomedia's anniversary celebrations (April 1, appropriately enough) or at their annual open-doors day in mid-September, you'll be greeted by the unusual sight of people unicycling, spinning plates, or swinging on trapezes below the elaborately decorated ceiling; you can also see the elegant interior during one of their performances (see p.132).

Ashton Court Estate

Long Ashton • Daily 8am–dusk **Visitor centre** Wed–Sun: March–Oct 10am–5pm; Nov–Feb 9.30am–4.30pm **Café** Daily 10am–5pm, Sat & Sun from 9am **Golf** Daily 7am–9pm, till 5pm in winter • Free • ⓦ ashtoncourtestate.com • On the A369, 2 miles from the city centre (bus #357/358/359)

Although it never feels crowded, the **Ashton Court Estate** attracts more visitors than anywhere else in the South West, welcoming over 1.5 million people into its landscaped grounds each year. Set around a rather grandiose Victorian mansion, the estate's 850 acres of woodland and open grassland – home to badgers, bats and, most noticeably, **deer** – make for one of the city's most enjoyable retreats. The park's foundations were laid as early as 1392, by Thomas de Lyons, but it was the wealthy Smyth family who, over four centuries of architectural tweaking, gave the focal **Ashton Court Mansion** its present appearance. The mansion is a private venue, but you can get an idea of its period decor from the *Coach House Café*, located in the stables courtyard.

In addition to the variety of **festivals** that are held here each year (see box, p.136), there are numerous events and **activities**, from open-air theatre to deer walks, as well as two eighteen-hole pitch-and-putt **golf courses** and a mountain-bike trail.

Blaise Castle Estate

Henbury Rd, Henbury • Daily 7.30am–dusk **Castle** summer Sun 2–4pm **Museum** mid-April to Oct Wed–Sun 10.30am–4pm, July & Aug also Mon; Nov to mid-April Sat & Sun only • Free • Ⓦ bristol.gov.uk/blaisecastleestate • Entrance on Kingsweston Rd (the B4057), 5 miles from the city centre (bus #1/40/40a)

The varied grounds of **Blaise Castle Estate** have all the ingredients for a perfect sunny afternoon excursion: a limestone gorge, woodland trails and a vast open expanse of picnic-friendly downs. The "**castle**" – described by Jane Austen in *Northanger Abbey* as "the finest place in England; worth going fifty miles at any time to see" – is actually a folly, and was used as a summer house; it's open when the flags are flying. Blaise House itself, built for John Harford in 1796, now serves as a charming **museum** of everyday objects from Victorian Bristol, including kitchen equipment, clothing and toys, and is markedly more interesting than it sounds.

Harford commissioned John Nash to design an idyllic little settlement in which to house his former servants, and **Blaise Hamlet** (NT), off Hallen Road, opposite the estate, is the epitome of idealized rural life, nine beautiful thatched cottages set around a figure-of-eight green. You can wander round the green but the cottages themselves aren't open; one is, however, available as a short-term let (see p.118).

ARRIVAL AND DEPARTURE   BRISTOL

Bristol is the busiest **transport hub** in the South West: it has the region's biggest airport, a major train terminus and excellent bus links. Sitting at the crossroads of the M4 and M5, it's also within easy reach of London, Devon, South Wales and the West Midlands if you're driving.

BY PLANE

Bristol Airport Bristol's modern, international airport is at Lulsgate, 8 miles southwest of the city on the A38 (Ⓣ 0871 334 4444, Ⓦ bristolairport.co.uk); the Airport Flyer bus service runs to and from Temple Meads and the Bus Station (#A1; every 10min; 40min; £6 single/£10 return) and, less regularly, direct to the city centre and the top of Park Street (#A2; every 20min; 45min; £7 single/£10 return). The airport also runs its own taxi service, Checker Cars (Ⓣ 01275 475000, Ⓦ checkercars.com), which charges around £20 to the city centre.

Destinations Aberdeen (0–3 daily; 1hr 45min–2hr 50min); Belfast (2–3 daily; 1hr 10min); Cork (daily; 1hr 20min); Dublin (5–6 daily; 1hr 15min); Edinburgh (1–4 daily; 1hr 15min); Glasgow (1–3 daily; 1hr 10min); Guernsey (6 weekly; 55min); Inverness (daily; 1hr 20min); Isles of Scilly (6 weekly; 1hr 15min); Jersey (5 weekly; 1hr); Knock (3 weekly; 1hr 5min); Leeds-Bradford (10 weekly; 1hr 10min); Manchester (5 weekly; 1hr), Newcastle (1–3 daily; 1hr 5min); Newquay (10 weekly; 40min); Shannon (6 weekly; 1hr 25min).

BY TRAIN

Bristol Temple Meads is served by First Great Western (Ⓦ firstgreatwestern.co.uk) a 20min walk east of the city centre, served by frequent buses #8, #8A and #9, which pass through the centre on their way to Clifton. Alternatively, from behind the train station you can make use of the cycle-way into town or the river ferry that leaves for the centre every twenty to forty minutes (see p.116).

Bristol Parkway is in Stoke Gifford, 7 miles north of the city centre, off Junction 1 of the M32, and is much less convenient than Temple Meads; bus #73 runs into The Centre.

Destinations Regular services from: Bath (15min); Birmingham (1hr 25min); Bradford-on-Avon (25min); Bridgewater (50min); Cardiff (50min); Cheltenham (40min–1hr); Chippenham (30min); Exeter (1hr); Gloucester (50min); London Paddington (1hr 40min); Oxford (1hr); Portsmouth (2hr 25min); Plymouth (2hr); Reading (1hr 15min); Salisbury (1hr 10min); Slough (1hr 10min); Southampton (1hr 40min); Swindon (30min); Taunton (35min); Westbury (40min); Weston-super-Mare (25–50min); Weymouth (2hr 25min); Worcester (1hr 35min); Yeovil (1hr 10min).

BY BUS

Bristol Bus Station is centrally located, on Marlborough Street, and is the destination for National Express (Ⓦ nationalexpress.co.uk) services from London; Megabus (Ⓦ uk.megabus.com), whose departures invariably leave at antisocial hours, stops opposite the Colston Hall, off The Centre.

Destinations Birmingham (4 daily; 2hr 5min–3hr); Cambourne (daily; 5hr 40min); Cardiff (3 daily; 55min–1hr 15min); Coventry (2 daily; 2hr 55min); Exeter (2 daily; 1hr 50min); Leeds (daily; 5hr 5min); London (frequent; 2hr 15min–2hr 45min); Manchester (daily; 4hr 50min); Middlesbrough (2 daily; 6hr 25min–7hr 30min); Newcastle (daily; 7hr 45min–8hr 50min); Newquay (daily; 4hr 50min); Paignton (daily; 3hr 10min); Penzance (daily; 6hr 5min); Plymouth (daily; 3hr 20min); Redruth (daily; 5hr 25min);

Rugby (daily; 3hr 15min); Salisbury (daily; 2hr 10min); Sheffield (daily; 4hr 20min); Southampton (daily; 2hr 55min); Sunderland (2 daily; 7hr 5min–8hr 10min); Swansea (6 daily; 2hr 20min–2hr 35min); Torquay (daily; 2hr 55min).

BY CAR

Via the M4 and M5 Bristol's position at the axis of the M4/M5 motorways makes it a very accessible city, and it's an easy drive along the M5 from the South West and the West Midlands, or the M4 from London and South Wales;

indeed, the city centre is just seven and a half miles from the M4, down the M32.

Park & Ride Bristol has three Park & Ride locations (w bristol.gov.uk/parkandride), with buses running to the city centre every ten to twenty minutes from Monday to Saturday from Portway (#902; 20min), just off the A4, near Junction 18 of the M4; Long Ashton (#903; 15min), just off the A370 towards Weston-super-Mare; and Bath Road (#904; 25min), just off the A4 towards Bath. Fares cost £2.50–3.50 return.

INFORMATION

Tourist information Bristol's Tourist Information Centre is in the E Shed on the Harbourside (April–Sept 10am–6pm; Oct–March 10am–5pm; ☎ 0906 711 2191, w visitbristol. co.uk) and provides bus timetables and cycling maps, sells City Sightseeing Bus and ferry tickets, and offers an accommodation booking service (£3). There are also information desks in At-Bristol (daily 10am–5pm), Cabot Circus (Mon–Sat 10am–8pm, Sun 11am–5pm), The Mall

in the Broadmead shopping centre (Mon–Sat 9am–5.30pm, Sun 11am–5pm) and at the *Aztec Hotel & Spa* off Junction 16 of the M5 (daily 10am–8pm).
Useful magazines and websites The free monthly listings magazine *Venue* is packed with reviews and features on local culture; you can check out their website w venue.co.uk, as well as w whatsonbristol.co.uk, for the latest openings and events.

GETTING AROUND

The city is served by a comprehensive network of **buses**, with most stopping around The Centre (the name given to the busy intersection at the heart of the modern city) and Cabot Circus; conversely, local **train** services are infrequent and of only real use to suburban residents. The **ferry** is a nifty (and cheap) way of exploring the city's waterways and gives access to major sights such as M Shed and the ss *Great Britain*. **Driving** is fun if you like traffic jams, particularly around The Centre; there are plenty of multi-storey car parks in central Bristol, though finding a place to park further afield, especially in Clifton, is notoriously difficult. The best way to see the city is by **bike** (Bristol is the UK's first Cycling City) or **on foot** – the major sights, perhaps with the exception of Clifton, are all within walking distance of each other.

BY BUS

Routes The majority of local services are run by First Group (see w firstgroup.com/ukbus/bristol_bath for timetables and network maps); the most useful are the #8 and #9, which depart from Temple Meads and pass the city centre

and Park Street on their way up to Clifton, and the #500, which circuits the Harbourside.
Travelcards and passes If you're going to be doing much travelling by bus, it makes sense to buy a FirstDay travelcard (from £4); note that you'll only really need to venture into

CITY TOURS

In addition to the recommended **tours** below, you can also download half a dozen **audio tours** from the Visit Bristol website (w visitbristol.co.uk), which explore the city's slave-trading past and literary connections, among others.

Bristol Packet ☎ 0117 926 8157, w bristolpacket .co.uk. Cruises around the harbour (£5.50), through the Avon Gorge (£14.50) and along the river to Bath (£25). Weekends May to mid-Dec.
City Sightseeing Bristol ☎ 0906 711 2191, w citysightseeingbristol.co.uk. Hop-on, hop-off, open-top bus tour of the city's key sights, including the ss *Great Britain*, St Mary Redcliffe and the Clifton Suspension Bridge. Daily April– Sept, plus weekends in February, March & Oct; £10.
Haunted and Hidden Bristol ☎ 07766 258407, w hauntedandhiddenbristol.co.uk. Spooky stories of

haunted inns, ghostly monks and other mysterious apparitions. Fri 8pm; £5.
Pirate Walks ☎ 07950 566483, w www .piratewalks.co.uk. Enthusiastic tours of the harbourside with Pete "The Pirate" Martin, covering the legend of Blackbeard, smuggling and Bristol's links with piracy. Sat & Sun 2pm; £6, children £3.50.
Walk Bristol ☎ 0117 968 4638, w bristolwalks .co.uk. A range of guided regional and themed walks, taking in medieval and maritime Bristol among others. Sat 11am; from £3.50.

2

THE BRISTOL AND BATH RAILWAY PATH

The UK's first off-road cycle route, the **Bristol and Bath Railway Path** (ⓦbristolbathrailwaypath.org.uk) traces the former Midland Railway Line for thirteen miles, cutting through the suburbs of Easton, Fishponds and Staple Hill before heading on past Warmley, Oldham Common, Bitton (home of the Avon Valley Railway; see p.135) and Saltford. Sculptures by local artists line the route, and there are plenty of cafés and pubs along the way; short detours from the path lead to Willsbridge Mill Nature Reserve (ⓦavonwildlifetrust.org.uk) and Saltford Brass Mill (May–Oct second & fourth Sat of the month 10am–1pm; ⓦtcsafety .co.uk). Moreover, it's a novel way of nipping between the two cities and is quite scenic in parts, particularly the final stretch, where it follows the River Avon as it meanders into Bath.

Zone 2 if you're visiting Blaise Castle Estate in Henbury or the Mall at Cribbs Causeway, just off the M5. If travelling by train to Bristol, you can buy a PlusBus pass (ⓦplusbus.info) at the same time as your train ticket, which gives you unlimited bus travel around Bristol, including Cribbs Causeway, from £3.50 a day.

NextBusBristol You can check live bus-departure times from any bus stop in Bristol at ⓦbristol.acislive.com.

Night buses At weekends, eight services run hourly through the night, departing from The Centre.

BY FERRY

Bristol Ferry Boat Co A daily ferry service (☎0117 927 3416, ⓦbristolferry.com) connects the various parts of the Floating Harbour including Temple Meads, The Centre, *ss Great Britain*, the CREATE Centre and numerous waterside pubs. Ferries leave twice hourly between 7.25am and 6.25pm; buy tickets on board (£1.60–3.30 single; £2.70–4.90 return; £7 all-day ticket).

BY CAR

Parking There are large NCP car parks at Frogmore Street and Nelson Street, an underground car park at Millennium Square (convenient for Harbourside), plus a huge car park at Cabot Circus, linked to the city centre by a series of pedestrian bridges. Parking elsewhere, especially in Clifton, can be tricky and will involve chucking lots of change at a parking meter for invariably very little time on the clock.

Taxis Reliable and reputable taxi firms include V Cars (☎0117 925 2626) and Yellow Cabs (☎0117 923 1515).

BY BIKE

Information See ⓦbristol.gov.uk/cycling for information on cycling in the city, and ⓦbetterbybike.info/cycle-maps for a range of downloadable route maps. You can stop by *Mud Dock* (see p.120) for repairs and a breather over a latte. **Bike rental** From Specialized Concept Store at 12–14 Park St (Mon–Sat 9am–5.30pm, Thurs till 7pm, April–Oct also Sun 11am–4pm; ☎0117 929 7368, ⓦspecializedconceptstore .co.uk); half-day (£7) and full-day (£12) hire. Also Blackboy Hill Cycles, 180 Whiteladies Rd, Clifton (Mon–Sat 9am–5.30pm, Sun 11am–4pm; ☎0117 973 1420, ⓦblackboycycles.co.uk).

ACCOMMODATION

With a few notable exceptions, quality **independent accommodation** in Bristol is surprisingly thin on the ground, and the emphasis at many of the big names is on **business** – although there are several at which you'd feel equally at home as a tourist. Hotels in the **Old City** and on the **Harbourside** are ideally located for the majority of the city's sights, while the grand Georgian terraces around chic **Clifton Village** offer a different kind of stay. Note that **parking** can be a problem, but most places can provide permits or offer discounts at a local car park (around £10 per day).

THE OLD CITY AND AROUND

Bristol Backpackers 17 St Stephen's St ☎0117 925 7900, ⓦbristolbackpackers.co.uk; map p.88. Friendly, independent hostel with mixed and single-sex dorms, a decent kitchen and a bar that stays open late; the surrounding area can get noisy at night, though, especially at the weekend. Good discounts on both short- and long-term stays. Dorms £15

★ **Brooks Guesthouse** St Nicholas St, entrance on Exchange Ave ☎0117 930 0066, ⓦbrooksguest housebristol.com; map p.88. This charming boutique guesthouse, superbly located in the midst of bustling St Nicholas Market (see p.87), was the first of its kind in Bristol when it opened in April 2011. Compact rooms, done out in designer wallpaper and with natty little shutters, benefit from comfy beds and even comfier pillows. The lavender-filled courtyard adds a touch of the Mediterranean. Organic breakfast – served in the rustic-chic downstairs diner – costs extra. £69

The Grand Broad St ☎0871 376 9042, ⓦthistle.com; map p.88. Ornate Victorian hotel on historic Broad Street, set back from the road and lavishly designed in Venetian Quattrocento style. The variety of crisp, modern rooms have spacious beds – king rooms cost the same as standards, as do family rooms that sleep three – and there's an indoor swimming pool, gym and spa. On-site car park. Breakfast is £10 extra. **£85**

★ **Hotel du Vin** The Sugar House, Narrow Lewins Mead ☎ 0117 925 5577, ✉ hotelduvin.com; map p.88. The city's best hotel is a stylish conversion of an eighteenth-century sugar factory, the last remaining one in Bristol. Contemporary decor (trademark *du Vin* dark woods and glinting chrome) is matched by modern comforts: hand-sprung mattresses, luxury linens, and a freestanding bath in every room. If you can afford it, the rich, wood-panelled Pommery/Pol Roger mezzanine suite (£280) is a stunner. The attached *Bistro* also happens to be one of the best places for fine dining in the Old City (see p.119). **£150**

Radisson Blu Broad Quay ☎ 0117 934 9500, ✉ radissonblu.co.uk/hotel-bristol; map p.88. The city's tallest hotel, housed in a striking glass tower that dominates The Centre skyline. Rooms vary in look, depending on the gimmicky design theme ("Chic", "Fashion" or "Fresh"), though the floor-to-ceiling windows mean you can make the most of the stunning views. Breakfast costs extra. **£90**

Rock & Bowl Motel 22 Nelson St ☎ 0117 325 1980, ✉ rocknbowlmotel.com; map p.88. Basic, budget digs in a variety of clean dorm rooms (4 to 12 beds) and student accommodation-style doubles. Its location above The Lanes, a multi-purpose venue that is nominally a retro bowling alley, American diner and karaoke joint but also hosts live music and club nights, is a mixed blessing – the club doesn't close until 3am but you do get decent discounts on bowling and booths. Dorms from **£13**, doubles **£36**

TEMPLE

Mint Hotel Temple Way ☎ 0117 925 1001, ✉ minthotel.com/bristol; map pp.94–95. Tucked away between Temple Church and the train station, this smart, modern hotel manages the tricky feat of appealing to people travelling both for business (there's an iMac, free wi-fi and Skype in every room) and pleasure – they're light and airy, and the attached restaurant (see p.119) is in the hands of one of the best chefs in the city. Flexibility with early/late checkout is an added bonus. **£69**

HARBOURSIDE

The Bristol Hotel Prince St ☎ 0117 923 0333, ✉ doylecollection.com; map pp.94–95. Deceptive hotel, with a grim exterior that would have swept the board at architectural prize-givings in the former Soviet Bloc, but a swishly renovated interior that's surprisingly pleasant, its smart little rooms big on amenities. **£87.12**

Bristol YHA 14 Narrow Quay ☎ 0870 371 9726, ✉ yha .org.uk; map pp.94–95. In a great location, occupying a refurbished grainstore right on the quayside, this relaxed hostel is almost as popular with families as it is with

backpack-toting twenty-somethings. Most dorms have four beds, and there's a chilled out café-bar attached. Dorms **£20.40**, doubles **£51**

Luxury Rooms Bristol Balmoral House, Canon's Way ☎ 0117 330 6850, ✉ luxuryroomsbristol.co.uk; map pp.94–95. Mix of en-suite rooms and serviced apartments in a modern block that forms part of the Canon's Marsh Harbourside development. Standard rooms are nice enough, but it's worth pushing the boat out for the superior penthouses (from £120), whose private wood-decked terraces offer sweeping views along the Floating Harbour. **£68**

Mercure Bristol Brigstow 5–7 Welsh Back ☎ 0117 929 1030, ✉ mercure.com; map pp.94–95. Rooms are bright but functional – this is another central Bristol hotel with the business traveller in mind – though the views along the eastern arm of the Floating Harbour are good, and the location is difficult to fault: it rises directly over the restaurants and bars along Welsh Back, while the historical pubs of King Street are a few minutes' walk away and the buzzing Harbourside a minute or so more. **£90**

PARK STREET AND THE WEST END

The Berkeley Square 15 Berkeley Square ☎ 0117 925 4000, ✉ cliftonhotels.com; map pp.94–95. Set on a regal-looking square, just metres from the indie boutiques of Park Street, this "art hotel" in a smart Georgian building has two permanent exhibition spaces and rotating works displayed on each floor. Rooms are smallish but well appointed – avoid those near the noisy basement bar. Breakfast costs extra. **£97**

Bristol Marriott Royal Hotel College Green ☎ 0117 925 5100, ✉ bristolmarriottroyal.co.uk; map pp.94–95. Overlooking College Green and right next to Bristol Cathedral, this Italianate-style Victorian hotel is by far the more attractive of the city's two *Marriotts* (the other is at the northeast end of Castle Park), with spacious rooms, two restaurants and a Champagne bar, and a lovely swimming pool. **£83**

CLIFTON

Avon Gorge Hotel Sion Hill ☎ 0117 973 8955, ✉ theavongorge.com; map p.108. Historic hotel, originally a spa fed by the spring waters of nearby Hotwells, perched on the edge of the Gorge. Rooms are homely and warmly decorated, but what really counts are the views: close-up, knock-you-down vistas of Brunel's mighty Suspension Bridge. If anything, they're even better from the hotel's popular terrace bar (see p.129). **£123**

The Clifton St Pauls Rd, Clifton ☎ 0117 973 6882, ✉ cliftonhotels.com; map p.108. The original Clifton Group hotel – others include *The Berkeley Square* (see above) and *The Rodney* (see p.118) – has a laidback vibe that takes its lead from the hip little ground-floor *Caffe Clifton*. The adjacent *Racks Bar & Kitchen* isn't quite so chilled, though. Book a month in advance and prices can fall as low as £25. **£75**

★ **Number 9. PB** 9 Princes' Buildings ☎0117 973 4615, ⓦ9pb.co.uk; map p.108. A short walk from the Suspension Bridge and handily located for the pubs around Sion Hill, this five-storey Georgian B&B, lovingly cared for by its easy-going owners, enjoys a grand vista over the Gorge from its antique-filled rooms. Great breakfasts, too. **£80**

The Rodney 4 Rodney Place ☎0117 973 5422, ⓦcliftonhotels.com; map p.108. Similar in style to *The Clifton*, though smaller, and occupying a Georgian terrace in the heart of Clifton Village. Rooms lack the historical grandeur of the exterior but have all the mod cons. **£85**

★ **Rosebery House** 14 Camden Terrace ☎0117 914 9508, ⓦroseberyhouse.net; map p.108. Intimate, homely B&B, with just three soothing en-suite rooms in a Georgian terrace on the Clifton/Hotwells border. The knowledgeable owners provide plenty of personal touches (home-made biscuits, fresh flowers) and serve up a tremendous breakfast in the refined first-floor dining room. **£89**

Victoria Square Victoria Square ☎0117 973 9058, ⓦvictoriasquarehotel.co.uk; map p.108. Some of the rooms in this Georgian hotel are on the petite side, but the location is great, on a leafy square near Clifton Village – and, for a Best Western, the interiors are subtly elegant. **£79**

SOUTH BRISTOL

The Greenhouse 61 Greenbank Rd ☎0117 902 9166, ⓦthegreenhousebristol.co.uk; map pp.84–85. At the end of a quiet cul-de-sac in Southville, a few minutes' walk from trendy North Street, this well-established B&B provides proper coffee (no sachets here) in the four pastel-shaded

guestrooms and delicious organic breakfasts. Some of the en-suite bathrooms are small, but friendly owners, wi-fi and – perhaps uniquely for accommodation in Bristol – easy parking out front are ample compensation. The centre is a 10min walk over the footbridge across the Avon. **£90**

Hotel24Seven 15 Acramans Rd ☎0844 770 9411, ⓦhotel24seven.com; map pp.84–85. Primarily aimed at business travellers, this automated-access set-up has some of the best-value digs in Bristol: thirty surprisingly respectable rooms, split between Acramans Road and adjoining Dean Lane, with a well-equipped shared kitchen and secure parking. **£45**

FURTHER AFIELD

The Base 564 Fishponds Rd, Fishponds ☎0117 902 3456, ⓦthebase.vg; 3 miles from the city centre (bus #48/49); map pp.84–85. It's a long way from the action, but this nine-room, strictly veggie B&B has built up a loyal customer base of repeat visitors, who come back for the friendly hosts and the freshly prepared veggie/vegan breakfast featuring fried halloumi and coriander pakoras. Try and snare room 4 (2nt minimum stay) or 8, at the rear of the property and with wood flooring and wrought-iron bedsteads. **£63.60**

Rose Cottage 6 Blaise Hamlet, Henbury ☎0844 800 2070, ⓦnationaltrustcottages.co.uk; 5 miles from the city centre (bus #1/40/40a); map pp.84–85. This cute little cottage – set on a green and with a private rear garden – forms part of historic Blaise Hamlet, otherwise off-limits to the general public. There's a decent-sized lounge/dining room, plus kitchen and bathroom; the first-floor bedrooms, including a pretty whitewashed double, sleep three. 3nt minimum stay costs £450, but prices can fall by up to fifty percent out of season. **£150**

EATING

Eating out is one of the real pleasures of a visit to Bristol. There's a strong **café culture** that very much reflects the local, relaxed way of life, and watching the world go by over a flat white on the **Harbourside** or in one of the cosy cafés in **Clifton Village** is as quintessentially a Bristol experience as poking around the *ss Great Britain*. **Park Street**, too, has a number of good coffee shops, which provide a particularly welcome respite from scaling the city's steepest shopping street. It's the **restaurants**, though, that really deliver. Their range, scope and quality is easily the best in the South West, and with the city at the forefront of all things eco, it's no surprise that many of its menus are built around fresh **local**, **seasonal produce**. *Casamia*, Bristol's only Michelin-starred establishment (see p.126), is famously Gordon Ramsey's favourite UK restaurant, though there are a number of other equally fine places at which to pamper your palate.

THE OLD CITY AND AROUND
CAFÉS AND SNACK BARS

The Bristol Sausage Shop The Glass Arcade, St Nicholas Market ☎07817 478302, ⓦbristolsausageshop.co.uk; map p.88. The gourmet bangers at this local sausage specialist are the real deal: prime cuts of pork, lamb, venison or buffalo, served with gravy and a soft, smooth mash, or stuffed into a "super sandwich" and plied with Tracklements mustards and sauces for munching on the move. Choice of three or four sausages daily from a range of around eighteen,

including the spicy Lucifer, Cumberland-style Pepper Pot and herby Cotswold. Mon–Sat noon–2pm.

Pieminister The Glass Arcade, St Nicholas Market ☎0117 302 0070, ⓦpieminister.co.uk; map p.88. The St Nick's outlet of this Bristol institution (see p.125) does a roaring lunchtime trade, with office workers and market browsers tucking into one of their ten heart-warming pies around a couple of tile-topped benches. Mon–Sat 10am–5pm.

★ **Source** 1–3 Exchange Ave ☎0117 927 2998, ⓦsource-food.co.uk; map p.88. This beautiful

BEST PLACES FOR...

Breakfast *Lockside* (see p.120); *Primrose Café* (see p.122); *Rocotillos* (see p.122).

Confirmed carnivores *The Bristol Sausage Shop* (see opposite); *Clifton Sausage* (see p.123); *The Cowshed* (see p.123).

Cuppa and a cake *Boston Tea Party* (see p.122); *Swinky's* (see p.122); *tart* (see p.124).

Historic surroundings *Bistro du Vin* (see below); *Lido* (see p.123); *The Rummer* (see below).

Local legends *Beeses* (see p.126); *Brunel Buttery* (see p.120); *Pieminister* (see p.125).

Local produce *Juniper* (see p.123); *The Pump House* (see p.120); *Source* (see opposite).

Organic goodies *The Better Food Company* (see box, p.123); *Bordeaux Quay* (see p.120); *Folk House Café and Bar* (see p.122).

Treating yourself *Bell's Diner* (see p.125); *Casamia* (see p.126); *The RockFish Grill & Seafood Market* (see p.124).

Veggies *Café Maitreya* (see p.126); *Café Kino* (see p.125); *Thali Café* (see p.124).

2

Bath-stone building on the fringes of St Nick's Market houses a great concept: an airy, high-ceilinged café that uses ultra-fresh ingredients from the adjoining deli/butchers/fishmongers. Look out for salt-marsh lamb, a tender meat with a distinctly sweet flavour that's derived from their diet of low-tide grasses in the Severn Estuary. Lunchtime mains around £10. Mon–Sat 8am–6pm.

RESTAURANTS

⭐ **Bistro du Vin** Hotel du Vin The Sugar House, Narrow Lewins Mead ☎0117 925 5577, ⓦhotelduvin.com; map p.88. French bistro-style dining in the elegant surroundings of a former sugar factory, using good seasonal West Country produce (poultry from Creedy Carver, fish and game from Severn and Wye Smokery) in its Modern European menu; mains from £12.50. Wines from the extensive list are stored in the factory's old engine house. Mon–Fri noon–2pm & 6–10pm, Fri till 10.30pm, Sat & Sun 12.15–2.30pm & 6–10.30pm.

El Puerto 57 Prince St ☎0117 925 6014, ⓦel-puerto.co.uk; map p.88. Authentic tapas bar, expertly covering all the essentials, as well as some more unusual dishes, such as *pinchos morunos* (marinated lamb kebab) and *alubias salteados* (plump alubia beans in a creamy tomato sauce); prices range between £2.95 and £6.70. Interesting Spanish wine list. Popular live flamenco on Sunday evenings. Mon–Thurs 12.30–3.30pm & 5.30pm till close, Fri–Sun 12.30pm till close.

Harvey Nichols Second Floor Restaurant & Bar Harvey Nichols, Philadelphia St, Quakers Friars, Cabot Circus ☎0117 916 8898, ⓦharveynichols.com; map pp.94–95. Well-heeled dining in a glitzy setting on the top floor of this flagship store, with a local-leaning menu that takes in the likes of seared Brixham scallops and pumpkin *pastilla* (mains from £13), all beautifully cooked and bursting with flavour. Make sure you leave room for dessert, though – it'd be a crime to miss the assiette of chocolate puds. Fixed-price menus (two courses £16.50, three courses £19.50) are good value, and there's live jazz

every third Sunday of the month. Mon noon–3pm, Tues–Sat noon–3pm & 6–10pm, Sun noon–4pm.

Kathmandu Colston Tower, Colston St ☎0117 929 4455, ⓦkathmandu-curry.com; map p.88. Seemingly propping up Colston Tower, this smart family-run restaurant is a bastion of quality Nepalese cooking, though the menu also ventures south of the border as well. Tasty dishes, including *mo mo* (Nepalese dumplings) and *chhoyla* (lamb cooked in a Tandoori oven with ginger and garlic), are pepped up by spices imported from the owners' home village just outside Kathmandu. Twenty-five percent discount on takeaway orders. Mon–Thurs noon–2pm & 6–11pm, Fri & Sat noon–2pm & 6–11.30pm, Sun noon–2pm & 6–10.30pm.

Renato's Taverna dell'Artista 33 King St ☎0117 929 7712; map p.88. Well located for the Old Vic and thence much-loved by theatrical folk, serving pizzas and pasta in the upstairs restaurant, and post-performance pints (including draught Moretti and Menabrea) at the ground-floor bar (until 2am). Tues–Sat 5.30pm–midnight.

The Rummer Hotel All Saints Lane ☎0117 929 0111, ⓦtherummer.net; map p.88. Atmospheric, historic inn – Samuel Taylor Coleridge launched *The Watchman* here in 1795 and it was the destination for the first stage coach from London – with friendly staff and a Modern British menu of pan-fried monkfish and the like (mains around £16.95). Classy "themed" evenings such as the Wagyu Beef Night and a monthly Heritage Tasting Menu (nine courses of medieval dishes cooked with a contemporary twist) are worth catching. Between them, the two bars probably stock the widest range of spirits in Bristol (see p.127). No unders-18s. Mon–Fri 11am–3pm & 6–10pm, Sat 11am–5pm & 6–10pm, Sun 1–5pm.

TEMPLE
RESTAURANT

City Café Mint Hotel, Temple Way ☎0117 910 2700, ⓦcitycafe.co.uk; map pp.94–95. This small but sophisticated hotel restaurant overlooking Temple Gardens is quite a find: very friendly staff and an interesting menu of skilfully prepared Modern British dishes (mains from £10.95). The lunchtime Market Menu (two courses £9.95, three courses £14.95) is excellent value and changes twice weekly. Mon–Fri noon–2.30pm & 6–10pm, Sat 1–3pm & 6–10pm, Sun 1–3pm & 7–9.30pm.

HARBOURSIDE
CAFÉS AND SNACK BARS

Brunel Buttery Wapping Wharf ☎0117 929 1696; map pp.94–95. This perennially popular red-brick hut just along from the *ss Great Britain* is something of a local institution. Forget your Five-A-Day for a few minutes and tuck into a good old-fashioned bacon buttie or sausage sandwich with a steaming mug of tea, and watch the boats go by on a wharfside bench out front. Mon–Fri 8am–4pm, Sat & Sun till 5pm.

★ **Lockside** 1 Brunel Lock Rd ☎0117 925 5800, ⓦlockside.net; map pp.84–85. It's easy to miss this contemporary little diner, wedged under the Cumberland Basin flyover, although the excellent, generous breakfasts (all 21 variations) should ensure that you don't. Lunchtime is equally buzzing, with regulars cramming the circular tables for bangers and mash, sardines on toast and other such standards; offbeat desserts include a bowl of Maltesers. Mon–Thurs 7am–4pm, Fri 7am–11pm, Sat 8am–11pm, Sun 9am–4pm.

Mud Dock 40 The Grove ☎0117 934 9734, ⓦmuddock.com; map pp.94–95. A bike-shop-café combo sounds odd until you see it in action – the large, open dining space makes a chic setting for a simple but satisfying lunch menu (mains from £5.25, more serious dinner fare from £9.95), while pedal-pushers can get their bike checked at the downstairs Cycleworks. The south-facing terrace, with great views over the Floating Harbour, is a sunny-day hotspot. Mon & Sun 10am–5pm, Tues–Thurs 10am–10pm, Fri 10am–11pm, Sat 9am–11pm.

No.1 Harbourside 1 Canon's Rd ☎0117 929 1100, ⓦno1harbourside.co.uk; map pp.94–95. Relaxed, great-value café-bar – every meal comes with free soup and home-made bread – from the guys behind *Canteen* (see p.125), which has quickly established itself as a Harbourside hub. The short but satisfying lunchtime menu stays local with Gloucestershire pork chop and Frampton lamb shepherd's pie (mains from £5); things really get going in the evening with a strong programme of events. Live music Mon–Thurs, DJs Fri & Sat. Daily 10am–midnight, Fri & Sat till 2am, Sun till 7pm.

★ **Watershed** 1 Canons Rd ☎0117 927 5101, ⓦwatershed.co.uk; map pp.94–95. Cool café-bar in a respected arts complex at the head of the Floating Harbour, as great for people-watching on the harbourfront below as it is for grabbing a post-flick drink. Much of the appetizing Plot to Plate menu is also available in kid-sized portions. Mon 10.30am–11pm, Tues–Thurs 9.30am–11pm, Fri 9.30am–midnight, Sat 10am–midnight, Sun 10am–10.30pm.

RESTAURANTS

★ **Bordeaux Quay** V–Shed, Harbourside ☎0117 943 1200, ⓦbordeaux-quay.co.uk; map pp.94–95. Steadfastly organic warehouse restaurant, brasserie and bar – these guys have even been accredited by the Bristol-based Soil Association – so expect a daily-changing menu of locally sourced dishes along the lines of Cornish mackerel with rhubarb (£7) and Frampton on Severn salt-marsh lamb with barley and beetroot (£19.50); lighter meals are available in the downstairs brasserie. There's also a good little on-site deli (see box, p.123). Restaurant Tues–Sat 6–10pm, Sun noon–3pm; brasserie and bar Mon–Fri 8am–11pm, Sat 9am–11pm, Sun 9am–4pm.

The Glass Boat Welsh Back ☎0117 929 0704, ⓦglassboat.co.uk; map pp.94–95. This vintage barge, moored near Bristol Bridge for a quarter of a century, was the city's first upmarket floating restaurant. It's still going strong, thanks to a recent (stylish) makeover and a continued dedication to good Mediterranean cooking, particularly fish dishes. Mains, such as red mullet and squid tortellini, cost around £15. Mon 5.30–10pm, Tues–Sat noon–2.30pm & 5.30–10pm, Sun 10am–4pm.

The Pump House Merchants Rd, Hotwells ☎0117 927 2229, ⓦthe-pumphouse.com; map pp.84–85. Part restaurant, part gastropub, this nicely renovated former pumping station is surprisingly relaxed given the quality of the cuisine on offer. The enterprising chef is committed to seasonal, local produce, and dishes such as spiced rump of Mendip lamb and Bath chap (a regional speciality of breadcrumb-covered pig's cheek) are packed with fresh flavours. The eight-course tasting menu (£45) should help if you're having difficulty deciding. Bar food daily noon–3pm (Sun till 3.30pm) & 6.30–9.30pm; restaurant Tues–Sat 7pm–midnight, Fri also noon–3pm.

riverstation The Grove ☎0117 914 4434, ⓦriverstation.co.uk; map pp.94–95. Two-storey former river-police station, with light bites at the relaxed ground-floor bar and kitchen and more refined dining upstairs, where mains such as Jerusalem artichoke risotto and wild sea bass run from £14.50 to £22.50. An emphasis on seasonal ingredients means the menu changes daily. Restaurant Mon–Sat noon–2.30pm & 6–10.30pm, Fri & Sat till 11pm, Sun noon–3pm; bar and kitchen Mon–Wed 9am–11pm, Thurs–Sat 9am–midnight, Sun 10am–5.30pm.

Severnshed The Grove ☎0117 925 1212, ⓦsevernshedrestaurant.co.uk; map pp.94–95. Housed in a former Brunel transit shed that dates to around 1865,

2

with one half a restaurant serving an arranged marriage of European-influenced cuisine and chargrilled "Shed Fire-sticks" (beef or tiger-prawn kebabs), and the other a bar. Wall-length windows look out over the Floating Harbour and what is apparently the UK's only "hover bar", which can rotate 360 degrees and glide along the front of the building. Daily 9am–10.30pm (bar till midnight), Fri & Sat till 11pm (bar till 1.30am).

PARK STREET AND THE WEST END

CAFÉS

The Boston Tea Party 75 Park St ☎0117 929 8601, ⓦbostonteaparty.co.uk; map pp.94–95. Excellent Fair Trade coffees and quality house teas define this popular student hangout and boho pit-stop, one of a family-run, West Country mini-chain – there are a couple more in Bristol (on Whiteladies Road, and on the corner of Princess Victoria Street in Clifton Village) and another in Bath. Among the upstairs hubbub, there's cheek-by-jowl seating at wooden tables or on a couple of leather couches; downstairs, you can grab a stool at the window-front counter or head out back to the heated terrace garden. Food runs the gamut from wraps, paninis and home-made muffins to lamb tagine and roasted squash and feta salad. Daily 7am–8pm, Sun from 8am.

Folk House Café & Bar 40a Park St ☎0117 908 5035, ⓦfolkhousecafe.co.uk; map pp.94–95. Hearty, home-cooked soups and savoury tarts in a friendly, no-frills café tucked down an alley halfway up Park Street; there's normally a good range of vegetarian options, and most of the produce is organic, right down to the baby food, soft drinks, wines and some of the local lagers. It's part of the Bristol Folk House, which hosts live music and runs workshops on everything from yogic medicine to Eastern European round dances. Mon–Thurs 9am–9pm, Fri & Sat 9am–5pm, also 7pm–midnight depending on events.

★ **Rocotillos** 1 Queens Row, Triangle South ☎0117 929 7207; map pp.94–95. The huge breakfasts at this authentically furbished 1950s-style American diner put the "full" in "full English" and are reckoned by some to be the best in Bristol. But it's the legendary ice-cream milkshakes that really make this a must-visit: thick, creamy concoctions that are big enough to share and come in a bounty of flavours, from peanut butter to Crunchie Bar and honey. Also triple-decker sandwiches, quesadillas and good old-fashioned, proper beef burgers. Breakfast is served all day, but get here before 10am to enjoy it for just £2.95. Mon–Wed 8am–5pm, Thurs–Sat 8am–10pm, Sun & bank hols 10am–5pm.

Swinky's 20 Park St ☎0117 929 7512, ⓦswinkysweets .co.uk; map pp.94–95. Twee teashop with a retro Great-Yarmouth-meets-Cath-Kidston look and feel. Most patrons, seated at dinky, brightly coloured tables, accompany their cuppa with one of the dozen or so deliciously elaborate cupcakes; innovative flavours include bouncing blue bubblegum and wild white chocolate and horseradish. If you can look beyond the frosted icings, they also serve home-made fudges, ice cream and confectionery. Mon–Sat 10am–6pm, Sun 11am–5pm.

RESTAURANTS

★ **Goldbrick House** 69 Park St ☎0117 945 1950, ⓦgoldbrickhouse.co.uk; map pp.94–95. Richly decorated Georgian beauty, with classic sandwiches and "Goldhouse Grazers" (English tapas) in the brasserie-style café-bar and refined but relaxed dining in the split-level restaurant upstairs; mains, such as cider-braised pork belly, start at £12.50. The roof terrace, overlooking St George's concert hall, is a great little spot in the summer; the moody cocktail bar (see p.128) is a great little spot all year round. Themed monthly Fabulous Food evenings (£25) cover lamb, rabbit, game birds and so on. Restaurant Mon–Sat noon–3pm & 6–10.30pm; café-bar Mon–Sat 9am–11pm.

Jamie's Italian 87–89 Park St ☎0117 970 0265, ⓦjamiesitalian.com; map pp.94–95. The Bristol branch of Jamie Oliver's burgeoning empire opened in spring 2011 and, like its predecessors, offers a comforting menu of Italian classics and surprisingly more adventurous fare (read scallop and squid ink angel hair) from around £9.50. The space, open and industrial with exposed brickwork and red-leather pews, has been stylishly refurbished – this used to be a bookshop – and includes a fresh pasta machine and an antipasti counter packed with hanging meats from Levoni. Daily noon–11pm, Sun till 10.30pm.

CLIFTON AND AROUND

CAFÉS

Meme Chocolat 19 The Mall, Clifton Village ☎0117 974 7000, ⓦmemechocolat.co.uk; map p.108. Cocoa heaven in Clifton Village, with over a dozen drinks (milk, dark or white; hot, with milk or iced) made with melted chocolate; the Ultimate Hot Chocolate lives up to its moniker. Pair your drink with a few of their creamy couverture chocolates – made in Somerset and supplied to Fortnum & Mason among others – handmade truffles or a melt-in-the-mouth brownie. Mon–Sat 8.30am–6.30pm, Sun 9am–6.30pm.

★ **Primrose Café & Bistro** Boyces Ave, Clifton Village ☎0117 946 6577, ⓦprimrosecafe.co.uk; map p.108. Bustling, homely café at the entrance of Clifton Arcade, known for its excellent breakfasts but really a top spot at any time of day, especially if the sun is shining. Light-hearted lunchtime sandwiches include fishfingers and onion bhaji and mango chutney; evening fare (from £13.50) is more elaborate. Good range of teas and organic fruit juices. Mon–Sat 9am–5pm, Tues–Sat also 7pm–1am, Sun 9.30am–3pm.

RICH PICNICKINGS

The locally leaning menus in many of the city's restaurants are mirrored by the variety of regional produce available in its **delis**, from bread baked on site to tangy Somerset cheeses, much of it organic, and all of it just a little bit too tempting to resist. Add specialist Italian produce imported from smallholdings in rural Tuscany and you've got picnic nirvana. The following should have you reaching for the paper plates and novelty napkins...

★ **Arch House Deli** Arch House, Boyces Ave, Clifton ⓦarchhousedeli.com; map p.108. The ultimate larder? This "jam"-packed deli, wedged into an arch between Clifton Village and Victoria Square, is what delicatessen dreams are made of. Just don't come here on an empty stomach or you'll blow a fortune on the stacks of cured meats and gourmet cheeses. Their tailor-made biodegradable hampers (from £8.95), filled with savoury tartlets, antipasto nibbles, home-made cakes and chutneys, make the perfect summer-picnic companions. There's also a little café (Mon–Sat till 4.30pm, Sun till 4pm) tucked behind the lavender oils and honeys at the back of the shop. Mon–Sat 9am–6pm, Sun 11am–5pm.

★ **The Better Food Company** 94 Whiteladies Rd, Clifton & Sevier St, St Werburghs ⓦbetterfood .co.uk; map p.108 & pp.84–85. Award-winning one-stop organic shop for local breads, cheeses, fruit and veg, and artisan wines and beers, plus other fresh produce from their own community farm based in the nearby Chew Valley. The original store in St Werburghs also has an eco-café that serves mostly organic breakfast and lunches. Mon–Sat 8am–8pm, Sun 10am–6pm.

C & T Licata & Son 36 Picton St, Montpelier ⓦlicata .co.uk; map p.111. Traditional Italian deli that has been trading on Picton Street since the family moved here from Sicily in 1959. It lacks the gloss of others of its ilk but is the real deal, with premium salami, antipasti, olives (over thirty kinds) and the like. Mon–Sat 9am–7pm, Sun 10am–1pm.

the deli @ Bordeaux Quay V–Shed, Harbourside ⓦbordeaux-quay.co.uk; map pp.94–95. Organic deli attached to the accolade-laden restaurant of the same name (see p.120), with handmade bread (eleven types, from spelt sourdough to potato bread, all baked on site) and pastries, plus regional cheeses, Somerset honey and so on. Mon–Sat 8am–6pm, Sun 9am–4pm.

Southville Deli 262 North St, Southville ⓦsouthvilledeli.com; map pp.84–85. The best deli south of the river stocks Herbert's artisan breads and does a good line in Somerset goats' cheese, camembert and brie; storing nuts, spices and organic cereals in old-school dispensers is a nice touch. The strong range of gluten-free, wheat-free, vegetarian and vegan products includes vegan wines. Mon–Sat 9.30am–5.30pm, Sun 10.30am–4.30pm.

RESTAURANTS

Brunel Raj 6–7 Waterloo St, Clifton Village ☎0117 973 2641, ⓦbrunelraj.co.uk; map p.108. Curry connoisseurs swear by this upmarket Indian, a dark, cosy setting for superior versions of all the usual suspects, from kormas to vindaloos, plus more interesting traditional dishes such as haras, hundis and rezalas. The enormous king prawns are worth trying but start at £14.50 (other mains from £6.50). There's a twenty-percent discount for takeaway. Daily noon–2pm & 6–11.30pm, Fri & Sat till midnight.

Clifton Sausage 7–9 Portland St, Clifton Village ☎0117 973 1192, ⓦcliftonsausage.co.uk; map p.108. Pork fingers are obviously the thing at this popular, candlelit place, and most are here for the sausage and mash with onion gravy, or the tasting plate of five regional varieties (£12.75). There are plenty of other fine traditional British dishes on offer, though, should you wish to bypass the bangers; they're mostly seasonal, and range from steamed mussels in cider to venison casserole. No under-14s. Tues–Sun noon–3pm & 6.30–10pm, Fri till 11pm, Sat till 5pm & 11pm, Sun till 4pm & 9pm.

The Cowshed 46 Whiteladies Rd, Clifton ☎0117 973 3550, ⓦthecowshedbristol.com; map p.108. A proper temple to the tenderloin: *The Cowshed* is serious about its steak, sourcing quality cuts from local suppliers and dry-ageing them for a month. Take a deep breath and tackle the sixteen-ouncer, or order Steak on a Stone, brought uncooked to your table so you can sear it yourself. Most steaks are around £15.95, though the finest cuts will set you back £30. Daily Mon–Sat noon–3pm & 6–10pm, Sun noon–4pm.

★ **Juniper** 21 Cotham Rd South, Cotham ☎0117 942 1744, ⓦjuniperrestaurant.co.uk; map pp.84–85. Lovely little neighbourhood restaurant, with deep purple decor, softly lit tables and an exciting menu dominated by regional produce: follow stuffed rabbit and artichoke salad (£6) with trio of locally reared pork, bubble and squeak cake and apple smoothie (£16). Add refined but informal service, and you've got all the ingredients of a class act indeed. Mon–Sat 7pm–midnight.

★ **Lido** Oakfield Place, Clifton; restaurant entrance on Southleigh Rd ☎0117 933 9533, ⓦlidobristol.com; map p.108. Set-piece venue given a stylish new lease of life as a restaurant/bar and pool/spa complex. The glass-walled restaurant overlooks the heated outdoor pool, which makes dining on dishes like wood-roast chicken slow cooked in yoghurt (£16.50) while others exercise a deliciously guilty affair. Much of the rustic food is foraged, so expect seasonal ingredients such as Somerset truffles, wood sorrel and wild onion. Restaurant daily noon–3pm & Mon–Sat 6.30–10pm; poolside bar Mon–Sat 8am–11pm, Sun 9am–6pm.

Planet Pizza 83 Whiteladies Rd ☎0117 907 7112 & 187 Gloucester Rd ☎0117 944 4717; ⓦplanetpizza .co.uk; map p.108 & map opposite. Hip little restaurant with local art decorating the walls and a range of great, planet-christened pizzas. "Neptune" (prawns and tuna) and the "Moon" (feta, blue cheese, mozzarella and parmesan) neatly reflect their names; luckily, "Uranus" does not (it's herb-roasted chicken). Twelve-inch pizzas average around £11, nine-inch £7.50; daytime deal of any nine-inch pizza for a fiver. Tasty salads, too. Ten-percent discount on takeaway. Daily 11am–11pm.

The RockFish Grill & Seafood Market 128 Whiteladies Rd ☎0117 973 7384, ⓦtherockfishgrill.com; map p.108. A rich, wonderful smell greets you at this upmarket but informal restaurant, owned by celeb chef Mitch Tonks and serving pricey but perfectly cooked fresh fish and seafood – the kitchen (and the adjoining fishmongers) get their delivery direct from the boats at Brixham each morning. Starters include fat Lyme Bay scallops, roasted with garlic and white port (£10), while for mains it's worth trying the catch of the day cooked over a charcoal grill, a speciality of the restaurant that lends fish such as wild sea bass (£19.50) a lovely smoky Mediterranean flavour. Tues–Sat noon–2.30pm & 6–10.30pm.

Sands 95 Queens Rd ☎0117 973 9734, ⓦsandsrestaurant.co.uk; map p.108. Authentic Lebanese restaurant in an impressive Georgian building at the start of Clifton proper, using traditional recipes to create a varied selection of hot and cold mezze, from smoky *baba ghanoush* to *arayes*, strips of grilled lamb served in Lebanese bread. There's also a choice of larger mains, many of them *kafta* kebabs, and over a dozen Lebanese wines. Hot and cold mezze from £3.75/£4.75, mains from £11.95. Daily noon–2.30pm & 6–11pm.

★**Thali Café** 1 Regent St, Clifton ⓦthethalicafe .co.uk; map p.108. Born in the fields of Glastonbury and the Big Chill, this eco-conscious concept has gone from strength to strength since the first café opened in 1999, winning Best Cheap Eats in the *Observer Food Monthly* Awards in 2010 and Radio 4's Best Takeaway the year before. This Clifton branch – there are three others in Bristol, including one on St Mark's Road in Easton and another on York Road in Montpelier – has the trademark deep-pink decor and range of tasty *thalis*, a balanced selection of dishes served on a stainless-steel platter (from £7.95; kids' Tiny Thali £2.95). Daily 5pm–close, Sat & Sun from 10am.

GLOUCESTER ROAD AND AROUND
CAFÉS

La Ruca 89 Gloucester Rd ☎0117 944 6810, ⓦlaruca .co.uk; map opposite. Cosy Latin American organic health-food shop with a warm and welcoming upstairs café. Good-value home-cooked food includes *chimichangas*, bean enchiladas, hummus-topped spinach tortilla and other simple but tasty delights, such as chunky lentil and sun-dried tomato stew with halloumi (around £4.99). Mon–Sat 9am–5.30pm.

★**tart** 16 The Promenade, Gloucester Rd ☎0117 924 7628, ⓦlovelytart.com; map opposite. This cute café and foodstore is the sort of place you'd picture yourself running if you didn't have to do your normal nine-to-five. It's a lovely spot for afternoon tea: generous portions of scones, their own jams and Somerset clotted cream, plus a selection of home-made sandwiches – they're supplied by *The Breadstore*, diagonally opposite – cakes and, of course, tarts. Tues–Sat 8.30am–5.30pm, Sun 10am–5.30pm.

RESTAURANTS

Bistro La Barrique 225 Gloucester Rd ☎0117 944 5500, ⓦbistrolabarrique.co.uk; map opposite. *Magnifique* little bistro built around the concept of *petits plats*, a French take on tapas. There's a wide range of miniature mains, including tomato *tarte fin* and snails baked in pernod and garlic butter, as well as chalked-up daily specials of more standard-sized meals. Plenty of wines to try by the glass, so you can mix and match. *Petits plats* from £4.95; mains from £9.95. Mon–Fri 6–10pm, Sat 11.30am–10pm.

Casa Mexicana 29–31 Zetland Rd ☎0117 924 3901, ⓦcasamexicana.co.uk; map opposite. Atmospheric, authentic Mexican offering chunky burritos, *chimichangas* and enchiladas (from £12.95) that go way beyond the nachos-and-guacamole fare you get at most Tex-Mex places. Sizzling fajitas (grilled rump steak or marinated chicken) are pricey at £25.95, but they're made to share; wash them down with a quality margarita or two. Daily 6.30am–10pm.

Greens' Dining Room 25 Zetland Rd ☎0117 924 6437, ⓦgreensdiningroom.com; map opposite. Elegant family-run eatery at the bottom of Zetland Road, and with a daily changing menu that consistently delivers cooking of the highest order. It's a set menu – much of it local – but you can expect an interesting choice of dishes such as fish soup with rouille, North Somerset pork with semolina gnocchi and wild mushroom lasagne with truffle oil. Two courses £23.50 (£10 at lunch), three courses £29.50. Tues–Sat 12.30–2.30pm & 6.30–10.30pm.

Plantation Caribbean Bar & Restaurant 221–223 Cheltenham Rd ☎0117 907 7932, ⓦplantationrestaurant .biz; map opposite. Probably the best place to get a taste of Bristol's West Indian heritage. It's run by a friendly Jamaican-British lady who deals in simple but delicious jerk chicken, urried goat, ackee and salt fish and the like (mains around £12.95); there's also a substantial buffet for £18.95.Open-mic nights and occasional live music at the weekend. Tues–Thurs 6–11pm, Fri & Sat 6–11.30pm, Sun 6–10pm.

EAST BRISTOL

CAFÉS

Café Kino 108 Stokes Croft ☎0117 924 9200, ⓦcafe-kino.com; map p.111. Vegetarian and vegan cooking with a passion from a not-for-profit workers' co-operative. The food is all ethically sourced – and ranges from Thai red curry and moussaka to veggie burger and chips – the lagers organic and the coffee Fair Trade. It's part café, part community centre, hosting regular events and discussion groups, including a monthly Vegan Emporium day (vegan marshmallows anyone?). Daily 9am–9.30pm.

Canteen Hamilton House, 80 Stokes Croft ☎0117 923 2017, ⓦcoexistuk.org; map p.111. Overlooked by Banksy's famous *Mild, Mild West* mural, a drab 1960s office block now accommodates this incredibly popular artsy collective-style bar. Take a seat at a graffitied table for a coffee or a pint, or try something from the good, cheap menu that changes twice daily and includes dishes such as beetroot rosti and Gloucestershire beef shin (dishes from £5.50). Live music from 10pm most nights (from 4pm on Sun). Daily noon–3pm & 5–10pm.

Zazu's Kitchen 45 Jamaica St, Stokes Croft ☎0117 922 2333, ⓦzazuskitchen.co.uk; map p.111. Attractive country-kitchen café, with wooden tables at the back and a deli counter and window seating at the front, overlooking the busy junction of Jamaica Street and Stokes Croft. The central, open kitchen uses fresh, ethically sourced ingredients to whip up yellow chickpea curry (£5.50), mashed swede with crispy pancetta and fried egg (£4.50) and a variety of other Mediterranean-inspired light bites, from superfood salads to soups. Mon–Wed 7.30am–5pm, Thurs 9am–4pm & 6–9pm, Fri 9am–4pm & 6.30–10pm, Sat 10am–4pm & 6.30–10pm, Sun 10.30am–2.30pm.

RESTAURANTS

★ **Bell's Diner** 1–3 York Rd, Montpelier ☎0117 924 0357, ⓦbellsdiner.com; map p.111. Intimate in feel, this destination restaurant is consistently one of the most creative in Bristol, forging its reputation on the back of some truly tastebud-teasing combinations: sea bass is paired with hibiscus-soaked bulgar wheat, and scallops with a smoked-haddock foam, while beef carpaccio with beetroot sorbet and horseradish cream is the epicurean epitome of great teamwork. Mains are around £19.50, but you can save the anguish of decision-making by plumping for the eight-course tasting menu instead (£49.50, optional wine flight £35; Mon–Thurs only). Exceptional wine list, with over 150 to choose from. Mon & Sat 7–9.30pm, Tues–Fri noon–2pm & 7–9.30pm.

GLOUCESTER ROAD AND AROUND

● CAFÉS	
La Ruca	3
tart	4

● RESTAURANTS	
Bistro La Barrique	1
Casa Mexicana	5
Greens' Dining Room	6
Planet Pizza	2
Plantation Caribbean Bar & Restaurant	7

● SHOPS	
Beast	2
Plastic Wax Records	3
RePsycho	1

■ BAR	
The Prom	1

Café Maitreya 89 St Mark's Rd, Easton ☎0117 951 0100, ⓦcafemaitreya.co.uk; map pp.84–85. The multicultural but rundown neighbourhood of Easton makes an unlikely setting for one of the country's best vegetarian restaurants, regularly rated as the UK's finest by a variety of national papers and, more importantly, the National Vegetarian Society. Despite the accolades, it's an easy-going place, with friendly staff and an innovative, seasonally changing menu of flavourful dishes such as potato galette, pistachio rissole and spinach roulade, many available in gluten-, wheat- and dairy-free versions. Two- and three-course set menus cost £19.95/£22.95. Tues–Sat 6.30–9.45pm.

★ **Pieminister** 24 Stokes Croft ☎0117 942 9372, ⓦpieminister.co.uk; map p.111. Headquarters of the Bristol-based pie empire that has gradually been making their goody-filled pastries a lifestyle choice. Fresh, home-made pies include Chicken of Aragon (with bacon and tarragon), Heidi Pie (goats' cheese) and Mr Porky Pie (with cider, sage and apple). Make it a meal by adding minty mushy peas, crispy shallots and a dollop of mash, then drench it all in rich gravy. There's also a stall at St Nick's Market (see p.118), while several outlets across the city sell their pies. Pie, mash and gravy around £5.80. Daily 11am–7pm, Sun till 5pm.

SOUTH BRISTOL
CAFÉS
Beeses Riverside Bar and Tea Gardens Wyndham Crescent, signed off the A4 in Brislington "To Conham Ferry" ☎0117 977 7412, ⓦbeeses.co.uk; map pp.84–85. Super summer-only spot that does what it says on the tin: afternoon tea or ales served in a tranquil riverside setting that feels a million miles from the nearby city centre. Food is simple but satisfying – quality burgers (a choice of nine; from £6.50), salads and home-made cakes – and there's regular music in the form of rock and blues, country and folk, plus brass bands on the occasional Sunday. It's a short drive from the centre, but it's even better to arrive by boat (see p.116). Easter–Sept Thurs 4–11pm, Fri & Sat noon–11pm, Sun 10am–7pm, bank hols noon–7pm.

Lounge 227–231 North St, Southville ☎0117 963 7340, ⓦthelounges.co.uk; map pp.84–85. The original *Lounge* – there are four others in Bristol, including one on Gloucester Road – is one of the mellowest joints around. It's pitched just right for trendy Southville, acting as a relaxed, family-friendly meeting place during the day and a chilled-out drinking destination come nightfall. Food is fairly classic – paninis, ciabattas, beer-battered fish and chips, plus a decent range of tapas – though they also serve up some of the best chocolate brownies in the city. Perfect weekend-brunch fodder. Daily 9am–11pm.

RESTAURANTS
Bocabar Paintworks, Bath Rd, Arnos Vale ☎0117 972 8838, ⓦbocabar.co.uk; map pp.84–85. Set in a huge, open warehouse at the heart of the Paintworks creative quarter, this art-filled café-restaurant and bar (see p.129) has quickly established a solid reputation for relaxed lunches and snazzy pizzas – authentic thin-crust beauties, made on site with Italian dough and stone-baked to perfection. There are over thirty to choose from, with nearly half of them available as veggie versions (from £9.50), though footy fans will find it hard not to go for a Zico, a Rivelino or a Maracana (chicken, roasted peppers,

gorgonzola and olives). Big appetites can alternatively kick-off the weekend with a Big Boca, a double full English (£11.50; till 11.30am). Daily 10am–11pm, Fri & Sat till 1am, Sunday till 10.30pm.

The Spotted Cow 139 North St, Southville ☎0117 963 4433, ⓦthespottedcowbristol.com; map pp.84–85. A nod to the area's pastural past, the *Spotted Cow* has quickly established itself as a Southville favourite, stylishly furnished and with a changing menu that utilises local ingredients where possible: Mark's Bread, freshly baked further up North Street, Tom Murray's butcher sausages (sausage and mash £7.95) and herbs and vegetables from their own roof garden. The pleasant area out back is more of a field than a pub garden. DJs, quizzes and nightly open mic sessions keep diners entertained beyond dinner. Mon–Thurs noon–3pm & 5–9pm, Fri–Sun noon–9pm; bar until midnight/1am.

Teohs Tobacco Factory, North St, Southville ☎0117 902 1122, ⓦteohs.net; map pp.84–85. Set within the Tobacco Factory theatre building, this vast Pan-Asian bistro has the *de rigueur* canteen-style set-up but a menu that's a little bit more adventurous than most: the thirty mains (all £7.50, and over half of them available as vegetarian or vegan) include Malaysian kajang chicken satay, Hainan chicken rice and Penang fried *ho fun*, a dish of noodles, fish cake, Chinese sausage and mussels. Half-day classes at their cookery school (£50), led by the eponymous owner himself, give an insight into their wok wizardry. Mon–Sat noon–2.30pm & 6–10.30pm.

FURTHER AFIELD
RESTAURANT
★ **Casamia** 38 High St, Westbury-on-Trym ☎0117 959 2884, ⓦcasamiarestaurant.co.uk; map pp.84–85. The rising star of the ambitious Sanchez-Iglesias brothers shows no sign of dimming. Since coaxing their parents' trattoria into a select Modern Italian diner, they have captured the city's only Michelin star and been voted Gordon Ramsey's favourite restaurant in the UK. But far from resting on their laurels, the brothers continue to conjure up well-sourced seasonal menus that combine sensationally simple dishes, such as beautifully cooked pig's cheek, with touches of real creativity: the crowd-pleasing pine-nut pannacotta and Amalfi lemon sorbet is sensory dining at its best. Five- and nine-course tasting menus £45/£68, wine flight £25/£40. Tues–Sat 7–9pm, Sat also 12.30–1.45pm.

DRINKING

Bristol's repertoire of drinking dens is almost as varied as its restaurants: traditional **pubs**, most obviously around the Old City; cool **cocktail bars**, particularly up Park Street; and well-worn **cider houses**, spread throughout. Most areas are welcoming and relaxed, though The Centre is perhaps best avoided late at night, when worse-for-wear revellers descend on the area's taxi ranks. Many pubs and bars feature **live music**, and several of the latter host **club nights** throughout the week (see p.130).

WHAT'S YOUR TIPPLE?

Cider *Coronation Tap* See p.128
Cocktails *Goldbrick House* See p.128
Home brew *Zerodegrees* See below

Real ale *Portcullis* See p.129
Rum *The Rummer* See below
Whiskey *The Woods* See p.128

THE OLD CITY AND AROUND

Big Chill Bar 15 Small St ☎0117 930 4217, ⊛bigchill net/bristol; map p.88. Funky, compact bar, with album lovers adorning one wall and pine benches spread around the main space. Good cocktails, including the sweet peach Big Chill Punch, plus Bath Ales Gem on draught, but it's the laidback atmosphere and the quality live music and DJs (Wed–Sat) that make this place. Mon–Wed & Sun noon– midnight, Thurs noon–1am, Fri & Sat noon–3am.

The Hole in the Wall 2 The Grove, Queen Square ☎0117 26 5967, ⊛theholeinthewallbristol.co.uk; map p.88. Robert Louis Stevenson allegedly based *The Spyglass* in *Treasure Island* on this historic boozer, now housing a thoroughly modern interior strewn with leather armchairs and couches. The "holes" – once used to detect approaching press gangs – are still there, a couple of slits in a "spy house" that juts out of the building's southern side; you can squeeze in here and watch the goings-on along The Grove with a pint of Butcombe or an Addlestones cider. In summer, tables fill the grass out front. Daily 11am–11pm, till 10.30pm on Sun.

The Llandoger Trow 1–3 King St ☎0117 926 0783; map p.88. Sloping, timber-framed drinking den on cobbled King Street, full of historical resonance (see p.89), with cosy nooks and armchairs. It's been expanded over the years – what is now known as the *Smugglers Bar* is the original inn. Cask ales include Butcombe and Black Sheep Bitter. Mon–Sat 11am–11pm, Sun noon–10.30pm.

The Rummer Hotel All Saints Lane ⊛therummer.net; map p.88. Stylish but relaxed restaurant bar, with ageing chesterfields set around a roaring fire and an enclosed medieval bar that heaves with the weight of some four hundred spirits, over a quarter of them rums. There's a globe-trotting range of bottled beers, too, plus a strong wine list. At the weekend, head downstairs to *The Cellars Bar*, a late-night gin den, for some quality cocktails. Bar Mon–Thurs 10am– midnight, Fri 10am–1am, Sat 11am–1am, Sun noon– 10.30pm; The Cellars Fri & Sat 7pm–1am.

Start the Bus 7–9 Baldwin St ☎0117 930 4370, ⊛startthebus.tv; map p.88. Innovative, feel-good indie hangout, with an eclectic choice of music and food (including Hippy Burgers and Po Boys). Art students have been let loose on the decor, and there are board games, comfy sofas and live music or DJs in the evening; regular offbeat events include jumble sales and alternative pub quizzes. Good range of draughts, including Leffe, Westons Organic and Fruli. Mon–Wed 10am–1am, Thurs–Sat 10am–3am, Sun 11am–1.30am.

Zerodegrees 53 Colston St ☎0117 925 2706, ⊛zerodegrees.co.uk; map p.88. Huge stainless steel vats take centre stage at this industrial-chic microbrewery at the top of Christmas Steps, which produces its own award-winning crisp pilsner, black lager, wheat beer and vegan-friendly pale ale. Tables are arranged over a number of terraces, most looking down over the vast, very open central space – it's normally buzzing in here, but when it's quiet, it feels *really* quiet. Daily noon–midnight, Sun till 11pm.

TEMPLE

King's Head 60 Victoria St ☎0117 927 7860; map pp.94–95. Snug old pub, squished into a row of shops that partly hide Temple Church – it's very narrow, and there can't be room for much more than a dozen or so people in here at any one time. The ornate interior is modelled on an old Bristol tramcar, prints of which adorn the walls. The bar is equally decorative; you can get draught lagers and ciders, but it's more of a cask-ale kind of place, with Doom Bar, Atlantic IPA and Sharp's Cornish Coaster on tap. Mon–Fri 11am–11.30pm, Sat 2–11.30pm, Sun noon–3pm & 7–11.30pm.

HARBOURSIDE

★ **The Apple** Welsh Back ☎0117 925 3500, ⊛applecider.co.uk; map pp.94–95. No prizes for guessing what this converted Dutch barge specializes in, though you may be taken aback by the range: nearly forty ciders, perries and other alcoholic, apple-related drinks, from cocktails to brandies; you can even order a jug of cider sangria if you're feeling in a Bristol-by-the-Balearics kind of mood. Food is simple but superb – the ploughman's lunch, the only thing on the menu, is (officially) the best in the country. You can put your own together from some 28 ingredients, including seven different cheeses, though you may need to polish off a couple before tackling the Old Bristolian cider; at 8.4 percent, it's only sold in halves. Daily noon–midnight, Sun till 10.30pm.

Grain Barge Mardyke Wharf, Hotwell Rd ☎0117 929 9347, ⊛grainbarge.com; map pp.94–95. Floating pub, café and restaurant near the mouth of the harbour, with a tranquil ambience and half a dozen real ales brewed at the Bristol Beer Factory just south of the river. Interesting calendar includes a Pie & Pint night (Wed) and regular live music on Friday evenings, plus monthly art exhibitions. Tues–Thurs & Sun noon–11pm, Fri & Sat noon–11.30pm.

The Orchard 12 Hanover Place ☎0117 926 2678; map pp.94–95. This dinky former CAMRA National Cider Pub of the Year, tucked behind some dockyards on Spike Island, punches well above its weight, with over twenty ciders,

2

LATE-NIGHT WEEKEND BARS

The Bank of Stokes Croft (closes 4am)
See opposite
The Elbow Room (closes 5am) See below

Hyde & Co (closes 3am) See below
The Park (closes 4am) See below
The Woods (closes 6am) See below

including Black Rat, Wilkins, Gwatkin and Orchard Pig; other rarities and specials regularly pop up on the bar-side blackboard. Thankfully, there's a handy *Hangover Café* on Saturday and Sunday mornings (9am–noon), whose fry-ups are just the ticket for soaking up the cider. Daily 10am–11.30pm, Fri & Sat till midnight.

PARK STREET AND THE WEST END

Browns 38 Queen's Rd ☎0117 930 4777, ⍵browns-restaurants.com; map pp.94–95. Spacious and relaxed place for an early evening drink, housed in the Venetian-style former university refectory – some nights, with the squadron of ceiling fans whirring in unison and the piano player tinkling the ivories, it can feel like you've stepped into a Colonial bar at the height of the Empire. Plenty of choice on the drinks front, with 45 wines and champagnes by the glass, the usual lagers on tap and some moreish cocktails (from 4pm). Food, along the lines of hamburgers and shepherd's pie, is served all day. Mon–Sat 10am–11pm, till midnight Thurs–Sat, Sun 11am–10.30pm.

The Elbow Room 64 Park St ☎0117 930 0242, ⍵theelbowroom.co.uk; map pp.94–95. Dark, laidback pool hall, good for playing a little eight-ball or for generally kicking back and enjoying some of the great drinks offers, including cool cocktails such as Weston-Super-Mud and West Country Ice Tea. Moves seamlessly into a trendy dance venue, with DJs playing through the night. Daily noon–2am, Fri till 4am, Sat till 5am.

Goldbrick House 69 Park St ☎0117 945 1950, ⍵goldbrickhouse.co.uk; map pp.94–95. This choice cocktail bar housed in an old Georgian building feels more like a suave gentleman's club, with original fireplaces, dark leather armchairs and polished parquet flooring. The lengthy list, which stretches to a dozen pages, tiptoes through vodkas, gins (you can make up your Martini from a dozen varieties), rums, bourbons and champagne, all using home-made syrups and fresh purees; enlightened Golden Hours (daily 4–8pm) see some prices drop to £4.50. Put together your own Flight of the Navigator at a monthly Wednesday-night cocktail crash-course (£17.50). Mon–Thurs noon–midnight, Fri & Sat noon–1am.

★ **Hyde & Co** Upper Byron Place ☎0117 929 7007, ⍵hydeandcobristol.net; map pp.94–95. Stylish speakeasy – look for the bowler-hat sign over the unmarked red door – with a mature but mellow ambience, just yards from the Triangle but feeling a world away. Moody lighting, tassel-fringed lampshades and dapper bar staff done up in 1920s vintage attire lend the place a Prohibition vibe, as do

the classic (quality) American cocktails, from sours, swizzles and fizzes to highballs, juleps and smashes. Live music Wednesday nights. Daily 7pm–1am, Thurs–Sat till 3am.

The Park 37 Triangle West ☎0117 940 6101, ⍵theparkbristol.com; map pp.94–95. Sassy late-night bar that's been running a smooth operation on the notoriously fickle Triangle for over a decade. Plenty of draughts (Peroni, Gem) and bottles (Kirin, Weston Organic) to choose from, plus quality cocktails. The line-up of local DJs keeps the crowd going with a mixture of funk, Northern Soul, rare groove and more, all under the gaze of some interesting *Last Supper* artwork. Daily 4.30pm–2am, Thurs till 3am, Fri & Sat till 4am.

The Woods 1 Park St Ave ☎0117 925 0890; map pp.94–95. It's whiskey-a-go-go at this classy all-night bar at the top of Park Street, with the choice of blends and malts topping out just shy of a hundred, easily the most comprehensive list in the city. The arty decor makes you feel like you're supping on Jack Daniels and his pals in the middle of a forest, but it enhances the concept rather than detracts from it. Draught beer includes the punchy Moretti, and there's a decent cocktail selection, but most drinkers don't look beyond the bourbon. Daily 4pm–3am, Fri till 4am, Sat till 6am.

CLIFTON AND AROUND

★ **The Coronation Tap** 8 Sion Place, Clifton ☎0117 97. 9617, ⍵thecoronationtap.com; map p.108. A legend in its own (long) lifetime, *The Cori Tap* has kept true to its roots for nearly three hundred years – one of the first buildings in Clifton, it began life as Clifton Farm, surrounded on all sides by acres of apple orchards. A proper cider house, it produces its own Exhibition "apple juice", which is sold by the half-pint only, and stocks a wide range of locally produced ciders, from still to sparkling, clear to cloudy and including Cheddar Valley and Taunton Traditional. Excellent live music has seen it shortlisted for UK Music Pub of the Year three years running. All draught ciders available in two-pint takeaways. Daily 5.30pm–close, Sat from 7pm, Sun from 2pm.

★ **Hausbar** 52 Upper Belgrave Rd, Clifton ☎0117 946 6081, ⍵hausbar.co.uk; map p.108. Sophisticated, one-of-a-kind German cellar-bar, bringing a bit of bohemian Berlin to Bristol, as much with its intimate ambience as its vintage set-piece decor. Quality ingredients plus quality bartenders equals quality cocktails, though those after a traditional German brew can also opt for the draught Flensburger. Daily 8pm–2am.

★ **The Highbury Vaults** 164 St Michael's Hill ☎0117 973 3203; map pp.84–85. It's a stiff climb up St Michael's ill to this historic boozer – impossible to miss, thanks to ick Walker's mural of a graffiti artist swinging from Rapunzel's hair – but it's worth the workout. Originally the ite of a gallows (condemned prisoners spent their last ights here), *The Highbury Vaults* is a lovely local in the most traditional of senses, with wall-to-wall wood and plenty of snugs in which to lose track of time while nursing a pint – it's a Young's pub, so you'll get Young's Bitter and Highbury Gold on tap, plus St Austell Tribute and Bath Ales' Gem. There's also bar billiards and a popular patio out back. Daily noon–midnight, Sun till 11pm.

Portcullis 3 Wellington Terrace, Sion Hill, Clifton ☎0117 908 5536; map p.108. A CAMRA favourite, this tiny pub, wedged into a graceful terrace on swanky Sion Hill, is a bastion of real ales in Clifton, with up to nine on tap at any one time, including – as a Dawkins pub – Brass Knocker and Green Barrel. The friendly landlords hold regular beer festivals that usually turn up a few punchy rarities. Mon–Thurs 4.30–11pm, Fri noon–2pm & 4.30–11pm, Sat noon–11pm, Sun noon–10.30pm.

White Lion Bar and Terrace Avon Gorge Hotel, Sion Hill, Clifton ☎0117 973 8955, ⓦtheavongorge.com; map p.108. Located on the very edge of the Avon Gorge, this modern bar draws in the crowds thanks to the magnificent views from its expansive terrace, where it feels like you're almost sitting underneath the Suspension Bridge; it's a spectacular spot on a sunny day. The bar menu features burgers, baked brie, pasta and pies. Daily 11am–11pm, Sun till 10.30pm.

GLOUCESTER ROAD AND AROUND

The Prom 26 The Promenade, Gloucester Rd ☎0117 942 7319, ⓦtheprom.co.uk; map p.125. This intimate bar is a café by day, offering a rare chance on Gloucester Road to chomp on burgers, jackets, tortillas and wraps alfresco, but really comes into its own at night – there's live music every evening (bar Tuesday, which is pop-quiz night), mostly blues and folk, but also jazz, country, soul and the occasional rock and ska set. Sunday is open-mic night; free entry except Saturday (£5). Mon–Wed 11am–midnight, Thurs 11am–1am, Fri 11am–2am, Sat 10am–2am, Sun 10am–midnight.

EAST BRISTOL
The Bank of Stokes Croft 84 Stokes Croft ☎0117 923

2565, ⓦthebankofstokescroft.com; map p.111. As it says on the tin, this former Allied Bank is now home to an achingly contemporary late-night bar, with graffiti daubed across its vaults. Run by a team with a strong pedigree – they also own the *Big Chill Bar* (see p.127) and the *Spotted Cow* across the river (see p.126) – it attracts hardworking arty types with a blend of laidback drinking and up-tempo DJs. Changing exhibitions decorate the walls, and there's a little garden hidden out the back. Mon–Wed & Sun 11am–1am, Thurs 11am–2am, Fri & Sat 11am–4am.

Bristol Cider House 8–9 Surrey St, St Pauls ☎0117 942 8196, ⓦwww.bristolciderhouse.co.uk; map p.111. The name says it all: this long-running CAMRA favourite on the edge of St Pauls is all about the apple, with nine draughts taking in Broadoak, Thatchers and Black Rat Cloudy, plus the speech-slurring Old Bristolian (sold by the half-pint only). Soak it all up with farmhouse stew, ploughman's lunch or a Gert Big Bap, the house speciality. Popular cider-tasting evenings, and a cider festival every Saturday. Tues & Wed 5–11pm, Thurs 5–11.30pm, Fri & Sat noon–midnight.

Cosies Wine Bar 34 Portland Square, St Pauls ☎0117 942 4110, ⓦcosies.co.uk; map p.111. They got half the name right: it's certainly cosy in here. But this bunker-esque basement is far from your average wine bar. Popular with local office workers during the day, it comes into its own at night, when the pews quickly fill with drinkers who drop by for the intimate atmosphere or the top-draw DJs spinning mostly hip-hop, drum 'n' bass and dubstep; the Reggae Sunday session is unmissable for many. Mon–Thurs 11am–10pm, Fri till late, Sat & Sun 9pm till late.

SOUTH BRISTOL

Bocabar Paintworks, Bath Rd, Arnos Vale ☎0117 972 8838, ⓦbocabar.co.uk; map pp.84–85. Breezy, easy-going warehouse hangout in the self-styled Paintworks creative quarter, which doubles as a café-restaurant (see p.126). Melt into a comfy sofa with one of their ever-changing bottled beers (think Kasteel Cru, Grolsch Weizen, Chimay Red) or try one of the mighty fine caipirinhas, given a kick with Leblon cachaça – the Green & Red cocktail neatly sums up their whimsical approach: "Some ingredients are green. Some ingredients are red. All ingredients are within their use-by-dates." Live music at the weekends, from Balkan footstompers to jive and contemporary jazz. Daily 10am–11pm, Fri & Sat till 1am, Sunday till 10.30pm.

NIGHTLIFE

As you might expect from such an urbane city, nightlife in Bristol is lively to say the least. Indeed, few places outside of London have as vibrant a **live music** scene, and the range of venues is almost as eclectic as the genres on offer, from hip-hop and reggae to jazz and folk – though the city is particularly renowned for drum 'n' bass and dubstep. The local **club** scene is equally dynamic, from old-timers *Lakota* and the *Thekla* to the new breed of super-venues such as *Motion*. Several places host both live bands and club nights – we've noted where this is the case in the reviews on p.130 – as do some bars, including *Big Chill Bar* (see p.127), *Start the Bus* (see p.127) and *Cosies Wine Bar* (see above); the *Bank of Stokes Croft* (see above) runs quality DJ sets, while the *Coronation Tap* (see opposite) and *The Prom* (see above) are also known for their live music.

Listings For the latest musical offerings and club happenings, check out *Venue*, the monthly listings magazine (ⓦ venue.co.uk), or consult ⓦ whatsonbristol. co.uk for details of events.

CLUBS

Basement 45 8 Frogmore St ⓦ basement45.co.uk; map pp.94–95. Small underground venue peddling big underground house, plus drum 'n' bass and dubstep. Club nights, student events and a range of weekend sessions hosted by the likes of Torque (first Fri of month) and Just Jack (second Sat). After-parties keep the vibe going till morning. Entry £5–10.

Dojo Lounge 12–16 Park Row ☎ 0117 925 1177; map pp.94–95. Intimate venue specializing in weekend all-nighters, where you can dance till dawn to techno and electronica at Revolution or Empathy, Bristol's longest-running club night. There's more breathing space on the outdoor terrace. Entry £5–8, though some events are free.

Lakota 6 Upper York St, Stokes Croft ⓦ lakota.co.uk; map p.111. The *grande dame* of Bristol's club scene – though recently improved and its soundsystems updated – and still serving up the goods, churning out hardcore, old skool and drum 'n' bass. Look out for Bad Bass and Tribe of Frog (last Sat of month). Entry £5–17.50, though some events are free.

Motion 74–78 Avon St, St Philips ⓦ motionbristol .com; map pp.84–85. It's worth the effort to reach this out-of-the-way warehouse near Temple Meads Station, for all-night raves and big-name acts pumping out dubstep, drum 'n' bass and electro. Organizes regular DJ match-ups, plus the monumental In:Motion, an underground music season that starts in October and runs through till New Year. Entry £5–16.

Oceana The South Buildings, Canons Rd ⓦ oceanaclubs .com; map pp.94–95. The Bristol franchise of this national chain – an ominous-looking, black-glass building on the Harbourside – is theme-park heaven, with seven very different mini-venues, ranging from the Moulin Rouge styling of "Parisian Boudoir" to the altogether airier "Sydney Harbourside", decorated with aboriginal art. The music isn't quite as globetrotting, though. Entry £4.50–8.50.

Thekla East Mud Dock, The Grove ☎ 0117 929 3301, ⓦ theklabristol.co.uk; map pp.94–95. Salvaged Baltic coaster that found a new calling as a live-music venue and club and never looked back. It's much loved round these parts, mostly for the varied club-night line-up, and the consistently fine acts that belt out tunes in the bowels of the boat. There's a great little bar, too.

Syndicate 15 Nelson St ⓦ thesyndicate.org; map p.88. A real super-club, the largest in Bristol, and home to Propaganda, the Wednesday-night indie session that has rolled out across the country to become the biggest of its kind in the UK. Guest DJs are some of the hottest names

Tickets In addition to the places themselves, you can buy tickets from the Bristol Ticket Shop at 26 Union St (Mon–Sat 10am–6pm, Thurs till 7pm; ☎ 0117 929 9008; ⓦ bristolticketshop.co.uk).

around, including the likes of the Arctic Monkeys. Eden, on Friday nights, is particularly popular with students. Entry £4–5, free in the week.

LIVE-MUSIC VENUES

Bristol Bierkeller The Pithay, All Saints ☎ 0117 926 8514, ⓦ bristolbierkeller.co.uk; map p.88. A dark dungeon of a venue, just right for hosting hard, hurts-your-head rock and heavy metal acts including the likes of Sepultura. Friday is Phuct; Saturday night is Oompah night a name-affirming Bavarian-style knees-up.

Colston Hall Colston St ☎ 0117 922 3686, ⓦ colstonhall .org; map p.88. Bristol's largest concert hall and probably the South West's premier venue, attracting the major players in pop and classical music. Catch acoustic sets from local bands in the revamped foyer several nights a week. Hosts the Bristol Folk Festival in late April.

The Croft 117–119 Stokes Croft ☎ 0117 987 4144, ⓦ the croft.com; map p.111. Nightly gigs from a varied mix of local and national talent – particularly punk but also hip-hop and dubstep – in both the main room and the front bar. Club nights sometimes pop up on the packed programme.

Fiddlers Willway St, Bedminster ☎ 0117 987 3403 ⓦ fiddlers.co.uk; map pp.84–85. Mainly live folk, world music and Afrobeat at this relaxed family-run venue south of the river, off Bedminster Parade.

The Fleece 12 St Thomas St ☎ 0117 929 9008, ⓦ thefleece.co.uk; map pp.94–95. Stone-flagged ex-wool warehouse, now a loud, sweaty pub for live rock, jazz, folk and more. An old-timer on the Bristol music scene, recently given a new lease of life, so expect a stronger programme of quality touring acts.

The Louisiana Wapping Rd, Bathurst Terrace ☎ 0117 926 5978, ⓦ thelouisiana.net; map pp.94–95. Established music pub with a well-earned reputation for helping break bands (The White Stripes, Elbow, Florence and the Machine) and promoting local artists; more recent acts to have played the upstairs room include Elbow and Mumford & Sons.

Mr Wolf's 33 St Stephens St ☎ 0117 927 3221, ⓦ mrwolfs.com; map p.88. Friendly, shabby-chic noodle-bar hosting nightly music sessions that run from funk to rockabilly and back again; live DJs take centre stage once the clock strikes midnight. Open-mic nights, graffiti sessions and quizzes add to the mix.

O2 Academy Frogmore St ☎ 0844 477 2000, ⓦ o2academybristol.co.uk; map pp.94–95. The Bristol branch of this national chain is a spacious, multi-level place that stages almost nightly live gigs, both the big guns and,

MASSIVE ATTACK AND THE BIRTH OF TRIP-HOP

You could be forgiven for thinking that **music** didn't exist in Bristol until the 1990s. Despite a healthy history of establishment-shaking bands such as The Pop Group and Strangelove, it wasn't until the release in 1991 of *Blue Lines*, the stunning debut album of local collective Massive Attack, that the city forced itself upon the nation's musical psyche. And for the following decade, Bristol seemed to rule the urban music scene.

Massive Attack – essentially Grant Marshall (Daddy G), Andy Vowles (Mushroom) and former graffiti artist Robert del Naja (3D), with whispered rapping from Adrian Thaws (better known as Tricky) – were born out of the city's New York-influenced underground scene, and their work, marked by mesmeric beats and a laidback but highly worked hip-hop style, was unlike anything that had gone before. Music journalists called it **trip-hop**, a concept the group themselves have never bought into, but the tag stuck, and was cemented as a genre with the release of **Portishead**'s *Dummy* in 1994; coupling slow-burning beats with cinematic scores, Portishead's equally unique sound was underwritten by the fragile vocals of Beth Gibbons, a technique unique Massive Attack had so effectively used with Shara Nelson on *Blue Lines*, and did so again with Tracey Thorne on *Protection* (1994) and Elizabeth Fraser on *Mezzanine* (1998). No sooner had Portishead picked up the Mercury Music Prize for *Dummy*, than **Tricky** released his *Maxinquaye* (1995) masterpiece, an unexpectedly complex solo triumph that took dark and down-tempo to a whole new level.

Portishead gained further acclaim with the self-titled *Portishead* in 1997, but didn't produce their next album, *Third*, until 2008. Massive Attack, in turn, waited five years before releasing *100th Window* (2003), a far more experimental and electronic album that had only 3D at the helm. Compared to his peers, Tricky has been prolific, producing another eight albums, four before the century was out, with each growing ever more anxious than the last. But where Tricky's most recent release, *Mixed Race* (2010), has been his poorest performing, Massive Attack have experienced something of a return to form, with *Heligoland* (2010), their first album in seven years, seeing 3D and Daddy G united once more.

n the more intimate 02 Academy 2 room upstairs, local cts. "Ramshackle" club night on Fridays.

Old Duke 45 King St ☎0117 927 7137, ☻theoldduke co.uk; map p.88. Trad-jazz and blues pub – *the* place in Bristol to catch freeform sax or a melancholy sawgrass set – with live music every night of the week, plus Sunday lunchtime. Plenty of real ales and ciders on tap, with seating on the historic cobbled street out front. Popular jazz Festival every August.

St George's Great George St ☎0845 402 4001, ☻stgeorgesbristol.co.uk; map pp.94–95. Elegant Georgian church with superb acoustics, staging a packed programme of lunchtime and evening concerts covering classical, world, folk and jazz music.

The Trinity Centre Trinity Rd, Old Market ☎0117 935 1200, ☻3ca.org.uk; map pp.84–85. Atmospheric old building with a lofty legacy, having played host to U2, Massive Attack and Public Enemy among others. Mostly music, but nights such as Teachings in Dub are a reminder of its historical clubbing clout.

ENTERTAINMENT

CINEMA

The Cube Dove St South ☎0117 907 4190, ☻cubecinema.com. Creative, volunteer-run, community cinema and arts centre, screening mainstream and independent films, plus an avant-garde schedule of music, cabaret, talks, performance art and kids' events. Refreshments include Cube-Cola, their home-made coke, and coffee shipped in direct from Central America.

Showcase Cinema De Lux Level 3 Cabot Circus ☎0871 220 1000, ☻cinemadelux.co.uk. Vast multiplex at the heart of the Cabot Circus shopping centre, with thirteen screens (four of them 3D) showing the latest releases in suitable comfort – particularly if you're in one of the two Director's Halls, which benefit from large reclining leather

chairs and an order-in-your seat policy.

Watershed 1 Canons Rd ☎0117 927 5100, ☻watershed.co.uk. A real Bristol landmark, delivering a consistently diverse programme of open-run films and one-off viewings across three screens, plus talks, Q&As, festivals and all manner of other events dedicated to the visual arts. The popular café-bar is worth a visit whether you're catching a movie or not (see p.120).

THEATRE

Alma Theatre *The Alma Tavern*, 18–20 Alma Vale Rd, Clifton ☎0117 946 7899, ☻almataverntheatre.co.uk. Intimate pub-theatre venue (there are less than fifty seats) that entertains local and touring companies, including the

2

Bristol Old Vic Theatre School. Expect a broad range of productions, with lots of leftfield, experimental theatre, from state-of-the-nation monologues to musical adaptations of Shakespeare.

Bristol Hippodrome St Augustine's Parade ☎0117 302 3310, ⓦbristolhippodrome.org.uk. Large traditional theatre that celebrates a hundred years of putting on performances in 2012. It's the favoured port of call for big West End shows heading to the West Country though is equally at home hosting opera, ballet, big-name touring comedians and concerts. Also runs Saturday-morning theatre tours.

Bristol Old Vic King St ☎0117 987 7877, ⓦbristololdvic .org.uk. Highly respected historical complex, home to the company of the same name and centred around the Theatre Royal, a beautiful Georgian theatre that's the oldest in the country. After a bit of a wobble a few years ago, it's back to its best under the auspices of Tom Harris, former artistic associate at the National Theatre, with new takes on old plays, spoken-word performances, social-media shows and outdoor events. Ambitious refurbishment and redevelopment plans are in the pipeline.

Tobacco Factory Raleigh Rd, Southville ☎0117 90 0344, ⓦtobaccofactorytheatre.com. Neighbourhood-defining theatre offering a broad spectrum of plays and other performing arts. The programme in the main theatre is Bard-focused, with four plays a year from much-admired theatre company Shakespeare at the Tobacco Factory (ⓦsattf.org.uk), supplemented with comedy courtesy of The Comedy Box (ⓦthecomedybox.co.uk) and theatre festivals; The Brewery studio theatre, just down North Street, has a more varied calendar of performances.

COMEDY AND PERFORMANCE ART

Circomedia The Church, Portland Square, St Paul ☎0117 924 7615, ⓦcircomedia.com. Gothic St Paul Church is the unlikely but enlightening venue for this groundbreaking circus school, which runs foundation degrees and workshops and also puts on occasional showcases that provide an unforgettable evening of Big Top tricks and physical theatre.

Hen & Chicken 210 North St, Southville ⓦhenandchicken.com. The upstairs room of this big open boozer is home to The Comedy Box

GAY BRISTOL

Bristol's dynamic gay scene is focused on **Old Market**, the area just east of Castle Park that was earmarked as a gay village by the city council a long time ago and is increasingly living up to the name – The Village is now home to a dozen or so gay bars and clubs, including the city's only bear bar. The area around **Frogmore Street**, sometimes referred to as Gay Central, is a smaller enclave whose venues include Bristol's original gay club.

   Pride Week (July or Aug; ⓦpridebristol.org), a varied programme of art, film and theatre that culminates in a parade and music festival in Castle Park, only started in 2010 but is already the biggest LGBT event in the South West.

INFORMATION

Bristol LGBT Forum ⓦbristol-lgb-forum.org.uk. Member-driven focus group concerned with local issues but also providing an up-to-date diary of regional LGBT events.

Out Bristol Magazine ⓦoutbristol.co.uk. Monthly mag for the LGBT community, covering the local bar and club scene, plus goings-on in Bath and Somerset.

BARS AND CLUBS

Flamingos 23–25 West St, Old Market ⓦflamingosbristol.co.uk; map pp.84–85. In the heart of The Village, this lively club is the biggest LGBT venue in the South West, with two "arenas", two chill-out areas and four bars, spread over three floors. Live PAs, club nights and occasional guest acts. Entry £5–8.

The Palace 2 West St, Old Market; map pp.84–85. The former *Gin Palace*, tarted up and then some, and now a friendly venue for cabaret, with plenty of drag. The owners also run the *Bristol Bear Bar* just over the road. Mon–Thurs

7–11.30pm, Fri & Sat 7pm–2am, Sun 3pm–11.30pm.
The Pineapple 37 St George's Rd ⓦthepineapplebristol.com; map pp.94–95. Bristol's longest-running gay bar and a popular pre-clubber, whether you're hitting nearby *OMG* or the *Queenshilling*. Drop by for Chillax (Tues), or Family Misfortunes (Sun) with Tray La Trash.

Queenshilling 9 Frogmore St ⓦthequeenshilling .co.uk; map pp.94–95. Freshly refurbished after twenty years of serving Bristol's LGBT community, this scene-goers' stalwart hosts a variety of nights, from cabaret to karaoke; Friday's Camp As Tits pumps out five hours of classic anthems. Entry £1–15.

The Retreat 16 West St, Old Market ⓦretreatbristol .com; map pp.84–85. Stylish gay bar, the largest in the South West, hosting a packed programme of events, from quizzes to club sessions, including drag DJ Amber Dextrous' Weekend Starts Here (Fri) and the Come To Daddy club night (second Sat of month). Daily 11am–midnight.

ART TRAILS

Many of Bristol's inner-city areas join forces for one weekend a year to put on a local programme of arts and entertainment – from pottery to poetry and stone carving to Shakespeare, and encompassing a range of open studios, workshops, theatre and live music. Trails to look out for include the **Southbank Arts Trail** (May; ⓦsbaweb.co.uk), at over fifty venues in Southville, Bedminster and Ashton, and the **Front Room Arts Trail** (Nov; ⓦfrontroom.org.uk), with over two hundred artists displaying works across Totterdown.

2

ⓦthecomedybox.co.uk), a popular comedy club that attracts an interesting range of local and national talent; bigger names that need a bigger venue play the Tobacco Factory (see opposite).

The Island Bridewell Island, Silver St ☎0117 929 1534, ⓦtheislandbristol.com. Former police station that's home to a far-reaching artist co-operative, whose performance wing, The Invisible Circus (ⓦinvisiblecircus .co.uk), has a well-earned reputation for groundbreaking physical-theatre shows, such as the extravagant Carny Ville. The adjoining building, a former fire station, is now home to a cutting-edge youth centre.

SHOPPING

The £500 million super-store "suburb" of **Cabot Circus** has bumped the city up the shopping charts, but while it offers all the convenience you'd expect from a one-stop retail centre, the real joy of shopping in Bristol is browsing its boutiques, particularly in **Park Street**, the arts quarter around **Christmas Steps**, **Clifton** and along **Gloucester Road**, whose diverse selection of shops has earned it the moniker of Bristol's Independent High Street. As well as the food shops listed below, you can pick up locally made breads, cheeses and other gourmet provisions at the **delis** (see box, p.123).

ARCADES, SHOPPING CENTRES AND MALLS

Cabot Circus ⓦcabotcircus.com; map pp.94–95. Ultra-contemporary shopping precinct filled with the usual big-name brands such as Hollister, Apple, Sony, Next and a three-floor House of Fraser; the adjoining piazza-style Quakers Friars is home to the only Harvey Nichols in the South West. There's also an upmarket cinema (see p.131), and the abundance of eating and drinking options includes the snazzy *Harvey Nichols Second Floor Restaurant & Bar* (see p.119). Mon–Sat 10am–8pm, Sun 11am–5pm, public hols 10am–6pm.

The Clifton Arcade Boyces Ave, Clifton ⓦcliftonarcade .co.uk; map p.108. Lovely little Victorian shopping arcade, refurbished to its original Venetian design – look out for the striking decorative window at its far end – and housing an eclectic collection of one-off shops, including antiques stores, an art gallery and the requisite Fair Trade Mexican-craft importer. Mon–Fri 10am–5.30pm, Sat 9.30am–5.30pm, Sun 11am–4pm.

Guild 68–70 Park St ⓦbristolguild.co.uk; map pp.94–95. Quality independent retailer that has been operating at the top of Park Street for over a hundred years, formerly as the Bristol Guild of Applied Art. Various departments, from designer kitchen goods to a gourmet food hall, plus an outside terrace for a quick coffee break. Changing exhibitions from regional artists on the second floor. Mon–Sat 10am–6pm.

The Mall at Cribbs Causeway Off Junction 17 of the M5 ⓦmallcribbs.com; bus #1/40/54/73/75 from The Centre; map p.83. Classic out-of-town, everything-under-one-roof retail destination, with 135 big-name brands such as John Lewis, Marks and Spencers, Apple and H&M. Over a dozen cafés and restaurants provide nourishment for a sustained bout of credit-card swiping. Mon–Fri 9.30am–9pm, Sat 9am–8pm, Sun 11am–5pm.

BOOKSTORES AND RECORD SHOPS

Arnolfini 16 Narrow Quay ⓦarnolfini.org.uk; map pp.94–95. Small but very browsable arts-centric bookshop just off the main gallery, with one of the UK's best collections of contemporary-art titles, from situationism to stencil graffiti (and including some interesting books for kids, too), plus magazines covering art, architecture and design. Tues 11am–6pm, Wed–Sat 11am–8pm, Sun 11am–7pm.

★ **Plastic Wax Records** 222 Cheltenham Rd ⓦplasticwaxrecords.com; map p.125. This is Bristol's largest record dealer, and it's wall-to-wall vinyl (some 10,000 LPs, allegedly), across all genres, and all of it crying out to be leafed through, pored over and ultimately added to your collection. Mon–Fri 9.30am–7pm, Sat 9am–6pm, Sun noon–4.30pm.

Rise 70 Queens Rd, The Triangle ⓦrise-music.co.uk; map pp.94–95. Independent mini-chain with a wide-ranging stock and admirable attention to the local scene; regular midweek in-store performances enhance the experience. Mon–Sat 10am–7pm, Sun noon–6pm.

Stanfords 29 Corn St ⓦstanfords.co.uk; map p.88. Dedicated travel bookshop stocking a good range of local-interest books, regional walking guides, and maps to the city and surrounding area. Mon–Sat 9am–6pm, Tues from 9.30am.

Wanted Records The Covered Market, St Nicholas Market ⓦwantedrecords.co.uk; map p.88. Compact,

2

relaxed and strictly vinyl, with a little bit of everything, from folk and jazz to reggae and hip-hop. Extra kudos for having their own weekly residency at the *Big Chill Bar* (see p.127). Mon–Sat 9.30am–5pm.

FASHION

★ **Beast** 224 Cheltenham Rd & St Nicholas Market, ⓦ beast-clothing.com; map p.125 & p.88. Amusing T-shirts, hoodies and hats emblazoned with snippets of the local lingo – choose from "Ginormous Innum", "Ark At Ee" and "Gert Lush" among others. Possibly the most authentic souvenir of Bristol you can get. The St Nick's branch closes an hour earlier. Mon–Sat 10am–6pm.

the boot room 22 Park St; map pp.94–95. Half shoe shop, half homeware emporium, where you can slip your size 5s into everything from Poetic License heels to designer wellies, pick up a vintage bag or belt, or shop for quirky Cath Kidston-style knick-knacks. Mon–Sat 10am–5.45pm, Sun noon–4pm.

Cooshti 57 Park St ⓦ cooshti.com; map pp.94–95. A treasure-trove of trendy streetwear, stocking the latest labels such as Silas, Gravis, Nixon and WeSC; it's usually a good bet if you're looking for old-school styles and limited-edition footwear. The regular sales make the price-tags much more palatable. Mon–Sat 10am–6pm, Sun noon–5pm.

RePsycho 85 Gloucester Rd; map p.125. Great little "retro superstore" when you can wade through racks of vintage clothing (on the ground floor) or pick up a vintage piece of furniture (upstairs); Prime Cuts, in the claustrophobic basement down possibly the steepest stairs in Bristol, has plenty of old records and CDs, too. Mon–Sat 10am–5.30pm.

★ **Shop** 19 Christmas Steps ⓦ shoptheshop.co.uk; map p.88. Charming "Social Enterprise" that specializes in retro clothing at retro prices, plus vintage homeware, books and records. It's all non-profit, so any extras go towards community art events including workshops, film screenings and a monthly record club. What's more, the incredibly friendly staff provide free coffee and cake to boot. Mon–Sat 11am–7pm.

FOOD AND DRINK

Averys 9 Culver St ⓦ averys.com; map pp.94–95. Trading since 1793, Averys stocks over a thousand wines from all corners of the globe, stacked up in crates in a network of historic vaulted cellars or – for the particularly fine vintages – stored in a locked metal cage. Also runs wine courses and monthly themed wine-tastings (Wed 7pm; £25). Mon–Sat 10am–7pm.

Bristol Cider Shop 7 Christmas Steps ⓦ bristol cidershop.co.uk; map p.88. Welcoming store stocking over fifty varieties of local cider and perry, with six on tap, including Rich's Farmhouse, Home Orchard and the legendary Wilkins. The knowledgeable staff organize talks, tastings and tours, and even make-your-own cider days if you fancy having a go at pressing the apples yourself. Mon–Sat 11am–7pm.

Guilbert's Foster Rooms, Small St ⓦ guilberts.com; map p.88. This little boutique is the last of its kind in Bristol crafting luxury handmade chocolates, many of which are based on the same recipes that Piers Guilbert used over a century ago at his store on Park Street. Decadent boxed collections, plus individual creams, fondants and truffles. Mon–Thurs 7.30am–4.30pm, Fri 7.30am–12.30pm.

MARKETS

As well as the markets listed below, there's a **Farmers' Market** on Corn Street every Wednesday and a very good **Slow Food Market** on the first Sunday of the month (see p.87).

Ashton Court Farmers' Market Ashton Court Estate, Long Ashton, on the A369, two miles from the city centre. Small monthly produce market that sets up stalls in a courtyard outside the mansion. Third Sun of the month 10.30am–2.30pm.

Harbourside Market Bordeaux Quay. Weekend market running outside *No.1 Harbourside* and the tourist office, with stalls selling food (charcuterie, artisan chocolates, baked goods), arts and crafts on the Saturday, plus books and records on the Sunday. Sat & Sun 10am–4pm.

Tobacco Factory Market Raleigh Rd, Southville. Weekly South Bristol community market, with around 25 stalls offering mostly organic and local goodies, from healthy farm food to cakes and crafts. Sun 10am–2.30pm.

MISCELLANEOUS

Bristol Blue Glass Unit 5, St Catherine's, White House Lane, Bedminster ⓦ bristolblueglass.com; map pp.84–85. Glass-blowing studio and factory shop where you can watch craftsmen teasing the soft, deep-blue resin into intricate (and expensive) stemware, tableware and centrepieces; you can even get your own hands cast in glass. The on-site museum is worth a quick browse, with some pieces dating back over 1800 years. Daily 10am–4pm.

Bristol Kite Store 39A Cotham Hill ⓦ kitestore.co.uk; map p.108. Impressive range of stunt kites and kitesurfing kit, but of most interest for its simple single-liners, including around thirty kids' kites (from £5), shaped, among others, like a dragon, a shark or a brilliant, iridescent-pink flamingo – great entertainment for a sunny day up on the Downs. Also stocks Frisbees, Aerobie rings and other picnic-activity essentials. Mon–Fri 10am–6pm, Sat 9.30am–5.30pm.

★ **Weapon of Choice** 8B Park St, entrance down the steps next to Fifty Fifty ⓦ weaponofchoicegallery .co.uk; map pp.94–95. Unique gallery-cum-design-store wedged "underneath" Park Street, celebrating the best of Bristol's subversive street culture and selling original works (some with ironically hefty price tags) from the city's top graffiti artists, including Inkie, Paris, Cheo and SEPR – if you've spent any time wandering Nelson Street or spray-painted Stokes Croft, you'll recognize many of the distinctive styles on show here. Mon–Sat 11am–6pm, Thurs till 7pm, Sun noon–4pm.

PORT

Bristol is perhaps most famous in sporting circles for being the biggest city in England without a Premier League football team – although City came desperately close when they lost 1-0 to Hull in the Championship Play-Off Final in 2008. The rivalry between its two clubs has waned since Rovers were relegated from Division Two in 2001, which was the last year they met in a league derby; City now play in the Championship, Rovers in League Two. The city is also home to professional **rugby** and **cricket** teams, though the county cricket team is by some way the more successful of the two.

FOOTBALL

Bristol City ☎ 0871 222 6666, ⊕ bcfc.co.uk. The Robins have played at Ashton Gate in South Bristol for over a century, although they may finally succeed in their long-running plan to move to a purpose-built stadium in nearby Ashton Vale. Tickets start at £25 (under-16s £10).

Bristol Rovers ☎ 0117 909 6648, ⊕ bristolrovers.co.uk. The Pirates, or The Gas (Rovers' old ground, Eastville stadium, was right next to Stapleton Gasworks, and their supporters are still known as Gasheads), play at the Memorial Stadium in Horfield. Tickets cost from £16 (under-16s £8).

RUGBY

Bristol Rugby ☎ 0871 208 2234, ⊕ bristolrugby.co.uk. Bristol share the Memorial Stadium in Horfield with Rovers; they play their rugby in the Championship, with tickets starting at £12 (under-16s £5).

CRICKET

Gloucestershire County Cricket Club ☎ 0117 910 8010, ⊕ gloscricket.co.uk. GCCC, the most successful one-day side of the last decade, play the majority of their County Championship and Friends Provident t20 games at The County Ground in Bishopston. Tickets start at £15 (under-16s £5).

ACTIVITIES

Although navigating the steep hills around Clifton and Cotham is a workout in itself, there are plenty of other, more official, activities to engage in, from sailing around the harbour to soothing your aches away in a city **spa**. Given the city's connections to **ballooning** and its status as the home of the biggest hot-air balloon festival in Europe (see box, p.136), taking to the skies in a gas-fired basket is a quintessentially Bristol experience.

Avon Valley Railway Bitton Station, Bath Rd, Bitton, six and a half miles southeast of Bristol, on the A431 ☎ 0117 932 5538, ⊕ avonvalleyrailway.org. Jump aboard a traditional steam or diesel locomotive for a five-mile trundle along the old Midland Railway Line to Oldham Common and back (about 25min in total); the station yard, scattered with engines and rolling stock in various states of repair, will also appeal to locophiles. Special events include a twice-monthly Steam 'n' Cuisine Sunday lunch (£35) and Thomas the Tank Engine days (£14, under-14s £10.50). £6.50, under-14s £5, ticket offers unlimited rides for the day.

★ **Bailey Balloons** ☎ 01275 375300, ⊕ baileyballoons.co.uk. Run by the Flight Director of the Balloon Fiesta, Bailey Balloons has a big fleet and offers champagne balloon flights (from £125) from Ashton Court and the chance to fly at the festival itself.

Bristol Balloons ☎ 0845 077 0730, ⊕ bristolballoons.co.uk. Similar operation to Baileys but also offering cheaper "Midi" flights (from £85).

Bristol Ice Rink Frogmore St ☎ 01179 292148, ⊕ jnlbristol.co.uk. Open sessions, events and ice-skating discos – timings vary, so check the website for details. From £7.75, including skate hire (£8 for a 15min lesson).

Lido Oakfield Place, Clifton ☎ 0117 933 9533, ⊕ lidobristol.com. Stylishly renovated Victorian lido with an infinity lap pool, sauna, steam room and trendy spa, offering facials and holistic treatments (both from £60), including a two-hour Manipura Full Body Massage (£108). Also home to a sleek café-bar and top-notch restaurant (see p.123). Spa daily 10am–9pm; swimming Mon–Fri 1–4pm; £15, under-16s £7.50.

Sanctuary Spa Bristol Quakers Friars, Cabot Circus ☎ 0117 370 2791, ⊕ thesanctuary.c.uk/bristol-spa .htm. The first Sanctuary Spa in the South West offers over 120 treatments, from an exfoliating salt scrub to a hydrating rose cocoon (from £20 for a 15min Lava Shell Massage), or you can spend some "Me Time" in the Champagne Nail Bar. Mon–Sat 10am–8pm, Sunday 11am–5pm.

CHILDREN'S BRISTOL

From the simple pleasure of kicking about in the fountains in Millennium Square to exploring the *ss Great Britain*, Bristol is an excellent city to discover with the kids in tow. **Harbourside** is the principal destination, home to many of the city's top children's attractions, and with plenty of pirate folklore to spice up the walks between them. All of the city council's **museums** are free, meaning you can take the family to half a dozen sights (including M Shed and the City Museum and Art Gallery) without spending a penny; most attractions offer substantial discounts for various age groups and often free entry for the under-3s. Bristol's many and varied **festivals** should also appeal, particularly its balloon and kite fiestas (see

2

TOP 5 FESTIVALS

Bristol's calendar is packed with some outstanding **festivals and events** (see p.33), but the following five – six if you count the brilliant **Ashton Court Festival**, which may make its musical return in 2012 after a four-year absence – are not to be missed.

Bristol Harbour Festival Harbourside; free; ⓦ bristolharbourfestival.co.uk. Hundreds of sailing vessels fill the harbour for this weekend event, one of the biggest free festivals in the country, which also takes in music, street theatre, cabarets and food markets in a variety of waterfront venues. End July.

Bristol International Balloon Fiesta Ashton Court Estate, Long Ashton; free; ⓦ bristolballoonfiesta .co.uk. Unique four-day festival celebrating Bristol's ballooning heritage with twice-daily mass ascents of over a hundred balloons – an incredible sight – and a visually stunning "night glow" performed to music and topped off with a fireworks finale. Mid-August.

Bristol International Festival of Kites and Air Creations Ashton Court Estate, Long Ashton; free; ⓦ kite-festival.org.uk. Novel two-day event, also held at Ashton Court, but on a far smaller scale than the

Balloon Fiesta. Choreographed routines, stunt display teams – including traditional Japanese fighting kites – and a medley of aerial oddities, from manta rays and monkeys to Wallace and Gromit. Early September.

BrisFest Harbourside; £8 per day, £16 for the weekend; ⓦ brisfest.co.uk. It might have only started in 2008, after the demise of the Ashton Court Festival, but this three-day, three-night jamboree across half a dozen stages and twice that number of nightclubs has quickly become an essential part of the late-summer cultural calendar. Mid- to end September.

St Pauls Carnival St Pauls; free; ⓦ stpaulscarnival .co.uk. Second only to Notting Hill for sheer Caribbean colour, this community carnival attracts over eighty thousand people to St Pauls for street parties, samba bands and sound systems; the legendary parade loops up Brigstocke Road and around. Early July.

---

box above), while the Harbour Festival features circus performances and street theatre, and sets up a children's area in Castle Park offering storytelling, face painting and the like. For more **information**, check out ⓦ whatsonbristol.co.uk/Kids Zone or pick up a copy of *Bristol & Bath Unlocked* (£8.99), a guidebook specifically aimed at kids.

ATTRACTIONS

At-Bristol Anchor Rd ☎ 0845 345 1235, ⓦ at-bristol .org.uk. Addictive hands-on science centre with planetarium shows, Live Lab sessions (daily 11am–noon, Sat, Sun & hols till 3pm) and a bounty of thought-provoking and interactive exhibitions. There's also an inviting section just for the under-7s, plus regular "Toddler Takeover" days. £11.35, under-15s £7.25, under-3s free. Daily 10am–5pm, Sat, Sun & hols till 6pm.

Bristol Aquarium Anchor Rd ☎ 0117 929 8929, ⓦ bristolaquarium.co.uk. Sharks, rays, a giant octopus, and a monster IMAX screen showing 3D marine-life movies. £13.50, under-14s £9.20, under-3s free. Daily 10am–5pm, Sat, Sun & school hols till 6pm.

City Museum and Art Gallery Queen's Rd ☎ 0117 922 3571, ⓦ bristol.gov.uk/museums. One more for the adults maybe, but kids should love the interactive Egyptian section, complete with ageing mummies, and the dinosaurs. You can explore the museum using one of several child-centric trails, and there are also a number of family areas, including the Curiosity zone (daily 10.30am–4.30pm), where you (or at least your kids) can "make" a pot, play with puppets or dress up as a character from one of the paintings upstairs. Free. Daily 10.30am–5pm, Wed till 8pm.

ss Great Britain Great Western Dockyard ☎ 0117 926 0680, ⓦ ssgreatbritain.org. An exciting destination in its

own right – with plenty of interactive displays in the Dockyard Museum – that can be even more fun for kids by giving them their own audio guides (which follow Sinbad the ship's cat as he explains what life was like for children on board ship). Educational programmes in the adjoining Brunel Institute (Tues–Sat 10.30am–4.30pm; free; ID required; ⓦ brunelinstitute.org) include "Future Brunels" for teenagers and "Sea Hear", storytelling for the under-5s (first Tues of the month; free). £12.50, under-16s £6.25, under-4s free. Daily 10am–5.30pm, Nov–March till 4.30pm.

FARMS AND ZOOS

Bristol Zoo Clifton ☎ 0117 974 7300, ⓦ www .bristolzoo.org.uk. As well as getting up close and personal with all creatures great and small, children visiting the city's first-rate zoological gardens can keep themselves busy at an activity centre, an adventure playground and Explorers' Creek, part water play area, part walk-through tropical birdhouse. The aerial assault course, ZooRopia (daily 10am–4pm, Nov to mid-March Sat, Sun & school hols only £7.50, under-14s £6.40, no under-5s), will appeal to older children and teenagers. £14, under-14s £8.50, under-3s free. Daily 9am–5.30pm, Nov to mid-March till 5pm.

Noah's Ark Clevedon Rd, Wraxall, six miles from the city centre, off junction 19 of the M5 ☎ 01275 852606, ⓦ noahsarkzoofarm.co.uk. Working farm and oo with over a hundred animal species, from gerbils to iraffes, plus adventure playgrounds, tractor rides and the biggest hedge maze in the world. £11.50, under-16s 9, under-2s free. 10.30am–5pm: Feb–Oct Mon–Sat; ov Sat only.

t Werburghs City Farm Watercress Rd, St Werburghs 0117 9428 241, swcityfarm.org.uk. Community arm that's home to pigs, goats, chickens and sheep, and as an adventure playground on site. The award-winning afé (open from 10am; closed Tues) serves healthy dishes hat include eggs, meat, vegetables and salad from the arm itself. Free. Daily 9am–5pm, till 4pm in winter.

PARKS

Ashton Court Estate Long Ashton, on the A369, two miles from the city centre ashtoncourtestate.com. Lovely expansive grounds, some of them home to deer, that make a great spot for a walk, a picnic or a bit of pitch and putt. £6.50. Daily 8am–dusk.

Blaise Castle Estate Henbury Rd, Henbury, entrance on Kingsweston Rd (the B4057), five miles from the city centre bristol.gov.uk/blaisecastleestate. Mix of open downs and wooded gorge – plus a fantastic children's playground – lorded over by its very own mock castle (summer Sun 2–4pm; free). Daily 7.30am–dusk.

DIRECTORY

Internet Free access at the Central Library, College Green Mon, Tues & Thurs 9.30am–7.30pm, Wed 10am–5pm, Fri & Sat 9.30am–5pm, Sun 1–5pm; book at 0117 903 7200) and the Watershed, 1 Canons Rd (Mon 10.30am–11pm, Tues–Thurs 9.30am–11pm, Fri 9.30am–midnight, Sat 10am–midnight, Sun 10am–10.30pm).

Medical care Hospital: Bristol Royal Infirmary, Marlborough St 0117 923 0000. Walk-in centres: 35

Broad St 0117 906 9610 (Mon–Sat 8am–8pm, Sun 10am–6pm); Boots chemist, 59 Broadmead 0117 929 3631 (Mon–Sat 8am–8pm, Sun 11am–5pm).

Police New Bridewell Police Station, Rupert St 0845 456 7000.

Post office 13 Castle Gallery, The Mall Bristol (Mon–Sat 9am–5.30pm).

The Chew Valley

Just the other side of Dundry Hill from Bristol, eight miles south of the city centre, the swathe of bucolic countryside that stretches to the foothills of the Mendips constitutes the fertile **CHEW VALLEY**, a cluster of contented villages set around man-made **Chew Valley Lake**. Like nearby **Blagdon Lake**, it was built to provide Bristol with a much-needed water supply but has since become a scenic spot for lakeside walks, fishing and other activities.

The most notable of the valley's many pretty villages are **Chew Magna** – named the best village in the UK by *The Sunday Times* in 2011, a decision no doubt influenced by its bounty of appealing pubs – and **Stanton Drew**, home to an intriguing set of Neolithic **stone circles**.

Chew Valley Lake

Visitor centre and teashop daily 10.30am–5.30pm, Nov to mid-March till 4.30pm • www.bristolwater.co.uk/leisure

On sunny days, its sparkling waters broken by the white specks of sailing boats, **Chew Valley Lake** is simply majestic. The largest lake in the South West, it was formed in 1956, flooding the village of Moreton in the process; during particularly dry summers, the arch of the old village bridge emerges, Excalibur-like, from the receding water, an occasional reminder of what lies beneath.

BIRD-WATCHING AT CHEW

Over 260 **bird species** have been recorded at Chew Valley Lake, including snipe, lapwing, reed warbler and even the occasional osprey, and the lake is the third most important site in Britain for wintering waterfowl. Popular spots include **Herons Green**, on the B3114 between Chew Stoke and West Harptree, and **Herriotts Bridge**, on the A368 between West Harptree and Bishop Sutton. You'll need a permit (£2.50/day, £1.50 children aged 10–18) to access the five **hides** at the lake's southern end (see cvlbirding.co.uk/birdingmap.html for locations), which are available from Woodford Lodge (see box, p.138) and, in summer, the teashop.

2

FISHING ON THE LAKES

Experienced anglers go all misty-eyed at the mention of the Chew Valley, whose two lakes provide the setting for some of the best still-water fishing in the country. **Blagdon Lake** is the more famous of the two, a name resonant throughout the world of fly-fishing for its hefty brown and rainbow trout, though **Chew Valley Lake** is equally as popular, and is regarded as the UK's premier pike-fishing venue.

The trout-fishing **season** runs from mid-March to November, with fishing for pike allowed on certain dates within that period. **Permits** start at £13.50 for an afternoon of bank fishing at Chew Valley and are available at Woodford Lodge, on the B3114 between Chew Stoke and West Harptree (mid-March to Oct daily 8.45am–4.45pm; Nov to mid-March Mon–Fri 8.45am–4.45pm; permits also available outside the building from one hour before sunrise until one hour after sunset; ☎ 01275 332339, ✉ woodford.lodge@bristolwater.co.uk); the lodge also has a fully stocked **tackle shop**. For advice on which spots to fish and what tactics to use, contact John Horsey (☎ 01761 490367, ⓦ johnhorsey.co.uk), a former World Champion with over twenty years' experience as a professional fishing **guide**.

Two **picnic areas** on the road between Chew Stoke and Bishop Sutton – the first with a small visitor centre and teashop – provide great views across the water. The one furthest from Chew Stoke has access to **trails** that cut through the corner of a nature reserve, where it's possible to spot kingfishers, great-crested grebes and (occasionally) bittern.

Stanton Drew Stone Circles

Daily 9am–sunset · £1 donation; EH · ⓦ english-heritage.org.uk

The megaliths that dot a farmer's field on the fringes of **STANTON DREW** enjoy a wonderfully low-key location that is all the more surprising given their status as the third most significant prehistoric standing stones in the country. The collection of stones – actually three separate sets of circles, as there's another to the southwest – are not, as local legend may have it, the petrified members of a wedding party, punished for celebrating on the Sabbath, but are instead part of an ancient ritual site dating back some four thousand years to the late Neolithic–early Bronze Age. Geophysical research has revealed that the largest of these, **The Great Circle**, contains a number of buried pits, and is itself set within a larger enclosure, or henge.

Further along the main road through Stanton Drew, you'll find **The Cove**, three stones erected around the same time as the Great Circle that now huddle together in the back garden of *The Druids Arms*, and are accessible to patrons of the pub only.

Blagdon Lake and around

Blagdon Lake predates neighbouring Chew by over half a century, and has been supplying much of Bristol's water since 1899. The original **pumping station** is still in good working order, and is open to visitors during the summer, though for many, the lake's chief attraction is its plentiful stocks of **trout**.

Blagdon Pumping Station

Station Rd, Blagdon · April–Aug Sun 2–5pm · Free · ⓦ bristolwater.co.uk/leisure

The two huge beam engines at the **Blagdon Pumping Station** are a reminder that the Victorians didn't do anything by half – the surviving set of four engines that operated under steam until 1949, they weigh 37 tonnes each, consumed nearly six tonnes of coal a day between them and took nine men to operate. One of them was given an electric motor in the 1980s, so you can now see it "in action".

The wildlife exhibit in the attached **visitor centre** is worth a look before heading out on one of the surrounding **trails**, though perhaps the most interesting nature experience is feeding the thousands of trout being bred in the two huge suction tanks outside.

The Organic Garden at Holt Farm

Bath Rd, Blagdon • May–Sept Thurs 10am–5pm, also first Sun in June, July, Aug & Sept 2–5pm • £4, children free; 1hr tour by arrangement; visits at other times by arrangement • £7 • ☎ 01761 461650, ⓦ theorganicgardens.co.uk

One of the first in the country, the creatively designed **Organic Garden at Holt Farm** has been twenty years in the making and is still constantly evolving, with around a dozen different areas spread over five acres including meadows, a gravel garden and a willow garden that takes its inspiration from the Somerset Levels.

You can finish off your visit with tea and home-made scones (all organic, of course) on the attractive terrace that overlooks Blagdon Lake.

ARRIVAL AND GETTING AROUND   THE CHEW VALLEY

By bus Two services run from Bristol to villages within the Chew Valley, the #67 (Mon–Fri daily) and the #672 (Mon–Sat 5 daily), taking about 35min to get to Chew Stoke, the nearest stop to the Chew Valley Lake Visitor Centre, and another 10min to Stanton Drew.

By car Having your own wheels is by far the best way of getting around; you can reach the Valley on the B3114 via Bishopsworth and Dundry, or the A37 via Totterdown and Whitchurch.

ACCOMMODATION

The Carpenter's Arms Stanton Wick, signed off the A368 ☎ 01761 490202, ⓦ the-carpenters-arms.co.uk. Ideally located midway between Chew Valley Lake and Stanton Drew Stone Circles, and offering a dozen stylish en-suite rooms, modern but comfortable, with spacious beds, duck-down duvets and flat-screen TVs. An even closer attraction is the recommended pub downstairs (see below). **£105**

★ **Harptree Court** East Harptree, on the B3114, half a mile beyond West Harptree ☎ 01761 221729,

ⓦ harptreecourt.co.uk. Distinguished B&B set on seventeen acres of parkland, with all the trappings of a regal country house, including a tennis court and croquet lawn. The friendly owners provide home-made afternoon tea on arrival (a nice touch), and you can complete the unwinding process with a holistic treatment in your room (from £50). The on-site yurt and treehouse – an incredible creation, complete with wood-burning stove and copper bath – are bookable through ⓦ canopyandstars.co.uk. No children under 12. **£120**

EATING AND DRINKING

★ **The Bear & Swan** Chew Magna, on the B3130, which arcs between the A37 and the A38 ☎ 01275 331100, ⓦ thebearandswan.co.uk. Well-respected open-plan gastro pub with lots of distressed wood and a romantic little restaurant at one end. The daily changing blackboard is usually strong on fish and often carries a tasty Butcombe beef and mushroom pie (£13.50). Daily noon–11pm, Sat till 11.30pm, Sun till 5pm.

The Carpenter's Arms Stanton Wick, signed off the A368 ☎ 01761 490763, ⓦ the-carpenters-arms.co.uk. Country-pub beauty – think low ceilings, open beams, exposed brickwork – serving consistently good food (mains from £12) in either The Coopers or the more segregated Dining Room. Sup on Butcombe, Doom Bar and Otter at the rich wooden bar or in the flower-festooned seating area out front. Mon–Thurs noon–2pm & 6–9.30pm, Fri & Sat noon–2pm & 6–10pm, Sun noon–9pm.

★ **New Manor Farm** North Widcombe, West Harptree, on the A368 near Herriots Bridge ☎ 01761 220172. Inviting farmyard tearoom that foregoes the frills for a focus on home-made soups, baguettes and paninis (from £3.75), plus good-value Sunday lunches. Much of it is made using produce from their excellent farm shop just across the courtyard, which also stocks local cheeses, honey, smoked salmon and the like. Daily 10am–5.30pm, Sun from 11am.

The Pony and Trap Knowle Hill, Newton, Chew Magna, signed off the A368 ☎ 01275 332627, ⓦ theponyandtrap .co.uk. The creative cooking of head chef Josh Eggleton has made this one of the most popular pubs in the Valley (sometimes a little too popular) and earned him a Michelin star in the process. The food – virtually all of it sourced locally and ranging from saffron, wild garlic and sheep-curd risotto to Chew Valley trout – is keenly priced considering, with mains around £13.95. Mon–Sat noon–2.30pm & 7–9.30pm, Sun noon–3.30pm.

2

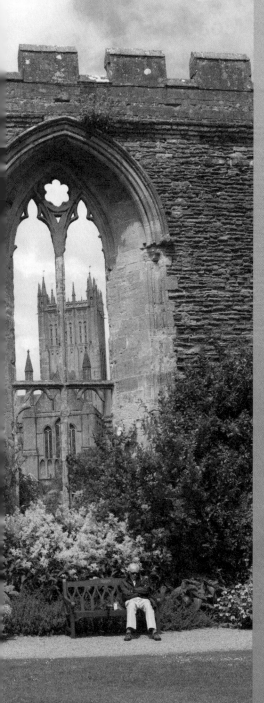

Wells and the Mendips

THE BISHOP'S PALACE, WELLS

Wells and the Mendips

The miniature cathedral city of Wells, 21 miles south of Bristol and the same distance southwest from Bath, has not significantly altered in eight hundred years. Charming and compact, it is eminently walkable, and a stroll around its tightly knit streets reveals a cluster of medieval religious buildings, archways and almshouses. This architectural ensemble – impressive in its own right – is capped by the city's stunning cathedral, its startling west front adorned with some of the finest medieval statuary in Europe.

3

From the first few years of the tenth century, the cathedral's bishops effectively ruled both the city and the greater portion of Somerset, their estates once extending as far south as Kingsbury Episcopi, between Taunton and Yeovil. It was these same bishops who created Wells as we know it today, building the walled **Bishop's Palace**, which houses the celebrated wells themselves, and the tidy **Vicars' Close** – the city's two other must-see sights – and establishing the oldest almshouses in the county.

Spreading northwest of Wells, the ancient woodland, exposed heaths and craggy gorges of the **Mendip Hills** provide the perfect backdrop to some lovely **walks**, as well as caving and climbing in the potholes and ravines that give the area its distinct geological character. The main **A371** traces the Mendips' southern escarpment, linking Wells with Cheddar and Axbridge and running on to Weston-super-Mare. The region's famed outdoor activities lie to the north – indeed, this is real get-up-and-go country, and you haven't really experienced the Mendips until you've squeezed through a cavern in **Wookey Hole**, scaled the cliffs at **Cheddar Gorge** or **Burrington Combe** and hiked through some of the reserves encircling the former mining land at **Charterhouse**.

Wells

WELLS owes its celebrity entirely to its spectacular **cathedral**, the presence of which makes what would otherwise be a beautiful little town into a beautiful little city – the smallest, in fact, in England. Approaching from **Brown's Gate**, the thirteenth-century archway cut through the old city walls on Sadler Street, slowly reveals its full glory: the dazzling west front is one of the visual highlights of Somerset.

The clerical houses on the surrounding **Cathedral Green** are mostly seventeenth- and eighteenth-century, though one, the **Old Deanery**, shows traces of its fifteenth-century origins; the chancellor's house, further along, is now the **Wells and Mendip Museum**, and beyond that a little arch leads into the cobbled medieval **Vicars' Close**, another of the city's architectural treasures. The archway on the green's southeastern corner, **Penniless Porch**, was built in the fifteenth century to provide alms for beggars and opens onto the attractive **Market Place**, focal point of the city and still the site of a twice-weekly market. The **conduit** here, from which water flows down the High Street

CHEDDAR GORGE

Highlights

❶ Wells Cathedral The wow factor of the cathedral's west front is continued on the inside, a combination that adds up to one of the finest buildings in Somerset. **See p.146**

❷ The Good Earth Something of a Wells institution, this easy-going and very enjoyable vegetarian restaurant has been serving up wholesome wholefood for decades. **See p.152**

❸ Walking in the Mendips Take your pick from hiking along the fringes of Cheddar Gorge, through the nature reserves around Charterhouse or up precipitous Crook Peak – or sling a pack on your back and visit the lot on the West Mendip Way. **See p.153**

❹ Cheddar Gorge A bounty of attractions, not least the gorge itself – towering, craggy and with a brooding, elemental presence. **See p.155**

❺ Cheddar cheese You could hardly come to Cheddar and not take home a truckle or two of the world's favourite cheese. **See p.156**

❻ Charterhouse Dotted with Roman remains, old Victorian mines and a World War II decoy town, the area around Charterhouse is one of the most intriguing on the Mendips. **See p.157**

❼ Axbridge Diminutive medieval market town that makes a great base at the western end of the range. **See p.159**

HIGHLIGHTS ARE MARKED ON THE MAP ON PP.44–45

in gutters, is served by the Scotland Spring that rises in the gardens of the **Bishop's Palace**, accessed through the **Bishop's Eye**, at the top of Market Place.

Many visitors – and there can be an awful lot at weekends in summer – content themselves with the big sights that are gathered together at this eastern end of the city, but a leisurely stroll down the bunting-strung High Street will cover the rest of Wells in little time at all, taking in Gothic **St Cuthbert's Church** and the dinky **almshouses** nearby.

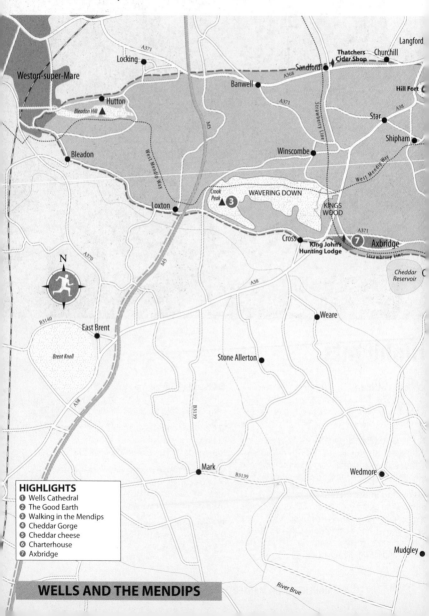

HIGHLIGHTS
1. Wells Cathedral
2. The Good Earth
3. Walking in the Mendips
4. Cheddar Gorge
5. Cheddar cheese
6. Charterhouse
7. Axbridge

WELLS AND THE MENDIPS

Brief history

People have been drawn to the city's **springs** (*wella* in Anglo-Saxon) since the Stone Age, although the earliest evidence of them assuming spiritual significance is a Romano-British mausoleum. The mausoleum was succeeded by a mortuary chapel, and the chapel by the **Saxon church of St Andrew**, founded in 705 AD by Ine, King of Wessex, in a spot that now lies in the gardens of the cathedral. In 909, St Andrew became the cathedral of the new diocese of Wells (which included all of Somerset), with Athelm its first bishop.

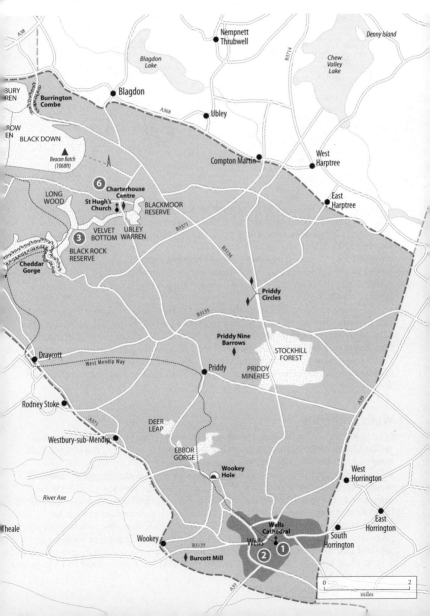

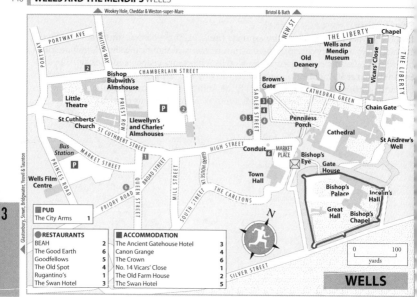

The city has been shaped by its **bishops** ever since. From 1219, they have held the powerful title of Bishop of Bath and Wells, a position that has historically enabled them to get things done, and much of Wells's appearance is owed to them: **Bishop Jocelin** (1206–1244) started work on the Bishop's Palace and **Bishop Ralph** (1329–1363) founded Vicars' Close, but it was **Bishop Bekynton** (1443–65) who was the busiest of the lot, building the city's three medieval gateways and the cathedral's Chain Gate bridge, and providing the precious water supply that is still pumped into the conduit on Market Place today.

Much more recently, Wells was the setting for **Hot Fuzz**, the Simon Pegg/Nick Frost cult comedy directed by local lad and former Wells Blue pupil, Edgar Wright. The city fondly remembers its brush with fame, and several places proudly brandish their fifteen minutes' worth: the exterior of *The Crown*, an ancient coaching inn on Market Place, bears two historical plaques, one denoting the arrest of William Penn in 1695 for illegal preaching, the other recalling its role in the *Hot Fuzz* shootout scene of 2006.

Wells Cathedral

Cathedral Green • Daily 7am–7pm, Nov–March till 6pm **Information desk** April–Oct Mon–Sat 9am–5pm Tours Mon–Sat 10am, 11am, 1pm, 2pm & 3pm; 1hr; book at least 2 weeks in advance **Chapter two café** Daily 10am–5pm, Sun from 11am • Suggested donation £6, children £3; photography permit £3 • ☏ 01749 674483, ⓦ wellscathedral.org.uk

Hidden from sight until you pass into its spacious close, **Wells Cathedral** presents a majestic spectacle, the broad lawn of its former graveyard providing the perfect foreground. The **west front** teems with some three hundred thirteenth-century figures of saints and kings, once brightly painted and gilded, though their present honey tint has a subtle splendour of its own. The sensational facade was constructed about eighty years after work on the main building was begun in 1175. The interior itself is a supreme example of early English Gothic, the long nave punctuated by a dramatic and very modern-looking "**scissor arch**", one of three that were constructed in 1338 to take the extra weight of the newly built tower.

The quire and the Lady Chapel

Beyond the arch, the **quire** is framed at its eastern end by a wonderfully vibrant **Jesse Window**, a fourteenth-century stained-glass masterpiece that shows the family tree of Christ sprouting from Jesse's hip. The Bishops' Throne here (the *cathedra*, which gives this, and all cathedrals, their name) is backed by an embroidery of St Andrew, Wells's patron saint – his image crops up throughout the cathedral, most notably in the row of disciples that adorn the top of the west front (he's in the middle, bearing a cross).

The gnarled old tombs in the aisles of the quire include the **chantry chapel of Bishop Bekynton**, Chancellor of England and the man who changed Wells's fortunes when he gave the city a public water supply in 1451 – the gesture is still acknowledged by the mayor each year.

At the far eastern end of the cathedral is the light-filled **Lady Chapel**, a star-shaped room dating to the fourteenth century. Its stained-glass windows, visible from the quire, were smashed during the Civil War, but the resulting collage of richly coloured pieces is mesmerizing nonetheless.

The transepts

Usually bypassed in the rush, the capitals and corbels of the **south transepts** hold some amusing narrative carvings – look out for the men with toothache (on the first column on the right) and an old man caught pilfering an apple (on the next one along). The stout-looking **font** is from the Saxon church that once occupied the site of the present-day Camery Garden (see p.148), and as such is the oldest object in the cathedral.

In the **north transept**, the 24-hour astronomical **clock** is almost as ancient, dating from 1390. From his seat high up on the right of the clock, a figure known as Jack Blandiver kicks a couple of bells every quarter-hour, heralding the appearance of a pair of jousting knights charging at each other – a little routine they haven't tired of in over six hundred years – and on the hour, he strikes the bell in front of him.

The Chapter House

Opposite the clock, a doorway leads to a graceful, much-worn flight of steps rising to the **Chapter House**, an octagonal room elaborately ribbed in the Decorated style. It was here that the members of the clergy met to discuss cathedral affairs and, from time to time, carry out legal proceedings. The door at the top of the steps (usually closed) leads to the Vicars' Hall and the **Chain Gate**, a covered walkway that loops over St Andrew's Street and down into Vicars' Close (see p.149), thus ensuring that the clergy could commute to work untempted by the distractions of a "sinful" city.

Below the Chapter House, the **undercroft** built to support its considerable weight now houses an **interpretation centre** covering the building's history and its life as a contemporary church.

HEAVENLY MUSIC

Regarded as one of the finest choirs in the world, **Wells Cathedral Choir** has been singing hymns here for over eight hundred years – although it wasn't until 1994 that they welcomed girl choristers into their ranks. Hearing their voices soaring through the vast, echoing nave is the closest most people will get to a divine experience: the traditional performance to catch is **Evensong** (Mon–Fri 5.15pm, Sun 3pm), though they also sing at the Sunday **Eucharist** (9.45am) and **Matins** (11.30am) services.

In addition to its world-class choir, the cathedral also serves as the occasional venue for evening **concerts**, orchestral performances and opera (box office ☎01749 672773), while local schools and visiting choirs regularly perform lunchtime concerts throughout the year (Tues, Thurs & sometimes Fri; 1pm; 45min; free).

Each summer, the cathedral hosts the six-day **new music wells festival**, a retrospective of choral and organ music held in May or June.

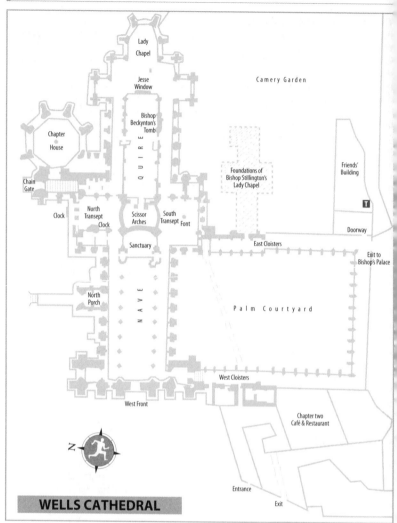

WELLS CATHEDRAL

The cloisters

The tranquil **cloisters**, laden with monuments, were substantially remodelled in the fifteenth century, when an extra storey was added to both the west (for a school) and east (a library) cloisters. The collection in the library (check website for opening times) features ancient tomes on theology, of course, but also science and mathematics – the library's set of Aristotle's works, published in 1497, has been uniquely annotated by Erasmus.

Just off the east cloister, the fifteenth-century foundations of **Bishop Stillington's Lady Chapel**, commissioned mainly to house his own tomb, poke through the grass of the Camery Garden; the chapel was itself built on the site of an earlier Saxon church.

Wells and Mendip Museum

8 Cathedral Green • Easter–Oct Mon–Sat 10am–5pm, Sun 1.30–4pm; Nov–Easter Mon–Sat 11am–4pm • £3, children £1 • ☎ 01749 673477, ⓦ wellsmuseum.org.uk

The former chancellor's house, adjacent to the cathedral, is now home to a tourist information centre (see p.150) and the **Wells and Mendip Museum**, displaying some of the cathedral's original statuary and a good geological section with fossils from the surrounding area. The exhibitions charting the history of caving are a nod to the museum's founder, Herbert Balch, who was something of a potholing pioneer, opening up several of the area's complex cave systems.

Vicars' Close

The word "quaint" might have been invented for **Vicars' Close**, two symmetrical rows of impossibly picturesque clergymen's cottages that make up the oldest continuously habited medieval street in Europe. The cottages were built in the mid-fourteenth century to house the Vicars' Choral (the men of the choir), and its members still make up most of their inhabitants today. A chapel was added to the northern end in the early fifteenth century, and the cottages themselves have undergone various alterations over the years – small front gardens created, chimneys extended into their current distinctive forms – though you can get a good idea of the street's initial appearance at no. 22, which was restored to its original proportions in 1863.

The Bishop's Palace

Feb half-term daily 10.30am–4.30pm; April–Oct daily 10.30am–6pm **Tours** Daily 11.30am (gardens), Mon–Fri also 2.30pm (buildings) **Restaurant** Daily 10.30am–5pm • £5.45, under-18s £2.25, under-5s free • ☎ 01749 988111, ⓦ bishopspalace.org.uk

The residence of the Bishop of Bath and Wells since 1206, the **Bishop's Palace** was walled and moated as a result of a rift with the borough in the early fourteenth century, and the imposing gatehouse still displays the grooves of the portcullis and a chute for pouring oil and molten lead on would-be assailants. The **moat**, fed by the famous wells, makes for a short but pleasant walk, with views over the Palace Fields; the bishop's **swans** that circuit it have learnt to feed on demand, ringing the little bell that hangs next to the drawbridge when it's time for more grain.

The Great Hall and the gardens

Through the gatehouse, across a well-trimmed croquet lawn, stand the scant but impressive remains of the **Great Hall**, built at the end of the thirteenth century and despoiled during the Reformation; Richard Whiting, the last Abbott of Glastonbury, was tried here before being martyred on Glastonbury Tor in 1539.

The trim, tranquil gardens predate the palace itself and contain the famous wells. Despite its placid appearance, **St Andrew's Well** – its waters gloriously reflecting the cathedral – is swollen by some 3.5 million gallons of spring water each day.

The Bishop's Chapel and Bishop Jocelin's Hall

Alongside the Great Hall are the thirteenth-century **Bishop's Chapel** and **Bishop Jocelin's Hall**, containing the *Undercroft* restaurant, the State Rooms and the Long Gallery, hung with portraits of former bishops – Bishop Mews (1672–1685), easily identified by the circular black patch on his cheek, pleaded the case of the Monmouth rebels at Judge Jeffries' Bloody Assizes (see box, p.218), and owed his nickname, "The Bombardier Bishop", to the fact that he fought in the English Civil War (the patch covers an injury sustained during the conflict).

At the time of writing, work was underway to move the restaurant and to develop the medieval undercroft as a historical **interpretation centre**, something previously lacking from the site.

St Cuthbert's Church and around

A short walk down the High Street from Market Place leads to Gothic **St Cuthbert's Church**, its lengthy spire visible above the rooftops from some way off. Despite its location at the opposite end of Wells to the cathedral, this was once the focus of city life – workers in the wool trade lived in nearby Tucker Street, and St Cuthbert's was the parish church of the trade guilds. The attractively carved (and recently repainted) ceiling is worth a fleeting glance, but otherwise the church's main interest today lies in its starring role in *Hot Fuzz* – it was a falling pinnacle from St Cuthbert's that squished over-inquisitive local journalist Tim Messenger at the film's characteristically gory church fête.

The almshouses

Facing St Cuthbert's across its cemetery, the compact Wells Old Almshouses include **Bubwith's Almshouses**, the oldest in Somerset, having been founded by the eponymous bishop in 1436. A chapel and guildhall, both still in use, make up the miniature complex, which fronts Chamberlain Street just behind.

The nearby **Llewellyn's and Charles's Almshouses**, on Priest Row, are even more petite, two opposing rows of traditional-looking almshouses that actually date from 1887.

ARRIVAL AND DEPARTURE
WELLS

By bus The bus station is on Princes Road, off Market Street.

Destinations Bath (#173; 1hr 15min); Bridgwater (#375 & #376; 1hr 25min); Bristol (#376; 1hr); Cheddar (#126; 25min); Frome (#161; 1hr 5min); Glastonbury (#29, #375, #376 & #377; 20min); Shepton Mallet (#161; 20min); Street (#29, #375 & #376; 30min); Taunton (#29 & #376; 1hr 20min); Weston-super-Mare (#126; 1hr 25min); Wookey Hole (#670; 10min); Yeovil (#376 & #377; 1hr 20min).

By train The nearest train station is at Castle Cary, 9 miles away, which serves London Paddington, Birmingham, Bristol, Bath, Taunton, Weymouth, Plymouth and smaller stations across the West Country. Bristol Temple Meads and Bath Spa have more regular services, and frequent bus connections on to Wells.

By car Wells is 21 miles from both Bristol (down the A37 and then the A39) and Bath (down the A39), and 8 miles from Glastonbury (up the A39). There are a couple of long-stay car parks, both west of the cathedral.

INFORMATION AND TOURS

Wells Visitor Information Service 8 Cathedral Green (Easter–Oct Mon–Sat 10am–5pm, Sun 1.30–4pm; Nov–Easter Mon–Sat 11am–4pm; ☎01749 671770, ✉visitwellsinfo@gmail.com). Offers an accommodation-booking service, discounted tickets to Wookey Hole and a *Hot Fuzz* trail for film enthusiasts.

Wells Walking Tours ☎01749 672438 or 07961 159122, ✇wellswalkingtours.co.uk. Market-day tours depart from outside *The Crown* (Easter–Sept Wed & Sat 11am; 1hr; £4, children £1; no booking required), or you can organize tailor-made tours of the city or the surrounding countryside.

ACCOMMODATION

The Ancient Gatehouse Hotel Sadler St ☎01749 672029, ✇ancientgatehouse.com. The newly refurbished rooms at this fourteenth-century hostelry got the Laura Ashley treatment in 2011, some more daringly than others – only take the pink four-poster bedroom if you've brought your eye mask with you. Several of the rooms look across Cathedral Green to the statuary of the west front, and one is set into the adjoining fifteenth-century Brown's Gate. **£115**

Canon Grange Cathedral Green ☎01749 671800, ✇canongrange.co.uk. Five spacious rooms, vastly different in design, on the western fringe of Cathedral Green, some facing that beautiful west front. Breakfast is accompanied by equally commanding views. **£60**

The Crown Market Place ☎01749 673457, ✇crownatwells.co.uk. Fifteenth-century inn enjoying a very central location, with 15 en-suite bedrooms, some of them four-posters. It's kiddy and canine friendly (extra £5 per dog), and there's a popular bar and on-site restaurant fronting Market Place. Free parking. **£95**

No. 14 Vicars' Close 14 Vicars' Close ☎01749 674483, ✇wellscathedral.org. Unique chance to stay on this historic cobbled street, right in the heart of the cathedral precinct. It's a self-catering set-up, with four bedrooms that can accommodate seven people in two doubles, a twin and a single. Available in 3, 4 & 7t stays. From **£115**

CLOCKWISE FROM TOP LEFT CHEDDAR CAVES (P.156); WELLS FARMERS' MARKET (P.152); WELLS CATHEDRAL (P.146); SOAY SHEEP, CHEDDAR >

WELLS MARKET

Market Place still fulfills its historical role twice a week, when around eighty stalls form the city's thriving **market** (Wed & Sat 9.30am–2.30pm). The general market is joined on the Wednesday by a **Farmers' Market**, selling a variety of local produce, such as honey, cheese, breads, and organic fruit and vegetable.

The Old Farm House 62 Chamberlain St ☎01749 675058, ✉theoldfarmhousewells@hotmail.com. Highly regarded B&B, opening onto an attractive walled garden and draped with wisteria. There's just two en-suite rooms (a double and a twin), each with a flat-screen TV, so you'll probably need to book well in advance. The entertaining hosts create an amiable atmosphere, and there's home-made bread and jam included in the breakfast spread. Min 2nt stay. **£75**

★ **The Swan Hotel** Sadler St ☎01749 836300, Ⓦswanhotelwells.co.uk. Rambling old coaching inn full of antique atmosphere, with stylish rooms and a lavish Cathedral Suite (£300), complete with free-standing brass bath. The warm interior – oak beams, open fires – is reflected in the friendly service. There's a restaurant in the hotel itself, and a terrifically positioned terrace just over the road (see below). **£120**

EATING AND DRINKING

BEAH 2 Union St ☎01749 678111, Ⓦbeah.co.uk. Unusually located in what is essentially the city's main car park, this bright and breezy restaurant does a mean tagine thanks to its Moroccan-born chef, as well as hearty English dishes such as slow-cooked beef and saddle of rabbit. Mains around £15. Mon–Fri 10am–2pm & 6pm–close, Sat 10am–4pm & 6pm–close, Sun 10am–3pm.

The City Arms 69 High St ☎01749 673916, Ⓦthecityarmsatwells.com. The old city jail – a single cell is still intact, with barred windows, in the centre of the pub – is a popular spot for a pint of Potholer, Hedgemonkey, or any other of the seven cask ales on tap. There's also outside seating in the plant-filled courtyard. Daily 9am–11.30pm, Sat till midnight, Sun from 10am.

★ **The Good Earth** 4 Priory Rd ☎01749 678600. Lovely wholefood restaurant that was making a name for itself with its delicious home-made quiches long before eco food was en vogue. Soups, salads (from £3.50), veggie pizzas and other organic goodies (mains from £5.50), plus Fair Trade coffee, available to eat in or take away. Mon–Sat 9am–6pm.

Goodfellows 5 Sadler St ☎01749 673866, Ⓦgoodfellowswells.co.uk. Top-notch diner serving innovative but pricey seafood at its upmarket restaurant and a range of superb sandwiches, pastries and (in the evening) game-centric dishes at the equally excellent streetside patisserie. Seafood mains, such as crayfish and seabass,

around £17.50; six-course tasting menu £55. Restaurant Tues–Sat noon–2pm & Wed–Sat 6.30–9.30pm, patisserie Mon–Sat 8.30am–5pm & Wed–Sat 6–10pm.

★ **The Old Spot** 12 Sadler St ☎01749 689099, Ⓦtheoldspot.co.uk. Much-lauded but easy-going little restaurant with a stylishly rustic interior, specializing in honest, no-frills Italian/French cuisine. The pithy two- and three-course lunch (£13.50/15.50) and dinner (£23.50/28.50) menus offer excellent value and are suitably meaty, featuring coarse pork terrine, braised shoulder of lamb, calf's liver and the like. Wed–Sun 12.30–2.30pm & Tues–Sat 7–10.30pm.

Rugantino's The Ancient Gatehouse Hotel Sadler St ☎01749 672029, Ⓦancientgatehouse.com. Italian-run restaurant serving quality Mediterranean cuisine in gorgeous medieval surroundings. You can enjoy a leisurely two-course lunch for £10.50, or dine more formally in the evening, when main courses (including home-made pasta) are around £16 and the three-course menu £23.50. Daily noon–2.30pm & 6–10pm.

The Swan Hotel Sadler St ☎01749 836300, Ⓦswanhotelwells.co.uk. Modern British dishes (mains from £14.50) in the handsome surrounds of oak-panelled *15c A.D.* or alfresco, in the *Walled Garden Café* out back or the *Swan Terrace*, facing the cathedral's west front. Daily noon–2pm (Sun till 2.30pm) & 7–9.30pm.

ENTERTAINMENT

Little Theatre Chamberlain St ☎01749 672280, Ⓦlittletheatrewells.org. Local players and enthusiastic amateurs come together for a variety of short-run plays, musicals and pantomimes.

Wells Film Centre Princes Rd ☎01749 673195, Ⓦwellsfilmcentre.co.uk. Independent family-run cinema showing mainly mainstream movies plus the odd arthouse flick on its three screens.

DIRECTORY

Banks Several, including an HSBC on the corner of Market Place and Sadler Street and a NatWest diagonally opposite, on the High Street.

Post office In Market Place, next to the Bishop's Eye (Mon–Fri 9am–5.30pm, Sat 9am–12.30pm).

The Mendips

Rising abruptly between the fertile fields of north Somerset and the marshy Levels to the south, the rolling **MENDIP HILLS** – commonly shortened to the Mendips (and by some locals even further to just Mendip) – forge a plateau of gorges, dry valleys and collapsed caverns that runs for 22 miles across the centre of the county.

Designated an Area of Outstanding Natural Beauty in 1972, the Mendips are a haven both for wildlife and walkers. Even on the shortest of jaunts, though, it's worth packing a fleece (it can get windy up here) and a rain jacket; as the local saying goes, "If you can see the Welsh hills, it's going to rain; if you can't see them, it's raining."

Aside from the medieval town of **Axbridge** – the best place to base yourself outside of Wells – settlements are few and far between, and only in **Cheddar Gorge** do you really encounter significant numbers of visitors.

Brief history

The Mendips were formed around 280 million years ago, when they were folded into their characteristic whaleback shape – though the coral-rich limestone that makes up Cheddar Gorge and **Burrington Combe** predates by some eighty million years. As meltwaters bored through this rock during the last Ice Age, they left behind them a network of caves, which sheltered hyenas, mammoths, woolly rhinos – the remains of which have been found in **Ebbor Gorge** and in caves in **Long Wood** – and, eventually, man. Settlements were established on the spring lines at the foot of the hills, then up on the plateau, at first in the area around modern-day **Priddy** and then further afield. **Charterhouse** developed with the discovery of lead (its open-cast mines were of such repute that the Romans headed here not long offer their sandaled feet touched British soil in 43 AD), and **mining** has left a lasting legacy on the hillsides – the very word Mendips is thought to stem from the medieval term for its deep mines, or "Myne-deepes".

Wookey Hole and around

Daily 10am–5pm, Nov–March till 4pm • £16, under-15s £11, under-3s free, 15% online discount • ☎ 01749 672243, ⦿ wookey.co.uk

Hollowed out by the River Axe a couple of miles outside of Wells, **Wookey Hole** is an impressive cave complex of deep pools and intricate rock formations, but it's folklore rather than geology that takes precedence on the guided tours. The highlight is the alleged petrified remains of the Witch of Wookey, a "blear-eyed hag" who was said to turn her evil eye on crops, young lovers and local farmers until the Abbot of Glastonbury Abbey intervened; a monk, dispatched from the abbey, sprinkled the witch with holy water, turning her to stone.

THE WEST MENDIP WAY

There are a lot of good walks on the Mendips, but none more so than the **West Mendip Way**, a thirty-mile hike that cuts in from the coast at Uphill, near Weston-super-Mare, and camelbacks the hills to Wells. Along the way, it serves as a vigorous dot-to-dot, connecting many of the area's best individual walks. The route's first proper climb is up **Bleadon Hill**, with good views back across the Bristol Channel, before it summits **Crook Peak** (see p.160). Cutting through the reserves around **Charterhouse** (see p.157), it then links up with the walk fringing **Cheddar Gorge** (see p.156); the last leg threads through **Ebbor Gorge** (see p.154) before finishing, in suitable style, at the west front of **Wells Cathedral**.

Tourist offices in Wells and Weston-super-Mare can provide you with details of the route, and stock **guides** such as *West Mendip Way*, a booklet by Andrew Eddy (£3.50), and the more comprehensive *The West Mendip Way*, by Derek Moyes (£5.95); two OS Explorer **maps**, 141 and 153, cover the route.

CAVING IN THE MENDIPS

The Mendip Hills are riddled with sinkholes and underground caverns, and the variety of complex cave systems in a relatively small area makes this one of the best **caving** destinations in the country, with plenty of boulders, waterfalls and canyons to negotiate. **Priddy Caves** alone contains over ten miles of passages, including **Swildon's Hole**, a phreatic cave (meaning it was carved out by water pressure), and **Eastwater Cavern**, which was Britain's first swallet cave (a depression formed by water washing soil through a cave system) when it was discovered by Herbert Balch (see p.149) in 1902.

Several companies run beginners' **trips** to caves around Priddy, as well as to Burrington Combe (see p.160) and Cheddar Gorge (see opposite) – try the Bristol Exploration Club (☎01749 672126, ⓦbec-cave.org.uk), Rocksport (☎01934 742343, ⓦcheddargorge.co.uk /x-treme) or Adventure Caving (☎01460 30102 or ☎07971 621946, ⓦadventurecaving.co.uk).

Following the tour, you can also visit a functioning Victorian paper mill and rooms containing speleological exhibits. Indeed, for families, the caves are likely to be just the start of the "Wookey Hole Experience", a melange of attractions that range from King Kong and the Valley of the Dinosaurs to a Fairy Garden and a Clown Museum. But no Chewbacca-themed displays – as yet.

Burcott Mill

On the B3139 · Easter–Sept Sat & Sun 11am–5pm · £2.50, under-15s £1.50, under-3s free · ☎01749 673118, ⓦburcottmill.com

One of only a handful of traditional flourmills still working in the country, **Burcott Mill**, two miles from Wells, hasn't changed its methods or machinery – including an immense waterwheel, powered by the River Axe – in a century and a half. The mill makes a pleasant diversion on the way to or from Wookey Hole, especially if you stop by the tearooms after the tour for a scone or cake, made with their own organic, stone-ground flour, of course.

Ebbor Gorge and around

Perched on the very edge of the Mendips, 2.5 miles northwest of Wells, **Ebbor Gorge** offers a wilder alternative to the more famous Cheddar Gorge, with tranquillity guaranteed on the wooded trails that follow its ravine up to the Mendip plateau. The mixture of ancient woodland and rocky cliffs, cloaked in unusual mosses, liverworts and lichen, attracts a variety of wildlife, including an abundance of butterflies. Lesser horseshoe bats roost in the gorge's caves, which – as fossil remains have revealed – sheltered reindeer and arctic lemming during the Ice Age. The main trails can be bumpy and quite steep in parts, but there's a two-mile loop near the car park that's accessible to pushchairs and wheelchairs.

Deer Leap

Half a mile or so up the road from Ebbor Gorge, a kissing gate off Pelting Drove leads to **Deer Leap**, an open-access site that rewards a short ramble with some staggering views: Glastonbury Tor, emerging from the Somerset Levels; the Quantocks; and, in the distance to the west, Brean Down, Steep Holm and the end of the Mendip Hills as they slip into the Bristol Channel.

Priddy

The rich agricultural land surrounding the dinky settlement of **PRIDDY** – essentially two pubs set around a village green some five miles from Wells – has provided summer pasture to shepherds working the Mendip plateau for nigh on eight hundred years, and its green has hosted an annual **Sheep Fair** for almost as long. The traders' fair (nearest Wed to Aug 21; ⓦpriddysomerset.org) has been going strong since 1348, a tradition commemorated by the **hurdle stack** on the focal green; **sheep racing** (June) and the well-respected **Priddy Folk Festival** (July; ⓦpriddyfolk.org) complete the social calendar.

Priddy Circles and Priddy Nine Barrows

The whole Priddy area was of ritual significance to tribal Britons, and two intriguing Neolithic monuments lie just northeast of the village. **Priddy Circles**, four unique henge-like enclosures believed to be contemporary to Stonehenge, are spread across private land, but you can wander among the dumpy mounds of **Priddy Nine Barrows**, an eyebrow-shaped row of Bronze Age tumuli; the latter are accessed from a public footpath off the B3135, or off Nine Barrows Lane, northeast of Priddy Green.

Priddy Pools

Behind Priddy Nine Barrows, and just off the B3134, the varied habitat of **Priddy Pools** supports a range of wetland wildlife, including dragonflies – among them downy emerald, found nowhere else on the Mendips, and four-spotted chaser – and all three species of British newt; pond-dipping for little sticklebacks is particularly fun. The pools were used in the nearby St Cuthbert's lead works, which now make up **Priddy Mineries** nature reserve, home to grass snakes, adders and a number of unusual plants that thrive in the lead-rich soil.

Cheddar Gorge

The deep fissure of **CHEDDAR GORGE** cuts a jagged gash across the Mendips, at times squeezing the road that bisects it through the narrowest of gaps. The first few rocky curves, with the cliffs towering almost five hundred feet above, hold the gorge's most dramatic scenery, though each turn of its two-mile length presents new, sometimes startling vistas. The gorge, the largest in Britain, was carved out by successive glacial meltwaters over a million years ago, and its toothy limestone crags are now the precipitous domain of primitive **British goats** (the archetypal Billy Goat Gruff) and feral **soay sheep**, introduced a couple of decades ago to keep invasive plants from killing off rare local wildflowers such as the Cheddar Pink. In summer, the RSPB runs a "Peregrine Watch" in one of the south-side lay-bys (April–Aug Wed, Sat & Sun 3–6pm; free), pointing out **peregrine falcons** that nest on the upper ledges.

Striking though it is, the gorge's natural beauty is undermined somewhat by the mile of tea shops, trinket stores and parking areas at its lower end, which cater for the half-million or so visitors that funnel through each year – the very bottom car park serves as the departure point for the **open-top bus** that runs through the gorge between March and October (free to Cheddar Caves ticket-holders). There's a slightly nagging theme-park feel to this area, enhanced by the branded bins that run along the pavements down here.

Jacob's Ladder and the Gorge Walk

The best way to experience Cheddar Gorge is from above. Climbing the 274 steps of **Jacob's Ladder** leads to a lookout tower offering vistas towards Glastonbury Tor and occasional glimpses of Exmoor and the sea – there are plans for a cable-car to ferry people up here by 2013.

> ### CLIMBING IN THE MENDIPS
> The limestone cliffs of Cheddar Gorge are one of the most popular places in the Mendips for **climbing**, its granite-grey walls cut by the coloured ropes of rock-hugging mountain types as they scale Acid Rock, Freaky Wall or any other of its four-hundred-odd routes. If you fancy having a go yourself, contact Rocksport (☎01934 742343, ⓦcheddarcaves.co.uk/x-treme) or Cave Climb (☎01934 741623, ⓦcaveclimb.co.uk), who can also take you up (and down) the equally impressive cliffs at nearby Burrington Combe (see p.160).

3

CHEDDAR'S CHEDDAR

The legacy of the rather mundane village of Cheddar, about a mile south of the gorge, is to have given its name to Britain's most famous cheese. **Cheddar cheese** has been handcrafted here for nearly 850 years, during which time it has cornered the cheese-and-pickle-sandwich market and become a country-pub staple throughout the land, providing ploughmen with an obvious choice of lunch. King Henry II was pretty partial to the stuff, ordering 10,000lb of Cheddar in 1170 (its earliest recorded reference), as was Charles I, under whose reign the cheese was the preserve of the king's court only.

Several factors determine whether a cheese can be Cheddar, including the amount of fat and protein it contains and the level of moisture – lower than 39 percent, according to law. But the thing that really makes Cheddar Cheddar is the practice of cutting the cheese into "bricks", stacking them and then turning them every ten minutes or so to squeeze out the whey – a process, understandably enough, known as **Cheddaring**. Slowly maturing the cheese (traditionally done in muslin cloth, and for up to eighteen months in some cases) hardens it and allows the strong, tangy flavour to develop.

Originally, cheese had to be made within thirty miles of Wells Cathedral to be called Cheddar, and while only cheese made in Somerset, Dorset, Devon and Cornwall can be called West Country farmhouse Cheddar, its name has not been protected to the same degree that, say, Melton Mowbray pork pies or Arbroath Smokies have, and most "Cheddar" is now mass-produced far from here. Only one Cheddar, though, can claim to be authentic.

From the tower, the three-mile **Gorge Walk**, a public footpath that circuits the summit, provides close-up views over the Pinnacles, the highest point in the gorge; distinctive Horseshoe Bend; and, further down the gorge towards Cheddar, the sheer cliff face of High Rock. A marked path at the top of the loop branches off to Black Rock reserve and, beyond that, Velvet Bottom, Blackmoor and Black Down (see opposite).

Cheddar Caves

Daily: July, Aug & school hols 10am–5.30pm; Sept–June 10.30am–5pm • £17.80, under-15s £11.80, under-5s free; combined ticket includes entry to the Museum of Prehistory, plus a ride on the Gorge Tour Bus • ☎ 01934 742343, ⓦ cheddargorge.co.uk

The network of caverns that lies beneath the gorge can be explored to some extent in the **Cheddar Caves**, which were scooped out by underground rivers in the wake of the Ice Age and subsequently occupied by primitive communities. Several important Stone Age discoveries have been made here, including the nine-thousand-year-old skeleton known as **Cheddar Man** – spookily, DNA tests have proved that a local schoolteacher is his direct descendant.

Gough's Cave

Discovered in 1890, **Gough's Cave** burrows deep into the Somerset countryside, following the former route of the River Yeo through a sequence of extravagantly gouged chambers. Just inside the entrance – where Cheddar Man was found – you're immediately swallowed up by the dank, dripping underground world that Richard Gough painstakingly revealed during eight years of exploration. The exhaustive audio tour, narrated by "Gough" in a thick West Country burr, does a good job of rekindling the excitement he must have felt emerging for the first time into caverns such as **St Paul's Cathedral** and **King Solomon's Temple**, their floors arrayed with tortuous rock formations and their walls "flowing" with banoffee-coloured calcite – it's easy to see how, after visiting on honeymoon in 1916, the caverns provided J. R. R. Tolkien with the inspiration for Rohan's Glittering Caves in *The Lord of the Rings*.

There's enough audio information to spend a couple of hours in the cave, though that would still leave you 129 days and 22 hours short of the World Underground Endurance Record, set here by David Lafferty in the 1960s.

Cox's Cave

Further down the main drag, the much smaller **Cox's Cave** is floodlit to pick out the subtle pinks, greys, greens and whites in the rock, as well as a set of lime blocks known as "the Bells", which produce a range of tones when struck. The caves were discovered by George Cox (Richard Gough's uncle) in 1837, and while the piped choral music is a bit OTT, they're still worth exploring in comparison, in some stages requiring you to squeeze between crevices and under rock ledges. **The Crystal Quest**, a "fantasy grotto" near the exit, may appeal to older children.

Museum of Prehistory

daily: July, Aug & school hols 10am–5.30pm; Sept–June 10.30am–5pm • £17.80, under-15s £11.80, under-5s free; combined ticket includes entry to the Cheddar Caves, plus a ride on the Gorge Tour Bus • ☎ 01934 742343, ⓦ cheddargorge.co.uk

The rather patchy **Museum of Prehistory** charts Cheddar Gorge's 40,000 years of human occupation, exploring the hunter-gatherer lifestyles of Mesolithic man with displays on tools, sex and cannibalism – five skeletons from Gough's Cave showed signs of butchering, which appears to be the cue for an enormous rotating model of a half-eaten skull. Children should, however, enjoy the "cave-painting" section and the outdoor demonstrations of flint-knapping, fire-lighting and other Stone Age survival skills (most days in summer).

Cheddar Gorge Cheese Company

Visitor centre Daily 10am–4pm • £1.95, under-16s free (max of 2 per paying adult) **Shop** Daily 10am–5pm • ⓦ cheddargorgecheeseco.co.uk

The last authentic producers of Cheddar cheese, the **Cheddar Gorge Cheese Company** still make their Cheddar the traditional way: by hand, using local, unpasteurized milk, and maturing it in muslins. You can watch part of the seven-hour process from a viewing gallery in their **visitor centre** out the back, which includes free tasters afterwards.

The street-front **shop** does a range of Cheddars – with cider, garlic and chives, or speckled with chilis, for example – though purists are unlikely to look beyond the classic mellow (buttery), mature (full-bodied and complex), vintage (a palate-tingler, and a previous Best Cheddar winner at the World Cheese Awards) or cave-matured Cheddars, the last of which is the real deal, aged for around a year in Gough's Cave.

Charterhouse and around

The fascinating former mining area of **Charterhouse** lies at the centre of a patchwork of nature reserves that, linked together, provide enough varied walks to keep even the most jaded of ramblers entertained. Long ago reclaimed by nature, this one-time industrial wasteland still bears the scars of nearly two thousand years of mining – within a few years of conquering Britain, the Romans were dispatching pigs of Mendip lead across the Empire, with lead mined at Charterhouse shaping the water pipes of Pompeii (their remains still poke out of the ashes) and, closer to home, lining the Roman Baths just up the road.

The legacy left on the landscape – and by the Victorian miners who followed them – is best seen at **Blackmoor Reserve** and the adjoining reserves of **Velvet Bottom** and **Ubley Warren**, where the swathes of furrowed ground are eerily treeless. From Blackmoor, paths lead north to **Black Down**, a gorse-covered heathland offering wonderful rural views, and on to **Rowberrow Forrest** and **Dolebury Warren**, the latter a medieval rabbit keep and home to the earthen ramparts of an enormous Iron Age fort.

Blackmoor Reserve

Charterhouse itself is little more than a crossroads and the Charterhouse Centre, an old school that now serves as a base for outdoor activities. Beyond this, **Blackmoor Reserve**, like much of the surrounding area, is covered with grassy humps known as "grooves" or **"gruffy"**

3

A WALK AROUND CHARTERHOUSE

You could spend days following the trails around Charterhouse, though the following six-mile circular **walk** (around 2hr 15min) is as good an introduction to the area as any, traversing four reserves and taking in Roman lead workings, World War II remains and the highest point in the Mendips along the way.

Starting from the car park at **Blackmoor Reserve**, follow the path as it curves around the site of the **Roman fort**, then head down the steps to the left and across the dam that bridges a slag-fringed pond, where the path traces a dry-stone wall up to the main road. Turn right at the main road, then take the first left: Raines Batch. The sign at the corner here ("Town Field") refers to the **Roman settlement** that once occupied this entire area – recent surveys indicate that the town was up to five times bigger than Roman Bath, though little archeological evidence has survived the ravages of mining. Where the road flattens out at the top of Raines Batch, the fenced-off depression in the field to the left – easily identified by the gorse bushes growing in its centre – marks the site of Town Field's **amphitheatre**.

At the **radio masts** at the top of the hill, follow signs to the left along a rutted bridleway. After about a quarter of an hour, the landscape opens out into the far-reaching blanket of heather and gorse that constitutes **Black Down**. Following the footpath (not the bridleway) straight ahead leads to the trig point at **Beacon Batch** – at 1068ft, the highest point on the Mendips, with dazzling panoramas of rolling fields, distant villages and the sliver of steely grey water that forms the Bristol Channel.

The path continues down the other side of the hill to **Burrington Combe** (see p.160), but return instead along the narrow trail (to the right of the one you just came up when looking back at it from Beacon Batch) that runs directly through the heather – the exposed path is a perfect sunbathing spot for adders, so watch your step. Believe it or not, the stone cairns, or "tumps", running either side of the trail are actually **anti-glider landing obstructions**, which, along with the remains of a **bunker** in the next field to the south (reached by turning left at the fence at the bottom of the tumps and then crossing the first stile on the right), formed part of the decoy town complex constructed on Black Down during World War II (see box opposite).

The path eventually runs to the bottom left-hand corner of this field; first, though, it cuts diagonally across to the stile halfway along the fence on the right, before following the fence downhill and then turning left, running parallel to the row of bushes that mark the field's southern boundary. At the bottom corner of the field, follow the trail south through a wooded coppice and then turn right at the stile on the main road, shortly forking left down Fir Lane; taking the first left (before the farm) picks up a trail as it wends through **Long Wood**, dappled on sunnier days and carpeted with bluebells in the spring – the little "gates" in the stone walls here enable badgers to move freely around the reserve.

Shortly after emerging from the woods, the path forks. Right leads to rocky **Black Rock Reserve** and **Cheddar Gorge** (see p.155), left (which is the route to take) through **Velvet Bottom**, where the soft ground staggers up over a series of settlement dams, remnants of the area's Victorian lead-mining industry. The trail runs past a number of large **buddles**, first on the left, and then on the right, and then some seriously bobbly **"gruffy" ground**, before rejoining the main road; turn left and, shortly after passing the old miners' church of **St Hugh's** (Sun afternoons May–Sept only) turn right at the crossroads to return to the Blackmoor Reserve car park.

ground, the result of lead ore being cut from veins directly beneath the surface. Blackmoor is the site of an old **Roman fort**, essentially a tussock-clumped bowl today, and, further along the path (and much more noticeable), the remains of two Victorian **lead-condenser flues**. The glassy slag heaps nearby date from around this time, when the miners resorted to resmelting slag from earlier operations to try and draw out the residual lead.

Velvet Bottom and Ubley Warren

The terrain at **Velvet Bottom**, accessed from the main road just south of the Charterhouse Centre, is the sort of spongy, rabbit-trimmed surface that characterizes

OPERATION STARFISH

Thanks to their prominent position and network of old mines, underground caverns and hidden gorges, the Mendips assumed an unusual role during **World War II**. The Home Guard stored weapons in caves at Burrington Combe, the Special Operations Executive had a secret hideaway in Ebbor Gorge, and St Hugh's Church at Charterhouse doubled as an anti-gas centre. But nothing was quite as elaborate as the **decoy town** on Black Down.

An important part of **Operation Starfish** – a countrywide system of dummy towns that distracted night-time German raids away from their intended targets – Black Down was one of a dozen sites set up to protect the docks at Bristol. The scaled-down city was a remarkable feat. Hundreds of lights were strategically placed around the hilltop to mimic key areas of Bristol, turning a bit of the Somerset countryside into Temple Meads Railway Station or the Pyle Hill Goods Yard. The whole system was carefully manipulated to resemble the comings and goings of "trams" and "trains" far below – you can see an old **control bunker**, one of the complex's few surviving remnants, in a field just south of Black Down (see box opposite). To further hoodwink the Luftwaffe, when bombs *were* dropped on the area, ground crews would ignite fire baskets, giving the impression to the pilots above that the city was ablaze.

Despite the ingenuity of the system – and the occasional "success", as scattered bomb craters testify – the decoy ultimately did little to protect Bristol, and the city was on the receiving end of some of the severest bombing of the Blitz (see box, p.91).

3

much of the walking on the Mendips. Small and slim, the reserve is dotted with circular pits known as **buddles**, settling beds that were used for washing the impurities out of lead ore.

Nearby **Ubley Warren**, rich in wildlife, harbours similar reminders, including, at Banwell's Shaft, a series of "**rakes**", lines of mineral veins that have been hacked into what look like rocky gullies, and the remains of a **horse whim**, a horse-drawn winch that hauled buckets full of ore to the surface.

Axbridge

Set at the foot of the Mendips' southern escarpment, sleepy **AXBRIDGE** still retains the look of a medieval market town, though the heady days it enjoyed when the town was important enough to have its own mint are long gone. A number of attractive, ancient-looking houses line the High Street, including the **old drugstore** and, diagonally opposite, the **old butcher's shop**, its studded wooden door making for a "magnificent entrance", as so aptly described by John Betjeman.

Axbridge's mercantile tradition continues on the first Saturday of the month, when a dozen or so stallholders congregate in the pretty little central square for the local **farmers' market** (9am–1pm).

King John's Hunting Lodge

April–Sept daily 1–4pm, first Sat of the month 10.30am–12.30pm • £2.50 • ☎ 01934 732012, ⓦ kingjohnshuntinglodge.co.uk

Sitting on the corner of The Square, the beautifully restored timber-framed **King John's Hunting Lodge** is home to Axbridge's local-history museum, with minor exhibits on its wool-trading past, the geology of the Mendips and scattered finds from a recently discovered Saxon site at Brent Knoll (see p.244).

Although the king used to hunt in the Royal Forest of Mendip (modern-day Axbridge and Cheddar), the building was actually built around 1460, a good two and a half centuries after John's reign, for a wealthy wool merchant – note the wooden arch braces that support the vertical beams, a structure found only in Somerset timber-framed houses, and the decorative upstairs windows, known as ogee-headed windows. The crowned figurehead on the corner is a remnant of the days when the house served as *The King's Head Inn*.

Burrington Combe

Dotted with Billy goats skittering about its upper ledges, **Burrington Combe** (pronounced *coom*) is a smaller version of nearby Cheddar Gorge, popular with cavers, climbers and walkers seeking a quieter alternative to its more famous neighbour. The limestone has been worn into sharp, serrated crags, most significantly at a crevice in the lower end of the combe (on the left if you're coming down from Wells), known as the **Rock of Ages**. It was here in 1762 that the Reverend Augustus Toplady sought refuge from a storm, inspiring him to pen the famous hymn ("Rock of Ages, cleft for me, let me hide myself in thee…"), though judging by the size of the crack, it can't have been much more than a damp drizzle.

About 275 yards back up the combe, on the same side, a trail leads after fifty yards or so to **Aveline's Hole**, the site of the oldest cemetery in Britain (its incumbents perished nearly 8500 years ago) and home to one of the UK's few examples of cave art. The cave belongs to the University of Bristol Speleological Society, and only experienced cavers can go beyond the gate two-thirds of the way in.

At the top of the combe, a path from the lay-by on the right weaves up heather clad Black Down (see box, p.158).

Crook Peak

The Mendips tail out as they approach the Bristol Channel, but rocky **Crook Peak**, two miles west of Axbridge and one of the last hills in the range, rewards hikers who struggle up its steep summit with great views over Brent Knoll and Brean Down (and the M5) and across the water to Wales. The shortest route to the top (about a mile one-way) starts from a path just opposite the car park on Webbington Road; the longer approach from the car park on Winscombe Hill, just off the A38 (around 2.5 miles one-way), follows the West Mendip Way (see box, p.153) through **King's Wood** and across **Wavering Down** before climbing up to the barrelling wave of rock that marks the peak itself.

GETTING AROUND — THE MENDIPS

By bus Public transport is essentially limited to the #126, the bus service that runs along the A371 from Wells to Weston-super-Mare; some of the smaller destinations are walkable from stops along this route.

Destinations Axbridge (#126; 35min); Cheddar (#126; 25min); Cross (for King's Wood; #126; 40min); Winscombe (for Crook Peak; #126; 45min); Wookey Hole (also for Ebbor Gorge; #670; 10min).

By bike Wookey Hole, Ebbor Gorge, Priddy and Charterhouse are on National Cycle Route 3. The Strawberry Line (ⓦ thestrawberryline.co.uk) follows the old GWR branch route that was used to ship strawberries from the fields of the Cheddar Valley; it currently connects Cheddar with Axbridge and Kings Wood, and passes through the orchards of Thatchers cider farm in Sandford (see box opposite).

INFORMATION

National Trust Office The Cliffs, Cheddar (10am–5pm: March–Oct daily; Nov to mid-Dec Sat & Sun only; ☎01934 844518, ✉ cheddargorge@nationaltrust.org.uk). Information point and outdoor centre, the first of its kind in the country when it opened in July 2010.

Useful websites Mendip Hills AONB (ⓦ mendiphillsaonb

.org.uk) has details of walking routes, events in the area and online editions of the latest *Mendip Times*.

Maps OS Explorer 141 (Cheddar Gorge & Mendip Hills West 1:25,000) and 153 (Weston-super-Mare & Bleadon Hill 1:25,000) cover the area.

ACCOMMODATION

Cheddar Gorge Youth Hostel Hillfield, Cheddar ☎0845 371 9730, ⓦ yha.org.uk. Clinically refurbished Victorian house in Cheddar village, not too far from the gorge but far enough to be away from the hustle and bustle. It's all very spick and span, with clean, spacious rooms – four- to six-bed dorms, en-suite doubles and

family rooms – and a decent kitchen. There's on-site laundry and a cycle store – the Strawberry Line cycle route to Axbridge passes nearby. Dorms **£21.40**, doubles **£46**
Compton House Townsend, Axbridge ☎01934 733944, ⓦ comptonhse.com. Georgian country-house hotel, whose five lovely bedrooms – two with tremendous

THERE'S GOLD IN THEM THAR HILLS

Thatchers Gold, that is. Plus Old Rascal, Cheddar Valley and the nine other varieties of **cider** that **Thatchers** produce at their farm in Sandford, four miles north of Axbridge on the A368. It's a big operation, capable of fermenting a million litres of apple juice at a time; on a more personal scale, you can taste their cider straight from the barrel at their shop (Mon–Sat 9am–6pm, Sun and bank hols 10am–1pm; ☎01934 822862, ✆thatcherscider.co.uk), or take a walk through their orchards nearby.

our-poster beds and stylish rolltop or claw-foot iron bath, all with flat-screen TVs and reading matter – offset the fact that it's located just off the A371, a walk west of town. The amiable host can whip up home-cooked evening meals from £16.50. **£100**

The Oakhouse Hotel The Square, Axbridge ☎01934 732444, ✆theoakhousehotel.com. Right in the heart of medieval Axbridge – and dating back to the eleventh century itself – the friendly *Oakhouse Hotel* has a variety of smartly designed modern en suites, including excellent-value family rooms, and a great little restaurant (see below). Breakfast (continental £5, full English £7) costs extra. **£50**

Warren Farm Charterhouse ☎01420 80804, ✆featherdown.co.uk. Family-run farm enjoying a fantastic

location slap bang in the middle of Charterhouse's prime walking territory. It's part of the Feather Down Farms set-up, so (pricey) tents are of the luxury safari-style mould, with wooden floors, wood-burning stoves and comfy beds. Slow-cook your own stew and then tuck into your own fried eggs for breakfast (private chicken coop from £10). Bike hire £8.50 (£5 for kids). Dogs £5 extra per night. 3nt minimum stay. **£125**

★ **The Wookey Hole Inn** Wookey Hole ☎01749 676677, ✆wookeyholeinn.com. Just down the street from the caves, this excellent inn has contemporary, fully equipped rooms – with low-slung beds, matt flooring and swish bathrooms – that belie its traditional exterior. And you get your continental breakfast delivered to your room. The restaurant and bar are also top choice (see below). **£90**

3

EATING AND DRINKING

Frank's Restaurant The Bays, Cheddar ☎01934 742761, ✆franksrestaurant.co.uk. Upmarket restaurant, with candle-lit tables come dinner, tucked away off the main drag at the bottom of Cheddar Gorge. The mostly Modern British dishes are, for the majority, based around locally sourced products such as rump of Somerset lamb and sirloin steak from a farm in nearby Priddy. Mains from £15.95, plus keenly priced one-, two- and three-course set lunches (£7.25/11.50/15.75). Mon–Fri noon–2pm & 6–9pm (Fri till 9.30pm), Sat 6.30–9pm.

The Lamb The Square, Axbridge ☎01934 732253, ✆lamb.butcombe.com. Traditional fifteenth-century coaching inn, with oak-beamed ceilings, a striking "bottle bar" and a pleasing pub-grub menu that features beef and Butcombe pie (£9.75). Butcombe's own cask ales dominate, including Bitter and Gold, plus seasonal brews such as Mendip Spring. Outside seating, on the square, looks directly across to King John's Hunting Lodge. Mon–Wed 11.30am–3pm & 6–11pm, Thurs 11.30am–11pm, Fri & Sat 11.30am–11.30pm, Sun noon–10.30pm.

★ **The Oakhouse Hotel** The Square, Axbridge ☎01934 732444, ✆theoakhousehotel.com. A simple setting – just six tables, nicely spaced out in the hotel's red-brick restaurant – but with a really good menu that's well executed, making parmesan-crusted scallop and Sharpham

Park organic spelt risotto taste as good as they sound (mains from £10.50). Refreshingly, the small kids' menu isn't an afterthought either, including the likes of a very tasty fishcake and chips (served in a mini fryer). There's a chilled little lounge bar next door for an after-dinner drink, with Axbridge Ale and Thatchers Gold on tap. Daily noon–2.30pm (bookings only Mon–Wed, min 4 people) & 6–11pm

The Queen Victoria Inn Pelting Drove, Priddy ☎01749 676385, ✆queenvictoria.butcombe.com. Cosy, characterful Butcombe pub, just off Priddy Green, with low ceilings, stone walls and a light, flagstone-floored restaurant (char-grilled meats a speciality; from £8). There's also a little children's playground. Mon–Fri noon–2pm & 6–8pm, Sat noon–4pm & 6–9pm, Sun noon–4pm.

The Wookey Hole Inn Wookey Hole ☎01749 676677, ✆wookeyholeinn.com. Expensive but memorable dishes, such as cider-soused mackerel with pickled vegetables, and a hit-list of tempting desserts (mains around £18). The bar serves a great selection of Belgian beers, plus local ales and ciders (including Wilkins); in fine weather, you can quaff them in the quirky sculpture garden. Also regular live music. Mon–Sat noon–2.30pm & 7–9.30pm, Sun noon–3pm.

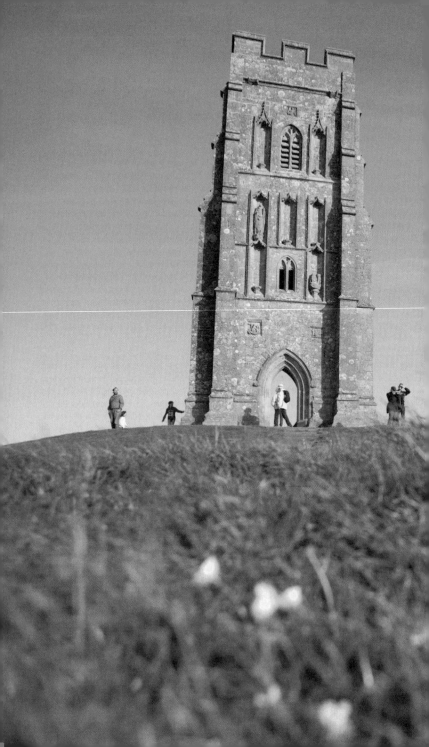

Glastonbury and the Somerset Levels

ST MICHAEL'S TOWER, GLASTONBURY TOR

Glastonbury and the Somerset Levels

In a county laden with legends, Glastonbury is king. For centuries a site of pilgrimage, its historical guestbook reads like a Who's Who of ancient mythology and religious lore, with everyone from St Patrick and King Arthur to Jesus Christ himself alleged to have passed through at some point; some say the Holy Grail is here, others that the Lord of the Underworld resides just outside of town. There's no disputing, however, the status of Glastonbury Abbey: the cradle of Christianity in the UK and the supposed final resting place of Arthur and Guinevere, its ruins make up one of the most evocative sights in Somerset. There are a couple of good regional museums in town – scattered among the sanctuaries and shops that form the country's most enthusiastic centre of New Age cults – though the other must-see sight, the humpback hill of Glastonbury Tor, lies just to the southeast, where more folklore (and fine views) await. The cluster of houses that almost runs into Glastonbury from the south is Street, a town whose link with Clarks shoes is the focus of a worthwhile little museum.

Beyond here spread the **Somerset Levels**, a curious patchwork of rivers, rhynes (pronounced *reens*), drains and ditches that constitute the largest area of low-lying wetlands in Britain. Topping out just a few feet above sea level, they are under constant threat of **flooding**, and for lengthy periods of the year vast areas can be submerged beneath a good 6ft of water – when the floodwaters rise and the fields go under, the countryside can resemble a disjointed lake, with the spindly silhouettes of pollard willows appearing to float above the surface. Its original settlers deserted the Levels during winter, prompting the Saxons to label them the *Sumor saete*, or **Land of the Summer People**, a name that over time has been co-opted to cover the entire county.

Some of Somerset's earliest signs of settlement have been found here, in the so-called **lake villages** preserved in peat-bogs near Glastonbury and Meare, and in the wooden walkways that carried tribal Britons across the marshes, most famously on the **Sweet Track**. Sections of this ancient footpath are preserved under **Shapwick Heath Nature Reserve**, the largest in a system of wildlife reserves that attract myriad birdlife to their shallow pools and densely packed reedbeds.

Most of the man-made sights – such as the assorted ruins of **Muchelney Abbey**, near the regional hub of **Langport** – are set on higher ground, though much of the area's appeal lies in simply ambling through its sweeping lowlands, the gentle rhythm of rhyne and river slowly ingraining itself until you can no longer imagine a horizon that isn't endless.

SWELL WOOD HERONRY, WEST SEDGEMOOR NATURE RESERVE

Highlights

❶ Glastonbury Abbey Somerset's most spectacular abbey is now the county's most spectacular ruin. **See p.167**

❷ Glastonbury Tor Steeped in legend and mired in myth, and offering views fit for a (legendary) king. **See p.172**

❸ Glastonbury Festival Buy your ticket eight months in advance, pack your wellies and enjoy the ride that is simply Britain's biggest, boldest and best music festival. **See p.176**

❹ The Avalon Marshes A magical wetland wilderness, home to some of the best bird-watching in the country. **See p.178**

❺ Muchelney Dinky village with a trio of fine medieval buildings, capped by the prominent remains of Muchelney Abbey. **See p.184**

❻ West Sedgemoor Nature Reserve Make a beeline for Swell Wood, where spiky-feathered heron chicks take their first tentative flights from the treetops in spring. **See p.185**

❼ Smoked eels A Levels delicacy, and at their tastiest when they've been whipped hot out of the smokery and plonked straight onto your plate. **See p.187**

HIGHLIGHTS ARE MARKED ON THE MAP ON P.166

Glastonbury and around

Six miles south of Wells, **GLASTONBURY** lies at the centre of the so-called **Isle of Avalon**, a region rich with mystical associations. At the heart of it all is the early Christian legend that the young Jesus once visited this site, a story that is not as far-fetched as it sounds. The Romans had a heavy presence in the area, mining lead in the Mendips (see p.153), and one of these mines was owned by **Joseph of Arimathea**, a well-to-do tin merchant said to have been related to Mary. It's not completely unfeasible that the merchant took his kinsman on one of his many visits to his property, in a period of Christ's life of which nothing is recorded – it was this possibility to which William Blake referred in his *Glastonbury Hymn*, better

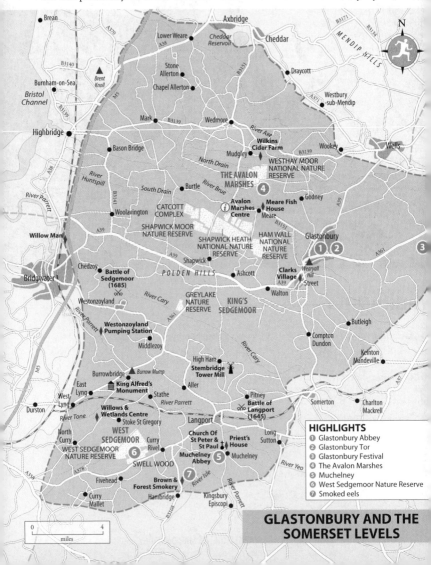

HIGHLIGHTS

1. Glastonbury Abbey
2. Glastonbury Tor
3. Glastonbury Festival
4. The Avalon Marshes
5. Muchelney
6. West Sedgemoor Nature Reserve
7. Smoked eels

GLASTONBURY AND THE SOMERSET LEVELS

known as *Jerusalem*: "And did those feet, in ancient times/Walk upon England's mountains green?"

Glastonbury's legends are much larger than the town itself, a few streets focused around Market Place and the walled square of grassy parkland that houses the **abbey** ruins. New Age mystics and spiritual healers dominate the esoteric **High Street**, running shops with names like The Cat and the Cauldron, Natural Earthling and The Psychic Piglet, and selling more crystals than you can shake a shaman stick at.

For a bit of a breather, away from the pungent waft of incense, head up the surrounding hillocks of **Glastonbury Tor** and **Wearyall Hill**, both steeped in legend themselves and offering, particularly in the case of the Tor, superlative panoramas of the surrounding Levels.

Brief history

It's difficult to separate fact from fiction in Glastonbury's past. Its history – a complex interweaving of ancient Celtic myth and religious legend – begins around 150 BC, when tribal Britons lived in the marshland huts that made up the **Glastonbury Lake Villages**. At that time, Glastonbury was surrounded by water and was known as *Ynis Witrin*, the Isle of Glass, or **Avalon**, the Island of Apples – though other myths link this name to the Celtic underworld (see box, p.172).

The lake villages were abandoned around the same time that **Joseph of Arimathea** landed here to convert the country in AD 63, establishing with his disciples – who according to some eighth-century chroniclers included Mary and her sister Martha, Mary Magdalene – the first church in Britain.

St Patrick was believed to have been made abbot of a Celtic monastery here in 443 (later visited by **St David**), and in the seventh century, Ine, the Saxon king of Wessex, built the stone church around which the abbey later grew.

Glastonbury was briefly awoken from the slumber that followed the abbey's demolition in the mid-sixteenth century when the waters of the **Chalice Well** were discovered to have curative properties – the **Old Pump House** was fashioned in a hurry in the early 1750s to deal with the influx of visitors, and the town was awarded its own charter a decade or so later, in 1765.

Glastonbury Abbey

Abbey Gatehouse, Magdalene St • Daily: Jan, Feb & Dec 10am–5pm; March–May 9am–6pm; June–Aug 9am–9pm; Sept–Nov 9am–5pm • Café mid-May to Sept • £6, under-16s £4, under-5s free • ☎ 01458 832267, ⦿ glastonburyabbey.com

Aside from its mythological origins, **Glastonbury Abbey** can safely claim to be the country's oldest Christian foundation, dating back to the seventh century and possibly earlier. Three kings (Edmund, Edgar and Edmund Ironside) were buried here, and in the tenth century, funded by a constant procession of pilgrims, the Saxon church was enlarged by St Dunstan (later archbishop of Canterbury), under whom it became the richest Benedictine abbey in the country. Further expansion took place under the Normans, though most of the additions were destroyed by fire in 1184. Rebuilt, the abbey was the longest in Europe when it was destroyed in the Dissolution of the Monasteries in 1539, and the ruins, now hidden behind walls and nestled among acres of well-tended grassland, can only hint at its former extent.

The Lady Chapel

The most complete set of remains is the shell of the **Lady Chapel**, at the west end of the abbey, with its carved figures of the Annunciation, the Magi and Herod. The chapel was built on the site of the wooden Saxon church, itself believed to have been erected around the "**First Church**", the small wattle and daub construction allegedly built by Joseph of Arimathea and his disciples in 63 AD, on a spot subsequently known as the "Holiest Earthe of England". With that legend in mind, venturing down into the now-open crypt below the chapel can make for a momentous few steps.

The choir

The abbey's **choir** – announced by the photogenic remains of the transept piers – introduces another strand to the Glastonbury story, for it holds what is alleged to be the **tomb of Arthur and Guinevere** (see box opposite). The discovery of two bodies in an ancient **grave** south of the abbey in 1191 was taken to confirm the popular identification of Glastonbury with Avalon; in 1278, the bones were transferred to the abbey but disappeared after the Dissolution of the Monasteries in 1539 – a plaque near the **High Altar** marks the spot where their black marble tomb lay.

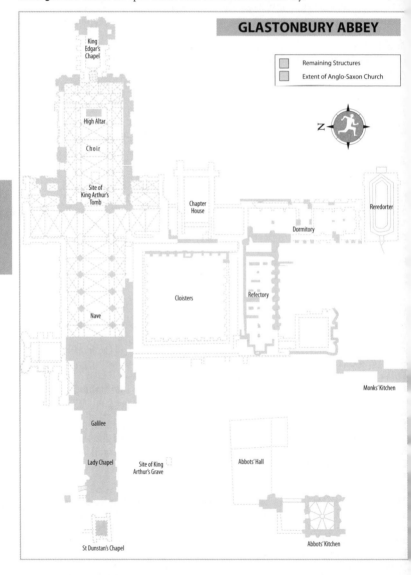

GLASTONBURY ABBEY

Remaining Structures

Extent of Anglo-Saxon Church

King Edgar's Chapel

High Altar

Choir

Site of King Arthur's Tomb

Chapter House

Reredorter

Dormitory

Cloisters

Refectory

Nave

Monks' Kitchen

Galilee

Lady Chapel

Site of King Arthur's Grave

Abbots' Hall

St Dunstan's Chapel

Abbots' Kitchen

KING ARTHUR AND THE ISLE OF AVALON

The West Country is sprinkled with sites relating to the legendary **King Arthur** but only in Glastonbury do you get the feeling that some of these tales might not be so tall. Arthur's name appears in historical texts as early as the ninth century, in the Welsh poem *Y Gododdin*, the *Historia Brittonum* (*History of the Britons*) and the *Annales Cambriae* (*Welsh Annals*), who tell of an Arthur (or Arturius) defending his lands against the Anglo-Saxons in the mid-sixth century. Flesh was added to these bones by **Geoffrey of Monmouth** in the mid-twelfth century, whose embellished *Historia Regum Britanniae* (*History of the Kings of Britain*) established most of the Arthurian legend that we know today, while the French writer **Chretien de Troyes** later brought Lancelot and Camelot into the mix...

The bastard child of Uther Pendragon, King of Britain, Arthur was raised by the wizard **Merlin**, and was crowned king himself aged just 15, a feat preordained when he pulled the sword **Excalibur** from its seemingly immovable position, wedged deep into a stone. Arthur married **Guinevere** and ruled his kingdom from **Camelot** (believed to be the sixth-century fort at Cadbury Castle; see p.195), but spent much of his time on a fruitless quest with his **Knights of the Round Table** to find the **Holy Grail** – though it would seem that they didn't have too far to look (see p.171).

Returning to England to quell a rebellion led by his nephew **Mordred**, Arthur was mortally wounded at the **battle of Camlann**; Excalibur was subsequently thrown into a lake – supposedly from Pomparles (or Pons Perilis) Bridge, which crosses the River Brue just south of Glastonbury – and his dying body brought to the **Isle of Avalon**. He lay buried at **Glastonbury Abbey** until the late twelfth century, when, shortly after its gutting by a great fire, monks "discovered" his body, along with Queen Guinevere's, under a leaden cross bearing the inscription "Here lies the renown King Arthur in the Isle of Avalon". Experts argue over how old the writing style is, and the cross itself was lost centuries ago, but there's no doubt that the resulting **influx of pilgrims** provided the finance necessary for the abbey's restoration. The bones were lost after the Dissolution of the Monasteries and have never been seen again.

4

The rest of the grounds

The fourteenth-century **Abbot's Kitchen** is the only monastic building to survive intact, with a great central lantern that funnelled smoke away from the four huge corner fireplaces. Henry III ate here in 1497, dining on fish that were dried and salted at the fish house in Meare (see p.179) and produce stored in barns throughout the abbey's estates, like the one at the Somerset Rural Life Museum (see p.170).

Behind the main entrance look out for the **Glastonbury Thorn** that is supposedly from the original thorn tree on Wearyall Hill (see p.172); only at Glastonbury do they flourish, it is claimed – everywhere else they die after a couple of years.

Glastonbury Lake Villages Museum

9 High St • Mon–Sat 10am–1pm & 2–4pm, Fri & Sat till 4.30pm • £2.50, children £1; EH • ☎ 01458 832954, ⓦ glastonburytic.co.uk

The bulging fifteenth-century **Glastonbury Tribunal** – long thought to be the abbots' court but actually a merchant's house – provides an atmospheric setting for the tourist office (see p.173) and the small but interesting **Glastonbury Lake Villages Museum**, with displays from the Iron Age settlements that grew up in the former marshland northwest of Glastonbury. Discovered by Arthur Bulleid in 1892, the villages consisted of conical wattle houses that were consistently rebuilt on layers of clay as they slowly submerged into the marshes – the finds, which were perfectly preserved in peat after the villages were abandoned in AD 53, include jewellery made from animal bones, carbonized cakes and a 3000-year-old wooden canoe.

St John the Baptist

High St • Mon–Fri 10.30am–12.30pm & 2–4pm • Free

The fifteenth-century church of **St John the Baptist**, halfway up the High Street, is worth a quick glance. The tower is reckoned to be one of Somerset's finest, and the interior has a fine oak roof and stained glass illustrating the legend of St Joseph of Arimathea, both from the period of the church's construction; the vessels in Joseph's hands are cruets, a variation of the Grail tale, with one containing the blood of Christ and the other his sweat. For the last 450 years or so, a sprig has been cut each winter from the **Glastonbury Thorn** that grows in the churchyard, and sent to the reigning monarch to place on the royal table come Christmas Day.

Somerset Rural Life Museum

Abbey Farm, Chilkwell St • Tues–Sat & Bank Holiday Mon 10am–5pm • Dairy Tearoom Easter–Oct 10.30am–4.30pm • Free • ☎ 01458 831197, Ⓦ somerset.gov.uk/museums

Centred round the fourteenth-century Abbey Barn, the engaging **Somerset Rural Life Museum** illustrates a range of local rural occupations, from cider-making and peat-digging to the unusual practice of mud-horse fishing, named after the wooden sledge shrimp-netters used to safely navigate the mudflats of Bridgwater Bay. A collection of heavy-duty farm machinery is on show in the courtyard outside the dirt-floored tithe barn, now home to a few clucking chickens but originally a produce storehouse for the abbey's 524 acres of arable estates. Today, the adjacent orchard holds twenty different types of cider apple trees, including Gennet Moyle, a local variety once thought to be extinct.

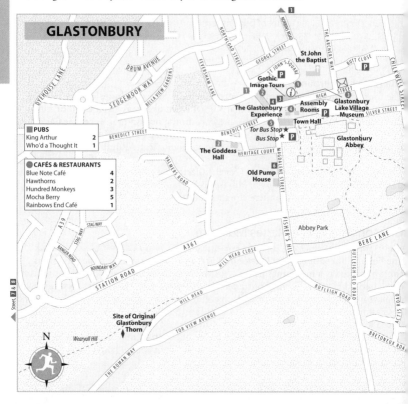

Chalice Well

Chilkwell St • Daily 10am–6pm, Nov–March till 4.30pm • £3.60, under-18s £1.80, under-5s free • ☎ 01458 831154, ⓦ chalicewell.org.uk

Standing amid a tranquil garden intended for quiet contemplation, the fabled **Chalice Well** is fondly supposed to be the hiding place of the Holy Grail. Legend has it that Joseph of Arimathea buried the Grail (the chalice from the Last Supper, in which the blood was gathered from the wound in Christ's side) at the foot of Glastonbury Tor; the spring of blood that miraculously flowed forth is now marked by the well, though the water's red colouring has more to do with its rich iron content than any sacred symbolism.

You can **sample the spring waters** at the Lion's Head fountain, near the top of the gardens – it's akin to sucking on a copper coin, and quite a different taste to the water flowing from the White Spring – or from the tap around the corner in Wellhouse Lane.

The White Spring

Wellhouse Lane • Mon, Tues & Fri–Sun 1.30–4.30pm • Free • ⓦ whitespring.org.uk

Just behind the Chalice Well, the Well House, a vaulted Victorian reservoir, is currently being converted into a temple in order to protect the **White Spring**, a natural well that drops 15ft into a series of pools. Legend links this place with the entrance to Gwyn Ap Nudd's Underworld in Glastonbury Tor (see box, p.172); less controversial is the fact that the reservoir itself was never used – the very waters it was built to store, sweet-tasting and tinged white with calcium, saw to that.

4

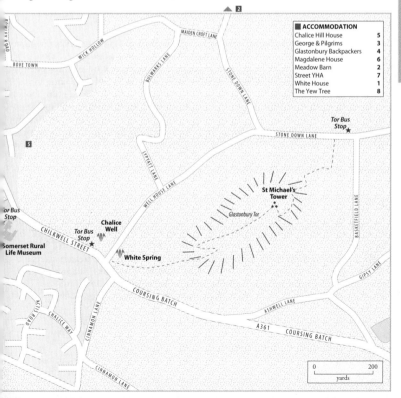

■ ACCOMMODATION	
Chalice Hill House	5
George & Pilgrims	3
Glastonbury Backpackers	4
Magdalene House	6
Meadow Barn	2
Street YHA	7
White House	1
The Yew Tree	8

PARADISE LOST?

One of Glastonbury Tor's earliest mythic incarnations is as a magic mountain that was home to **Gwyn ap Nudd**, the Celtic Winter King and Lord of the Underworld, and in later legends the King of the Fairies. As the **Winter King**, Nudd rode through the sky each autumn, leading his pack of phantom hounds (the *Cŵn Annwn* in Celtic mythology, known locally as the Gabble Retchet) in the "Wild Hunt", seen as a sign of imminent death – but more likely a primitive explanation for storms, or the night-time honking of migrating geese. Likewise, it was his Tor-top battle with the Summer King each year that represented the changing of the seasons.

As the **Lord of the Underworld**, Nudd protected the dead on their way to *Gwynfa*, or Paradise – the road that runs around the base of the Tor is called Paradise Lane – and ruled over the inner realm of *Annwn*, or Avalon, the Meeting Place of the Dead. To this day, some people still believe that the Tor is hollow, though no one knows what exactly lies inside.

Wearyall Hill

A five-minute walk up Hill Head leads to **Wearyall Hill**, with good views of Glastonbury Tor and across the surrounding Levels to the Mendips and the Polden and Quantock hills. It was here that a tired Joseph of Arimathea, with his disciples ("Weary, All"), was said to have stuck his thorn staff into the ground to rest; by morning, it had taken root. Descendants of this original **Glastonbury Thorn** are dotted about town and still bloom twice a year (Easter & Dec); the thorn on Wearyall itself was vandalized in December 2010, and only its sad stump remains, still surrounded by Tibetan-style prayer flags, as it slowly attempts to grow once more.

Glastonbury Tor

From Chilkwell St, turn left into Wellhouse Lane and immediately right for the footpath that leads up to the Tor; the shorter, steeper path is accessed from the top of Wellhouse Lane and is served by the half-hourly Tor Bus • Free • ⓦ nationaltrust.org.uk

Towering over the Somerset Levels, a lone pinnacle in an open expanse of marshland, the 521ft-high conical hill of **Glastonbury Tor** has invited myth and conjecture for centuries, serving (allegedly) as everything from the Land of the Dead (see box above) to a meeting point for UFOs. Topped by the dilapidated **St Michael's Tower**, sole remnant of a fourteenth-century church, it is visible for miles around and commands stupendous views, encompassing Wells, the Quantocks, the Mendips and, on very clear days, the Welsh mountains. Pilgrims once embarked on the stiff climb here with hard peas in their shoes as penance – nowadays, people come to picnic, fly kites or feel the vibrations of crossing ley-lines.

Street

The one-road town of **STREET**, two miles south of Glastonbury, could only be better named if it was called Clarksville, such is the impact the shoemaking magnates **C. & J. Clark** have had on its fortunes since they first started stitching soles here in 1825. Clarks stopped making shoes in Street in the early 1990s, but their headquarters are still here, and their legacy lives on: in the **Shoe Museum**, the **Clarks Village** shopping centre and the focal **Crispin Hall**, built by the Quaker brothers in 1885 as a community centre and named after the patron saint of – yep, you guessed it – shoemakers.

The Shoe Museum

40 High St • Mon–Fri 10am–4.45pm • Free • ☎ 01458 842169

The old Clarks factory clock-tower now houses the quirky **Shoe Museum**, whose dazzling collection of slip-ons, knee-highs and strap-up sandals, dating back to Roman

BY HECKS: CIDER IN STREET

Street might not seem like the kind of place you'd find **traditional farmhouse cider**, but that's exactly what **Hecks** have been producing here since 1840. Stop by the family's cider barn, on the corner of Middle Leigh and Ivythorn Road (it's signed down Stone Hill off the High Street), and sample some straight from the barrel (Mon–Sat 9am–5.30pm, Sun 10am–12.30pm, spring/summer bank hols 10am–1pm, closes half an hour earlier in winter; ☎ 01458 442367, ⓦ hecksfarmhousecider.co.uk).

They're particularly noted for their **Kingston Black** (medium sweet), a former CAMRA National Gold Winner, but also produce several other single-variety ciders, including the ultra-dry Maid of Devon (cider from £2.20 a litre, up to £31.50 for five gallons). There's also a choice of their own Torside apple juice (18 varieties in total), plus a perry or two.

times, would make Imelda Marcos blush – compare the extravagant diamante-studded 1930s evening wear with the comfy looking sheepskin slippers that got the ball rolling over a century before. Such is the bond between company and town that the displays of clunky foot measurers, fashion plates and sepia photographs make this as much a history of Street as it is of shoemaking.

Clarks Village

Mon–Sat 9am–6pm (Thurs till 8pm), Sun 10am–5pm • ☎ 01458 840064, ⓦ clarksvillage.co.uk

When shoe manufacturing in Street ended in 1993, the derelict warehouses were transformed into **Clarks Village**, the first discount shopping outlet in the UK. The "village" – a clever concept at the time but one that has since snowballed into the scourge of small-town stores across the country – is home to ninety shops, including GAP, Coast, Bench, Sony, Nike and, of course, Clarks (the biggest of the lot), as well as a tourist information centre (see below) and a children's play area.

4

ARRIVAL AND DEPARTURE
GLASTONBURY AND AROUND

By bus National Express runs a daily service from London Victoria to Glastonbury, departing at 7pm (3hr 50min) and returning at 6.45 or 7am (4hr 20min–4hr 35min). Local First Group buses drop you off outside the abbey on Magdalene Street.
Destinations Bridgwater (#375 & #376; 1hr 5min); Bristol (#376; 1hr 30min); Street (#29, #375, #376 & #377; 10min); Taunton (#29 & #376; 55min); Wells (#29, #375, #376 & #377; 20min); Yeovil (#376 & 377; 1hr 10min).
By train The nearest train stations are Bridgwater, on the Bristol–Exeter line, and the more useful Castle Cary, which serves London Paddington, Birmingham, Weymouth and Plymouth among others (both are about 15 miles away), though Bristol Temple Meads, Bath Spa and Taunton have more regular services and better bus connections.
By car Glastonbury is 29 miles from both Bristol (down the A37 and then the A39) and Bath (down the A39), 8 miles from Wells (also down the A39) and 22 miles from Taunton (up the A39). There are several car parks in town, one right next to the abbey.

GETTING AROUND

By bus The Glastonbury Tor Bus runs from the abbey car park to the base of the Tor every 30min with stops at the Somerset Rural Life Museum and Chalice Well (daily: April–Sept 9.30am–7pm; £3, under-16s £1.50, under-5s free, ticket valid all day).
By taxi Mike's Taxis ☎ 07754 538284 or ☎ 07783 978001.
Bike rental The *Hundred Monkeys* café rents bikes, handy for exploring the surrounding Somerset Levels (☎ 01458 833386; from £5 per half-day).

INFORMATION AND TOURS

Glastonbury TIC The Tribunal, 9 High St (Mon–Sat 10am–1pm & 2–4pm, Fri & Sat till 4.30pm; ☎ 01458 832954, ⓦ glastonburytic.co.uk). Plenty of info on the town, the wider area and Somerset in general, plus discounted tickets to the Cheddar Caves, Wookey Hole and other local attractions.
Street TIC Clarks Village, Farm Road (daily 10am–5pm, Sun from 11am; ☎ 01458 447384, ⓦ streettic.co.uk).
Town Crier Tours Daily historic tours with Glastonbury's town crier (£5, under-16s £2.50; 1hr 30min), bookable through the TIC.
Gothic Image Tours A mystical look at Glastonbury's

4

HEALING HANDS

It can seem that every other shop in Glastonbury offers some sort of crystal healing or shamanic training, but if you're interested in developing your soul armour, want to find out more about runic sound work or just fancy getting your chakra balanced, then drop into **The Glastonbury Experience**, a New Age hub at the western end of the High Street that's home to some of the town's longest-established practitioners.

Try the **Isle of Avalon Foundation** (☎01458 833933, ⓦisleofavalonfoundation.com), for an introduction to tarot reading and shamanic self protection; **The Bridget Healing Centre** (☎01458 833317, ⓦbridgethealingcentre.co.uk) for reflexology and Reiki healing; or **The Goddess Temple** (☎01458 831518, ⓦgoddesstemple.co.uk), for worshipping the Divine Feminine (Dan Brown would have a field day), and whose Goddess Hall, behind St Benedict's Church, runs regular drop-in healing days. Only the truly committed, though, sign up for their Priestess of Avalon training, an in-depth course that takes around three years to complete.

legends – including Gog and Magog, the "Oaks of Avalon", which were once part of a Druidic avenue – with the guys behind the Gothic Image Bookshop at 7 High St (£70, much cheaper if you can get a few people together, entrance fees to the abbey are extra; 2hr 30min; ☎01458 831281, ⓦgothicimagetours.co.uk).

ACCOMMODATION

★ **Chalice Hill House** Dod Lane ☎01458 830828, ⓦchalicehill.co.uk. Handsome from the outside and even more dramatic within, this gorgeous Georgian manor has three individually styled en suites, including the Oak Room, a twin with beautifully carved beds, and the wonderfully light Sun and Moon Room. Breakfast is served in the grand dining room or, in summer, a Rajasthani-style tent in the sweeping grounds. **£100**

George & Pilgrims 1 High St ☎01458 831146, ⓦrelaxinnz.co.uk. Built by Abbot Selwood in the fifteenth century, this oak-panelled inn brims with medieval atmosphere, though unless you go for a frilly four-poster (£110) – from one of which Henry VIII is rumoured to have watched the abbey burn – the rooms themselves are less characterful than the public areas downstairs. **£85**

Glastonbury Backpackers 4 Market Place ☎01458 833353, ⓦglastonburybackpackers.com. Centrally located former coaching inn (it's in *The Crown*) with lively bar (regular drinks promos and live sport on the big screen), kitchen, pool table, internet access and no curfew. Advance booking recommended. Dorms **£16.50**, doubles **£45**

Magdalene House Magdalene St ☎01458 830202, ⓦmagdalenehouseglastonbury.com. Grade II-listed former convent directly opposite the abbey, whose three stylish but homely rooms (one with views over the abbey itself, the others to Wearyall Hill) make a great place to retreat to at the end of the day. Comfy beds and a generous breakfast. No children under 3. **£80**

Meadow Barn Middlewick Farm, Wick Lane ☎01458 832351, ⓦmiddlewickholidaycottages.co.uk. The best of ten self-catering cottages converted from old outbuildings on a farm a few miles down the A361 from Glastonbury. Stone walls, oak floors and a wood burner set the scene (helped by the lovely rural views), and there's also an indoor pool and steam room on site, plus a resident therapist (Swedish massage from £40 for 1hr). Sleeps four. Minimum 3nt stay, longer in July & Aug. **£115**

Street YHA The Chalet, Ivythorn Hill, Street ☎0845 371 9143, ⓦyha.org.uk. Quirky Swiss-chalet-style accommodation a couple of miles south of Glastonbury (bus #29 or #377; alight at Marshall's Elm crossroads and follow signs), with brightly decorated rooms – three- to six- bed dorms, plus a few family rooms – and a kid-friendly attitude. Camping pitches also available. Dorms **£17.40**

White House 21 Manor House Rd ☎01458 830886, ⓦtheglastonburywhitehouse.com. Lovely B&B with just two en-suite rooms, one with a king-size bed and rolltop bath. Everything is eco-friendly and organic, including the optional veggie breakfast (£5–7) – which can be served in your room and is well worth taking. Aromatherapy and reflexology treatments are available for guests of the Master Bedroom (from £35), and there's free internet access. No credit cards. **£60**

The Yew Tree Church Farm, School Lane, Compton Dundon, four miles south of Glastonbury ☎01458 274891, ⓦyewtreebnb.co.uk. Four stylish doubles occupying a cream stone annexe off the main farmhouse – it's all very nicely done, with a touch of chic throughout, particularly in the first-floor loft apartment (£100). Breakfast served until 11am is an added bonus. Picnic hampers available on request. No credit cards. **£69**

CAMPSITE

The Isle of Avalon Godney Rd ☎01458 833618; map p.178. Clean, friendly campsite, a 10min walk

GLASTONBURY FESTIVAL

Glastonbury Festival takes place most years over four days in late June, with happy campers braving the predictable mudfest at Worthy Farm, outside Pilton, six miles east of Glastonbury itself – some locals refer to it, perhaps more accurately, as the Pilton Pop Festival. Having started in the 1970s, "Glastonbury" has become the biggest and best-organized festival in the country, without shedding too much of its alternative feel. Much more than just a music festival, large parts of the sprawling site are given over to themed "lifestyle" areas, from the meditation marquees of Green Fields to campfire-filled Strummerville and futuristic Arcadia. Bands cover all musical spectrums, from up-and-coming indie groups to international superstars – recent headliners have included U2, Coldplay and Beyoncé, while more eccentric acts, such as Rolf Harris and his wobble board, often make an appearance. Despite the steep price (£195), tickets are invariably snapped up within hours of going on sale around October of the previous year. The next festival takes place in 2013; for tickets and general information, see ⓦ glastonburyfestivals.co.uk.

from Northload Street and within sight of the Tor. The pitches are spacious and there's a well-stocked shop, plus decent washing facilities and a freezer for cool-box ice-packs. **£12**

EATING AND DRINKING

Blue Note Café 4 High St ☎ 01458 832907. A relaxed place to hang out over inexpensive coffees and cakes or such satisfying veggie bites as halloumi burgers and falafel (mains from £5). It backs on to The Glastonbury Experience (see box, p.174), with some seating in the shared courtyard. Daily 9am–5pm.

★ **Hawthorns** 8 Northload St ☎ 01458 831255, ⓦ hawthornshotel.com. Homely bar and restaurant whose big draw is its eclectic menu, including a lunchtime curry buffet, a regional Curry Night (Thurs; £12.45) and other globetrotting specials, from Iraqi *murag* to Brazilian *xinxin* (£12.50). Lunch Thurs–Sun noon–2.30pm, dinner Mon–Thurs 6.30–9.30pm, Fri & Sat 6.30–10pm.

Hundred Monkeys 52 High St ☎ 01458 833386. Mellow contemporary café-restaurant whose wholesome snacks include a renowned seafood soup, as well as gourmet spelt sarnies (from £6) and varied salads (from £9). Try one of their thirty different varieties of tea with a home-made cookie. Mon, Tues & Thurs 10am–8pm, Wed 10am–4pm, Fri & Sat 10am–9pm, Sun 11am–4pm.

King Arthur 31–33 Benedict St ☎ 01458 831442. Wood-floored freehouse near St Benedict's Church, open for breakfast and lunch (pies, burgers and home-made pizza; £4.95) and running live-music nights on Thursdays and most weekends. Drinks are reassuringly local: beer from Glastonbury Ales, cider from Wilkins. Mon–Wed 10am–3pm & 5–11pm, Thurs & Fri 10am–3pm & 5pm–midnight, Sat 10am–midnight, Sun noon–midnight.

Mocha Berry 14 Market Place ☎ 01458 832149. Small café with a buzzy feel, right in the heart of Market Place, serving up traditional grub such as sausage and mash, and bubble and squeak for around £6. Daily 9.30am–6pm, Sun till 5pm.

★ **Rainbows End Café** 17A High St ☎ 01458 833896. Classic Glastonbury café, accessed down a narrow arcade and through a vintage clothes shop. Very laidback and very appealing, serving huge wedges of cheese and broccoli quiche, shepherd's pie, mezze and other assorted mains (around £7), topped up with heaps of unusual salads (£1.25 a pop). Cute garden out back. Daily 10am–4pm.

Who'd a Thought It 17 Northload St ☎ 01458 834460. Quirkily decorated place with garden, serving solid pub grub for lunch (pork and herb meatballs, Ploughman's Lunch) and more adventurous dishes in the evening, including sesame-coated duck leg and Cornish mussels (mains around £9). Daily noon–2pm & 6–9pm, Sat & Sun till 9.30pm.

ENTERTAINMENT

The Assembly Rooms High St ☎ 01458 834677, ⓦ assemblyrooms.org.uk. Regular talks and musical and theatrical performances.

Chalice Well Chilkwell St ☎ 01458 831154, ⓦ chalicewell.org.uk. Various events, healings and workshops throughout the year.

Glastonbury Abbey ☎ 01458 832267, ⓦ glaston buryabbey.com. Big-name concerts, miracle plays and exhibitions staged in the abbey grounds.

DIRECTORY

Banks Several on the High Street, including a Lloyds, and a Barclays further up towards Chilkwell Street.
Internet The Assembly Rooms (Tues–Sat noon–6pm; 50p for 15min), or Glastonbury TIC (£1 for 15min).
Markets There's a small monthly farmers' market in the

car park behind St John the Baptist (last Sat of the month 9am–1pm) and a weekly artists' market at the Assembly Rooms (Tues 11am–4pm).
Post office At the eastern end of the High Street (Mon–Fri 9am–5.30pm, Sat 9am–1pm).

The Somerset Levels

Stretching over 250 square miles from the Mendips to the Quantocks, the vast marshy flatness of the **SOMERSET LEVELS** is a region apart: sparsely populated, flooded in winter and characterized by the silvery fingers of **rhynes** that chase the horizons. The natural area of the **Somerset Levels and Moors** (to give them their full, seldom-used, title) is defined by a huge basin, marked in the east by a zigzagging depression that runs between Nailsea, Weston-super-Mare, Cheddar, Glastonbury and Langport, and to the west by the Bristol Channel. The "**Levels**" part refers to the clay areas along the coast; the peat-heavy, lower-lying area inland that makes up most of the region covered in this chapter is technically the "**Moors**" but is almost never referred to as such.

The Levels were created – and the area given its crazy-quilt pattern – in the eighteenth and nineteenth centuries, when the River Brue was irrigated and the fields were drained for peat-digging and enclosed for farming; this system of "wet fencing" is still in use today, though the government is intent on phasing out peat extraction completely by 2030. The result is a highly distinctive landscape, at its most evocative around the old peat workings of the mist-draped **Avalon Marshes**, which are being carefully converted into a series of terrific nature reserves. There are a few breaks in the flatness, most obviously at **Burrow Mump**, where the views are understandably stellar, but also at elevated outcrops like the **Isle of Wedmore** and the **Isle of Athelney**, which were once islands "surrounded on all sides by very great, swampy and impenetrable marshes". In some cases, you can plot the lie of the land simply by the names on a map: villages containing the word "zoy" (such as **Westonzoyland**, where the Duke of Monmouth's

---

4

> ### BIRD-WATCHING ON THE LEVELS
>
> One of the most important wetlands in the world, the waterlogged expanse of the Somerset Levels is simply *the* best place in the country for inland **bird-watching**, its dykes and ditches, seasonal lakes and sodden fields providing a vast haven for countless bird species, their numbers ebbing and flowing with the changing of the seasons. A network of excellent **nature reserves** (five in the Avalon Marshes alone) not only preserves their habitat but in many cases has extended it, returning abandoned peat workings and former farmland back into flooded meadows or boggy mire.
>
> Spring and early summer are the **best times** for birding in the Levels: the vegetation isn't too thick, the courtship season is in full swing, and you can see stellar species such as hobby at **Shapwick Moor** (see p.180), marsh harrier at **Catcott** (see p.180) and the rare bittern at **High Ham** (see p.179). In April and May, herons and their young gather in the treetops of Swell Wood at **West Sedgemoor** (see p.185), and you may even catch a glimpse of a recently reintroduced **crane** (see box, p.183). Winter, though, can be equally rewarding, with migrants from Northern and Eastern Europe holing up in the waters here. Wildfowl are abundant, and you'll probably see hen harriers at **Greylake** (see p.182), but the big event is the arrival of the **starlings** in November (see box, p.180); although their major roosting sites vary from year to year, **Westhay Moor** (see p.180) is more often than not *the* place to be.
>
> You'll be able to tick off a fair few species with just a pair of binoculars, a field guide and a bit of patience, but you'll get much more out of birding here if you can tell your warblers from your widgeons – check the relevant reserve websites for details of **guided walks** and bird-watching introductions throughout the year.

attempted rebellion was emphatically crushed at the **Battle of Sedgemoor**) were also formerly islands, as were places ending in "ey" – **Muchelney**, for example, is Anglo-Saxon for "Great Island", an obvious setting for a religious building on the scale of **Muchelney Abbey**.

Perhaps as a result of the demands such a landscape places on its populace, the area remains one of Somerset's most traditional. Eels are still fished from the Parrett using hand-held dip-nets, as they have been for centuries, and withies harvested by hook and trussed into bundles for use at basket-making workshops like the one at the **Willows and Wetlands Centre** in Stoke St Gregory. The local importance of this time-honoured industry, a quintessentially Somerset craft, was recognized in 2001 with Serena de la Hey's 40ft-tall **Willow Man**: chest puffed, pointy arms outstretched as he strides beside the M5 near Bridgwater, the wicker figure has become something of an *Angel of the South*.

The Avalon Marshes

The curve of the A39 around Glastonbury effectively marks the eastern boundary of the **Avalon Marshes**, a broad wedge of wetlands rich in wildlife and currently conserved in a patchwork of **nature reserves** that stretches for several miles to the west. Cut through by forgotten roads edged with the occasional pile of freshly dug peat, it's a quite magical landscape, at its most beguiling in the first rays of sunlight, when cotton-budded wisps of mist hang lazily above the waters.

The area's few scattered villages are set on higher ground, either on the **Polden Hills**, which cut the Levels cleanly in half, or on what were once "islands" within the marshes themselves. Nearly six thousand years ago, when this low-lying area was under water,

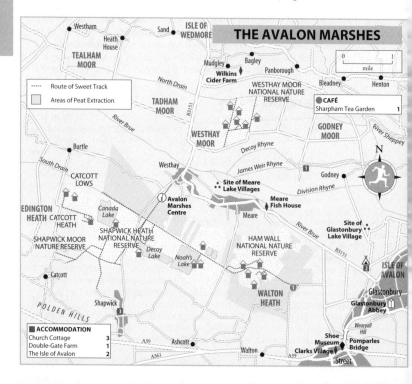

Neolithic man fashioned some of Europe's first **wooden walkways** to connect the communities at Westhay, Burtle and the Isle of Wedmore (see box below); the "**lake villages**" that were later established near Glastonbury and Meare remain the best-preserved prehistoric villages ever discovered in the UK.

Meare Fish House

Key available at any reasonable time from Manor House Farm, 350 yds up the road, just behind the church and visible from the Fish House itself • Free • ⓦ english-heritage.org.uk

The B3151 shadows a rhyne for 3.5 miles west of Glastonbury to the strung-out village of Meare, where the **Meare Fish House** once provided a bounty of roach and pike for the monks of Glastonbury Abbey. Built in 1330 by Abbot Adam of Sodbury (whose figure stands above the front door of the nearby Manor House), it was gutted by a fire in the nineteenth century but remains the only surviving monastic fishery building in England, with a central storage area, used for drying and salting fish, and an upstairs bedroom where the abbot's water bailiff slept. Up to 25,000 fish and 5000 eels were netted each year in a vast **pool** – the "mere" that gives the village its name – which stretched for four miles beyond what is now the River Brue.

Shapwick Heath National Nature Reserve

Entrances on the Meare–Ashcott and Westhay–Shapwick roads • Daily dawn–dusk • Free • ☎ 01458 860120, ⓦ www.naturalengland .org.uk

The former commercial peat bogs of **Shapwick Heath National Nature Reserve**, four miles west of Glastonbury, make up the largest reserve in the Somerset Levels, its trails cutting through a variety of hay meadow, reedbed and marshy fen. Together with adjacent Ham Wall (see below), Shapwick forms a near-unbroken block of superb birding country: it's home to over sixty species of **birds**, including marsh harriers, lapwing and water rail, easiest to see around the open waters of Noah's Lake and Canada Lake, as the woodland enclosing the meadows gives that part of the reserve a much denser feel.

The otherwise elusive **otter** is common here, and you've got a very good chance of spotting one from the lakeside hides in the early morning. Look out, too, for the unusual **hairy dragonfly**, a chunky insect with a furry thorax.

Ham Wall National Nature Reserve

Entrances on the Meare–Ashcott road and from Sharpham village • Daily dawn–dusk • Free • ☎ 01458 860494, ⓦ rspb.org.uk/hamwall

Directly opposite the eastern entrance to Shapwick Heath, the more compact **Ham Wall National Nature Reserve** is a good place to spy great-crested grebes and kingfishers feeding among the ribbed reedbeds of Walton Heath and Loxton's Marsh, which vibrate with the rasping croak of **marsh frogs** in summer. Its most prized resident, however, is the **bittern**. Thanks to some sterling conservation work (in the mid-1990s, only eleven males were left in the whole of the UK), Ham Wall now hosts the country's

---

THE SWEET TRACK

One of the oldest roads in Europe lies hidden a few feet beneath Shapwick: the **Sweet Track**, a timber routeway built in 3806 BC to cross the mile or so of marsh that lay between the Polden Hills and Westhay. Named after Ray Sweet, who discovered it in 1970, the walkway was made by driving pairs of slanted stakes diagonally into the ground and then resting oak planks on the resulting V-shaped cradle; about 500m of the track is preserved today, buried in the peat under a boggy trail to keep it from drying out and ultimately disintegrating.

The Sweet Track – the most famous of at least thirty separate ancient tracks that cut through the Levels – was believed to be the oldest in Britain until another wooden walkway (the **Post Track**) was discovered beneath it, whose timber predated it by just thirty years. The Post Track itself lost that title when a causeway dating from around 4100 BC was unearthed in the grounds of London's Belmarsh Prison in 2009, eclipsing them both by a good 250 years.

largest breeding population of this cautious bird, but even here they can be difficult to spot, so well do they blend in with the surrounding reeds – their fog-horn "boom", though, is a familiar sound in spring, and can be heard up to a mile away.

Shapwick Moor Nature Reserve

Entrance on the Meare–Ashcott road; also accessed via a trail from the Canada Lake hide in Shapwick Heath National Nature Reserve • Daily dawn–dusk • Free • ☎ 01761 490458, ⓦ hawkandowl.org/shapwickhome

Since 2007, acres of former arable land at the southwestern fringe of Shapwick Heath have slowly been returning to their natural state in order to create **Shapwick Moor Nature Reserve**, one of only three in the country to cater specifically to **birds of prey**. Three trails cross the rhynes at present, on which you might see barn owls, buzzards, kestrels or (in summer) hobbies; the tussocked ridge of grass that parallels the reserve's southern boundary is a good place to spot sparrowhawks hunting for bullfinches.

Catcott Complex

Entrance on the Burtle–Catcott road • Daily dawn–dusk • Free • ☎ 01823 652400, ⓦ somersetwildlife.org/catcott.html

Two reserves make up the **Catcott Complex**: the wet meadows of **Catcott Lows** – which, as the name implies, occupies one of the lowest parts of the Brue Valley – and the more varied habitat of **Catcott Heath**, to the southeast. The seasonal changes at Catcott are perhaps even more defined than those of its neighbours, the wafting summer grasslands here deep under water come winter.

There are only two hides in the Lows (and one on the Heath), but you might still catch sight of a **whimbrel**, or pick out the distinctive "ping" of a **bearded tit**. Panicky **water voles** are also sometimes seen, though that often amounts to little more than a quick glimpse of fur as the startled critter scurries across the drove in front of you and hurls itself into the nearest rhyne.

Westhay Moor National Nature Reserve

Entrance on the Westhay–Godney road, signed off the B3151 between Westhay and Wedmore • Daily dawn–dusk • Free • ☎ 01823 652400, ⓦ somersetwildlife.org/westhay_moor.html

The flagship **Westhay Moor National Nature Reserve** is something of a celebrity in the bird-watching world: old-time twitchers whisper its name in reverential tones and Chris Packham and Kate Humble are regulars down here, scanning the skies for their seasonal series on the BBC. Even for the uninitiated, Westhay can be quite enchanting, especially in summer, when the sun glints off the pools and the dried reeds crackle in the breeze; it's in winter, though, that the reserve really comes into its own, when the skies literally darken with millions of **starlings** returning to the reedbeds to roost (see box below). There are six hides to watch the action from, including one perched on its own island and another up an atmospheric rickety tower, with views across the bulrushes.

MURMUR ON THE DENSE MOOR

Seeing a couple of **starlings** squabbling in your back garden might not be the most thrilling of wildlife encounters, but watching millions of them come together in an orchestrated swarm above the Somerset Levels is one of Britain's great natural spectacles. From November to February each year, the starlings gather together in great cacophonous clouds (known as a **murmuration**), swirling back and forth before darting down to roost between the reeds. Local populations are swollen by migrants from as far afield as Eastern Europe and Russia, with half a dozen or more birds often clinging to a single reed.

The best places to see this phenomenon are usually **Westhay Moor** or **Ham Wall** and **Shapwick Heath**, but check the **Starling Hotline** (☎ 07866 554142) to find out exactly where they're roosting. And wait for sunny weather – the birds go straight to roost on rainy days.

CIDER ON THE EDGE

Up on the Isle of Wedmore's southern edge, **Roger Wilkins** has been making cider at his suitably named Lands End Farm for nearly sixty years. More than a local legend, his simple attitude to the apple – pick it, press it, taste it, sell it – has seen him become one of the best-known traditional cider-makers in the country. Stop by his cider barn (daily 10am–8pm, Sun till 1pm; ☎01934 712385, ⓦwilkinscider.com) for a (generous) tasting or two: no fuss, no frills, just good old-fashioned farmhouse cider from a barrel (from £2.10 for one litre up to £34 for five gallons).

ARRIVAL AND DEPARTURE   **THE AVALON MARSHES**

By bus From Glastonbury, the regular #375 to Bridgwater runs via Ashcott (for Shapwick Heath and Ham Wall; 20min) and Catcott (for the Catcott Complex; 30min), while the #29 to Taunton (12 daily) also passes Ashcott (20min).
By bike National Cycle Route 3 traces the old Somerset and Dorset Railway through Shapwick Heath and Ham Wall.

INFORMATION

Avalon Marshes Centre On the road between Westhay and Shapwick (daily 9am–5pm; ☎01458 860120, ⓦwww.naturalengland.org.uk). The Natural England office has displays on local nature and information on events and activities in the reserves, particularly at Shapwick Heath; there's also a shop selling traditional Somerset crafts (from 10am). It is hoped that the old Peat Moors Centre here will have reopened by 2013.

ACCOMMODATION AND EATING

Church Cottage Station Rd, Shapwick ☎01458 210904, ⓦchurchcottageshapwick.co.uk. Reassuringly stereotypical stone cottage, dating back four centuries, with flagstone floors, a huge inglenook fireplace and plenty of fresh flowers about the place. Only two (smart) doubles, one of which is in the "potting shed" in the lovely garden (£85, min 2nt stay), so advanced booking recommended. The friendly owner bakes fresh bread for breakfast. **£70**
Double-Gate Farm Godney, near the Sheppey Inn ☎01458 832217, ⓦdoublegatefarm.com. Traditional farmhouse offering traditional B&B: cute rooms, a communal lounge and a generous breakfast spread (sausage, kippers, pancakes) that will set you up for the day. Free wi-fi, and a well-equipped games room with snooker and table tennis. Accessible riverside rooms (£100) would also suit families. **£70**
Sharpham Tea Garden Sunnyview, Sharpham ☎01458 442050. What is essentially a garden shed provides the perfect pit-stop for a cream tea and cake after a walk in nearby Ham Wall, though they also serve breakfast (Wed–Sat 10am–noon) and baguettes, as well as home-made curries. Sunday roasts and Bank Holiday BBQs. April–Oct Wed–Sun 10am–5pm; Nov to mid-Dec & early Feb–March Wed–Fri 11am–4pm, Sat & Sun 10am–4.30pm.

Westonzoyland and around

The biggest village hereabouts, **WESTONZOYLAND** lies at the westerly end of what was once an island in a sea of peaty marsh – with Middlezoy and Chedzoy to the east. It secured its place in the annals of English history on July 6, 1685, when the Duke of Monmouth's rag-tag rebels were routed by James II's Royal Army in the fields a few hundred yards to the north: the **Battle of Sedgemoor** turned out to be the last fought on English soil.

St Mary's Church
Main Rd • Free

After the Battle of Sedgemoor, some five hundred rebel prisoners were held in central **St Mary's Church** while they awaited trial and, more often than not, punishment at the end of a rope, a particularly severe retribution that came to be known as the **Bloody Assizes** (see box, p.218). The church, notable for its fine timber roof, features displays on the battle and a painstakingly crafted diorama showing a chastened Monmouth fleeing from the battlefield.

The Sedgemoor Inn
19 Main Rd • Mon 6–11pm, Tues–Thurs noon–2.30pm & 5–11pm, Fri & Sat noon–11pm, Sun noon–10.30pm • ☎01278 691382

Rich in battle lore, the **Sedgemoor Inn**, just down the road from St Mary's Church, hosted Lord Faversham, commander of the Royal Army, the night before Monmouth's

THE BATTLE OF SEDGEMOOR

Cornered at Bridgwater, his rebellion in tatters (see box, p.218), the **Duke of Monmouth**'s only hope of escape lay in taking the fight to the Royal Army, camped outside **Westonzoyland**, five miles to the southeast. But only in an ambush, and at night, when the greater size of Monmouth's forces might just outweigh their inferior organization and experience. Monmouth's guide lost his way trying to lead the rebels across **Langmore Rhine**, the alarm was sounded and the Royal Army – although outnumbered – drove them back into the cornfields around **Chedzoy**, slaughtering them as they went. Nearly 1300 of the 3500-strong rebel force were killed.

Some of the rebels escaped, including Monmouth (and a certain Daniel Defoe, who had joined the rebellion with a few of his old colleagues from Morton's Academy for Dissenters in London – most of whom were not so lucky). Monmouth himself was captured in a field in Hampshire two days later and beheaded in London on July 15. His hapless executioner, **Jack Ketch** – who famously delivered five blows with his axe, asked for help from the crowds and then had to finish the job with his knife – is remembered as the Hangman in Punch and Judy shows throughout the land.

attack, and was a popular drinking den for Royalist troops – the stone on the left-hand side of the fireplace was allegedly used to sharpen their swords. You can sup on a pint (see opposite) amid a wealth of "memorabilia", including a *List of Rebels*, which details the four hundred or so men who were subsequently executed and hung from gibbets throughout the West Country.

The Battle of Sedgemoor Memorial

Information panels around Westonzoyland culminate in a **memorial** in the middle of the battlefield (now farmers' fields and a series of grass-lined droves), dedicated to those who, "doing the right as they gave it", were killed on July 6, 1685, executed, or later transported as slaves to the West Indies. To reach the battlefield, head up Standards Road, on the corner by the post office, then turn right into Broadstone and right again into Kings Drive; after half a mile, a drove on the left leads to the memorial.

Westonzoyland Pumping Station

Hoopers Lane, signed from Westonzoyland • Sun 1–5pm, in steam first Sun of the month from April to Nov • £3, children £2; steam days £5/2.50 • ☎ 01275 472385, ⓦ wzlet.org

Standing on the banks of the River Parrett just southwest of Westonzoyland, the red-brick chimney that's visible for miles around houses Somerset's first steam-driven pumping station. Now the Soviet-sounding **Westonzoyland Pumping Station Museum of Steam Power and Land Drainage**, the station was built in 1830 when Westonzoyland became part of a Parliament-instigated "drainage district", set up to try and stem the perpetual problem of flooding. The station is still home to the old racing-green Easton Amos drainage machine that served the area until its closure in 1951, as well as a large collection of various other steam engines – the best time to visit is when the Easton is "in steam", when it's quite literally all hands to the pump.

Greylake Nature Reserve

Signed off the A361 between Greinton and Othery • Daily dawn–dusk • Free • ☎ 01458 252346, ⓦ rspb.org.uk

Like Shapwick Moor to the north, **Greylake Nature Reserve** was arable farmland not so long ago, and the gradual reversion of this small wildlife sanctuary into seasonally flooded marshes, fringing reedbeds and water-filled "scrapes" has provided the ideal habitat for a host of waders and other wildfowl. A short (accessible) boardwalk leads to the comfy modern hide, where you're likely to tick off lapwing and snipe, yellow wagtail and maybe even a crane or two.

THE GREAT CRANE PROJECT

In the autumn of 2010, 21 **cranes** were released into the protected environment of the Somerset Levels after an absence of nearly 400 years, the first part of a major project (W thegreatcraneproject.org.uk) to re-establish this graceful waterbird back into Britain's wetlands. Most **sightings** so far have been made in an area northeast of Langport, between the A372 and Stathe, though the odd crane has turned up at Greylake; as more birds are released (around twenty each year until 2015, by which time the first batch are due to be nesting), their distribution should spread further afield. The chicks are initially reared at a "Crane School" at Slimbridge Wetlands Centre, 26 miles north of Bristol, then acclimatized on the Levels before being set free, aged around five months. Incidentally, if the bird you've got lined up in your binoculars is flying on its own, with its neck bent, then it's actually a heron. Not that the folks back home would ever know…

Burrow Mump and King Alfred's Monument

Rising up by the side of the A361 at Burrowbridge, just before it crosses the River Parrett, **Burrow Mump** looks much like a miniature Glastonbury Tor, a conical hill topped by a ruined church of St Michael – though unlike the Tor, not one that you can venture inside. Burrow Mump translates as "Hill Hill", an emphasis that's easy to understand after making the short walk to the top, such are the views of pancake-flat farmland for miles around.

The mump acted as an outpost of the nearby fort at the Isle of Athelney, now **Athelney Hill**, at the end of the ninth century. King Alfred is said to have sheltered here from the Danes in 878 (it was in the Athelney marshes that he famously burnt his cakes), before repelling them at the Battle of Ethandun and signing the subsequent peace treaty that effectively saved the Anglo-Saxon kingdom of Wessex. A **monument** to Alfred on the hill (now private land) marks the site of the abbey he founded in thanks.

4

Willows and Wetlands Visitor Centre

Meare Green Court, Stoke St Gregory **Visitor centre** Mon–Sat 9.30am–5.30pm; café 10.30am–4.30pm • Free **Guided tours** Mon–Fri 11am & 2.30pm • £3, under-5s free • ☎ 01823 490249, W englishwillowbaskets.co.uk

The countryside around Stoke St Gregory, south of Athelney, is prime willow-growing territory, perfect fodder for a deeply traditional Somerset skill that you can explore in more depth at the engaging **Willows and Wetlands Visitor Centre**. The Coates family have been growing willow here since 1819 and teasing it into baskets for almost as long. There's an **exhibition** on the history of the industry, and their **museum** – containing wicker beehives, eel traps (known as kypes), a child's potty and a coffin among others – is well worth a wander. Try and coincide your visit with one of their hour-long **tours** where you get to watch the experts at work, deftly twining and weaving the withy sticks into a range of log baskets, picnic hampers and desk tidies ready for the on-site **shop**.

ARRIVAL AND DEPARTURE

By bus The #29 from Glastonbury to Taunton (12 daily) runs via Burrowbridge (for Burrow Mump; 35min), while #51 from Taunton (6 daily) passes North Curry (20min) and Athelney Bridge (25min) on its way to Stoke St Gregory

WESTONZOYLAND AND AROUND

(35min). From Westonzoyland, buses run to and from: Bridgwater (#16; 6 daily; 10min), Langport (#16; 6 daily; 20min) and Huish Episcopi (#16; 2 daily; 25min).

ACCOMMODATION AND EATING

North Curry Community Coffee Shop The Pavement, North Curry ☎ 01823 490191. Welcoming café-cum-craft-shop at the western end of North Curry, serving home-made soup, cakes, and, of course, coffee. Tues–Sun 10am–5pm.
Rose and Crown Woodhill, Stoke St Gregory ☎ 01823 490296, W browningpubs.com. Light, airy modern-looking place, completely renovated after a fire, with three simple but

pretty en-suite rooms decked in bright cushions and comfy throws. Good food at the downstairs pub includes crispy pressed Somerset pork belly with spiced apple and gravy (mains from £8.75). Keen single rates. **£85**
Sedgemoor Inn 19 Main Rd, Westonzoyland ☎ 01278 691382. Historic boozer that played a central role in the Battle of Sedgemoor and is now decorated with tidbits

from the time, including a proclamation from the King rewarding £5000 for "whoever shall bring in the *perfon* of James, Duke of Monmouth". Rotating local ales and a skittle alley out the back. Mon 6–11pm, Tues–Thurs noon–2.30pm & 5–11pm, Fri & Sat noon–11pm, Su noon–10.30pm.

Langport and around

The self-proclaimed "heart" of the Somerset Levels, **LANGPORT** fans out from a nook in the languid River Parrett, broadened here by its tributaries, the Sowy, Isle and Yeo, either side of town. Focused around the neat strip of houses that fall back from central Bow Street, today's town seems a world away from the busy river port that once operated its own customs house and needed a good twenty inns to cater for the number of crews that ran barges here from Bridgwater.

The town was torched by retreating royalists after the **Battle of Langport** in 1645, and a short stroll up the hill from central Cheapside will tick off the two main sights. Langport's real appeal, however, lies in its location: there's pleasant walking in the surrounding countryside – you can follow the bucolic **River Parrett Trail** (see box, p.208) two miles south to the medieval ruins of **Muchelney Abbey** – a smattering of fine traditional **pubs** and a fantastic little **smokery**.

All Saints Church
The Hill • Daily 10am–2pm, key available from Langport Information Centre (see p.186) • Free

Crowning the top of the steep hill that slopes up from Cheapside, disused **All Saints Church** is decorated with contorted gargoyles (known locally as "hunky punks") and, in its glorious east window, houses the finest collection of medieval stained glass in Somerset, some remarkably well-preserved fifteenth-century work that depicts Joseph of Arimathea and other saints.

The Hanging Chapel
Just beyond All Saints Church, bridging the road down to Muchelney, the distinctive **Hanging Chapel** is set on top of a fourteenth-century gateway that was once part of Langport's old town wall; the chapel is now home – as the square and compasses on the wall outside testify – to a Masonic lodge.

Muchelney Abbey and around
Muchelney • Daily: April–June & Sept 10am–5pm; July & Aug 10am–6pm; Oct 10am–4pm • £4.20, under-15s £2.50, under-5s free; EH • ☏ 01458 250664, 🌐 www.english-heritage.org.uk/muchelney

The teeny village of **MUCHELNEY**, two miles south of Langport, punches way above its diminutive weight. Within a few yards, it has some of the finest medieval buildings in the area: an unusual priest's house, a distinctive parish church and the atmospheric ruins of Benedictine **Muchelney Abbey**, second only to Glastonbury until Henry VIII flattened it in the 1530s. It was founded in 939 by Athelstone on the remains of a Saxon church but mostly dates to the mid-twelfth century – start in the **south cloisters**, one of only three sections to survive the Dissolution, where exhibitions chart the story of the abbey and the well-preserved Abbot's House.

The Abbot's House
Just inside the **Abbot's House**, characterfully worn steps lead up to the lodge's late fifteenth-century **Abbot's Great Chamber**. The intricately carved grapes hanging from the lion-topped medieval fireplace denote its use as a room for entertaining, while the small but beautifully rich stained glass – which bears the signature of former abbot Thomas Broke – is an indication of the abbey's wealth. The expensive white oak beams here hint at the lodge's esteem, an impression further enhanced in the **Painted Chamber** next door, where the pomegranates on the wall and the barrel-vaulted ceiling depict the coat of arms of Catherine of Aragon, and the spider-like symbols (actually ermine)

epresent the king. The adjoining **East Room** has a patch of very faded wall painting, hough it's still possible to get an idea of its quality.

Downstairs, the thirteenth- and fourteenth-century **kitchens**, once one room – look up between the two to see the blackened chimney soaring towards the open sky – lead o the **Stewards Room**, accessed via an impressive medieval door, and a display of ornamental gargoyles (or "hunky punks") carved in local hamstone.

Outside the Abbots' House, and originally joined to the abbey, the thatched **reredorter** (monastic latrine) is the most complete example of its kind in the country; it was built in 1256 and still clearly features the close-knit cubicles that the monks once lined up in, cheek by jowl.

Church of St Peter and St Paul
Muchelney • Tea served April–Sept Sun from 2.30pm • Free

Though just yards from the ruins of Muchelney Abbey, the village's **Church of St Peter and Paul** fares well in comparison, thanks mostly to its incredible painted Jacobean ceiling, each panel bursting with bare-chested angels and arch-winged cherubs. The church, unusually, was built by the abbey and now houses some of its earliest decorated tiles, moved here from the Lady Chapel and relaid around the altar. They date back to the twelfth century but are still quite vivid – look out for knights on horseback, howdah-backed elephants and, near the bottom left-hand corner of the altar, the two west towers of the abbey itself.

The Priest's House
Muchelney • Mid-March to Sept Mon & Sun 2–5pm; admission by guided tour only, last tour at 4.30pm • £3.80, children £1.90; NT • ☏ 01458 253771, Ⓦ nationaltrust.org.uk

Squatting opposite the Church of St Peter and Paul, the sweet-looking **Priest's House** was built of local blue lias stone in 1308 for Muchelney's parish priest, who certainly didn't have too far to walk to work. One of the National Trust's first projects when they requisitioned it in 1911, the medieval hall-house is now a private home; a tour of the inside reveals a huge fifteenth-century fireplace and other aspects of an interior that has barely changed in over four hundred years.

Stembridge Tower Mill
Windmill Road, High Ham **Exterior** March–Oct daily 11am–4pm • Free **Interior** Open three times a year; check website for dates • £3.80, children £1.90; NT • ☏ 01935 823289, Ⓦ nationaltrust.org.uk

Completely repointed in 2009, the bulbous stone-and-timber **Stembridge Tower Mill**, three miles north of Langport, is the archetypal Somerset flourmill. Built in 1822, its thatched roof, the last of its kind in the country, could be rotated to ensure that the sails (now bereft of canvas) could always catch the wind that whips up over High Ham; you can share the interior on certain days of the year with the long-eared and lesser horsehoe bats that now call the mill home. The pretty adjoining cottage is available as a holiday let (see p.186).

West Sedgemoor Nature Reserve
Swell Wood Daily dawn–dusk • Free **Moor** Access by guided walks in spring, summer & winter only; book well in advance during peak winter times • £4.50 • ☏ 01458 252805, Ⓦ rspb.org.uk/westsedgemoor

Few places in spring can top **West Sedgemoor Nature Reserve**, when the treetops of **Swell Wood** reverberate with the squabbling of baby grey herons in what is one of the UK's biggest heronries. Over a hundred pairs nest here, with the bristle-covered chicks emerging in early April (visible from the hide); little egret chicks follow in late May.

You're free to walk the trails and visit the hide at Swell Wood but access to the **moor** is limited to pre-booked guided walks – well worth doing, especially in winter, as these wet meadows are home to the largest population of breeding wading birds (among them lapwing, curlew and golden plover) in southern England. Alternatively, you can get good views across the meadows from the **footpath** that runs west from Curry Rivel, further up the A378 towards Langport.

ARRIVAL AND GETTING AROUND

By bus Langport has fairly decent bus connections, both to local destinations and to Yeovil and Taunton.

Destinations Bridgwater (#16 & #624; 7 daily; 30–40min); Chard (#624; Mon–Fri 7.50am; 30min); Curry Rivel (#54; 12 daily; 5min); East Lambrook (#850; Thurs 12.15pm; 30min); High Ham (for Stembridge Tower Mill; #903 Mon & Wed 4–5 daily, #850 Thurs 11.15am; 20min); Ilminster (#624; Mon–Fri 7.50am; 20min); Kingsbury Episcopi (#850; Thurs 12.15pm; 15min); Muchelney (#850; Thurs 12.15pm; 5min); Pitney (#54; 12 daily; 5min); Taunton

(#54; 12 daily; 35min); Westonzoyland (#16; 6 daily; 25min); Yeovil (#54; 12 daily; 40min).

By bike Bow Bridge Cycles at the Langport & River Parrett Visitor Centre, just over the Great Bow Bridge at the western end of Langport (Tues–Sun 10am–5pm, Oct–March till 4pm, also Mon in Easter & summer school hols ☎01458 250350), rents out bikes for 3hr (£7, children £5.50) and by the day (£10, children £7), and also has tandems, trailers and tandem wheelchair bicycles; it's an easy 1.5 miles along the Parrett Cycleway to Muchelney.

INFORMATION

Langport & River Parrett Visitor Centre Just across the Great Bow Bridge, at the western end of Langport (Tues–Sun 10am–5pm, Oct–March till 4pm, also Mon in Easter & summer school hols ☎01458 250350). Various displays on regional history, wildlife and the make-up of the Somerset Levels, plus information on local walks,

including the River Parrett Trail. Also home to a bike-rental shop (see above).

Langport Information Centre Little Bow, Bow Street (daily 9.30am–4pm; ☎01458 253527, ✉ langportinfo @btconnect.com). Helpful advice on accommodation and attractions in Langport and the surrounding area.

ACCOMMODATION

As well as the below, places listed around Martock (see p.207) and Somerton (see p.200) are also within reach, as are The Pilgrims at Lovington (see p.198) and The Yew Tree at Compton Dundon (see p.174).

Cherry Orchard Cottage Townsend, Curry Rivel, two miles southwest of Langport on the A378 ☎01458 252545, ⓦ cherryorchardcottage.com. Good, old-fashioned homely B&B filled with antiques and featuring just two (comfy) first-floor rooms, both with king-sized beds, flat-screen TVs and DVD players. Sit out in the attractive garden in summer, gather round the wood-burning stove in winter, and head down the road to the recommended Old Forge Inn for a drink at any time of the year. No credit cards. **£65**

The Devonshire Arms Long Sutton, 3.5 miles from Langport on the A372 ☎01458 241271, ⓦ thedevon shirearms.com. Slick, contemporary gastropub-with-rooms – all creams and beiges, with dark-wood furnishings (including canopied four-posters in some rooms) and wide-screen TVs. The special rates including dinner for two in the quality restaurant (see opposite) can be a good deal if you're in one of the larger, more expensive rooms. No singles Fri & Sat nights. **£85**

★ **Gypsy Caravan** Marsh Farm, Pitney, three miles from Langport on the B3153 ☎01458 270044, ⓦ gypsycaravanbreaks.co.uk. Thoroughly romantic gypsy wagon, lovingly restored and beautifully finished, set in an old cider apple orchard on a farm just outside

Pitney. You'll need a hearty supper, cooked-up over the open fire (you can stock up on organic goodies at nearby Pitney Farm Shop; see opposite), to tackle the scramble up into the bow-top bed. Don't forget the folk guitar and Tarot cards. Fri & Sat nights extra £10. Closed Nov–March. **£95**

★ **The Parsonage** Muchelney, two miles south of Langport ☎01458 259058, ⓦ parsonagesomerset.co.uk. Perfectly located for Muchelney Abbey, just 300 yards from the ruins, this top B&B ticks all the boxes: welcoming, committed owners; three simple, sweet rooms; and an inglenook fireplace so large that it's effectively another room. There's also a little library for the evenings, and four-course dinners from the Cordon Bleu-trained lady of the house (£30, £47.50 with wine). Generous breakfast includes fresh figs from the tree outside in season. Good rates for singles. **£85**

Stembridge Cottage High Ham, three miles north of Langport ☎0844 800 2070, ⓦ nationaltrust holidaycottages.co.uk. Pretty miller's cottage dating to the early 1800s, with the unusual bonus of having a windmill (see p.185) at the end of the garden path. The four bedrooms (sleeping 7) are well furnished, there's a lovely lounge with a vast inglenook fireplace, plus a smart, spacious kitchen. 3nt minimum stay (£689). **£230**

EATING AND DRINKING

In addition to the following places, it's also worth travelling a little further to enjoy a meal at The Pilgrims at Lovington (see p.198) and The Red Lion near Babcary (see p.200), or a pint at the Wyndham Arms in Kingsbury Episcopi (see p.207).

artteazen 105 Cheapside, Langport ☎01458 250635. There's art on the wall, tea on the shelves (several Tea Pig

varieties) and plenty of good karma running through this chilled-out café at the top of Langport's high street. The

EEL BE BACK: THE GREAT ELVER MIGRATION

Each spring, thousands of baby **eels** (elvers) wriggle their way up through the rhynes and ditches of the Somerset Levels, having spent the previous year drifting across the Atlantic Ocean from their breeding grounds in the Sargasso Sea near Bermuda. No one really knows why they make such a mammoth journey, only to return when fully mature, to spawn and die, or indeed what triggers the transformations on the way that take them from larvae to "glass" eel to elver. In fact, not much is known about this mysterious creature at all, other than they don't half taste good – eels have been a central Somerset delicacy for hundreds of years, covered in flour and deep-fried, cooked with bacon and served in an omelette or, best of all, smoked.

distressed-textile armchairs and benches are perfect for relaxing over a carrot and coriander soup or cold pesto pasta (£4.95), while making the most of the free wi-fi. Breakfast served till 10am, lunch noon–3pm. Mon–Sat 9am–5pm, Sun 10am–4pm.

★ **Brown & Forrest** Bowden Farm Smokery, Hambridge, four miles southwest of Langport on the B3168 ☎01458 250875, ⍵smokedeel.co.uk. Tuck into succulent Somerset eels (see box above), hot-smoked over beech (to bring out their delicate flavour) and apple wood (which gives them a mellow sweetness) and served straight from the smokery. Starters include smoked eel on rye bread and smoked trout pâté (£4.95), and mains smoked salmon steaks (£9.75), though there are no smoked puddings as yet. Add a pinch of pepper – or, for the smoked-eel aficionado, a dash of horseradish. You can pick up some vacuum-packed smoked goodies at the next-door deli. Mon–Sat 10am–4pm.

The Devonshire Arms Long Sutton, 3.5 miles from Langport on the A372 ☎01458 241271, ⍵thedevonshirearms.com. Beautiful pub – a former hunting lodge, lording it over Long Sutton green – that runs a stylish (and busy) restaurant serving original, well-presented dishes, such as Dorset crab crème brûlée and rare-breed beef chuck slowly cooked in ruby port (mains from £9.50). Relax among the scatter cushions in the bar next door with a pint of draught Moor Revival or a shot of local Somerset Cider Brandy. Daily noon–3pm & 6–11pm, Sun till 10.30pm.

The Famous Parrett Café Bow St, Langport ☎01458 251717. Popular, cheery caff, "famous" throughout Langport for its all-day breakfasts (£4.95) and thick Milkshake Mayhem, using crushed Flakes, Rolos and the like – if they haven't got the chocolate you want, they'll nip out and buy it. Serves other staples such as jackets, salads and sandwiches (around £5.50), plus a decent cup of coffee, too. Mon–Thurs 9.30am–3.30pm, Fri & Sat 9am–3.30pm.

★ **The Halfway House** Pitney Hill, Pitney, 2.5 miles northeast of Langport on the B3153 ☎01458 252513, ⍵thehalfwayhouse.co.uk. This low-lit, flagstone-floored village pub, "halfway" between Langport and Somerton, is the sort of place you'd love to call your local. Music is a no-no and there's little in the way of decor, but it oozes character, with the lengthy list of real ales – sometimes ten or more at any one time, including Butcombe, Otter Bright and Moor Beer Peat Porter – drawn from barrels out the back. Plenty of lagers, too, plus Ashton Press, Hecks, Wilkins and Gurt Dog for cider-drinkers. Big open fires and simple, honest pub grub. Mon–Sat 11.30am–3pm & 5.30–11pm (Thurs–Sat till midnight), Sun noon–3pm & 7–10.30pm.

Rose and Crown Huish Episcopi, half a mile east of Langport on the A372 ☎01458 250494. Don't be put off by the "seems to be shut" exterior. This friendly, flagstone-floored local legend – universally known as *Eli's* – is a great place for a drink, with a "walk-through" bar connecting the appealing front parlours. The range of real ales on tap includes a couple of Teignworthys, while local cider comes from nearby Burrow Hill (see p.206). One of the two back gardens has a children's play area. Mon–Thurs 5.30–11pm, Fri, Sat & Sun 11.30am–3pm & 5.30–11pm.

SHOPPING

★ **Muchelney Pottery** Muchelney, 2.5 miles south of Langport ⍵johnleachpottery.co.uk. Quality stoneware from John Leach, a master potter with over 45 years' experience, hand-crafted at his pretty thatched workshop in Muchelney. There's usually something going on – throwing, glazing or the bi-monthly firing of the kiln – plus regular exhibitions at the next-door John Leach Gallery. Phone in advance for workshop viewing. Mon–Sat 9am–1pm & 2–5pm.

★ **Pitney Farm Shop** Glebe Farm, Woodsbirds Hill Lane, Pitney, three miles northeast of Langport, off the B3153 ⍵pitneyfarmshop.co.uk. Award-winning organic farm shop selling freshly picked veg, dry-cured meats from their own herd of saddleback pigs, and home-made pies and pastries, plus Somerset cheeses, local ciders and beers, and organic fruit wines. Walk, cycle or ride your horse over here and take advantage of the five-percent "green" discount. Mon, Tues & Thurs–Sat 9am–5.30pm.

4

South Somerset

MONTACUTE VILLAGE

5

South Somerset

Staggering slowly downwards as it runs west along the border with Wiltshire,
Dorset and Devon, verdant South Somerset matches the county's rural
image more so than any other region. Rolling fields are broken by the
occasional isolated farm, while the backcountry lanes that link them are
plied by tractors loaded with hay. This is an area of hamstone hamlets and
"Honey for sale" signs, of stately homes and traditional pubs, where villages
bearing names like Haselbury Plucknett and Hardington Mandeville have
barely changed in centuries.

The region's towns developed on the back of flourishing textile trades, first wool and
then later flax, linen and lace, prosperity that endowed places like **Crewkerne**, **Bruton**
and **Ilminster** with the kind of handsome, grandiose churches that Somerset has
become famous for. There is much more appeal in wandering the streets of towns such
as **Somerton** and **Castle Cary** than there is in the bigger, more industrial sprawls of
Yeovil and **Chard**, though even these find it hard to compete with South Somerset's
glorious **hamstone villages**, made in a beautiful soft stone that glows the colour of
flapjacks. The buildings of Martock, Montacute and the "sub-Hamdons" (Stoke and
Norton) seem to soak up the sun and – in the late afternoon especially – really take
some visual beating.

Similar in size to some of the smaller villages in the region, the destination museums
of **Haynes International Motor Museum** in Sparkford and the **Fleet Air Arm Museum** at
Yeovilton hold hours of interest for younger travellers, while South Somerset's
numerous National Trust properties – from antiques-heavy **Lytes Cary Manor** to
Montacute House, the most magnificent of manor houses – will keep their parents
(and grandparents) happy for even longer.

INFORMATION

Tourist offices In addition to the local information centres listed with the towns below, there's a regional information centre at Cartgate Picnic Site, off the A303/ A3088 near Stoke-sub-Hamdon (April–Oct daily 10am–5pm; Nov–March Mon & Fri 10am–3pm; ☎01935 829333).

GETTING AROUND

By car Having your own wheels is by far the best way to see South Somerset, and the ever-present A303 – here, unlike further west, a fairly free-flowing dual carriageway – can make getting between places quicker than you might think.
By bus Numerous bus services run by Southwest Coaches (☎01963 33124, ⓦsouthwestcoaches.co.uk) connect many of the towns and villages in South Somerset, but the significant majority of them depart just one afternoon a week and will typically make dozens of stops before the one you need – a cheap way to see the region but hardly the most convenient. However, Nippy Bus (☎01935 823888, ⓦwww.nippybus.co.uk), which regularly runs between Yeovil and towns such as Ilminster, Wincanton, Castle Cary and Bruton may prove more useful, as you can book specific pick-up and/or drop-off points in advance.

A day at the races See p.195
King Arthur's Camelot? See p.196
Manors from heaven See p.199
The follies of Barwick Park See p.202
How do you like them apples? See p.204
The River Parrett Trail See p.208

BURROW HILL CIDER FARM

Highlights

1 Country cooking South Somerset is blessed with some quality places to eat – *At The Chapel*, *The Pilgrims at Lovington* and *Little Barwick House* in particular will do your palate proud. **See p.197, p.198 & p.204**

2 Montacute House A stately home worthy of the title, stuffed with fine furniture and tapestries and housing an impressive collection of paintings from the National Portrait Gallery. **See p.200**

3 Hamstone villages Nothing says South Somerset quite as much as a hamlet of houses carved from golden stone – Martock and Montacute are two of the most harmonious. **See p.200 & p.205**

4 Fleet Air Arm Museum Step inside Concorde or take a "ride" on a helicopter at this brilliant interactive aircraft museum. **See p.203**

5 Cider farms South Somerset is real cider country: work your way through the vintages at Bridge Farm, Burrow Hill and Perry's. **See p.204, p.206 & p.209**

6 River Parrett Trail Follow the Parrett as it lazily meanders for fifty bucolic miles across South Somerset and beyond. **See p.208**

7 Lord Poulett Arms The perfect marriage of relaxing bar and fine-dining restaurant, stylish bedrooms and traditional hospitality. And in one of the region's prettiest villages to boot. **See p.211**

HIGHLIGHTS ARE MARKED ON THE MAP ON PP.192–193

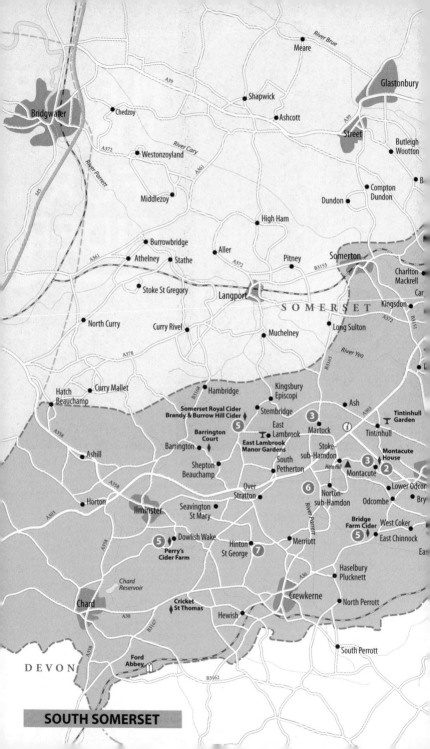

SOUTH SOMERSET

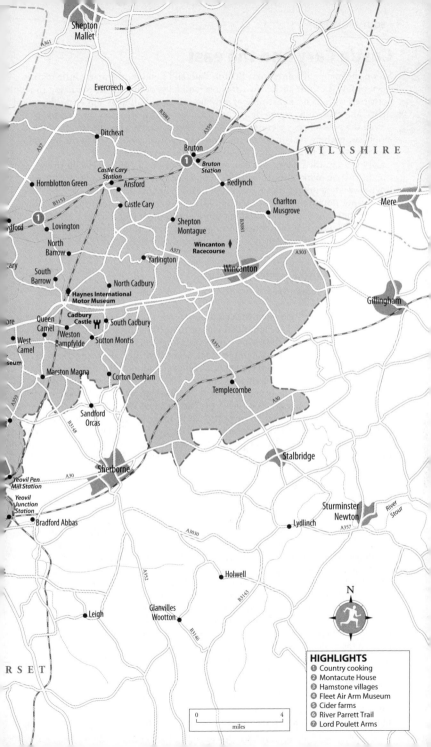

WILTSHIRE

Shepton Mallet

Evercreech

Ditcheat

Bruton

Bruton Station

Castle Cary Station

Ansford

Hornblotton Green

Castle Cary

Redlynch

Charlton Musgrove

Mere

Lovington

...dford

Shepton Montague

North Barrow

Yarlington

Wincanton Racecourse

Wincanton

...cary

South Barrow

North Cadbury

Gillingham

Haynes International Motor Museum

Cadbury Castle

Queen Camel

South Cadbury

West Camel

Weston Bampfylde

Sutton Montis

...seum

Marston Magna

Corton Denham

Templecombe

Sandford Orcas

Stalbridge

Yeovil Pen Mill Station

Sherborne

Sturminster Newton

River Stour

Yeovil Junction Station

Bradford Abbas

Lydlinch

Holwell

Leigh

Glanvilles Wootton

...R S E T

N

HIGHLIGHTS

1. Country cooking
2. Montacute House
3. Hamstone villages
4. Fleet Air Arm Museum
5. Cider farms
6. River Parrett Trail
7. Lord Poulett Arms

0   4

miles

5

Castle Cary and the east

Set on the main rail routes from Bristol, Bath and London, the pretty little market town of **CASTLE CARY** makes an attractive (and fairly authentic) introduction to South Somerset, with its neat ensemble of mustard-coloured buildings and minor historical sights, and everything set on or around the main road that snakes through town – even the post office is picturesque. "Cary" means "castle", but despite the double emphasis, nothing remains of the twelfth-century stronghold, though the hill on which it was set, to the south of town, offers pleasant enough views.

Cary was awarded its market charter by Edward IV in 1468; the stalls moved to the distinctive **Market House** in 1855, a practice that continues today with the town's weekly **market** (Tues 8.30–11.30am). Up behind Market House, the dinky pepper-pot **Round House** was used as a lock-up for a short time at the end of the eighteenth century. Several **walking routes** run through and around Cary: the local Leland Trail and the much longer Monarch's Way and Macmillan Way, the latter named after the cancer charity's founder, who was born here in 1884.

Castle Cary and District Museum

First Floor, Market House • April–Oct Mon–Fri 10.30am–12.30pm & 2–4pm, Sat 10.30am–12.30pm • Free • ☎ 01963 350680, ⓦ castlecarymuseum.org.uk

The two-floor **Castle Cary and District Museum** is most notable for its striking setting, the mid-Victorian Market House that's propped up at the front by an arch-lined colonnade, under which the town's traders used to go about their business. There's the usual assortment of agricultural implements, plus storyboards depicting the local industries of rope-making and **horsehair weaving**, a tradition that survives at John Boyd Textiles, whose work has graced Number 10 Downing Street and the White House. Displays chart the lives of local lads **Douglas Macmillan**, the founder of Macmillan Cancer Support, and the diarist **Parson James Woodforde**, whose father was vicar of Castle Cary; the diary he kept for nearly 45 years was universally uneventful but painted a (highly) detailed picture of rural clergy life in the late eighteenth century.

At the time of writing, the museum was awaiting the results of a geophysics survey on the **castle**'s hidden foundations, which should shed light on its appearance and ultimate demise – and help create its newest exhibit, a 3D "look-around" model.

Bruton

The tranquil town of **BRUTON**, four miles northeast of Castle Cary, is allegedly the smallest in England, an unhurried place cut through by the River Brue and dominated by King's School, established in 1519 and now occupying most of the town's old buildings. It's worth popping into the courtyard of **Sexey's Hospital**, an attractive quadrangle of Jacobean almshouses founded by Hugh Sexey, auditor to both Elizabeth I and James I, and into two-towered **St Mary's Church**, notable for the striking eighteenth-century Rococo plasterwork in its chancel.

Most appeal, though, lies in simply wandering. Narrow alleyways, known as "bartons", run down to the river – winding Elliott's Barton pops out at the fifteenth-century **Packhorse Bridge** – while turning up Park Road (on the left just after the railway bridge) leads to the hilltop **dovecote**, the town's most notable landmark; originally part of Bruton Abbey, it's peppered by dove holes but is more endearing from afar.

Bruton Museum

Dovecote Building, 26 High St • Mon–Fri 11am–1pm, Sat 11am–3pm, Sun 2–4pm • Free • ☎ 01749 813513

The handful of antique-looking display cases that constitute the one-room **Bruton Museum** chart the town's thousand-year history, from its Augustinian priory – long

> **A DAY AT THE RACES**
> **Horseracing** has been held at Wincanton's immaculate **Kingwell Farm** course for nearly
> ninety years, and providing you don't get carried away on the betting front, the current
> programme of National Hunt races provides one of the best-value days out in the area, with
> tickets costing from £11 for the Grandstand and from £16 for the Premier Enclosure, cheaper
> for under-25s (under-17s are free throughout). The season runs from October to May; call
> ☎01963 32344 or see ⓦwincantonracecourse.co.uk for details and dates of meetings.

gone but still remaining, in spirit at least, in the brickwork of houses throughout town
– to its railways, including the now defunct Somerset & Dorset Joint Railway (the
S&D, or "The Slow and Dirty"), a once-important line for Bruton businesses. Pride of
place, though, goes to the writing desk of **John Steinbeck**, who lived in nearby
Redlynch in 1959 while penning the (incomplete) *Acts and Deeds of King Arthur and
His Noble Knights*; the Pulitzer Prize-winning novelist considered the time he spent at
Discove Cottage the happiest of his life, telling a friend, "The peace I have dreamed
about is here, a real thing: thick as a stone and feelable."

Wincanton

Sitting virtually atop the A303, near the border with Wiltshire and Dorset,
WINCANTON shows few signs of its former life as an important staging post on the road
from London to the west, and is regularly dismissed as a bit of a peculiar place
– thanks, in no small part, to its twinning with a city that doesn't even exist. In 2002,
presumably feeling that the French town of Gennes-Les Rosiers and its German
counterpart Lahnau just weren't cutting it on their own anymore, Wincanton officially
twinned with **Ankh-Morpork**, the fictional city-state of Sir Terry Pratchett's fantasy
Discworld novels; the tie was strengthened in 2009 when roads on the Kingwell Rise
estate, southeast of the centre, were given Discworld-inspired names, such as Peach Pie
Street and Treacle Mine Road. Although a blatant marketing ploy, the twinning does at
least (with the closure of its museum in 2010) provide Wincanton with its one
year-round attraction – and the occasional sight of a fancy-dress "troll" wandering
around town is certainly something to savour.

Discworld Emporium
41 High St • Mon, Tues, Fri & Sat 10am–4pm, Sun by appointment only • ☎01963 824686, ⓦdiscworldemporium.com
Since *The Colour of Magic* was published in 1983, Terry Pratchett's 39 Discworld novels
have sold over seventy million copies. The books inspire a fanatical following, and there's
no greater pilgrimage for fans than to Wincanton's unique **Discworld Emporium**. Lovingly
assembled into a one-stop-shop for Pratchett memorabilia, it is chock-full of artefacts,
mementoes and trinkets. There are Discworld-themed models and stamps (accepted by
Royal Mail, so you can use them to send letters from the on-site Ankh-Morpork Post
Office), Assassins' Guild college scarves and even Ankh-Morpork passports – which you
can get stamped here, this being the official **Ankh-Morpork Consulate** and all.

Cadbury Castle
South Cadbury • South West Coaches' #40/40A from Bruton to Yeovil
Occupying a prominent hill just half a mile south of the A303, **Cadbury Castle** is not a
castle at all, and never has been. All that remains today are the concentric rings of
earthen ramparts, a mixture of banks and ditches that have served as a defensive outpost
since 3000 BC. The Iron Age Durotriges tribe established a significant town here, but it
is the sixth-century hill fort – which lends some credence to Cadbury's claim to be the
site of King Arthur's **Camelot** – that draws people to this windswept hilltop.

5

KING ARTHUR'S CAMELOT?

"At the very South Ende of the Chirch of South-Cadbyri standith Camallate... The People can telle nothing ther but that they have hard say that Arture much resortid to Camalat."

The Itinerary of John Leland the Antiquary, 1542

At least half a dozen places in the UK claim to be the site of **Camelot**, the legendary court of King Arthur, but Cadbury Castle is the most convincing of the lot. The connection was first established by the antiquarian John Leland in the mid-sixteenth century, but it wasn't until the 1950s that there was any form of physical evidence to support it, when pottery shards similar to those found at Tintagel, Arthur's reputed birthplace, were unearthed within the enclosure. These finds were sufficient enough for further excavations to be carried out in the late 1960s, and the **Camelot Research Committee** – with a name like that, clearly a group confident of finding *something* – uncovered a gatehouse and a wooden hall that also dated to the sixth century. More importantly, it was found that the surrounding bank had been refortified on a scale that only a king could command, and that the enclosure once housed a thousand-strong army. Whether the king was Arthur and the army his, is anybody's guess. But there could be a further clue in the names of nearby villages, for just a few miles down the road lie the hamlets of Queen Camel and West Camel...

Arthurian legends (see box, p.169) originate from a mid-sixth century Briton who battled with invading Anglo-Saxons, and Cadbury certainly enjoys a strategic military position; following the uppermost ring around its perimeter, it's obvious why this spot was chosen, with its commanding 360-degree views of central Somerset. The remnants of the complex – a central **timber hall** and a 16ft-thick **dry-stone wall** – lie buried beneath the turf, though the original entry to the fort, marked by a break in the earthworks' southwest side, is easy enough to make out; in a legend not too dissimilar to the Wild Hunt (see box, p.172), folklore has it that once a year the sound of galloping horses fills the sky as Arthur and his Knights of the Round Table ride down through the gateway and into the village of Sutton Montis below.

Haynes International Motor Museum

Sparkford, just off the A303 • April–Sept daily 9.30am–5.30pm, till 6pm in summer hols; Oct–March daily 10am–4.30pm • £9.95, under-16s £4.95, under-4s free • ☎ 01963 440804, ⓦ haynesmotormuseum.com • South West Coaches' #1/1A & 2/2B from Castle Cary to Yeovil

Every petrol-head's dream, the **Haynes International Motor Museum** opened in 1985 with the private collection of John Haynes – the man behind the *Haynes Owners Workshop Manual*, the amateur car mechanic's Bible – and now houses nearly four hundred gleaming automobiles. Some of the classiest cars in history are here – the **Lamborghini Countach**, with its gullwing "coleopter" doors (found in the Red Room), the **Rolls-Royce Shadow**, the **Jaguar XJ220** – interspersed with oddities like the Heinkel Cabin-Cruiser, a *Ghostbusters*-style Pontiac ambulance and the Sinclair C5, perhaps motoring's most famous flop. There are currently a dozen halls (more are planned as part of the redevelopment project that started in September 2011), with a few given over entirely to British cars and motorbikes. Among them all, it's worth seeking out the **1905 Daimler Limousine**, in Hall 5, whose one careful owner was George V (making this the first car to be driven by a royal), and the rare **1931 Duesenburg**, elevated on a podium at the far end of the same hall and worth a cool £1.25 million.

Kids are kept entertained with a Top Trumps Trail, soft-play "Fun Bus" and mini go-kart track (£1 a go), though as the museum is essentially a super-sized car showroom – albeit the ultimate one of its kind – it lacks the interactivity of the nearby Fleet Air Arm Museum (see p.203); to see some of the cars in action, try and coincide your visit with one of the many themed **events** detailed on the website.

ARRIVAL AND DEPARTURE

BY TRAIN

Castle Cary Station is just north of town, on the B3153, and served by trains on both the "Heart of Wessex" line and the main route from London.

Destinations Bath Spa (4–8 daily; 1hr); Bradford-on-Avon (4–8 daily; 50min); Bristol Temple Meads (4–8 daily; 1hr 10min); Bruton (5–8 daily; 5min); Dorchester (5–8 daily; 40min); Exeter (10 daily; 50min); Frome (5–8 daily; 20min); London Paddington (10–12 daily; 1hr 35min–2hr); Newbury (8 daily; 1hr 5min); Plymouth (8 daily; 1hr 55min); Reading (10–12 daily; 1hr 5min–1hr 30min); Taunton (10 daily; 20min); Weymouth (5–8 daily; 1hr

CASTLE CARY AND THE EAST

5min); Yeovil Pen Mill (5–8 daily; 1hr 5min).

Bruton Station is a few minutes' walk southeast of town, off the B3081; the "Heart of Wessex" line runs here eight times daily (4–5 on Sun) from Bristol to Weymouth.

Destinations Bath Spa (50min); Bradford-on-Avon (1hr); Bristol Temple Meads (1hr); Castle Cary (5min); Dorchester (50min); Frome (10min); Weymouth (1hr 15min).

BY BUS

Wincanton Bus Station is served by Berry's Coaches' twice-daily service to and from London (Hammersmith Bus Station; 2hr 5min).

INFORMATION

Castle Cary The Market House, Market Place (April–Sept Tues–Fri 9.30am–12.30pm & 2.30–4.30pm, Sat 9.30am–12.30pm; Oct–March Tues–Fri 9.30am–12.30pm; ☎ 01963 359631).

Bruton 26 High St (Mon–Wed & Fri 9.30am–12.30pm, Thurs 10am–noon; ☎ 01749 812851).

Wincanton Town Hall, Market Place (Mon–Thurs 9am–1pm & 2–4pm, Fri 9am–1pm; ☎ 01963 31693).

ACCOMMODATION

★ **Clanville Manor** Signed off the B3153, two miles northwest of Castle Cary ☎ 01963 350124, ⓦ clanvillemanor.co.uk. Set on a working farm, this beautiful Georgian B&B ticks all the right boxes, from the four comfortable bedrooms (one of which is a single) to the antique-filled lounge and the hospitable hosts. There's free wi-fi, and a smashing heated outdoor pool. The farm's two self-catering cottages sleep up to six; minimum 2nt stay, longer in summer hols (from £75). No children under 10 in the manor house. **£90**

High House Bruton 73 High St, Bruton ☎ 01749 813015, ⓦ highhousebruton.co.uk. Centrally located Victorian townhouse – a short walk from the river and an even shorter walk to Bruton's cafés and restaurants – with two tastefully furnished rooms, both with flat-screen TVs, DVD players and wi-fi. **£70**

Lower Farm Shepton Montague, off the A359 between Castle Cary and Bruton ☎ 01749 812253, ⓦ lowerfarm .org.uk. Stylishly converted eighteenth-century granary barn, which can be rented on a B&B or self-catering basis. The beds are rather grand, but it's the open-plan lounge-diner that gets the plaudits, with exposed beams, wood-burning stove and floor-to-ceiling windows at one end that let the light come flooding in. 2nt minimum stay unless on one of their organic gardening courses (see ⓦ www.charlesdowding.co.uk). B&B **£90**, self-catering (for 4) **£150**

The Pilgrims at Lovington Lovington, 4.5 miles west of Castle Cary, off the B3153 ☎ 01963 240600, ⓦ thepilgrimsatlovington.co.uk. Five modern rooms in the pub's old cider barn, all with good-sized beds (one with a French sleigh bed, another with a leather double), flat-screen TVs and DVD players and big new bathrooms with sleek bath tubs and a wet-room shower. A great breakfast served in the adjoining restaurant (see p.198), a meal at which is worth an overnight stay on its own. No under-14s. **£105**

The Queens Arms Corton Denham, about 2.5 miles past South Cadbury ☎ 01963 220317, ⓦ thequeensarms .com. A range of chic twins and doubles, with a similar set-up but all individually styled; two of the "Executive" rooms (£110) have lovely baths, either slipper or deep, cast-iron tubs. **£85**

Yarlington Yurt Yarlington, signed off the A371 between Castle Cary and Wincanton ☎ 01275 395447, ⓦ canopyandstars.co.uk. Glamp it up at this very spacious yurt in the grounds of Yarlington House, whose period decor – Victorian luggage cases, globes, rugs and paintings – has come from the Georgian manor house itself. There's a king-size double in the main dome and two singles in a connecting pod; the kitchen and bathroom are set in a neighbouring tent. Guests have use of the family pool. Breakfast £10 extra. 3nt weekend stays, 4nt mid-week stays. **£390**

EATING AND DRINKING

★ **At The Chapel** High St, Bruton ☎ 01749 814070, ⓦ atthechapel.co.uk. Contemporary gem in sleepy Bruton, making the most of its spacious setting with seating around the gallery, spread-out refectory tables and

a cocktail bar where the altar used to be. Tuck into quality dishes such as ham hock and parsley terrine or Cornish sardine Nicoise salad (mains from £10.50), or try one of their tempting wood-fired pizzas, served all day – the chefs

5

perfected their skills in Venice. Superb wine list. Artisan breads baked on site. Mon–Sat 9am–noon & 6–9.30pm (bar till 11pm), Sun 9am–4pm.

The Camelot Chapel Rd, South Cadbury ☎01963 440448, ⓦthecamelotpub.com. A good place to grab a bite to eat after circuiting Cadbury Castle, with a pretty, ivy-clad exterior and various cubbyholes leading off the main bar. Honest, tasty food includes oven-baked courgette stuffed with stilton and walnuts (£9.25) and duck breast with black-cherry sauce (£12.75). Daily noon–2.30pm & 6–9.30pm, Sun till 9pm.

Holbrook House Signed off the A371 about a mile north of Wincanton ☎01963 824466, ⓦholbrookhouse .co.uk. Handsome country-house hotel whose formal restaurant was named best in the county in the 2011 Taste of Somerset Awards. A la carte starts at £17.50 for Arborio herb risotto, though the short lunch menu features similar dishes at more affordable prices (two/three courses £14.50/19.50). Afternoon tea from £8.50. Mon–Thurs 7–9.30pm, Fri & Sat noon–2.30pm & 7–9.30pm, Sun noon–2.30pm.

Matt's Kitchen 51 High St, Bruton ☎01749 812027, ⓦmattskitchen.co.uk. Novel little restaurant serving authentic home-cooked food (*Matt's Kitchen* is in Matt's house) to a few in-the-know diners. The ad-hoc menu revolves around a single dish of the day, such as slow-braised pork shoulder or pan-fried whiting (all £10), plus sides. BYO. No credit cards. Thurs–Sat 12.30–2.30pm & 6.30–10.30pm.

The Old Bakehouse High St, Castle Cary ☎01963 350067. Unusual but successful combination of coffeehouse and Thai restaurant, with lattes and the like served all day and authentic pad Thai and chili-packed pad ka-ree spicing up the lunch and dinner menus (mains around £8.25). Tues–Sat 9.30am–4pm (lunch noon–2pm), Fri & Sat also 7pm–late.

★ **The Pilgrims at Lovington** Lovington, 4.5 miles west of Castle Cary, off the B3153 ☎01963 240600, ⓦthepilgrimsatlovington.co.uk. A real find, this fantastic place combines the relaxed atmosphere of a country pub with the elegant cooking of a fine-dining restaurant. The commitment to quality (local) cuisine is evident in dishes such as the cider-infused pork in a blanket and monkfish and scallops with black rice (mains from £16); just make sure you leave room for the superb Somerset cheese board. The Sunday roast (£18) is a labour of love, with the gravy alone taking three days to make. Tues 7–11pm, Wed–Sat noon–3pm & 7–11pm, Sun noon–3pm.

★ **The Queens Arms** Corton Denham, about 2.5 miles past South Cadbury ☎01963 220317, ⓦthequeensarms.com. Hidden away in the back roads south of Cadbury Castle, near the border with Dorset, this attractive former AA Pub of the Year is incredibly popular thanks to its solid but sophisticated food, from ham, egg and chips through to venison steak with mushroom and raspberry gnocchi; there are normally some great fruity desserts on the pudding menu, too. Excellent selection of bottled beers (around 45 in total) and ciders. Daily noon–3pm & 6–10pm, Sun till 9.30pm.

SHOPPING

Affinity Fine Art 3 High St, Castle Cary ⓦaffinityarts .com. Varied selection of interesting contemporary art, mostly by local artists, with prints, paintings, sculpture and some quality ceramics, plus regular exhibitions. Tues–Sat 9.30am–5.30pm.

Somerton and around

It is difficult to picture quiet, unassuming **SOMERTON** as a county town, let alone the ancient capital of Wessex, but it has been both, the latter allegedly for a short period in the seventh century, when King Ina's royal council, or *witan*, met here – it is in Somerton that Ina reputedly drew up the oldest written laws in English.

The town's spell as an important crossroads on the road to London and the south coast bequeathed it a number of fine seventeenth- and eighteenth-century buildings, most notably its **church** and **Market Cross,** which was built by Sir Edward Hext from local blue lias stone. Hext also gave Somerton its oldest **almshouses,** the ancient-looking building down West Street, established in 1626 and still in use today.

St Michael and All Angels

Market Place • Free • ⓦstmichaels-somerton.org.uk

The stout octagonal tower of **St Michael and All Angels** shelters one of the finest Jacobean altars in the country, but it's the church's sixteenth-century oak roof that catches the eye.

Constructed from some seven thousand different pieces, its elaborate carvings include a pair of dragons at each spandrel, mouths agape and growing ever bigger as they approach the altar. Among the many motifs – including a greyhound, a cat, pomegranates and a devil with a pig's nose – look out for the full-relief cider barrel in the north aisle; it's lying on a leaf on the fourth horizontal beam above the second window from the left.

Lytes Cary Manor

About three-quarters of a mile from the A372, near the A37/A303 junction • **House & gardens** Mid-March to Oct daily except Thurs 11am–5pm • £7.30, under-18s £3.70; gardens only £5.20, under-18s £2.65; under-5s free; NT **Estate** Daily dawn–dusk • Free • ☎ 01458 224471, ⓦ nationaltrust.org.uk/main/w-lytescarymanor• South West Coaches' #665 from Yeovil to Street

Of the many stately homes in South Somerset, **Lytes Cary Manor** offers perhaps the most personal insight into period country living: a private, unpretentious home that just happens to have belonged to particularly wealthy owners. William le Lyte was feudal lord of the manor in 1286, and for the next five hundred years it bounced between the Lyte family members until it was sold to an MP in the eighteenth century; it fell into disrepair, and when Sir Walter Jenner bought the house in the early 1900s the Great Hall was being used as a cider press.

Each room at Lytes Cary is stuffed with Dutch paintings, Flemish tapestries and period furniture, much of it – including the mahogany bed of William Pitt the Elder – purchased by Sir Walter. The entrance room, the **Great Hall**, built in 1453 purely as a place for entertainment, has the most interesting exhibit in the house, a first edition (1578) of the *Lytes Herbal*, an updated translation of the Flemish *Cruydeboeck* by botanist Henry Lyte. It's closely followed by the pair of creepy mannequins in the **Great Parlour** next door; known as "Good Companions", they were believed to have bumped up "unlucky" dinner parties that would otherwise have numbered thirteen.

Outside, beyond the topiary of the trim Arts and Crafts **garden**, you can head off on several **walks** that lead round the wider estate and along the river.

MANORS FROM HEAVEN

While it's all very enlightening to spend a few hours nosing around stately homes such as Lytes Cary Manor, it's not quite the same as **staying the night** – but that's exactly what you can do at some of the National Trust's finest mansions in the area. The period properties can be rented for between three and seven nights, with lets starting on a Thursday (Friday for Lytes Cary Manor). The prices given below are for the six-week high season from mid-July to end August; it's significantly cheaper at other times of the year, and up to sixty percent less in low-season months.

1 Strode House Barrington Court ☎ 0844 800 2070, ⓦ nationaltrustcottages.co.uk. The rooms in this red-brick former stables overlook Barrington Court (see p.206) and were built a century after the house itself; the bedrooms are quite plain, though the sitting room is grander. The gardens here are some of the most attractive in the county. Sleeps 6. 3nts <u>£707</u>

Lytes Cary Manor Charlton Mackrell ☎ 0844 800 2070, ⓦ nationaltrustcottages.co.uk. The best choice if you really want to feel like the lord of all you survey. Set in the west wing, authentically baronial rooms – one with a four-poster bed – look out over the well-kept gardens; the surroundings of the fantastic wood-panelled dining room, heavy with portraiture, can make dinner a very grand affair. There's a private terraced garden, plus croquet lawn and grass tennis court (June–Sept). Sleeps 14. 3nts <u>£1709</u>

South Lodge Montacute House, Montacute ☎ 0844 800 2070, ⓦ nationaltrustcottages.co.uk. This sixteenth-century lodge stands at the entrance to Montacute House (see p.200), and so enjoys easy access if not the *exact* same setting. It's built from the same lovely hamstone, though, and has a slate-floored dining room (with piano), very big (if sparsely furnished) bedrooms and a private rear garden. Sleeps 6. 3nts <u>£862</u>

Tintinhull House Farm St, Tintinhull ☎ 0844 800 2070, ⓦ nationaltrustcottages.co.uk. Beautiful seventeenth-century manor house with antique beds and original roll-top baths, a cosy lounge with monumental open fire and a lovely country kitchen. Best of all, you can have Tintinhull Garden (see p.203) to yourself come closing time. Sleeps 8. 3nts <u>£1352</u>

Tourist office Somerton Local Information Centre, Market Cross Antiques, West Street (Mon–Sat 10am–4pm).

ACCOMMODATION AND EATING

As well as the below, there's also accommodation at *The Yew Tree* in Compton Dundon (see p.174), *The Devonshire Arms* at Long Sutton (see p.186) and *The Pilgrims at Lovington* (see p.198). The latter two both also do good food, while *The Halfway House* at Pitney (see p.187) is the most atmospheric drinkers' pub for miles.

Cary Fitzpaine House Cary Fitzpaine, 4 miles east of Somerton, off the A37 ☎ 01458 223250, ⓦ caryfitzpaine .com. Attractive farmhouse B&B, with three sweet bedrooms, one with a four-poster that can sleep up to five, and a homely drawing room in the main house, plus a couple of tastefully converted self-catering barns (weekly rental), each with their own private garden. Evening meals are available on request (from £8), and the considerate owners can also provide packed lunches (£5) and storage for wet walking/cycling kit. Pet-friendly – and not just dogs and horses, either. B&B **£60**, self-catering **£280**

Emma B Coffee Shop West St, Somerton ☎ 01458 077332. Occupying the back of a gift shop in central Somerton, this relaxed spot does paninis, sandwiches, toasted teacakes and the like, and opens out onto a tidy courtyard. Daily 9.30am–5pm.

Lynch Country House Hotel Somerton ☎ 01458 272316, ⓦ thelynchcountryhouse.co.uk. Archetypal Georgian country house, with cropped ivy hugging the walls and pretty grounds; it's in a residential area on the fringes of Somerton but overlooks the Cary Valley. The rooms – particularly the first-floor "Premiere" ones – are equally classic, with plenty of floral furnishings; the cheapest are in the eaves of the main house, while there are four more in a converted coach house. **£80**

The Red Lion Babcary, a mile off the A37 ☎ 01458 223230, ⓦ redlionbabcary.co.uk. Homely thatched corner pub, charmingly decorated and offering a varied, ever-changing menu that ranges from their own fish pie to sag paneer (mains from £8.75) and is consistently well delivered; draught drinks include Teignworthy Reel Ale and Lilly's Apples & Pears cider. There's a pleasant garden for good-weather dining. Mon–Sat noon–2pm & 7–9.30pm, Sun 11am–4pm.

SHOPPING

★ **Somerset Guild of Craftsmen** The Courthouse Gallery, Market Place, Somerton ☎ 01458 274653, ⓦ somersetguild.co.uk. The old town courthouse makes a grand setting for this long-established guild, with up to sixty artists at any one time displaying a wide range of work, from stained glass, woodcarving and art quilts to watercolours, prints and intricately embroidered wall pictures. Mon–Sat 10am–5pm.

Yeovil and around

The largest town in South Somerset by some way, **YEOVIL** disproves the theory that appearances can be deceptive, its fringe of hum-drum suburbs and business parks giving way to a uniformly bland central shopping precinct. Consequently, it does have the best facilities in the area, which, combined with its central location can make it a fairly convenient base for exploring other parts of the region, particularly **Montacute House**, four miles to the west, and the excellent **Fleet Air Arm Museum**.

In town, the small green facing the fourteenth-century church of **St John the Baptist** is a pleasant enough place to rest your legs, and the church itself – known as the Lantern of the West due to its abundance of windows – is quite a sight when the sun streams through its (modern) stained glass. Yeovil's main attraction, though – ironically, given the miles of surrounding countryside – is the sizeable **Yeovil Country Park**, the Ninesprings area in particular providing plenty of trails and a handy children's playground.

Montacute House

Montacute • **House & gardens** Mid-March to Oct daily except Tues 11am–5pm (also Tues in Aug), gardens till 5.30pm & also rest of year Wed–Sun 11am–4pm • £9.30, children £4.40; gardens only £5.70, children £2.90 (£4/2 in winter); NT **Parkland** Daily 5am–9pm • Free • ☎ 01963 440804, ⓦ nationaltrust.org.uk/montacutehouse • South West Coaches' #81 from Yeovil to South Petherton

Set in the picture-postcard hamlet of the same name, majestic **Montacute House** still makes the striking statement that Sir Edward Phelips intended when he built it from local hamstone in the late sixteenth century. The mansion, a beautifully designed and lavishly filled status symbol, was intended to help further Phelips's progress at court and deliver him his dream of entertaining Elizabeth I – an ambition he never achieved as the queen died just two years after the house was completed.

Phelips would have appreciated the attention his mansion attracted in 1995, when it was used as the Palmer residence in Ang Lee's adaptation of *Sense and Sensibility* – it was after running through the gardens in the rain here that Kate Winslet's character, Marianne Dashwood, fell ill.

The house
Among the assorted period furniture and paintings that decorate the first-floor rooms (including pictures by Gainsborough and Reynolds), there's an interesting frieze in the **Great Hall** depicting the public humiliation of a cuckolded husband and several vibrant tapestries, most significantly *The Hunter*, in the **Parlour**, a late-eighteenth-century piece based on a set woven for Louis XIV.

Upstairs, the windows in the grand **Library**, originally the Great Chamber, showcase the stained-glass coats of arms of the Phelips family and their well-to-do associates; the Phelips's crops up throughout the house and is often topped by a fire-basket – the family's motto was "homes and hearths". The centrepiece of the neighbouring **Crimson Bedroom** is its central four-poster, richly carved with foliage and figures and surrounded by embroidered bed hangings; the bed was built in 1612, hence the royal arms of James I above its headboard, showing a lion (for England) and a unicorn (for Scotland), the first time the supporters of the United Kingdom had appeared together in a monarch's coat of arms.

Sixty or so of the National Portrait Gallery's vast collection of Tudor and Jacobean portraits are on permanent loan in the top-floor Elizabethan **Long Gallery**. Admittedly, most are by unknown artists or are copies of more famous works, but there are still some fine pieces here, particularly George Gower's 1588 *Armada Portrait* of Elizabeth I, where the monarch is tellingly decked in pearls, diamonds and jewels in a typically ostentatious show of wealth.

The gardens and parkland
The formal **gardens** are most notable for their bulbous hedges, while a couple of waymarked walks lead through the estate's three hundred acres of **parkland** and to a tower on St Michael's Hill that marks the site of a motte and bailey castle. Regular **events** in the grounds include a monthly Gardeners Q&A (April–Oct Wed 2–4pm) and the Levels' Best farmers' market (March–June & Sept–Dec Sat 10am–2pm); the pleasant **courtyard café** uses fruit and vegetable from the kitchen gardens at Tintinhull (see p.203) and Barrington Court (see p.206).

Montacute TV, Radio and Toy Museum
1 South St, Montacute • Easter–Oct Wed–Sat 11am–5pm, Sun noon–5pm (summer hols also Mon & Tues 11am–5pm); check website for winter opening hours • £6.50, children £4.50 • ☎ 01935 823024, ⓦ montacutemuseum.co.uk

Just a few yards from Montacute House, but an altogether different proposition, the **Montacute TV, Radio and Toy Museum** is a nostalgic trip down memory lane, as much – you get the impression – for its curator as for the parents who try to kid themselves that they're only here for the children. The collection started with a few vintage radios and TVs (which now number around five hundred) and today features a labyrinth of display cases crammed with annuals, games and all the associated memorabilia that has sprung up over the last eighty years around programmes ranging from *Dixon of Dock Green* and *Dad's Army* to *The Simpsons* and *CSI*, via *Skippy*, *Bonanza*, *Dr Kildare* and all those other childhood favourites.

5

THE FOLLIES OF BARWICK PARK

Marking the boundaries of Barwick House estate, just south of Yeovil, the four whimsical and triumphantly pointless **follies of Barwick Park** were built in the 1770s for no reason other than as a bit of decadent decoration – an easy, one-and-a-half-mile walk along public footpaths leads past three of the follies, with views across to the fourth.

From Barwick Village Hall (to get here, follow signs for *Little Barwick House* off the A37, a mile south of Yeovil), turn left into Rex's Lane and head up past Barwick House and through an "avenue" of high-banked trees until you come to an overgrown by-way on your left. Along here, on the left, stands **Jack the Treacle Eater**, an arch of ragged stones topped by a round lock-up tower with a conical roof; the statue of Hermes at its tip recalls the eponymous messenger whose journeys to and from London were allegedly sustained only by tins of the sticky stuff. Follow the by-way for three-quarters of a mile to Two Tower Lane, turn left, and after a while you'll see **The Fish Tower** on your left-hand side; it originally peaked with a fish-shaped weather vane but now looks more like a bung-topped test tube. Beyond here, a gate signed "Barwick Park" cuts diagonally across the field, the path giving good views of the **Rose Tower** (also known as Messiter's Cone, after the family who once owned Barwick House), which appears on the ridge to the right like a pock-marked pixie hat; in the distance, in a line of trees just up from the A37 and almost behind Barwick House, **The Needle** is a much less fanciful obelisk. Follow the path to the driveway of Barwick House, turn left past the house – looking up to see Jack the Treacle Eater from its western side – and then right at the end of the driveway back onto Rex's Lane; Barwick Village Hall is a third of a mile down the road.

Ham Hill Country Park

Rising 260ft above the surrounding countryside, six miles northwest of Yeovil, **Ham Hill Country Park** is the source of all South Somerset's honeyed houses. This is the only place in Britain where **hamstone** is thick enough to quarry, and every Crunchie-coloured community in the region can trace its roots to here, including Montacute, Stoke-sub-Hamdon and Norton-sub-Hamdon, the picturesque trio of hamstone hamlets that lie at the foot of the hill. As well as providing the uniform foundation for entire villages, the golden stone was used in stately homes such as Barrington Court, Tintinhull and Montacute House.

Ham Hill has also served as the location for an Iron Age fort, a Roman military base and a medieval village; following the **ramparts** of the hill fort for three miles around its contours affords great views over South Somerset and leads past a "stone circle" (erected by a quarrying company) and into a deep, fissured quarry site, now a Geological Site of Special Scientific Interest.

Stoke-sub-Hamdon Priory

North St, Stoke-sub-Hamdon • March–Sept daily 11am–5pm • Free • ☎ 01935 823289, ⓦ nationaltrust.org.uk/main/w-stokesubhamdon priory• South West Coaches' #81 from Yeovil to South Petherton

Hidden behind a heavy wooden gate, the attractive but crumbling hamstone ensemble of **Stoke-sub-Hamdon Priory** sees few visitors bar the house martins that nest in the drafty rafters of its hall. The buildings were erected around the chantry of the Beauchamp family, the thirteenth-century lords of Stoke Manor who gave their name to some of the villages around here. The barn and its bulging, thatch-roofed stables are well and truly closed, and the ruined dovecote and granary are off limits and awaiting funds for restoration, but you can poke around the main hall, kitchen and what appears to be a small larder while enjoying the likely solitude.

Tintinhull Garden

5

Farm St, Tintinhull, 5 miles northwest of Yeovil on the A3088 and half a mile south of the A303 • Mid-March to Oct Wed–Sun & bank hols 11am–5pm • £5.55, under-16s £2.75, under-5s free • ☎ 01935 823289, ⓦ nationaltrust.org.uk/main/w-tintinhullgarden• First's #52 from Yeovil to Martock

The half-dozen interconnecting "outdoor rooms" that make up orderly **Tintinhull Garden** are largely the work of Felicity (Phyllis) Reiss, who spent nearly thirty years tweaking its aesthetics after moving into the seventeenth-century manor house in 1933. Avid gardeners will find interest in the careful combinations of colour and texture, and in the busy kitchen garden (which provides fruit and veg for the restaurant at Montacute House), but you don't need green fingers to appreciate the overriding air of tranquillity here – Tintinhull is a place to unwind, and it's not uncommon to see people idling through a paperback at the edge of the Pond Garden's lily pool.

Fleet Air Arm Museum

RNAS Yeovilton, on the B3151 near the junction of the A303 and the A37 • April–Oct & school hols daily 10am–5pm; Nov–March Wed–Sun 10am–4.30pm • £9.95, under-16s £4.95, under-4s free • ☎ 01935 840565, ⓦ fleetairarm.com • Nippy Bus N11 from Yeovil

Set on RNAS Yeovilton, seven miles north of Yeovil, the **Fleet Air Arm Museum** boasts Europe's largest collection of naval aircraft, as well as the first Concorde ever built in Britain. But despite the superlatives, it's the interactive displays throughout – from touch-screen simulations to mini-wind turbines that show how an aircraft banks, pitches or yaws – that set this museum apart. That and the age-old adage of location, location, location: the Fleet Air Arm is slap bang in the middle of Europe's busiest military air base, and the whirring of rotor blades makes for an exciting welcome as Lynx helicopters buzz back and forth over the car park.

The halls

Hall 1 deals with over a century of British naval aviation, from the bullet-ridden Short 5184, the first plane to take part in a naval battle, to a BAE Sea Harrier that saw action in the Falklands; the exhibits in **Hall 2** span World War II and Korea, with a chilling Kamikaze exhibition, complete with a Yokosuka MXY7 "flying bomb". But it's the last two halls that elevate the Fleet Air Arm from an interesting museum to an excellent one: in the Aircraft Carrier Experience in **Hall 3**, accessed by a juddering helicopter "flight", a noisy Phantom fighter launch from the plane-packed flight deck (a replica of HMS *Ark Royal*) is followed, via a tour of the Island control rooms, by the equally dramatic rescue of a Buccaneer bomber. The biggest draw (literally) in **Hall 4** is a climb-aboard Concorde, a test prototype that was used to run experiments before the first commercial models could roll off the production line. It's a suitably grand finale before you head outside to the whirring of helicopters once again.

ARRIVAL AND INFORMATION   **YEOVIL AND AROUND**

BY TRAIN

Yeovil Junction is in Stoford, 2 miles south of the centre and served by regular trains from Basingstoke (1hr 40min); Crewkerne (10min); Exeter St Davids (1hr); London Waterloo (2hr 30min); and Salisbury (1hr).

Yeovil Pen Mill is a mile east of town, just off the A30 and on the "Heart of Wessex" line that runs eight times daily from Bath (1hr 15min); Bradford-on-Avon (1hr 5min); Bristol (1hr 35min); Bruton (25min); Castle Cary (15min); Dorchester (35min); Frome (35min); and Weymouth (50min).

BY BUS

Yeovil Bus Station is on several national routes: Berry's Coaches operates a twice-daily service to and from London (Hammersmith Bus Station; 2hr 40min), while National Express runs daily services to Bristol (1hr 35min), Bournemouth (2hr 25min), Dorchester (45min), London Victoria (4hr 40min), Poole (2hr), Salisbury (1hr 30min) and Weymouth (1hr 5min).

INFORMATION

Yeovil Information Centre Petters Way (Mon–Thurs 9am–5pm, Fri till 4.45pm; ☎ 01935 462781).

5

ACCOMMODATION

★ **Brympton House** Brympton D'Evercy, half a mile off the A3088, just west of Yeovil ☎01935 862528, ⓦ www.brympton-accommodation.co.uk. Quirky, atmospheric and utterly unique B&B, in a stately home dating back to 1220 and once described by *Country Life* magazine as "the most incomparable house in Britain". The fifteen spacious bedrooms (some with lovely clawfoot baths) are dispersed among the D'Evercy Tower – reached by a winding stone staircase – the 1680 Restoration Wing and the ground-floor medieval complex; all rooms bar those in the latter have access to a sitting room with Sky TV and plenty of kids' toys. Its grounds take in the fifteenth-century "Castle House" (complete with arrow slits) and Lady Fane Lake, and are roamed by a range of rescue animals, including Lrnie the cockerel. Breakfast in the 1350 Star Chamber, provided by cheery staff and warmed by a monumental fireplace, is also memorable. **£80**

The Lanes High St, West Coker, two miles southwest of Yeovil ☎01935 862555, ⓦ laneshotel.net. Enclosed by walled gardens, the soft hamstone exterior of this former rectory belies the boutique hotel within. The rooms are suitably contemporary, as are the public spaces – the restaurant is pretty much a glass cube. Facilities include a gym, sauna, Jacuzzi and "experience shower", with plenty of treatments available at the on-site spa (ⓦ spatherapyatlanes.com). There are also one- and two-bedroom apartments, with stylish standalone baths (from £150). **£130**

Little Barwick House Rex's Lane, Barwick, signed off the A37 a mile south of Yeovil ☎01935 423902, ⓦ littlebarwickhouse.co.uk. Intimately grand Georgian dower house set in attractive grounds. The half-dozen rooms are individually furnished and enjoy nice touches such as home-made shortbread – but you're really here for the divine three-course dinner at the downstairs restaurant (see below), included in the rate. Occasionally 2nt minimum stays at the weekend. **£240**

The Masons Arms 41 Lower Odcombe, about a mile off the A3088 west of Yeovil ☎01935 862591, ⓦ masonsarmsodcombe.co.uk. The oldest building in the hamstone village of Lower Odcombe, with spacious modern doubles (and smart bathrooms) in an extension off the back of the pub (see below); rooms overlook the pub garden and have (quiet) ceiling fans, digital TV and free wi-fi. The good breakfast includes eggs from their own chickens. Camping is also available in the field behind, with sparkling facilities. Doubles **£85**, camping **£12**

Slipper Cottage 41 Bishopston, Montacute ☎01935 823073, ⓦ slippercottage.co.uk. Seventeenth-century hamstone cottage in the charming village of Montacute, a few hundred yards from Montacute House itself, recently renovated but still with plenty of low beams and open fireplaces, plus a lovely long cottage garden. There are just two rooms, both with inviting double beds and, of course, slipper baths. Very good-value single rates (£27). Credit cards not accepted. **£50**

EATING AND DRINKING

The Art Gallery Café 8 Church St, Yeovil ☎01935 433292. Simple café overlooking St John the Baptist church, with art for sale on the wall and soups, salads, bagels and jackets on the menu. Some more substantial dishes, too, such as fish pie (£8.50). Daily 8am–5pm.

★ **Little Barwick House** Rex's Lane, Barwick, signed off the A37 a mile south of Yeovil ☎01935 423902, ⓦ littlebarwickhouse.co.uk. White-washed Georgian restaurant with rooms, run by a husband-and-wife team whose enviable skill is to provide quality cooking in a refreshingly relaxed environment – locally sourced produce makes up the majority of a tastebud-teasing menu,

featuring the likes of pink roasted wild roe deer and free-range duck with wild mushroom risotto. Very good (and very good-value) wine list, too. Lunch: two courses £21.95, three courses (Wed–Sat) £25.95. Dinner: two courses £34.95 (available Mon–Fri), three courses £39.95. Closed Sun dinner, Tues lunch & all day Mon.

The Masons Arms 41 Lower Odcombe, about a mile off the A3088 west of Yeovil ☎01935 862591, ⓦ masonsarmsodcombe.co.uk. Lovely looking thatch-roofed inn whose friendly owners keep their regulars coming back for more thanks to a combination of classic pub grub and an à la carte menu (from £11.50) of dishes

---

HOW DO YOU LIKE THEM APPLES?

There are several low-key cider producers in the deep south of Somerset, pressing apples on a smaller scale than neighbouring Perry's (see p.209) and Burrow Hill (see p.206) but still crafting a quality traditional farmhouse cider or two. One of the best is **Bridge Farm Cider**, on the A30 just out of East Chinnock, on the way from Yeovil to Crewkerne (9.30am–6.30pm: May–Sept daily; Oct–April Fri, Sat & Sun only; ☎01935 862387). The owner, Nigel Stewart, makes award-winning dry, medium and sweet cider (from £4 for two litres up to £32 for a five-gallon barrel), a bottle-fermented sparkling cider and a number of single-variety apple juices; he has also recently added his own cider brandy to the range.

uch as baked whole sea bass with saffron risotto, and sun-
lushed tomato and vodka tagliatelle – all in generous
ortions. The pub's own microbrewery produces five Real
les, including the deep, dark Roly Poly. Daily noon–2pm
& 6.30–9.30pm, bar till midnight.

Prezzo Old Sarum House, 49 Princes St, Yeovil ☎ 01935
426381, ⓦ prezzorestaurants.co.uk. Sleek Italian chain
with dark decor, set in a 1730 clothier's house that was
home to Yeovil's first mayor. Expect mushroom risotto, spicy
meat calzone and the like (from £6.95). Daily 11am–11pm.

Martock and around

Set around Church Street and its continuation, North Street, the grand village of
MARTOCK is chock-full of pretty hamstone buildings. Many date from the sixteenth
and seventeenth centuries, literally the town's golden age, when it prospered thanks
to the fertile fields nearby – according to one seventeenth-century writer, Martock
was "seated in the fattest place of the Earth of this Countie". Any walk around the
village should start at the **Treasurer's House** and the church, just opposite, but it's
also worth exploring North Street and the eighteenth-century **Market House**, which
used to shelter the village's horse-drawn fire engine and is still in use as the local
tourist information centre; on the way there, you'll pass possibly the prettiest
NatWest bank in the country.

Treasurer's House

Church St, Martock • Mid-March to Sept Mon, Tues & Sun 2–5pm • £3.80, under-16s £1.90, under-4s free; NT • ☎ 01935 825015,
ⓦ nationaltrust.org.uk/main/w-treasurershousemartock

The oldest inhabited private house in Somerset, the **Treasurer's House** was built for
Hugh, Treasurer of Wells Cathedral, not long after the Bishop of Bath and Wells had
acquired the village in 1226; up until then, Martock had belonged to the Abbot of
Mont St-Michel in Normandy. In 1293, John de Langton, at that time Chancellor of
England, tagged the high-ceilinged **Great Hall** onto its northern end; among several
later alterations, a medieval **kitchen** was constructed alongside.

The manor house itself later became a vicarage and then, by the mid-nineteenth
century, a series of individual tenements. Its oldest part is the upstairs **solar block**, the
Treasurer's private apartment, one side of which is covered with a rare wall-painting
depicting the Crucifixion (with St Mary, St John – clasping his gospel inside his robe
– and Christ); the picture dates to around 1262 but was only discovered in 1995, when
the whole house was extensively restored.

All Saints Church

Church St, Martock • Free

The thing that grabs your attention most as you enter Martock's bold and beautiful **All
Saints Church**, the second largest in Somerset, is its bold and beautiful oak nave **ceiling**,
dating to 1513 and exquisitely carved with open-winged angels hovering from its cross
beams – if it's dark, a light switch by the pulpit helps illuminate the work. Musket shot
found embedded in the wood dates to when Cromwell and his Parliamentarian troops
were billeted here after the battle for Bridgwater in 1645; it's alleged that they were
trying to pick off the angels.

Almost as striking as the ceiling are the canopied **niches** spaced among the aisle
windows, which contain seventeenth-century paintings of (uniquely) all twelve
apostles. They're believed to have been based on contemporary bigwigs, with St James
the Less – on the north side, the fourth one in from the eastern end – bearing an
uncanny resemblance to Charles I.

5

Somerset Distillery and Burrow Hill Cider Farm

Pass Vale Farm, Burrow Hill, signed from Kingsbury Episcopi, about three miles northwest of Martock • Mon–Sat 9am–5.30pm • Free • Tours by arrangement • ☏ 01460 240782, Ⓦ ciderbrandy.co.uk

Lying at the foot of Burrow Hill, a local landmark topped by a single sycamore, the **Somerset Distillery** is the only one of its kind in the county. Its five varieties of smooth, rich **Somerset Cider Brandy** are produced in old French copper stills (which you can see behind armoured glass) before being aged in oak barrels for between three and twenty years – reviving this monastic tradition earned its charismatic owner, Julian Temperley, the freedom of the city of London.

Their award-winning dry and medium **Burrow Hill Cider** is pressed from around forty varieties of cider apple but is perhaps eclipsed by their two single-variety, bottle-fermented sparkling ciders, produced using the *méthode champenoise*, whereby the cider is matured within the bottle, its sediment frozen in the neck and then removed. The method might carry a controversial name round these parts – nearby Montacute House was producing sparkling cider back in 1664, long before the French had ever dreamt about their bottles of bubbly – but the resulting punchy Kingston Black and bone-dry Stoke Red are a revelation.

Pre-arranged **tours** among the vast cider vats (some holding up to eighty thousand pints) and copper stills add insight into the workings of a 150-year-old cider farm, as does the twenty-minute **self-guided walk** around the sheep-grazed orchards. The old, dark **ciderhouse**, crammed with oak barrels, is as atmospheric a place for tasting as any, though you'll need a designated driver if you want to sample the full range of ciders, aperitifs, eaux de vie, pomonas and apple brandies on offer (cider from £3.70 for two litres, brandy from £13.80 for a half-bottle of three-year-old).

East Lambrook Manor Gardens

East Lambrook, near South Petherton, 2 miles north of the A303 • Feb, May, June & July daily 10am–5pm; March, April & Aug–Oct Tues–Sat 10am–5pm • £5.50, under-16s free • ☏ 01963 240328, Ⓦ eastlambrook.co.uk

The busy terraces of charming, Grade-I listed **East Lambrook Manor Gardens** are the country's finest example of a cottage-style garden, mainly because this is where it all began. In 1938, when **Margery Fish** moved here from London with her husband, the editor of *The Daily Mail*, she had no experience of gardening whatsoever, just a notion that it needn't be the preserve of the wealthy few whose huge landscaped grounds required tending by paid gardeners.

After thirty years of fine-tuning, development and innovation – and a writing career that included the cottage-garden classic *We Made A Garden* (see p.326) – Margery Fish died a gardening icon in 1969. The garden today is essentially the same one she left behind, and now serves as a sort of pilgrimage site for pruners. Themed areas include the Silver Garden, the White Garden and the Ditch, where you'll find East Lambrook's famous hellebores and snowdrops (there are over eighty varieties on show in spring), plus hardy geraniums, a Fish favourite. You can pick up some of the plants you'll see at the **Margery Fish Plant Nursery**, which the great lady started in the 1950s.

Barrington Court

On the B3168 in Barrington, signposted from the A303 and the A358 • March–Oct daily except Wed 11am–5pm, also some weekends in Nov & Dec; Strode House Restaurant noon–3pm • £8.60, under-16s £3.75, under-4s free; NT • ☏ 01460 241938, Ⓦ nationaltrust.org.uk/barrington

In 1907, sixteenth-century **Barrington Court** became the first major manor-house project of a fledgling National Trust, but was in such disrepair that it nearly ruined the organization. Only the intervention of Colonel Arthur Lyle (of Tate & Lyle fame) in 1920 saved Barrington – within five years, he had completed the restoration of the focal Court House. The house served as the Lyle family home until 1991, and the rooms, now empty of furniture again, are filled with the history of three generations, their memories brought to life in occasional audio snippets. The Great Hall and the Master Bedroom, with its 1625 Strode fireplace, are highlights, though the most notable feature throughout is the Colonel's collection of delicately carved wood panelling – salvaged from historic houses across the country – which he installed in the Buttery, the Long Gallery and in adjoining Strode House.

Outside, you can wander the varied Gertrude Jekyll-inspired **gardens** and, at the far end of the estate, **orchards**, apples from which (along with Montacute, Tintinhull Garden and Glastonbury Tor) are pressed to make the National Trust's South Somerset apple juice and cider; produce from the sizeable **Kitchen Garden** is used in the restaurant in **Strode House**, a later red-brick building that makes a vivid contrast to the muted hamstone of Court House itself.

ARRIVAL AND INFORMATION   MARTOCK AND AROUND

By bus Berry's Coaches' twice-daily service runs between London (Hammersmith) and South Petherton (3hr); local First buses link Martock with Yeovil (#52) and Taunton (#632).
Martock LIC Market House (Mon–Fri 10am–1pm, also

second Sat of the month 9.30am–12.30pm; ☎01935 310040).
South Petherton LIC Market Square (Mon–Sat 10am–noon & 2–4pm, closed Wed & Sat afternoons; ☎01460 249171).

ACCOMMODATION

As well as the places below, there are also some good accommodation options in the villages around Yeovil (see p.204), not forgetting *The Devonshire Arms* at Long Sutton (see p.186).

Ash House Country Hotel Main St, Ash, 1.5 miles northeast of Martock ☎01935 822036, ⓦ ashhousehotel .co.uk. There's a warm welcome at this Georgian manor house, whose unfussy rooms have comfortable beds and fresh milk in their fridges – a nice touch. The informal brasserie overlooks an attractive garden, which is atmospherically lit at night. **£95**
Burrow Hill B&B Orchard View, Burrow Way; follow the "Distillery & Cider Mill" signs from Kingsbury Episcopi ☎01460 240288, ⓦ burrowhillbandb.co.uk. Pretty little Grade II-listed cottage with just two doubles, one of which (Hill View) has a gorgeous double-ended bath and, unsurprisingly, views over Burrow Hill itself. As an added bonus, the B&B is right next door to the Somerset Distillery and Burrow Hill Cider Farm (see opposite). Keen single rates (£40). No credit cards. **£70**
★ **Farndon Thatch** Puckington, less than a mile west

along the B3168 from Barrington Court ☎01460 259845, ⓦ bandbinsomerset.com. Top-notch B&B that seems to do everything just right, though the setting – a lovely fifteenth-century, reed-thatched cottage – certainly helps. The two doubles, one with exposed beams, both with great views, are comfy in the extreme, while the charming guest areas feature woodburning stoves and plenty of exposed beams. And anyone that calls their cats Crinklechops and Mr Blobby is bound to be a hospitable host. The lovely gardens open as part of the National Garden Scheme. Afternoon tea from 4pm. No under-12s. **£70**
Rock House 5 Palmer St, South Petherton ☎01460 240324, ⓦ unwindatrockhouse.co.uk. Two modern split-level apartments, with well-equipped lounges and a shared garden. There's a fridge for perishables, though rates include breakfast – served in the apartment – and afternoon tea can be arranged. **£90**

EATING AND DRINKING

In addition to the below, *The Devonshire Arms* at Long Sutton (see p.186) does good meals, while some of the best food in the area is to be found at the delightful *Lord Poulett Arms* (see p.211); few pubs can better *The Halfway House* at Pitney (see p.187) for character.

New Farm Restaurant Over Stratton, just off the A303 near South Petherton ☎01460 240584, ⓦ newfarmrestaurant.co.uk. Great setting – a converted hamstone barn – for a family-run restaurant, where global starters are followed by Modern British mains (from £11.90), finished off with a choice of "Jane's delicious desserts". Thurs–Sat from 7pm, also open for lunch every second Wed & Thurs of the month.
★ **Provender** 3 Market Square, South Petherton

☎01460 240681, ⓦ provender.co.uk. Chic spot at the tip of South Petherton's pretty Market Square, with a square-side deli offering farmhouse cheese, smoked meats and speciality breads, and a light-filled café at the back, with art for sale and soups, savoury tartlets and deli platters to eat. Plus a mean cup of coffee. Mon 10.30am–3pm, Tues–Fri 9am–4.30pm, Sat 9am–3pm; lunch served noon–2.30pm, from 10am on Sat.
The Wyndham Arms Kingsbury Episcopi ☎01935

5

823239, ⓦwyndhamarms.com. Attractive local, both outside and in, with a warm welcome and a decent range of regional brews – Butcombe and Otter for ale drinkers, Burrow Hill and Ashton Press Still for cider lovers. Also does

comfortable pub staples such as steak and ale pie, scampi and chips and the like (from £8.95). Daily noon–2pm (Sat & Sun till 3pm) & 7–9pm (Fri & Sat 6.30–9.30pm), bar till 11pm, 10pm on Sun.

SHOPPING

The Trading Post The Old Filling Station, Lopenhead, just off the A303 near South Petherton. Well-stocked farm shop, selling their own organic veg, pork sausages and eggs, and trading various goodies from over eighty

local suppliers, including Burrow Hill cider vinegar Sharpham Park Speletto and ham, bacon and chicken from Langport. Mon–Sat 8.30am–6pm, Sun 9am–1pm.

Crewkerne and the west

The ancient market town of **CREWKERNE** (pronounced "crook-un", from *crug*, meaning "hill") still retains many of its fine hamstone buildings, huddled – as its history would suggest – around Market Square and adjoining Market Street, where the weekly market still takes place (Wed 9am–1.30pm). The town's original wealth was earned through wool, its prosperity reflected in the size and splendour of fifteenth-century **St Bartholomew's church**, at the end of Church Street. The subsequent success of its textile industry brought a second wind of wealth and added a Georgian flavour to its architectural ensemble.

The old part of town is a pleasant place to wander, with a cluster of attractive townhouses up **Court Barton** and on Abbey Street, where the **Church Hall** (in its former life as Crewkerne Grammar School) educated Sir Thomas Masterman Hardy, Nelson's flag-captain, to whom the admiral turned during his dying moments at the Battle of Trafalgar and uttered the immortal line, "Kiss me, Hardy".

Crewkerne Museum

Market Square • Mid-April to Oct Wed–Fri 10.30am–4pm, Sat 10.30am–1pm • £1 • ☎ 01460 77079

Housed in a noble Georgian building, the diminutive **Crewkerne Museum** charts the town's two boom periods, particularly the growth enjoyed by the flax and linen industries during the eighteenth and nineteenth centuries – aside from Hardy hailing from Crewkerne, the town's flax mills also produced the sails for HMS *Victory*, Nelson's flagship at Trafalgar. Hardy's school is also covered; one of the earliest grammar schools in England, it was founded in 1499 and also counted the explorer William Dampier, the first Englishman to set foot in Australia, among its pupils.

THE RIVER PARRETT TRAIL

The fifty-mile-long **River Parrett Trail** traces the route of the river from its source at Chedington in Dorset, just southeast of Crewkerne, to where it finally spills into the Bristol Channel near Steart. It's an easy amble, much of it across the flat Somerset Levels, and can be tackled in one four- or five-day hike or broken down into a series of shorter walks. As a snapshot of Somerset, it's difficult to beat, traversing apple orchards, running through hamstone villages and crossing withy beds and wetlands before ending at a nature reserve in Bridgwater. **Attractions** along the way include Ham Hill, East Lambrook Manor Gardens, Muchelney Abbey (see p.184), Burrow Mump (see p.183), Westonzoyland Pumping Station (see p.182) and the Bridgwater and Taunton Canal (see box, p.221), which the trail follows for a few miles towards its end. A trail **map** and directions can be downloaded from ⓦwww .riverparrett-trail.org.uk; OS Explorer maps #116, 129 and 140 cover the route.

Perry's Cider Mills

5

Dowlish Wake, signed from Crewkerne, Ilminster and Chard • Mon–Fri 9am–5.30pm, Sat 9.30am–4.30pm, Sun 10am–1pm; café Mon–Fri 10.30am–4.30pm, Sat 10.30am–4pm • Free • ☎ 01460 55195, ⓦ perryscider.co.uk

The apple harvest at **Perry's Cider Mills** is still pressed in the farm's creaking thatched barn, just as it has been since the sixteenth century. Now in their fourth generation of cider-makers since starting in 1920, the Perry family craft a dozen farmhouse and single-variety ciders, available from the farm shop – either straight from the barrel (from £5.20 for two litres) or, for the single varieties such as Somerset Dabinett, Morgan Sweet and Somerset Redstreak, in bottles. The small rural **museum** in the barn teems with old cider-making equipment and farm tools, as well as a working cider press and mills, which are in action in the autumn; a short video and display boards chart the process involved.

Ilminster

For its compact size, modestly handsome **ILMINSTER** is quite a social hub, with a vibrant arts centre, a well-established local theatre company, and a number of independent shops and galleries along Silver Street. The central **Market House**, rebuilt in the early 1800s, still holds Ilminster's weekly market (Thurs 9am–1pm), though the main site is, of course, **The Minster**, which – along with the River Il – gives the town its name. The tourist information centre can provide leaflets on local walks, some passing tank traps and pill boxes that formed part of the **Taunton Stop Line**, a coast-to-coast defensive system that was built in 1940 to hinder a potential German invasion of the South West.

The Minster

Silver St • Free

Raised above Silver Street, the golden, fifteenth-century church of St Mary's, better known as **The Minster**, is architecturally one of the finest in Somerset, cathedral-like in appearance and dominated by its fine Perpendicular tower. The Duke of Monmouth attended services here in 1680 as part of a recruitment drive ahead of his failed rebellion – over fifty Ilminster men fought with Monmouth five years later, an action that was later to cost a dozen of them their lives at the hands of the infamous Judge Jeffreys (see box, p.218). Today, the Minster is most notable for its elaborate **reredos**, carved from Caen stone and covered in statues of religious figures (and little critters); look out for the caterpillar to the left of Abraham and his ram, and the snail eating a grape just to the right of Moses.

Cricket St Thomas Lakes and Gardens

Cricket St Thomas, 5 miles west of Crewkerne on the A30 • Easter–Oct 10am–4pm • £4.95, dogs £1 • ⓦ warnerleisurehotels.co.uk/cricketgardens

The famous Cricket St Thomas Wildlife Park closed in 2009, dispatching its animals to various zoos across the country, and so a wildlife park without its wildlife has become **Cricket St Thomas Lakes and Gardens**, 160 acres of landscaped grounds, woodland walks and – as the name suggests – themed gardens and lakes, some of it accessed on a (free) miniature train. Nineteenth-century Cricket House, designed by Sir John Soane and used as Grantleigh Manor in the TV series *To The Manor Born*, is now an overpriced hotel, but you can take afternoon tea in *Hamilton's Tea Rooms*, a reference to the fact that Admiral Nelson and his Lady were frequent guests here.

Forde Abbey

Signed off the B3162, 5 miles southwest of Crewkerne and 3 miles southeast of Chard • **House & gardens** April–Oct Tues–Fri, Sun & bank hols noon–4pm; gardens daily 10am–6.30pm, last admission 4pm • £10.50 (gardens only £8.50), under-15s free **Tearoom** March–Oct daily 11am–4.30pm **Fruit farm** April–Oct daily 9.30am–6pm **Nursery** March–Oct daily 10am–5pm • ☎ 01460 220231, ⓦ fordeabbey.co.uk

Lying right on the border with Devon, **Forde Abbey** was founded as a Cistercian monastery in 1148 and remained a place of worship until Edmund Prideaux, Oliver

5

Cromwell's Attorney General, turned it into a private home in the middle of the seventeenth century. Prideaux shortened the Great Hall and converted the chapter house into a chapel, though both are still overwhelmingly monastic – you can still see the twelfth-century vaulting in the latter. Of the so-called State Rooms, the Saloon is the main draw, with its colour-saturated **Mortlake Tapestries**, "woven frescoes" that were made in London in 1620. Based on cartoons that Raphael created for the Sistine Chapel – now on display at the Victoria & Albert Museum in London – they show scenes from the lives of St Peter and St Paul.

The surrounding **grounds** contain a rockery, a bog garden, a huge arboretum and numerous ponds, one of which is dominated by the Centenary Fountain, at 160ft the highest in England (it's switched on each day at noon, 1.30pm & 3pm). The estate also runs a pick-your-own **fruit farm** and a **nursery**, and keeps herds of Ruby Red Devons and milking goats – produce from all these, and from the walled kitchen garden, is served in the vaulted *Undercroft Tearoom*.

Chard

The sizeable town of **CHARD** is the highest in Somerset, and its most southerly, clinging onto the last mile of the county before it slips into Dorset and Devon. Its long history dates back nearly eight hundred years – which is plenty of time for it to have lost any charm it may have once had. There are several survivors of the town's lace-making past – including Holyrood Lace Mill, on Holyrood Street, and Boden Mill – but other than its enjoyable little **museum**, the most intriguing aspect of Chard today is the streams on its High Street, one of which flows north into the Bristol Channel, the other south into the English Channel.

Chard and District Museum

Godworthy House, High St • Mid-April to Oct Mon–Fri 10.30am–4.30pm, Sat 10.30am–1pm • £3, children free • ☎ 01460 65091, ⓦ chardmuseum.co.uk

Staffed by enthusiastic volunteers, the Tardis-like **Chard and District Museum** is a rabbit warren of rooms, its main displays focusing on **John Stringfellow**, who invented powered flight when his 9lb aircraft flew 22 yards in an old lace mill here in 1848. It's also worth venturing into the barn out back to the exhibition on his fellow Chardian **James Gillingham**, a shoemaker who used his skills to better the lives of local amputees at the end of the nineteenth century; his assorted creations – wooden hands and clodhopper feet – look rudimentary now but were pioneering at the time. The carnival costumes upstairs in the New Inn building give a flavour of the pageantry if you're not around for the real thing in autumn (see box, p.34).

ARRIVAL AND INFORMATION

CREWKERNE AND THE WEST

By train Crewkerne Station, a mile south of town on the A356, is served by regular trains from Basingstoke (1hr 50min); Exeter St Davids (50min); London Waterloo (2hr 40min); Salisbury (1hr 10min); and Yeovil Pen Mill (10min).

By bus Berry's Coaches runs a twice-daily service between London (Hammersmith) and Ilminster (3hr 10min).

Crewkerne LIC Town Hall, Market Square (Mon–Wed 9am–1pm & 2–5pm, Thurs & Sat 9am–1pm, Fri 9am–1pm & 2–4pm; ☎ 01460 75928).

Ilminster LIC The Meeting House, East Street (April–Oct Mon–Fri 10am–1pm; ☎ 01460 57294).

Chard LIC The Guildhall, Fore Street (Mon–Fri 10am–4pm, Sat 10am–1pm; ☎ 01460 260051).

ACCOMMODATION

As well as the below, the lovely *Farndon Thatch* in Puckington (see p.207) is just under 3 miles up the B3168 from Ilminster, while the places southwest of Yeovil (see p.204) are within six or so miles of Crewkerne.

The Five Dials Goose Lane, Horton ☎ 01460 55359, ⓦ thefivedials.co.uk. Tastefully furnished, contemporary

rooms – two doubles (one small), a twin and a good-sized family room (£100) – that are stylish yet homely, with smart bathrooms and soft throws draped across the beds. Good food and local brews, too (see below). **£60**

★ **Lord Poulett Arms** Hinton St George ☎01460 73149, ⓦlordpoulettarms.com. Set in the drop-dead gorgeous hamstone village of Hinton St George, the *Lord Poulett Arms* is one of the best places to stay in Somerset, with the kind of rooms you'd want to live in – classy but comfortable, with antique beds, seagrass floors, and gilded mirrors set against exposed hamstone or Osbourne and Little wallpaper. Some rooms have a slipper bath in the middle, all have the sort of thoughtful touches that only come with small-scale lodgings: Roberts radios rather than satellite TV, home-made biscuits in place of tartan-packet shortbread. What's more, there's a fantastic pub-restaurant at the bottom of the stairs (see below). Minimum 2nt stay at weekends. **£85**

EATING AND DRINKING

Barleymow's On the A30, half a mile west of Chard ☎01460 62130, ⓦbarleymowsfarmshop.co.uk. Incredibly popular with families, *Barleymow's* gets most of its ingredients from the adjoining farm shop, so dishes like lamb and apricot casserole (£7.95) and goats' cheese quiche (£6.25) are most definitely made on site. In the summer holidays, there's a maize maze and an adventure playground (daily 9.30am–5pm; £4.50). Daily 8.30am–5pm, Sun & bank hols till 4pm.

The Five Dials Goose Lane, Horton ☎01460 55359, ⓦthefivedials.co.uk. Smart, modern pub with welcoming owners and a choice of tables either round a buzzing Shaker-style bar up front or in the more open (and less atmospheric) restaurant behind. There's a strong specials board, but you can't go far wrong with the tasty pan-roasted chicken with broad bean and bacon cream (£10.50). Draught Otter Ale and Perry's cider, from just down the road (see p.209). Tues–Sun noon–2pm & 6.30–9pm (Sun till 8.30pm), bar till 11pm (11.30pm Fri & Sat).

★ **Lord Poulett Arms** Hinton St George ☎01460 73149, ⓦlordpoulettarms.com. Award-winning restaurant – one half bare flagstones, the other polished wooden floorboards – serving game from Exmoor and fish from Dorset, with lunch running along the lines of gourmet sarnies with triple-cooked chips or home-made herb gnocchi, and dinner featuring cider-soused mackerel or pan-roasted lamb (mains from £11). The cosy bar, decked in dried hops and lit with flickering candles, serves Somerset ale from the barrel, cider from a jug and, in season, home-made sloe gin or mulled wine. In summer, regulars play boules on the lavender-fringed piste out back; in winter, open fires crackle with contentment. Daily noon–2pm & 7–9pm, bar till 3pm & 6.30–11pm.

no. 7 the café 7 Market St, Crewkerne ☎01460 74194. Chose from nearly forty sandwiches – home-cooked gammon, ox tongue, and Somerset Brie and coleslaw among them – plus a range of daily specials and lighter bites such as home-made quiches and smoked salmon salads. Everything that goes into their breakfasts and lunches (from 11.30am) is freshly sourced from *no. 5 the deli*, their sister operation two doors down the road. Mon–Fri 9am–5pm, Sat 9am–3pm.

The Tea Tree 11 West St, Ilminster ☎01460 55958, ⓦtheteatree.co.uk. Elegant Mediterranean-style café with a bare-brick interior and a simple but interesting menu of sweet potato and ginger soup, beetroot burger, steak and stilton salad, and the like (mains around £6.75). There's an attractive little garden out back. Tues–Sat 9.30am–5pm, Sun 10am–2pm.

ENTERTAINMENT

Arts Centre at the Meeting House East St, Ilminster ☎01460 55783, ⓦthemeetinghouse.org.uk. Housed in a former chapel, this is a great little venue, with changing exhibitions in the Main Gallery and Café Gallery, plus regular music sessions (mainly jazz and classical) and craft demonstrations. Mon–Fri 9.30am–4.30pm, Sat 10am–2.30pm.

SHOPPING

Crewkerne Antiques Centre 16 Market St, Crewkerne ⓦcrewkerneantiques.co.uk. Fifty antiques dealers under one roof, with a treasure-trove of prints, jewellery, china goods and furniture that should turn up something for patient browsers. Mon–Sat 9.30am–4.30pm.

Gresham Books 31 Market St, Crewkerne. Probably the best of the town's many antiquarian bookshops, with higgledy-piggledy stacks of local-interest and unusual books, from *The Pouletts of Hinton St George* to *The Illustrated Guide to Horse Tack*. Mon–Sat 10am–5pm.

Taunton, Bridgwater and the Quantocks

HORSERIDING ON THE QUANTOCKS

Taunton, Bridgwater and the Quantocks

6

The two major towns of western Somerset, Bridgwater and Taunton, offer a few specific attractions, notably Bridgwater's Blake Museum and the new Museum of Somerset housed in Taunton's castle, but few people linger long in either place, and they are primarily useful as transport hubs and bases for excursions to the nearby Quantock Hills. Covered by heathland, woods and steeply sloping meadows, this wedge of uplands slanting northwest towards the Bristol Channel is home to snug villages nestled among scenic wooded valleys or "combes".

Designated England's first AONB (Area of Outstanding Natural Beauty) in 1956, the Quantocks offer an alluring alternative to the more famous expanses of Exmoor – less dramatic perhaps, but equally panoramic. The hills hold literary interest in the home of Samuel Taylor Coleridge, who lived in **Nether Stowey** for three years, but the main recreation hereabouts lies in the great outdoors, specifically hiking, biking and riding. The best areas, however, are remote from the public transport network, which sticks to the main A39, running west from Bridgwater, and A358 from Taunton, the two roads meeting near the northwestern end of the range at Williton. You can get a taster, though, on the private, steam-hauled **West Somerset Railway** between **Bishops Lydeard**, a village north of Taunton, and the coastal resort of Minehead (see p.249), with stops close to some of the thatched, typically English hamlets along the west flank of the Quantocks.

If you're not tempted by the **accommodation** choices at Bridgwater and Taunton, you'll find good options in the smaller centres, such as Nether Stowey, **Combe Florey** and **Crowcombe**, while refreshment is provided at some excellent pubs tucked away in these and other unspoiled rural outposts. There are **horseriding** facilities at many local farms, and a good network of bridleways and walking routes throughout the hills.

GETTING AROUND

Bridgwater and Taunton are both on the main **train** line between Bristol and Exeter. Apart from the steam and diesel trains of the private **West Somerset Railway**, however, **public transport** in the Quantocks area is limited to **bus** services running along the A39 between Bridgwater and Minehead and A358 between Taunton and Minehead, with stops at or near the main Quantock villages. Traveline (☎0871 200 2233, ⊛traveline.org.uk) has full **schedules** for the whole region.

By train Hourly trains link Taunton and Bridgwater, taking 20min. Wellington has no station. Between late March and early November (plus some dates in Feb & Dec), the West Somerset Railway (☎01643 704996, ⊛west-somerset-railway.co.uk) plies between Bishops Lydeard (with bus connections to the nearby main-line station at Taunton) and Minehead (see p.249), with stops at Crowcombe, Heathfield, Stogumber, Williton, Watchet (see p.246), Washford and Dunster (see p.266).

By bus The major bus company in these parts is First (☎0845 602 0156, ⊛firstgroup.com), but Stagecoach (☎01392 427711, ⊛stagecoachbus.com) and Webberbus (☎0800 096 3039, ⊛webberbus.com) also operate routes. Webberbus #15A connects Taunton, Wellington and

BRIDGWATER & TAUNTON CANAL

Highlights

❶ Museum of Somerset The county's history – and plenty more – is imaginatively encapsulated in this newly opened collection housed in Taunton's old castle, especially strong on the Roman and pre-Roman eras and the seventeenth century. **See p.217**

❷ Bridgwater & Taunton Canal Walk or cycle along the fourteen or so miles of this tranquil waterway to explore a range of wildlife, with pubs and other refreshment stops along the way. **See p.221**

❸ Bridgwater Carnival There's not a lot of action on show in this small provincial town unless you come at Carnival, when the whole

place explodes in an exuberant outburst of sound and spectacle. **See p.227**

❹ Coleridge Cottage, Nether Stowey Once home to Samuel Taylor Coleridge, this modest dwelling in the Quantock Hills is now an absorbing museum devoted to the poet and the birth of the English Romantic movement. **See p.227**

❺ The walk to Wills Neck The Quantock Hills offer quiet, undemanding hikes in secluded combes, but the payback is immensely satisfying, with steep, scenic dips and folds and stunning vistas. **See p.228**

HIGHLIGHTS ARE MARKED ON THE MAP ON P.216

Bridgwater hourly (not Sun). There are regular connections to Minehead from Bridgwater and Taunton. Service #14 runs every couple of hours (not Sun) from Bridgwater to Nether Stowey and Holford, while #28 and #X28 run once or twice an hour between Taunton and Bishops Lydeard, continuing along the A358 to Combe Florey, Crowcombe and Watchet and Minehead, sometimes involving short walks from the stops to the village centres.

Taunton and around

Somerset's county town of **TAUNTON** lies in the fertile Vale of Taunton, watered by the surrounding Quantock, Brendon and Blackdown hills. The region is famed for its

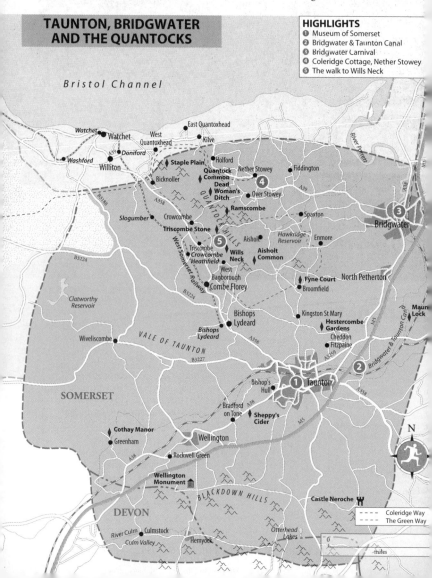

TAUNTON, BRIDGWATER AND THE QUANTOCKS

HIGHLIGHTS
1. Museum of Somerset
2. Bridgwater & Taunton Canal
3. Bridgwater Carnival
4. Coleridge Cottage, Nether Stowey
5. The walk to Wills Neck

roduction of cider, while Taunton itself is host to one of the country's biggest cattle markets. The town's much restored castle holds the newly opened **Museum of Somerset**, while, a few steps from the county cricket ground and the **Cricket Museum**, are the pinnacled and battlemented towers of the town's two most important churches: **St James** and **St Mary Magdalene**, both fifteenth-century though remodelled by the Victorians.

Out of town, both **Hestercombe Gardens** and **Fyne Court** would make splendid spots for a picnic, while you can delve into the finer points of cider-making at **Sheppy's Cider**.

Taunton Castle

Castle Green

Started in the twelfth century, **Taunton Castle** became one of the most important strongholds in the county. Here was staged the trial of royal claimant Perkin Warbeck, who in 1490 declared himself to be the Duke of York, the younger of the "Princes in the Tower" (the sons of Edward IV, who had been murdered seven years earlier). It was also the venue of one of the bloodiest of Judge Jeffreys' assizes following the Duke of Monmouth's rebellion (see box, p.218), at which 514 prisoners were tried for treason, of whom 144 were sentenced to be hanged, drawn and quartered. Some of the structure was demolished in 1662, and much of the rest has been altered, but you can still get a good idea of its once-imposing keep and inner bailey (courtyard).

Museum of Somerset

Taunton Castle • Tues–Sat 10am–5pm • Free • ☎ 01823 255088, ⓦ www.somerset.gov.uk/museums

The castle building now houses the **Museum of Somerset**, a well-organized and creatively displayed collection that opened in 2011. Centring on the castle's original Great Hall, the museum focuses mainly on the history, prehistory and geology of the county, starting with one of the largest ammonite fossils found in Britain and a complete plesiosaur skeleton discovered by fishermen in 2003. The human presence is represented by such items as the **Shapwick Canoe** (c.350 BC), suspended from the ceiling and made from a hollowed-out tree trunk preserved in peat; a wooden toy axe (possibly Britain's earliest known toy), and the **"God dolly"** from around 2500 BC, showing both male and female characteristics (and claimed to be the country's oldest carving of a human figure). The most spectacular Roman exhibits include the **Shapwick hoard** of 9,238 silver coins from the third century AD, the even greater **Frome hoard** of more than 52,000 coins unearthed in 2010, and the magnificent **Low Ham mosaic**, from around 350 AD, depicting the story of Dido and Aeneas. Exhibits from Somerset's Middle Ages include the vivid **Congresbury carving**, probably from the shrine of St Cyngar dating from around 1000, and a graphic collection of church carvings, but it is the seventeenth century that receives most attention, not least in the world's largest collection of (of all things) cauldrons and skillets – many of them dangling overhead. There are arms and armour from the Civil War, and the Monmouth Rebellion is brought to life in the very room that held captured rebels before their execution. Modern times are sparsely covered, but a separate section houses the **Somerset Military Museum**, which tells the story of Somerset regiments in combat in the Zulu and Boer wars, the Afghan War of 1919 and World War II. Elsewhere in the museum you can view and listen to recordings of various local figures – such as Glastonbury Festival organizers Michael and Emily Eavis – talking about their experience of Somerset life.

St Mary Magdalene

Church Square • Mon–Fri 10am–4pm, Sat 9am–1pm • Free • ⓦ stmarymagdalenetaunton.org.uk

Grandly set at the end of the Georgian-era Hammet Street, the church of **St Mary Magdalene** has seen many changes over a period of some 1300 years. An Anglo-Saxon church here was replaced in the thirteenth century by a more solid construction, which

6

became the parish church of Taunton in 1308, but was itself much altered and rebuilt in the Perpendicular style between 1480 and 1514. In this form, with its four aisles giving it width almost as great as its length, the church became the model for others throughout this part of Somerset. When this structure in turn was deemed unsafe, the church was completely rebuilt in 1858–62, though faithfully in keeping with its previous appearance. Thus, the richly sculpted **tower**, an iconic image in Taunton and at 163ft the highest church tower in Somerset, is a replica of the original tower of around 1510, while the roof walls and pillars of the church are the main features surviving from the sixteenth century.

The interior
The earliest survivors of its previous history lie inside on the north aisle: two pink columns from the church's thirteenth-century construction. Below lie the foundations of the even earlier wooden church probably built by King Ine of the West Saxons in the eighth century. The magnificent stained glass of the West Window is from the 1860s, as is most of the glass of the church, the original windows having been smashed by Cromwell's troops in the seventeenth century. The hammer-beam roof and roof-bosses carved with medieval masks have survived more or less intact from the sixteenth century. Looking around, you'll see angels everywhere – 133 in all, on the roof, the capitals and the walls.

St James
Coal Orchard • Open for services , plus Mon–Sat 10am–3.30pm • Free • ⓦ stjamestaunton.co.uk

A less ambitious structure than St Mary Magdalene, the church of **St James** was rebuilt around 1840 but still retains its medieval lines and barrel roof, and has remnants of the early fourteenth-century building that stood on the site. The elaborate, fifteenth-century font is probably the single most interesting feature, with carved panels on its eight sides showing figures of Christ and his disciples. The pulpit, carved with mermaids and suns, dates from 1633, and the chancel holds a copy of a Rubens painting on its north side. Soaring above the adjacent cricket ground, the **tower** (120ft) is smaller and slightly older than that of St Mary Magdalene, and was replaced – again, in the original style – in the 1870s. If you stand by it while the bells are rung for services, you can feel the structure actually rocking.

Somerset County Cricket Ground
Priory Ave • **Museum** April–Oct Tues–Fri 11am–4pm • Closed to non-spectators on match days • £1 • ⓦ somersetcricketmuseum.co.uk •
Matches Tickets for one-day matches around £20 in advance, £25 on the day; for county cricket matches £10 in advance, £15 on the day
To buy tickets, call ☎ 0845 337 1875, or visit ⓦ www.somersetcountycc.co.uk, or buy at the Andrew Caddick Pavilion

Somerset is one of England's great cricketing counties, and it's particularly hard to escape

---

THE MONMOUTH REBELLION

Somerset and Dorset were the scene for one of England's last significant popular **uprisings**. Having landed in Lyme Regis from his base in Holland in June 1685, the Protestant **Duke of Monmouth**, an illegitimate son of Charles II, was proclaimed king in Taunton's Market Square followed by an equally enthusiastic reception in Bridgwater. Resentment against the Catholic James II at this time was high, and Monmouth knew that if he could take Bristol, a potential source of mass support, the campaign could swing in his favour. However, in a botched night attack on the royal forces at Westonzoyland, near Bridgwater, his untrained rebel army was routed at the **Battle of Sedgemoor** – the last pitched battle to be fought on English soil (see box, p.182). Monmouth himself was later captured while trying to escape the country in the guise of a shepherd, and beheaded on London's Tower Hill. Meanwhile, a period of savage repression was unleashed in the West Country under the infamous Judge Jeffreys, whose **Bloody Assizes** resulted in gibbets and gutted corpses displayed around Somerset.

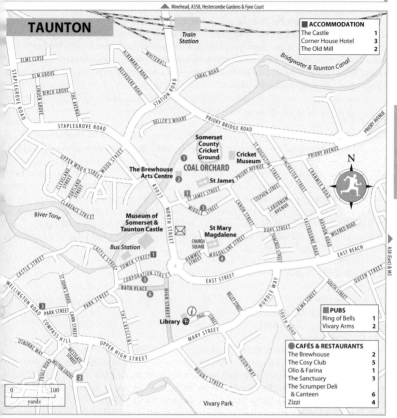

Minehead, A358, Hestercombe Gardens & Fyne Court

TAUNTON

6

some reference to the game in Taunton, home to Somerset County Cricket Club – which has numbered Ian Botham and Viv Richards among its members – as well as England's Women's Cricket Association. Located just north of the centre of town, the **County Ground** is open to view on non-match days, and includes a **museum** dedicated to the sport, housed in what was once part of a sixteenth-century priory. Here fans can feast on ancient equipment, black-and-white photos of players, examples of the evolution of the cricket bat and a plethora of caps, badges and blazers, among other memorabilia. Non-cricket oddities include Queen Victoria's walking stick, but first and foremost the museum is a celebration of the game, and an opportunity for non-fans to dip into the arcane world of cricket.

Hestercombe Gardens

Cheddon Fitzpaine • Daily 10am–6pm, last admission at 5pm • £9.50 • ☎ 01823 413747, ⓦ hestercombe.com • By car or bike, head north of the town centre along Cheddon Rd to Rowford and Cheddon Fitzpaine, following the brown signs; by public transport, take bus #23 (not Sun) from Taunton to Kingston St Mary and walk a couple of miles southwest towards Cheddon Fitzpaine

Three miles north of Taunton, **Hestercombe Gardens** grew from a Georgian landscape garden laid out along a combe in the eighteenth century by Hestercombe's then owner, the marvellously named soldier and artist Coplestone Warre Bampfylde. Later additions were made on the south side of the house: a Victorian Terrace from the 1870s, and the Edwardian Formal Garden designed by Edwin Lutyens and Gertrude Jekyll in 1904–1908, both enjoying serene views over the Vale of Taunton.

The **landscaped park** behind the house, which was discovered in its overgrown state in 1992 and subsequently restored, is the place for longer strolls, taking in ponds, a cascade, a Chinese bridge, a temple arbour, a "Witch House" and a Gothic alcove. Near the entrance there's also a **bat roost**, viewable through a video link, where rare Lesser Horseshoe bats congregate in summer. The house itself is occupied by council offices and not open to the public.

6 Fyne Court

Broomfield • Early Jan to late Dec Mon–Fri 9am–5pm, Sat & Sun 10am–5pm • Free; NT • ☎ 01823 451587, ⓦ nationaltrust.org.uk /fynecourt • To reach Broomfield by public transport from Taunton, take bus #23 to Kingston St Mary (not Sun), from where it's a 3-mile walk up Lodes Lane

On the southern edge of the Quantock Hills, five miles north of Taunton, stands **Fyne Court**, famous as the home of Andrew Crosse (1784–1855), a child prodigy who had mastered ancient Greek at the age of eight and became a pioneer in the new science of electricity. Crosse first became obsessed with the potential of electricity while at school in Bristol, and on inheriting the family estates and fortune in 1805 he set up a laboratory in Fyne Court – much to the consternation of the local yokels, for whom he became the "Wizard of Broomfield" and the "Thunder and Lightning Man" on account of his noisy experiments. Crosse's renown grew, and it has been suggested that the seeds of the Frankenstein story were first planted when Percy Bysshe and Mary Shelley attended one of his lectures in London. He continued his electrical studies until the end; his last reported words were: "The utmost extent of human knowledge is but comparative ignorance."

The grounds

Of Fyne Court itself there are scant remains – the building was mostly destroyed by a fire in 1894. A former barn next to the courtyard café displays some of Crosse's notes and items from his laboratory, as well as information about the Quantocks, with examples of the rocks that make up the range. The main attraction, however, is Fyne Court's former leisure gardens, now largely overgrown and consisting of woodland and meadows. You can follow various trails around the park (pick up pamphlets at the café); look out too for details of open-air drama productions occasionally held here.

A left turn out of Fyne Court will bring you to the local churchyard, which has an obelisk in memory of Crosse. The church itself, **St Mary's and All Saints**, dates in parts from 1320, and has a table supposed to have come from Crosse's laboratory, along with some good specimens of the carved bench-ends that are so characteristic of Quantock churches.

Sheppy's Cider

Three Bridges, Bradford-on-Tone • Mon–Sat 8.30am–6pm, July & Aug also Sun 11am–4pm • Museum £2 • ☎ 01823 461233, ⓦ sheppyscider.com

Here in the heart of cider country, you can explore the process of cider-making at **Sheppy's Cider**, 3.5 miles southwest of Taunton (and the same distance northeast of Wellington) on the A38. The complex combines a shop, restaurant, museum and orchards. You can taste the apple juices and ciders while pondering a purchase in the farm shop, stroll around the orchards to view the resident herd of pedigree longhorn cattle as well as other farm animals, and learn the nuts and bolts of cider-making in the Rural Life Museum, which shows the tools and equipment not only for producing the stuff – wooden presses and mills – but those used in farming, blacksmithing, thatchering and coopering. There's also a replica of a typical farm kitchen of former days and a film of the cider-maker's year.

ALONG THE BRIDGWATER & TAUNTON CANAL

Opened in 1827, the **Bridgwater & Taunton Canal** was the only section to be completed of a major complex of waterways planned to reach as far as Bristol, a scheme abandoned with the advent of the railways. Today, the well-maintained 14.5-mile stretch makes a splendid walking or biking route (part of National Cycle Route 3), taking in some pubs along the way. You can access the canal from the River Tone that runs through Taunton's centre, for example near the Brewhouse arts complex – the canal runs off the river at Firepool Lock, a short way northeast past the cricket ground. **Maunsel Lock**, halfway along, offers refreshments and, between Easter and October, boat trips (⊛ maunsellock.co.uk).

6

ARRIVAL AND DEPARTURE TAUNTON AND AROUND

By train Taunton's station lies a few minutes' walk north of town on Kingston Road. There are frequent services between Taunton and Bridgwater (1–2 hourly; 12min), Bristol (2–3 hourly; 55min) and Weston-super-Mare (hourly; 30min) to the north, and Exeter (3–4 hourly; 50min) to the southwest. There's also the West Somerset Railway (see p.230) which terminates at Bishops Lydeard.

By bus Taunton's bus station is off Castle Green. National Express and Berry's (⊛ berryscoaches.co.uk) operate a fast service from London (9–10 daily; 3–4hr). National Express

also operates buses to Exeter (3 daily; 45min–1hr). Within the region, there are services to and from: Bishops Lydeard (Mon–Sat 2–3 hourly, Sun hourly; 30min); Bridgwater (Mon–Sat every 30min, Sun every 2hr; 45min); Burnham-on-Sea (Mon–Sat every 30min, Sun 5 daily; 1hr 15min); Glastonbury (5–6 daily; 50min); Minehead (Mon–Sat every 30min, Sun hourly; 1hr 30min); Watchet (Mon–Sat every 30min, Sun hourly; 1hr); Wells (Mon–Sat 1hr 25min; 1hr 20min); and Yeovil (Mon–Sat hourly; 1hr 15min).

INFORMATION AND GETTING AROUND

Tourist information In the library building on Paul Street (Mon–Sat 9.30am–4.30pm; ☎ 01823 336344, ⊛ heartofsomerset.com). Provides information and publications on the whole area, including the Quantocks.

By bus Webberbus runs the Taunton Flyer, a cheap and frequent service (not Sun) between Taunton's two Park-and-Ride car parks (at Silk Mills, west of town, and Taunton

Gateway, near the M5 on the east side of town) and the centre.

By bike You can rent bikes at Six Cycles, Coal Orchard, next to the Brewhouse arts centre (Mon–Sat 8.30am–5.30pm, Sun 10.30am–4pm; ☎ 01823 323130, ⊛ sixcycles.co.uk). Hybrid bikes cost £12 per hour, £22.50 per half-day, £40 per full day.

ACCOMMODATION

The Castle Castle Green ☎ 01823 272671, ⊛ the-castle-hotel.com. The town's most atmospheric hotel is an upmarket choice, a wisteria-clad, three-hundred-year-old mansion next to Taunton Castle, exuding an old-fashioned baronial style. The appropriately plush rooms come in different sizes so it's worth viewing before booking. Breakfast costs £15.50 on top of room rates. **£190**

The Corner House Hotel Park St ☎ 01823 284683, ⊛ corner-house.co.uk. This functional place is geared towards business-folk, but provides a handy base close to the centre of town. It's smart and efficient, with a popular bistro on the ground floor. Rooms are plain but clean and

modern, with fridges and free wi-fi. Breakfast is £6–8 extra. Noise from the busy road outside doesn't impinge too much. From **£90**

The Old Mill Netherclay, Bishops Hull ☎ 01823 289732, ⊛ bandbtaunton.co.uk. Right on the River Tone, this peaceful B&B in a village 2 miles west of town only has a couple of rooms, the larger one worth the slightly higher price for its idyllic river views. Restored pieces of the old mill machinery lend the place the air of a small museum. Netherclay is a right turn off the A38 heading west. No credit cards. From **£65**

EATING AND DRINKING

The Brewhouse Coal Orchard ☎ 01823 283244, ⊛ thebrewhouse.net. This arts centre by the river has a snack bar and a restaurant, *Edwardo's*, for more formal meals, where you can pick up set-price menus (£14 for two courses, £18 for three before 7pm, otherwise £18 and £22). There are tables inside and out. Mon–Sat 10am–6pm, closes 11pm when there are evening performances,

Sun bar open 2hr before performances.

The Cosy Club Hunts Court, Corporation St ☎ 01823 253476, ⊛ cosyclub.co.uk. In a converted ex-art college, this bar occupies several rooms on two floors, with comfy chairs and sofas, distressed brick walls and quirky bits and pieces scattered about. Come for a coffee or tea during the day, or tuck into a brunch, salad or sandwich; tapas are £8

6

for three, and burgers are £8–9, available all day until 9pm. Mon–Wed 9am–11pm, Thurs–Sun 9am–12.30am.

Olio & Farina Coal Orchard ☎01823 257466, ⊛olioefarina.com/taunton. On the riverfront next to the Brewhouse arts centre, this elegant Italian deli and restaurant has coffees, a nice range of simple, healthy snacks and fuller evening meals (Thurs–Sat only). The evening menu includes such dishes as *caprese* salad, lasagne, vegetable *girasole* and choice Italian desserts, with main courses £10–15. If you don't want to eat here, buy olives, cheese and wine to take away. Mon–Wed 9am–7pm (last orders), Thurs–Sat 9am–10pm (last orders).

Ring of Bells 16–17 St James St ☎01823 288487, ⊛theringofbells.co.uk. Next to St James church, this traditionally styled freehouse has more character than most of Taunton's pubs, serving a range of West Country ales which you can enjoy in the beer garden. Mon–Wed 11am–11pm, Thurs–Sat 11am–midnight, Sun noon–10.30pm.

The Sanctuary Middle St ☎01823 257788, ⊛sanctuarywinebar.co.uk. Snug corner bistro with subdued lighting, a low ceiling and polished wooden floors. The menu is modern and eclectic, for example brie fritters with a spicy tomato coulis, and chicken marinated with yoghurt and Asian spices with a couscous salad. Lunchtime mains are £8–10, in the evening £15–20. Mon–Sat noon–3pm & 6.30–11.30pm.

The Scrumper Deli & Canteen 19b Bath Place ☎01823 337234, ⊛thescrumper.com. In a tiny lane off the main shopping street, this modern place with small wooden tables inside and out makes a great stop for coffees or teas with cakes, a fresh and crusty sandwich, or a full lunch, which might be a charcuterie platter, quiche, or one of the daily specials, such as baked stuffed aubergine (most dishes £6–8). Beers, ciders and wines are also available, and there are deli items to take away. Mon 8.30am–4pm, Tues–Sat 8.30am–5pm.

Vivary Arms Wilton St ☎01823 272563, ⊛vivaryarms.com. Said to be Taunton's oldest pub, this traditional place in the Wilton neighbourhood – once a rural settlement – has a suitably villagey feel. Unpretentious bar food is served (around £9) and there's a small beer garden. Daily noon–2.30pm & 6/7–11pm; food served daily noon–1.30pm & 7–9pm.

Zizzi Magdalene St ☎01823 333110, ⊛zizzi.co.uk. This outlet of a chain of Italian eateries has a decent menu of Mediterranean staples, including a range of pizzas (£9–13), but its main selling point is the setting, in a Tudor-era schoolhouse linked to St Mary Magdalene opposite. There are fabulous views of the church, and the whole place has a lively, pleasantly airy feel. If it's too noisy in the main room, choose a spot in one of the quieter, smaller side rooms; there are also a few tables outside. Booking at weekends recommended. Mon–Sat noon–11pm, Sun till 10.30pm.

DIRECTORY

Internet Free access at the library on Paul Street (Mon, Tues & Thurs 9.30am–5.30pm, Wed & Fri 9.30am–7pm, Sat 9.30am–4pm).

Market Local produce is sold at the Farmers' Market in the High Street (Thurs 9am–3pm; ⊛tauntonfarmersmarket.co.uk).

Wellington and the Blackdown Hills

Six miles southwest of Taunton, **WELLINGTON** has an appealingly sleepy, old-fashioned air, almost detached from modern life. It merits a glance for its town museum, and makes a useful base for visiting nearby attractions. The Duke of Wellington who triumphed at the Battle of Waterloo took his title from this town in 1809, though he had no obvious link with it; apparently, he chose the place as it sounded like his family name, Wellesley. More recently, the top-drawer Wellington School, founded in 1837, has produced such alumni as the chef Keith Floyd, the actor David Suchet and the author, ex-Tory MP and ex-con Jeffrey Archer.

Heading west from Wellington, in one of the remotest corners of the Vale of Taunton, you can step back in time at the perfectly preserved **Cothay Manor**. To the south, the **Blackdown Hills** form an enticing yet overlooked area, well furnished with walking routes.

Wellington Museum

28 Fore St • Easter–Sept Mon–Fri 10am–4pm, Sat 10am–1pm; Oct to mid-Dec Sat 10am–1pm • Free • ⊛wellingtonmuseum.org.uk

Run by enthusiastic volunteers of the local history society, **Wellington Museum** squeezes plenty into its one room, a mix of diverse mementoes and historical relics, all carefully belled. As such, it provides a nice insight into how small provincial centres in the West Country were touched and occasionally buffeted by the tides of national history. The earliest items include an axehead from the area's prehistory, and there are finds from skirmishes that took place during the Civil War. The Duke of Wellington's tangential and tenuous links with the town are summarised – the victor of Waterloo is thought to have visited once, if at all – and there is some background to the monument erected outside town in his honour (see box below). More recent times are covered by a then-and-now photo gallery, a cabinet of relics of the two world wars including a French helmet, plumed and spiked, and a scale model of the town's Art Deco Wellesley Cinema from 1937 (still operating on Mantle Street). The stewards are more than willing to provide the back-story of each item, and there are pamphlets and books available for sale.

Cothay Manor

near Greenham, 5 miles west of Wellington • **House tours** June–Sept Sun 11.45am & 2.15pm • £13.50 including gardens **Gardens** Early April to Sept Tues–Thurs & Sun 11am–5pm, last entry at 4.30pm • £7 • ☎ 01823 672283, ⓦ cothaymanor.co.uk

Well off the beaten track, reached by winding country lanes, **Cothay Manor** is a hidden gem of a place, little altered since its construction in the late fifteenth century. The building is privately owned and occupied, hence the restricted opening hours, but it's worth going out of your way to join a house tour on a Sunday to appreciate the treasures within, notably the Great Hall with wingless angels on the corbels of its massive roof trusses, the exquisitely carved chimney pieces, the tiny oratory and the authentic period furnishings. At other times, only the terraced gardens are accessible, but these too are remarkable: a succession of hedged "rooms" running off a yew walk, with ponds and the occasional sculpture to add interest.

You'll need your own transport to get here, turning right off the A38 westward from Wellington, signposted Greenham.

The Blackdown Hills

Straddling the border with Devon, the **Blackdown Hills** are a sparsely populated region between Wellington and Honiton in East Devon, largely wooded with oak, ash and beech. Rising to 1033ft, the Blackdowns are ideal for aimless wandering, though there are numerous opportunities for more targeted walks along the Herepath Trails – old military roads dating from the wars between Anglo-Saxons and Vikings. Some of these bring you to archeological sites, for example **Castle Neroche**, a late Iron Age hill fort on the northeastern edge of the range south of Taunton.

THE WELLINGTON MONUMENT

You don't even need to venture into the Blackdown Hills to view their most prominent feature: the soaring **Wellington Monument**, 2.5 miles south of Wellington. The 175ft obelisk, which celebrates the Iron Duke's rather arbitrary link with the town, was initiated in 1817, two years after the Battle of Waterloo, but not completed until 1854, two years after the Duke's death. However, funded by public subscriptions and consequently built on the cheap, the monument required drastic repairs and didn't assume its present form until the 1890s. Even then, it continued to suffer from structural problems – indeed, it's currently closed until the money is stumped up for a further major renovation. When it's open to the public, a **viewing platform** near the top affords dizzying views across Somerset and Devon, taking in the Blackdown and Quantock hills, Taunton Deane and Exmoor. The steps to reach the platform are steep and extremely tight. Leaflets outlining the walk from town are available from Wellington's tourist office and museum, an easy stroll, with a steep final approach through woods. By car or bike, take South Street, then Hoyles Road and Monument Road.

Individual beauty spots include the **Culm Valley**, five miles south of Wellington, and the **Otterhead Lakes** off the B3170 south of Taunton, part of a Local Nature Reserve that centres on the River Otter. The lakes are much prized for their fishing, wildlife and general air of tranquillity; dippers, kingfishers, grey wagtails, moorhens and herons are among the birds to be spotted.

One local event worth noting is the **Blackdown Hills Beer & Music Festival**, over two days in mid-August (blackdownbeerfestival.com; £10–12 per day). The festival takes place in a huge field at Cherry Hayes Farm, near Smeatharpe, and brings together a range of ales, mostly from Devon and Somerset, and music ranging from folk to funk. Camping facilities are on hand.

ARRIVAL AND DEPARTURE

WELLINGTON AND THE BLACKDOWN HILL

By bus Services run by First, Stagecoach and Webberbus connect Wellington with Taunton (Mon–Sat 5–6 hourly, Sun 1 hourly; 25min). For onward travel to Exeter (1hr 45min–2hr 20min in all), it's easiest to return to Taunton and take a bus or train from there. Public transport links with the Blackdown Hills are sketchy; bus #20 fro Wellington goes to Culmstock, for the Culm Valley (Mon Sat 6 daily; 20min), and the frequent #99 goes fro Taunton to Castle Neroche (Mon–Sat hourly; 30min).

INFORMATION AND ACTIVITIES

Tourist information 30 Fore St (Mon–Fri 9.30am–4pm; 01823 663379, visitsomerset.co.uk).
Walking in the Blackdown Hills Ordnance Survey Explorer 128 is the best map for the Blackdown Hills area. See blackdownhillsaonb.org.uk or nerochescheme.org for hiking and biking routes, or pick up itineraries from the tourist offices at Wellington or Taunton, which can also supply lists of stables and riding schools. You can pick up digital guide to one of the longer routes, the fourteen-mi Staple Fitzpaine Herepath, on handsets available free fro Taunton's office.
Cycling You can rent bikes from King's Cycles, 7 Corn Hi North Street (01823 662260, kingscycles.co.u Mon–Sat). Mountain bikes £15 per day.

ACCOMMODATION

The Blue Mantle 2 Mantle St 01823 662000. Good-value, no-frills B&B in the centre of town. It's friendly and clean, with all rooms en suite, and provides a decent breakfast in the large bay-windowed front room. **£60**
The Cleve Mantle St 01823 662033, clevehotel.com. Guests at this country house hotel can take full advantage of its main attractions – the gym, the indoor pool, various spa and beauty treatments, and a decent restaurant. Despite some modern touches, the rooms are a bit outdated, and it's worth paying extra for a more spaciou premier room. It's out of town, half a mile west off the A38 next to the Texaco garage (bus #22A or #92). From **£90**
Old Vicarage 8 Exeter Rd, Rockwell Green 0182 661376, theoldvicarage-rockwellgreen.co.uk. A mi west of town on the A38 (simply follow Mantle Street), th wi-fi-enabled Victorian place offers three en-suite rooms large gardens to front and rear, and award-winnin breakfasts. No credit cards. From **£55**

EATING AND DRINKING

The Cheese and Wine Shop 11 South St 01823 662899, thecheeseandwineshop.co.uk. There's a great choice of goodies sold at this deli, not just delicious pies, pastries, artisan breads and local cheeses, but also Belgian chocolates, fruit smoothies and ice cream in such flavours as stem ginger and coffee crunch. Mon–Sat 9am–5.30pm.
Flavours 59 High St 01823 662006, flavourslicensedrestaurant.co.uk. The menu intersperses traditional English dishes such as Gressingham Duck and fillets of sea bass with more exotic choices, for example pork goulash (all £10–14). At lunchtime, tasty platters of mezze (£7.50) and tapas (£8.50 for three) come with a drink included. Tues–Sat noon–2pm & 7–9pm.
Garden Café 17 High St 01823 660896. A handy spot in the centre of town for a range of panini, salads, jacke potatoes and fry-ups, all under £5, or more substantia dinners at weekends. There's a spacious garden at the back Mon–Sat 8.30am–4.30pm, until 4pm in winter, Su 11am–3pm, Fri closes 8pm in summer.
The Vintage 24 Fore St 01823 662369 thevintagewellington.co.uk. Traditional pub with paved beer garden, good for a pint of West Country ale There are snacks, bar meals, live bands on Saturda evenings (also some Fridays) and occasional summe barbecues. Top-floor accommodation is also availabl (£50). Mon–Thurs & Sun 11am–12.30am, Fri & Sat til 1.30am; food served Mon–Sat noon–2.30pm an 6–9pm, Sun noon–2.30pm.

Bridgwater

Sedate **BRIDGWATER** has seen little excitement since the seventeenth century, when it was first besieged then almost completely destroyed by Parliamentary forces during the Civil War, lying derelict for almost a century afterwards. What little of the town survived was then embroiled in the events surrounding the Monmouth Rebellion of 1685 – the Duke of Monmouth and his army spent their last night here before their catastrophic defeat at the Battle of Sedgemoor (see box, p.182). The nineteenth century saw a partial revival of fortunes when the town became a centre for roofing tiles and brick production, but the Industrial Revolution largely by-passed Bridgwater, and recent times have seen the town further marginalized in the life of the county and country. Nowadays, the place is most associated with the **Bridgwater Carnival**, though this also takes in other Somerset towns (see box, p.227).

Bridgwater's major attractions are the excellent **Blake Museum** on Blake Street and the magnificent church of **St Mary's** in the centre. Less essential but equally absorbing, Bridgwater's **Brick and Tile Museum** throws light on this once-thriving local industry. Elsewhere, much of the town has a run-down look, and is overrun with traffic, though traces of its eighteenth-century prosperity are visible in some handsome architecture around East Quay and West Quay (alongside the River Parrett), in King Square and in Castle Street, where every entrance of the otherwise uniform row of early Georgian houses is different. On Dampiet Street, the red-brick Unitarian **Christ Church** is where Coleridge preached in 1797 and 1798, while nearby on Cornhill (at the top of Fore Street), the elegantly colonnaded **Rotunda** dates from 1844, originally part of the old market hall and now a restaurant (see p.226).

Bridgwater lies at one end of the **Bridgwater & Taunton Canal** (see box, p.221), and on the River Parrett Trail, a fifty-mile route from the river's source in the Dorset hills to its mouth at Stert Point on the Bristol Channel (see box, p.208).

Blake Museum

Blake St • Tues–Sat 10am–4pm • Free • ☎ 01278 456127, ⓦ bridgwatermuseum.org.uk

The probable birthplace of local hero Robert Blake (see box below) stands by the River Parrett, a sixteenth-century building now housing the **Blake Museum**. Most of the ground-floor exhibits are related to him, or place him in context with such items as model ships and a contemporary sea chest. Other rooms show local fossils, including a large ichthyosaurus, and illustrate the town's Roman and medieval history. Upstairs, the Battle Room focuses on the Monmouth Rebellion and the Battle of Sedgemoor, while the Maritime Room displays shipbuilding and rope-making artefacts. Lastly, the Bygones Room brings together everything from agricultural tools to an old boneshaker bicycle, and has a section devoted to the local brick and tile industry.

BLAKE IN BRIDGWATER

Bridgwater's most feted native son is **Robert Blake** (1598–1657), a swashbuckling soldier and naval hero who won glory during the English Civil War and then against the Dutch and Spanish fleets. Fighting on the Parliamentary side, he distinguished himself as a commander in the field during the defence of Bristol in 1643 and in subsequent engagements in Lyme Regis and Taunton. In 1649, Blake was appointed General-at-Sea, in which role he created a permanent, well-disciplined navy, adept in such techniques as blockades and amphibious landings. Blake went on to win outstanding victories in the English Channel and the Mediterranean, and at his death he was afforded the rare privilege of a state funeral and burial in Westminster Abbey. A **statue** of Blake surveys the modern shopping centre on Cornhill – one of the country's very few monuments to a Republican.

6

St Mary's

St Mary St • Open for services, plus Thurs 10am–1.30pm • Free • ⓦ saintmaryschurchbridgwater.org.uk

Bridgwater's most striking monument is the thirteenth- to fourteenth-century church of St Mary's, immediately identifiable by its polygonal, slightly angled, red-sandstone steeple (175ft), soaring above the town centre like a medieval rocket. Much of the interior was rebuilt in the 1840s and 1870s, but there is plenty to admire here, including a black oak pulpit from 1490 and a seventeenth-century Italian altarpiece – the impressive hammer-beam roof, however, was added in the 1850s. Sadly, the church is usually locked up, so you'll need to time your visit carefully.

Somerset Brick and Tile Museum

East Quay • Tues–Thurs 10am–4pm • Free • ☎ 01278 426088

Bridgwater's brick- and tile-making industry petered out in the 1960s, but this former mainstay of the local economy is celebrated at the Somerset Brick and Tile Museum, housed in the county's only surviving industrial kiln on the banks of the Parrett. The various stages of the manufacturing process are explained, from excavation through to weathering, pugging, extrusion, moulding, drying and finally firing. You can view numerous examples, enter the "pinnacle" kiln and, under instruction, try your hand at tile-making.

ARRIVAL AND DEPARTURE BRIDGWATER

By bus There are services to: Glastonbury (Mon–Sat hourly, Sun 4 daily; 50min–1hr 10min); Taunton (Mon–Sat every 30min, Sun every 2hr; 45min); and Wells (Mon–Sat hourly; 1hr 30min). For the northern Quantocks, bus #14 (Mon–Sat 5–7 daily) stops at: Nether Stowey (30–45min), Holford (50min); Kilve (40–50min); and Watchet (50min–1hr 10min).

ACCOMMODATION

Admiral's Rest 5 Taunton St ☎ 01278 458580, ⓦ admiralsrest.com. Showing little evidence of its former role as a Victorian workhouse, this is a useful if unremarkable B&B, well-placed for the centre and with reasonable rates. It's cycle-friendly and has private parking. No credit cards. **£60**

The Old Vicarage 45–51 St Mary St ☎ 01278 458891, ⓦ theoldvicaragebridgwater.com. This central choice right opposite St Mary's church is one of Bridgwater's oldest buildings (you can see a section of its wattle-and-daub fabric on the left of the archway). Rooms are mainly small and modern, with the exception of the Somerset Room, a grand, beamed chamber complete with four-poster bed, at around £160. There's a bistro (see below), and a nice garden for an evening drink. Opt for a room away from the street to avoid the noise of weekend carousers. From **£97**

The Tudor 21 St Mary St ☎ 01278 422093, ⓦ tudorhotel.co.uk. Though the building dates from 1610, when it started life as a bakery, this hotel has shed most of its historic character and is primarily used by business-folk. It's not exactly over-modernized, however, its rooms furnished in a low-key, traditional style. There's a little more atmosphere in the restaurant and bar, and there's free wi-fi. **£66.50**

EATING, DRINKING AND ENTERTAINMENT

Bridgwater Arts Centre 11–13 Castle St ☎ 01278 422700, ⓦ bridgwaterartscentre.co.uk. Worth seeking out for exhibitions, concerts, films, plays and comedy, not to mention the agreeable bar where there are regular free music sessions. Bar Tues–Sat 7–11pm.

The Nutmeg House Angel Crescent, behind the shopping centre off Fore St ☎ 01278 457823. This casual café makes a useful refreshment stop, offering coffees and cakes as well as all-day breakfasts, pastas, soups, steaks and grills, and there are some outdoor tables. Hot dishes are mostly £6–9. Mon–Sat 7.30am–5pm, Sun 10am–3pm.

The Old Vicarage 45–51 St Mary St ☎ 01278 458891. The beamed, traditional restaurant attached to this hotel (see above) is the place for classic English dishes such as slow-roasted duck and seafood grill (£10–15). Also opens during the day as a café. Mon–Sat: café 10.30am–3pm, restaurant 6.30–8pm (last orders).

Prezzo 30 Cornhill, off Fore St ☎ 01278 433600, ⓦ prezzorestaurants.co.uk. Though this restaurant is part of a so-so chain of Italian eateries, the location alone makes eating here something of an event, in the Victorian Rotunda building with grand views from the tall windows. Pizzas, pastas and grills dominate the menu, all around £7–11, and you can come here for just coffees and teas during the day. Daily 11am–11pm.

THE BRIDGWATER CARNIVAL

In a country that has never made a big deal about **carnival**, Bridgwater puts on a pretty spectacular show. The **Bridgwater Carnival** (Ⓦbridgwatercarnival.org.uk) claims to be the largest illuminated procession in Europe, attracting up to 150,000 people and traffic queues for miles around. Dating from 1605, when local people celebrated the failure of **Guy Fawkes** to blow up the Houses of Parliament in the Gunpowder Plot (one of the Catholic conspirators hailed from nearby Nether Stowey), the Carnival has expanded in recent years and now takes in various other local towns and villages, including Glastonbury and Wells. In Bridgwater, the festivities usually take place on the first Saturday of November, the procession starting at 7pm and taking more than two hours to trundle past on its 2.5-mile route. The grandly festooned floats belonging to Somerset's seventy-odd carnival clubs are accompanied by samba bands, majorettes and masqueraders. Festivities kick off the evening before, with a grand fireworks display at 7pm; there are more fireworks for the finale, when, following an age-old tradition, the High Street is lined with "squibbers" who set off their "squibs" (fireworks) simultaneously – a spectacular sight worth sticking around for. Visitors to the area in early November should book way ahead for accommodation and be prepared for massive crowds in Bridgwater itself.

The Quantock Hills

West of Bridgwater, crossed by clear streams and grazed by red deer, the **Quantock Hills** measure just twelve miles in length and are mostly 800–900ft high. Most of the secluded settlements lie on the edges of the range, linked by a tangle of narrow lanes and connected to Bridgwater and Taunton by regular **bus** services, and with a restored **steam railway** tracking the western flank of the range. Many of the Quantock villages – notably **Bishops Lydeard**, **Combe Florey** and **Crowcombe** – boast beautifully preserved churches with superb examples of medieval wood-carving.

The Romantic poets Coleridge and Wordsworth were famous denizens of the area around 1800, and they brought with them such celebrated acquaintances as Hazlitt, with whom they trudged indefatigably over the hills. Today, the Quantocks are notorious for confrontations between hunting parties and anti-hunt activists, but if you want to indulge in less contentious **pony-trekking**, the tourist office in Taunton can supply a list of stables.

Nether Stowey

On the northeastern edge of the hills, eight miles west of Bridgwater on the A39, the pretty village of **NETHER STOWEY** is best known for its association with **Samuel Taylor Coleridge**, who walked here from Bristol at the end of 1796 to join his wife and child at their new home (see box, p.228). In **Coleridge Cottage** (mid-March–Oct Thurs–Sun 11am–5pm; £5; NT; Ⓣ01643 821314, Ⓦnationaltrust.org.uk) you can see the parlour, kitchen, bedroom and an exhibition room containing letters, early editions and various locks of the poet's hair. The house has changed considerably since Coleridge lived here – rooms have been added and it even served as an inn during the later nineteenth century – but it's easy to get a real feel for the man and his imagination. In the reading room, you can clamp on some headphones to hear readings of his work while browsing books on Romanticism and the Quantocks.

You can pick up leaflets here on the **Coleridge Way** (Ⓦwww.coleridgeway.co.uk), a walking route that supposedly follows the poet's footsteps between Nether Stowey and Porlock on the Exmoor coast (see p.269). Waymarked with quill signs, the 36-mile hike takes you through some of the most scenic parts of the Quantocks and Exmoor.

The eastern Quantocks

From Nether Stowey, a minor road winds west off the A39 through **Quantock Common**, a Site of Special Scientific Interest on account of its maritime heath – an

6

COLERIDGE AND WORDSWORTH IN THE QUANTOCKS

Shortly after moving into their new home – or "miserable cottage", as Sara Coleridge called it – in Nether Stowey, the Coleridges were visited by William Wordsworth and his sister Dorothy, who soon afterwards moved into the somewhat grander Alfoxden House, near Holford, a couple of miles down the road. The year that **Coleridge and Wordsworth** spent as neighbours was extraordinarily productive – Coleridge composed some of his best poetry at this time, including *The Rime of the Ancient Mariner* and *Kubla Khan*, and the two poets in collaboration produced the *Lyrical Ballads*, the poetic manifesto of early English Romanticism. Many of the greatest figures of the age made the trek down to visit the pair, among them Charles Lamb, Thomas De Quincey, Robert Southey, Humphry Davy and William Hazlitt, and it was the coming and going of these intellectuals that stirred the suspicions of local authorities in a period when England was at war with France. Spies were sent to track them and Wordsworth was finally given notice to leave the area in June 1798, shortly before *Lyrical Ballads* rolled off the press.

Scenes from Julien Temple's film *Pandaemonium*, narrating a version of Coleridge and Wordsworth's poetic relationship, were shot hereabouts.

endangered habitat mainly composed of heather, gorse and whortleberry (better known as bilberry) – and the wildlife that resides here. Among the species that may be spotted are Dartford warblers, nightjars, adders and red deer. An Iron Age earthwork runs across **Dead Woman's Ditch** – despite the name a lovely open space for a picnic. From here, paths trail off, including one leading eventually to the highest point on the Quantocks, **Wills Neck** (1260ft). Drivers can most easily access this point by parking at **Triscombe Stone**, on the edge of Quantock Forest, from where a footpath leads to the summit about a mile distant.

Stretching between Wills Neck and the village of Aisholt is the bracken- and heather-grown moorland plateau of **Aisholt Common**. The best place to begin exploring this central tract is near **West Bagborough**, where a five-mile path starts at Birches Corner. Lower down the slopes, outside Aisholt, the banks of **Hawkridge Reservoir** make another scenic picnic stop.

Bishops Lydeard and the western Quantocks

The terminus for the West Somerset Railway (see box, p.230), the relatively large village of **BISHOPS LYDEARD** is worth a wander, not least for the church of **St Mary**. Built in the local red sandstone, the church has a splendid, pinnacled tower in the Perpendicular style from around 1450, with five carved dragons on the corners, one with a stone in its mouth – these decorative gargoyles are known as "hunky punks" in Somerset. Inside is a renowned set of carved bench-ends, the work of itinerant Flemish craftsmen in the sixteenth century; look out for Green Men, a ship, a windmill and a pelican feeding its young with blood from its own breast – a symbol of the redemptive power of Christ's blood. Victorian renovation accounts for the appearance of much of the rest of the church, including all the stained glass.

Combe Florey

The pretty village of **COMBE FLOREY**, a couple of miles northwest of Bishops Lydeard, is almost exclusively built in the local red sandstone. Its centrepiece, fronted by a neat lawn, is the beautifully preserved church of **St Peter and St Paul**, originating in the thirteenth century, though it was largely rebuilt in around 1480, from when the tower, windows, roof and carved pews date. Some of the effigies and memorials lining the aisles date back to 1300. For over fifteen years (1829–45), the rector here

WALKING IN THE QUANTOCKS

The Quantocks offer some great walks of differing lengths and terrain, many of them waymarked trails. The most ambitious of these, the **Quantock Greenway**, traces a figure-of-eight that takes in the Quantock villages of Holford, Crowcombe and Triscombe. The route can be tackled in two-day-long circular walks, or sampled on shorter sections. Alternatively, head for such specific areas as **Lydeard Hill**, southeast of Wills Neck and surrounded by woods and heathland, with far-reaching views across the Vale of Taunton; **Staple Plain**, for access to Beacon Hill and the northern end of Quantock Common; **Holford Combe**, thickly wooded with protected sessile oaks; and **Ramscombe**, north of Triscombe Stone, with barbecues and picnic tables in the midst of woodland.

6

was the unconventional cleric **Sydney Smith**, called "the greatest master of ridicule since Swift" by the essayist Macaulay; he was also a champion of parliamentary reform and at one time Canon of St Paul's Cathedral. More recently (1956–1966), Combe Florey House was home to **Evelyn Waugh**. He and his wife are buried near the northeast side of the church, and his son, the journalist Auberon Waugh, is also buried in the churchyard. Last on the literary roster, the playwright Terence Rattigan lived in the village as a boy.

Crowcombe

CROWCOMBE, a little over three miles along the A358 from Combe Florey, is another typical cob-and-thatch Quantock village, with a well-preserved Church House from 1515. Opposite, the red-stone parish church of the **Holy Ghost** has a superb collection of pagan-looking carved bench-ends from around the same time, intricately woven with vines, leaves and Green Men – well worth a look. The tower and part of the northern wall date from the fourteenth century.

GETTING AROUND   THE QUANTOCK HILLS

The cycle, hike or drive across the Quantocks from Crowcombe to Nether Stowey takes in some of the range's loveliest wooded scenery, including some very steep stretches.

By bus All bus services in the northern Quantocks run between Bridgwater and Minehead, primarily the #14 (Mon–Sat hourly), which stops at Nether Stowey, Holford and Kilve. For the Western Quantocks, the #28 and #X28 (Mon–Sat every 30min, Sun hourly) run from Taunton to: Bishops Lydeard (30min); Combe Florey (35min); Crowcombe (45min); Bicknoller (50min); Watchet (1hr); Dunster (1hr 20min); and Minehead (1hr 25min).

By train Vintage steam and diesel trains of the West Somerset Railway run between Bishops Lydeard and Minehead up to 8 times a day between late March and October; stops include Crowcombe Heathfield on the edge of the Quantocks, a 10- to 15min ride. Note that the station of Crowcombe Heathfield lies 1.5 miles south of Crowcombe.

INFORMATION

Tourist information There are no tourist offices in the Quantock Hills, but the office in Taunton (see p.221) can provide information, maps and advice. See also

ⓦ thequantockhills.co.uk and ⓦ quantockonline.co.uk, where you can download walking itineraries.

ACCOMMODATION

BISHOPS LYDEARD

The Mount 32 Mount St ⓣ 01984 431897, ⓦ themount-accommodation.co.uk. One room is available in this B&B at the centre of the village (and near some good pubs), but it's spacious, has its own entrance and includes a seating area where locally sourced breakfasts are served. No credit cards. **£70**

CROWCOMBE

Quantock Orchard Caravan Park Flaxpool, just off the A358 and a few minutes' walk from the West Somerset Railway stop at Crowcombe Heathfield ⓣ 01984 618618, ⓦ www.quantock-orchard.co.uk. This small, neat site is convenient for walks around Wills Neck. It offers a gym and heated outdoor pool (May–Sept),

THE WEST SOMERSET RAILWAY

The main road route fringing the western side of the Quantocks – the A358 heading northwest from Taunton – is accompanied for most of the way by the **West Somerset Railway** (☎01643 704996, ⚳west-somerset-railway.co.uk), a restored branch line running some twenty miles between the station outside the village of Bishops Lydeard, five miles out of Taunton, to Minehead on the Somerset coast (see p.249). Between late March and October (plus some winter dates), up to eight steam and diesel trains depart daily from the terminus near Bishops Lydeard, stopping at renovated stations on the way. The total journey to Minehead takes around 1hr 15min, for which the ticket costs £10.40 one way, £15.60 return. Rover tickets, allowing multiple journeys, cost £15.60 for one day, £29 for two days; bikes travel at 25 percent of the adult rate. The station outside Bishops Lydeard can be reached on bus #28 from Taunton's centre and train station.

and has static caravans to rent (£55 per night or £385 per week in high season). There's a small shop but no restaurant facilities. Bike hire available. Pitches from £25

FIDDINGTON

Mill Farm Caravan and Camping Park A couple of miles east of Nether Stowey, signposted outside the village of Fiddington ☎01278 732286, ⚳millfarm.biz. This family-friendly site has indoor and outdoor pools, a boating lake, a gym and pony rides. The bar, restaurant and evening entertainment (in peak season) meet all other needs, and facilities are clean. It can get crowded though, and booking is essential at peak times. Pitches from £21

HOLFORD

Combe House Hotel ☎01278 741382, ⚳combehouse .co.uk. Hidden away in a combe a few minutes' walk above the village, this is the place to come for a little pampering, with a range of spa treatments and massages on offer, plus a classy restaurant. Rooms are quietly luxurious, and trails lead directly into the hills. £165

NETHER STOWEY

The Old Cider House 25 Castle St ☎01278 732228, ⚳theoldciderhouse.co.uk. Five fully equipped rooms, great evening meals (£15–20) and a microbrewery on site. Themed walking breaks taking in good pubs in the area are run from here. From £60

★ **The Old House** St Mary's St ☎01278 732392, ⚳theoldhouse-quantocks.co.uk. Once owned by the printer Thomas Poole, this house in the centre of the village accommodated Coleridge in 1807. The two rooms – Sara's Room and the huge Coleridge Suite – are furnished with antiques, and there's an acre of garden for unwinding with a book after tramping the Coleridge Way. Self-catering cottages are also available. From £70

OVER STOWEY

★ **Parsonage Farm** Over Stowey, about a mile south of Nether Stowey ☎01278 733237, ⚳parsonfarm .co.uk. Set next to a lovely old Quantock church, this B&B with its own orchard and walled kitchen garden has three rooms and heaps of character. Run organically and sustainably by a native of Vermont, it offers a Vermont breakfast among other options, and simple candlelit suppers are also available for £10. No credit cards. From £60

TRISCOMBE

★ **The Blue Ball Inn** Below Wills Neck, Triscombe ☎01984 618242, ⚳blueballinn.info. This secluded inn has two comfortable B&B rooms – one with a gorgeous bathroom up a spiral staircase in the attic – and a self-catering cottage that can accommodate up to four, all tastefully decorated, and with meals, good ales and a pleasant pub garden on hand. From £75

EATING AND DRINKING

BICKNOLLER

Bicknoller Inn Three miles northwest of Crowcombe ☎01984 656234, ⚳bicknollerinn.com. Great country pub serving Palmer's ales (from Dorset) and baguettes, ploughman's lunches and light bites in a separate restaurant. There's a patio and garden, a skittles alley used in winter and an outside boules area for summer. Mon noon–2pm & 6–11pm, Tues–Sun noon–11pm; food served daily noon–3pm & 6.30–9.30pm.

COMBE FLOREY

Farmers Arms Signposted off the A39 just south of Combe Florey ☎01823 432267, ⚳farmersarmsat combeflorey.co.uk. This is a lovely old place, tidily thatched, with log fires, a garden and a good menu that's strong on lamb and poultry (main dishes £8.50–9.50 at lunchtime, £14–16 in the evening). Booking is advised at peak times. Daily noon–11pm; food served Mon–Sat noon–2.30pm & 7–9pm, Sun noon–2.30pm.

CROWCOMBE

★ **Carew Arms** ☎ 01984 618631, ⊛ thecarewarms
.co.uk. Don't be put off by the stags' heads covering the
walls and the riding boots by the fire – this is a delightful
rustic pub with a skittles alley and a spacious garden. Local
ales are served as well as top-notch food (£12–17). Rooms
also available (£64–84). Daily noon–11pm; food served
noon–2pm & 7–9pm; in winter closes 3–6pm, no food
Sun eve & all Mon.

HOLFORD

Plough Inn Five miles west of Nether Stowey along
the A39 (a stop on the #14 bus from Bridgwater)
☎ 01278 741232. This place was the unlikely setting for
Virginia and Leonard Woolf's honeymoon in 1912 (before

they travelled to Spain). Today it serves simple pub grub
(mains around £9), local beers and ciders, and there's a
small beer garden. Cream teas feature home-made scones.
Mon–Sat 11am–11pm, Sun noon–10.30pm; food
served Mon–Thurs noon–3pm & 6–9pm, Fri & Sat
noon–9pm, Sun noon–3pm.

NETHER STOWEY

Rose and Crown St Mary's St ☎ 01278 732265,
⊛ roseandcrown-netherstowey.co.uk. Local and guest
ales, plus excellent bar meals are served at this cosy village
inn (en-suite rooms are available, £65), and there's a nice
walled garden. Curries and steaks feature on the menu
(£7–9). Mon–Sat noon–11pm, Sun noon–10.30pm;
food served daily noon–2pm & 6–8.30pm.

6

The coast

CLEVEDON PIER

The coast

Somerset's **coast** is dotted with Victorian resorts from the heyday of seaside holidaymaking, and though these have been brought up to date to greater or lesser degrees, they preserve a prosaic, old-fashioned air. The chic makeover that has given a fashionable edge to such resorts as Brighton and Falmouth has not happened here. Nonetheless, there is much to like about these time-warped towns, and a certain frisson in the collision between the holiday culture concentrated on their seafront esplanades and the more reserved, essentially staid life of the calmer neighbourhoods away from the sea. You don't have to go far along the coast to discover unspoilt and genuinely picturesque bays and beaches in between the resorts that most people never see, with long views across the Bristol Channel to Wales.

Of the resorts, **Weston-super-Mare** is the brashest, a full-on bucket-and-spade affair with two piers (one derelict) and acres of sand – though this turns into endless mud when the tide's out. On either side are two much lower-key towns: to the north, **Clevedon**, armed with a much more traditional pier, and **Burnham-on-Sea**, set in an especially atmospheric stretch of coast. Clevedon also boasts a fourteenth- and fifteenth-century manor house, **Clevedon Court**, a couple of miles inland, and is within easy reach of the much more flamboyant **Tyntesfield**, a Victorian-Gothic mansion, beautifully restored by the National Trust and surrounded by gorgeous parkland.

The coast turns a sharp corner westward at the River Parrett estuary, from where it extends along a tract of bleak flatlands, rising to low cliffs around **Kilve Beach**, part of the Quantocks Hills Area of Outstanding Natural Beauty. **Watchet** is the first settlement of any size along this section of coast, a low-key fishing port that makes a nice place to hole up for a few days. Inland are a couple of intriguing distractions from the sea: the quirky **Bakelite Museum** at Williton and the medieval remains of **Cleeve Abbey**.

To the west, **Minehead** has all the trappings of the quintessential British seaside resort, whose proximity to both Exmoor and the medieval wool town of Dunster (see p.266) makes it a useful base for its accommodation and transport links. Minehead also marks one end of the **South West Coast Path**, Britain's longest national trail, which follows the southwest peninsula's coast to end up in Dorset.

The **Bristol Channel**, which separates the Somerset coast from Wales, has the second-highest tidal range in the world (up to 49ft; the highest is the Bay of Fundy in eastern Canada), with the result that half the time what was a beach becomes an extensive mud-flat with the sea a distant ribbon up to a mile out. Given this, the grey-brown Channel doesn't always inspire great enthusiasm for anyone wanting a dip, though there are a few appealing sandy **beaches** which are good for a picnic or just a runaround, even if you're not tempted to take to the water.

Accommodation is abundant in Weston and Minehead, surprisingly scarce in Clevedon and Burnham, with much of it falling into the tired and dreary seaside-resort category. There are a few gems, though, which we've recommended in the listings.

GETTING AROUND

By train The main train line between Bristol and Exeter runs through Weston-super-Mare and Highbridge & Burnham (outside Burnham-on-Sea). Heritage trains of the private West Somerset Railway (see box, p.230) stop at Williton, Watchet, Washford, Blue Anchor Bay and Minehead between late March and early November. The eastern terminus is Bishops Lydeard in the Quantock Hills. For all stations and a full schedule, see ⓦ west-somerset-railway.co.uk.

Boat trips from Clevedon p.236
Weston's Sand Sculpture Festival p.240
Exploring Flat Holm and Steep
  Holm p.242

Haile Selassie in Burnham p.244
A walk from Kilve Beach p.246
Fossicking p.247
The South West Coast Path p.249

SAND BAY

Highlights

❶ Clevedon Court On the outskirts of Clevedon, this well-preserved manor house merits a lingering visit, as much for its fine collections of glassware and pottery as for the Tudor architecture and seventeenth- and eighteenth-century furnishings. **See p.238**

❷ Tyntesfield This Victorian mansion is a repository of aesthetic delights – every detail is a masterpiece of art and craftsmanship, and there are terrific walks in the grounds. **See p.238**

❸ Sand Bay The next bay up from Weston-super-Mare presents a calm contrast to that bustling resort, with a broad sandy beach and bracing panoramic walks. **See p.242**

❹ Kilve Beach One of the most atmospheric stretches of Somerset's coast centres on this foreshore embellished with beautiful rock formations; it's a good starting point for coastal walks and fossil hunts along the beach. **See p.245**

❺ Watchet Coleridge's Ancient Mariner supposedly set off from this unspoiled harbour town, a peaceful spot with a couple of great museums and within easy reach of some absorbing sights inland. **See p.246**

❻ Cleeve Abbey Largely intact, this Cistercian house has afforded valuable insights into medieval monastic life; its showpieces are the vaulted refectory and polychrome tiled floor. **See p.247**

HIGHLIGHTS ARE MARKED ON THE MAP ON P.237

By bus Weston-super-Mare, Clevedon and Burnham-on-Sea have National Express connections to London (wnationalexpress.com). Local buses link these towns to each other and to Bristol. West of the Parrett, bus #14 runs to Kilve, Watchet, Washford and Williton from Bridgwater, and the more frequent #18 and #28 services stop at Williton, Watchet, Washford and Minehead en route from Taunton. The main operators are First (☎0845 602 0156, wfirstgroup.com) and Webberbus (☎0800 096 3039, wwebberbus.com).

Clevedon and around

Fifteen miles west of Bristol, **CLEVEDON** is centred on hills slightly inland from the sea, but its jaunty seafront promenade is the most compelling part of town, with wind-bent trees and views across the Bristol Channel to the isles of Steep Holm and Flat Holm, and beyond to the coast of Wales. The focal point is, naturally, the elegant Victorian **pier**, but the whole beachfront invites a stroll, not least the promontory at its southern end, where the **Poet's Walk** offers a pleasant perambulation round the headland. The path, which was supposed to have provided inspiration for Tennyson and Coleridge, winds round Church Hill, passing St Andrew's churchyard and climbing Wain's Hill, taking in some bracing views en route – about a mile in all. There's a panel at the beginning of the walk providing a bit of background, and leaflets are sometimes available at the pier's Tollhouse.

Away from the sea, the higher reaches of Clevedon exude a genteel and prosperous air, not least around **Hill Road**, where there are rows of salubrious villas as well as trendy shops and the town's best choice of eateries (see p.239); head up Alexandra Road or Marine Parade from the pier to reach the area. The main shopping zone lies around the Triangle, marked by its clock-tower, located at the bottom of Chapel Hill from the southern end of Hill Road.

Clevedon Pier

The Beach • Late March to late Oct Mon–Fri 10am–5pm, Sat & Sun 10am–6pm; late Oct to late March Mon–Fri 10am–4pm, Sat & Sun 10am–5pm • £1.50 • w clevedonpier.com

Opened in 1869, **Clevedon Pier** is one of the best-preserved of Britain's 78 seaside piers, and was the setting for a scene from the 2010 film *Never Let Me Go*. Its construction was spurred by the arrival of the railway and the possibility of a faster route to South Wales than the route via Gloucester allowed before the construction of the Severn Tunnel in 1886: passengers would travel by train to Clevedon's station (now gone), and from the pier board a paddle-steamer to cross the Bristol Channel. The sides of the pier are studded with more than ten thousand brass plates inscribed with the names of individual sponsors of the restoration following the collapse of part of the structure in 1970. At the pier's end, the Edwardian-style *Pagoda* café serves teas and cakes.

The Tollhouse at the base of the pier holds the ticket desk and shop, where you'll find a few leaflets on local visitor attractions (the staff are also happy to help with

---

BOAT TRIPS FROM CLEVEDON

Summer offers the opportunity to participate in a very traditional seaside amusement, in the form of **boat trips** aboard period vessels in and across the Bristol Channel. On selected dates between early June and early September, cruises from Clevedon Pier go to Porlock Bay, Ilfracombe and Clovelly on the Devon coast, around the Holm islands and Lundy Island in the Bristol Channel, Bristol (via the River Avon) and over to Wales. Cruises either take place on the *Waverley*, claimed to be the world's last sea-going paddle steamer, and the *Balmoral*, a classic old motorized pleasure boat. **Tickets**, which range from £15 for South Wales to £43 for Lundy Island, can be obtained from Waverley Excursions (☎0845 130 4647, wwaverleyexcursions .co.uk) or from Clevedon Pier's Tollhouse (☎01275 878846). Some cruises also depart from Weston-super-Mare, Watchet and Minehead.

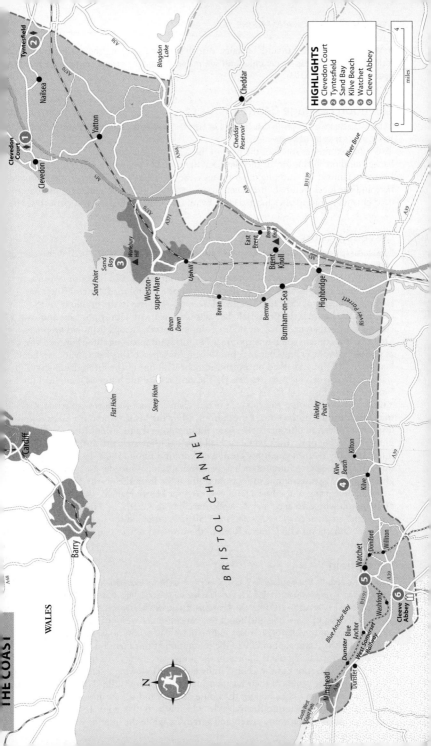

WALES

Cardiff

Barry

A48

BRISTOL CHANNEL

Flat Holm

Steep Holm

Minehead

South West Coast Path

Dunster

Blue Anchor Bay

Blue Anchor

Washford

West Somerset Railway

Watchet

Williton

Doniford

Cleeve Abbey

Kilve

Kilve Beach

Kilton

Hinkley Point

B3191

A39

A39

River Parrett

Highbridge

Burnham-on-Sea

Berrow

Brent Knoll

Brent Knoll

East Brent

Brean

Brean Down

Sand Point

Weston-super-Mare

Worlebury Hill

Sand Bay

Uphill

A371

A370

A38

River Brue

Cheddar Reservoir

Cheddar

A368

Blagdon Lake

A368

A38

Clevedon Court

Clevedon

Nailsea

Yatton

Tyntesfield

A370

A369

B3139

B3139

M5

M5

N

HIGHLIGHTS
1 Clevedon Court
2 Tyntesfield
3 Sand Bay
4 Kilve Beach
5 Watchet
6 Cleeve Abbey

0   miles   4

information on the area), and, upstairs, a small gallery displaying changing exhibitions of local art, photographs, ceramics and sculpture. A modern visitor centre is planned to open alongside in 2013.

Clevedon Heritage Centre

The Beach • Late March to late Oct Tues–Fri 10am–5pm, Sat & Sun 10am–6pm; late Oct to late March Tues–Fri 10am–4pm, Sat & Sun 10am–5pm • 50p, free to pier ticket-holders

Two hundred metres south of the pier on the seafront, you can glean a bit of background on the locality at the **Clevedon Heritage Centre**, which offers some historical context on – among other things – the pier, the paddle steamers that stopped here and the local picture house, a century old and said to be the oldest continuously used cinema in Europe (it's located close by on Old Church Road if you want to see it).

7   Clevedon Court

Tickenham Rd • April–Sept Wed, Thurs & Sun 2–5pm • House & garden £6.30, garden only £3; NT • ☎ 01275 872257, ⊛ nationaltrust.org .uk • Bus #361

Clevedon's greatest treasure is **Clevedon Court**, a fourteenth- and fifteenth-century manor house lying less than two miles inland on the Bristol road. Since 1709 it has been the property of the Elton family, who continue to live in the building. At the centre of the house is the **Great Hall**, its walls plastered with family portraits and with a curious Elizabethan carved stone doorway in one corner, created from old fireplaces. Other rooms contain some fine specimens of furniture spanning three hundred years, as well as portraits of and drawings by William Makepeace Thackeray, who, as a guest here in the 1840s, embarked on a platonic affair with one of the Elton daughters who was already married (as was Thackeray). The author used the house as the model for Castlewood in his novel *Henry Esmond*.

Elsewhere in the house you can see the tiny chapel whose window with reticulated tracery is a feature of the house's south front, while the Justice Room (or Glass Room) displays a collection of Nailsea glassware, multi-coloured and fashioned in the shapes of pipes and rolling pins. The Old Great Hall holds "Eltonware", the distinctive and internationally renowned pottery created by Edmund Elton (1846–1920), using unusual shapes and techniques such as platinum glazing. Outside, the terraced gardens give good views seaward, but suffer from traffic noise from the nearby M5 motorway.

Another offspring of the Elton family was Arthur Henry Hallam – the bosom friend of Tennyson who died aged just 22 while travelling in Austria, and the subject of the poet's grief-stricken elegy, *In Memoriam*. Hallam is buried in the family vault in St Andrew's church, off Old Church Road in the west end of Clevedon.

Tyntesfield

Wraxall • **House** March–Oct Mon–Wed, Sat & Sun 11am–5pm; early Nov to late Nov Sat & Sun 11am–3pm• £12.20 including gardens; £2 reduction if arriving by public transport by bike or on foot; NT **Gardens** March–Oct daily 10am–6pm or dusk if earlier; Nov–Feb 10am–5pm or dusk if earlier • £9; NT • ☎ 0844 800 4966, ⊛ nationaltrust.org.uk/tyntesfield • Buses #354 and #361

Seven miles east of Clevedon and about the same distance west of Bristol, **Tyntesfield** represents one of the National Trust's most triumphant renovations, made possible by a huge fundraising campaign in 2002. The restoration of this mansion is ongoing, with meticulous efforts being made to present the house according to its final appearance, the fruit of four generations of the Gibbs family faithfully following a single aesthetic vision.

Largely with the profits of their business importing guano (seabird droppings) for use as fertiliser, William Gibbs bought the house in 1843 and set about its complete rebuilding in a florid Gothic-Revival style, which was completed in 1865. The structure was embellished with towers, turrets and gargoyles, while the interior was given high

Gothic ceilings, copious oak panelling and grand staircases, and was filled by successive members of the family with a treasure-trove of decorative artwork, making this a must-see for Arts and Crafts fans. Every detail is eye-catching, from the ornate fireplaces of Venetian marble and exuberantly carved doorways to the intricate cabinets and statuettes liberally sprinkled around. The library and drawing room have vaulted ceilings, and the billiards room impresses with its tiger-skin rug and numerous stag-head trophies. The upstairs bedrooms are less opulent, as are, of course, the servants' quarters.

Alongside the house, the imposing High Victorian **chapel** is also worth a look, while you could spend a pleasurable day traipsing over the 500-acre **estate**, spread over a ridge with marvellous views over the fertile Yeo Valley, and including a fine set of landscaped gardens and a croquet lawn.

Note that Tyntesfield is a popular attraction, and tickets available on a first-come-first-served basis soon sell out – so get here early.

ARRIVAL AND DEPARTURE — CLEVEDON AND AROUND

By bus Service #361, with a stop on Old Street, near the Triangle, connects Bristol with Clevedon, with stops at or near Clevedon Court and Tyntesfield. On Sunday, #362, #363 and #657 run to Bristol, stopping at Clevedon Court (#657 stops near Tyntesfield). Service #X25 runs to Weston-super-Mare.

Destinations Bristol (hourly; 45min–1hr); Weston-super-Mare (Mon–Sat hourly; 45min).

INFORMATION

Visitor Centre There's a desk with limited tourist information in Clevedon Library, 37 Old Church Rd (Mon & Thurs 9.30am–5pm, Tues & Fri 9.30am–7pm, Sat 9.30am–1pm & 2–5pm; ☎01934 426020, ⊛visitsomerset.co.uk).

ACCOMMODATION

Highcliffe Hotel Wellington Terrace ☎01275 873250, ⊛highcliffehotel.com. In keeping with Clevedon's overall flavour, this is an old-fashioned choice with uninspiring decor, but the rooms are spacious and most enjoy great sea views. It's a 10min walk north of the pier. **£70**

★ **The Limes** Kenn Moor Rd, Kenn ☎01275 342235, ⊛limesbb.co.uk. With Clevedon's dearth of decent accommodation, this rural B&B 2 miles southeast of town, between the villages of Kenn and Yatton, offers an excellent alternative. Sustainability and self-sufficiency are key, with solar-powered electricity and most of the food produced within the radius of a bike ride (the jams and free-range eggs come from the smallholding itself). A good pub, the *Drum and Monkey*, lies close by in Kenn. Pick-ups available from Yatton train station. **£59**

Moon & Sixpence 15 The Beach ☎01275 872443, ⊛moonandsixpenceclevedon.co.uk. Right opposite the pier, these small, functional rooms above a pub are perfectly adequate for an overnight stop. Only one of the rooms, though, has any view of the sea – the largest, no. 4. The pub has real ales, mediocre bar meals and free wi-fi. **£65**

Walton Park Hotel Wellington Terrace ☎01275 874253, ⊛waltonparkhotel.co.uk. The posher of Clevedon's two central hotels occupies a prime clifftop position with views over the sea from its bar, restaurant, garden and back bedrooms. It needs an overhaul but it's fine for a night or two, and the rates are reasonable. Free wi-fi. **£80**

EATING AND DRINKING

The Cellar 36 Hill Rd ☎01275 340340, ⊛thecellarclevedon.com. Located in a former pharmacy, with the old labelled drawers in the counter, this wine bar and bistro has a range of tapas to nibble (around £3) while you sample the generous selection of beers, ciders, whiskeys and wines. Tues–Sat 10am–10pm.

Little Harp Elton Rd ☎01275 343739, ⊛www.little-harp-avon.co.uk. This large pub above the seafront, a few minutes' walk south of the main beach, makes a great drink or snack stop, with panoramic views and outdoor tables. There's a full menu of such standards as beef and ale pie and gammon steak (£8–9). Daily noon–11pm.

★ **Murrays** 87 Hill Rd ☎01275 341555, ⊛murraysofclevedon.co.uk. This rustic-looking Italian deli/café/restaurant with hams and salamis suspended from the ceiling is a good place for picnic goodies – olives, home-made bread, wines and cheeses – and snacks. The sandwiches are fresh and delicious, and hot dishes include pizzas (£5–8) and a lip-smacking ham and mushroom lasagne (£9.50). Mon 10am–4pm, Tues, Wed & Sat 8.30am–5pm, Thurs & Fri 8.30am–8pm.

Scoozi 18 Hill Rd ☎01275 877516, ⓦscooziclevedon .co.uk. Buzzy modern Italian with a dozen pizzas to choose from (£7–11), pastas and risottos (£9–12) and grills such

as swordfish (£13). The chicken breast stuffed with gorgonzola and Parma ham is amazing. Mon–Sat noon– 2pm & 6pm–late.

Weston-super-Mare

Eight miles south of Clevedon, and the major resort on this coast, **WESTON-SUPER-MARE** was a tiny fishing village at the beginning of the nineteenth century, but boomed after the arrival of the Great Western Railway in 1841 to become one of the West Country's chief seaside resorts of the Victorian and Edwardian eras. Much of the town is rather moth-eaten today, and the dramatic retreat of the sea at low tide to more than a mile out from Marine Parade creates a forlorn, sometimes surreal picture, but with the tide in, its sandy beaches can look positively Mediterranean, and the town, with its shiny new **pier**, continues to attract busloads of trippers.

Traditional seaside amusements are still very much in evidence on the beach, such as donkey rides and Punch and Judy puppetry, and there are even cockles and whelks on sale at stalls. There's a sand sculpture festival every summer (see box below), and if you're looking for entertainment, you can take a turn on the **Wheel of Weston**, a giant Ferris wheel, or view marine life at the **Seaquarium**. Other indoor attractions include the **Weston-super-Mare Museum**, and, some way inland, the **Helicopter Museum**.

North of the pier, you can take in the views from Knightstone Island, which once held public baths, and stroll beside the Marine Lake beyond, a sheltered, non-tidal, salt-water swimming spot. A short walk up to the point brings you to Weston's second pier, the ruined **Birnbeck Pier**, looking like a shamefully neglected poor relation of the comparatively glamorous Grand Pier.

The town is sandwiched between two hills that offer possibilities for more adventurous walking. To the south, **Uphill** has views over the cliffy promontory of Brean Down (see p.244), a spindly finger of land pointing towards the isle of Steep Holm. Uphill marks one end of the **West Mendip Way** (see box, p.153), a long-distance trail which follows the Mendip Hills for thirty miles to Wells (take bus #5A from Regent St to Links Rd for the start of the route). North of town is **Worlebury Hill**, with some Iron Age remains and thick woods crossed by trails. Beyond Worlebury Hill, the wide arc of **Sand Bay** provides a quiet tonic to Weston's exuberance, ideal for a picnic or a nap.

Grand Pier

Marine Parade • Daily 10am–dusk • Pier free, amusements £1–5 • ⓦgrandpier.co.uk.

The single object that for decades drew the crowds from London and Birmingham to Weston – almost its *raison d'être* – is its **Grand Pier**. It's had a chequered history: built in 1904, it burned down in 1930 and again in 2008, after which the resort was almost ready to close down. However, the pier was rebuilt and, following its reopening in 2010, has restored the fortunes of this grand-aunt of resorts. Weston-super-Mare's Grand Pier can

---

WESTON'S SAND SCULPTURE FESTIVAL

Forget puny sand castles; if you don't want sand kicked in your face, aim high and try your hand at sand-sculpting. You can find inspiration at Weston-super-Mare's **Sand Sculpture Festival** (ⓦwestonsandsculpture.co.uk), an annual event taking place all summer on Weston's main beach (entry £3.50). The festival follows a theme every year; recent ones have been fairy tales, with evocations of Cinderella and Snow White among other tales, and Great Britain, which included everything from London's Tower Bridge to Henry VIII. The ideal ratio is roughly eight parts sand to one part water, but different sand requires different mixes; there's a useful how-to guide at ⓦsandsculptureice.co.uk.

ow boast a gleaming new fun palace, all twenty-first-century glass, steel and wavy lines of
lue neon, within which there are attractions ranging from the traditional (mirror maze,
odgems, helter-skelter, shooting galleries and penny arcade) to up-to-date thrills (a
Robocoaster, which thrashes passengers around at high speed in a giant claw; a split-level
go-kart circuit; a laser maze, involving retrieving jewels without crossing laser beams; and a
-D cinema, in which you're sprayed by rain and lashed by wind). Concerts and other
vents are held in the **Great Hall** and the pirate-themed *Captain Jack's* bar.

If the cacophony and crowds don't appeal, content yourself with simply treading the
boards – following the length of the pier deck promenade. If it's windy or wet, you can
use a central covered walkway.

Wheel of Weston

Beach Lawns • Mon–Thurs 10am–6pm, Fri 10am–8pm, Sat 10am–9pm, Sun 10am–7pm • £6.50; tickets available from Weston's tourist
office • Ⓦ greatcityattractions.com

Thirty metres tall, with thirty air-conditioned glass pods, Weston's giant Ferris wheel,
the **Wheel of Weston**, was built to provide a new beachside attraction when the old pier
burned down in 2008. Each circuit lasts thirteen minutes and affords lofty views over
the town, coast and across the Bristol Channel to Wales.

SeaQuarium

Marine Parade • Daily 10am–5pm, last admission at 4pm • £7.99 • ☎ 01934 613361, Ⓦ seaquarium.co.uk

It may not be as impressive as some big-city aquariums, but Weston's **SeaQuarium**, on
the beach south of the pier, is a well-presented and informative display, and makes a
good rainy-day retreat. Tropical Reef and Rainforest Zones bring you up close to
graceful red-bellied piranhas, freshwater stingrays and moray eels, and a walk-through
tunnel allows you to view local species including sharks and rays. There are regular
presentations, feeding times usually attract a crowd, and if you attend a ray talk you get
to touch one of the critters.

Weston-super-Mare Museum

Burlington St • Mon–Sat 10am–4pm • £3.80 • ☎ 01934 621028

Housed in an old gasworks plant, the **Weston-super-Mare Museum** takes you on a
whirlwind tour of the town's history, natural history and geology, taking in local
prehistoric finds, some Roman and medieval knick-knacks, and material on life during
World War II. A brief survey of seaside culture includes an entertaining selection of
still-operating vintage penny arcade machines, one of them with the self-explanatory
title "American Execution". **Clara's Cottage**, a separate building at one end of the
museum, holds a reconstructed front parlour, kitchen and bedroom from around 1900.

Helicopter Museum

Locking Manor Rd • April–Oct Wed–Sun 10am–5.30pm; Nov–March Wed–Sun 10am–4.30pm; last admission 1hr before closing; daily
during Easter and summer school hols • £6 • ☎ 01934 635227, Ⓦ helicoptermuseum.co.uk • Buses #120, #121 and #126 from Grand Pier

Every shape and size of whirlbird is represented at the **Helicopter Museum**, on the
corner of an old airfield three miles inland of Weston. More than eighty helicopters
and autogyros are on display here, the country's only helicopter museum and claimed
to be the world's largest, including Eastern European, US and veteran models. Open
Cockpit Days take place once a month (usually the second Sun), allowing access to
helicopter controls, and Helicopter Air Experience flights are offered on specified dates
with prior booking (£40 including museum entry) – a memorable way to view the
coast on a fifteen-mile excursion lasting around eight minutes.

7

EXPLORING FLAT HOLM AND STEEP HOLM

You really feel like you've left the world behind on landing at Flat Holm or Steep Holm, the two isles that are a constant feature of the view across the Bristol Channel around these parts. Circular **Flat Holm** is the larger of the two, measuring less than half a mile across and consisting mainly of gently sloping rock and maritime grassland. The island is the most southerly point of Wales and was as a smuggling base in the eighteenth century; today, apart from some rare flora found here – rock sea lavender and wild leek among them – you can see four gun emplacements dating from the 1860s, a derelict isolation hospital, a lighthouse and a handful of Soay sheep. As its name implies, **Steep Holm** is, at 256ft, the taller island, and forms part of England. Like its sister isle, it has a few Victorian gun batteries to explore and is a similarly protected nature reserve, with Muntjac deer among its denizens, and there's a visitor centre.

Boats to each island leave about four times monthly in summer from Knightstone Harbour. For day-trips to Flat Holm, contact MW Marine (sailings mid-May to mid-Oct; ☎01934 636734, ⬤mwmarine.org; £30 including landing fees). For Steep Holm, contact the trust that owns the island (sailings mid-July to mid-Oct; ☎01934 522125, ⬤steepholm.org .uk; £25). The whole excursion to either island takes ten or eleven hours, including seven or eight hours ashore. Refreshments are available on both islands. Bring non-slip shoes, waterproofs and, if possible, binoculars.

Worlebury Hill and Sand Bay

Bus #1 from train station and Royal Parade

If Weston's crowds get oppressive, you can always climb up to **Worlebury Hill**, a breezy, much quarried and mined limestone elevation to the north of the main beach, reachable from around the point on Kewstoke Road. Here you can see the scant remains of an Iron Age hill fort and hut circle, and there are numerous trails running through **Weston Woods**, which thickly cover a large part of the hill. Continuing further north will bring you to **Sand Bay**, virtually undeveloped and a nice contrast to the bustle of Weston Bay. The beach here is bounded to the north by Sand Point, a headland maintained by the National Trust.

ARRIVAL AND INFORMATION

WESTON-SUPER-MARE

By train Weston's train station lies a 10min walk from the seafront on Station Road.
Destinations Bridgwater (Mon–Sat hourly, Sun 9 daily; 20min); Bristol (2–4 hourly; 30min); Taunton (Mon–Sat 1–2 hourly, Sun 12 daily; 35min).
By bus Most buses arrive at and depart from High St, Regent St and Marine Parade. Buses #X1 and #353 run to

and from Bristol from High St (Mon–Sat every 30min, Sun hourly; 1hr); bus #X25 runs to Clevedon from Marine Parade (Mon–Sat hourly; 45min).
Tourist office Winter Gardens Pavilion, Royal Parade (daily: Easter–Sept 9am–6pm; Oct–Easter 10am–4pm; ☎01934 417117, ⬤visitsomerset.co.uk).

ACCOMMODATION

★ **Church House** 27 Kewstoke Rd ☎01934 633185, ⬤churchhousekewstoke.co.uk. With grand views over Sand Bay, this elegant Georgian rectory offers five airy and spacious rooms with minimalist decor and smart modern bathrooms. You can soak up the panorama from the conservatory or patio. It's on the #1 bus route, and a pick-up can be arranged from Weston's station. Wi-fi available. **£85**
Country View Sand Rd, Sand Bay ☎01934 627595, ⬤cvhp.co.uk. Just five minutes' walk from the beach at Sand Bay, this small, clean campsite has an outdoor pool, a shop and a bar, plus spotless facilities and free hot water. Closed Feb. Pitches **£25**
Oak and Glass 1 Uphill Rd North ☎01934 641874,

⬤oakandglass.co.uk. The highly regarded restaurant here has three rooms upstairs that count among Weston's finest accommodation. The Uphill Suite has its own sitting room and a balcony overlooking the garden, the Beach Room features deck-chair colours and the Putting Room is more muted but equally smart. The food in the restaurant is fab, but you should book for evening meals as it's popular (Thurs–Sat & Sun lunch). **£80**
Ormond House 19 Uphill Rd North ☎01934 412315. Near the quiet end of the beach, this Edwardian building built for the head of Bristol Zoo offers B&B in spacious, cream-coloured rooms (one with a spa bath) and its own indoor pool and sauna. **£80**

phill Manor 3 Uphill Rd South ☎01934 644654, ⓦuphillmanor.co.uk. Castellated country house with a arge garden, in the quieter, southern end of Weston, though only a few minutes from the beach. There's a snooker room, a well-stocked library and charming rooms with garden views and free wi-fi. **£90**

EATING AND DRINKING

★ **The Cove** Marine Lake, Birnbeck Rd ☎01934 418217, ⓦthe-cove.co.uk. This sleek, modern restaurant takes full advantage of its position right by Weston's saltwater Marine Lake, lending it a romantic feel. There are tables outside and a fine menu that includes Cornish mussels, baked fish and rib-eye steaks (most mains £14–19), and there are good-value lunch and early evening menus. If you don't want a full meal, just come for a relaxed drink. It's not well marked from Birnbeck Road: take the steps down from beside the *Claremont Vaults* pub. Tues–Sat 9.30am–9.30pm, Sun 9.30am–7.30pm.

Demetris Taverna 18 Richmond St ☎01934 620187, ⓦdemetristaverna.co.uk. This place has the smack of authenticity, with refreshingly few trappings of Greek-holiday kitsch. Kleftiko and souvlaki are on the menu, of course (£12–14), but grilled chops, steaks and the daily specials are also worth sampling. Book ahead for the music and dancing shenanigans on the last Friday of the month. Mon–Sat 7–10.45pm.

Dr Fox's Tearoom Knightstone Island ☎01934 707411. North of the Grand Pier, this place occupies one of the best vantage-points in Weston, with views from the outdoor tables straight across to the pier and beyond. It's full of old-time atmosphere without succumbing to tweeness, a great spot for breakfasts, snack lunches such as Ploughman's (£7.50) and quiche (£5.50), and do-it-yourself hot chocolates, where you melt a stick of the chocolate of your choice into hot milk. Daily 8.30am–6pm.

Imperial Brasserie 14 South Parade ☎01934 621815, ⓦimperialbrasserie.co.uk. This bar and brasserie makes an agreeable place for a drink in the evening or a full meal in the restaurant, for example imperial fish pie and duck à l'orange (most mains £8–10). There are good-value lunch and early evening menus (£12 for two people), a Supper Club Tues (£10 for three courses) and live music Wed & Sun. No food Sun eve & Mon eve. Daily 11am–late.

Yo-Ji 25–27 St James St ☎01934 620800, ⓦyo-ji.co.uk. First-class Japanese restaurant where you can order a sushi platter or tempura scallops (£5–15), and pork, tuna and prawns are cooked in front of you (£12–18). The menu is long, portions are large and the staff are helpful. Mon–Thurs & Sun noon–3pm & 5–11pm, Fri & Sat noon–11pm.

Burnham-on-Sea and around

Weston seems almost metropolis-like when compared with **BURNHAM-ON-SEA** eight miles south, a rather neglected resort in need of a charm injection. There's some charm though in its seafront, where the Esplanade offers views over a long, flat expanse of sand, stretching north as far as **Brean Down** and west along Somerset's north coast. Immediately south of the town is the estuary of the River Parrett, where, in the river mouth, tiny **Stert Island** is the nesting place for innumerable seabirds, and is also the halfway point of the annual **Stert Island Swim**, when eighty or so intrepid swimmers race from Burnham's beach to the island and back, a distance of around 1.5 miles; the swim usually takes place on the third or fourth Sunday of July.

Like other resorts along this coast, Burnham's seafront can look delightful or depressing, according to the state of the tide in the Bristol Channel and the weather. Even in the worst conditions, though, the view across the sands to Wales has an intensely still, almost mesmerising quality. The Esplanade itself is nothing special, though it does boast what is claimed to be Britain's shortest pier, dating from 1911–1914, now entirely occupied by an amusement arcade. Further up the beach, you'll spot what is Burnham's oddest feature, the Low Lighthouse, also known as the Lighthouse-on-the-Sands or the **Lighthouse-on-Legs** due to its construction on stilts on the beach.

St Andrew's

Victoria St • Free • ⓦstandrewsbos.org

Burnham has little of any great age, one notable exception being **St Andrew's church**, right by the seafront, dedicated in 1316 but remodelled in subsequent centuries. Its showpiece is a marble altar-piece carved in 1686 by master-carver Grinling Gibbons, originally intended for the chapel at Whitehall Palace, later transferred to Westminster Abbey, and finally installed here in 1820. Other sculpted figures by Gibbons are in the nave windows and in the baptistery. Outside the church, note the distinct slant of the square, castellated tower, the result of faulty foundations.

Brean Down

Bus #112 from Burnham-on-Sea or Weston-super-Mare (not Sun)

North of Burnham, an unbroken succession of bungalows and caravan parks trails through Berrow and Brean. The beach, though, preserves an appealingly wild feel, backed by miles of grassy dunes – especially grand at **Berrow Dunes** – and ending at the cliffy peninsula of **Brean Down**. Maintained by the National Trust, this outcrop of the Mendips has steps leading up to the ridge, from where there are splendid coastal views, Iron Age remains and an abandoned Palmerston Fort (one of the defences thrown up around Britain's coasts under prime minister Lord Palmerston), dating from 1865. North of Brean Down, a saltmarsh spreads soupily around the mouth of the River Axe, cutting off access to Weston's beach. The currents around the headland can be ferocious, so don't attempt a swim.

There's a car park at the base of Brean Down, but if you're dependent on public transport you'll have a half-hour walk from the nearest bus stop.

Brent Knoll

Bus #102 from Burnham-on-Sea or Weston-super-Mare to Brent Knoll and East Brent villages (not Sun)

A couple of miles northeast of Burnham, the round elevation of **Brent Knoll** appears more interesting the closer you get to it. Though not particularly high at around 450ft, it rears imposingly above the surrounding flatlands, and was an island before the Somerset Levels were drained. Its geographical prominence has given it a recurring role in history: Iron Age remains lie on the summit; for the Romans it was the "Mount of Frogs"; it was a refuge from invading Vikings; and it may even have been the site of a significant victory by Alfred the Great over the Danes.

A walk to the top is strongly recommended, which can be tackled from either of the two villages at its base, **East Brent** and **Brent Knoll**. While you're in the area, take a few minutes to look at the churches in both of these villages, which sport some remarkable examples of bench-carving. The bench-ends in **St Mary's** in East Brent are in better condition, and the church also has a graceful seventeenth-century plaster ceiling over the nave, a timber one over the north aisle and a gallery from 1637. The fourteenth-century carvings at **St Michael's** in Brent Knoll include a darkly amusing sequence showing the local abbot as a fox being arrested and hanged by his geese parishioners.

ARRIVAL AND INFORMATION

BURNHAM-ON-SEA AND AROUND

By train Highbridge & Burnham train station lies a couple of miles south of Burnham-on-Sea's seafront, linked by frequent local buses.

Destinations Bridgwater (Mon–Sat hourly, Sun 8 daily;

10min); Bristol (Mon–Sat 1–2 hourly, Sun 11 daily; 45min); Weston-super-Mare (Mon–Sat hourly, Sun 11 daily; 10min).

By bus Most buses arrive at and leave from Vicarage Street, at the north end of the Esplanade, or nearby Manor

oad or its extension Berrow Road. Burnham is connected
y services #15, #21 and #21A with Bridgwater, by #102
with Brent Knoll, by #X2 and #102 with East Brent, and #X2,
102 and #112 with Weston-super-Mare.

Destinations (Mon–Sat 3 hourly, Sun 6 daily; 40min);
Brent Knoll (Mon–Sat 3 daily; 15min); East Brent

(Mon–Sat 8 daily; 20–25min); Weston-super-Mare (Mon–
Sat 2–3 hourly, Sun hourly; 40min–1hr).
Tourist office South Esplanade (April–Oct daily
10am–4pm, reduced hours in winter; ☎01278 787852,
ⓦburnham-on-sea.com).

ACCOMMODATION

Cheriton Lodge 4 Allandale Rd ☎01278 781423,
ⓦcheritonlodge.com. Late Victorian B&B in one of
Burnham's most agreeable neighbourhoods, where the three
light and airy rooms have en-suite or private facilities and
wi-fi access. The beach is right at the end of this quiet cul-de-
sac. No credit cards. No under-5s. Closed Nov–April. **£55**
Warren Guest House 29 Berrow Rd ☎01278 786726,
ⓦthewarrenguesthouse.co.uk. Next-door to *Cheriton
Lodge*, very close to the beach, this B&B has large,

period-furnished rooms, fresh fruit and home-made jams
at breakfast, plus a peaceful garden. **£60**
Yew Tree House Hurn Lane, Berrow ☎01278 751382,
ⓦwww.yewtree-house.co.uk. Parts of this house date
back to the seventeenth century, but the rooms – some in
converted stables in a courtyard garden – are spacious with
modern bathrooms. It's on a secluded lane a few minutes'
walk from the dunes, three miles north of Burnham. Bus
#112 from Burnham and Weston stops nearby. **£60**

EATING AND DRINKING

@cks 1 The Esplanade ☎01278 238646. Burnham has
no shortage of cafés, most a bit downbeat, but this one is
modern, airy and child-friendly, a welcome spot for a
fry-up, burger or steak (most dishes £5–9), or just a cup of
tea. It stays open in the evening for wines and beers. Mon–
Thurs & Sun 9am–6pm, Fri & Sat 9am–9pm; closes
around 10pm in summer.
La Vela 4 Abingdon Rd ☎01278 782707, ⓦlavela.co.uk.
It's not exactly cutting edge, but you'll find all your old
favourites in this sober, 1970s-style Italian eatery, including
risottos, pastas and pizzas (£8–9). There are some good

salads too (try the *Pollo Cesare*, with grilled chicken), and
succulent steaks (around £15). Daily 5–11pm.
The Mitre 13 College St ☎01278 782752. This
unprepossessing, old-fashioned French bistro brings classic
provincial French cuisine to the English seaside. If frog's legs
don't appeal, indulge in such dishes as *poulet au tarragon*,
filet de boeuf au stilton or vegetable *provençale*, washed
down by a bottle of Fleurie. Mains are £10–15, and there
are lunchtime and early evening menus for £6.75 (Tues–
Thurs). Tues–Fri from 11.45am & 6pm, Sat from 6pm.

Kilve and around

An alien presence hangs over the otherwise flat and featureless landscape west of the
Parrett estuary, lending it a spooky air of menace – **Hinkley Point**, a complex of nuclear
power stations (Hinkley A and Hinkley B, with a third being mooted). The
installations dominate the coast west of Steart Point, though with your back to them,
following the coast path west, the shore assumes a more benign air, with modest cliffs
rising above the sea.

There's an especially atmospheric stretch of sand and rock at **Kilve Beach**, where the
strata of shale and lias (limestone) form beautiful geometric patterns and it's not hard
to spot ammonites and other fossils (see box, p.247). The beach here was once much
used for conger-eel hunting, or "glatting", which took place during the low spring
tides. The remains of a brick retort stand behind the beach, once used to extract oil
from the shale, and there are also the remains of a lime kiln and stone jetty nearby. The
West Somerset Path provides easy walking here along the cliffs overlooking the shore;
don't, however, be tempted to walk for any length along the beach itself at low tide
– there are few opportunities to reach higher ground when the tide comes in.

KILVE itself lies a mile or so inland, little more than a huddle of shops on the A39,
linked to Kilve Beach by an easily missed turn-off, Sea Lane. On the way to the beach,
you'll pass the propped up ruins of a **chantry** built in 1329 for the recitation of prayers
for the local squire. Legend has it that it was used to store contraband liquor landed on
the nearby shore.

A WALK FROM KILVE BEACH

From Kilve Beach, you could make an easy **circular walk** of five miles or so, that takes in a couple of attractive Somerset churches. Head east along the coast, following the clifftop path for around 1.5 miles towards the distant, rather sinister landmark of Hinkley Point power station. At Lilstock Beach, at the end of a stretch of loose, sharp-edged stones, a gravel track heads inland to meet a tarmac road. Past Lilstock Farm, look out on the left for **St Andrew's chapel**, a small, simple and much restored fourteenth-century structure topped by a bellcote. The derelict and deconsecrated church was saved from demolition and restored by a local rector in 1993, and is now almost empty save for a pair of elegant stone memorials from the early eighteenth century, one carved from slate. Further up the road, easily visible on the brow of the hill, lies the much larger church of **St Nicholas**, mostly Victorian though sections (the chancel arch and lower part of the tower) date back to the fourteenth century. Among the curiosities within is a dusty collection of fossils and oddments picked up from the coast. Carry on through the scattered hamlet of Kilton; just before Hilltop Lane look out for a signposted footpath on the right leading through fields. Following the path westwards for a mile or so will bring you back to Sea Lane, at the bottom of which is the car park at Kilve Beach.

7

ACCOMMODATION AND EATING

Chantry Tea Gardens Sea Lane, Kilve Beach ☎01278 741457. After exploring the coast, you'll find restorative refreshments at this tea garden beside the ruin of Kilve chantry, just up from the car park at Kilve Beach. Refuel with soups, sandwiches and ploughman's lunches, or treat yourself to home-made cakes or thirteen flavours of Devon ice cream. Daily 10.30am–5pm, may close some days in winter.

Hood Arms Kilve ☎01278 741210, ⓦthehoodarm .com. Although it's right on the A39, this seventeenth century coaching inn in the village has quiet rooms, a different, some with modern showers. The bar area i bedecked with hunting jackets and boots, and offers loca beers and ciders and a full menu (mains £14–19); there's a large garden too. **£95**

Watchet and around

Two miles northwest of Williton, Somerset's only port of any size, **WATCHET**, seems to have little in common with the coast's other holiday-focused centres, though it too gets its share of tourism. There has been a town here since at least 988, when a Viking raid was recorded, and it later became a highly active smuggling centre. **Samuel Taylor Coleridge**, on his perambulations around this area from his base in the Quantock village of Nether Stowey (see p.227), supposedly modelled the port from which his Ancient Mariner embarked on his doomed voyage on Watchet, an association recalled by the modern statue on the Esplanade of the Mariner himself, gazing out over a harbour now filled with yachts.

Seated close by the Ancient Mariner is a second statue that portrays another renowned local figure, that of John Short, or **Yankee Jack**, as he was known (1839–1933), a sailor famed for his powerful voice with which he sang rousing sea shanties. He was interviewed and recorded by the great collector and transcriber of English folk songs, Cecil Sharp, and had a colourful career, sailing the world and running the blockade during the American Civil War before becoming Watchet's town crier in his retirement.

Watchet has a couple of small but absorbing **museums**, and makes a good base for visiting **Cleeve Court**, outside the inland village of Washford, and the unique **Bakelite Museum**, near Williton. You could also make an easy excursion three miles west along the coast to one of Somerset's best beaches, the broad, sandy **Blue Anchor Bay**, a stop on the West Somerset Railway and reached by road from Watchet on the B3191.

Watchet Boat Museum

Harbour Rd • Easter & mid-May to Sept daily 2–4pm • Free • ⓦ wbm.org.uk

Somerset is not known for its maritime tradition, but Watchet has been a fishing and trading port for centuries, while the Levels have seen constant boat activity inland. The **Watchet Boat Museum**, housed in an old goods shed next to the WSR station, presents an overview of life afloat in times gone by, illustrated by an absorbing collection of old photographs, models and full-size examples of boats: coracles; punts; "flatners", the flat-bottomed vessels used for fishing on Somerset's inland waters; turf boats, for carrying the cut and dried blocks of peat; and withy boats, for carrying young willows. Other curiosities include a salmon butt (basket) for catching salmon, and a "mud-horse", a sort of barrow for use on mud-flats, alongside an array of net-making and boat-building tools. It's a fascinating collection, and worth the donation visitors are asked to make.

Market House Museum

Market St • Easter–Oct daily 10.30am–4.30pm • Free • ⓦ watchetmuseum.co.uk

Just up from the harbour, Watchet's old market building from 1820 now houses a chapel upstairs, and on the ground floor an old lock-up at one end and the **Market House Museum** at the other. This low-key but engaging display of local mementoes in one large room includes fossils and molluscs from the surrounding shores, fragments of tools and weapons from the Paleolithic, Neolithic and Bronze ages and Romano-British pottery shards. From more recent times are navigational instruments, a "glatting" spear for the hunting of conger eels, and dozens of black and white photos of the local fishing population.

Cleeve Abbey

Abbey Rd, Washford • Daily: April–June & Sept 10am–5pm; July & Aug 10am–6pm; Oct 10am–4pm • £4.20; EH • ☎ 01984 640377, ⓦ english-heritage.org.uk • Bus #18 or #28, or West Somerset Railway to Washford

Signposted off the A39 at Washford, three miles southwest of Watchet, **Cleeve Abbey** holds one of the country's finest sets of monastic remains, the source of much information about pre-Reformation monastic life. Founded as an abbey in the late twelfth century, this was Somerset's only Cistercian monastic house until the abbey church was razed during the Dissolution of the Monasteries in the 1530s and remaining buildings adapted for domestic and farm use. Beside a stream, the tall arched **gatehouse** is particularly well preserved, as are the monks' **dormitory**, the low-roofed **chapter house** and part of the **cloisters**. Highlight of the site is the superb fifteenth- and sixteenth-century **refectory**, its lofty wagon roof carved with angels. There are also remains of an earlier, thirteenth-century refectory, paved with delicate polychrome **tiles** showing heraldic shields, foliage and combat scenes. You can join a free 45-minute **guided tour** of the site on Tuesdays at 2pm between late July and the end of August (but check first), and open-air plays are occasionally staged in summer.

FOSSICKING

In geological terms, the coast around **Kilve Beach** and **Watchet** is where sedimentary beds of the Jurassic period merge with those of the Upper Triassic, and has proved a fertile spot for "**fossicking**" (the word is probably Cornish in origin). Daniel Defoe, journalist and author of *Robinson Crusoe*, spent time on the fossil trail at Watchet in 1724, and countless others have followed in his footsteps. If you're interested, be aware that the crumbly cliffs on this coast pose a threat, and hard hats are recommended. The best time is after a high tide or a stormy sea. See ⓦ www.kilve.ukfossils.co.uk, and enquire about occasional guided excursions at Watchet's tourist office.

The abbey is just five minutes' walk from the Shepherd's Corner bus stop in Washford, a little longer from Washford's WSR station.

Bakelite Museum

Orchard Mill, Williton • Easter–Oct Thurs–Sun 10.30am–6pm, daily during school hols • £5 • ⓦ bakelitemuseum.co.uk • Bus #18 or #28

Among Somerset's various museum collections, the **Bakelite Collection** has to be the unlikeliest: a bizarre but fascinating collection of British plastic – chiefly Bakelite, but also vulcanite, celluloid, shellac and other synthetics. Tightly packed, randomly but artistically arranged, these gadgets, ornaments, utilities and appliances are an unashamed, affectionate nostalgic wallow in the minutiae of domestic life. Bakelite, developed by a Belgian chemist from 1907 to 1909, was primarily useful for its heat resistance and non-conductivity, and its wide range of applications is illustrated here by the rows of hefty TV sets, gramophones and radios, the shelves of clocks and telephones, and the cases of egg cups and other kitchenware. Among the many curiosities are a couple of Bakelite coffins, a set of plastic teeth and several cream-makers used to make "mock cream" during postwar rationing. In theory, the collection takes in the century 1850–1950, though there are a few anachronisms – always in the same spirit – such as the odd plastic Homer Simpson and dozens of Snoopies, and there's even an old Trabant in the yard, from 1980 but looking much older. There are few labels or explanations, but this only enhances the experience.

A rickety flight of steps leads to the loft, which holds the completely separate but equally nostalgic **Rural History Museum**, displaying a diverse and often mysterious array of cobbler's tools and agricultural devices such as turnip choppers and thistle paddles. The collections are located beside a pretty stream half a mile outside Williton, off the A39, and housed in a water-mill dating from 1616 but in use until the 1960s. The owner, curator and artist Patrick Cook, is usually out of sight but is on hand to answer any questions. The building also houses the *Crafty Cuppa*, serving **snacks and teas**.

ARRIVAL AND INFORMATION

By train Trains of the West Somerset Railway (see box, p.230) stop at Williton, Watchet, Washford and Blue Anchor Bay on their run between Bishops Lydeard and Minehead (late March to early Nov; ⓦ west-somerset-railway.co.uk). Watchet's station is on Harbour Rd, five minutes from the seafront.

By bus Buses pull in outside Watchet's WSR station on Harbour Road.

WATCHET AND AROUND

Destinations Blue Anchor Bay (Mon–Sat 5 daily; 15min); Bridgwater (Mon–Sat 5 daily; 1hr 15min); Minehead (Mon–Sat 2–3 hourly, Sun 9 daily; 25min); Taunton (Mon–Sat 3 hourly, Sun 9 daily; 45min–1hr); Washford (Mon–Sat 3 hourly, Sun 9 daily; 10min); Williton (Mon–Sat 3 hourly, Sun 9 daily; 10min).

Tourist office Volunteer-run office at 6 The Esplanade (Easter–Sept daily 10.30am–4.30pm; ⓦ visit-watchet.co.uk).

ACCOMMODATION

Ivy House 3 Harbour Rd ☏ 01984 633359, ⓦ theivyhousewatchet.co.uk. Right opposite the WSR station, this B&B has friendly owners, clean, traditionally furnished rooms and free wi-fi. Room 2 is biggest, with a roll-top bath and regular sightings of the steam trains from the large windows. Fresh and dried fruits and yoghurt are on the breakfast menu, which uses mainly local ingredients. __£65__

Warren Bay On the B3191 ☏ 01984 631460, ⓦ pringsholidayparks.co.uk. A mile or so west of Watchet on the coast road, this campsite overlooking the sea is set in a large, sloping field, though some flat pitches can be found. There's an indoor pool (50p) and access to a muddy, pebbly beach with rock pools. Watchet is a 25min walk along the coastal path, Blue Anchor Bay about twice that. Closed Nov to mid-March. Pitches __£13__

White House 11 Long St (A39), Williton ☏ 01984 632306, ⓦ whitehousewilliton.co.uk. Within this B&B's imposing white Georgian exterior are chic, modern rooms, some (costing less) in an old stables block, with modern bathrooms. Aga-cooked breakfasts include veggie options. __£74__

ATING AND DRINKING

★ **Binham Grange** Old Cleeve ☎ 01984 640056, ⊕ binhamgrange.co.uk. A little over half a mile inland of Blue Anchor Bay, signposted on the road leading to the village of Old Cleeve, this handsome Jacobean manor house sits next to a cattle farm that helps to provide the top-notch cuisine served in the Great Hall (£37 for three courses). The house is also open for morning coffees, snack lunches and cream teas, which you can have on the terrace with views over the delightful gardens and the fields beyond. There are also a couple of luxurious rooms (£120 & £168), one with its own sitting area. March–Jan daily 10am–late.

Somerset Farmhouse North St, Williton ☎ 01984 632450, ⊕ www.somersetfarmhouse.co.uk. Drop into this quality deli for everything you might need for a snack on the go. You'll find wholesome pies, pasties, meats, cheeses and olives in abundance. It's on the corner of the A39. Mon–Fri 8.30am–5pm, Sat 8.30am–4pm.

Star Inn Mill Lane, Watchet ☎ 01984 631367. Near the harbour, this award-winning freehouse dates back to the eighteenth century, and preserves a richly traditional feel. The menu stretches from ploughman's lunches and pasties to gammon steak, pork ribs and suet pudding, with all meat Exmoor-sourced (most dishes £8–10), and there's a small garden. No credit cards. Daily noon–3pm & 6.30–11pm.

Minehead

West Somerset's chief resort, **MINEHEAD**, is a smaller, smarter and more relaxed version of Weston-super-Mare, but equally devoted to holiday-making. The presence here of one of the country's three remaining Butlin's holiday parks seems only natural, though this venerable institution has in recent years been yanked into the twenty-first century by its staging of one of the UK's most fashionable music festivals, **All Tomorrow's Parties** (⊕ atpfestival.com).

Minehead certainly doesn't have Weston's share of mud, and its wide, sandy beach even at low tide makes an attractive sight. Backing the beach is a jaunty promenade, which can become frantically busy in the holiday season. Away from the sea, the town preserves some residue of its Victorian character in the well-to-do area of **Higher Town** on the slopes of North Hill, holding some of the oldest houses and offering splendid views across the Bristol Channel. Steep lanes link the quarter with **Quay Town**, the harbour area at Minehead's western end, where a few fishing vessels still operate.

Though this traditional family resort has little in common with the windswept uplands of Exmoor, the moor is only a hop away, accessible from North Hill, and the town's good range of shops, services and accommodation makes it a useful base for excursions. Minehead is also a terminus for the West Somerset Railway (see box, p.230), with a station practically on the

THE SOUTH WEST COAST PATH

Minehead marks one end of Britain's longest National Trail, the **South West Coast Path** (⊕ southwestcoastpath.com), which tracks the coastline along Somerset and Devon's northern seaboard, round Cornwall, back into Devon, and on to Dorset, where it finishes close to Poole Harbour. Although it's much used, it counts as one of the country's hardest trails, at least in parts, as little of it is level for very long. The path was conceived in the 1940s, but it was only some forty years ago than – barring a few significant gaps – the full **630-mile route** opened, much of it on land owned by the National Trust, and all of it well signposted with the acorn symbol of the Countryside Agency.

Some degree of **planning** is essential for any long walk along the South West Coast Path, and **accommodation** should be considered too: don't expect to arrive somewhere late in the day in season and immediately find a bed – even campsites can fill to capacity. Bone up on local transport schedules, and, to lighten your load, ask at local tourist offices or look online for **luggage-transfer** operators.

Aurum Press publishes four **National Trail Guides** describing different parts of the path and using 1:25,000 Ordnance Survey maps, Cicerone Press publishes a one-volume edition using 1:50,000 Ordnance Survey maps, while the **South West Coast Path Association** (☎ 01752 896237, ⊕ swcp.org.uk) publishes an annual guide (£10, plus postage) to the whole path, including accommodation lists, ferry timetables and transport details, but without maps.

seafront. If you're here for the **South West Coast Path** (see box, p.249), head west to Quay Street, where huge sculptured hands holding a map stand on the seafront; opposite the sculpture, a path between cottages ascends North Hill onto the coast path.

ARRIVAL AND DEPARTURE

MINEHEA[

By train Trains of the West Somerset Railway (see box, p.230) connect Minehead with Bishops Lydeard in the Quantock Hills (late March to early November; ⓦ west-somerset-railway.co.uk). The station is just off The Esplanade.

By bus Most bus stops are on or around The Parade, at the southern end of The Avenue.

Destinations Dunster (Mon–Sat 3–4 hourly, Sun hourly 20min); Porlock (Mon–Sat hourly, Sun early April to la[Oct 3 daily; 20min); Taunton (Mon–Sat 2 hourly, Sun daily; 1hr 10min–1hr 25min); Watchet (Mon–Sat 2 hourly, Sun 9 daily; 30min).

INFORMATION

Tourist office Warren Road, on the seafront close to the West Somerset Railway station (Mon, Tues, Fri & Sat 10am–5pm, Wed & Thurs 10am–2.30pm, Sun 11am–4pm ☎ 01643 702624, ⓦ visit-exmoor.co.uk).

ACCOMMODATION

The Anchorage Quay West ☎ 01643 704814. Close to the start of the coast path, this B&B has just two rooms and they're both fairly plain, with louvre doors connecting the small en-suite bathrooms. Go for the larger, fron[room for its terrific sea views (£60). No credit cards Closed Oct–April. **£50**

MINEHEAD

Baytree 29 Blenheim Rd ☎01643 703374, ✉derekcole@onetel.com. This Victorian B&B facing public gardens offers spacious rooms with private bathrooms, including a family suite. The science fiction author Arthur C. Clarke was born a few doors along at no. 3. Closed Nov–March. No credit cards. **£60**

Kildare Lodge Townsend Rd ☎01643 702009, ✉kildarelodge.co.uk. This small hotel has more character than most: a reconstructed faux-Tudor inn designed by a pupil of Edwin Lutyens and strongly influenced by him. It's got an impressive, high-ceilinged bar, a courtyard and garden. There are a few single rooms, but book early for a double, as there are only three (two with four-poster beds). **£70**

Old Ship Aground Quay St ☎01643 702087, ✉theoldshipaground.co.uk. Rooms are basic but modern and clean, and a couple have sideways views over the harbour. The more expensive ones are huge, but all bathrooms are on the small side. **£55**

YHA Minehead Midway between Minehead and Dunster, signposted from the A39 at Alcombe ☎0845 371 9033, ✉minehead@yha.org.uk. This well-run hostel is beautifully situated in a secluded combe on the edge of Exmoor. Most rooms have four beds, and there are family rooms as well as a kitchen, restaurant and a nice garden. Bus #28 from Minehead, Dunster and Taunton stops a mile away at Alcombe. Dorms from **£19**

CAMPSITES

★ Minehead Camping and Caravanning North Hill ☎01643 704138, ⓦ campingandcaravanningclub.co.uk. High above town on the edge of Exmoor, this clean and well-equipped site is well placed for hiking excursions. Pitches are slightly sloping, but it's reasonably well-sheltered, surrounded by trees with the occasional glimpse of Blue Anchor Bay and the town below. A footpath leads through trees to town in 20–30min. Turn up Martlet Road off Blenheim Road to get here. Closed late Sept to mid-April. Pitches **£7.10**

Minehead and Exmoor Caravan and Camping Park Porlock Rd (A39) ☎01643 703074, ⓦ minehead andexmoorcamping.co.uk. A mile or so west of town on the A39 (look out for the sign, on the right-hand side heading west, as it's tricky to see), this is a small but fully equipped site arranged in a series of "bays," or woody glades. There's some traffic noise from the adjacent main road, but it's quiet enough at night. Closed Oct–Feb. **£9** per person.

7

EATING AND DRINKING

Bistro 16 16 Park St ☎01643 705222. This cosy little restaurant has a Spanish-influenced menu, with ciabattas and pies at lunchtime and exquisite tapas (£3–6) or fuller meals in the evening, for example pork tenderloin with mozzarella and sweet piquillo peppers, and butternut squash with apricot tagine (mains £10–13). Leave space for tasty desserts. No credit cards. Mon–Wed 10am–3pm, Thurs–Sat 9/10am–3pm & 6.30–9.30pm.

Old Harbour House 11a Quay St ☎01643 705917. Traditional and slightly twee, this seafront restaurant specializes in seafood, including crab and lobster, with a solid selection of meat and vegetarian options as back-up (mains £13–17). There are set menus (evenings £23–25 for four courses, Sun lunch £12 for two courses), and you should call first to pre-order. No credit cards. Tues–Sat 7–9pm (last orders), Sun 12.30–3pm.

Quay Inn Quay St ☎01643 707323, ⓦ quay-inn.co.uk. On the seafront, this convivial pub has a traditional bar and a nice garden. There's a full bar menu (three courses for £20) and cream teas in summer. B&B also available (£80–100). Daily 11am/noon–11pm/midnight, food served noon–8.45pm, reduced hours in winter.

Queen's Head Holloway St ☎01643 702940. West Country ales are dispensed at the bar of this large central tavern, which also has darts and pool. There's the usual selection of seafood, curries and steaks (£6–13), as well as a good-value carvery (Tues, Thurs & Sun; £7.75). Mon–Thurs & Sun 11am–11pm, Fri & Sat till midnight, food served noon–2pm & 6–9pm.

Sashes 11a Quay St ☎01643 709890, ⓦwww .sashesgoodfood.co.uk. Intimate and a bit posh, but not formal, this small place has a romantic ambience to accompany some of Minehead's finest food, including such dishes as roast loin of lamb and fresh seafood (£15–19). Food served Tues–Sat 7–8.30pm (last orders).

★ Toucan Café 3 The Parade ☎01643 706101. In a mustard-coloured room above a natural food store, with mellow background music, you can tuck into falafels, bean burgers and quesadillas (£4–7), or just a Fair Trade tea or organic coffee. Also offered are healthy smoothies and fruit juices with names like Ginger Spice and Spinach Spectacular. Mon–Sat 9am–5pm.

DIRECTORY

Bike rental Exmoor Cycle Hire, 6 Parkhouse Rd ☎01643 705307, ⓦ exmoorcyclehire.co.uk (£9 per half-day, £14 per day); Pompy's Cycles, Mart Road ☎01643 704077, ⓦ pompyscycles.co.uk (£14–30 per day).

Internet Exmoor Printers, Tregonwell Road ☎01643 704799. Mon–Fri 9.30am–5pm.

Taxis Rank outside the town hall on The Parade, or call Webber Cabs ☎01643 703344 or Exmoor Taxis ☎01643 863355.

Exmoor

LYNMOUTH HARBOUR

Exmoor

A high, bare plateau sliced by wooded combes and splashing streams,
Exmoor boasts tracts of wilderness every bit as forbidding as the South
West's other great National Park, Dartmoor, but is smaller, with greater
expanses of farmland breaking up the bare moorland. Its long seaboard,
from which mists and rainstorms can descend with alarming speed, add to
its distinctive character, affording compelling views over the Bristol Channel.
Most of the park is privately owned – including about ten percent held by
the National Trust – but there's good access along an extensive network of
footpaths and bridleways.

Apart from around the moor's famed beauty spots, you'll generally find complete
isolation here – with the exception of the occasional group of hikers, photographers,
and hunting and shooting folk who often descend at weekends. Drivers, incidentally,
should beware of sheep and ponies straying over Exmoor's roads, including the
relatively fast coastal A39; after dark, you may even come across sheep lying down on
the tarmac.

Inland Exmoor lacks any major road running through it, though you'll almost
certainly make use of the B3223, B3224 and B3358, traversing the moor in an
east–west direction and providing access to some of the best walking country. Basing
yourself at **Dulverton**, on the moor's southern edge and site of the park's main
information office, or at **Exford**, at the centre of the moor, you'll be well placed for
some of the choicest areas, including such celebrated beauty spots as **Tarr Steps** and the
moor's highest point of **Dunkery Beacon**. The hamlets of **Winsford** and **Simonsbath** are
smaller, less frequented starting points for excursions.

The **Exmoor coast**, which includes Britain's tallest sea cliffs, is more easily accessible
for visitors, with the A39 running parallel to the sea to link the pretty small towns and
villages nestled between the steep bluffs. Consequently, you'll find more tourist activity
here, not least around the well-preserved medieval village of **Dunster** with its impressive
castle, on the northeastern edge of the moor. Nearby **Minehead** marks one end of the
South West Coast Path, which offers the best way to get acquainted with Exmoor's
seaboard.

Working west along the coast, a string of coastal villages including **Porlock**,
Lynmouth, **Lynton** and **Oare** make up part of what's known as "**Doone Country**", an
indeterminate area that includes some of Exmoor's wildest tracts, and which is now
inextricably tied to R.D. Blackmore's tale, *Lorna Doone*. Following its publication in
1869, this romantic melodrama based on local outlaw clans in the seventeenth century
quickly established itself in Exmoor's mythology, and is still frequently recalled today,
despite the fact that the book is not as widely read as it once was.

Walking is the most popular activity on the moor. You can pick up good, simple route
cards of "Golden Walks" (£1) from Visitor Centres, while the National Park Authority
has a full programme of **guided walks** (see box, p.264) aimed at all abilities. Stables

DUNSTER CASTLE

Highlights

❶ Riding on the moor Discover the moor on horseback for a memorable and exhilarating experience. Stables are plentiful, catering to all ability levels. **See p.258 & 277**

❷ Dunster Castle Looming above Dunster's tapering main street, this romantic castle is filled with sixteenth- and seventeenth-century furnishings and works of art. **See p.266**

❸ Coastwalking The hogback cliffs at Exmoor's northern edge can be tough going, but the ever-changing views more than compensate. **See p.272**

❹ Valley of Rocks West of Lynton, this area is overlooked by crags and inhabited by feral goats – a great spot for a wander. **See p.272**

❺ The cliff railway at Lynton and Lynmouth A steep cliff separates these scenic sister towns, but the water-powered funicular makes for an effortless and eco-friendly way to move between the two. **See p.273**

❻ Watersmeet Two rivers merge at this renowned beauty spot, from where paths radiate in every direction. **See p.275**

HIGHLIGHTS ARE MARKED ON THE MAP ON P.256

EXMOOR

B R I S T O L   C H A N N E L

Watchet

Minehead

Dunster

Dunster Castle 2

Clatworthy Reservoir

Wimbleball Lake

Brendon Hills

Brompton Regis

Bridgetown

Wheddon Cross

River Exe

Winsford

Caratacus Stone

Dulverton 1

The Punchbowl

Winsford Hill

Tarr Steps

Withypool

Two Moors Way

Winsford Hill

Exford

Edgcott

River Exe

River Barle

Simonsbath

Cow Castle

North Molton

SOMERSET

Dunkery Beacon

Selworthy Beacon

Selworthy

Allerford

Luccombe

South West Coast Path

Hurlstone Point

Bossington

Porlock

Porlock Weir

Culbone Church

Oare

County Gate

Malmsmead

EXMOOR NATIONAL PARK

Foreland Point

Watersmeet 6

Lynmouth

Lynbridge

Barbrook

Lynton

Valley of Rocks 4

3

5

Hoar Oak Water

West Lyn River

Pinkworthy Pond

Challacombe

Brayford

DEVON

Woody Bay

Heddon's Mouth

Great Hangman

Little Hangman

Hangman Point

Wild Pear Beach

Combe Martin

Ilfracombe

TRENTISHOE DOWN

Holdstone Hill

EXMOOR FOREST

South West Coast Path

Parracombe

Blackmoor Gate

Arlington

Barnstaple

South Molton

River Taw

West Somerset Railway

N

0   miles   2

cattered across the moor provide opportunities for **riding** – we've mentioned the best ones – while adventure-seekers will find a range of other organized activities available, such as **wildlife safaris**. Despite some serious-looking hills, there are also **cycling** possibilities: see ⓦactiveexmoor.com for details of the sixty-mile on-road **Exmoor Cycle Route**. Biketrail Cycle Hire, based at Fremington, near Barnstaple (☎01271 372586 or 07788 133738, ⓦbiketrail.co.uk), rents out bikes and provides a delivery and collection service with free route maps. It's worth doing some research on guided walks, wildlife safaris and adventure sports on Exmoor (see box, p.264). Be aware that winter, especially, is the time when you'll run into the **organized hunts** for which Exmoor is notorious – despite the statutory restrictions on hunting with dogs.

INFORMATION

VISITOR CENTRES

Dulverton National Park Visitor Centre on Fore Street (daily: April–Oct 10am–1.15pm & 1.45–5pm; Nov–March 10.30am–3pm; ☎01398 323841, ⓦwww.exmoor-nationalpark.gov.uk) provides information on the whole moor. Other visitor centres are at Dunster (see p.267) and Lynmouth (see p.274).

USEFUL WEBSITES

ⓦ**activeexmoor.com** Useful resource for activities, from mountain-biking to fly-fishing, as well as events, accommodation, and food and drink.

ⓦ**everythingexmoor.org.uk** Wide-ranging, community-based directory and encyclopedia on all things Exmoor, from adders to youth hostels – though not always up to date.

ⓦ**exmoor.com** Useful for accommodation, attractions, food, drink and events.

ⓦ**exmoor-accommodation.co.uk** Efficient directory of all types of accommodation, including campsites and self-catering.

ⓦ**www.exmoor-nationalpark.gov.uk** Official National Park site – comprehensive and reliable.

ⓦ**visit-exmoor.co.uk** Official tourist website, useful for all aspects of Exmoor.

ⓦ**whatsonexmoor.com** General information on transport, places to visit and activities, including riding and fishing, plus links for accommodation, eating out and weather forecasts.

GETTING AROUND

Apart from the steam and diesel trains of the **West Somerset Railway**, public transport around Exmoor is limited to a sketchy **bus** network. You can flag down a bus anywhere in the national park, providing it is safe for it to stop. If you're planning to use bus services on Exmoor, it's worth checking routes beforehand, as services can be withdrawn or changed, depending on annual local transport budgets. Consider buying a money-saving all-day **FirstDay South West pass** (£7–8), valid for travel on services operated by First. The other main bus company in these parts is **Quantock Motor Services** (☎01823 430202, ⓦquantockmotorservices.co.uk). Traveline (☎0871 200 2233, ⓦtraveline.org.uk) has full **schedules** for the whole region.

BY TRAIN

The nearest main-line stations for Exmoor are Taunton and Tiverton. There's also the West Somerset Railway (see box, p.230), a heritage line operating from late March to early November between Bishops Lydeard (near Taunton) and Minehead, with a stop near Dunster .

BY BUS

Connections between Exmoor's coastal centres are fairly regular, but services to small inland villages are sporadic at best. Some lines run in the summer only; all services are greatly reduced in the winter months, and few buses run on Sundays at any time.

Bus #398 runs between Minehead, Dunster, Wheddon Cross, Dulverton and Tiverton runs throughout the year (not Sun).

Bus #400 "Exmoor Explorer" vintage bus runs useful but limited seasonal services. It's open-top in fine weather and loops between Minehead, Dunster, Wheddon Cross, Exford and Porlock (twice daily on Tues, Thurs, Sat & Sun between late July and early Sept and on Sun early to late Sept). There are also a few once- or twice-weekly community buses connecting Dulverton, Minehead and Lynton.

Bus #300 On the coast, the (usually) open-top "Exmoor Coastlink" connects Lynmouth with Porlock, Allerford, Selworthy and Minehead daily in summer (early April to late Oct), and with Combe Martin and Ilfracombe daily in summer (late May to mid-Oct) and weekends only in winter.

Bus #39 runs roughly every hour between Minehead, Selworthy, Allerford, Porlock and Porlock Weir (not Sun).

8

Inland Exmoor

Watered by 325 miles of river, the upland plateau of inland Exmoor reveals a rich spectrum of colour and an amazing diversity of wildlife. The cheapest and best way to appreciate the grandeur of the moor is on foot, and endless permutations of **walking routes** are possible along a network of some six hundred miles of public footpaths and bridleways. **Pony trekking** is another option for getting the most out of Exmoor's desolate beauty, and stables are dotted throughout the area. **Kayaking** and **mountain biking** are also increasingly popular pursuits. Whichever of these you are pursuing, bear in mind that over seventy percent of the National Park is privately owned and that access is theoretically restricted to public rights of way; special permission should certainly be sought before doing anything like camping or fishing.

There are four obvious bases for excursions: **Dulverton**, in the southeast and connected by bus #25B to Taunton and by #398 to Tiverton and Minehead, makes a good starting point for visiting the seventeen-span medieval bridge at Tarr Steps, about five miles to the northwest; you could also reach the spot from **Winsford** via a circular walk that takes in the prehistoric Wambarrows on the summit of Winsford Hill, and the ancient Caratacus Stone; on the B3224, **Exford** makes a useful base for the heart of the moor; and further west, **Simonsbath** is an excellent starting point for hikes in the Barle valley, despite holding only a couple of hotels. Dulverton and Exford have most of inland Exmoor's accommodation – and it's not uncommon for all of this to be filled by the various walkers, hunters, shooters and fishers who frequent these parts.

8

Dulverton

On the banks of the River Barle on Exmoor's southern edge, **DULVERTON** is one of the main gateways to the moor, and, as home to the National Park Authority's headquarters, makes a useful port of call before further explorations. The town is grouped around Fore Street and High Street, which run parallel from the river towards the hilltop parish church. Fore Street has most of the shops and pubs, plus the post office, a bank with a cash machine and the Exmoor Visitor Centre. Behind the visitor centre, and accessible from it, the **Guildhall Heritage Centre** (Easter–Oct daily 10am–4.30pm; free) has an absorbing museum of the village, including an art gallery, a reconstructed Victorian kitchen and bedroom, and an archive room holding an extensive photographic collection, tapes of oral history and films. The centre also holds regular exhibitions.

ARRIVAL AND DEPARTURE

DULVERTON

By bus Buses run to and from: Dunster (Mon–Sat 6–7 daily; 50min); Exford (Mon–Fri 2 daily, Sat 1 daily; 40min); Minehead (Mon–Sat 6 daily; 1hr); & Winsford (Mon–Fri 2 daily, Sat 1 daily; 25min).

INFORMATION AND ACTIVITIES

Exmoor Visitor Centre Shares premises with the public library at 7 Fore St (daily: April–Oct 10am–1.15pm & 1.45–5pm; Nov–March 10.30am–3pm; ☎ 01398 323841, ⓦ www.exmoor-nationalpark.gov.uk). The centre has information on the whole moor and a small exhibition on life on Exmoor with a film showing aspects of moor management. The library has internet access.

Horseriding Moorland horseriding is offered at West Anstey Farm (☎ 01398 341354), a couple of miles west of Dulverton.

ACCOMMODATION

Exe Valley Caravan Site Bridgetown ☎ 01398 323602, ⓦ exevalleycamping.co.uk. This clean and spacious adults-only site sits by the Exe, some five miles north of Dulverton on the A396. Pitches are a generous size, and the *Badgers Holt* pub is just two minutes' walk away. Closed mid-Oct to mid-March. Pitches <u>£15.50</u>

Lion Hotel Bank Square ☎ 01398 324471, ⓦ lionhoteldulverton.com. This inn should suit anyone hankering for beams and four-posters; rooms 9 and the slightly larger 11 have a nice prospect over the street. 2nt inimum stay at weekends. **£82**

orthcombe Farm A mile north of Dulverton, past the ock House Inn ☎ 01398 323602, ⓦ woodsdulverton o.uk. There are two YHA-affiliated camping barns here ith cooking facilities, hot showers and bed mats (but no ien), charging £8.50 per person per night. Dorms **£8.50**

★ **Tongdam** 26 High St ☎ 01398 323397, ⓦ tongdamthai.co.uk. Above this Thai restaurant (see elow) you'll find excellent, modern and tastefully

furnished accommodation: two doubles with shared bathroom, and a suite with a separate sitting room and balcony. From **£56**

★ **Town Mills** High St ☎ 01398 323124, ⓦ townmillsdulverton.co.uk. A burbling stream runs through the garden of this elegant Georgian millhouse at the bottom of the High Street. The good-size, pine-furnished bedrooms include a family room and are all spotlessly clean. Free wi-fi. No under-12s. **£90**

EATING AND DRINKING

ewis's Tea Rooms 13 High St ☎ 01398 323850. Serves ot and cold snacks, including a range of rarebits made vith ham, brie and local cider (£5–8). There's a choice of ream teas, best of them the Dulverton (£10.50), including reshly made sandwiches and cake. There's a courtyard arden. Daily 9.30am–5.15pm.

★ **Tongdam** 26 High St ☎ 01398 323397, ⓦ tongdamthai.co.uk. Take a break from English country ooking at this Thai outpost, where dishes such as narinated duck and prawn curry go for £10–15. Mediterranean dishes like dolmades and pastas are sold at unchtime, and there's a takeaway service. You can eat

alfresco on the small patio in warm weather. Daily noon–3pm & 6–10pm.

★ **Woods** 4 Bank Square ☎ 01398 324007. With wooden tables, chairs and floor, and a scattering of antlers, boots and riding whips, this gastropub has a smart-rustic feel. The menu features traditional, French-influenced dishes, such as grilled sole, slow-roast shoulder of pork and guinea-fowl (mostly £14–17 in the evening). The bar dispenses draught ales from Devon and Cornwall, and there's a small garden. Mon–Sat 11am–3pm & 6–11pm, Sun noon–3pm & 7–11pm.

8

Tarr Steps and around

Nestling in the deeply wooded Barle valley seven miles northwest of Dulverton, the **Tarr Steps** clapper bridge is one of Exmoor's most famous beauty spots. Many prefer to walk here (from Dulverton Bridge, simply follow the riverside track upstream); by road it's a left turn from Dulverton's Fore Street, and another left five miles along the B3223. If you're driving, leave your vehicle in the car park and walk the final 500m downhill, or else you can follow a tributary of the Barle to the bridge signposted from the car park.

The ancient **woodland** around Tarr Steps largely consists of sessile oak – formerly coppiced for tan bark and charcoal production – and a sprinkling of beech, but you'll

---

A WALK FROM TARR STEPS

Tarr Steps makes a great destination on foot from Dulverton or Winsford (see p.260), and you can extend the trip by combining it with this exhilarating five-mile circular walk, which takes in Winsford Hill, near Winsford. It's not excessively challenging, and you should be able to complete the circuit in around four hours.

Follow the riverside path upstream from Tarr Steps, turning right about half a mile along Watery Lane, a rocky track that deteriorates into a muddy lane near Knaplock Farm. Stay on the track for three-quarters of a mile until you reach a cattle grid, on open moorland. Turn left here, cross a small stream and climb up **Winsford Hill** for the 360-degree moorland views and the group of Bronze Age burial mounds (see p.260). If you want a refreshment stop, descend the hill on the other side to the village of Winsford (see p.261).

A quarter of a mile due east of the Barrows, via any of the broad grassy tracks, the ground drops sharply by over 190ft to the **Punchbowl**, a bracken-grown depression resembling an amphitheatre. Keep on the east side of the B3223 which runs up Winsford Hill, following it south for a mile to the Spire Cross junction, where you should look out for the nearby **Caratacus Stone** (see p.261), partly hidden among the gorse. Continue south on the east side of the road, cross it after about a mile, and pass over the cattle grid on the Tarr Steps road, from where a footpath takes you west another one-and-a-half miles back to the river crossing.

also see a mix of downy birch, ash, hazel, wych elm and field maple, often with a thick covering of lichen. The hazel coppice forms an important habitat for dormice, and you may spot red deer on the riverbanks. Birds breeding hereabouts include redstart, wood warbler and pied flycatcher, and you'll probably catch sight of dippers, grey wagtails and kingfishers. There's a choice of **walks** to embark upon, either onto Winsford Hill (see box, p.259); upstream of the river as far as Withypool (4 miles); or downstream to Dulverton. The visitor centre at Dulverton sells itineraries for waymarked circular walks taking in Tarr Steps.

The bridge

Positioned next to a ford, the ancient **bridge** is said to be the finest of its type in Britain, constructed of huge gritstone slabs that are fixed onto piers by their own weight – which can be as much as two tonnes. Over 180ft long with seventeen spans, it's normally about 3ft above water level – much lower than when originally built due to the river silting up. Floodwaters now frequently cover the bridge, often causing damage – all but one of the slabs were washed away on the night of the 1952 Lynmouth deluge (see p.273). When this happens, however, the stones seldom travel far, and they are now numbered for easy repair; they're also protected by upstream cables that help to arrest flood debris charging down.

The bridge's age has been much disputed, with some claiming prehistoric origins, apparently backed up by the Bronze Age tracks found converging on the crossing, and its name, derived from the Celtic *tochar* meaning causeway. But there's no proof of a previous construction to this one, the earliest record of which is from Tudor times. Most now agree that, like the clapper bridges on Dartmoor, it is likely to be medieval. According to legend, however, the bridge was made by the devil as a place to sunbathe. The Prince of Darkness vowed to destroy any creature attempting to cross, and when a parson was sent to confront him he was met by a stream of profanities. When the abuse was returned in good measure, the devil was so impressed he allowed free use of the bridge.

ACCOMMODATION AND EATING   **TARR STEPS AND AROUND**

Tarr Farm ☎01643 851507, **✆**tarrfarm.co.uk. Above the Steps, this sixteenth-century riverside inn, restaurant and tearoom provides an excellent spot to contemplate the river, and also serves light lunches and teas, as well as evening meals (mains around £17), for which you should book. Upmarket accommodation is available in modern, fully equipped rooms. No under-10s. **£150**

Winsford

Five miles north of Dulverton, and signposted a mile west of the A396, **WINSFORD** lays good claim to being the moor's prettiest village. A scattering of thatched cottages ranged around a sleepy green, Winsford is watered by a confluence of streams and rivers – one of them the Exe – giving it no fewer than seven bridges. Dominated, as it has been for centuries, by the rambling, thatched *Royal Oak Inn*, the village was the childhood home of the great trade union leader and Labour politician Ernest Bevin (1881–1951) – his birthplace, bearing a plaque, is across from the post office and shops.

Winsford Hill

Once you've admired the village's obvious charms, the best plan is to abandon them in favour of the surrounding countryside. The obvious walking excursion from the village is the climb up **Winsford Hill**, a heather moor cut through by the B3223 that's reached on foot by taking the Tarr Steps road past the *Royal Oak*; turn off onto the moorland where it turns sharp left after about three-quarters of a mile. About the same distance further west, the hill's round 1400ft summit is invisible until you are almost there, but once you're at the top, your efforts are repaid by views as far as Dartmoor, and you can clamber around three Bronze Age burial mounds known as the **Wambarrows**.

EXMOOR WILDLIFE

The establishment of the National Park has done much to protect Exmoor's diverse **wildlife**, from dormice and fritillary butterflies to otters and buzzards. The management of the coastal heath that makes up most of the terrain has allowed certain species of bird to thrive, while the gorse covering large parts of it has especially favoured the diminutive blue Dartford warbler and the orange-breasted stonechat. Most celebrated of the moor's mammals, though, are **Exmoor ponies**, a unique species closely related to prehistoric horses. Most commonly found in the treeless heartland of the moor around Exmoor Forest, Winsford Hill or Withypool Common, these short and stocky animals are not difficult to spot, though fewer than twelve hundred are registered, and of these only about 170 are living free on the moor. You probably won't get close to them, but if you do, don't try to feed them, and bear in mind that their teeth are sharp enough to tear up the tough moorland plants. Much more elusive is the **red deer**, England's largest native wild animal, of which Exmoor supports the country's only wild population. Over the centuries, hunting has accounted for a drastic depletion in numbers, but red deer have a strong recovery rate – about three thousand are thought to inhabit the moor today, and their annual culling by stalking as well as hunting is a regular point of issue among conservationists and nature-lovers. Porlock Visitor Centre (see p.271) organizes "Rutting Weekends" in autumn, a good opportunity to view the deer – advance booking essential.

The Caratacus Stone

A mile southeast of the summit, near the turning for Tarr Steps, the B3223 runs close to the **Caratacus Stone**, an inscribed monolith thought to date from between 450 and 650 and referred to in medieval documents as the Longstone. It is not immediately easy to spot among the vegetation, though you'll probably pick out the roof of the comic "bus shelter" canopy built over it in 1906. The damaged inscription on the greyish-green monolith, four feet high, reads "Caratatci Nepos" – that is, "kinsman of Caratacus", the last great Celtic chieftain who was defeated by the Romans in 46 AD. It's an easy walk from here to Tarr Steps (see box, p.259).

8

ARRIVAL AND DEPARTURE · WINSFORD

By bus Buses run to and from: Dulverton (Mon–Sat 2 daily; 25min); Dunster (Mon–Sat 1–2 daily; 50min); Exford (Mon–Sat 1–2 daily; 15min); and Minehead (Mon–Sat 1–2 daily; 1hr).

ACCOMMODATION AND EATING

Halse Farm Campsite A mile southwest of the village, reached from Halse Lane ☎01643 851259, ⓦ halsefarm.co.uk. Not very well sheltered and with fairly basic but clean facilities, this smallish site is located on the edge of the moor, convenient for walkers. Closed Nov to mid-March. Pitches **£14**

Karslake House Halse Lane ☎01643 851242, ⓦ karslakehouse.co.uk. Traditional, upmarket B&B close to the village centre (100m behind the *Royal Oak Inn*). The owners can arrange shooting, fishing, wildlife safaris and relaxation therapies, and provide picnic lunches and cream teas. Rooms are all en suite or with private bathrooms, and there's a self-catering cottage. No under-12s. From **£90**

Royal Oak Village centre ☎01643 851455, ⓦ royaloakexmoor.co.uk. This thatched and rambling old inn dominating Winsford offers Exmoor ales, snacks and full restaurant meals (most mains £10–14). The accommodation is plush but rooms vary so check first – the four-poster rooms are spacious but expensive; cheaper ones are less appealing. From **£80**

Exford

At an ancient crossing point on the River Exe, **EXFORD**, four miles northwest of Winsford, preserves an insular air, its sedate cottages and post office ranged around a tidy village green. A part of the Royal Forest of Exmoor from Saxon times until the early thirteenth century, Exford prospered as a junction for packhorse trains carrying wool and cloth. During the nineteenth century, it grew as a **sporting centre** and today, as the base of the Devon and Somerset Staghounds, local life is intimately involved with the **hunt**, particularly during the long season, which lasts from early August to late April.

HUNTING ON EXMOOR

For many, outdoor sports on Exmoor means hunting and shooting, practices which have been at the heart of local communities for centuries. Shooting mainly takes place between September and January, but **hunting** can go on all year – though mostly in winter – and plays a large part in the lives of many of Exmoor's inhabitants. Socially, too, the institution is central, since most hunts have full calendars of events. The voice of local hunt supporters is loud and clear: the **Countryside Alliance** (ⓦ countryside-alliance.org) pro-hunting lobby has strong support and "Fight Prejudice" stickers are evident everywhere.

In contrast, the true number of local **opponents** to the hunt will never be known – few want to risk taking a stand in Exmoor's close-knit communities. Alongside the cruelty argument, the two reasons most often cited for opposing hunting are the damage caused to farmland and gardens by dogs and horses, and the chaos created by the hunt followers – many of them city-folk – whose cross-country manoeuvrings can block up roads and show scant regard for either countryside or property. The National Trust's ban on stag-hunting on its land has added more fuel to the debate, since it has virtually ended the practice in many places.

What cannot be denied is the heavy dependence of Exmoor's economy – more than most other hunting areas in Britain – on the sport, not least in such villages as Exford, home to the kennels and stables of the Devon and Somerset Staghounds. If you're looking for a quiet time in these parts, you're best off keeping your views on the matter to yourself, since feelings run high.

You can find out about meets of the Devon and Somerset Staghounds in the local press or at ⓦ devonandsomersetstaghounds.net, alongside news of the hunt's puppy and horse shows, point-to-point races and other summer events. For the case against hunting, see the **League Against Cruel Sports**' website ⓦ league.org.uk.

Dunkery Beacon

Exford is a popular starting point for the hike to **Dunkery Beacon**, Exmoor's highest point at 1704ft (map ref SS891415). A four-mile hike to the northeast, the route is clearly marked along a track that starts from Combe Lane, just past the post office (turn right at the end of the playing fields). The bridleway here eventually becomes a rough track, which winds slowly round to the summit of the hill – a steady uphill trudge. A substantial cairn sits at the top, from where a majestic vista unfolds, with lonely moorland all about and South Wales often visible; there's also easy access by car, with a road passing close to the summit.

ARRIVAL AND DEPARTURE
EXFORD

By bus Buses run to and from: Dulverton (Mon–Sat 2 daily; 40min); Dunster (Mon–Sat 1–2 daily; 35min); Minehead (Mon–Sat 1–2 daily; 50min); and Winsford (Mon–Sat 2 daily; 15min).

ACCOMMODATION

Crown Hotel ☎ 01643 831554, ⓦ crownhotelexmoor .co.uk. With friendly staff and a log fire in the lounge, this elegantly old-fashioned, rather upper-crust inn is at the heart of local sporty life. Some of the quiet and spacious rooms have views over the green. Rates are negotiable. From **£135**

Exmoor Lodge Chapel St ☎ 01643 831694, ⓦ exmoor-lodge.co.uk. Small, plain and friendly B&B backing onto the village green, with most rooms en suite, and lots of local information on hand. Packed lunches and evening meals can be arranged. No credit cards. From **£50**

Westermill Farm Edgcott ☎ 01643 831238, ⓦ exmoorcamping.co.uk. Two and a half miles northwest of Exford, this tranquil campsite has grass pitches on the banks of the Exe. There are free hot showers and waymarked walks over the five-hundred-acre farm, plus a small, seasonal shop selling local meat. Self-catering cottages are available too. **£6.50** per person

White Horse Inn ☎ 01643 831229, ⓦ exmoor-whitehorse.co.uk. Large, impressively timbered and creeper-covered coaching inn right by the bridge, less exclusive than the *Crown* but similarly traditional in style, and with the huntin' and shootin' crowd equally in evidence (there are stables right next door). Some rooms are on the small side, and some have four-posters. **£160**

YHA Exford ☎ 0845 371 9634, ⓔ exford@yha.org.uk. Exmoor's main YHA hostel occupies a gabled Victorian house near the centre of the village on the banks of the Exe. Most rooms have four to six beds, and family rooms and facilities for campers are also available, along with kitchen and restaurant. Dorms **£18.40**, doubles **£46**

EATING AND DRINKING

Crown Hotel ☎01643 831554. You can choose between the bar menu or classier modern dishes in the restaurant (evenings only), though classic local favourites such as roast loin of venison are also offered. Set-price menus are £24 and £29 for two or three courses. Also a nice spot for afternoon tea, but the bar rather lacks atmosphere. Bar daily noon–11pm.

White Horse Inn ☎01643 831229. Basic bar meals popular with walkers, hunters and hostellers are offered here for around £9, alongside a pricier restaurant menu with "typsy pheasant" and salmon steak going for around £14.50. Serves afternoon teas and some 150 malt whiskies, and there are tables outside by the river. Daily 11am–11pm.

Exmoor Forest and Simonsbath

At the centre of the National Park, **Exmoor Forest** is the barest part of the moor, scarcely populated except by roaming sheep and a few red deer – the word "forest" denotes simply that it was formerly a hunting reserve. It's also one of the moor's wettest and boggiest zones – walkers should carry waterproofs whatever the weather, and take note of local weather reports.

In the middle of the area, and just over five miles west of Exford on the B3223, the village of **SIMONSBATH** (pronounced "Simmonsbath") consists of little more than a couple of hotels, a pottery and a sawmill at a crossroads between Lynton, Barnstaple and Minehead on the River Barle. The village was home to Midlands ironmaster John Knight, who purchased the forest in 1819 and, by introducing tenant farmers, building roads and importing sheep, brought systematic agriculture to an area that had never before produced any income. The Knight family also built a wall around their land – parts of which can still be seen – as well as the intriguing dam at Pinkworthy (pronounced "Pinkery") Pond, part of a scheme to harness the headwaters of the River Barle, though its exact function has never been explained.

You can visit the restored Victorian **Simonsbath Sawmill**, below *Simonsbath House*, on a ninety-minute guided tour (£3), usually taking place on the last Sunday of the month; there's no booking, just turn up at the Ashcombe car park (above the *Exmoor Forest Inn*) at 10.30pm. Dulverton's tourist office has more details.

Paths radiate from Simonsbath across epic moorland, for which park visitor centres can supply walking itineraries. One easy waymarked route starts from opposite the *Exmoor Forest Inn* (see below) and leads through Birchcleave Wood, running more or less parallel to the Barle for a couple of miles to **Cow Castle**, site of an old hill fort, and four miles further to Withypool. In the opposite direction, you can follow the River Barle upstream from Simonsbath for about four miles to the dark, still waters of **Pinkworthy Pond** – keep a lookout for red deer drinking here in summer. If you don't want to walk all the way, the B3358 passes within a couple of miles of the lake.

8

ACCOMMODATION

EXMOOR FOREST AND SIMONSBATH

Exmoor Forest Inn ☎01643 831341, ⓦexmoorforestinn.co.uk. This friendly moorland inn has plain but clean, comfortable and good-sized rooms with decent bathrooms. There's a field for camping but no camping facilities. The bar and restaurant are popular with locals (see p.264). **£95**

★ **Simonsbath House** ☎01643 831259, ⓦsimonsbathhouse.co.uk. Former home of the Knight family and now a cosy, upmarket bolt-hole offering plush, spacious rooms with glorious moorland views. Self-catering cottages in a converted 350-year-old barn are also available, and there's a good restaurant (see p.264). **£110**

EATING AND DRINKING

Black Venus Five miles west of Simonsbath, Challacombe ☎01598 763251. This traditional, award-winning pub with a garden has real ales and a range of excellent local food – from ciabattas and ploughman's lunches to hot dishes costing around £10. Daily Noon–2.30pm & 6–11pm, closes 10.30pm Sun.

Boevey's ☎01643 831622. In a converted barn next to *Simonsbath House*, this is a handy restaurant and café that will refuel hungry hikers with everything from baguettes to salads and pasta dishes, all around £5–8. Daily 10.30am–5pm, till 4.30pm in winter; closed Dec to mid-Feb.

EXMOOR ACTIVITIES

One of the best ways to enjoy the full range of outdoor activities on Exmoor is as part of an organized group. Park visitor centres can supply a full list, but the most appealing options include the partly off-road **Land Rover tours** to view Exmoor ponies, red deer and other wildlife. The main operators are: Barle Valley Safaris (☎01643 851386, ⓦexmoorwildlifesafaris. co.uk), which leave from Dulverton and Dunster; Exmoor Safari (☎01643 831229), which start their tours at the *White Horse Inn* in Exford, where you can also book; Red Stag Safari (☎01643 841831, ⓦredstagsafari.co.uk), leaving daily from various departure points; and Discovery Safaris based in Porlock (☎01643 863444, ⓦdiscoverysafaris.com), leaving from outside Porlock's tourist office (or any other prearranged spot). Excursions generally last 2 to 3 hours and cost £25–35 per person.

The National Park Authority and other local organizations have also put together a programme of **guided walks**, graded according to distance, speed and duration and costing £3–5 per person depending on the length of the walk. For more details contact any of the Exmoor visitor centres or see the *Exmoor Visitor* free newspaper or ⓦwww.exmoor-nationalpark.gov.uk.

Exmoor Forest Inn ☎01643 831341. The bar serving Exmoor ales and snacks is the hub of this scattered community, while the restaurant offers local classics such as braised lamb shank and "Exmoor burgers", made with lamb or beef (£9–15). Daily 11am–11pm, closes 3–6pm in winter.

Poltimore Arms A couple of miles southwest of Simonsbath off the Brayford road, Yarde Down ☎01598 710381. This classic country pub serves excellent food, including a renowned fish pie. It's on a tiny lane, and not easy to find. Tues–Sun noon–2.30pm & 5.30–11pm.

Simonsbath House ☎01643 831259. Treat yourself to a quality dinner in a romantic, refined setting at this restaurant, where set-price three-course dinners cost £20 and three courses à la carte will set you back £30–35. The menu is local, seasonal and imaginative, and might include rack of lamb, guinea fowl and venison, followed by some fabulous puddings. Booking essential. Orders taken 7–8.30pm.

The Exmoor coast

The thirty-odd miles between Minehead and Combe Martin form Britain's highest section of **coastline**, with cliffs rising to 1043ft. With gentle upper slopes, the hogbacked hills still make for some fairly strenuous hiking if you're following the **South West Coast Path**, and long stretches of woodland add variety to an already diverse landscape. The narrow, stony strips of beach here don't compare with those in other parts of the West Country, but the **sea** is still the central attraction, with an ever-changing shoreline and constant views across the Bristol Channel to the Welsh coast. Tracking the coast, the A39 frequently affords sublime sea views, especially between Porlock and Lynmouth.

Though a couple of miles inland, **Dunster**, a typically genteel and quaint Somerset village crowned by a flamboyant castle, is an unmissable stop for anyone travelling along the coast and makes a more appealing place to stay than Minehead, three miles northwest (see p.249). Travelling west on the A39, Selworthy and Allerford score highly on the charm scale, and the latter has a diverting museum of rural life. **Porlock** has a stronger flavour of Exmoor and also makes a great base for excursions to places such as **Culbone Church**, deeply hidden in the woods west of the village, and around the so-called Doone Country south of Oare and Malmsmead. West of Foreland Point, there are more terrific walks to be enjoyed from **Lynton** and **Lynmouth** – sibling villages which occupy a niche in the cliff wall with woodland and moorland on all sides. Two of the easiest excursions present Exmoor's most contrasting faces: west to the dramatic **Valley of Rocks** and inland to **Watersmeet**, where two of the moor's rivers merge. Nine miles west, **Combe Martin** marks the edge of the moor and the end of one of the toughest sections of the coastal walk.

Dunster

On the northeastern edge of the moor, **DUNSTER** has a very separate identity from most Exmoor settlements, closer to the classic medieval Somerset village with its broad main thoroughfare. The well-preserved High Street is dominated by the towers and turrets of **Dunster Castle**, the main attraction here, but there is plenty else to see in and around the village to justify a leisurely wander before or after a tour of the historic house.

As an important cloth centre, Dunster reached its peak of wealth in the sixteenth century, and the octagonal **Yarn Market** in the High Street, dating from 1609, is the most evocative of a handful of relics of its wool-making heyday, with a conical roof supported by hefty oak rafters.

Sprouting out of the woods at the northern end of Dunster's High Street, the hilltop folly, **Conygar Tower**, dating from 1776, is worth the brief ascent from the Steep for the excellent views. There are also longer walks from here, for which you can get route maps from the tourist office: **Grabbist Hill**, a mile or so west from the village via a path that starts near the school opposite St George's, or eastwards for about a mile to the sandy and rocky **Dunster Beach** – not great for swimming but with a long foreshore that makes an attractive spot for a picnic.

Dunster Castle

Castle Mid-March to early April, late April to mid-July & late Aug to Oct Mon–Wed & Fri–Sun 11am–5pm; early April to late April & mid-July to late Aug daily 11am–5pm • £8.50 with grounds; NT **Grounds** Daily: mid-March to Oct 10am–5pm; Nov to mid-March 11am–4pm • £4.70; NT • ☏ 01643 821314, ⊕ nationaltrust.org.uk/dunstercastle

The site of **Dunster Castle** was once a Saxon frontier post against the Celts and was rebuilt by the Normans, but almost nothing of these earlier constructions survived the thorough pasting the building received during the Civil War. Inherited by Lady Elizabeth Luttrell in 1376, the property remained in her family for six hundred years until the National Trust took over in the 1970s. It owes its present castellated appearance to a drastic remodelling it received around 1870, though this itself was little more than a veneer on what remains essentially a stately home, predominantly Jacobean within. Dating back to 1420 and flanked by a pair of squat towers that formed part of the Norman construction, the formidable battlemented **gatehouse** smacks of authenticity, while beyond here, the irregular design of the main building reflects the various changes it has undergone over the years.

Note that on Wednesdays between April and October, travellers on the West Somerset Railway (see box, p.230) can buy an inclusive train-plus-castle ticket which includes a bus connection from and to Dunster station; the ticket is valid for the train from Bishops Lydeard that arrives at Dunster at 11.33am and departs at 4.12pm.

The interior

The highlights of the interior are all seventeenth century: most obvious is the grand oak and elm **staircase**, magnificently carved with hunting scenes – a recurrent theme throughout the house. Alongside the stags' heads, numerous portraits of the Luttrells gaze across the rooms, including one showing the sixteenth-century John Luttrell wading Triton-like across the Firth of Forth. Much of the furniture and artwork dates from the sixteenth and seventeenth centuries, such as the odd "thrown" chairs of ash, pear wood and oak in the Inner Hall, and the rare **gilt-leather hangings** in the upstairs Gallery, which vividly depict the story of Antony and Cleopatra.

The gardens

Outside, it's well worth a stroll round the sheltered terraced **gardens**, where oranges and lemons have been growing since 1700 (including what is claimed to be Britain's oldest lemon tree), and there's a renowned collection of strawberry trees. Mimosas and palm trees contribute a subtropical ambience, and picturesque paths lead down to the River Avill.

St George's

Church St • Daily 9am–5pm • Free

Originally a Norman priory church, **St George's** has a fine, bossed wagon roof and a magnificent rood screen (said to be the longest in the country) from about 1500 with its own miniature fan vaulting. Among the tombs of various Luttrells, look out for a group at the top of the south aisle which includes the alabaster floor slab inscribed to Elizabeth Luttrell, from 1493. The sloping chest here is thought to be unique, and was probably used by the Benedictine monks of the priory in the fifteenth century.

Behind St George's church, the sixteenth-century **Tithe Barn** has been renovated as a community centre. The **Priory Garden** next to it would make a pleasant spot for a picnic, and opposite you can peek into the circular **dovecote** that may date back to the fourteenth century. Doves damaged farmers' crops, so monks were the only people allowed to keep these birds.

Dunster Water Mill

Mill Lane, off West St • April–Oct daily 11am–4.30pm • £3.25; NT (though members must pay entry fees) • ☎ 01643 821759, ⓦ dunsterwatermill.co.uk

A few yards beyond St George's on West Street, turn down Mill Lane to reach the three-hundred-year-old **Dunster Water Mill**, still used commercially for milling the grain that goes into the flour and muesli sold in the shop. There isn't a great deal to see or do here once you've absorbed the mysteries of milling and viewed the small array of agricultural tools, but the riverside café and garden make a good spot for refreshment.

A path along the Avill from the mill soon brings you to **Gallox Bridge**, a quaint packhorse bridge from the eighteenth century surrounded by woods.

8

ARRIVAL AND DEPARTURE

DUNSTER

By train and bus Although Dunster is a stop on the West Somerset Railway, its station is inconveniently located a mile north of the village, near Dunster Beach. Minehead is the nearest transport hub, connected to Dunster by bus #28 (Mon–Sat 3–4 hourly, Sun hourly; 20min) and other less frequent services. There are a few other direct services from Dunster, including buses to Dulverton (1 daily; 50min), Porlock (1 daily; 50min), Selworthy (1 daily; 1hr) and Winsford (Mon–Sat 2 daily; 50min).

INFORMATION

Exmoor Visitor Centre By the main car park at the top of Dunster Steep (Easter–Oct daily 10am–5pm; Nov & Feb–Easter Sat & Sun 10.30am–3pm; ☎ 01643 821835, ⓦ www.exmoor-nationalpark.gov.uk). Has information on Exmoor generally, including details of guided walks on the moor, and a leaflet for a self-guided walk around the village. The centre also houses a free exhibition focusing on the peculiarities of the moor, with hands-on activities and background on the local wool and timber industries, and conservation issues. To find the Centre, follow the High Street round to the north. Information on Dunster is also available at ⓦ visitdunster.co.uk.

ACCOMMODATION

Exmoor House 12 West St ☎ 01643 821268, ⓦ exmoorhousedunster.co.uk. This elegant Georgian B&B offers airy, refreshingly untwee en-suite rooms in pastel colours. Guests get their own front-door key, and there's wi-fi, fresh milk on the landing and a choice of breakfasts stretching to Quorn sausages and rashers. From **£72**

Luttrell Arms 25–31 High St ☎ 01643 821555, ⓦ luttrellarms.co.uk. Right by the Yarn Market, this traditional and atmospheric fifteenth-century inn has open fires and beamed rooms, some with four-posters and some with views towards the castle. Standard rooms are more ordinary and lack views. From **£100**

★ **Old Priory** Priory Green ☎ 01643 821540, ⓦ theoldpriory-dunster.co.uk. Parts of this B&B behind St George's church date back to the twelfth century, otherwise it's mainly from 1660, when it was converted into a farmhouse. It's all immaculately preserved (there's no TV anywhere), including the gigantic fireplace in the guests' sitting room. The three bedrooms are all different; one has an arched roof and a four-poster. The pretty garden has its own door to the next-door church garden. No credit cards. **£90**

Yarn Market Hotel 25–33 High St ☎ 01643 821425, ⓦ www.yarnmarkethotel.co.uk. Traditional, family-run hotel overlooking the Yarn Market, offering fairly bland but clean and comfortable rooms (some with four-posters). There's a restaurant, and a range of themed short breaks for guests, from music workshops to murder weekends. From **£110**

EATING AND DRINKING

Cobblestones 24 High St ☎01643 821595. Unpretentious, agreeable little restaurant with a nice garden and a fairly basic menu including sausage and mash, and beef and ale stew, with occasional more exotic dishes (vegetable and apricot tagine). Prices are relatively low for Dunster, at £7.50–11 for mains. Daily 10.30am–3.30pm & 6.30–10.30pm, reduced hours in winter.

Luttrell Arms 25–31 High St ☎01643 821555. Serving local ales, the bar here once served guests of the local abbot and oozes medieval atmosphere, with black-framed windows and huge fireplaces. The same menu is served here and in the rather stuffy restaurant, a roster of English classics (mains £14–19). Bar 10am–11pm, restaurant 7–9.30pm.

Reeves 20 High St ☎01643 821414. This chic restaurant with a low beamed ceiling and smart wooden tables offers locally sourced dishes such as steamed pollock and roast rump of lamb (£15–19), and delicious desserts including raspberry shortbread tower. It's popular, so advance reservations are essential. You can dine alfresco in the garden in summer. Easter to late Oct Tues–Sat noon–2pm & 7–9pm, Sun noon–2pm; late Oct to Easter Tues–Fri 7–9pm, Sat noon–2pm & 7–9pm, Sun noon–2pm.

Selworthy

The National Trust-owned village of **SELWORTHY**, five miles west of Dunster, is a sequestered nook of custard-coloured thatched cottages and a church with a notable barrel-vaulted ceiling. The limewashed cottages were originally built in the 1820s for retired workers of the local Holnicote Estate, which was taken over by the National Trust in 1944. Predictably it's all very syrupy and picturesque, and a bit too Hansel-and-Gretel to swallow whole, but there's genuine charm in the tidy dwellings with their immaculate gardens, and the views across to Dunkery Beacon are undeniably lovely.

Downhill from the church stands a fourteenth-century **tithe barn** (now holiday accommodation) and paths through to the enclosed village green. There are walking routes everywhere, including a signposted path leading through thick woods to **Selworthy Beacon** (1012ft; map ref SS918479); the Macmillan Way (see p.31) and Coleridge Way (see p.227) also pass through the estate.

All Saints church

Daily 9am–8pm • Free

Crowning the village, Selworthy's church of **All Saints** is unusual for Somerset in being limewashed a brilliant white, and its square battlemented tower has little in common with the elaborate church towers elsewhere in the county. Most of the building dates from the fifteenth century, with the large windows, slim pillars and airy interior of the late Perpendicular style. Apart from its striking barrel roofs over the nave and aisles, the church is full of interest. The graceful south, or Steynings aisle is the most impressive section, its roof decorated with angels and bosses carved with symbols of the Passion. Dominating the west end of the nave, the classically inspired gallery was designed in 1750 to hold musicians but now holds a massive organ. The wooden structure projecting like a theatre box above the church's entrance was installed at the start of the nineteenth century as a balcony pew for the local Acland family, former lords of the manor. At the east end, behind the high altar, is a reredos (ornamental screen) fashioned from leather in 1900.

ARRIVAL AND DEPARTURE   SELWORTHY

By bus There's a stop at the turn-off for Selworthy on the A39, on the #39 and #300 bus routes, from which it's a ten-minute walk to the village. There are services to and from: Allerford (Mon–Sat hourly, Sun early April to late Oct 3 daily; 15min); Lynmouth (early April to late Oct 3–4 daily; 50min); Lynton (early April to late Oct 3–4 daily; 1hr 5min); and Porlock (Mon–Sat hourly, Sun early April to late Oct 3 daily; 20min).

ACCOMMODATION AND EATING

Periwinkle Tearooms Selworthy Green ☎ 01643 862122. This National Trust tearoom ticks all the right boxes, not least with its cream teas made with locally renowned scones (£4.30–5.40). There are also sandwiches, pasties (both £3.50–6) and salads (£8), and a picnic rug available for borrowing. March–Oct daily 10.30am–5pm.

Selworthy Farm ☎ 01643 862577, ⊛ selworthyfarm-exmoor.co.uk. You'll find true tranquillity at this elegant farmhouse from 1870, offering two traditionally furnished rooms with private or en-suite facilities. It's below the church, on the way into the village. No kids, and no credit cards. **£60**

Allerford and around

Just off the A39 a mile or so west of Selworthy, the unspoiled village of **ALLERFORD** is famed for its pretty, cobbled packhorse bridge next to a ford across Aller Brook. Old school buildings now hold a museum of local memorabilia. Following the minor road through the village will bring you eventually to another picture-postcard hamlet, **Bossington**, and beyond to **Bossington Beach**, a shingle beach backed by salt marshes where you'll spot egrets and peregrine falcons.

West Somerset Rural Life Museum

The Old School • April–Oct Tues–Fri 10.30am–4pm, Sun 1.30–4.30pm • £2 • ☎ 01643 862529, ⊛ allerfordmuseum.org.uk

An absorbing collection of domestic and farming knick-knacks fill two former schoolrooms in Allerford's **West Somerset Rural Life Museum**. Don't expect spectacular displays – this focuses on the nitty-gritty of everyday life, from a crib from around 1850 to an array of typewriters and a wall of equestrian accessories. There's plenty here for a nostalgic wallow, and some of it is genuinely intriguing, particularly those objects that have no modern equivalent such as a foot-warmer for carriage passengers, pawnshoes worn by horses and a knife-cleaning drum. Other items are more pedestrian: displays of teapots, police truncheons and carpenter's tools. There's a fascinating photo archive, and one of the rooms has been restored to its Victorian appearance as a schoolroom. In the yard are reconstructions of a dairy and a cobbler's workshop, complete with glassy-eyed dairy maid and cobbler.

ARRIVAL AND DEPARTURE   ALLERFORD

By bus Buses #39 and #300 stop at Allerford. Services run to and from: Lynmouth (early April to late Oct 3–4 daily; 40min); Lynton (early April to late Oct 3–4 daily; 1hr); Porlock (Mon–Sat hourly, Sun early April to late Oct 3 daily; 10min); and Selworthy (Mon–Sat hourly, Sun early April to late Oct 3 daily; 15min).

Porlock and around

The real enticement of **PORLOCK**, a mile or so west of Allerford, is its extraordinary position in a deep hollow, cupped on three sides by Exmoor's hogbacked hills. The thatch-and-cob houses and dripping charm of the village's long High Street, with its succession of hotels, cafés, antique shops and stores selling outdoor gear, have led to invasions of tourists. Some are also drawn by the place's literary links: according to Coleridge's own less than reliable testimony, it was a "man from Porlock" who broke

---

A WALK AROUND ALLERFORD

The much-photographed packhorse bridge at **Allerford** makes a starting point for a varied five-mile circuit. A path leads northwest through the Allerford Plantation and later emerges into the open before reaching **Hurlstone Point**. From there, the coast path climbs southeast onto the rolling moor reaching its highest point at Selworthy Beacon (308m), with sweeping views across to Wales and far inland. From there, a choice of tracks leads down into a wooded combe and into the village of **Selworthy**, at the bottom of which a track leads west back down to Allerford.

8

the opium trance in which he was composing *Kubla Khan*, while the High Street's ancient *Ship Inn* prides itself on featuring prominently in the Exmoor romance *Lorna Doone* and, in real life, having sheltered the poet Robert Southey, who staggered in rain-soaked from a ramble on Exmoor, and wrote a sonnet here ("Porlock, thy verdant vale so fair to sight..."). Aside from its atmosphere and charm, the village has some specific attractions, spaced along its winding High Street, in the form of its fifteenth-century church, St Dubricius, and a couple of museum collections.

Porlock stands at one end of the **Coleridge Way**, a 36-mile route that takes in a good stretch of the Quantock and Brendon Hills and Exmoor from Coleridge's former home in Nether Stowey (see p.227). A free leaflet describing the walk is available at the tourist office.

Dovery Manor Museum

Doverhay • Easter–Sept Mon–Fri 10am–1pm & 2–5pm, Sat 10.30am–1pm & 2–4pm • Free • ⓦ doverymanormuseum.org.uk

Porlock's main appeal is its atmosphere and charm, but it does have a specific attraction at the eastern end of the High Street in the form of the **Dovery Manor Museum**, housed in a fifteenth-century cottage. A couple of cramped rooms show traditional domestic and agricultural tools of Exmoor – including a mantrap – together with some material on the local wildlife and a few photos and portraits, though the most impressive items here are the building's beautiful mullioned window and huge fireplace on the ground floor.

Exmoor Classic Cars

High St • Easter–Sept Fri–Sun 11am–4pm • £3 • ⓣ 01643 841476

There isn't much that's specifically Exmoor about this collection of vintage cars, but the nostalgic tone of **Exmoor Classic Cars** fits in nicely with Porlock's old-fashioned feel. In this period garage you can ogle at a 1927 Bugatti, a Singer "Porlock Sports Special" from 1930, a stately Rolls and an Austin taxi from 1938, not to mention various ancient motorbikes, including a cluster of bright red BSA Bantams used by the Post Office. All are polished up a treat, and most of the vehicles are in working order. There are also numerous models, for example of past winners of Le Mans, but it's not all motoring memorabilia for petrol-heads – you'll also find old posters, advertising signs and even a wall of paintings by the museum's owner.

Porlock Weir

Porlock gets very busy in high season, but you can escape the crush by heading two miles west along reclaimed marshland to the tiny harbour of **PORLOCK WEIR**, whose sleepy air gives little inkling of its former role as a hard-working port trafficking with Wales. With its thatched cottages and lovely stony foreshore, it's a peaceful, atmospheric spot, giving onto a bay that enjoys the mildest climate on Exmoor. A rambling old pub and a classy restaurant (see opposite) share prime position. A room at one end of the toilets in the car park houses the **Natural History Centre** (mid-May to July & early Sept Wed & Thurs 1.30–5pm; Aug Wed & Thurs & Sat 1.30–5pm), with pictures and panels showing the local fauna and flora.

An easy two-mile stroll west from Porlock Weir along the South West Coast Path brings you to **Culbone Church** (always open), a tiny church – claimed to be the country's smallest – sheltered within woods once inhabited by charcoal burners.

Oare and Doone Country

West of Porlock, the A39 climbs over 400m in less than three miles – cyclists and drivers might prefer either of the gentler and more scenic **toll roads** to the direct uphill trawl, one from Porlock (a right turn off the A39, after the *Ship Inn*; cars £2.50, bikes £1), the other narrower and rougher going from Porlock Weir (cars £2, bikes free), both passing mainly through woods. Just before the Devon–Somerset border at **County Gate** (site of a café and car park), the hamlet of **OARE** shelters a minuscule church that's famous in the annals of Lorna Doonery as being the scene of the heroine's marriage, and where she was shot. R.D. Blackmore's grandfather was rector here, and it's likely that the author derived much of the inspiration for his border tale from the local stories told to him on his visits. Accordingly, the surrounding area, particularly Badgworthy Water and the valleys of Lank Combe and Hoccombe Combe, identified as the heart of "**Doone Country**", is rich with echoes of Blackmore's fictional Doone Valley. If you want to explore further, head three-quarters of a mile west to the hamlet of **Malmsmead**, from where you can follow the Badgworthy Water river upstream; Porlock's tourist office can supply a detailed route.

ARRIVAL AND INFORMATION   PORLOCK AND AROUND

By bus Service #39 connects Porlock and Porlock Weir with Minehead (not Sun), and #300 runs daily between Porlock, Allerford, Selworthy, Lynmouth and Minehead (early April to late Oct only). There are direct services to: Allerford (Mon–Sat hourly, Sun early April to late Oct 3 daily; 10min); Lynmouth (early April to late Oct 3–4 daily; 35min); Minehead (Mon–Sat hourly, Sun early April to late Oct 3 daily; 20min); Selworthy (Mon–Sat hourly, Sun early April to late Oct 3 daily; 20min); and Porlock Weir (Mon–Sat 8 daily; 5min).
Tourist office Helpful spot at West End, High St (March–Oct Mon–Fri 10am–12.30pm & 2–5pm, Sat 10am–5pm, Sun 10am–1pm; Nov–Feb Tues–Sat 10am–1pm; ☎01643 863150, ⓦporlock.co.uk). Internet access available.

ACCOMMODATION

Andrews on the Weir Porlock Weir ☎01643 863300, ⓦandrewsontheweir.co.uk. This "restaurant with rooms" offers rather plain bedrooms with magnificent sea views. The food is first-class, and there's an excellent pub next door (see below). Closed late Dec to late Jan. From **£70**
Burrowhayes Farm West Luccombe ☎01643 862463, ⓦburrowhayes.co.uk. A mile or so southeast of Porlock, off the A39, this well-equipped rural campsite has pitches for tents and motorhomes, and static caravans to rent. There's a shop, and escorted pony treks are also available (not Sat). Closed Nov to mid-March. Pitches **£16**
The Gables Doverhay ☎01643 863432, ⓦthegables porlock.co.uk. Classically thatched seventeenth-century cottage near Porlock's museum, with restful rooms, including a family suite, all with bathrooms and wi-fi connection, and there's a garden. Abundant breakfasts include muesli, yoghurt and fruit. Self-catering accommodation is also available. No credit cards. **£65**
★ **Glen Lodge** Hawkcombe ☎01643 863371, ⓦglenlodge.net. A few minutes from the High Street (up Parson's St), you'll find perfect seclusion plus comfort and

character at this beautifully furnished Victorian country B&B. There are distant sea views from the rooms and access to the moor right behind, plus healthy breakfasts and wi-fi. No credit cards. From **£90**
Lorna Doone Hotel High St ☎01643 862404, ⓦlornadoonehotel.co.uk. Conspicuously sited on the main drag, this thoroughly Victorian lodging is a bit run-down but retains period atmosphere. Three sizes of room are on offer, all clean, comfortable and en suite, with wi-fi access. From **£48**
Sparkhayes Farm Sparkhayes Lane ☎01643 862470. This small campsite is little more than a field with basic washing facilities, but it's extremely handy for the village, signposted off the High Street near the Lorna Doone Hotel. Hook-ups available. **£7** per person
Sparkhayes Farmhouse Sparkhayes Lane ☎01643 862765. Handsome, centrally located seventeenth-century lodging offering tastefully furnished rooms with en-suite or private facilities. There's a guest sitting room with a log fire in winter. No credit cards. Closed Nov–Easter. **£60**

EATING AND DRINKING

★ **Andrews on the Weir** Porlock Weir ☎01643 863300, ⓦandrewsontheweir.co.uk. Top-notch contemporary cuisine using local ingredients is available in this swanky restaurant (main courses £15–20), or you can settle for a light lunch of sandwiches, quiches and salads (£6–12). Teas are also served. Daily 10am–7pm (last orders); closed late Dec to late Jan.
Lorna Doone Hotel High St ☎01643 862404. This comfortingly old-fashioned hotel has a tearoom and restaurant that concentrates on local dishes but is also known for its Thai curries (all £13–15, though there are

set-price mid-week menus for under £10). Real ales are dispensed in the small bar. Flexible opening, meals usually served daily 5.30–8.15pm.
Ship Inn High St ☎01643 862507. Exmoor ales, bar billiards, darts, skittles and occasional folk evenings are the draw in this old tavern, locally known as the "Top Ship". The food's not bad either, with sandwiches and hot dishes for around £10. Accommodation also available (£60). Bar daily 9.30am–11pm, food served noon–2.30pm & 6/6.30–9pm.
Ship Inn Porlock Weir ☎01643 863288. Crab salads (£9)

8

are a lunchtime favourite in the "Bottom Ship", an oak-beamed pub by the harbour at Porlock Weir, with a range of other bar food and outdoor tables. Three guestrooms are also available (£50). Food served noon–3pm & 5.30–8.30pm; bar daily 10am–11pm (Jan & Feb closes 6pm Mon–Fri), food served noon–2.30pm & 6–8.30pm.

Whortleberry Tearoom High St ☎ 01643 862337.

Soups, savoury scones, quiches and sandwiches are among the home-made goodies you can tuck into here, not to mention whortleberry (bilberry) jam, thickly spread on scones and muffins. The courtyard garden is open in summer. Tues–Sat 9am–4/5pm; closed Tues in winter and all Jan.

Lynton and Lynmouth

On the Devon side of the county line, eleven miles along the coast from Porlock, the Victorian resort of **LYNTON** perches above a lofty gorge with dramatic views over the sea and its sister resort of **LYNMOUTH**, down at sea level. Encircled by cliffs, both places were pretty isolated for most of their history, but struck lucky during the Napoleonic Wars when frustrated Grand Tourists unable to visit their usual continental haunts discovered here a domestic piece of Swiss landscape. Coleridge and Hazlitt trudged over to Lynton from the Quantocks, but the greatest spur to the area's popularity was the 1869 publication of *Lorna Doone*, which led to swarms of literary tourists in search of the book's famous settings. Most of the present-day visitors are similarly attracted by the natural beauty of the place, while the existence of a number of walks radiating out from here onto Exmoor and along the coast are a major bonus.

Lynton

A prosperous Victorian-Edwardian air imbues **Lynton**, epitomized by the imposing faux-medieval **town hall** from 1900 on Lee Road. It was the gift of publisher George Newnes, who also funded the nearby **cliff railway**, and holds the local tourist office.

WALKS FROM LYNTON AND LYNMOUTH

The major year-round attraction in these parts is **walking**, not only along the coast path but inland. Most trails are waymarked, and you can pick up walkers' maps of the routes from the tourist office or Park Visitor Centre. One of the most popular walks is about two miles eastward, either along the banks of the River Lyn or high up above the valley along the Two Moors Way to **Watersmeet** (see p.275), itself the starting place for myriad trails; from Lynmouth, the path starts from the Lyndale car park opposite *Shelley's Hotel*. An easy expedition takes you west out of Lynton along the North Walk, a mile-long path leading to the **Valley of Rocks**, a steeply curved heathland dominated by rugged rock formations. The poet Robert Southey summed up the raw splendour he found here when he described it as "the very bones and skeleton of the earth, rock reeling upon rock, stone piled upon stone, a huge terrific mass". At the far end of the valley, herds of wild goats range free as they have done here for centuries; a short climb up Hollerday Hill yields a terrific view over the whole area.

Lynmouth is the best starting point for coastal walks eastwards, including to the lighthouse at **Foreland Point**, a little over two miles away, via a fine, sheltered shingle beach at the foot of Countisbury Hill – one of a number of tiny coves that are easily accessible on either side of the estuary – while the route west towards Combe Martin (see p.276) traces some of Devon's most majestic and unspoiled coastline.

The deep, wooded **Heddon Valley**, halfway between Lynton and Combe Martin, is another focus for scenic walks. The coast path crosses the River Heddon a short way upstream of **Heddon's Mouth**, site of an old lime kiln and ringed by treacherous rocks. By road you can reach the spot from the *Hunter's Inn*, signposted off the A399 and offering good refreshments. Either direction along the coast path is amply rewarding for views. Eastwards it contours halfway up the coastal slopes to Woody Bay, where you can climb up and return on a parallel path that wiggles its way round a higher contour. Westwards you can head to Trentishoe Down and the summit of **Holdstone Hill** for a breezy all-round view.

Cliff railway

Daily mid-Feb to early April & early Oct to late Oct 10am–5pm; early April to early May, late May to late July & late Aug to mid-Sept
10am–7pm; early May to late May & mid-Sept to late Sept 10am–6pm; late July to late Aug 10am–9pm; late Oct to early Nov 10am–4pm
• £3 return • Ⓦ cliffrailwaylynton.co.uk

Opened in 1890, the **cliff railway** is the most practical way of moving between Lynton
and Lynmouth, 150m below. The ingenious hydraulic system consists of two carriages
on separate rails, counterbalanced by water tanks which fill up at the top from a natural
water supply (piped from the West Lyn River). As the bottom carriage empties its load
(sometimes the weight of passengers at the top makes this unnecessary), the water-
powered brakes are released and the top carriage descends. Requiring no external power
source, it's fast, scenic, virtually noise-free and completely eco-friendly.

Lyn and Exmoor Museum

Market St • Easter–Oct Mon–Fri 10am–4pm, Sun 2–4pm • £1, Sun free

A short distance below Lee Road, opposite the school, one of Lynton's oldest houses
– probably from the early eighteenth century – holds the **Lyn and Exmoor Museum**, a
must for fans of small and quirky local collections. The whitewashed cottage is stuffed
to the gills with a miscellany of relics from the locality, and has a reconstructed Exmoor
kitchen from around 1800 on the ground floor. Upstairs you'll find displays of history,
geology and wildlife, including samples of local rocks, fossils and minerals, stuffed birds
and small animals. Old paintings and prints illustrate the domestic and social life of
former times, and agricultural tools recall how most locals made a living before the
advent of tourism.

Lynmouth

Directly below Lynton, **Lynmouth** lies at the junction and estuary of the East and West
Lyn rivers, in a spot described by Gainsborough as "the most delightful place for a
landscape painter this country can boast". Shelley spent his honeymoon here (see box,
p.274) – two different houses claim to have been the Shelleys' love-nest – and R.D.
Blackmore, author of *Lorna Doone*, stayed in **Mars Hill**, the oldest part of the town,
whose creeper-covered cottages are framed by the cliffs behind the Esplanade.

Lynmouth's peace was shattered in August 1952 when nine inches of rain fell onto
Exmoor in 24 hours and the village was almost washed away by **flood waters** raging
down the valley. Huge landslips carried hundreds of trees into the rivers, all the bridges
in the area were swept away, houses were demolished and 34 people lost their lives. Since
the disaster, rumours have circulated regarding one possible cause of the inundation, in
particular that secret tests were then being carried out by the Ministry of Defence in the
Exmoor area, which involved sending pilots to "seed" clouds with dry ice to make them
rain. The story has been denied by the MoD, but the suspicions remain.

Lynmouth is the start (or end) of the **Two Moors Way**, a 103-mile walking route
which runs to Ivybridge in South Devon thereby linking Exmoor with Dartmoor, and
also running along part of North Devon's Tarka Trail (the walking and cycling route
that follows the travels of Tarka the Otter in the book of the same name). Leaflets and
other publications on both routes are available at tourist offices.

Glen Lyn Gorge

Easter–Oct daily 10am–6pm, closes 3pm in winter • £5 • ☎ 01598 753207, Ⓦ www.theglenlyngorge.co.uk

There are numerous reminders of the 1952 flood around Lynmouth, the most vivid being
the boulders and other rocky debris still strewn about the **Glen Lyn Gorge**, a steep wooded
valley through which the destructive torrent took its course. Entered from the main road
at the back of the village, the gorge has a deeply tranquil air, making it difficult to
imagine the fury of that stormy night. The walks and waterfalls upstream make ideal
picnic spots, and there are also displays on the uses and dangers of water power, including
a small hydroelectric plant which provides electricity for the local community.

ARRIVAL AND DEPARTURE

LYNTON

By bus There are services to and from: Barnstaple (Mon–Sat 10 daily; 55min); Combe Martin (late May to mid-Oct 3 daily, mid-Oct to late May Sat & Sun 2 daily; 40min); Ilfracombe (late May to mid-Oct 3 daily, mid-Oct to late May Sat & Sun 2 daily; 1hr); and Porlock (early April to late Oct 3–4 daily; 50min).

LYNMOUTH

By bus There are services to and from: Barnstaple (Mon–Sat 10 daily; 1hr 10min); Combe Martin (late May to mid-Oct 3 daily, mid-Oct to late May Sat & Sun 2 daily; 45min); Ilfracombe (late May to mid-Oct 3 daily, mid-Oct to late May Sat & Sun 2 daily; 1hr 10min); and Porlock (early April to late Oct 3–4 daily; 35min).

INFORMATION

National Park Visitor Centre Opposite *Shelley's Hotel* in the Lyndale car park, Lynmouth (Easter–Oct daily 10am–5pm, Nov & mid-Feb to Easter Sat & Sun 10.30am–3pm; ☎01598 752509, ⓦwww.exmoor-nationalpark.gov.uk).

Tourist office Town hall, Lee Rd, Lynton (Easter–Sept Mon–Sat 10am–5pm; Oct–Easter Mon–Sat 10am–4pm, Sun 10am–2pm; ☎0845 660 3232, ⓦlynton-lynmouth-tourism.co.uk). Offers internet access.

ACCOMMODATION

LYNTON

Channel View Manor Farm, Barbrook ☎01598 753349, ⓦchannel-view.co.uk. Useful site just east of Barbrook on the A39, 2 miles south of Lynton (linked by a footpath through woods). A café serves all-day breakfasts. Caravans available for weekly rent. Closed mid-Nov to mid-March. Pitches **£13**

North Walk House North Walk ☎01598 753372, ⓦnorthwalkhouse.co.uk. Top-quality B&B in a panoramic position overlooking the sea, and convenient for the coast path. The spacious, stylish rooms have rugs, wooden floors and free wi-fi. Breakfasts are filling and delicious and great organic dinners are available to guests for £24 per person. From **£106**

★ **St Vincent House** Castle Hill ☎01598 752244, ⓦst-vincent-hotel.co.uk. This whitewashed, Georgian guesthouse has elegantly furnished, light and airy rooms, all en suite. Breakfast includes home-made yoghurt and fruit compotes, and packed lunches and Belgian beers are also available. No under-16s. Closed Nov–March. From **£75**

Southcliffe 34 Lee Rd ☎01598 753328, ⓦsouthcliffe.co.uk. One of a row of guesthouses near the centre, this has clean and crisp rooms, helpful owners and complimentary wi-fi. It's worth paying a little extra for a balcony room. Breakfast is a fantastic spread, including "Southville Sundaes" and good veggie options. **£64**

★ **Sunny Lyn** Lynbridge ☎01598 753384, ⓦcaravandevon.co.uk. You can camp next to the West Lyn River at this tranquil spot halfway between Lynton and Barbrook off the B3234, but it's small so booking is essential. There's an on-site shop and café (closed in low season). Closed Nov to mid-March. **£7.75** per person

LYNMOUTH

Hillside House 22 Watersmeet Rd ☎01598 753836, ⓦhillside-lynmouth.co.uk. Teddy bears aside, this simple B&B is refreshingly free of the tweeness that affects most of the establishments hereabouts. Rooms are spacious, and all but one enjoy views over the East Lyn River. Free wi-fi. From **£56**

Rising Sun Harbourside ☎01598 753223. Rooms in this fourteenth-century inn have all the requisite beams and sloping floors. It's touristy and expensive but steeped in atmosphere and with a superb location by the harbour. From **£130**

SHELLEY IN LYNMOUTH

In the summer of 1812, **Percy Bysshe Shelley**, aged 20, stopped in Lynmouth in the company of his 16-year-old bride Harriet Westbrook, Harriet's sister Eliza, and Dan Healy, their Irish servant. This, Shelley decided, would be the place to establish the commune of free-thinking radicals that he had long contemplated. Although this vision never materialized, Shelley used his nine-week stay – allegedly in what is now *Shelley's Hotel* (see opposite) – to work on his polemical poem *Queen Mab* and to compose his seditious manifesto, or *Declaration of Rights*, which declared, among other things, that "titles are tinsel, power a corrupter, glory a bubble, and excessive wealth a libel on its possessor". Copies of the *Declaration* were attached to balloons, inserted into bottles launched from Lynmouth's harbour and distributed in nearby Barnstaple (for which Healy was arrested and imprisoned). Now under observation, Shelley and his entourage took flight soon after, hiring a boatman to ferry them to Wales, where the poet continued to work on *Queen Mab*.

HARBOUR BOAT TRIPS

Look out for boards at Lynmouth's harbour advertising **boat trips** with Exmoor Coast Boat Cruises (April–Sept; £10; ☎01598 753207). Usually setting off at 11am or noon, depending on the tides, the hour-long excursions to Woody Bay and back allow you to view the abundant birdlife on the cliffs.

Rock House Hotel Harbourside ☎01598 753508, ⓦrock-house.co.uk. Splendidly sited by the beach and river mouth, this has fantastic views from its smart but smallish rooms (some have four-posters). The pub, restaurant and garden here are popular (see below), so don't expect seclusion. Closed early Jan to early Feb. **£93**

Shelley's Hotel 8 Watersmeet Rd ☎01598 753219, ⓦshelleyshotel.co.uk. Adjacent to the Glen Lyn Gorge, this traditional small hotel has friendly owners, a great location and literary credentials – the poet Shelley was supposed to have honeymooned here. Rooms are bright and clean, some with great views, and you can sleep in the very one claimed to have been used by Shelley himself (who apparently left without paying his bill). **£149**

EATING AND DRINKING

LYNTON

The Crown Market St ☎01598 752253. Former coaching inn that's still at the heart of local life, with real ales, bar snacks, stir fries and other diverse dishes (£8–13), as well as regular live music Fri & Sat. Tables on the front patio. Mon–Thurs 11am–midnight, Fri–Sun 11am–1am.

Ethel Braithwaites 1 Castle Hill. This should be your first stop for superior picnic food, all fresh and locally produced. The sandwiches and baguettes are made to order, and there's a range of pasties. You'll be further tempted by jams, scones, Exmoor ice cream, smoothies and flagons of cider. Daily 9am–5pm.

The Oak Room Lee Rd ☎01598 753838. Convivial, Spanish-styled restaurant with small wooden tables and a sofa or two. Such tasty dishes as meatballs or pan-fried king prawns can be served as tapas (£5–7) or as a main course (£9–15). Daily 10.30am–4.30pm, also 6–9.30pm March–Oct.

Vanilla Pod 10–12 Queens St ☎01598 753706. Good wholesome meals are served at this friendly, modern eatery, with a large choice of daily specials. Evening mains such as duck cassoulet and steak entrecôte are £10–16. Vegan and gluten-free diets accommodated. Daily 10.30am–9.30pm.

LYNMOUTH

Le Bistro 7 Watersmeet Rd ☎01598 753302, ⓦlebistrolynmouth.co.uk. This small, traditional place specializes in fresh fish, including a hearty *bouillabaisse*, though there are plenty of meatier options, including Exmoor classics like roast rump of lamb and rib-eye steak. Mains £12–16. 6.30–10pm: Feb & March Thurs–Sat; Easter–Oct Mon–Sat.

Rising Sun Harbourside ☎01598 753223. Ancient and atmospheric inn with local ales. You can have sandwiches at lunchtime (£7) or sample the menu of classic English dishes, mainly lamb, duck and seafood (around £15), but few vegetarian options. Eat in the bar rather than the more congested restaurant if there's a choice. Mon–Sat 11am–11pm, Sun 11am–10.30pm.

Rock House Hotel Harbourside ☎01598 753508. Set by the harbour, this place has a garden and a bar serving snacks and meals (£5–10), and a restaurant where seafood and Exmoor lamb are the specialities (£10–16). Daily 10am–9pm; closed early Jan to early Feb.

Watersmeet and around

The East Lyn River is joined by Hoar Oak Water one and a half miles east and inland of Lynton and Lynmouth at **Watersmeet**, one of Exmoor's most celebrated beauty spots. Try to avoid visiting in peak season or at weekends to see this thickly wooded location at its best. Even without other visitors present, the tranquillity can be utterly transformed after a bout of rain, when the rivers become roaring torrents and the water that is usually crystal clear is stained brown with moorland peat. Drivers can leave vehicles at a car park off the A39, and follow the path down through oak woods to the two slender bridges where the rivers merge.

A mile south of Watersmeet, **riding**, **bike rental** and **camping** are all offered at Doone Valley Holidays, Hallslake Farm (☎01598 741234, ⓦwww.doonevalleyholidays.co.uk); turn off the B3223 Simonsbath road near Hillsford Bridge where it's signposted.

WALKS AROUND WATERSMEET

Watersmeet is surrounded by signposted **paths**, many of which were established as donkey tracks when the local charcoal and tanning industries flourished in the nineteenth century. One short route from the bridge takes you south up Hoar Oak Water to **Hillsford Bridge**, the confluence of Hoar Oak and Farley Water, while the Fisherman's Path leads east along the East Lyn River, climbing and swooping through the woods above one of the river's most dramatic stretches. Another marked route strikes off from the Fisherman's Path after only a few hundred metres, zigzagging steeply uphill to meet the A39, about a mile north of Watersmeet and 100m east of the *Sandpiper Inn*. Opposite the pub, a path leads a quarter-mile north to meet the coast path and gives access to **Butter Hill** which, at over 300m, affords stunning views of Lynton, Lynmouth and the North Devon coast. You can pick up pamphlets with full details about all the various routes at Watersmeet House.

Watersmeet House

Daily: Mid-March to April & Oct 10.30am–4.30pm; May–Sept 10.30am–5pm • Free • ☎ 01271 850887, ⓦ nationaltrust.org.uk /watersmeet

On the far side of the bridges, the only building in sight is **Watersmeet House**, an old fishing lodge now owned by the National Trust, which operates a tearoom and shop in summer. You can consume teas, salads and soups on the pleasant veranda, and there's a small exhibition of photos of the 1952 Lynmouth floods in the back.

8

Combe Martin

At the western edge of Exmoor's seaboard, **COMBE MARTIN** has little of the spirit of the moor but has some diversions that merit an hour or two of your time. Sheltered in a fertile valley, the village is famous for its prodigiously long and straggling main street, which follows the combe for about a mile down to the seafront, and holds the unusual *Pack o' Cards Inn* (see opposite), supposed to have been built by a gambler in the eighteenth century with his winnings from a card game. Originally possessing 52 windows (some were later boarded up), the building has four storeys – decreasing in size as they get higher – each with thirteen doors, and chimneys sprouting from every corner; it's now a pub.

Follow the High Street down to reach Combe Martin's **beach**, a good swimming spot which is sandy at low tide, with rock pools and secluded coves on either side. A spectacular stretch of coast extends east of Combe Martin, notably round Wild Pear Beach to Little Hangman and Hangman Point, part of the **Hangman Hills**. The waymarked path – a section of both the South West Coast Path and the Tarka Trail – is signposted off the north end of the car park behind the *Foc's'le Inn* (see opposite). It's a gruelling route, involving a two-mile uphill slog, with no refreshment stops on the way, to the great gorse-covered headland of **Great Hangman** – at 1043ft, the highest point on the South West Coast Path. The payback is the incredible panorama, occasionally taking in glimpses of the Gower peninsula in Wales. From here you can retrace your steps back or complete a circle by veering inland round Girt Farm and west down Knap Down Lane to Combe Martin, the whole well-marked circuit adding up to about six miles.

Combe Martin Museum

Cross St • Daily: Easter–Oct 10.30am–5pm; Nov–Easter till 3pm • £2.50 • ☎ 01271 889031, ⓦ www.combe-martin-museum.co.uk

Just behind the seafront next to the tourist office, the **Combe Martin Museum** is more modern and child-friendly than most collections on Exmoor. Distributed on three floors are a diversity of items that illustrate the silver-mining that has taken place here since Roman times, as well as displays on lime-quarrying, agriculture, horticulture and maritime history. There are some nostalgic old photos of the local rabbit-catcher, and naps of tourist charabancs and paddling holiday-makers from the 1920s and 1930s. Elsewhere you'll see items from the arcane (a "seed-fiddle" for scattering seeds) to the banal (fishing rods).

ARRIVAL AND DEPARTURE COMBE MARTIN

By bus There are bus services to and from: Barnstaple (Mon–Sat 5 daily; 1hr); Ilfracombe (Mon–Sat 1–2 hourly, Sun 3 daily; 25min); Lynmouth (late May to mid-Oct 3 daily, mid-Oct to late May Sat & Sun 3 daily; 50min); and Lynton (late May to mid-Oct 3 daily, mid-Oct to late May Sat & Sun 3 daily; 40min).

INFORMATION AND ACTIVITIES

Tourist office Next to the museum on Cross Street (Easter–Sept daily 10am–5pm; Oct till 2pm; Nov–Easter Fri & Sat till noon; ☎01271 883319, ⓦ visitcombemartin.co.uk).

Riding Dean Riding Stables, Dean, near Parracombe

☎01598 763565, ⓦ deanridingstables.co.uk. Instruction and escorted hacks provided at this riding centre four miles southeast of Combe Martin, with novices welcome. Self-catering accommodation also available. No credit cards.

ACCOMMODATION

Mellstock House Woodlands ☎01271 882592, ⓦ mellstockhouse.co.uk. Just a couple of minutes from the beach and coast path, this guesthouse has superb views from some of its spacious, wi-fi-enabled rooms, a bar and veranda, and tasty evening meals (£10–13) with gluten-free options. From **£70**

Pack o' Cards Inn ☎01271 882300, ⓦ packocards .co.uk. Has more conventional rooms than its appearance might suggest – some with four-posters – and there's a riverside garden and a skittle alley with a small exhibition of the history of the building. It's a bit far from the seafront though. From **£75**

EATING AND DRINKING

Foc's'le Inn Off Cross St ☎01271 883354. Overlooking the beach, this is the top choice for a drink and also does snacks and bar meals (£10–15), which you can eat on the outdoor benches. Basic rooms also available (£65). Daily 11.30am–11.30pm, Sun till 10.30pm.

Harbour Deli Borough Rd ☎01271 883688. Drop in to this deli, with a bright interior and modern art on the walls, for breakfasts, excellent baguettes and home-baked bread, scones and cakes, to eat in or take away. It's on the main road near the seafront. Mon–Sat 9am–5pm.

8

East Somerset

NUNNEY CASTLE

9

East Somerset

The **East Somerset** region covers a disparate mix of historical themes and styles, from prehistoric burial sites to eighteenth- and nineteenth-century sophistication, and from ruined medieval castles to the whimsical trappings of the Italian Renaissance. What ties it all together is the hilly green landscape, whose deeply rural appearance belies its industrial past. Coal was discovered here in 1763, and the area was soon transformed by pitheads and "batches", or slagheaps. The coalmining centre was **Radstock**, in and around which some thirty pits were operating in 1900, though, due to the technical difficulties of coal extraction – the narrow seams and other local geological peculiarities – these had dwindled to fourteen in the 1930s, and the five remaining collieries in 1960 had been abandoned fifteen years later. Radstock's excellent mining museum tells the story and illustrates the reality of life underground.

Northeast of Radstock are a pair of sights evoking the area's remoter past: **Stoney Littleton**, one of the country's best-preserved Neolithic long barrows, and the ruins of fourteenth-century **Farleigh Hungerford Castle**. From the latter it's an easy walk to one of East Somerset's hidden surprises: **Iford Manor**, where an Italian Renaissance garden has been lovingly and convincingly created on a series of terraces.

The region is crossed by the **Fosse Way**, the Roman thoroughfare that traversed England from Lincoln to Exeter, running through the agricultural centre of **Shepton Mallet**, south of Radstock. Though Shepton's medieval layout can still be discerned, you'll find more historic character at **Frome**, which has recently become a thriving centre for arts and crafts, chic shopping and trendy hotels. The town lies at the hub of a handful of engaging sights, most notably **Stourhead** across the county boundary in Wiltshire, and the brasher stately home at **Longleat**, an unlikely hybrid of safari park and exquisitely furnished Elizabethan palace. Both feature first-rate landscaped parks – artificially improved versions of nature that became a favoured mode of display among the grandest landowners of the eighteenth century.

West of Frome, the unsung, pretty villages of **Nunney** and **Mells** strike a humbler note, the former holding a small but highly romantic ruined castle, the latter harbouring one of Somerset's loveliest churches. To the east of the region, one of Wiltshire's famed white horses is carved into a hillside outside **Westbury**, also the site of an Iron Age hill fort.

GETTING AROUND

By train Frome and Westbury are served by trains on the London–Reading–Taunton line, and Westbury is also on the Bath–Salisbury line.

By bus There are good bus connections to Radstock, Shepton Mallet and Frome from Bath but you'll normally have to change if you're arriving from Bristol.

By bike or on foot You can take advantage of a couple of sections of the National Cycle Network: Route 24, of which the Colliers Way (see box, p.283) forms a part, connects the Avon and Kennet Canal at Dundas with Stoney Littleton, Radstock, Frome and Longleat, where it links with Route 25 going south to Stourhead. See ⓦ sustrans.org.uk for further details. Two long-distance walking trails also pass though the region, the Macmillan Way (ⓦ macmillanway.org), connecting Bradford-on-Avon (see p.69), Iford Manor, Farleigh Hungerford and Castle Cary (see p.194), and the Mendip Way, from Weston-super-Mare through Cheddar, Wells, Shepton Mallet and Frome.

LONGLEAT SAFARI PARK

Highlights

❶ Stoney Littleton Long Barrow It takes some effort to reach, but the journey along narrow lanes and across fields is half the fun, and its remoteness from modern life is entirely appropriate for this site, one of the country's best examples of Neolithic burial chambers. **See p.283**

❷ Farleigh Hungerford Castle Much of this classic old castle is in ruins, but there's enough here to evoke its glory days, and a well-presented museum fills out the picture. **See p.283**

❸ Longleat There's a feast of rollicking entertainment to suit all tastes in the range of attractions here, not to mention a taste of the savanna in the attached safari park, but beyond all this is one of the country's finest Elizabethan mansions. **See p.291**

❹ Stourhead Eighteenth-century landscape gardening reached its apogee in this meticulously planned park, whose studied harmonies are matched by the fine furnishings and art displayed inside the house. **See p.293**

HIGHLIGHTS ARE MARKED ON THE MAP ON P.282

9

Radstock and around

The centre of the Somerset coalfield was at **RADSTOCK**, but long before the last pit closed in 1973 the place had lost much of its sense of identity beyond the label of "ex-mining town". The mining heritage of Radstock and the surrounding area is fully explored in its museum, though apart from this there's little else to detain you here. Even the shops are all in **MIDSOMER NORTON**, its more attractive sister village a mile and a half west (reachable via a riverside track), which also hosts a **farmers' market** on the first Saturday morning of every month (in Hollies Garden, off the High Street). The town lies within a short distance of a trio of more alluring, if rather remote, sights, for which you'll need your own transport or some stout walking shoes.

Radstock Museum

Waterloo Rd • Feb–Nov Tues–Fri & Sun 2–5pm, Sat 11am–5pm • £4 • ☎ 01761 437722, ⓦ radstockmuseum.co.uk

Housed in the town's Victorian market hall, **Radstock Museum** is East Somerset's major museum collection, mainly dedicated to the local **mining industry**. One of the highlights is the recreation of a pit, showing the appalling conditions that miners had to endure, including dragging carts laden with rocks through passages that were too narrow and uneven for ponies to negotiate – a job usually undertaken by boys as young

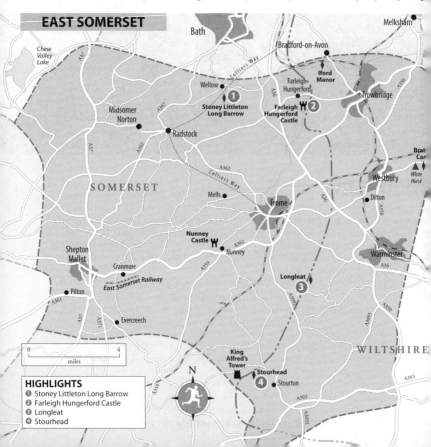

EAST SOMERSET

HIGHLIGHTS
❶ Stoney Littleton Long Barrow
❷ Farleigh Hungerford Castle
❸ Longleat
❹ Stourhead

THE COLLIERS WAY

One of the most pleasurable ways to experience the rolling landscape of East Somerset is on foot or by bike along the **Colliers Way** (𝕨 colliersway.co.uk), part of Route 24 of the National Cycle Network. The route partly follows the disused Somerset and Dorset Railway, which itself was built over the Somerset Coal Canal, and extends for eighteen miles between Dundas, on the Avon and Kennet Canal (and therefore within easy distance of both Bath and Bradford-on-Avon), and Frome, passing close to the site of Stoney Littleton Long Barrow (see below) and through Radstock en route. Eleven miles are completely traffic-free, and most of the remainder is on country lanes. Route 24 continues on southeast from Frome to Longleat (see p.291), Warminster and Salisbury (see p.298).

Unfortunately there are no places to **rent bikes** on the route itself; the nearest outlets are in Bradford-on-Avon (see p.72) and Bath (p.61).

...s 12 years old. The museum encompasses much more than just the mining industry, however, casting an eye over the culture and social life of the area and the wider activities of the mining families. There are reconstructions of a miner's cottage kitchen and scullery, a grocery and a blacksmith's workshop. Besides the collieries, other local employers in the town were boot manufacturers, brewers and foundries, all catering to the workers and their families and all represented here. Space is also given to such leisure pastimes as rugby, quoits and pigeon-racing, as well as brass bands, ale jugs and Methodism.

Volunteers and staff are on hand to add personal reminiscences, and the museum shop sells leaflets outlining four self-guided **heritage walks** that can be followed to the pit sites and quarries around Radstock.

Stoney Littleton Long Barrow

One mile south of Wellow, off A367 • Free • 𝕨 www.english-heritage.org.uk • Bus #757 (Wed only) to Wellow

One of Britain's finest examples of Neolithic long barrows – prehistoric chambered graves or shrines – lies on a peaceful hillside 3.5 miles northeast of Radstock as the crow flies, about twice that by road. Covered by a grassy mound, **Stoney Littleton** is thought to date from around 3500 BC, and probably served as both a burial site and a place of worship. Following its discovery by a farmer in 1760, most of its contents disappeared, though excavations in 1816 yielded human bones, some burnt. The interior stretches for 42ft, with a height of about 4ft, necessitating some awkward stooping for exploring within, but it's worth the effort even if there's little specific to see. A torch will allow you to peer into the three pairs of chambers leading off the main passage and one at its end, all probably once containing bodies. In any case, it's the place itself that constitutes the real pleasure here, reached via a narrow lane between Wellow and Shoscombe, then across a bridge and up through fields (all well signposted).

It's not straightforward to arrive by **public transport**: unless you can use the weekly #757 service between Radstock and Bath, which stops nearby, the best bet is to take any bus to Peasedown St John and walk 2.5 miles east.

Farleigh Hungerford Castle

Farleigh Hungerford • April–June & Sept daily 10am–5pm; July & Aug 10am–6pm; Oct daily 10am–4pm; Nov to late Dec & Jan–March Sat & Sun 10am–4pm • £4 • 𝕨 www.english-heritage.org.uk

Nine miles northeast of Radstock, the ruins of **Farleigh Hungerford Castle** strike a discordant note, incongruously evoking the threat of war amid the unruffled valleys and meadows of deepest Somerset. The castle was the abode of the mighty Hungerford dynasty until 1686, abandoned soon after, and ruined by the early 1700s. The original

9

structure, dating from around 1380, was enlarged in the following century with a ring of outer walls, where the **East Gatehouse**, the main entry to the site, still bears the sickle insignia of the Hungerfords and the family's coat of arms. Inside, an expanse of green leads to the flattened remains of the **Inner Gatehouse**, giving access to the castle's original core. On either side two towers still stand, but its counterparts on the northern wall have long since disappeared. Within this area you can discern traces of the inner courtyard, the great hall, kitchen and garden.

But the most impressive surviving parts of the complex lie between the East and Inner gatehouses, chiefly the **chapel**, dating from the original fourteenth-century construction of the castle and later enclosed within the new walls. The interior is full of interest, holding well-preserved Hungerford tombs to the right of the altar and a set of **wall paintings** probably dating from the 1440s, the most vivid showing a giant figure of St George slaying the dragon. The side chapel to the left of the altar also holds paintings of cherubs and flowers on the walls, commissioned by Lady Margaret Hungerford – connected with Corsham (see p.73) – in the mid-seventeenth century and once covering the entire side chapel. Below the chapel, accessed by a separate entrance, the **vault** holds the unusually shaped lead coffins of various Hungerfords, probably including Lady Margaret herself.

Behind the chapel, the **Priests' House**, built in 1430 and later converted into a dairy, and later still a farmhouse, holds displays relating to the site, including a model of the castle as it once looked, seventeenth-century arms and armour, and pictures. To immerse yourself in the day-to-day life of the castle as it once was, pick up a free audioguide at the ticket office.

Iford Manor

1.5 miles north of Farleigh Hungerford off the A36 and B3109 • April–Sept Tues–Thurs, Sat & Sun 2–5pm; Oct Sun only • £5 • ☎ 01225 863146, ⓦ ifordmanor.co.uk

Set alongside the Somerset–Wiltshire border, **Iford Manor** occupies an idyllic corner of the English countryside, a Palladian-fronted house just steps away from the River Frome, where a statue of Britannia stands sentinel atop a pretty stone bridge. All the more surprising, then, to find transposed here an outpost of Italy, in the form of a Roman or Tuscan garden, rising on terraces up the hillside behind the house. The **Peto Garden** is named after its creator, Harold Peto, an architect (Lutyens was briefly his pupil) and garden designer who was besotted with the Italian Renaissance and lived here from 1899 to 1933. A strong believer in the importance of architecture in garden design, Peto set about recreating an amalgam of the finest Italian Renaissance gardens he had seen while living and working abroad. Rather than herbaceous borders and gaudy colours – though the luxuriant swathes of wisteria in May and June are a brilliant exception – the emphasis here is on gravel walks, classical statuary and fountains splashing into lily-strewn ponds, amid Mediterranean herbs, junipers and statuesque cypress trees.

Iford Manor lies on the **Macmillan Way** cross-country walking route (ⓦ macmillanway .org), a useful link between the garden and Farleigh Hungerford Castle (see p.283). The house is about 1.5 miles' steep walk from Avoncliff train station.

The garden's monuments

On entering the garden, the Mediterranean theme is evoked straightaway by the **Loggia** that Peto added to the side of the house (which is far older than its eighteenth-century facade). From here paths ascend to the **Conservatory Terrace**, adorned with marble lions and columns from around 1200, and the **Great Terrace**, with its bronze wolf suckling Romulus and Remus (made from a mould of the original sculpture in Rome's Capitol Museum) and a Greek sarcophagus from the second or third century AD.

CLOCKWISE FROM TOP FROME (P.289); PARROT AT LONGLEAT (P.291); HOUSE IN NUNNEY (P.290) >

9

The Cloisters

Past the eighteenth-century Garden House are the **Cloisters**, completed by Peto in 1914 in the style of an Italian Romanesque cloister of around 1200, very authentic in feel, and filled with antique fragments. The Cloisters form the highly atmospheric setting of the **Iford Festival** (ⓦ ifordarts.co.uk), taking place between mid-June and mid-August every year, featuring opera, world music and classical performances. It's a magical venue on a summer's eve, but prices are steep: around £10 for opera, £30 for everything else. There are also free **concerts** by local amateur groups on selected Sundays between 3 and 4pm; see the website for dates.

ARRIVAL AND DEPARTURE

By bus Most buses arrive at and depart from The Street, Wells Rd and Kilmersdon Rd, near the museum. Destinations Bath (Mon–Sat 3 hourly, Sun 1–2 hourly; 40min); Bristol (Mon–Sat hourly, Sun 3 daily; 1hr 30min); Frome (Mon–Sat 1–2 hourly; 45min 1hr 5min); Midsomer Norton (Mon–Sat 4 hourly, Sun 2 hourly; 20min); Shepton

RADSTOCK AND AROUND

Mallet (Mon–Sat hourly with change, Sun 1 daily; 1hr–1hr 45min); Wells (Mon–Sat hourly, Sun 6 daily; 50min).
By bike or on foot Radstock lies on the Colliers Way between Dundas (near Bath and Bradford-on-Avon) and Frome (see box, p.283).

ACCOMMODATION

Babington House Babington, 3 miles south of Radstock ☎ 01373 812266, ⓦ babingtonhouse.co.uk. Anyone aspiring to rub shoulders with the moneyed elite will feel right at home in this private club-cum-hotel. There's no end of pampering, with a cinema, indoor and outdoor pools, and top-notch spa facilities, but leave your suits and furs behind as this trades on its cool, informal image. From **£390**

★ **Old Priory** Church Square, Midsomer Norton ☎ 01761 416784, ⓦ moodygoose.co.uk. In a building dating back to the twelfth century, this upmarket B&B has oak beams, flagstone floors and a peaceful walled garden. Breakfasts are superb, and it's home to a top-quality restaurant, the *Moody Goose* (see below). From **£100**

Old Vicarage Church St, Kilmersdon ☎ 01761 436926, ⓦ theoldvicaragesomerset.co.uk. Two chic suites are available at this guesthouse 1.5 miles south of Radstock, with free-standing baths and views of the garden and adjacent church. Breakfast can be taken in your room, with home-produced eggs. **£95**

Ston Easton Park Hotel Ston Easton ☎ 01761 241631, ⓦ stoneaston.co.uk. The perfect spot for a secluded country-house splurge, this Regency mansion has sumptuous drawing rooms and guest rooms, with swags and swirls, antique furnishings and log fires. The grounds were landscaped by Humphrey Repton. It's 3 miles west of Midsomer Norton, at the end of a drive off the A37. From **£200**

EATING

★ **Moody Goose** Church Square, Midsomer Norton ☎ 01761 416784, ⓦ moodygoose.co.uk. Set in the medieval *Old Priory* B&B (see above), this place serves up seriously good food, contemporary Anglo-French in style, on set-price menus (£32.50 for two courses, £39.50 for three). Items might include fennel panna cotta to start, followed by poached rabbit and, for dessert, passion fruit meringue roulade. Mon–Thurs 7–9pm (last orders), Fri & Sat noon–1.15pm (last orders) & 7–9pm (last orders).

No. 6 6 The Island, at the end of the High St, Midsomer Norton ☎ 01761 410693, ⓦ no6restaurant.com. This casual but smart café is the best choice for snacks, teas and reasonably priced meals. Tuck into a soup or a sandwich, or

choose from an eclectic evening menu that takes in roasted monkfish with crab mash (£15) and griddled Moroccan chicken (£11.50). Mon & Tues 9.30am–5pm, Wed–Sat 9.30am–11pm, Sun 10am–4pm; food served 9.30/10am–2.30pm & 6.30–9pm (last orders).

Radstock Hotel Market Place, Radstock ☎ 01761 420776. If you don't fancy the café in Radstock's museum, you can find refreshment across the road in this inn, which has a skittle alley and garden seating. Bath Ales are on tap, and you can order from the fairly standard selection of pub grub from baguettes to casserole (most hot dishes £6–8), and there's a popular Sunday carvery. Mon–Sat 11am–11pm, Sun noon–10.30pm; food served noon–2.30pm & 6–9pm.

Shepton Mallet and around

Today a sleepy market town, **SHEPTON MALLET** has a rich industrial history, with some thirty mills once operating along the banks of the River Sheppey, producing ool and silk, while nearby quarries provided stone for Glastonbury Abbey and Wells Cathedral. In the nineteenth century, when two railways intersected here, he town was a brewing centre – its Anglo-Bavarian Brewery was the first in the ountry to brew lager. The imposing, tall-chimneyed building is now a trading state, though Shepton's brewing days are not over, with cider still produced in the rewery on Kilver Street.

Shepton Mallet is still known as an agricultural centre, the home of the **Royal Bath nd West Show**, held in late May/early June – primarily an agricultural fair but now atering to all tastes (see box below). The **Mid-Somerset Show** is a more local and more rictly farming affair, taking place on the third Sunday of August, while a more orkaday weekly market is held on Fridays at Market Place at the bottom of the partly edestrianized High Street. Market Place is also the site of an elegant **Market Cross** fifteenth-century, but rebuilt in 1841) and the remains of the wooden **Shambles**, here butchers once displayed their wares. Following the failure of the Duke of Monmouth's rebellion in 1685 (see p.218), twelve men were hung, drawn and uartered here in one of Judge Jeffreys' Bloody Assizes.

Shepton Mallet is just three miles northeast of Pilton, site of Glastonbury Festival (see ox, p.176), making it a useful stop before or after the festival, or a base for festival-oers unable or unwilling to camp.

St Peter and St Paul

hurch Lane • Daily 8.30am–3pm • Free • W peterpaul.co.uk

Shepton Mallet's jewel is its parish church of **St Peter and St Paul**, accessed from the High Street but mostly hidden behind an ugly 1970s development. With giant gargoyles around its exterior, its most distinctive feature is the **tower**, dating from the ate fourteenth century though never completed, explaining its oddly truncated ppearance. The church's airy **interior** is the real highlight, flooded with light from its arge Perpendicular windows topped by a clerestory added in around 1500. Statues that originally stood in the clerestory's niches were destroyed by Puritans, as was the stained glass in the windows. Soaring above it all is the nave's intricate **wagon roof** made up of 350 oak panels, each different, and interspersed by an array of bosses. The octagonal stone **pulpit**, from around 1550, is also outstanding, carved with classical and Gothic motifs. Effigies of two knights, probably killed while crusading, have been laid on windowsills on the church's north aisle.

Fans of Somerset churches should also seek out the one at **Evercreech**, three miles south of Shepton, whose slender pinnacled tower is reckoned to be one of Somerset's best examples of the genre.

ROYAL BATH AND WEST SHOW

One of the foremost agricultural shows in the West Country, the **Royal Bath and West Show** was created by the Royal Bath and West of England Society in 1780, and first held at Weston, outside Bath. Since 1965 it has had a permanent home outside Shepton Mallet, regularly attracting some 160,000 visitors over four days in late May/early June. Pigs, livestock and cider are very much to the fore, and dog-handling, sheep-shearing and champion beef competitions attract the farming folk, but there's also air displays, live music and such crowd-pullers as the smelliest cheese competition. Ticket prices are around £17 in advance, £20 at the gate.

The showground, located three miles south of Shepton on the A371, hosts numerous other events, from car boot sales and antiques fairs to the National Gardening Show in early September. In 1970, it was the venue of the famed Bath Blues and Progressive Music Festival, whose stellar lineup included Pink Floyd, Led Zeppelin, the Byrds, Santana and Frank Zappa. For information on current events, call ☎01749 822200 or see W bathandwest.com.

9

Kilver Court Gardens

Kilver St • Daily: April–Oct 10am–5pm; Nov–March 10am–4pm; last entry 1hr before closing • £5 • ☎ 01749 340410, ⓦ kilvercourt.com

Shepton Mallet has two areas of greenery close to the centre, ideal for a picnic or a runaround: **Collett Park**, a spacious public garden accessed from Park Road or Charlton Road, east of the High Street, and **Kilver Court Gardens**, a more formal space with a delightful rockery, waterfalls, a lake and the dramatic backdrop of the Charlton railway viaduct slicing across. The gardens were laid out in the 1880s for factory workers, remodelled in 1960–61 by local entrepreneur Francis Showering (who owed his fortune to Babycham) and reopened by the founders of the Mulberry clothing and accessories brand, whose headquarters are in Shepton. As well as a nursery and café, the site includes a farm shop, with organic local produce, and the Emporium, selling designer brands at discounted prices, while the Mulberry factory shop is 200m away.

ARRIVAL AND DEPARTURE

SHEPTON MALLET AND AROUN

By bus Most buses stop on Paul Street and by the Cenotaph at the southern end of the High Street.
Destinations Bath (Mon–Sat 1–2 hourly with change, Sun 1 daily; 1–2hr); Bristol (Mon–Sat 2–3 hourly with change,

Sun 1 daily; 1–2hr); Frome (Mon–Sat 9 daily; 50min); Glastonbury (Mon–Sat hourly; 30min); Wells (Mon–S hourly; 25min); Yeovil (Mon–Sat 8 daily, Sun 1 daily; 1 20min).

INFORMATION

Tourist Information and Heritage Centre 70 High St (Mon–Fri 10am–4pm, Sat 10am–1pm; ☎ 01749 345258, ⓦ sheptonmallet-touristinfocentre.co.uk). The annexed

Heritage Centre has a few local history displays, including child's coffin from the fourth century and collections cider tankards and Babycham glasses.

ACCOMMODATION

Belfield House 34 Charlton Rd ☎ 01749 344353, ⓦ belfieldhouse.com. Good-value B&B within a few minutes' walk of the centre. Rooms, most en suite, are plain and a bit dated, and include a family room and some singles. There's free wi-fi, and a £5 discount for stays of more than one night. **£60**

★ **Bowlish House** Corner of Coombe Lane and Wells Rd ☎ 01749 342022, ⓦ bowlishhouse.com. An old cloth merchant's house from 1732 has been adapted to provide spacious accommodation that retains its Georgian elegance but comes with contemporary bathrooms, minibars and internet connection. Smaller, cheaper rooms are available in the attic. Top-quality cuisine is available for evening meals (booking required). From **£80**

Charlton House Charlton Rd (A361), 1 mile east of

centre ☎ 01749 342008, ⓦ bannatyne.co.uk. This "styl" hotel" set in its own grounds caters mainly to urba refugees or anyone else seeking a posh but inform country-house retreat. Service is attentive and friendly, th contemporary rooms (some with balconies) are we equipped, and guests have free use of the gym and sp facilities – though these are on the small side. From **£95**
Thatched Cottage 63–67 Charlton Rd ☎ 0174 342058, ⓦ thatchedcottageinn.com. Dating from th seventeenth century, this inn on the outskirts of town ha been extensively renovated, but its beams and ope fireplaces still provide a cosy atmosphere. Rooms are good size and quiet – despite the proximity of the mai road – and there's a decent restaurant. It's a 15min wal from the centre. **£89**

EATING AND DRINKING

Blostin's 29–33 Waterloo Rd ☎ 01749 343648, ⓦ www.blostins.co.uk. Shepton's finest dining can be found in this relaxed restaurant five minutes' walk from the High Street, with warm orange walls and bright modern paintings. Dishes such as oven-baked salmon and fillet of pork are expertly prepared, and the inventive desserts include iced ginger meringue with cappuccino cream. £18 for two courses, £21 for three. Tues–Sat 7pm–late.

Lisboa Café 6 Town St. Members of the local Portuguese community flock to this authentic Portuguese-run café with football scarves festooning the walls and news from Lisbon on a TV set in the corner. Have a glass of wine or caipirinha,

or a strong coffee with a home-made pastry. Salted cod anc octopus rice feature on the menu (£8–10), or order a very reasonably priced steak sandwich (£2). Daily 8am–6pm.
Oakhill Inn Fosse Rd, Oakhill ☎ 01749 840442, ⓦ theoakhillinn.com. This gastropub 3 miles north of town (off the A37) offers local ales in its smart-rustic bar (there's an open fire in winter and a courtyard garden for fine weather). In the separate restaurant, all ingredients in dishes such as venison, lamb chops, beef burgers anc mushroom risotto with grilled asparagus (all £12–16) are seasonal, organic, free-range, or all three. Finish off with a Somerset cider brandy. Five stylish double rooms are

EAST SOMERSET RAILWAY

The time when this area of Somerset was criss-crossed by railway lines is long past, but you can relive this golden era on the small **East Somerset Railway** (☎01749 880417, ⓦeastsomersetrailway.com), based in the village of Cranmore, three miles east of Shepton Mallet. The line, with a length of just 2.5 miles, extends west to Mendip Vale station. The steam-driven trains operate April to Sept Saturdays, Sundays and bank holidays; they also run on Wednesdays between June and early Sept, and on Thursdays during August. There are at least four departures a day (currently at 11am, 12.30pm, 2pm & 3.30pm from Cranmore); the five-mile round trip takes around forty minutes, and tickets (£8.50) are valid all day. There's a stop at Merryfield Lane Halt, and on the return journey at Cranmore West station, where you can visit the workshop and Engine Shed, providing an insight into the amount of work it takes to keep these grand old locomotives running. The broad-gauge line continues east of Cranmore, eventually meeting the main line between Frome and Castle Cary, though this stretch is now only used for freighting stone from Merehead Quarry. The village of Cranmore is served by an hourly #161 bus between Frome, Shepton Mallet and Wells (not Sun); the station is a few minutes' walk from the stop.

so available (£90–120). Mon–Thurs noon–3pm & –11pm, Fri noon–3pm & 5pm–midnight, Sat 10am–midnight, Sun 10am–11pm; food served daily noon–3pm & 6–9pm.

★ **Peppers** 2–4 Town St ☎01749 346640. This wholefood shop and café-restaurant offers the best of local, seasonal produce, either to take away – crusty rolls, cheeses, hams, fruits and juices – or to eat in the adjoining restaurant, where the menu includes salmon fishcakes and Moroccan lamb (around £8) as well as salads and sandwiches. Mon–Fri 8.30am–4.30pm, Sat 9am–2.30pm, lunch served until 2.30pm (2pm on Sat).

Frome and around

Combining a traditional, mainly unspoiled aspect with a lively, happening vibe, **FROME** (pronounced "Froom"), about seven miles northeast of Shepton Mallet, is one of Somerset's most attractive towns, with yellow-stone weavers' cottages and Georgian rows above a bustling centre. There's not much in the way of specific sights, but plenty of scope for exploring the town's steep cobbled lanes and getting lost in its quaint nooks and alleys. In particular, seek out pedestrianized **Catherine Hill**, with its vintage stores and shops selling "upcycled" furniture, and **Cheap Street**, with a leat (stream) flowing through its open conduit, and cafés and delicatessens to either side.

The **Cheese & Grain** hall in Market Yard (ⓦcheeseandgrain.co.uk) has regular **markets** (antiques and second-hand goods on Wednesdays and the first Saturday of the month, country produce on Thursdays, Farmers' Markets on the second Saturday of the month, crafts on the fourth Saturday of the month) as well as **live music**. Black Swan Arts on Bridge Street (ⓦblackswan.org.uk) and Rook Lane Arts on Bath Street (ⓦrooklanearts.org.uk) also host live shows as well as exhibitions, and all three places are among the chief venues of the **Frome Festival**, a wide-ranging cultural jamboree over ten days in July (ⓦfromefestival.co.uk).

The tourist office can provide a Heritage Trail pamphlet and map for discovering Frome's many historical buildings on a circular walk. The town has a good selection of lodgings, eateries and atmospheric pubs too, making this a great base for excursions to such nearby attractions as Nunney Castle, Longleat and Stourhead. Frome also marks the eastern end of the **Mendip Way**, a fifty-mile trail extending to Uphill, near Weston-super-Mare, and connecting with the Macmillan Way.

St John the Baptist

Church St • Mon–Fri 9.30am–2.30pm • Free • ⓦ sjfrome.co.uk

Perched above Cheap Street, Frome's tall-steepled parish church of **St John the Baptist** is a grand affair, mostly a Victorian replacement of a twelfth- to fifteenth-century

9

structure that itself stood on the site of a Saxon church. Unusually for an Anglican church, it has a Via Crucis, depicting the stations of the cross, leading uphill to the north porch, and roundels above the nave arches based on Christ's parables and miracles. The tomb of the hymn-writer and ecclesiastic Bishop Thomas Ken (1637–1711) lies in a curious cage-like crypt outside the east end of the church.

Frome Museum

1 North Parade • March–Nov Tues–Sat 10am–2pm • Free • ☎ 01373 454611, 𝕎 fromemuseum.org

Just over the town bridge from Market Place (at the bottom of Cheap Street), **Frome Museum** crams into two rooms exhibits illustrating local history, geology, archeology and industry, with a generous helping of those random items that are a staple of small-town museums everywhere. The collection has more of a bias towards technology than most, with a significant proportion devoted to the local firm of J.W. Singer, whose heyday was in the late nineteenth and early twentieth centuries, specializing in ornamental statuary and monuments. Their biggest customers were churches, but their productions included such iconic pieces as the statue of Boadicea on London's Victoria Embankment and "Justice" on the Old Bailey, and their commissions extended to South Africa.

Other items on display include a selection of old maps of the town and surrounds, rocks from the Mendip Hills, fossils found in local quarries (including bison teeth), a push-barrow fire engine and an equally ancient penny-farthing. All in all, it's an enjoyable diversion for half an hour or so.

Nunney Castle

Nunney • Free • 𝕎 www.english-heritage.org.uk

Well hidden in the pretty village of **NUNNEY**, 3.5 miles southwest of Frome off the A361, is Somerset's finest castle ruin, rearing dramatically over the surrounding cottage gardens. Dating from the late fourteenth century and modernized two hundred years later, **Nunney Castle** still stands within its moat, its exterior in remarkably good condition, all things considered, with the four corner turrets and three walls still presenting a formidable sight, though the north-facing wall has collapsed and the interior is gutted. The castle was constructed in the 1370s by the local baron, Sir John de la Mere (or Mare), who had gained favour fighting for Edward III in the Hundred Years' War and later became Sheriff of Somerset. During the Civil War it was besieged by Cromwell's forces who pounded it with cannon, destroying the interior and generally weakening the structure, though the north wall did not finally collapse until Christmas Day, 1910. You can still see traces of some of the original rooms: on the ground floor was a kitchen, above were a hall and private chambers, with a chapel leading off these.

Across a footbridge from the castle, Nunney's **All Saints** church holds tombs belonging to John de la Mere's family, the effigies of knights and their consorts laid out serenely in the northeast corner.

Mells

Roughly two and a half miles north of Nunney and three and a half miles west of Frome, the dreamy, unspoiled village of **MELLS** is worth a brief diversion, most of all for the beautiful old church standing at the end of a medieval row of cottages. The mainly fifteenth-century **St Andrew** has a yellowy, pale-grey exterior, a superb pinnacled and battlemented four-decker tower, and a fan-vaulted porch. The interior is less striking but holds a memorial by Edward Burne-Jones under the tower, and an equestrian statue by Alfred Munnings honouring his close friend Edward Horner, killed in World War I. The local Horner family, who occupied the Elizabethan manor

JACK, JILL AND LITTLE JACK HORNER

The hazy origins of most nursery rhymes are lost in centuries-old folklore, but two of the best-known rhymes have been linked to the parishes of **Mells** and **Kilmersdon** (south of Radstock). "**Little Jack Horner**" is said to have been a member of the Horner family whose Elizabethan manor neighbours Mells church; according to this version, the "plum" that he extracted from a Christmas pie turned out to be the house deeds – the gift of Richard Whiting, last Abbot of Glastonbury. Kilmersdon is said to be where **Jack and Jill** came to a sorry end while going to fetch water. There is no evidence for why Kilmersdon should be the site of this drama, but the steep hill behind the village is now called Jack and Jill Hill and is waymarked with lines from the rhyme.

adjacent to the church, was claimed (probably wrongly) to be associated with the nursery rhyme *Little Jack Horner* (see box above).

The churchyard holds the graves of a clutch of twentieth-century celebrities, including Violet Bonham-Carter, Liberal politician, diarist and grandmother of Helena Bonham-Carter; the Roman Catholic priest and crime writer Ronald Knox; and the World War I poet Siegfried Sassoon, who had asked to be buried close to Knox, an influence in Sassoon's decision to convert to Catholicism.

Mells also has a fine old tavern, the *Talbot Inn* (see p.295), good for a drink, meal or sleepover. The village lies just over a mile from the Colliers Way (see box, p.283), and about the same distance east of Vobster, an old mining settlement whose quarry has been turned into the region's best inland **diving** centre (⊕vobster.com).

Longleat

Four miles southeast of Frome off the A362 • **House** Late Feb & March Sat & Sun 10am–4pm; April to late July & early Sept to late Oct Mon–Fri 10am–5pm, Sat & Sun 10am–6pm; late July to early Sept daily 10am–7.30pm; late to end Oct daily 10am–5pm; early Nov daily 10am–4pm; last entry to house 30min before closing **Safari park** March–Easter Sat & Sun 10am–4pm; Easter–Oct Mon–Fri 10am–4pm, Sat, Sun & school hols 10am–5pm; check winter opening; last entry to safari park 1hr before closing • House and grounds £12.90; one-day multiple entry to all attractions including safari park £26; single entry to all attractions including safari park over more than one day £28.50; house, grounds, safari park and Cheddar Caves (see p.155) £34.50; safari bus £4 • ☎ 01985 844400, ⊕ longleat.co.uk • Bus #53 (not Sun) shuttles roughly every hour between Warminster and Frome train stations, both about four miles from Longleat – though the house is 2.5 miles from the stop; National Cycle Routes 24 and 25 meet at Longleat

One of the country's most magnificent stately homes, joined improbably to a safari park, lies just over the Wiltshire border. Apart from the house and park, **Longleat** offers a huge range of entertainment for all ages, not to mention its formal gardens and acres of grounds – enough to fill at least one full day. In fact, given its combined attractions, you might consider one of the ticket options allowing entry over more than one day.

The Great Hall

The **house**, an imposing three-storey construction topped with a panoply of ornamental statuary and cupolas, has been owned by the Thynne family since the site of an Augustinian priory was bought in 1541 by Sir John Thynne, steward to the Duke of Somerset. The house was more or less complete by Sir John's death in 1580, though it was further altered and embellished by succeeding generations. The **Great Hall** is the least changed part of the building, a lofty, cavernous space with a hammerbeam roof, galleries and enormous canvases showing hunting scenes above a grand Elizabethan fireplace, and wood-panelling from which giant prehistoric antlers from Ireland are hung. A waistcoat worn by Charles I at his execution is displayed in one corner.

The rest of the house

The rest of the house is a dizzying succession of fine furnishings and works of art. The central **staircase** was added, like much else here, by Jeffrey Wyatville in the early

9

eighteenth century, while the state rooms were altered beyond recognition in the 187
and 1880s when the fourth marquess, returned from a tour of Italy, employed the
celebrated designer J.D. Crace and a team of Italian craftsmen to create painted
ceilings, gilded cornices and other extravagances that really elevate Longleat's interior
a palatial level. There are paintings everywhere, many of them family portraits, but the
best works are reserved for the **State Drawing Room** where a range of Old Masters are
displayed, including Titian's "Rest on the Flight into Egypt" and a scene from Ovid's
Metamorphoses painted by Tintoretto. The works here are poorly displayed, however,
not helped by the dim lighting (most of the state rooms are heavily curtained to limit
damage from daylight).

Art of a very different order can be viewed in a separate suite of rooms containing
vivid, sometimes steamy **murals** by the current Lord Bath (the seventh marquess).
According to his own description, these offer "keyhole glimpses into my psyche",
encapsulating his interpretations of life, the universe and everything. A separate ticket
for a tour of these rooms (£4; no under-14s) is bookable at the front desk. You can als
join a private hour-long **tour** of rooms not normally open, scheduled once or twice a
month during the main season (£10) – check the website for details.

The grounds and safari park

The magnificence of the house is complemented by the 1100 acres of **grounds**, largely
created in 1758–62 by Capability Brown, who installed the walled kitchen garden and
the Pleasure Walk, planted prolifically (giving the park its heavily wooded appearance)
and enhanced the lakes fed by the serpentine river, or "leat", from which the house
takes its name. In 1966, the sixth marquess of Bath (father of the present Lord Bath),
who had already raised eyebrows among his peers twenty years earlier by opening his
house to the paying public (the first stately home owner to do so on a regular basis),
caused even more amazement when he turned Brown's landscapes into a drive-through
safari park – again, the first in the country. Today, this features lions, giraffes, rhinos,
elephants, wildebeest, zebras and famously meddlesome monkeys, among other
animals, which you can view at close quarters from your car or in a Safari Bus (places
on this should be booked at the ticket booths at the entrance).

Adventure park

Once set on the commercial route, the bosses of Longleat knew no limits: the
Adventure Park behind the house includes such attractions and curiosities as mirror
and hedge mazes, a Bat Cave, a zoo, motion simulators and the sixth marquess's
collection of Churchill and Hitler memorabilia. Look out too for regular **seasonal
events** such as fireworks in late October and early November, and ice-skating and other
Christmassy activities between mid-November and early January.

Westbury

The Wiltshire village of **WESTBURY** is best known for the **white horse** etched into a
nearby hillside, and as a railway junction where the Bath–Salisbury line meets the line
between Reading, Taunton and Exeter. But Westbury itself is worth a stop for a flavour
of its attractive old centre, with Georgian houses around its Market Place and circling
its handsome, fourteenth-century (though much restored) church of **All Saints**, which
holds a chained copy of the Paraphrase of the New Testament by Erasmus.

There's another, more compelling church a couple of miles southwest of Westbury in
the hamlet of **Dilton** (also known as Old Dilton), signposted off the A3098. **St Mary's**,
which has not been in use since 1900, feels as if its Georgian congregation has only just
left. Probably dating from the fourteenth or fifteenth century, the church is preserved
in immaculate condition, with a white-painted interior, galleries, a triple-decker pulpit
and tall box pews crowding the small space.

WILTSHIRE'S WHITE HORSES

Wiltshire's chalk downs have proved ideal for large and vivid hill-carvings, so much so that the county holds eight of Britain's twenty-three **white horses**, with several more overgrown and now invisible. The practice of carving figures into English hillsides is an ancient one, as the priapic Cerne Giant in Dorset testifies, but Wiltshire's white horses were probably all carved within the last three hundred years, as were all the rest in the country with the one exception of the sinuous horse at Uffington, Oxfordshire, thought to be 3000 years old. The background and purpose of the authentically old hill carvings has never been established – and probably never will be – but the more recent creations were usually the fruit of whimsy and fashion. Apart from Westbury's, some of the best examples can be seen outside Cherhill, Broad Town (outside Wootton Bassett) and Marlborough; the newest is outside Devizes, carved in 1999 to mark the millennium. For background on all of Wiltshire's carved horses, see ⓦ wiltshirewhitehorses.org.uk.

Westbury White Horse

Perfectly positioned for maximum visibility on Westbury Hill, a couple of miles east of town, the **Westbury White Horse**, one of several in Wiltshire (see box above), probably has its origins in the late seventeenth or early eighteenth century, though there are suggestions that there was a carved horse in Saxon times, possibly cut to commemorate Alfred the Great's victory over the Danes at Ethandun in 878. The carving we see today, however, is quite a different creature, as the original horse was judged to be a poor work and redesigned in 1778 by one G. Gee, a local steward. The figure was enlarged and possibly turned to face in the opposite direction, then further modified a hundred years later, and in the twentieth century it was stabilized with concrete and painted white.

The result is a vivid but rather inert affair, lacking the dynamic grace of some of Wiltshire's other hill carvings, though it still presents a strange and wonderful apparition when seen from afar (you'll get a brief glimpse of it from the train between Westbury and Trowbridge). The best view is from the B3098, where a parking area has been cleared for taking in the scene. If you want to get closer, follow the minor road signposted for Bratton Camp. Just above the carving, **Bratton Camp** is an Iron Age hill fort, one of a series of fortified encampments edging Salisbury Plain. Enclosed within the deep ditches and banks is a substantial **long barrow** (burial mound) some 5000 years old.

Stourhead

Stourton • **House** Mid-Feb to early March Sat & Sun 11am–3pm; mid-March to late July and early Sept to mid-Oct Mon, Tues & Fri–Sun 11am–5pm; late July to early Sept and mid-Oct to early Nov daily 11am–5pm; early Dec to mid-Dec Fri–Sun 11am–3pm • £7.30, £12.10 with grounds **King Alfred's Tower** Mid-March to Oct Mon, Tues & Fri–Sun 11am–5pm • £2.90 **Grounds** Daily 9am–6pm or dusk • £7.30, £12.10 with house• Half-price entry if you arrive by public transport, on foot or by bike • ☎ 01747 841152, ⓦ nationaltrust.org.uk Stourhead • Stourton is difficult to reach without your own transport; the nearest train station is at Gillingham, over 6 miles away

Eight miles south of Frome, off the B3092, **Stourhead** is like a slightly slimmed-down version of Longleat (see p.291), but here the style of the house is predominantly Georgian and formal rather than Elizabethan and flamboyant, and instead of a safari park Stourhead is best known for its grounds, among the most accomplished surviving examples of the eighteenth-century craze for landscape gardening.

The grounds

The Stourton estate was bought in 1717 by Henry Hoare, who commissioned Colen Campbell to build a new villa in the Palladian style. Hoare's heir, another Henry, returned from his Grand Tour in 1741 with his head full of the paintings of Claude and Poussin, and determined to translate their images of well-ordered, wistful classicism into real life. In the **grounds**, he dammed the Stour to create a lake, then

9

planted the terrain with blocks of trees, classical temples and statues, all mirrored vividly in the water of the lake, which is crossed by a modest, grass-carpeted **Palladian bridge** modelled on one in Vicenza. The most impressive of the lakeside monuments is the **Pantheon**, a domed and porticoed structure originally named the Temple of Hercules for the muscly statue that dominates the interior – a masterpiece by the Flemish sculptor John Rysbrack. The whole park forms a kind of travel scrapbook, with an assortment of eye-catching features poetically jumbled together: a grotto built of volcanic rock imported from Italy; a soaring obelisk at the end of an avenue of firs; and a "Gothic cottage". In 1772, the folly of **King Alfred's Tower** was added at the far western end of the park (nearly three miles from the house), and today affords fine views across the estate and into neighbouring counties. The rhododendrons and azaleas that now make such a splash in early summer are a later addition to this dream landscape. A circuit around the lake and woods (not including King Alfred's Tower) adds up to around two miles.

The house

In contrast to the magnificent grounds, the exterior of the **house** is fairly run-of-the-mill, though the artistic treasures inside more than compensate. The spacious **Entrance Hall** makes a fitting introduction, a thirty-foot cube with regal doorways and fireplace, and walls decked with a parade of family portraits. The **Library** is just as imposing, a long, barrel-ceilinged room furnished with rare volumes on the shelves and more work by Rysbrack on show: two busts of Milton as a youth and an old man, and a terracotta model of the Hercules statue in the Pantheon, displayed on a magnificent Chippendale desk carved with the heads of philosophers and ancient Egyptians. This room survived a fire that devastated much of the house in 1902 – though most of the works of art and furnishings were rescued.

There's more fine furniture in the other rooms, notably the **Music Room**, with another exuberant chimneypiece, and the ornately plastered **Dining Room** and **Saloon**, the latter once used for theatrical performances, balls and other social occasions. The last stop on a tour of the house is the **Picture Gallery**, another room that escaped the 1902 conflagration, displaying a mix of Old Masters and landscapes.

ARRIVAL AND DEPARTURE   FROME AND AROUND

By train Frome's station is at the eastern end of town, off Portway.
Destinations Bath (Mon–Sat 8 daily, Sun 4 daily; 40–50min); Bradford-on-Avon (Mon–Sat 8 daily, Sun 4 daily; 20–35min); Bruton (Mon–Sat 8 daily, Sun 3 daily; 10min); Castle Cary (Mon–Sat 8 daily, Sun 3 daily; 20min); Westbury (Mon–Sat 14 daily, Sun 4 daily; 10min).
By bus Stops are on Market Place, Cork St and

Christchurch St West.
Destinations Bath (Mon–Sat every 30min, Sun 4 daily; 45min–1hr); Lacock (Mon–Sat 1–2 hourly; 1hr 10min); Mells (Mon–Sat hourly; 20min); Nunney (Mon–Sat hourly; 15min); Shepton Mallet (Mon–Sat hourly; 50min); Radstock (Mon–Sat 1–2 hourly; 50min–1hr 10min); Wells (Mon–Sat hourly; 1hr 10min); Westbury (Mon–Sat 4 daily; 40min).

INFORMATION

Tourist office Library, Justice Lane (Mon–Fri 9.30am–5pm, Sat 9.30am–4pm; ☎01373 465757,

ⓦ frome-tc.gov.uk). Internet facilities are available in the library.

ACCOMMODATION

★ **Archangel** 1 King St, Frome ☎01373 456111, ⓦ archangelfrome.com. This up-to-the-minute hotel, bar and restaurant has helped to put Frome on the map. Converted from an old coaching inn in a contemporary industrial style, it has boldly coloured rooms featuring large Renaissance murals and free-standing zinc baths. Smiley staff and a buzzing café, bar, restaurant and

courtyard garden complete the picture, making this a great stop for meals and refreshment too. **£120**
Garden House Hotel 26 Edward St, Westbury ☎01373 859995, ⓦ thegardenhotel.co.uk. Formerly a post office, this small, central hotel makes for a handy stopover in Westbury, offering traditional rooms, some more spacious ones with separate sitting areas (ask for 1, 3 or 4). There's a

ar and restaurant, and free wi-fi. **£95**

he Lantern Tytherington, 1.5 miles south of Frome ☎01373 453585, ⓦlighthouse-uk.com. If you're ooking for a wholesome country retreat, this "healing entre" outside town is just the ticket. As well as the various eatments on offer, it has modern B&B rooms opening nto a central patio, a heated outdoor pool (open in ummer) overlooking the fields and fishing lake, and dairy- nd gluten-free breakfasts. **£80**

albot Inn Mells ☎01373 812254, ⓦtalbotinn.com. 'onderful old coaching inn near Mells church, full of haracter, offering traditional-style rooms named after

local figures. Two more luxurious rooms (costing more) have four-posters. There's Butcombe beer in the bar and good food on the menu (the Sunday carvery is renowned), making this an excellent refreshment stop too. **£95**

★ **Trinity House** Goulds Ground, Frome ☎01373 451547, ⓦthepaintedhome.co.uk. Two delightful rooms are available in this ex-Victorian school, the larger family room overlooking the garden, the other in the basement with its own entrance. The friendly owners have created a B&B with a cosy, individual feel, full of tasteful knick- knacks and with a secret bookcase door into the breakfast room. Closed Dec–Feb. No credit cards. **£75**

ATING AND DRINKING

ath Arms Horningsham, near Longleat ☎0844 815 099, ⓦbatharms.co.uk. Conveniently located outside he exit from Longleat, this upmarket Georgian inn shares ome of the same jaunty spirit. The food is traditional, local nd good quality; you can have sandwiches or main meals t lunchtime (£7–10) or more sophisticated dinners £24.50 for two courses). There's outdoor seating, and uxury accommodation upstairs (£140). Daily 0am–11pm; food served Mon–Thurs & Sun noon– 2.30pm & 7–9pm, Fri & Sat noon–2.30pm & 7–9.30pm.

Garden Café 16 Stony St, Frome ☎01373 454178, ⓦgardencafefrome.co.uk. The paved garden provides a leasant haven from Frome's bustling centre, where you an sip coffee or sample the tasty organic, ethical and ocally sourced vegetarian dishes – for example stone- aked pizza (£6.50–9), cashew nut and bean patties (£9), Thai burger (£10) or tapas (£4 each or a platter to share for £18.50). Mon–Thurs 8.30am–7pm, Fri & Sat 8.30am– ate, Sun 10.30am–5pm.

Madame Butterfly 16 Maristow St, Westbury ☎01373 228512, ⓦmadamebutterfly.biz. Snug tearoom and restaurant in the heart of this quiet village, providing a relaxed environment for baguettes, jacket potatoes, salads and Wiltshire ham, egg and chips (all

around £5). Check out the specials board, and leave room for the home-made cakes and desserts. There's garden seating too. May open some evenings. Tues–Sat 9.30am–4pm, Sun 11am–3pm.

Olive Tree 6 Christchurch St West ☎01373 467140. Agreeable pub with a large decked garden and authentic Thai food in a separate restaurant. Fresh ingredients and subtle flavours infuse dishes such as Pad Thai (noodles, king prawns and beansprouts) and green curry, both around £7.50. Mon–Thurs noon–3pm & 5.30–11pm (Tues afternoon only), Fri & Sat noon–3pm & 5pm–midnight, Sun noon–3pm & 6–10.30pm; food served Mon & Wed–Sat noon–3pm & 6–10pm, Sun till 9.30pm.

Spread Eagle Inn Stourton ☎01747 840587, ⓦspreadeagleinn.com. Part of the Stourhead estate, this slate-floored pub and restaurant is pricey but atmospheric, and the food is of a high standard. You can order generous sandwiches (around £7) or a full meal of robust English fare such as slow-cooked stew and Creedy Carver duck breast (£12–14 at lunchtime, £11.50–20 in the evening), washed down with West Country beers. Coffees and cream teas are also served, and five rooms with period furnishings provide accommodation (£115). Mon–Sat 9.30am–11pm, Sun noon–10pm; food served noon–3pm & 7–9pm.

Salisbury and Stonehenge

SALISBURY PLAIN

Salisbury and Stonehenge

The distant past is perhaps more tangible in neighbouring Wiltshire than in any other part of England. The chalky uplands of Salisbury Plain are littered with Bronze Age burial mounds and the remnants of ancient ceremonial structures, tell-tale signs of five millennia of pagan worship that reaches its enigmatic zenith at Stonehenge, Europe's greatest Neolithic monument and a legendary site in every sense of the word.

10

At a sprightly eight hundred years of age, the great cathedral city of **Salisbury** is youthful in comparison, but has more than its fair share of old-world atmosphere. The medieval Close and ensemble of half-timbered houses provide an aesthetic backdrop to the towering **cathedral**, while its compact core still bears the hallmarks of a deep-rooted mercantile tradition. Salisbury is an attractive city, small but spacious, cut through by the clear-flowing Avon and fringed by water meadows that slouch towards Harnham from the cathedral's southern edge.

There's a hat-trick of museums in the city itself, plus a varied calendar of cultural events, but most visitors also find time to make the short walk or bus ride to **Old Sarum**, the city's precursor. Its unusual double-ditch appearance – something akin to a grassy wedding cake – is just as much an attraction as the remains of the Norman castle that crowns it. In the other direction, and a model of accomplishment in comparison, lies sixteenth-century **Wilton House**, a real crowd-puller and one of Wiltshire's finest stately homes.

Just north of Salisbury begins the sea of swaying wheatfields and wildflower meadows that constitute **Salisbury Plain**. Much of it falls under the jurisdiction of the Ministry of Defence: signs warn motorists of tank crossings ahead, while flags deter casual trespassers from MoD firing ranges. Though now largely deserted except by forces families living in ugly barracks quarters, the Plain once positively throbbed with communities who lived, built, worshipped and died at Durrington Walls, Normanton Down and the other henges and barrows now conserved as the **Stonehenge World Heritage Site**. At the centre of this rich tapestry of ritualistic landmarks stands the famous circle of **Stonehenge** itself, an unmissable, frustrating, secretive and genuinely awe-inspiring monument that – some 3500 years after it was abandoned – still has the finest minds in archeological science scratching their heads and wondering what on earth it was used for.

Salisbury and around

SALISBURY, huddled below Wiltshire's chalky plain in the converging valleys of the Avon and Nadder, looks from a distance very much as it did when Constable painted his celebrated view of it from across the water meadows, its tranquil **Close** cradled by a kink in the River Avon and focused around the city's magnificent **cathedral**. Stern-looking medieval gates (which are still locked every night) shelter the Close from the

Highlights

❶ **Salisbury Cathedral** The city's sensational cathedral is literally its standout sight. **See p.301**

❷ **Old Sarum** The ruined remains of Salisbury's forerunner enjoy a dramatic setting on a hill just north of the city. **See p.304**

❸ **Wilton House** The pure panache of Inigo Jones's lavish "cube" rooms almost steals the show from the superb art within. **See p.304**

❹ **Haunch of Venison** Lovely wood-panelled pub, small but perfectly formed, and with a large dose of quirkiness. **See p.306**

❺ **Stone Circle Access** Watching the sun rise from inside the sarsens, with only birdsong for company, is the only way to do Stonehenge justice. **See p.308**

❻ **Walking the World Heritage Site** There's more to Stonehenge than the stone circle – get out among the surrounding barrows, henges and processional pathways for an altogether different experience. **See p.311**

HIGHLIGHTS ARE MARKED ON THE MAP ON P.300

rest of the city; **North Gate** opens onto the centre's older streets, where narrow pedestrianized alleyways bear names like Fish Row and Salt Lane, indicative of their trading origins.

Many half-timbered houses and inns survive all over the centre, and the last of four market crosses, **Poultry Cross**, stands on stilts in Silver Street. Nearby **Market Square** is gradually being refurbished after much of its southern side was gutted by a fire in March 2011, though the **market** itself (Tues & Sat 8am–4pm) continues unabated, and still serves a large agricultural area, as it did in earlier times when the city grew wealthy on wool. A farmers' market adds some local organic produce to the mix on the first and third Wednesday of the month (10am–2pm).

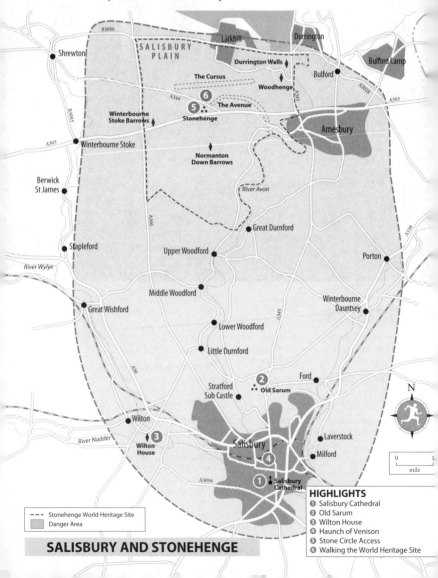

HIGHLIGHTS
1. Salisbury Cathedral
2. Old Sarum
3. Wilton House
4. Haunch of Venison
5. Stone Circle Access
6. Walking the World Heritage Site

- - - Stonehenge World Heritage Site
Danger Area

SALISBURY AND STONEHENGE

Salisbury sprang into existence in the early thirteenth century, when the bishopric was moved from **Old Sarum**, an Iron Age hill fort settled by the Romans and their successors. The current cathedral's location was allegedly determined by an arrow shot from atop the hill (from the bow of presumably the world's strongest archer, given the distance of nearly two miles). The deserted remnants of Salisbury's precursor now stand on the northern fringes of the city and are – along with **Wilton House**, to the west – well worth working into your itinerary.

10

Salisbury Cathedral

The Close • Daily 7.15am–6.15pm (recommended visiting times Mon–Sat 9am–5pm, Sun noon–4pm) • Suggested donation £5.50, under-18s £3, under-5s free • Regular free tours (45min) • Tower tours (1hr 30min) £8.50, under-17s £6.50, no under-5s; call ☎ 01722 555156 for times and to book (max 12 people) • ☎ 01722 555120, ⓦ salisburycathedral.org.uk

Begun in 1220, **Salisbury Cathedral** was mostly completed within forty years and is thus unusually consistent in its style, with one extremely prominent exception – the **spire**, which was added a century later and at 404ft is the highest in England. Its survival is something of a miracle, for the foundations penetrate only about six feet into marshy ground, and when Christopher Wren surveyed it he found the spire to be leaning almost two and a half feet out of true; he added further tie rods, which finally arrested the movement. You can get a better idea of how it all remains in place on one of the recommended tours of the **tower**, which take visitors up the 332 steps to the spire's base, offering offer sublime views of the city along the way.

The interior

The cathedral's **interior** is over-austere after James Wyatt's brisk eighteenth-century tidying, but there's an amazing sense of space and light in its high nave, despite the sombre pillars of grey Purbeck marble, which are visibly bowing beneath the weight they bear. Monuments and carved tombs line the walls, most notably the large marble memorial to Edward Seymour and Lady Catherine Grey (Lady Jane's sister) in the **Trinity Chapel**, and the colourful tomb of Richard Mompesson and his wife, facing the "wrong way" on the south side of the huge **quire**.

The chapter house

Mon–Sat 9.30am–4.30pm (Nov–March from 10am), Sun 12.45–3.45pm • Free • No photography allowed

The largest cathedral cloisters in the country lead to the octagonal **chapter house**, with a beautiful vaulted ceiling fanning out above walls that are decorated with a medieval frieze of scenes from the Old Testament. The room displays a rare copy of the original *Magna Carta*, the best preserved of only four surviving from 1215. The "great charter"

CONSTABLE IN SALISBURY

Though inextricably linked with the landscapes of Suffolk, **John Constable** (1776–1837) was greatly inspired by Salisbury and produced some of his finest work on the back of various visits to the city in the early half of the nineteenth century. A pencil drawing of *St Ann Gate* from his first trip here in 1811 – when he stayed with his uncle, John Fisher, the Bishop of Salisbury – hangs in the Salisbury and South Wiltshire Museum (see p.303), but it's his later paintings that are more compelling. After honeymooning in the city in 1816, Constable returned to paint *Salisbury Cathedral and Leadenhall from the River Avon* (1820) and *Salisbury Cathedral from the Bishop's Grounds* (1823), which show the daring use of colour that made *The Hay Wain* such a revelation at the Paris Salon in 1824 – though his uncle famously made him redo the clouds in the "Bishop's Grounds" version. The contrast between these and Constable's later works, produced after the death of his wife Maria, is stark: his second *Salisbury Cathedral from the Meadows* (1831), painted a year after the first, is a raw, pain-filled picture, one whose sentiment, as he wrote in a letter to his friend David Lucas, "is that of solemnity".

established a national scheme for weights and measures, trial by jury and other civil liberties, though the 1215 version only lasted three months thanks to a controversial section (dubbed Clause 61) that gave great power to the barons over their king.

The Close

Surrounding Salisbury Cathedral, **the Close** is a peaceful precinct of lawns and mellow old buildings, their pathways lined with lavender. A slow circuit enables you to

10

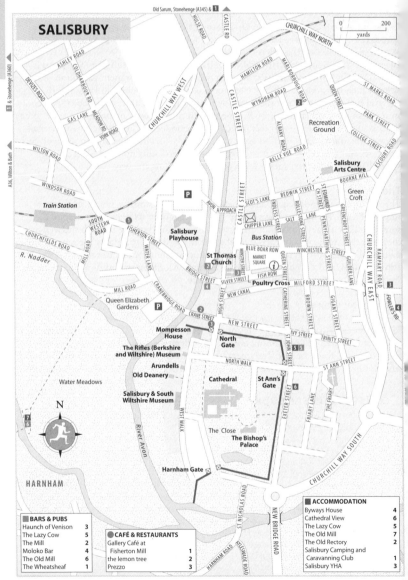

SALISBURY

Old Sarum, Stonehenge (A345) & █ ▲

CHURCHILL WAY NORTH

0   200
yards

█ & Stonehenge (A360) ▲

A36, Wilton & Bath ▲

ASHLEY ROAD
COLDHARBOUR RD
DEVIZES ROAD
GAS LANE
MEADOW RD
YORK ROAD
WILTON ROAD
WINDSOR ROAD
CHURCHILL WAY WEST
HAMILTON ROAD
MARLBOROUGH ROAD
WYNDHAM ROAD
CASTLE STREET
ALBANY ROAD
BELLE VUE ROAD
QUEEN STREET
ST MARKS ROAD
PARK STREET
COLLEGE STREET
ESCOURT ROAD

HULSE ROAD
CASTLE RD

Recreation Ground

Salisbury Arts Centre

BOURNE HILL
Green Croft

Train Station

CHURCHFIELDS ROAD
MILL ROAD
R. Nadder
SOUTH WESTERN ROAD
FISHERTON STREET
WATER LANE
MILL ROAD
CRANEBRIDGE ROAD
BRIDGE STREET
SILVER STREET
NEW CANAL
HIGH STREET
CRANE STREET

AVON APPROACH
SCOT'S LANE
CASTLE STREET
CHIPPER LANE
BLUE BOAR ROW
MARKET SQUARE
FISH ROW
Poultry Cross

BEDWIN STREET
ENDLESS STREET
SALT LANE
ST EDMUND'S CH STREET
ROLLESTONE STREET
PENNYFARTHING STREET
GREENCROFT STREET
GUILDER LANE
RAMPART ROAD
CHURCHILL WAY EAST
FOWLER'S RD

P

Salisbury Playhouse ❶

St Thomas Church ❷

WINCHESTER STREET
QUEEN STREET
CATHERINE STREET
BROWN STREET
GIGANT STREET
IVY STREET
TRINITY STREET

Bus Station ❸

ℹ

MILFORD STREET

NEW STREET

Queen Elizabeth Gardens
P
❷
❸
Mompesson House
North Gate
The Rifles (Berkshire and Wiltshire) Museum
Arundells
Old Deanery
Salisbury & South Wiltshire Museum

Water Meadows

N

WEST WALK
Cathedral
St Ann's Gate
The Close
The Bishop's Palace
ST JOHN STREET
❹ ❺
❻
NORTH WALK
EXETER STREET
FRIARY LANE
THE FRIARY
ST ANN STREET

River Avon

Harnham Gate ⊠

❼ ❻

HARNHAM

CHURCHILL WAY SOUTH
ST NICHOLAS ROAD
NEW BRIDGE ROAD
HARNHAM ROAD
AYLESMEAD ROAD

█ **BARS & PUBS**
Haunch of Venison   3
The Lazy Cow   5
The Mill   2
Moloko Bar   4
The Old Mill   6
The Wheatsheaf   1

● **CAFÉ & RESTAURANTS**
Gallery Café at
  Fisherton Mill   1
the lemon tree   2
Prezzo   3

█ **ACCOMMODATION**
Byways House   4
Cathedral View   6
The Lazy Cow   5
The Old Mill   7
The Old Rectory   2
Salisbury Camping and
  Caravanning Club   1
Salisbury YHA   3

ppreciate the cathedral from a variety of aspects – much like Constable did in the arly 1800s (see box, p.301) – and to take in many of the city's finest houses along the vay. Most of them have seemly Georgian facades, though some, like the **Bishop's Palace**, the **Old Deanery** and **the Wardrobe** (once used as the bishops' clothes store and ow home to the Rifles Museum), date from the thirteenth century. The stately home artly shielded by gates on the western side of the Close is **Arundells**, a medieval anonry that was the home of former prime minister Sir Edward Heath for twenty ears until his death in 2005. Heath decreed that his foundation open the house to the ublic so that everyone could "share the beauty of Arundells" but prohibitive running osts enforced its closure in 2011.

10

Mompesson House

he Close • Mid-March to Oct Mon–Wed, Sat & Sun 11am–5pm • £5.20, children £2.60; garden only £1; NT • ☎ 01722 335659, ⓦ nationaltrust.org.uk/main/w-mompessonhouse

On the northern side of Choristers' Green, facing Salisbury Cathedral in the distance, Mompesson House was built by a wealthy merchant in 1701 and contains some beautifully furnished eighteenth-century rooms and decorative ceilings throughout, even on the underside of the carved oak staircase in the main entrance hall. It still looks very much like it did in the 1700s, a fact not lost on the location team of Ang Lee's 1995 *Sense and Sensibility*, who used it for Mrs Jennings' London home.

The Rifles (Berkshire and Wiltshire) Museum

he Wardrobe, 58 The Close • Mon–Sat 10am–5pm, Sun noon–4.30pm, Feb & Nov closed Mon & Sun, March & Oct closed Sun except half-term week; closed Jan & Dec • £3.95, children £1.15; garden only £1.50 • ☎ 01722 419419, ⓦ thewardrobe.org.uk/museum

Backing onto a pretty, memorial-filled garden, the four rooms of **The Rifles Museum** house the collections of Berkshire and Wiltshire's infantry units; the Gloucester regiments, also part of the Rifles, are kept elsewhere. Its huge archive – the two thousand or so pieces on display at any one time constitute just five percent of the total collection – spans the regiments' 250-year history, with uniforms, medals, weapons and other military regalia adding colour to campaigns like the American War of Independence (from which they kept a cannon ball), the little-known nineteenth-century battles of Ferozeshah (India) and Tofrek (Sudan), and more recently the conflicts in Northern Ireland and Afghanistan.

Salisbury and South Wiltshire Museum

he King's House, 65 The Close • Mon–Sat & bank hols 10am–5pm, June–Sept also Sun noon–5pm • £5.45, under-17s £1.82, under-5s free • ☎ 01722 332151, ⓦ salisburymuseum.org.uk

At the southwestern corner of the Close, **The King's House** – so named because James I stayed here in the early seventeenth century – is home to the **Salisbury and South Wiltshire Museum**, an absorbing account of local history. Its enlightening section on Stonehenge includes five-thousand-year-old carved chalk plaques and the remains of the **Amesbury Archer**, originally from central Europe; his 4300-year-old grave is the richest "Beaker" burial site ever found in Britain and contained the country's first objects made of gold.

The museum also focuses on the life and times of Lieutenant-General Pitt-Rivers, the father of modern archeology, who excavated many of Wiltshire's prehistoric sites. The collection of paintings and prints is extensive, though only one, a pencil drawing of St Ann Gate, is by John Constable, despite his affiliation with the city (see box, p.301).

Church of St Thomas

St Thomas's Square • Free • ⓦ stthomassalisbury.co.uk

Tucked behind Bridge Street, the dark, peaceful **church of St Thomas** – named after Thomas à Becket – is worth a look inside for its carved timber roof, decorated with

Somerset angels (there are nearly 250 dotted around the church), and its "Doom Painting" over the chancel arch. Dating from 1475, it depicts Christ presiding over the Last Judgment and is the largest of its kind in England.

The water meadows

Enclosed by the Nadder and Avon, on an island to the west of the cathedral, the **water meadows** (Ⓦwww.salisburywatermeadows.org.uk) reward walkers with the defining image of Salisbury: the cathedral's inspiring silhouette and the view made famous by Constable. It takes about twenty minutes to cross Town Path, the pathway that bisects them, and reach **Harnham**, where the riverside *Old Mill* (see p.306) serves refreshments to set you up for the return journey.

Old Sarum

Castle Rd, off the A345 • Daily: Jan, Nov & Dec 11am–3pm; Feb 11am–4pm; March & Oct 10am–4pm; April–June & Sept 10am–5pm; Jul & Aug 9am–6pm • £3.70, under-16s £2.20, under-5s free; EH • ☏ 01722 335398, Ⓦ www.english-heritage.org.uk

The ruins of **Old Sarum** cap a bleak hilltop two miles north of Salisbury city centre. Possibly occupied up to five thousand years ago, then developed as an Iron Age fort (whose double protective ditches remain), it was settled by Romans and Saxons before the Norman bishopric of Sherborne was moved here in the 1070s. Within a few decades, a new **cathedral** had been consecrated at Old Sarum, and a large religious community was living alongside the soldiers in the central **castle** founded by William the Conqueror fifty years before.

Old Sarum was an uncomfortable place, parched and windswept, and in 1220 the dissatisfied clergy – additionally at loggerheads with the castle's occupants – appealed to the pope for permission to decamp to Salisbury (which is still known officially as New Sarum). When permission was granted, the stone from the cathedral was commandeered for Salisbury's gateways; once the church had gone, the population waned, and by the sixteenth century Old Sarum was deserted. Today, the dominant features of the site are its ditches, banks and huge, two-tiered earthworks, with a broad trench encircling the rudimentary remains of the Norman palace, castle and cathedral.

Wilton House

Wilton • April to early Sept Mon–Thurs, Sun & bank hol Sat 11.30am–4.30pm; grounds April to early Sept daily 11am–5pm, also weekends in Sept • £14, under-16s £8, under-5s free; grounds only £5.50, under-16s £4, under-5s free • ☏ 01722 746700, Ⓦ wiltonhouse.com

Dominating its eponymous village five miles west of Salisbury, splendid **Wilton House** is home to the eighteenth Earl of Pembroke, whose descendants have occupied its stately rooms since the mid-sixteenth century. The original Tudor house, built on the site of a dissolved Benedictine abbey, was damaged by fire in 1647. It was rebuilt by Inigo Jones, whose hallmark Palladian style can be seen in the sumptuous Single Cube and Double Cube rooms, so called because of their precise dimensions. The **Double Cube Room**, in particular, is breathtakingly grand; it was designed specifically with the Fourth Earl of Pembroke's Van Dyck paintings in mind, and portraits such as *The Three Elder Children of Charles I* fit seamlessly onto its walls. The room hosted royalty from the get-go and is still used to entertain minor members of the monarchy today.

It's these easel **paintings** that make Wilton really special – in addition to Van Dyck, the collection includes works by Rembrandt, two of the Brueghel family, Poussin, Andrea del Sarto and Tintoretto, spread through only slightly less extravagant rooms throughout the first floor. In the grounds, the famous **Palladian Bridge** has been joined by various ancillary attractions including an excellent **adventure playground** and, in the **Old Riding School**, a film on the colourful earls of Pembroke.

ARRIVAL AND DEPARTURE

By train First Great Western and South West Trains serve Salisbury train station, half a mile west of the city centre, on South Western Road.

Destinations Basingstoke (every 30min; 30min); Bath Spa (hourly; 1hr); Bristol Temple Meads (hourly; 1hr 10min); Cardiff (hourly; 2hr); Crewkerne (hourly; 1hr); Exeter St Davids (hourly; 1hr 45min); London Waterloo (every 30min; 1hr 30min); Portsmouth (hourly; 1hr 20min); Southampton (every 30min; 30–40min); Woking (every 30min; 50min); Yeovil Junction (hourly; 45min).

By bus National Express and the Wilts & Dorset Cross Country buses run to and from the station on Endless Street, a short way north of Market Square.

SALISBURY AND AROUND

Destinations Bournemouth (frequent; 1hr 15min); Bristol (daily; 2hr 10min); London (3 daily; 2hr 45min–3hr 30min); Portsmouth (daily; 1hr 35min); Southampton (regular; 1hr 5min–1hr 35min).

By car The main roads into Salisbury can get clogged with traffic, making the five Park & Rides that ring the city (Mon–Fri 7.15am–7.30pm, Beehive from 6.45am, Sat 7.45am–7pm) a sensible option. They're at the Beehive (north of Salisbury, on the A345); London Road (northeast, on the A30); Britford and Petersfinger (southeast, on the A338/A354 and A36 respectively); and Wilton (west, on the A36/A30/A360). If you do drive into the centre, there are convenient car parks at Old George Mall and on Crane Bridge Road.

10

GETTING AROUND

Old Sarum Cross Country buses #5 and #8 run to Old Sarum every half-hour, while the hop-on-hop-off Stonehenge Tour bus (£11, children £5; ⓦ thestonehengetour.info) passes the ruins on its way to and from the stones.

Wilton House Local bus #3 takes less than 10min to get to Wilton from the city centre, stopping right outside Wilton House (every 20min).

INFORMATION AND TOURS

TOURIST INFORMATION

Tourist office Fish Row, just off Market Square (Mon–Sat 10am–5pm; ☏ 01722 334956, ⓦ visitsalisbury.com).

WALKS AND TOURS

Salisbury City Guides Informative daily city walks (April–Oct 11am; £4, children £2) and weekly ghost walks (May–Sept Fri 8pm; same prices), departing from the tourist office

(☏ 07873 212941, ⓦ salisburycityguides.co.uk).

Salisbury and Stonehenge Guided Tours Recommended city walks and food tours, plus tours of Stonehenge (see p.308) and Old Sarum (☏ 07775 674816, ⓦ salisburyguidedtours.com).

Harnham Water Meadows Trust Guided walks of the water meadows in summer (July & Aug Sat 2.30pm; £3; ☏ 01722 328162, ⓦ www.salisburywatermeadows.org.uk).

ACCOMMODATION

Byways House 31 Fowler's Rd ☏ 01722 328364, ⓦ bywayshouse.co.uk. Large guesthouse, more akin to a small hotel than a B&B, with 23 rooms of various shapes and sizes (singles from £39) and a little garden out the back. En-suite doubles cost £10 extra. **£55**

★ **Cathedral View** 83 Exeter St ☏ 01722 502254, ⓦ cathedral-viewbandb.co.uk. Welcoming B&B in a Georgian townhouse just a few minutes' walk from the Close – which perhaps explains why the thoughtful hosts have such a good knowledge of what to do in town. Comfortable en suites (one with a bath) have comfortable beds; as the name suggests, some street-facing rooms have views of the cathedral spire. Great choice at breakfast. No children under 10. No credit cards. **£75**

★ **The Lazy Cow** 9–13 St Johns St ☏ 01722 412028, ⓦ thelazycowsalisbury.co.uk. Sixteen creatively designed rooms, stylish with a large dose of fun – choose from Black & Gold (very bling), the Log Shack (a nice, natural look, with hefty wooden fittings) or the Moo Room, the most apt, given the steakhouse downstairs (see p.306), and with friesian throws and wall-length prints of highland cattle. All rooms have king-size beds and huge TVs, and

there's free wi-fi throughout. **£110**

The Old Mill Town Path, West Harnham, half a mile southwest of Salisbury ☏ 01722 327517, ⓦ simonandsteve.com. Wood-beamed riverside inn dating to the fifteenth century. Rooms are cute in a country-cottage kind of way, with some boasting great views across the meadows to the cathedral. **£75**

The Old Rectory 75 Belle Vue Rd ☏ 01722 502702, ⓦ theoldrectory-bb.co.uk. Once home to the rector of nearby St Edmund's Church (now Salisbury Arts Centre), this pleasant B&B, a short walk north of the centre, has three light, airy rooms, with one that can be made up as a twin and one a single (from £50). Breakfast is served in the conservatory overlooking the spacious back garden. Wi-fi throughout. No children under 12. No credit cards. **£64**

Salisbury Camping and Caravanning Club Hudson's Field, Castle Rd, a mile and a half north of Salisbury ☏ 01722 320713, ⓦ campingandcaravanningclub.co.uk. Full-scale but friendly campsite close to Old Sarum (and Old Sarum Airfield), with plenty of room for kids to run around in the field next door (Hudson's Field itself). It's a good set-up, though many of the pitches are on sloping ground. **£18**

SALISBURY INTERNATIONAL ARTS FESTIVAL

Arty Salisbury gets even artier for two weeks every summer when it hosts the themed **Salisbury International Arts Festival** (May/June; www.salisburyfestival.co.uk), a fortnight of events – many of them interactive – that celebrate the theatre, dance, film and food of a different country each year. Recent nations to get the treatment include India, Russia and China.

10

Salisbury YHA Milford Hill ☎01722 327572, w yha .org.uk. Atmospheric, two-hundred-year-old lodgings, slightly tired inside but nice enough, and with a range of dorms and rooms (four-bed family rooms from £66). Rate include breakfast. Camping pitches available in summe Dorms **£20.40**, under-18s **£15.50**

EATING AND DRINKING

★ **Gallery Café at Fisherton Mill** 108 Fisherton St ☎01722 500200, w fishertonmill.co.uk. Set in a rustic old grain mill that's now home to a very browsable art gallery, this is a top spot for a light but tasty lunch – bacon and Swiss cheese tart (£9.50), coconut and coriander broth (£9.95) or cheaper sandwiches – or a cuppa and a home-made cake. Also opens for dinner one weekend a month (mains, with a French feel, from £11). Tues–Fri 10am–5pm (lunch noon–2.30pm), Sat 9.30am–5.30pm.

★ **Haunch of Venison** 1 Minster St ☎01722 411313, w haunchofvenison.uk.com. Tiny, richly atmospheric boozer, where you could easily lose an hour or two cradling a pint of Hopback's GFB or Summer Lightning. Creaky wooden stairs lead to a first-floor restaurant serving lamb tagine, home-made Scotch egg and salad, and "old English dishes" like liver and onions; mains start at £8.50, though the haunch of venison itself will set you back £16.50. The pub's famous mummified hand of a nineteenth-century card player (still clutching his cards) has become a little bit too famous and was stolen (again) in 2011. Daily 11am–11pm, Sun noon–10.30pm.

The Lazy Cow 9–13 St Johns St ☎01722 412028, w thelazycowsalisbury.co.uk. Large, sleek steakhouse that sources its beef from Knightsbridge; grilled meats run from pavé of Black Angus steak (£10) through to a 28oz porterhouse for two (£50). Burgers, beef noodles and baby back ribs also available, plus a decent line in fresh shellfish (lobster, crab, Atlantic prawns). They're also open for breakfast – the steak and eggs (£9.25) is enough to set anyone up for the day. Mon–Fri 7am–3pm & 6–10pm, Sat 7am–10pm, Sun 7am–8pm.

the lemon tree 92 Crane St ☎01722 333471, w thelemontree.co.uk. Relaxed bistro just down from the North Gate, serving Mediterranean-influenced meals in the softly lit main room or the conservatory (mains, such as cod in blanket and stuffed courgette, from £9.50); slightly cheaper lunch menu (from £8.50). There's also a nice little patio for sunnier days. Mon–Sat 10am–3pm & 5.30–10pm.

The Mill 7 The Maltings ☎01722 412127. Centra riverside spot, with a vast, industrial-chic interior, an outdoor seating above the rushing weir. Pub gru includes good burgers such as red Leicester and spinach (£6.45), while the seasonal specials board features the likes of sweet potato, apricot and red pepper kebabs (£7.75). Daily 11am–11pm, Fri & Sat till midnigh (food served till 9pm).

Moloko Bar 5 Bridge St ☎01722 507050 w themolokobar.co.uk. Dark, modern joint, with two bars spread over three floors. Coffee is brewed all day, but this is more a place to end an evening, with vodkas (some fifty flavours) served till late. Tues, Wed & Sun 7pm–midnight, Thurs & Fri 5pm–late, Sat 1pm–late.

The Old Mill Town Path, West Harnham, half a mile southwest of Salisbury ☎01722 327517, w simonandsteve.com. Harnham's fifteenth-century paper mill enjoys a wonderful location on the Avon, and makes a good halfway stop for a pint of Abbot on a round-trip across the water meadows. Daily 11am–11pm.

Prezzo 52 High St ☎01722 341333, w prezzo restaurants.co.uk. Italian staples – pizza, risotti, a range of grills including crab cake and chicken gorgonzola – in an attractive timber-framed Tudor building close to the cathedral. Alfresco diners can enjoy sweeping views from the upstairs terrace. Pizza from £6.95, mains around £12. Daily noon–midnight.

The Wheatsheaf Lower Woodford, two miles from the A360 ☎01722 782203, w wheatsheaflowerwoodford .co.uk. There's a warm feeling to this Hall & Woodhouse pub, tucked away at the bottom of the lovely Woodford Valley on the back road to Old Sarum. The food – jackets and baguettes, larder boards for sharing (£11.95) and pub classics branded here as "Heritage Cooking" (from £7.45) – is simple but satisfying, the interior varied (open in parts, cosier in others) and the service friendly. Daily 11am–11pm.

NTERTAINMENT

s well as the events staged at the two venues below, there's a busy calendar of musical performances throughout the city at the cathedral, Sarum St Martin (ⓦsarumstmartin.org.uk) and St Thomas, among others. For a diary of lunchtime oncerts, organ recitals, opera and the like, see ⓦmusicinsalisbury.org.

alisbury Arts Centre St Edmund's Church, Bedwin St ⓟ01722 321744, ⓦsalisburyartscentre.co.uk. The old hurch of St Edmund's makes a great venue for an eclectic rogramme of music, theatre, film and dance, including everal interesting Family Day events.

alisbury Playhouse Malthouse Lane ⓟ01722 20333, ⓦsalisburyplayhouse.com. Respected regional theatre producing a wide range of contemporary plays, plus costume dramas, pantomimes and comedies. Extras

include behind-the-scenes Theatre Days, post-show discussions and backstage tours.

Salisbury Racecourse Netherhampton, 4 miles west of the city ⓟ01722 326461, ⓦsalisburyracecourse .co.uk. One of the oldest racecourses in the country, hosting fifteen flat races a season (May to mid-Oct), which normally attract a quality field. Tickets (£6–20; under-16s free) are cheaper when booked in advance.

10

Stonehenge

No ancient structure in England arouses more controversy than **Stonehenge**, a mysterious ring of monoliths ten miles north of Salisbury. While archeologists argue over whether it was a place of ritual sacrifice or sun worship, an astronomical calculator or a royal palace, the guardians of the site struggle to accommodate its year-round crowds. Conservation of Stonehenge is an urgent priority, and unless you arrange for special access (see box, p.308), you must be content with walking around rather than among the stones, equipped with handsets that dispense a range of information.

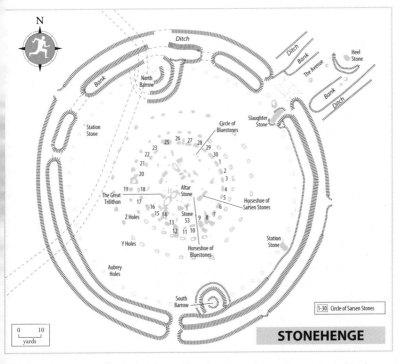

1-30 Circle of Sarsen Stones

STONEHENGE

10

> A **henge** consists of a circular ditch enclosed by a bank, a feature best seen at Woodhenge (see p.313) and Durrington Walls (see p.313) – but not, ironically, at Stonehenge, which despite giving rise to the name in the first place is not actually a henge at all.

INFORMATION

Opening hours Daily: mid-March to May & Sept to mid-Oct 9.30am–6pm; June–Aug 9am–7pm; mid-Oct to mid-March 9.30am–4pm.

Entry fee £7.50, children £4.50; NT & EH.

Tours Numerous companies run tours to Stonehenge, including The Stonehenge Tour Company (ⓦstonehenge tours.com), Salisbury and Stonehenge Guided Tours (☎07775 674816, ⓦsalisburyguidedtours.com) and HisTOURies (☎020 7193 6065, ⓦhistouries.co.uk), with departures from Salisbury, Bath, Glastonbury and London, among others. Several also incorporate the highly recommended Stone Circle Access in their itineraries (see

box below), though it's easy enough to book this direc[t] with English Heritage.

Contacts EH ☎0870 333 1181, ⓦwww.english-heritag[e] .org.uk/stonehenge; NT ☎01960 664780, ⓦnationaltru[st] .org.uk/stonehengelandscape.

Getting there You can reach Stonehenge from Salisbur[y] on either the A345 (via Amesbury) or the A360. The hop[-] on-hop-off Stonehenge Tour bus (£11, children £[5] ⓦthestonehengetour.info) picks up from Salisbury tra[in] and bus stations and from Old Sarum (see p.304), takin[g] just over half an hour from the train station.

The site

What exists at Stonehenge today is only a part of the original prehistoric complex, as many of the outlying stones were plundered for building materials, while posts have rotted away and ditches filled in over time. The site's **construction** is thought to have taken place in phases, starting with the surrounding earthworks and ending – nearly 1500 years later and with a few lengthy periods of inactivity in between – with the fina[l] adjustments to the great stone circle.

Specific dates within that timescale are open to debate, and archeologists still struggle to agree on the timings of some pretty significant events, including at what stage the first bluestones arrived from Wales and when the sarsen circle was actually erected. Thanks to advances in geophysical technology, our knowledge of Stonehenge is constantly evolving. In the mid-1990s, new discoveries aged the whole structure a thousand years overnight, while excavations of the Aubrey Holes in 2008 showed that the bluestones may have been here by 3000 BC, some five hundred years earlier than was originally thought. Incredibly, as the site enters its fifth millennium, the story continues...

The first Stonehenge (c.3015–2935 BC)

The creation of Stonehenge began over 5000 years ago with the bank and outer ditch that still surround the stones today. There were at least two entrances into the circle:

INSIDE THE CIRCLE

Since 1978, a low, looping rope has encircled Stonehenge, keeping visitors at bay and, to a certain extent, adding to its general sense of mystery. While the path that runs around the perimeter is perfect for taking in the scale of its construction, you can only appreciate the primordial power of Stonehenge from within. Venturing inside the sarsens, wandering among the bluestones and getting close enough to make out the etchings of ancient graffiti is an experience to turn even the sternest of sceptics.

English Heritage's one-hour **Stone Circle Access** (book well in advance on ☎01722 343834; £15.30, under-16s £9.20, under-5s free; EH; no visits Tues or Wed mornings, no visits Oct or Nov) allows you to do exactly that. As the name implies, it's not a guided tour, just a chance to visit outside of hours (the earliest "access" is at 5am in summer, the latest 8.45pm), when the site is quiet, the crowds have all gone home or are yet to arrive, and the A303 is merely an occasional hum in the background.

STONEHENGE TODAY: A "NATIONAL DISGRACE"?

Few people forget their first sight of Stonehenge: hemmed in by busy roads, cordoned off by rope and shielded by a high chain-link fence, and – at the time of writing, at least – lacking an interpretation centre of any kind. To round things off, the A344 ploughs right through the Avenue, virtually clipping the Heel Stone on its way to the car park. Is this really the way to treat the most important Neolithic site in the world?

Of course not, but then the powers that be have spent the best part of thirty years trying to agree on a solution to this long-running dilemma, an embarrassing state of affairs that once led a parliamentary committee to condemn the site as "a national disgrace". A whole range of ideas were toyed with and eventually discarded – it wasn't too long ago that plans were afoot to tunnel the A303 under the Plains completely, though the £550 million price tag ultimately put paid to that. At last, though, in June 2010, Wiltshire council gave the go-ahead for a **new visitor centre** and car park to be built at Airman's Corner, from where a transit system will ferry visitors the mile and a half down to the stones. The section of road between Airman's Corner and the A303 will be closed and grassed over, reconnecting Stonehenge with the Avenue and finally fulfilling a commitment made to UNESCO when Stonehenge was inscribed as a World Heritage Site back in 1986.

At the time of writing, work was scheduled to start in April 2012, with the centre to be completed by October 2013. For more on the plans, and for the latest updates, see ⓦ stonehengevisitorcentre.org.

10

one aligned with the midsummer sunrise, to the northeast (which became the **main entrance**), and the other to the south, by the South Barrow. Just inside the banks is a ring of 56 pits (a sacred number), now marked by little concrete plaques; known as **Aubrey Holes** after the antiquarian John Aubrey, who discovered them in the seventeenth century, these are now thought to have contained **bluestones** from the Preseli Hills in Wales, which were later moved inside the sarsen circle.

The timber phase and the bluestones (c.2900–2600 BC)

Post holes show that not long after the banks were dug **wooden posts** were irregularly erected around the two entrances and in a zig-zagging passageway that ran from the southern entrance into the centre. Despite numerous excavations, nothing has been found in these – the wooden posts themselves disintegrated hundreds of years ago – though it was during this same period that the Aubrey Holes were filled with a mixture of earth and human ash, proving that one of Stonehenge's first uses was as a ceremonial monument and cemetery.

According to the most recent excavations, it was also during this phase that a double arc of approximately eighty great blocks of **bluestone** (a collective name for the various "foreign" stones at Stonehenge) was raised within the enclosure itself. Some archeologists have suggested that these monoliths were found lying on Salisbury Plain, having been borne down from the Welsh mountains by a glacier in the last Ice Age, but the lack of any other glacial debris on the plain would seem to disprove this theory. It really does seem to be the case that the stones were cut from quarries over 150 miles away and dragged or floated here on rafts, a prodigious task which has defeated recent attempts to emulate it.

The sarsens (c.2580–2470 BC)

The crucial phase in the creation of the site came during the next hundred years, when the bluestones were replaced with colossal **sarsens**, the "precious unhewn stones of Eden" according to William Blake's *Jerusalem*. Shaped from Marlborough Downs sandstone, they were erected in a circle of thirty stones (seventeen of which remain), topped by lintels, and carefully dressed and worked – for example, to compensate for perspectival distortion, the uprights have a slight swelling in the middle, the same trick the builders of the Parthenon were to employ hundreds of years later.

Four **Station Stones**, only two of which survive, were also raised at this time (the positions of the other two are marked by the North and South Barrows), as were the three sarsens that marked the main entrance to the circle. These all stood upright, meaning the remaining stone, now known as the **Slaughter Stone**, could never have fulfilled the role of sacrificial altar that the Victorians so theatrically bequeathed it. The **Heel Stone**, standing in the middle of the Avenue (see p.313), was originally one of a pair, the gap between them aligning precisely with the rising sun on midsummer's morning.

10

The trilithons

Within the sarsen circle itself, a matching perimeter of bluestones was constructed around a horseshoe of five mammoth **trilithons** (two uprights crossed by a lintel), one – known as **stone 53** – carved with images of Bronze Age axeheads and a dagger resembling those from ancient Mycenae in Greece. The lintels in both the main circle and the sarsen horseshoe were held in place by mortise and tenon joints; the bobble topping the surviving upright of the **Great Trilithon** (45 tonnes of stone on its own) is a very visible example of the woodworking techniques that still keep some of the circle together.

Realigning the stones (c.2280–1930 BC)

The final phase of building at Stonehenge saw the bluestones rearranged a number of times, finishing with a horseshoe setting that reflected the surrounding horseshoe sarsens. At their enclosed end – and partly hidden under the fallen upright and lintel of the Great Trilithon – lies the **Altar Stone**, a huge block of sandstone discovered by Inigo Jones during the first study of Stonehenge in 1620. Jones was markedly more adept at architecture than archeology, and named the stone to fit in with his theory that the site was once a Roman temple, rather than after any concrete archeological evidence.

The Z & Y Holes (c.2020–1740 & c.1630–1520 BC)

The last work carried out at Stonehenge was the creation of two concentric rings outside the circle, known as the **Z Holes** and the later **Y Holes**. The holes were never filled, so whether this phase – coming at a very late stage in Stonehenge's ceremonial life – was left unfinished, or whether the pits were used for something entirely different, remains unknown.

Their purpose – and indeed, the purpose of all the work at Stonehenge – remains baffling. The symmetry and location of the site (a slight rise in a flat valley with even views of the horizon in all directions), as well as its alignment towards the points of sunrise and sunset on the summer and winter solstices, tend to support the supposition that it was some sort of temple to the sun or a time-measuring device – though it has come to mean much to druidic orders, their association with the circle was a mid-eighteenth-century invention. Whatever it was, Stonehenge ceased to be used at around 1600 BC, and by the Middle Ages it had become a "landmark".

THE SUMMER SOLSTICE

Heralding sunrise on the longest day of the year, the **summer solstice** (W www.english-heritage .org.uk) was once a guaranteed flashpoint between New Age travellers and the police. But since 2000 – fifteen years after open access was withdrawn following the notorious Battle of the Beanfield – it has been a relaxed and trouble-free event, despite drawing a mixed crowd of thirty thousand or so druids, hippies, travellers and interested observers.

The site opens at 7pm the evening before the summer solstice (usually around June 21) and closes at 8am the following morning, with the sun creeping up over the stones at around 5am. Buses ferry people from Salisbury train station to West Amesbury, about a mile from Stonehenge (departing every 10min between 6.30pm and 1.15am, returning less frequently between 4am and 9.45am; 20min; £9 return). You can park at the site, about half a mile from the stones themselves.

Stonehenge World Heritage Site

Only a fraction of the visitors who pull into the car park at Stonehenge explore beyond the famous circle, and while the burial mounds and earthworks that make up the rest of the **Stonehenge World Heritage Site** can't match its visual drama, they hold just as much interest as the stones – with many, including **the Cursus**, predating them by over a thousand years. This is one of the richest ceremonial landscapes in Europe, yet despite the finds at **Durrington Walls** and **Woodhenge** and the obvious presence of dozens of round barrows dotted among the wild-flower meadows, archeologists have only scratched the surface.

10

INFORMATION

It's easy enough to visit the main attractions around Stonehenge on your own, but a guided tour will give you a much deeper insight into the history of this ancient landscape. The Cursus, the Cursus Barrows and the Avenue are accessed off the A344; Durrington Walls and Woodhenge are on the A345; and the Winterbourne Stoke Barrows and Normanton Down Barrows are reached via footpaths leading off the A303. There are car parks at Stonehenge and Woodhenge.

Access The Stonehenge World Heritage Site is owned by a hotchpotch of organizations and individuals, including English Heritage and the National Trust, the Ministry of Defence, local farmers and private homeowners. The Cursus, the Cursus Barrows, the Avenue and King Barrows Ridge are on National Trust open-access land, while the other sites covered below can be reached by public footpath.

Tours Some of the best tours are with Salisbury and Stonehenge Guided Tours (☎07775 674816,

ⓦ salisburyguidedtours.com), whose tailor-made trips around Durrington Walls, the Cursus and other major sites are led by an informative guide with experience of working on excavations in the area. The National Trust runs an extensive programme of popular walks, including a highly recommended quarterly guided trip with an expert NT archeologist (£15; 5hr); for details, call ☎01960 664780 or see ⓦ nationaltrust.org.uk /stonehengelandscape.

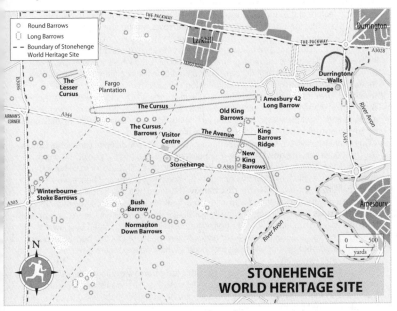

STONEHENGE WORLD HERITAGE SITE

The Cursus

Daily dawn–dusk • Free

The huge, drawn-out ellipse of **the Cursus**, or Greater Cursus (there's a Lesser Cursus nearby), stretches for nearly two miles across the fields north of Stonehenge. A 500ft-wide wedge, framed by two parallel sets of banks and ditches, it starts just beyond the trees of the Fargo Plantation (the gap between the copses is the Cursus) and finishes at a long barrow on King Barrows Ridge, a fact not properly established until 2008, when the Stonehenge Riverside Project discovered an enclosing ditch at its eastern end.

The Cursus was kept clean, but the few finds that have been made date it to around 3500 BC, some four hundred years before Early Neolithic man had even started thinking about constructing the first phase of Stonehenge. William Stukeley, the antiquarian who discovered it in 1723, believed it had been used for chariot racing – *cursus* is Latin for racetrack. Modern-day archeologists aren't much closer to the truth, but the fact that it was too long and too low to be used as a defensive structure makes it likely to have been a ceremonial monument.

The Cursus Barrows

Daily dawn–dusk • Free

Running partway along the southern side of the Cursus – and a useful landmark for finding it in the first place – **the Cursus Barrows** are the closest group to Stonehenge and one of the few features in the wider landscape to receive significant numbers of visitors. Like many of the barrows around Stonehenge (see box below), they are Bronze Age Beaker burial mounds, a mixture of bowl barrows and bell barrows that revealed fragments of pottery and amber beads when they were excavated by William Stukeley in 1723 and William Cunnington a century later.

BARROWS: THE LONG AND THE ROUND OF IT

A defining feature of the landscape around Stonehenge, the conical humps that surge through the fields alongside the A303 are **round barrows**, Bronze Age burial mounds that appeared after the circle itself was built. Although often found alone, many round barrows were constructed in groups, with up to half a dozen individuals (usually family members) interred in satellite graves around a central primary mound, the whole acting as a kind of vertical cemetery. The vast majority were excavated during the eighteenth and nineteenth centuries by William Stukeley, William Cunnington and Sir Richard Colt Hoare, the owner of Stourhead. Their discoveries of grave goods – pottery, arrowheads, and jewellery made of gold and jet – has shaped much of our understanding of Beaker culture, but their rudimentary methods and incomplete digs (lacking the technology to analyze human remains, they simply reburied them) effectively ruined the sites for later archeologists.

On closer inspection, it is fairly easy to distinguish between the different varieties of barrow. The most common, the **bowl barrow**, resembles an upturned pudding bowl and is usually surrounded by a ditch. The similar-looking **bell barrow** (generally used for male burials) is separated from its ditch by a gently sloping shelf (known as a berm), and hence has a very vague bell-like shape to it, while the **disc barrow** is defined by a much smaller mound and therefore a much wider shelf, and with an external bank enclosing its ditch. The mounds on **saucer barrows** (generally used for female burials) are much less distinct, while rarer **pond barrows** have no mound at all, with a hollow (rather than a ditch) enclosed by a lower bank than you'd find on a saucer barrow. Pond barrows were often used for "sky burials", wooden platforms supported by stilts and piled with bodies, which were exposed to the elements until only the bones remained.

The area contains far fewer examples of Neolithic **long barrows**, oblong-shaped burial mounds that often widen and rise at one end and were – unlike the later round barrows – used as communal burial chambers; there are notable examples at the western end of the Winterbourne Stoke group and behind King Barrows Ridge.

King Barrows Ridge

Daily dawn–dusk • Free

The various burial mounds on **King Barrows Ridge** are some of the largest in the area – normally an indication of age, but as these date from around 2500 BC, more likely a symbol of their occupants' importance, particularly as they run right across the route of the ceremonially significant Avenue. On the winter solstice, the area's inhabitants would have crossed the ridge after celebrating the sunset at Stonehenge on their way to watching the midwinter sunrise at Durrington Walls. The beech trees that surround the **New King Barrows** inadvertently saved these from inquisitive Victorian archeologists, meaning that they may still hold valuable clues to unlocking some of Stonehenge's secrets.

The track running behind the ridge (and leading down to Woodhenge) traces the top of **Amesbury 42 Long Barrow**, which dates to the same time as the Cursus but has been added to over time; ironically, the track protected the barrow from the ravages of ploughing and continues to keep the roots of trees at bay.

10

The Avenue

Daily dawn–dusk • Free

Despite its measured appearance, **the Avenue** is largely a natural feature, its almost imperceivable gully (marked by two parallel ditches) the result of detritus being dragged across the landscape during the last Ice Age. By remarkable coincidence, it was carved in a position that aligned exactly with both the midsummer sunrise and midwinter sunset – it is because of the Avenue, therefore, that Stonehenge was built here at all. Used as a ceremonial pathway, it was lengthened in the later Bronze Age and now doglegs over King Barrows Ridge and down to the River Avon; in 2009, the Stonehenge Riverside Project (see box, p.314) discovered a series of post holes by the river, a ring (dubbed "**Bluestonehenge**") that once held several of the Preseli stones that now stand inside the main circle itself.

Walking the original section back from King Barrows Ridge is by far the **best approach to Stonehenge**, and will be even more so when the A344 is grassed over (see box, p.309); the stones intermittently pop in and out of view until you crest the hill and see them looming directly ahead, the Avenue running past the Heel Stone and on into the circle.

Woodhenge

Daily dawn–dusk • Free

Compared to the mighty sarsens of Stonehenge, there's a lot less charisma about the reputedly significant Bronze Age site of **Woodhenge**, two miles to the northeast. The site consists of a circular bank about 220ft in diameter enclosing a ditch and six concentric rings of post holes, which would originally have held timber uprights, possibly supporting a roofed building of some kind; in 2006, it was discovered that standing stones were later erected on the same site. The holes are now marked more durably (if less romantically) by concrete pillars – those with black tops signify where a hole was found that did not fit into the regular pattern. A child's grave was discovered at the centre of the rings, suggesting that it may have been a place of ritual sacrifice.

Durrington Walls

Daily dawn–dusk • Free

In a landscape of burial mounds and ritual sites to the dead, **Durrington Walls**, the largest complete henge in Britain, is unique. Various finds of grooved-ware pottery and half-eaten animal bones (known as "feasting assemblages") had already established this

10

ALL IN THE NAME OF RESEARCH

With only a fraction of the World Heritage Site excavated so far, the one thing we know about Stonehenge that everyone can agree on is that we don't really know that much. A catalogue of key discoveries made by the **Stonehenge Riverside Project** over the last few years has gone a long way to increasing our knowledge but has also meant rewriting several parts of the story. The SRP, a supergroup of British archeologists led by Professor Mike Parker Pearson from Sheffield University, found that the Avenue was actually a periglacial feature that was extended rather than constructed completely, while their work around Durrington Walls proved that this was a year-round town and not simply a place for seasonal feasts. Their excavations of the Aubrey Holes around Stonehenge (see p.309), meanwhile, have turned conventional thinking on its head, pointing to the fact that Stonehenge has been a stone monument for a lot longer than we thought.

as a place where people *lived* when, in 2005, archeologists working on the Stonehenge Riverside Project (see box above) discovered the chalk floors of houses near the River Avon. They were so well preserved that even the hearthside indents remained where the occupants had kneeled down to rake out the ashes.

The houses were part of a vast village, the largest late Neolithic settlement in northern Europe, dispelling the notion that Durrington Walls was a temporary gathering place for ceremonial feasts. Given that they dated to the exact time the sarsens were going up at the great circle a couple of miles to the southwest, it is now thought that Durrington was in fact home to the builders of Stonehenge. The theory is lent more credence by the discovery that the earthworks were built after the houses, almost as if its creators wanted to seal it off as a kind of memorial.

The houses were covered up after the dig, and today Durrington Walls is again little more than the remains of a ditch and bank, albeit an enormous one, spreading for 550yds in a sweeping arc that is now partly cut through by the A345. You can't really get an idea of its size until you're standing inside it, in the area that was originally used for rituals and that once contained a number of timber circles, now mostly buried under the tarmac. The entrance to one of these, the **Southern Circle**, is aligned with the midwinter sunrise, the mirror image of Stonehenge. Like Stonehenge, Durrington Walls was connected to the River Avon by an "avenue", the river therefore effectively linking the land of the living with the resting place for the dead.

Normanton Down Barrows

Daily dawn–dusk • Free

Just west of Stonehenge, a turning left off the A303 leads half a mile down a bumpy, progressively rutted byway to **Normanton Down Barrows**, a fifty-strong round-barrow cemetery that contained the richest haul of Bronze Age grave goods found on Salisbury Plain. In 1808, while excavating a huge burial mound known as **Bush Barrow**, William Cunnington discovered the skeleton of an adult male, dating to around 1800 BC, who was surrounded by a treasure-trove of weapons and ornamentation: a bronze axe; bronze and copper daggers (traced back to Brittany); a fossil mace head, similar to those found at burial sites in Greece and Spain; and, most lavish of all, two diamond-shaped gold "lozenges" and a unique gold belt hook. All the gold objects were very delicately worked, with the same parallel patterns of engraved lines on each; they're now on display at the Wiltshire Heritage Museum in Devizes.

Most of the barrows are on private land, but a few (including Bush Barrow) can be accessed on public footpaths.

Winterbourne Stoke Barrows

Daily dawn–dusk • Free

West of Stonehenge, a path from the A303 leads briefly through woodland to **Winterbourne Stoke Barrows**, over twenty barrows that encompass some two thousand years of ritual burial practices. The round barrows – bowl, bell, disc and the much rarer pond barrow – run in a line northeast from a well-preserved long barrow and are topped with shaggy wildflower meadow. You can climb the one closest to the road for far-reaching views of Salisbury Plain and the grey dots of Stonehenge in the distance, though the noise from the adjoining roads detracts from the ambience somewhat.

10

RED DEER, EXMOOR

Contexts

History

For much of the last 500,000 years Somerset was covered by ice and snow, though this period was interspersed with warmer phases. The oldest evidence of human life in the region – and probably in the whole of Britain – is worked flints found in Westbury-sub-Mendip, from around 480,000 years ago, while Taunton's Museum of Somerset has examples of hand-axes from up to 400,000 years ago. Remains from about 12,000 BC have been found in the Cheddar Gorge, and a skeleton known as Cheddar Man has been dated to around 7000 BC – making him Britain's oldest complete skeleton.

Farming began about 6000 years ago, allowing people to settle year-round in permanent dwellings rather than being on the move in pursuit of prey and with the changing of the seasons. Funerary and religious shrines acquired special significance during this era, marked by numerous barrows (burial mounds) – such as that at **Stony Littleton** – and stone cairns, many found on the Mendip and Quantock hills and on Exmoor. Stone circles such as those at **Stanton Drew** and **Stonehenge** appeared in the late Neolithic and early Bronze Age (around 3500–2000 BC), though our knowledge about the purpose and function of these sites remains frustratingly slender. Pottery developed, important for the storage of food, metalworking began around 2500 BC, and the Bronze Age (roughly 3200–600 BC) saw the development of trade that extended beyond the British Isles.

During the late Bronze and early Iron Age (which began in the region around 650 BC), tribal territories became more defined and hill forts proliferated – important centres of crafts, trade and industry as well as power-bases. The most significant ones were at **Ham Hill** – one of the biggest in Europe – and **Cadbury Castle**, though this site had been occupied for centuries beforehand. Smaller hill forts have been excavated at **Dolebury Warren**, in the Mendips; **Worlebury Hill**, outside Weston-super-Mare; **Solsbury Hill**, outside Bath; and **Brent Knoll**, near Burnham-on-Sea. Later on, lowland settlements became more established, for example the **Glastonbury Lake Villages** – settlements built on man-made islands in the Somerset Levels and specializing in jewellery and crafted artefacts.

In the course of the **Iron Age**, the territory was dominated by Celtic tribal groupings: the **Dobunni**, occupying the area now approximately covered by Gloucestershire and North Somerset, with their capital at present-day Cirencester; the **Belgae** and **Durotriges** to the south; and the **Dumnonii** in what is now West Somerset and Devon. These peoples were primarily farmers, shepherds and craftsmen, not warlike, and for the most part they quickly submitted to Roman rule, blending easily into the new Romano-British culture.

7000 BC	4000 BC	47 AD	410
Cheddar Man (now preserved as Britain's oldest complete skeleton) dies.	Farming develops in Somerset. Permanent settlements are established, replacing nomadic communities.	The Romans reach Somerset; Bath is developed as a Roman spa town soon after.	The Romans leave Britain, but Romano-British culture survives.

Romans, Saxons and Danes

The peaceful integration of present-day Somerset into the Roman Empire was effected soon after the **Roman invasion** in 43 AD. The new regime undertook some major changes, including the deforestation of large areas and the building of such roads as the **Fosse Way**, which bisected Somerset on its route between Lincoln and Exeter. Roman Somerset was governed from **Ilchester**, a town on the Fosse Way, and Romano-British villas and bath complexes were scattered from **Pitney** to **Bruton**, though none so elaborate as the one at **Bath** itself, the only hot springs in Britain. The Romans also greatly expanded the mining activity that was already underway in parts of the region, particularly lead mining in the **Mendip Hills**.

Little is known about the region in the period following the Roman departure from Britain in around 410, but it is likely that the Romano-British culture endured for some decades afterwards. Eventually, though, Angles, Saxons and other Germanic peoples rushed in to fill the void during the sixth and seventh centuries. The shadowy figure of **King Arthur** – connected at least in myth with Glastonbury (see box, p.169) and Cadbury Castle (see box, p.196) – may have lived during this time, leading the Celtic Britons in their resistance to the newcomers. What is more certain is that the Britons suffered a major defeat at **Dyrham**, north of Bath, in 577, and the Saxons reached the River Parrett by around 660. By 845, Somerset formed part of the West Saxon kingdom of **Wessex**, whose capital was Winchester.

By this time, however, the **Danes** were already making incursions into the area, causing the Wessex king, **Alfred the Great**, to withdraw to **Athelney**, protected by the marshes of the **Somerset Levels**. In 878, Alfred rallied his forces to win a historic victory at Edington, near Westbury in eastern Wiltshire, blocking the Danish advance. The same year, a treaty dividing up southern England between Alfred and Guthrum, the Danish leader, was agreed at **Wedmore**, on the northern fringes of the Levels.

Wessex was the major bulwark against the Danes during the tenth century, but despite constant harassment Somerset itself was relatively unscathed. Edgar was crowned king of England in Bath Abbey in 973, and Christian foundations flourished, most notably **Glastonbury Abbey**, whose abbot Dunstan (909–988) was responsible for reforming the English monastic system and became Archbishop of Canterbury. The now-Christianized Danes tightened their grip on Wessex, culminating in the coronation of Cnut (or Canute) as king of England in 1016.

The Middle Ages

Having conquered England in 1066, the **Normans** maintained control by means of a chain of motte-and-bailey fortifications – essentially a mound surmounted by a keep and surrounded by a wall – throughout their new realm, including at **Dunster** and **Montacute**. Somerset, once at the heart of national life, found itself marginalized as William I established his capital in London rather than Winchester. As well as centralizing the government, the Normans consolidated trade and opened up European markets. Much of Somerset's growing wealth in the Middle Ages derived from the flourishing **wool and cloth industry**, centred in such towns as **Bradford-on-Avon**, **Frome**, **Yeovil** and **Taunton**. Landowners, merchants and other beneficiaries flaunted their prosperity by building and enriching churches, especially in the late medieval period

577	**878**	**1066**
The Britons suffer an overwhelming defeat by the Saxons at Dyrham, allowing the Saxons to occupy the Somerset region, which eventually becomes part of Wessex.	Alfred rallies his forces to win a decisive victory over the Danes at Edington. The Danish threat to Wessex is temporarily averted.	William, duke of Normandy, conquers England and moves capital from Winchester to Lon Somerset loses its central role.

- most of Somerset's exquisitely carved church towers, for example, date from 1450 to 1540. As well as parish churches, great cathedrals and abbeys were erected or rebuilt in Bristol, Bath, Wells, Glastonbury and Salisbury, their magnificence often funded with money accrued from the huge landholdings they possessed – Glastonbury Abbey, for example, became one of the richest monastic houses in the country.

Many of the great treasures acquired by these institutions were destroyed during the **Dissolution of the Monasteries** – Henry VIII's radical appropriation of church property in the 1530s – while some houses were completely demolished. Parish churches, too, were vandalized in the puritanical zeal of the **Reformation**, losing much of their stained glass and statuary – though some items survived, such as the marvellous oak bench-ends still to be seen in the churches of the **Quantock Hills**. The landed gentry benefited from the decline of ecclesiastical power, with many former church estates converted into grand houses such as that at **Lacock Abbey**, taken over by Sir William Sharington in 1540.

Somehow, through all of these tumultuous events, trade continued to prosper. Warfare and commerce together engendered a strong seafaring tradition, and **Bristol** was fast becoming one of England's foremost ports. It was from here in 1497 that **John Cabot** sailed on the *Matthew* to what is now thought to have been Newfoundland – the first European to have set foot in North America since the Norsemen (see box, p.97). Claiming the land on behalf of the crown, the Anglo-Italian sailor set in motion a long relationship between Bristol and the New World, for which the Bristol Channel became a major trading thoroughfare.

The English Civil War and the Monmouth Rebellion

In the Elizabethan and Jacobean periods, the wealthy directed their resources away from churches and castles and to their own abodes, and some of the region's greatest palaces, such as **Longleat**, date from this period. In the 1640s, Somerset was embroiled in the **Civil War**; most of the region's towns supported the Parliamentary cause, but many local families were divided in their loyalties. Large centres such as Bristol, Taunton and Bridgwater changed hands several times, and there were major engagements at **Langport**, in the Somerset Levels, **Dunster Castle** and **Lansdown**, outside Bath. Fortunes oscillated, but by 1645 almost the whole county was held by Parliament.

The reconciliation brought about by the **Restoration** of Charles II in 1660 proved all too brief. Like all of the king's other progeny, Charles's favourite son, James, duke of Monmouth, was illegitimate and so could not inherit the throne, but this did not prevent him from becoming the focus of Protestant opposition to the new king, the Catholic James II. Returning from exile in Holland in 1685, Monmouth landed unopposed in Lyme Regis to launch the **Monmouth Rebellion** (see box, p.218). Assured of support in Somerset, he gathered forces en route and was proclaimed king in Taunton. However, the venture ended soon after with the duke's catastrophic defeat at **Sedgemoor** (or more accurately Westonzoyland), near Bridgwater, the last pitched battle on English soil, when more than three hundred rebels died and a further thousand were slaughtered as they fled (see box, p.182). A wave of oppression against the rebels was unleashed under Judge Jeffreys, who held two of his so-called **Bloody Assizes** in Wells and Taunton. Altogether, more than 1400 were tried, at least 300 were sentenced to be hanged and nearly 750 were transported to the West Indies. Three years later, James II

1536–39	1642–1649	1685
Henry VIII orders the Dissolution of the Monasteries, one of the defining events of the Reformation in England.	The Civil War breaks out between the Royalists, led by Charles I, and Parliament, ending with the execution of the king.	The Monmouth Rebellion led by the Protestant Duke of Monmouth against his Catholic uncle, James II, is crushed, and Bloody Assizes are set up across the county.

was faced with another insurrection and was forced to flee the country when William of Orange landed in Torbay in the near-bloodless **Glorious Revolution** of 1688.

Bristol, meanwhile, was continuing to thrive as one of the country's great maritime cities. As well as its important trading role, it contributed to the settlement and colonization of the New World. Admiral William Penn, for example, took possession of Jamaica for the Lord Protector, Oliver Cromwell, in 1655, and his son, also called William Penn, established the Quaker colony of Pennsylvania in 1681, to which he (unwillingly) gave his name. Increasingly, however, Bristol's relations with the New World hinged on the **slave trade** – specifically the "triangular trade", whereby manufactured goods were exported to West Africa, the ships then transporting slaves to the West Indies from where they would bring sugar, tobacco and rum back to Bristol (see box, p.105).

The Georgian era

In contrast to the strife of the previous hundred years, the eighteenth century saw an extended period of peace – at least at home – and the growth of polite society. Bristol's burgeoning New World markets and the profits of the slave trade helped to finance grand mansions throughout the city, not least in its **Clifton** suburb. An even more dramatic transformation took place in Bath at about the same time, as the alleged health benefits of its spa waters made it an essential stop for England's fashionable elite. Its new status was reflected in a complete renovation of the city, filling it with architecture that revived classical Greek and Roman designs as filtered through the Italian Renaissance (courtesy of the sixteenth-century architect Andrea Palladio). During **Bath's Golden Age** (see box, p.55), the city became a centre for the arts – drawing writers such as **Jane Austen** and portrait painters such as **Thomas Gainsborough** – as well as sciences, at least in the person of **William Herschel**, who discovered (along with his sister) the planet Uranus in 1781.

It wasn't just the cities that witnessed significant changes during the eighteenth century: Somerset's grandees enhanced their rural seats with the help of some of the finest architects of the era, as at **Stourhead**, while designers such as **Capability Brown** were called in to apply the latest landscaping techniques to the parks of the great houses, as at **Longleat**. Elsewhere in the county, coalfields were opened up around **Radstock** in the 1760s, and a brick- and tile-manufacturing industry was established in **Bridgwater**. In the latter part of the century, large tracts of central Somerset were reclaimed from the marshes, increasing the productivity of the land, while agricultural reforms also helped to revive rural areas.

The Victorian age

Bath lost much of its kudos during the **nineteenth century**, but Bristol forged ahead. While the abolition in 1807 of the slave trade that had underpinned much of the city's prosperity seriously dented its commercial strength, the city was reinvigorated by **Isambard Kingdom Brunel**'s construction of the broad-gauge Great Western Railway between London and Bristol in 1841 (it was extended to Bridgwater and Taunton in the same year). Improved communications also came about through canal- and road-building, ending the isolation of much of the county. Somerset was soon criss-crossed by a dense network of railway lines owned by different companies (though

1700–1750	1720–1760	1763	1807
Bath experiences a "Golden Age", becoming a hub of high society, and is rebuilt along Palladian lines.	Bristol's slave trade reaches its peak, with Bristol vessels carrying one third of Britain's total slave shipments in 1756.	Collieries start operating around Radstock, part of the great expansion of the Somerset coalfield.	Abolition of the slave trade, leading to the collapse of Bristol's trade with the West Indies.

these were cut to the bone in the 1960s). This greater ease of travel facilitated the growth of mass tourism in the later nineteenth century, leading to the development of Somerset's major seaside resorts, **Weston-super-Mare**, **Clevedon** and **Minehead**. Brunel also applied his genius to other engineering feats in Bristol, such as the first iron-clad ocean-going ship, the **ss Great Britain**, built in Bristol in 1843, and the city's **Clifton Suspension Bridge**, inaugurated after his death in 1864.

The expansion of the railways boosted the local economy in other ways, for example by encouraging businesses to invest in provincial centres. The town of **Shepton Mallet** became known for cider production in the 1860s, while iron ore was mined in West Somerset's **Brendon Hills** towards the end of the century, reviving the fortunes of West Somerset's only port of any size, **Watchet**, from where the ore was shipped out.

Modern times

World War I affected Somerset much as it did the rest of Britain, bequeathing a trail of bleak war memorials in towns and villages throughout the county. Many local industries closed down during the first half of the century, such as the Brendon Hills mines, and while production peaked in Somerset's coalfields in the 1920s, coalmining in the region disappeared completely over the next fifty years, priced out by the global market.

During **World War II**, Bristol became one of Britain's most bombed cities, losing much of its historic core (see box, p.91), and Bath too did not escape bombardment. The postwar rebuilding of Bristol added some architectural horrors to the city's skyline, including the bland **Broadmead** shopping precinct and a clutch of tasteless office blocks that catered to Bristol's burgeoning new role as a centre for business, finance and technology. The city's manufacturing base was sustained by the engineering works at Filton, including the Rolls-Royce factory that provided engines for the supersonic aircraft Concorde in the 1960s and 1970s. **Yeovil**, in South Somerset, similarly established itself with its Westland aircraft plant, which specialized in helicopter manufacture after World War II.

The construction of the **M5** motorway through Somerset in the 1970s and the expansion of **Bristol airport** in the 1990s further improved the region's infrastructure. However, an ill-advised reorganization of local government in 1974, whereby parts of Somerset were amalgamated with Bristol and parts of Gloucestershire to form the county of Avon, was faced with almost universal opposition, and the experiment was ended in 1996 with the creation of the unitary authorities of Bristol, North Somerset, Bath and Northeast Somerset (BANES), and South Gloucestershire.

The trip-hop "Bristol sound" of the 1990s and the city's street art from the 1980s onwards has helped to raise Bristol's profile, while impressive new museums focusing on the local area were opened in Bristol and Taunton in 2011. But the creation and consumption of culture has taken second place to shopping in recent years; the construction of the **Cribbs Causeway** retail complex outside Bristol in 1998 symbolized a shift of emphasis away from manufacturing to service and retail industries. Both Bristol and Bath celebrated the twenty-first century with the building of bold new inner-city shopping centres, respectively at **Cabot Circus** (2008) and **SouthGate** (2010). But the economic future remains uncertain, as the region as a whole – with the rest of Britain – continues to suffer the effects of the **financial crash** of 2008, which among other consequences has led to the radical slashing of Somerset's arts budget.

1841	1941	1978	2011
The Great Western Railway reaches Bristol, Bridgwater and Taunton, largely financed by Bristol merchants.	Severe bombing of Bristol in World War II; the medieval quarter is gutted.	Louise Joy Brown, the world's first test-tube baby, is born to a couple from Easton in Bristol.	M-Shed and the Museum of Somerset open in Bristol and Taunton respectively.

Wildlife

Watching wildlife in Somerset is rewarding throughout the year, with spring offering the chance to catch mating displays, and summer the time to spot seasonal visitors such as nightjar and hobby; while many mammals and reptiles hibernate in winter, it can be a particularly good time for birdwatchers, when resident populations are boosted by arrivals from the Continent. The following field guide should help you identify some of the more common animals that you might see; notes give clear pointers about the kinds of habitat favoured by each species, their appearance and behaviour and tips on spotting them.

MAMMALS

RED DEER
Cervus elaphus
Habitat Dense woodland and forest, and moorland, particularly Exmoor and the Quantock Hills.
Appearance and behaviour Magnificent beast, weighing over 440lb, with shaggy reddish-brown coat (grey-brown in winter); male has impressive highly branched antlers, the more branches the older the deer; eats shoots, berries and leaves; volatile during rutting, when you should steer clear of males.
Sighting tips Most impressive during the October "rut", a breeding season characterized by warning bellows and occasional clashing of antlers.

BADGER
Meles meles
Habitat Undisturbed woodland.
Appearance and behaviour Stocky creature – the heaviest British carnivore – with two black stripes running from nose to back of neck and powerful front paws (name derives from *becheur*, French for "digger"); social, with large family groups living together in number of setts; varied diet, from mice to bluebells.
Sighting tips Mostly nocturnal; shy, though fierce if cornered, hence local saying "as mad as a badger"; if spotted, keep downwind – keen sense of smell is around eight hundred times better than man's.

STOAT
Mustela erminea
Habitat Woodland and farmland, particularly the Mendips.
Appearance and behaviour Reddish-brown fur, with cream belly and black-tipped tail; shorter and stouter than weasel; eats mostly rabbits and game birds, which it kills with bite to back of neck.

Sighting tips Most easily seen on morning hunts, particularly on open land that's attractive to rabbits.

OTTER
Lutra lutra
Habitat Rivers, lakes, marshland and coastal regions.
Appearance and behaviour Long brown furry body, with powerful tail and webbed feet; males slightly larger than females but both usually over 3ft long; can stay under water for over 3min; eats fish and crabs.
Sighting tips Usually swimming, with only head on view, though sometimes seen playing on the riverbank; tracks are fairly small, with only four of the five toes leaving an imprint.

WATER VOLE
Arvicola terrestris
Habitat Wetlands and fields around ponds, lakes and slow-flowing rivers and streams.
Appearance and behaviour Largest vole in Britain, growing to 1ft in length; name stems from Norwegian for "field" (*voll*), their preferred habitat; also known as water rat; eats aquatic plants.
Sighting tips Nervy animals, so sightings are brief; look around riverbanks (where they live in burrows) and pathways between water.

LESSER HORSESHOE BAT
Rhinolophus hipposideros
Habitat Caves and buildings, particularly on the Mendips.
Appearance and behaviour At ten inches, wingspan around six times length of body; name comes from horseshoe-shaped nose tip; locates food (moths and beetles) by echolocation.
Sighting tips Fairly rare, but between April and October can be seen inside caves or emerging from roosts half an hour or so after sunset.

BIRDS

GREY HERON
Ardea cinerea
Habitat Estuaries, rivers, ponds and wetlands, particularly Swell Wood in West Sedgemoor Nature Reserve.
Appearance and behaviour Largest European heron, measuring around 3ft, with uniform grey back and white breast, sinuous neck and black crests above eyes; long legs end in long toes, which help disperse weight across floating vegetation; usually solitary, though gathers to nest in single tree or group of trees (known as a "heronry").
Sighting tips Common; most often seen motionless on riverbank or in shallow water, stalking prey (mainly fish but also frogs and eels); flies with bent neck and bowed wings, which it beats very slowly.

BITTERN
Botaurus stellaris
Habitat Dense reedbeds, particularly Ham Wall.
Appearance and behaviour Squat, chunky member of the heron family, its sandy brown plumage mottled with dark streaks; eats fish, amphibians and insects; growing in numbers since critical point in 1990s (when less than a dozen males in entire country) but still one of most threatened species of bird in UK.
Sighting tips Elusive and shy, and difficult to spot due to camouflaged plumage; call, a far-reaching "boom", can be heard in spring, though birds themselves are more visible during winter.

LAPWING
Vanellus vanellus
Habitat Wet meadows, worked farmland and marshes, particularly nature reserves in the Avalon Marshes.
Appearance and behaviour Iridescent purple and green back and wings, with red legs, white breast, black band around neck and distinctive crest; dithering flight, hence name; eats worms and insects; declining in recent years, and now on Red List.
Sighting tips Numbers swollen by autumn arrivals from northern Europe, with one of the largest groups of lapwing in the country wintering on the Somerset Levels; listen for high-pitched "pee-wit" call.

KINGFISHER
Alcedo atthis
Habitat Ponds, lakes, canals, slow-flowing rivers and streams, and (in winter) estuaries along the coast.
Appearance and behaviour Unmistakable sapphire blue and orange bird; dagger-like beak around a third the length of body – male's is all black, females have a reddish-orange lower beak; nests in riverside banks; eats mostly fish.
Sighting tips Usually darting above water surface, though sometimes spotted hunting fish from riverside branches; in summer, parents can be seen bringing fish (up to 100 a day) back to their burrows.

GREAT CRESTED GREBE
Podiceps cristatus
Habitat Lakes, reservoirs, gravel pits and slow-moving rivers, particularly Chew Valley Lake.
Appearance and behaviour Graceful-looking bird with black body and long white neck, easily recognized in early spring when it grows distinctive orange-and-black ruff and elaborate crest for the breeding season; builds floating nests, carrying chicks on back for first few weeks.
Sighting tips Clumsy on land due to legs set far back on body, so rarely seen out of water – even prefers to dive to escape trouble, rather than fly; head-shaking courtship displays performed in February, when mating pairs hold themselves out of water by rapidly paddling.

WATER RAIL
Rallus aquaticus
Habitat Reedbeds, marshes, ditches and wetlands.
Appearance and behaviour Small, rounded body, with black-and-white striped flanks separating mottled brown back and grey underparts and face; long, slightly curving red beak; eats mainly small fish, snails and insects.
Sighting tips Fairly common but very secretive, though easier to see in winter, when more numerous and forced to break cover in search of food; more often heard than seen – odd-sounding call akin to squealing piglet.

SNIPE
Gallinago gallinago
Habitat Moors and wetlands.
Appearance and behaviour Squat, with striped brown back, dark streaks on chest and cream underparts; head has "humbug" streaking and long, arrow-straight bill; eats small invertebrates, including worms and insect larvae.
Sighting tips Most often seen on moorland during spring and summer, and round wetland pools in winter; performs acrobatic aerial displays during breeding season – thin whistling noise that accompanies these (known as "drumming") produced by male's tail feathers.

NIGHTJAR
Caprimulgus europaeus
Habitat Heathland, moors and woodland clearings, particularly Quantock Hills.
Appearance and behaviour Similar in shape to cuckoo, with grey-brown, mottled and streaked bodies, tapered wings and long tail; nocturnal; Latin name translates as "European Goatsucker", from belief it stole milk from goats during night; notes that make up male's strange song

– rising and falling "jar" or "churr", which gives bird its English name – emitted up to forty times a second.

Sighting tips Summer migrant, in Somerset late April or mid-May to September; difficult to spot due to camouflaged plumage, but most likely seen on warm, still evenings, hunting moths on the wing.

BUZZARD
Buteo buteo

Habitat Farmland, moors, woodland, scrub and hills, particularly Mendips and Quantocks.

Appearance and behaviour Large raptor with short neck and tail, which it regularly fans out when soaring; variable brown plumage, with yellow legs and talons; eats birds, small rodents and rabbits, but will resort to earthworms and insects if necessary.

Sighting tips Commonest bird of prey in Somerset, most often seen soaring, though will also perch on fence posts and pylons; distinctive "pee-o" call can sound like a cat.

PEREGRINE FALCON
Falco peregrinus

Habitat Cliffs, quarries and rocky areas, particularly Cheddar Gorge.

Appearance and behaviour Medium-sized falcon with blue-grey back (dark brown in young) and head, spotted white chest and barred underparts, with distinctive black "moustache" across white face; eats small birds.

Sighting tips Most likely seen when at nest, in upper cliff ledges; incredibly agile flier, reaching speeds of up to 180mph.

MARSH HARRIER
Circus aeruginosus

Habitat Wetlands, marshes, reedbeds and surrounding farmland, particularly Catcott Lows and Shapwick Heath.

Appearance and behaviour Slightly bigger than buzzard, with streaked head and long grey tail (females larger than males and much darker brown, with cream-coloured heads); nests on ground among reedbeds; has recovered from near extinction but still on Amber List.

Sighting tips Largest of harriers, easily identified in flight due to black wing tips; noticeable aerial displays during spring, when male inverts in mid-air to pass food to female.

SPARROWHAWK
Accipiter nisus

Habitat Woodland and open countryside.

Appearance and behaviour Small raptor, with blue-grey back and wings (less mottled than peregrine) and orange streaks on chest – females have browner back and wings, and brown barred underparts, both have long white "eyebrows"; eats small birds, mice and sometimes bats.

Sighting tips Common but secretive; flies close to ground, with several wing beats followed by a glide; males perform "rollercoaster" aerial displays in early spring.

REPTILES AND AMPHIBIANS

GRASS SNAKE
Natrix natrix

Habitat Ponds, ditches and wetlands.

Appearance and behaviour Largest UK snake, males measuring around 3ft, females another nine inches or so; olive or dark green with yellow collar and black bars along flanks; strong swimmer, feeding on fish, frogs and newts.

Sighting tips Usually seen in or around water; hibernates under logs November to March.

ADDER
Vipera berus

Habitat Heathland and dunes.

Appearance and behaviour UK's only venomous snake, also called "viper"; dark zig-zag pattern running down back, males are silvery-grey, females browner; eats small rodents and lizards.

Sighting tips Usually seen basking on exposed areas such as paths; hibernates underground November to February.

COMMON LIZARD
Lacerta vivipara

Habitat Grassland, heathland and dunes.

Appearance and behaviour Up to six inches long; olive-green, speckled with black, brown and yellow markings; also known as viviparous lizard, as female hatches eggs moments before young are born.

Sighting tips Often seen basking on flat stones or logs, sometimes around water (they're good swimmers); hibernates between November and February.

GREAT CRESTED NEWT
Triturus cristatus

Habitat Ponds, pools and streams.

Appearance and behaviour Up to 6.5 inches long; has bright orange belly and bumpy skin (also known as warty newt); eats insects, worms and slugs; protected species, so is illegal to catch or handle one.

Sighting tips Name comes from large crest male grows along back during spring, which tells it apart from smooth and palmate newts, UK's other, similar-looking newts (smooths have spotted throat, palmates webbed back feet); fairly easy to see (solitary) eggs laid on underside of aquatic plants; hibernates on land between November and February.

Books

FICTION

Jane Austen *Northanger Abbey* This tale follows 17-year-old Catherine Morland as she negotiates the sophisticated, vain and sometimes dishonest society of Bath, populated by characters you love and others you love to hate. Both a coming-of-age story and a satirical poke at the then-current vogue for Gothic literature.

Jane Austen *Persuasion* This is the more worldly-wise of Austen's two novels set (partly) in Bath, though the themes and narrative arcs are familiar – a young single woman in a world full of snobbery, social-climbing and frustrated romance – and it's drenched with the usual Austen wit.

★ **R.D. Blackmore** *Lorna Doone* Swashbuckling Exmoor yarn of romance and inter-clan warfare during the time of the seventeenth-century Monmouth Rebellion. Don't let the archaic language and antiquated style put you off this page-turner, which was televised by the BBC in 2000.

Moyra Caldecott *The Waters of Sul* Immerse yourself in the shenanigans of Roman Bath in this historical novel by a Bath resident, in which competing cultures and cults vie for supremacy in the year 72 AD. Undemanding but well researched and entertaining, this is a perfect holiday read.

Jennie Finch *Death of the Elver Man* Confident crime-thriller debut that beautifully evokes the haunting scenery and deep-rooted traditions of the Somerset Levels, as an outsider attempts to track down a killer amid the unusual setting of the eel-poaching underworld.

HISTORY AND ARCHITECTURE

H.G. Brown and P.J. Harris *Bristol England* If you're looking for a straight-up, no-nonsense history of the city, look no further. It's pretty ancient (taking us up to 1967) and long out of print, but you'll find it in libraries and online, and it provides the full low-down on Bristol, its people and its buildings.

Bryan Little *Bath Portrait* It's getting on a bit (first published fifty years ago, updated in 1980), but this remains a first-class history of the city and the colourful characters who created it. Written in an easy, unpompous style, it's an entertaining and informative read, guaranteed to enrich anyone's visit to the spa town.

Timothy Mowl and Marion Mako *Historic Gardens of Somerset* This well-illustrated study of the county's gardens follows a thematic arrangement that imaginatively links gardens that share ideas, associations and physical features. Some of the places covered are well known, such as Prior Park, Montacute House, Hestercombe and Tyntesfield, others less so, including Marston Bigot, Crowcombe Court, Poundisford Park and Camerton Court, but all are treated equally according to their significance. The appendices provide a helpful map, and a gazetteer gives visiting details and websites.

★ **Nikolaus Pevsner, et al** *The Buildings of England* Indispensable for anyone seriously interested in architecture and historic buildings in general, but a dry academic read for anyone else. The Pevsner guides were first written in the postwar years but updated and expanded by modern experts with greater resources. The editions on Bath; Bristol; Somerset: North and Bristol; and Somerset: South and West are authoritative and tell you everything you want to know about every building of note in the county – and plenty that you probably don't – but they're expensive.

GUIDES

WALKING

AA *50 Walks in Somerset* Handy little book describing walks of three to ten miles, with all the practical details you need and clear, large-scale maps. The walks are annotated with descriptions of local points of interest to visit along the way, plus tearooms and pubs, and there are suggestions for background reading on Somerset's history and wildlife.

Sue Gearing *Walking on the Mendip Hills* Subtitled "Twelve Circular Walks of Discovery", this is an excellent handbook for Mendip walkers, with most walks around five miles, though options are given for extending or shortening the walk. There's plenty of background information on the history, topography, flora and fauna of the landscape.

John Gilman *Exmoor Rangers' Favourite Walks* Thirty circular walks to get the most out of Exmoor, originally written by a former head ranger and subsequently updated by National Park staff and volunteers. The routes vary from two to eight miles.

Derek Moyes *The West Mendip Way* Readable account of the thirty-mile walking route from Uphill, near Weston-super-Mare, to Wells. It's a bit old-fashioned in style, and the maps are appalling, but there are interesting asides on the countryside.

James Roberts *Walking in Somerset* This Cicerone guide has dozens of circular walks of three to twelve miles, of varying levels of difficulty, plus a chapter on the county's long-distance trails. There's plenty of information on places en route, with accommodation suggestions for every walk and at least one pub listed in most accounts. The directions are admirably detailed, though the maps are a bit sketchy.

★ *South West Coast Path* The official National Trail Guide to the coast path in four pocket-friendly volumes, with excellent 1:25,000 Ordnance Survey maps, copious information on background and things to see, and details of circular walks en route.

Woodland Trust *Exploring Woodland: The South West of England* One of a series of illustrated guides with maps and lots of descriptions of what there is to see, historical background and wildlife.

CYCLING

Nick Cotton and John Grimshaw *The Official Guide to the National Cycle Network* Covers all the routes of the National Cycle Network opened in the UK so far. Well presented with good maps and pictures, the guide also

GENERAL

Banksy *Wall and Piece* Published in 2005 but still the definitive introduction to Britain's most notorious street artist. The text – at turns humorous and unflinching – nicely complements the stinging satire of his work.

★ **Felix Braun** *Children of the Can: 25 Years of Bristol Graffiti* Lavishly illustrated journey through Bristol's street-art scene, penned by a graffer, and full of no-holds-barred insights from all the major players.

Paul Cresswell *Bath in Quotes* An enjoyable romp through the literary impressions of various visitors to Bath from Anglo-Saxon times onwards. The prose and verse extracts are arranged chronologically and include pieces from Pepys, Defoe, Thackeray and Dickens, with more recent contributions by Jan Morris and U.A. Fanthorpe.

Margery Fish *We Made a Garden* Charmingly detailed autobiographical account of East Lambrook Manor Gardens, and how a resolute Fleet Street secretary created the concept of cottage gardening.

★ **Rosemary Hill** *Stonehenge* Perhaps the most accessible account of Stonehenge, clearly presenting the myriad theories that have grown up around the great stone circle – it includes ideas by everyone from antiquarians to astrologists – and its wider portrayal in (and influence on) art and architecture.

Maggie Lane *A Charming Place* Here's one for Jane-ites, a portrait of Bath seen through Jane Austen's life, books and

provides info on surfaces, traffic hazards and refreshment stops, and has useful advice for families.

Max Darkins *Mountain Bike Rides in & around Exmoor & Dartmoor* Beautifully produced guide to off-road biking in the region – not just the two moors but as far afield as Saunton and Truro – in a ring binder that can accommodate "expansion packs" (available from ⓦ roughrideguide .co.uk). The OS maps and directions are first class.

Nigel Vile *On Your Bike Around Bristol and Bath* and *On Your Bike in Somerset* These spiral-bound cycling guides are clearly designed, well illustrated and beautifully produced on glossy paper, though you'll need a back-up map for some of the trickier routes. Each of the rides – most around twenty miles – has sections about some of the features en route.

letters. Sections include "Taking the Waters", "Public Entertainments" and "Shopping". Comes with a pull-out map of Bath in Jane's time.

James Russell *The Naked Guide to Cider* Knowledgeable and passionate introduction to the history of cider and the intriguing culture that surrounds this West Country staple – though Somerset is just one of several cider-producing regions covered. Plenty of mouthwatering photos, plus a cider-making guide for those who really get bitten by the bug.

Robin and Romey Williams *The Somerset Levels* Excellent volume that tells you everything you might want to know about this fascinating landscape. The story of human interaction with the wetlands is set against descriptions of the fauna and flora, and there are brief accounts of towns in the area – Wells, Glastonbury and Bridgwater, among others – and historical or semi-historical characters (including King Arthur and Alfred the Great), plus plenty of photos and illustrations.

David Worthy *The Old Quantocks: People and Places* Wonderful compendium of stories, photographs and paintings of the Quantock Hills by a local author. There are features on Nether Stowey, Kilve Priory and Fyne Court, among many others, all in full colour. If you haven't been there already, this will make you want to go.

Small print and index

A ROUGH GUIDE TO ROUGH GUIDES

Published in 1982, the first Rough Guide – to Greece – was a student scheme that became a publishing phenomenon. Mark Ellingham, a recent graduate in English from Bristol University, had been travelling in Greece the previous summer and couldn't find the right guidebook. With a small group of friends he wrote his own guide, combining a highly contemporary, journalistic style with a thoroughly practical approach to travellers' needs.

The immediate success of the book spawned a series that rapidly covered dozens of destinations. And, in addition to impecunious backpackers, Rough Guides soon acquired a much broader readership that relished the guides' wit and inquisitiveness as much as their enthusiastic, critical approach and value-for-money ethos.

These days, Rough Guides include recommendations from budget to luxury and cover more than 200 destinations around the globe, as well as producing an ever-growing range of eBooks and apps.

Visit **roughguides.com** to see our latest publications.

Rough Guide credits

Editor: Lara Kavanagh
Layout: Sachin Gupta
Cartography: Deshpal Dabas
Picture editor: Rhiannon Furbear
Proofreader: Stewart Wild
Managing editor: Monica Woods
Assistant editor: Dipika Dasgupta
Production: Rebecca Short
Cover design: Nicole Newman, Jess Carter
Photographers: Lydia Evans
Editorial assistant: Lorna North

Senior pre-press designer: Dan May
Design director: Scott Stickland
Travel publisher: Joanna Kirby
Digital travel publisher: Peter Buckley
Reference director: Andrew Lockett
Operations coordinator: Becky Doyle
Operations assistant: Johanna Wurm
Publishing director (Travel): Clare Currie
Commercial manager: Gino Magnotta
Managing director: John Duhigg

Publishing information

This first edition published March 2012 by
Rough Guides Ltd,
80 Strand, London WC2R 0RL
11, Community Centre, Panchsheel Park,
New Delhi 110017, India
Distributed by the Penguin Group
Penguin Books Ltd,
80 Strand, London WC2R 0RL
Penguin Group (USA)
375 Hudson Street, NY 10014, USA
Penguin Group (Australia)
250 Camberwell Road, Camberwell,
Victoria 3124, Australia
Penguin Group (NZ)
67 Apollo Drive, Mairangi Bay, Auckland 1310,
New Zealand
Rough Guides is represented in Canada by Tourmaline
Editions Inc. 662 King Street West, Suite 304, Toronto,
Ontario M5V 1M7
Printed in Singapore
© Robert Andrews & Keith Drew 2012

Maps © Rough Guides
No part of this book may be reproduced in any form
without permission from the publisher except for the
quotation of brief passages in reviews.
336pp includes index
A catalogue record for this book is available from the
British Library
ISBN: 978-1-84836-605-3
The publishers and authors have done their best to
ensure the accuracy and currency of all the information in
The Rough Guide to Bath, Bristol & Somerset, however,
they can accept no responsibility for any loss, injury, or
inconvenience sustained by any traveller as a result of
information or advice contained in the guide.
1 3 5 7 9 8 6 4 2

MIX
Paper from
responsible sources
FSC™ C018179
www.fsc.org

Help us update

We've gone to a lot of effort to ensure that the first edition
of **The Rough Guide to Bath, Bristol & Somerset** is
accurate and up-to-date. However, things change – places
get "discovered", opening hours are notoriously fickle,
restaurants and rooms raise prices or lower standards. If
you feel we've got it wrong or left something out, we'd like
to know, and if you can remember the address, the price,
the hours, the phone number, so much the better.

Please send your comments with the subject line
"**Rough Guide Bath, Bristol & Somerset Update**" to
✉ mail@uk.roughguides.com. We'll credit all contributions
and send a copy of the next edition (or any other Rough
Guide if you prefer) for the very best emails.
Find more travel information, connect with fellow
travellers and book your trip on ⓦ roughguides.com

ABOUT THE AUTHORS

Keith Drew grew up on the edge of the Mendips and spent his Saturday afternoons at the Rec in Bath, which he fondly recalls, and his Saturday nights on Park Street in Bristol, which he can't really remember at all. Executive Editor at Rough Guides, he is also co-author of the *Rough Guide to Costa Rica*, which has a similarly friendly populace but significantly more volcanoes.

Robert Andrews is the author of the *Rough Guide to Devon and Cornwall*, among other titles. Based for twenty years in Bristol, he is a connoisseur of campsites, seaside piers and bacon sarnies. When not tramping or pedaling the highways and byways of Somerset, he loiters in public houses and strums on his uke.

Acknowledgements

Keith Drew would like to thank: Alex & Naomi Matthews; Alan & Kathleen Burbridge; Lucy Weaver; Kimberley Holder; Anna Simms; Carla Brooks; Dagmar Smeed; Kerrie Grist; Heather Holve; Chris Chalkey; Katy Bauer; the Pensford Posse (Guilly Jones, Linda Newey & Alison Patey); Jo Ladd & Abi Mallaban; Stefanie Martini; Elly Milln; Sarah Jackson; Charlotte Sangway; Tony Whitehead; Jools & Sally; Paula & Drew; Sara Glossop; Paul & Sarah; Jon Jefferies; Clair Holt; Mike Werkmeister; Joy Kaarnijoki; Lucy Evershed; Jane Stevens Smith and everyone else who helped along the way. Thanks, too, to the excellent team at Rough Guides, especially to Jo, for giving me the gig; Sachin, for tight typesetting; Deshpal, for map magic; Rhiannon, for sourcing some superb images; and to Lara, for enthusiastic and erudite editing and for generally being a legend in her own lifetime. Most of all, though, a huge and heartfelt thanks to my mum, my dad and especially my wife, Kate, for their unwavering support; and to Maisie and Joe, for lending their little hands.

Robert Andrews would like to thank the hard-worked staff and volunteers at the various tourist offices of the region for their friendly cooperation, also QBC for prodigious navigational skills, dauntless footslogging and tireless sightseeing above and beyond the call of duty. Grateful acknowledgement is also due to our editor, Lara Kavanagh, for sympathetic, knowledgeable and amazingly efficient editing, helping to make this guide such a pleasure to write.

Index

Maps are marked in grey

Map symbols

The symbols below are used on maps throughout the book

⊠	Post office	⌣	Bridge	⌒	Cave	✈	Airport
ⓘ	Tourist information	⊠	Gate	🏚	Windmill	⛵	Boat
⊞	Hospital	⛫	Tower	⍕	Radio mast	⚓	Ferry/boat stop
🅃	Toilets	🏛	Abbey	∿	Spring	⚓	Church
🅿	Parking	♦	Museum	✂	Battle site		Building
♦	Place of interest	🏛	Monument	∴	Ruin	⬭	Stadium
@	Internet access	♜	Castle	⌒	Hills		Park
⍏	Gardens/fountain	⌂	Observatory	▲	Peak		Beach
⊙	Statue	⚠	Campsite	★	Transport stop		Cemetery

Listings key

■	Accommodation
●	Restaurant/café
■	Bar/pub/club
●	Shop